ORGANIZED CRIME

Ninth Edition

Howard Abadinsky
St. John's University

WADSWORTH
CENGAGE Learning

Australia • Brazil • Japan • Korea • Mexico • Singapore • Spain • United Kingdom • United States

Organized Crime, Ninth Edition
Howard Abadinsky

Senior Acquisitions Editor: Carolyn Henderson Meier

Assistant Editor: Meaghan Banks

Editorial Assistant: John Chell

Technology Project Manager: Bessie Weiss

Marketing Manager: Michelle Williams

Marketing Assistant: Jillian Myers

Marketing Communications Manager: Tami Strang

Project Manager, Editorial Production: Jennie Redwitz

Creative Director: Rob Hugel

Art Director: Maria Epes

Print Buyer: Becky Cross

Permissions Editor: Bobbie Broyer

Production Service: Sara Dovre Wudali, Buuji, Inc.

Text Designer: Burl Sloan/Diane Beasley

Photo Researcher: Terri Wright

Copy Editor: Linda Ireland

Illustrator: Buuji Inc.

Cover Designer: Christopher Harris, Riezebos Holzbar Design Group

Cover Images: Top: © Graeme Robertson/ Getty Images; middle: © Nicolas Asfouri/Getty Images; bottom left: © Darren McCollester/ Getty Images; bottom right: © Pauline Breijer/RF Fotolia

Compositor: Macmillan Publishing Solutions

For product information and technology assistance, contact us at **Cengage Learning Customer & Sales Support, 1-800-354-9706.**

For permission to use material from this text or product, submit all requests online at **www.cengage.com/permissions.** Further permissions questions can be e-mailed to **permissionrequest@cengage.com.**

Library of Congress Control Number: 2008937862

ISBN-13: 978-0-495-59966-1

ISBN-10: 0-495-59966-2

Wadsworth
10 Davis Drive
Belmont, CA 94002-3098
USA

Cengage Learning is a leading provider of customized learning solutions with office locations around the globe, including Singapore, the United Kingdom, Australia, Mexico, Brazil, and Japan. Locate your local office at **www.cengage.com/international.**

Cengage Learning products are represented in Canada by Nelson Education, Ltd.

To learn more about Wadsworth, visit **www.cengage.com/wadsworth**

Purchase any of our products at your local college store or at our preferred online store **www.ichapters.com.**

Printed in the United States of America
2 3 4 5 6 7 13 12 11 10

BRIEF CONTENTS

CONTENTS

SECTION I: INTRODUCTION TO ORGANIZED CRIME

CHAPTER 1
The Definition and Structure of Organized Crime   1

CHAPTER 2
Explaining Organized Crime   17

SECTION II: ORGANIZED CRIME IN THE UNITED STATES

CHAPTER 5

Organized Crime in Chicago   **109**

SECTION III: INTERNATIONAL ORGANIZED CRIME

CHAPTER 6

Italian Organized Crime and the Albanian Connection   **133**

CHAPTER 7

Latin American Organized Crime   **159**

SECTION IV: BUSINESS OF ORGANIZED CRIME

SECTION V: FIGHTING ORGANIZED CRIME

INTRODUCING THE WADSWORTH CENGAGE LEARNING CRIMINAL JUSTICE ADVISORY BOARD

The entire Criminal Justice team at Wadsworth Cengage Learning wishes to express its sincere gratitude to the hardworking members of our Criminal Justice Advisory Board. This group of skilled, experienced instructors comes together once a year to further their driving mission, which can be summed up as follows:

> This collaborative group of publishing professionals and instructors from traditional and nontraditional educational institutions is designed to foster development of exceptional educational and career opportunities in the field of criminal justice by providing direction and assistance to the faculty and administrators charged with training tomorrow's criminal justice professionals. The Advisory Board offers peer support and advice, consults from both the academic and publishing communities, and serves as a forum for creating and evolving best practices in the building of successful criminal justice programs.

The members of our Advisory Board have the wisdom, expertise, and vision to set goals that empower students, setting them up to capitalize on the field's tremendous growth and expanding job opportunities. According to the U.S. Bureau of Labor Statistics, employment for correctional officers, law enforcement officers, investigators, and security officers is projected to increase at a rate of 9–26% over the next eight years. Add to that the growing number of jobs available in other parts of the criminal justice system—case officer, youth specialist, social services, and more—and one can begin to get a true sense of the vast employment opportunity in the field. Helping today's students unlock the door to exciting and secure futures is the ultimate goal of everyone associated with the Wadsworth Cengage Learning Criminal Justice Advisory Board.

Included on the board are faculty and administrators from schools such as:

Brown College
Florida Metropolitan University
Globe University/Minnesota School of Business
Hesser College
Kaplan University
Keiser University
John Jay College of Criminal Justice
Rasmussen College
South University
Western Career College
Western Carolina University
Westwood College

Again, the Wadsworth Cengage Learning Criminal Justice Team would like to extend our personal and professional thanks for all that the Advisory Board has enabled us to accomplish over the past few years. We look forward to continuing our successful collaboration in the years ahead.

We are always looking to add like-minded instructors to the Advisory Board; if you would like to be considered for inclusion on the Board, please contact Michelle Williams (michelle.williams@cengage.com).

Preparing Students for a Lifetime of Service

PREFACE

In 1964, fresh out of college, I was sworn in as a New York State parole officer. Soon afterward, equipped with a badge and a .38, I was assigned to the waterfront section of South Brooklyn known as Red Hook. As I struggled to become familiar with the neighborhood, I noticed that my presence on certain streets seemed to generate a great deal of curiosity (in those days I was six feet, one inch tall and weighed an athletic 200 pounds) and, at times, activity—windows opening and closing, people on the streets suddenly melting into doorways or shops. I discussed Red Hook with my more experienced colleagues and some of the naiveté faded.

Red Hook was dominated by a faction of one of New York City's five organized crime "Families." Prior to my arrival, this faction had been involved in a conflict with the rest of the Family, and Red Hook had been the scene of a great deal of violence. A tentative truce was in effect when I appeared on the scene. I became familiar with such terms as "wiseguy" and "made guy," *capo* and *consigliere*, and names like "Crazy Joey," "Blast," "the Snake," "Punchy," and "Apples."

After fifteen years as a parole officer and supervisor, I left New York for Western Carolina University and an academic career. My interest in organized crime continued, and I began to teach a course on the subject. However, a single text, one that was both comprehensive and accurate, was unavailable. Like so many others presenting courses on organized crime, I had students purchase the classics by Francis Ianni (1972), Donald Cressey (1972), Joseph Albini (1971), and Humbert Nelli (1976). Nevertheless, there were still gaps, particularly with respect to emerging organized crime and the statutes and techniques used in organized crime law enforcement.

The first edition of this book (1981) was the result of a need for a basic text that covered all of the important dimensions of organized crime and its control. But organized crime changed; hence a second edition was published in 1985, when I was teaching at Saint Xavier University/Chicago and becoming familiar with organized crime through contacts developed as a (part-time) Cook County deputy sheriff/inspector.

Ever dynamic, organized crime continues to change, with efforts to combat one aspect of the phenomenon, the American Mafia, reaching new levels of prosecutorial success. Meanwhile, emerging groups of criminals have become more sophisticated and more threatening, and additional crime groups have been added to the pantheon we refer to as organized crime. This new edition reflects changes that have occurred and updates information and analyses of organized crime and efforts to deal with it.

"Globalization and growing economic interdependence have encouraged and promoted the transformation of crime beyond national borders in all parts of the world. Improved communications and information technologies, increased blurring of national borders, greater mobility of people, goods, and services across countries, and the emergence of a globalized economy have moved crime further away from its domestic base" (United Nations Centre for International Crime Prevention 2000: 44).

The collapse of the Soviet Union was a pivotal historical event that intertwined with the rapid expansion of global markets: "money, goods and people have circulated with a rapidity and facility which were once unthinkable" (Violante 2000: x). "Whether in the developed or in the developing world, criminal organizations' scope of action and range of capabilities are undergoing a profound change" (Godson and Olson 1995: 19). Furthermore, as Roy Godson and William Olson (1995: 19) noted, the decline in political order and deteriorating economic circumstances have led to a growing underground economy that habituates people to working outside the legal framework.

Easy access to arms, the massive flow of emigrants and refugees, and the normal difficulties involved in accomplishing meaningful international cooperation are working to the advantage of criminal organizations. And the "rise of better-organized, internationally based criminal groups with vast financial resources is creating a new threat to the stability and security of international systems" (Godson and Olson 1995: 19). "Many international and transnational criminal organizations are continuing to expand their networks and links with other criminal organizations throughout the world, allowing the larger organizations to become increasingly powerful, technically sophisticated and global in their approach" (*INTERPOL at Work* 2003: 17). Added into this mix is the global problem of terrorism.

ORGANIZATION

Organized Crime is divided into five parts. Section I, Introduction to Organized Crime, serves as the book's foundation, exploring the definition of organized crime and the attributes and structures of criminal organizations, and offering explanations for their existence. Section II, Organized Crime in the United States, details the development of organized crime in America with a focus on its connection to politics and the importance of Prohibition. Section III, International Organized Crime, explores the globalization of organized crime with a worldwide journey that highlights the criminal organizations operating in various regions and countries. Section IV, Business of Organized Crime, covers the wide array of activities that are part of the business of criminal organizations, including gambling, trafficking in persons, drugs, and arms, and labor racketeering. Section V, Fighting Organized Crime, is concerned with the laws and techniques used to combat organized crime.

More specifically, here is what the reader will find in each chapter.

- Chapter 1, The Definition and Structure of Organized Crime, opens with a discussion of the problems inherent in defining organized crime; compares and contrasts organized crime with terrorist organizations; reviews the attributes that are requisite for determining whether a group is to be considered "organized crime"; and discusses the manner in which criminal organizations can be structured.
- Chapter 2, Explaining Organized Crime, explores social science theories that provide insight into explaining the existence of and understanding organized crime.
- Chapter 3, Development of Organized Crime in the United States, provides a history of organized crime that connects its growth to political machines in urban America and Prohibition and discusses the work of various investigative committees and commissions looking into the phenomenon.
- Chapter 4, Organized Crime in New York, provides a history and analysis of organized crime in New York with particular focus on the Jewish and Italian contributions to the phenomenon.
- Chapter 5, Organized Crime in Chicago, examines the unique history of organized crime in the Windy City and the current state of its premier organization, the "Outfit."
- Chapter 6, Italian Organized Crime and the Albanian Connection, begins with a discussion of the globalization of organized crime and examines the criminal organizations of Southern Italy: Mafia, Camorra, 'Ndrangheta, and *Sacra Corona Unita* and its connection to Albanian crime groups.
- Chapter 7, Latin American Organized Crime, looks at the drug trafficking cartels of Colombia and Mexico, as well as those of the Dominicans and *Mara Salvatrucha* (MS-13).
- Chapter 8, Black Organized Crime, explores African American, Jamaican, and West African organized crime.
- Chapter 9, Asian Organized Crime, explores the variety of criminal groups that constitute Asian organized crime, including *yakuza*, Triads, and tongs.

- Chapter 10, Russian Organized Crime, examines the criminal organizations that emerged from the former Soviet Union.
- Chapter 11, International Outlaw Motorcycle Clubs, discusses the international growth of outlaw motorcycle clubs including the Hell's Angels, Bandidos, and Outlaws.
- Chapter 12, Gambling, Loansharking, Theft, Fencing, Sex, and Trafficking in Persons and Arms, begins an examination of the business of organized crime with a discussion of organized crime as both a provider of illegal goods and services and an extorter from illegal entrepreneurs.
- Chapter 13, The Drug Business, details the most lucrative business of transnational organized crime, drugs, examining the mix of politics and foreign policy implications of major sources in Latin America, the Far East, and the Middle East.
- Chapter 14, Labor, Business, and Money Laundering, examines the history of organized crime involvement in the labor movement, legitimate business, and money laundering.
- Chapter 15, Organized Crime Statutes and Law Enforcement, reviews the problems inherent in responding to organized crime; the various statutes used in this effort, in particular, RICO; and the agencies and techniques for combating organized crime.

Terrorism and Organized Crime

Terrorism and organized crime often share a style of organization, geography, an overlapping membership, and techniques. They differ on their goals, however. The ninth edition discusses similarities and differences between terrorism and organized crime in Chapter 1 and also focuses on the topic of terrorism in the following chapters:

- Chapter 6: Connections between Albanian organized crime and terrorism in the former Yugoslavia
- Chapter 7: Narco-terrorism in Latin America

- Chapter 10: Overlapping of organized crime and Chechen nationalism
- Chapter 13: The business side of the mix of narcotics trafficking and insurgencies in Latin America, the Golden Triangle, and the Golden Crescent
- Chapter 15: The impact of terrorism on organized crime law enforcement

NEW IN THIS EDITION

In addition to the above changes, each chapter in the text has been carefully revised. Crucial updates include the following.

- **Chapter 1, The Definition and Structure of Organized Crime,** has an expanded discussion of the similarities and differences between organized crime and terrorism. The characteristics that define organized crime have been reduced from nine to eight, reflecting changes in the nature of the phenomenon.
- **Chapter 2, Explaining Organized Crime,** now includes the psychology of organized crime.
- **Chapter 3, Development of Organized Crime in the United States,** has been reorganized and material on Jewish organized crime has been moved to Chapter 4 for simplicity of presentation/pedagogical reasons.
- **Chapter 4, Organized Crime in New York,** has been updated to reflect changes that have occurred in organized crime since the last edition.
- **Chapter 5, Organized Crime in Chicago,** contains material that was in Chapter 4 (but which made that chapter too long and too complicated). The material has been updated to reflect changes that have occurred since the last edition.
- **Chapter 6, Italian Organized Crime and the Albanian Connection,** has been updated to reflect the increased importance of the Camorra and its role in the production

and distribution of counterfeit consumer goods as well as Albanian organized crime.

- **Chapter 7, Latin American Organized Crime,** has been expanded to include the structure of FARC, a terrorist group whose primary support is from the cocaine business. The material on M-13 has been expanded to reflect the growing importance of this group.
- **Chapter 8, Black Organized Crime,** has been revised to include a discussion of West African organized crime, which reflects its growing importance on the international scene. There is additional material on Frank Lucas to reflect public interest as a result of the popularity of the Denzel Washington motion picture *American Gangster*. Material on Nicky Barnes has been added to reflect public interest in his life as the result of a popular documentary on his life.
- **Chapter 9, Asian Organized Crime,** has been updated to reflect changes that have occurred since the last edition, with additional material on the Japanese *yakuza*.
- **Chapter 10, Russian Organized Crime,** has been updated and expanded to reflect the growing importance of Russian organized crime; material from several new and excellent books on the topic has been incorporated.
- **Chapter 11, International Outlaw Motorcycle Clubs,** has been expanded and updated to include a number of recent publications and my own experience as an expert witness on the subject. The chapter now centers on clubs that have an extensive international presence. Interest in the outlaw motorcycle club—not gang—will increase with series on FX and HBO on the phenomenon.
- **Chapter 12, Gambling, Loansharking, Theft, Fencing, Sex, and Trafficking in Persons and Arms,** has been updated and material on Internet gambling and the discussion of trafficking in persons have been expanded.
- **Chapter 13, The Drug Business,** has been updated and where necessary expanded to reflect changes in the drug business.
- **Chapter 14, Labor, Business, and Money Laundering,** includes expanded material on New York City's efforts to curb racketeering in the private solid waste hauling industry (Tony Soprano's business).
- **Chapter 15, Organized Crime Statutes and Law Enforcement,** has combined anti–organized crime statutes and law enforcement in one chapter to keep the book at 15 chapters, matching the typical college course. There is additional material on money laundering and human trafficking as well as the impact of terrorism on organized crime law enforcement.

LEARNING AIDS

The ninth edition features learning aids designed to help students understand the vast amount of information being conveyed. Figures and tables illustrate key concepts at appropriate points in the text, and boxed sidebars in chapters provide interesting background reading and help bring the material even more to life. Each chapter begins with a brief overview and ends with a summary and review section. End-of-chapter questions provide a basis for review of material and test students' knowledge of the chapter. End-of-book matter includes an author index, subject index, and an extensive references/bibliography section.

SUPPLEMENTS

Supplements are available to qualified adopters. Please consult your local sales representative for details.

For the Instructor

Instructor's Manual with Test Bank An improved and completely updated *Instructor's Manual with Test Bank* has been developed by Erin Heil of University of Illinois at Chicago. The manual includes learning objectives, a chapter summary, detailed chapter outlines, key terms, review questions, class discussion exercises, and Internet activities. Each chapter's Test Bank contains questions in multiple-choice, true-false, fill-in-the-blank, and essay formats, with a full answer key. Finally, each question in the Test Bank has been carefully reviewed by experienced criminal justice instructors for quality, accuracy, and content coverage. Our *Instructor Approved* seal, which appears on the front cover, is our assurance that you are working with an assessment and grading resource of the highest caliber.

PowerPoint Slides These handy Microsoft® PowerPoint® slides, which outline the chapters of the main text in a classroom-ready presentation, will help you make your lectures engaging and reach your visually oriented students. The slides may be downloaded from the eBank resource; contact your local Cengage Learning representative for assistance.

The Wadsworth Criminal Justice Video Library So many exciting new videos—so many great ways to enrich your lectures and spark discussion of the material in this text. Your Cengage Learning representative will be happy to provide details on our video policy by adoption size. The library includes these selections and many others:

- *ABC® Videos*: ABC videos feature short, high-interest clips from current news events as well as historic raw footage going back 40 years. Perfect for discussion starters or to enrich your lectures and spark interest in the material in the text, these brief videos provide students with a new lens through which to view the past and present, one that will greatly enhance their knowledge and understanding of significant events and open up to them new dimensions in learning. Clips are drawn from such programs as *World News Tonight*, *Good Morning America*, *This Week*, *PrimeTime Live*, *20/20*, and *Nightline*, as well as numerous ABC News specials and material from the Associated Press Television News and British Movietone News collections.

- *The Wadsworth Custom Videos for Criminal Justice*: Produced by Wadsworth and Films for the Humanities, these videos include short five- to ten-minute segments that encourage classroom discussion. Topics include white-collar crime, domestic violence, forensics, suicide and the police officer, the court process, the history of corrections, prison society, and juvenile justice.

- *Oral History Project*: Developed in association with the American Society of Criminology, the Academy of Criminal Justice Society, and the National Institute of Justice, these videos will help you introduce your students to the scholars who have developed the criminal justice discipline. Compiled over the last several years, each video features a set of Guest Lecturers—scholars whose thinking has helped build the foundation of present ideas in the discipline. Vol. 1: Moments in Time; Vol. 2: Great Moments in Criminological Theory; Vol. 3: Research Methods.

- *Court TV Videos*: One-hour videos presenting seminal and high-profile cases such as the interrogations of Michael Crowe and serial killer Ted Bundy, as well as crucial and current issues such as cybercrime, double jeopardy, and the management of the prison on Riker's Island.

- *A&E American Justice*: Forty videos to choose from on topics such as deadly force, women on death row, juvenile justice, strange defenses, and Alcatraz.

- *Films for the Humanities*: Nearly 200 videos to choose from on a variety of topics such as elder abuse, supermax prisons, suicide and the police officer, the making of an FBI agent, domestic violence, and more.

For the Student

Current Perspectives: Readings from InfoTrac® College Edition These readers, designed to give students a closer look at special topics in criminal justice, include free access to InfoTrac

College Edition. The timely articles are selected by experts in each topic from within InfoTrac College Edition. They are available for free when bundled with the text and include the following titles:

- *Cybercrime*
- *Victimology*
- *Juvenile Justice*
- *Racial Profiling*
- *White-Collar Crime*
- *Terrorism and Homeland Security*
- *Public Policy and Criminal Justice*
- *New Technologies and Criminal Justice*
- *Ethics in Criminal Justice*
- *Forensics and Criminal Investigation*

Internet Guide for Criminal Justice, Second Edition Internet beginners will appreciate this helpful booklet. With explanations and the vocabulary necessary for navigating the Web, it features customized information on criminal justice–related websites and presents Internet project ideas.

Internet Activities for Criminal Justice, Second Edition This completely revised 96-page booklet shows how to best utilize the Internet for research through searches and activities.

ACKNOWLEDGMENTS

The author would like to extend his thanks to Senior Acquisitions Editor Carolyn Henderson Meier of Cengage Learning for her confidence in the author; to Sara Dovre Wudali, a most proficient production editor; and to copyeditor Linda Ireland for her attention to detail, and to the following reviewers for their thoughtful suggestions:

Robert Brooks, Worcester State College
Susan Craig, University of Central Florida
Pat Kinkade, Texas Christian University
Richard Mangan, Florida Atlantic University
Gary Potter, Eastern Kentucky University
Hugh Snyder, St. Joseph's University
Harrison Watts, Cameron University
Richard Wiebe, Fitchburg State College

ABOUT THE AUTHOR

HOWARD ABADINSKY is professor of criminal justice at St John's University. He was an inspector for the Cook County, Illinois, Sheriff for 8 years and a New York State parole officer and senior parole officer for 15 years. He is the founder of the International Association for the Study of Organized Crime and served as a consultant to the President's Commission on Organized Crime. The author has a B.A. from Queens College of the City University of New York, an M.S.W. from Fordham University, and a Ph.D. in sociology from New York University. He is the author of several books, including *The Criminal Elite: Professional and Organized Crime; The Mafia in America, Probation and Parole*, 10th edition; *Law and Justice*, 6th edition; and *Drug Use and Abuse*, 6th edition.

Dr. Abadinsky encourages comments about his work and can be reached at St. John's University, 8000 Utopia Parkway, Jamaica, NY 11439. abadinsh@stjohns.edu.

Carolyn Bishop-Abadinsky

C H A P T E R

1

The Definition and Structure of Organized Crime

Conventional wisdom recognizes that garden variety/conventional crime is different from *organized* crime; that Jesse James and Al Capone—criminals both—are remarkably different. The James Gang ended with Jesse's death in 1882, while the Capone organization—the Chicago Outfit—despite his imprisonment in 1932 and subsequent death as an invalid in 1947—is with us in the twenty-first century. Thus, perpetuity is a variable that can distinguish organized from conventional crime. While the crime portfolio of Jesse James and his ilk was rather limited (robbing banks, stagecoaches, and trains), "the criminality of persons in organized crime differs from that of conventional criminals because their organization allows them to commit crimes of a different variety [labor racketeering, for example] and on a larger scale [smuggling planeloads of cocaine, for example] than their less organized colleagues" (Moore 1987: 51).

Criminals who are part of a recognizable (by other criminals) organization are in a position to negotiate transactions that those without an organizational affiliation would find difficult if not impossible to accomplish. In the dangerous and anarchic world of crime, organizational affiliation provides a form of *credentialing* by reputation, encouraging networking that facilitates cooperation between criminals that might not otherwise occur. In the dangerous environment in which organized crime exists, the willingness of criminals to cooperate requires a level of trust that can explain the need for bonding rituals used by groups as diverse as the Mafia, Triads, and outlaw motorcycle clubs (von Lampe and Johansen 2004).

In the Hobbesian world inhabited by criminals, an organization with sufficient martial capacity—the *value of a bad reputation*—can offer services typically reserved for government such as contract enforcement and adjudication of disputes. Indeed, the degree of sophistication characterizing a criminal organization can be measured by the degree to which it provides contract and arbitration services to criminals and sometimes legitimate entrepreneurs looking for a swifter, more reliable form of justice. In places where the legal system places onerous burdens on plaintiffs, such as Russia and Japan, the collection of legitimate debts is frequently contracted out to members of criminal organizations whose reputation for violence can expedite the collection process.

Members of criminal organizations are also in a position to enforce extralegal social norms ranging from restraining boisterous behavior to requiring a young man to marry the young lady he impregnated. In Chicago, when the police failed to adequately respond to complaints about reckless driving by youngsters in the Grand Avenue section, several residents went to see their neighbor "Judge Joey"—Joseph ("The Clown") Lombardo. This ranking member of the Outfit resolved the problem with a few carefully chosen words. In British Columbia, the son of a friend of a member of the Hell's Angels was being harassed by a gang of students at his high school. The harassment quickly ended when the motorcycle club member, wearing the full regalia of the Hell's Angels, visited the school.

In order to understand how the varied and large-scale tasks of criminal organizations can be accomplished, we need to examine the structures that contemporary organized crime can manifest. In this chapter, we will examine the problem of defining organized crime and then consider two contrasting organizational models. The *bureaucratic/corporate* model and the *patron-client network* represent two ends of a continuum; criminal groups, if they are to be defined as *organized*, can be located somewhere along this continuum.

DEFINING ORGANIZED CRIME

Attempts to define organized crime (OC) have met with only limited success, and no generally accepted definition has emerged. Although there is a great deal of discussion about organized crime groups and their activities, a review of the subject in the law enforcement and academic literature reveals it is difficult to determine what exactly is being discussed (Loree 2002).

Donald Cressey (1969: 319) presented a definition that for many decades was used by the Federal Bureau of Investigation (FBI): "An organized crime is any crime committed by a person occupying, in an established division of labor, a position designed for the commission of crimes providing that such division of labor includes at least one position for a corrupter, one position for a corruptee, and one position for an enforcer." In

1970, the U.S. Department of Justice defined the term as "all illegal activities engaged in by members of criminal syndicates operative throughout the United States and all illegal activities engaged in by known associates and confederates of such members." The FBI currently defines organized crime "as any group having some manner of a formalized structure and whose primary objective is to obtain money through illegal activities. Such groups maintain their position through the use of actual or threatened violence, corrupt public officials, graft, or extortion, and generally have a significant impact on the people in their locales, region, or the country as a whole."

In 1998, an international conference in Warsaw on the problem of organized crime used a definition offered by the host country: "Group activities of three or more persons, with hierarchical links or personal relationships, which permit their leaders to earn profits or control territories or markets, internal or foreign, by means of violence, intimidation or corruption, both in furtherance of criminal activity and to infiltrate the legitimate economy." This definition was followed by a list of "typical" activities (Jamieson 2000: 169). The entrepreneurial conception of organized crime was originally proposed by Dwight Smith (1978) and, as Letizia Paoli (2003) suggests, avoids the ethnic overtones inherent in the term *organized crime*. It also discounts the subcultural dynamics of organized crime—those of outlaw motorcycle clubs, for example—that frequently serve to attract members.

Michael Maltz (1976: 346) points to a semantic problem, noting that we call a specific behavior or act organized crime, but when we refer to organized crime in the generic sense, we usually mean an entity, a group of people: "An organized crime is a crime in which there is more than one offender, and the offenders are and intend to remain associated with one another for the purpose of committing crimes." In its 1967 report, the Task Force on Organized Crime noted that these crimes typically involve the providing of "illegal goods and services" for which there is widespread demand: gambling, loansharking, and narcotics. The definition offered by the state of California adds theft and fencing, and no list of organized criminal activities would be complete without business and labor racketeering and extortion.

The Criminal Code of Canada states that a "criminal organization" means "a group, however organized, that (a) is composed of three or more persons in or outside Canada, and (b) has as one of its main purposes or main activities the facilitation or commission of one or more serious offences that carry a five-year or higher maximum sentence that, if committed, would likely result in the direct or indirect receipt of a material benefit, including financial benefit, by the group or by any of the persons who constitute the group." It does not include a group of persons that forms randomly for the immediate commission of a single offense.

The United Nations Convention Against Transnational Organised Crime, meeting in Palermo, Italy, in 2000, established an international definition of organized crime. The Convention states, at Article 2(a), that an "organised criminal group shall mean a structured group of three or more persons, existing for a period of time and acting in concert with the aim of committing one or more serious crimes or offences established in accordance with this Convention, in order to obtain, directly or indirectly, a financial or other material benefit."

Although there is no generally accepted definition of organized crime—indeed, the federal Organized Crime Control Act of 1970 fails to define *organized crime* (an issue discussed in Chapter 15)—a number of attributes have been identified by law enforcement agencies and researchers as indicative of the phenomenon. Offering these attributes has a practical dimension: the attributes provide a basis for determining if a particular group of criminals constitutes *organized crime* and, therefore, needs to be approached in a way different from the way one would approach terrorists or groups of conventional criminals. Organized crime:

1. Has no political goals
2. Is hierarchical
3. Has a limited or exclusive membership
4. Constitutes a unique subculture

5. Perpetuates itself
6. Exhibits a willingness to use illegal violence
7. Is monopolistic
8. Is governed by explicit rules and regulations

Let us examine each of these attributes.

1. *No political goals.* The goals of an organized crime group are money and power whose procurement is not limited by legal or moral concerns. An organized crime group is not motivated by social doctrine, political beliefs, or ideological concerns. Although political involvement may be part of the group's activities, the purpose is usually to gain protection or immunity for its illegal activities. This distinguishes organized crime from groups of persons who may be organized and violating the law to further their political agenda—for example, the Ku Klux Klan or terrorist groups (discussed later). As distinguished from terrorists, organized crime members are not potential suicide bombers.

A group whose primary goal is political or ideological may consider their mission no longer relevant and, rather than disband, become an organized crime group. A group, or simply some of its members, may find personal and pecuniary goals outweighing ideology and drift across the amorphous divide between political and organized crime, for example, groups in Northern Ireland supporting (loyalists) and opposing (republicans) British rule.

2. *Hierarchical.* An organized crime group has a vertical power structure with at least three permanent ranks—not just a leader and followers—each with authority over the level beneath. The authority is inherent in the position and does not depend on who happens to be occupying it at any given time.

3. *Limited or exclusive membership.* An organized crime group significantly limits membership. Qualifications may include ethnic background, kinship, race, criminal record, or similar considerations. Those who meet the basic qualification(s) for membership usually require a sponsor,

typically a ranking member, and must also prove qualified for membership by their behavior—for example, willingness to commit criminal acts, obey rules, follow orders, and maintain secrets. There is a period of apprenticeship that may range from several months to several years. If the group is to remain viable, there must be considerably more persons who desire membership than the organized crime group is willing to accept. Exclusivity of membership serves to indicate that belonging is indeed something to be valued.

Although membership can refer to being part of a specific group, such as the Genovese Family or the Hell's Angels, it can also entail a more amorphous attachment to a criminal network, such as that which characterizes Russian organized crime in the United States (discussed in Chapter 10). Membership indicators include such bonding rituals as initiation ceremonies and distinctive group icons on clothing, jewelry, and tattoos. In the absence of specific indicators, the question of membership can be viewed subjectively: Do the people view themselves as being part of a particular criminal organization? Membership provides a basis for the credentialing discussed earlier.

4. *Constitutes a unique subculture.* Sometimes referred to as the "underworld," members of organized crime view themselves as distinct from conventional society, which they frequently view with derision if not contempt, and therefore not subject to its rules.

5. *Perpetuates itself.* An organized crime group constitutes an ongoing criminal conspiracy designed to persist through time, that is, beyond the life of the current membership. Permanence is assumed by the members, and this provides an important basis for attracting qualified persons to the group, thus perpetuating the group's existence. The strength of this attribute often depends on the depth of the subcultural orientation manifested by the group. Cressey (1969: 263) states that in order for an organized crime group to survive, it must have "an institutionalized process for inducting new members and inculcating them with the values and ways of behaving of the social system."

6. *Willingness to use illegal violence.* In an organized crime group, violence is a readily available and routinely accepted resource. Access to private violence is an important dimension that allows the group to actively pursue its goals. The use of violence is not restricted by ethical considerations but is controlled only by practical limitations.

7. *Monopolistic.* An organized crime group eschews competition. It strives for hegemony over a particular geographic area (a metropolitan area or section of a city); a particular "industry," legitimate or illegitimate (for example, gambling, trucking, loansharking); or a combination of both (for example, loansharking in a particular area or the wholesale cocaine market in a city). A monopoly, of course, restrains "free trade" and increases profits. An organized crime monopoly is maintained by violence, by the threat of violence, or by corrupt relationships with law enforcement officials. A combination of both methods, violence and corruption, may be employed.

Although an organized crime group may strive for a monopoly, this may not be possible given the nature of competing groups or the type of industry—for example, drug trafficking (discussed in Chapter 13). In 1995, when Maurice ("Mom") Boucher, head of Nomads chapter of the Montreal Hell's Angels, attempted to assert control over the city's drug market, he encountered a serious impediment—Phil Rizzuto, a Bonnano crime Family captain with his own murderous Montreal crew. Given the danger of conflict, Boucher chose diplomacy and negotiated a deal with Rizzuto (Lamothe and Humphreys 2006).

Moreover, territoriality is more closely associated with localness rather than the broader reach of transnational criminal organizations (Reuter and Petrie 1999). In Chapter 7, for example, we will examine Mexican organizations that, although associated with a particular geographic area—for instance, the "Juarez cartel," do not expend resources defending geographic hegemony.

8. *Governed by rules and regulations.* An organized crime group, like a legitimate organization, has a set of rules and regulations that members are expected to follow. In organized crime, however,

a rule-violating member is not fired but, more likely, fired upon.

These attributes are arrayed in a structure that enables the organized crime group to achieve its goals—money and power. A number of criminal organizations have many, if not all, of the attributes that have been discussed. Some are domestic, while most are transnational in scope or have important organizational or business ties overseas. Some have links to terrorism.

ORGANIZED CRIME AND TERRORISM

If we were to limit our definition of organized crime to two essential characteristics, they would be willingness to use illegal violence and devoid of political goals. The latter characteristic, however, is sometimes blurred, the result of ties between members of organized crime groups and terrorist groups. In some parts of the world—such as the Balkans, breakaway areas of the former Soviet Union, and Latin America—organized crime and terrorist organizations share the same geography, usually conflict zones, and membership can overlap with individuals belonging to both terrorist and organized crime groups (Shelley et al. 2005).

In some cases, the terrorists imitate the organized criminal behavior they see around them, borrowing techniques. This can lead to more intimate connections, particularly in places of poor governance, ethnic separatism, and/or a tradition of criminal activity, such as in failed states, war regions, prisons, and some urban neighborhoods (Shelley and Picarelli 2005). "It is not particularly uncommon for terrorist groups to recruit some of their members among criminal elements, particularly among individuals who may have special skills or common criminals who can contribute to its goals in instrumental, training, and other matters" (Préfontaine and Dandurand 2004: 16). Terrorist and organized criminal groups share some attributes, in particular organizational structure such as compartmentalization (discussed later). Terrorist groups and criminal organizations often have similar requirements for moving people, money, matériel, and weapons across borders and often operate under a similar set of contingencies.

Once terrorists and other criminals start to work together, they naturally begin to buy and sell services and goods from each other—it is more efficient to outsource a service (such as passport forgery) to an established specialist than to try to master the necessary techniques. If these business relationships progress beyond individual transactions, in the next stage the two groups begin working together more regularly and begin to share each other's goals as well as working methods. A symbiotic relationship, as seen in the Russian region of Chechnya, discussed in Chapter 10, develops where there is no hard-and-fast line between Chechen organized crime and Chechen rebels fighting a terrorist war against Russian sovereignty over their homeland (Shelley and Picarelli 2005). The Albanian Kosovo Liberation Army (KLA) in the former Yugoslavia forged links with drug traffickers and international criminals. The KLA used these connections, as well as contributions from Albanian emigrant communities abroad, to fund its paramilitary campaign against Serbian authorities.

Although the Revolutionary Armed Forces of Colombia (FARC)–controlled safe haven, or "despeje," situated between two of Colombia's largest coca cultivation areas, is not considered a major area for coca cultivation or drug trafficking, many FARC units throughout southern Colombia raise funds through the extortion ("taxation") of both legal and illegal businesses, the latter including the drug trade (discussed in Chapters 7 and 13). Similarly, in return for cash payments, or possibly in exchange for weapons, some FARC units protect cocaine laboratories and clandestine airstrips in southern Colombia. FARC units may be independently involved in limited cocaine laboratory operations, and some are more directly involved in local drug trafficking activities, such as controlling cocaine base markets. At least one prominent FARC commander has served as a source of cocaine for a Brazilian trafficking organization. FARC cocaine was also shipped to the Hell's Angels in Amsterdam via Curacao in the Dutch Antilles (Sher and Marsden 2006).

Taliban insurgents in Afghanistan have been using heroin to finance their efforts. In 2005, Afghan drug lord Baz Mohammad was extradited to the United States where he is accused of heading an organization that controlled poppy fields in Afghanistan, heroin-processing plants in Pakistan, and a trafficking network that smuggled millions of dollars worth of drugs into the United States. In partnership with the Taliban, Mohammad told supporters they would be committing jihad by selling heroin to Americans (Zambito 2005b; McFadden 2005). A tribal warlord allied with the Taliban, Bashir Noorzai, was tricked into traveling to New York where in 2008 he was convicted of smuggling $50 million dollars worth of heroin into the United States (Associated Press 2008).

In Southeast Asia's Golden Triangle, there is a long-standing tradition of using heroin trafficking to support insurgencies (discussed in Chapter 13). According to the Director of the Office of National Drug Control Policy: "Almost half of the State Department's list of known terrorist organizations are known to have, at one point or another, trafficked in drugs" (Walters 2003: 9). This gives rise to the term *narcoterrorism*, terrorist acts carried out by groups directly or indirectly involved in cultivating, manufacturing, transporting, or distributing illegal drugs. The links between terrorist organizations and drug traffickers can take many forms, ranging from facilitation—protection, transportation, and taxation—to direct trafficking by the terrorist organization itself in order to finance its activities. Traffickers and terrorists have similar logistical needs in terms of matériel and the covert movement of goods, people, and money.

Relationships between drug traffickers and terrorists are mutually beneficial. Drug traffickers gain from access to terrorists' military skills and weapons supply; terrorists gain a source of revenue and expertise in illicit transfer and laundering of proceeds. Both bring corrupt officials whose services provide mutual benefits, such as greater access to fraudulent documents, including passports and customs papers. Drug traffickers may also gain considerable freedom of movement when they operate in conjunction with terrorists who control large amounts of territory (Beers and Taylor 2002).

Like Colombian drug cartels, terrorist groups are frequently organized along compartmentalized lines (discussed later in this chapter). Similar to Italian and Asian organized crime groups, terrorist organizations such as al-Qaeda use sponsorships, apprenticeships, and initiation ceremonies. Like organized crime, terrorist groups have a need to launder their financial assets. The Provisional Irish Republican Army, for example, is reported to have become expert at money laundering through a portfolio of front businesses in Belfast (Chrisafis 2005).

The differences between terrorist organizations and organized crime groups rest on means and ends. While both engage in organized criminal activity to support themselves, terrorists use their funds to further political ends, to overthrow governments and impose their worldview. Organized crime instead seeks to form a parallel government while coexisting with the existing one. Organized crime groups are not motivated by an ideology, while terrorist groups try to give their activities an altruistic aura to justify their acts and to solicit

The Weapons of Mass Destruction Connection

There is concern that organized crime groups, particularly Russian criminal organizations, have become involved in smuggling nuclear material that they are willing to sell to the highest bidder. However, few actual cases of sale of nuclear contraband have been recorded in the former Soviet Union or in the West, and even fewer of them involved the confiscation of material that could actually be used to make nuclear weapons. "Nevertheless, there is the possibility that finished nuclear material might actually exist on the black market or that non-weapon grade material might still be used destructively by terrorists" (Préfontaine and Dandurand 2004: 14).

Another concern is the use of biological and chemical weapons by terrorists. In practice, however, these weapons are difficult to build and to use, and only a small subset or terrorist groups is likely to possess the technological sophistication to effectively carry out chemical and biological attacks. There are suggestions that criminal organizations could play a role in helping terrorist groups acquire the weapons or the technology. "Such suggestions are not based on any hard evidence, nor do they seem to be based on an appreciation of the many reasons why a criminal organization would normally be quite reluctant to take the kind of risk involved in such transactions" (Préfontaine and Dandurand 2004: 15).

people's sympathy for their cause. Frank Hagan (2006) refers to this as *political* crime, committed for ideological purposes. Organized crime groups prefer to carry out their activities secretly, while terrorists seek to maximize media coverage and to promote their message and publicize their goals. While organized crime groups typically place significant restrictions on membership, terrorists actively recruit and typically enjoy sympathy from a segment of the population that identifies with their goals. Thus, whether an individual—ranging from George Washington to Osama bin Laden—is a patriot or a terrorist is not a relevant issue with respect to organized crime.

Terrorism: What Is It?

Just as there is no accepted definition of organized crime, *terrorism* also defies a universally accepted definition. Indeed, "many definitions of terrorism are, in fact, encoded political statements" (Combs 2003: 7). As opposed to organized crime, terrorism is inherently political—the ultimate political statement—and as such it is relative to one's political view. Since the term is pejorative, terrorism is a label most likely to be attached to the violent activities of political opponents: One person's terrorist is another person's freedom fighter—for example,

the British view of George Washington in contrast with that of revolutionary Americans.

There is also confusion over the terms *terror* and *terrorism*: "The object of military force, for example, is to strike terror into the heart of the enemy, and systematic terror has been a basic weapon in conflicts throughout history" (White 2006: 3). While the tactics of terrorists can appear to be the same as those of military action, such as bombings and hostage taking, their targets are frequently noncombatants. (Of course, the same can be said of the nuclear bombs dropped on Japanese cities in 1945.) For the terrorist, injury to the innocent "is not an undesirable accident or by-product [euphemistically called "collateral damage"], but the carefully sought consequence of a terrorist act" (Combs 2003: 12).

Terrorists often choose their targets at random, and thus there is little if any precautions that potential victims can take—victims are defenseless. Terrorism exploits death as a means to advertise their cause. Terrorists do not expect governments to capitulate; indeed, their activities are frequently designed to elicit an overreaction that will aid in winning hearts and minds (Danner 2005). Although a number of American Mafia Families probably benefited from the building of the World Trade Center, they were not looking to advertise their role or make a political statement. And with the exception of Colombia, "rarely do the large established crime organizations link with terrorist groups, because their long-term financial interests require the preservation of state structures" (Shelley et al. 2005: 1). Indeed, many traditional organized crime groups are politically quite conservative and supportive of their host governments, for example, Japanese *yakuza* (discussed in Chapter 9), Sicilian Mafia (discussed in Chapter 6), and the American Mafia (discussed in Chapters 4 and 5). The infamous Medellín drug cartel in Colombia used terrorist tactics in their battle with the Marxist revolutionary group known as M-19.

However defined, the various categories of terrorism may overlap, such as domestic and international, left- and right-wing, separatist and religious. The Ku Klux Klan and other hate groups, self-styled militia groups, and survivalists are domestic and right-wing, while the right-wing "Skinheads" and Neo-Nazis are active in Europe. The Weather Underground in the United States used violence during the 1970s to express left-wing views, while the Red Army did the same in 1970 in Germany, Italy, and Japan; and the separatist *Euzkadita Askatasuna* (ETA) uses violence against Spain in an effort to establish a Marxist independent Basque state. Al-Qaeda is the best-known example of a religious and international terrorist group whose activities often begin in one country and take place in another.

Some terrorists defy easy categorization, such as Theodore Kaczynski, the "Unabomber," and "ecoterrorists" like the Earth Liberation Front and Animal Liberation Front who use violence to promote animal rights and preserve wilderness. Some observers refer to state- or state-sponsored terrorism such as the Khmer Rouge slaughter in Cambodia during the 1970s, the Serbian militia massacres of Muslim men and rape of Muslim women in Bosnia during the 1990s, and the massacres of Tutsis by government-supported Hutus militias in Rwanda during the 1990s. But terrorism can be carried out by a single person—such as Ted Kaczynski, the "Unabomber" who was arrested in 1996—while organized crime by definition requires organization.

Similarity of Methods

Terrorist groups and drug trafficking organizations often rely on cell structures to accomplish their respective goals (discussed later). This enhances security by providing a degree of separation between the leadership and the rank-and-file. In addition, terrorists and drug traffickers use similar means to conceal profits and fundraising. They use informal transfer systems such as "hawala" (discussed in Chapter 14), and also rely on bulk cash smuggling, multiple accounts, and front organizations to launder money. Both make use of fraudulent documents such as passports and other identification to smuggle goods and weapons. Both fully exploit their networks of trusted couriers and contacts to conduct business. They use multiple cell phones and encrypted e-mails and are careful about what they say on the phone to increase communications security. The methods used for moving and laundering money for general criminal purposes are similar to those used to move money to support terrorist activities. Countries and jurisdictions that have poorly regulated banking structures allow both terrorist organizations and drug trafficking groups to use online transfers and accounts that do not require disclosure of owners (Beers and Taylor 2002).

One striking dissimilarity is the suicide bomber frequently used by Jihadist terrorists—unlikely (understatement) to be used by organized crime. A radical British Muslim is quoted as saying: "Even if my own family were killed by a Jihadist bomb, I would say it is the will of Allah" (Powell 2005: 56). "Organized crime's business is business. The less attention brought to their lucrative enterprises, the better. The goal of terrorism is quite the opposite. A wide-ranging public profile is often the desired effect" (Cilluffo 2000: Internet). Organized crime groups enjoy the shadows and do not seek to publicize their activities for public consumption. Al-Qaeda, on the other hand, distributed a video-tape depicting their second-in-command cutting off the head of an American journalist.

In sum, terrorist organizations and organized crime groups differ on means and ends. Both engage in organized criminal activity such as drug trafficking to support themselves, but terrorists use their funds to further political ends—to overthrow governments and impose their worldview. Organized crime instead seeks to corrupt government to gain immunity for their crimes. Rather than destruction, criminal organizations frequently form a parallel government while coexisting with the existing one. While members of organized crime are not motivated by an ideology and generally identify themselves as criminals, terrorist groups try to give their activities an altruistic aura to justify their acts and to solicit people's sympathy for their cause. Organized crime groups prefer to carry out their activities secretly, while terrorists seek to maximize media coverage to promote their message and publicize their goals.

Law enforcement resources diverted to fighting terrorism dilute government efforts against organized crime. But greater surveillance of our borders to fight terrorism also benefits efforts against drug smuggling. There is a parallel between the Organized Crime Control Act of 1970 and the USA Patriot Act (both discussed in Chapter 15) enacted in the wake of the September 11, 2001, destruction of the Twin Towers. Both provide the federal government with extraordinary powers

justified by "clear and present dangers," and both have been used against persons devoid of ties to organized crime or terrorism. For example, a Patriot Act provision that authorizes "secret warrants"—permits federal agents to search a home without immediately notifying the target that they have been there—has "been used in a wide variety of cases beyond terrorism, including child pornography, drug trafficking and organized crime" (Lichtblau 2005b: 19).

A terrorist group may abandon its political goals or the use of violence to achieve these goals. In either instance, some members no longer restrained by ideological ends may find that their skills lend themselves to achieving more personal goals. A transformation occurs as individual skills developed as terrorists and the advantages of organization are mobilized in the pursuit of pecuniary interests: terrorists become organized crime. There is evidence of this transformation in Northern Ireland where the Irish Republican Army has relinquished violence as an organizational tool. Glenn Curtis and Tara Karacan (2002: 4) refer to this as "fighters turned felons." If, for example, "narcotics trafficking proves lucrative beyond the immediate goal of paying for arms, the 'pure' ideology of a terrorist group such as the ETA may be diluted and some parts of the organization may 'wander off' into conventional criminal activity."

THE STRUCTURE OF ORGANIZED CRIME

The eight attributes of organized crime that we have examined can fit two contrasting organizational models: the *bureaucratic/corporate* and the *patron-client network*. Each organized crime group approximates one of these models viewed as a continuum. Thus, while international outlaw motorcycle clubs (discussed in Chapter 11) are clearly on the bureaucratic side of our continuum, the American Mafia (discussed in Chapters 4 and 5) is best understood according to the patron-client network model. Criminal organizations can be located

FIGURE 1.1 *Structure of an Organized Crime Group*

Patron–client network

Bureaucratic/corporate

along this continuum—for example, Colombians (discussed in Chapter 7) tend to organize along bureaucratic (that is, compartmentalized) lines, while Russians in the United States (discussed in Chapter 10) have a fluid structure that tends toward the patron-client network (see Figure 1.1).

The Bureaucratic/Corporate Model

The corporation, the police, and the military are examples of bureaucracies, that mode of organization essential for efficiently carrying out large-scale tasks. All bureaucracies are rational organizations sharing a number of attributes:

- A complicated hierarchy
- An extensive division of labor
- Positions assigned on the basis of skill
- Responsibilities carried out in an impersonal manner
- Extensive written rules and regulations
- Communication from the top of the hierarchy to persons on the bottom, usually in written (memo) form

Whenever an entity—club, business, crime group—continues to expand, at some point it will have to adopt the bureaucratic style of organization. For example, a "mom and pop grocery" need not have any of the attributes of a bureaucracy. The owners and workers are related, and

the structure is informal and kinship based. If the business expands—the owners establish many groceries—a formal hierarchy becomes necessary, as do skilled persons and a division of labor: there will be extensive written rules and regulations, and directives will be via the hierarchy. Thus, the model of organization adopted by an entity—legitimate or criminal—will depend on the scope of its operations and the organizational experience of its leaders. In Chapter 11, we will examine the structure of the international outlaw motorcycle club best explained by the military experience of its early members—the military is *the* quintessential bureaucracy.

A criminal organization structured along corporate/bureaucratic lines has inherent weaknesses:

- Communication from top management to operational-level personnel can be intercepted.
- Generating and maintaining written records endangers the entire organization.
- Successful infiltration at the lower level can jeopardize the entire organization.
- Death or incarceration of command personnel leaves dangerous gaps in operations.

These deficiencies can be countered by the use of the compartmentalized form of bureaucracy (see Figure 1.2). Members at the operational/street level are organized into cells and know only other members of their cell. If a cell is lost, the

FIGURE 1.2   *Compartmentalized Criminal Organization*

Central command: Located in a relatively safe haven, the central command oversees and coordinates operations through the controllers.

Controller: Responsible for overall operations of the several cells within a region, the controller reports to central command via cell phone or Internet.

Cell: Compartmentalization involves cells with about ten members, each operating independently—members of one cell typically do not know members of other cells. Operating within a geographic area, the head of each cell reports directly to a controller.

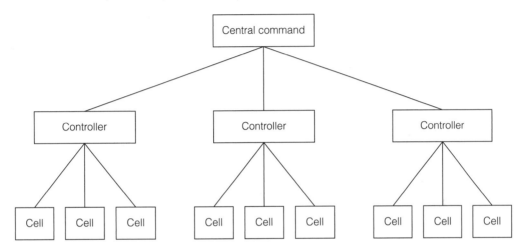

organization continues to function uninterrupted and the cell is eventually replaced. Cells are bundled under the direction of a controller who is not in direct contact with and may not even know the other controllers. A controller who is lost is quickly replaced by the central command that operates out of an area of relative safety.

Patron-Client Networks

Many aspects of bureaucracy are impractical for criminal organizations because they must be concerned with the very real possibility that communications are being monitored. The use of the telephone must be limited (often only to arrange for in-person meetings), and written communication is avoided. Information, as well as orders, money, and other goods, is transmitted on an intimate, face-to-face basis. Lengthy chains of command, characteristic of modern bureaucracy, are impractical for organized crime, and this limits the span of control. Randall Collins (1975) points out that control is a special problem for which bureaucracies develop to overcome. In the absence of bureaucracy, when the geographic range becomes too great, an organization collapses into feudalism. In organized crime, this can have deadly consequences: When Lucchese crime Family boss Vittorio ("Little Vic") Amuso and underboss Anthony ("Gaspipe") Casso found out that they had lost control of the New Jersey crew of the Family headed by capo Anthony Accetturo, they ordered Accetturo and his loyalists executed. They, in turn, ran to the authorities for protection, effectively shutting down Lucchese Family operations in the Garden State (Carlo 2008).

In fact, says Mark Moore (1987: 53), a highly centralized organization "tends to make the enterprise too dependent on the knowledge and judgment of the top management, and wastes the knowledge and initiative of subordinate managers who know more about their own capabilities and how they fit into a local environment of risks and opportunities." But the very informality of organized crime can bring other dangers. In 1977, for example, Ruby Stein, a major loan shark for the Gambino crime Family, was murdered by the Westies, a group of Irish-American criminals from New York's West Side, because the Westies owed Stein a considerable sum of money. The murderers dismembered their victim and stole his "black book" containing records of Stein's loans. Because there were no duplicate or backup records, the Gambino Family was unable to claim millions of dollars in outstanding loans (English 1990).

Decentralization in a criminal organization can be advantageous for both business and security reasons, notes Joseph Albini (1971: 285). He points out that the bureaucratic model would be a relatively easy target to move against: "All that would be necessary to destroy it would be to remove its top echelon." Instead, Albini argues, the syndicate's real power lies in its amorphous quality: "If a powerful syndicate figure is incarcerated, all that has really been severed is his position as a patron to his clients." If it so happens that another individual is in a position to assume this role, the clients may continue in the enterprise. The alternative is to find a new patron or to develop their own enterprises. Albini's point is supported by the deputy administrator of the Drug Enforcement Administration, who notes that the bureaucratic structure of Colombian cocaine cartels makes them vulnerable. The need to exercise effective command and control over a far-flung criminal enterprise "is the feature that law enforcement can use against them, turning their strength into a weakness. The communications structure of international organized crime operating in the United States is, therefore, the prime target for drug law enforcement" (Marshall 1999: 5).

A network consists of a collection of connected points or junctures. Every person is embedded in a social network, notes Jeremy Boissevain (1974: 24), "the chains of persons with whom a given person is in contact." Since contact can be through a chain of persons, an individual can send "messages" to far more people than he or she actually knows directly. These are the "friends of friends," a phrase that in Sicily refers to mafiosi: "Every individual provides a point at which networks interact. But not everyone

displays the same interest in and talent for cultivating relationships with strategic persons for profit" (Boissevain 1974: 147). To be successful, a member of organized crime, just like Sicilian mafiosi, must display such interest and talent. This is done by acting as a patron.

When a social exchange relationship (see Homans 1961; Blau 1964) becomes unbalanced, we have a patron-client relationship. The patron "provides economic aid and protection against both the legal and illegal exaction of authority. The client, in turn, pays back in more intangible assets"—for example, esteem and loyalty—and may also offer political or other important support, thus making the relationship reciprocal (Wolf 1966: 16–17). The patron acts as a power broker between the client and the wider society, both legitimate and illegitimate.

The member of the American Mafia, acting as a patron, controls certain resources as well as strategic contacts with people who control other resources directly or who have access to such persons. The member-as-patron can put a client "in touch with the right people." He can bridge communication gaps between the police and criminals, between businesspeople and syndicate-connected union leaders; he can transcend the world of business and the world of the illegitimate entrepreneur. He is able to perform important favors and be rewarded in return with money or power. There is a network surrounding the patron, a circle of dyadic relationships orbiting the organized crime member in which most clients have no relations with one another except through the patron.

The patron needs a great deal of time to manage his network adequately, develop and maintain contacts, provide services, enhance power and income, and keep well informed (Boissevain 1974). Since organized crime members do not usually have to maintain conventional schedules, they are free to "hang around," to pick up and disseminate important information. An organized crime patron may dominate a particular geographic area or industry. He will have available a network of informants and connections—for example, with the police and other officials, as well as with specialized criminal operatives such as papermen (persons who convert stolen "paper," such as stocks, bonds, and checks, into cash), *torches* (professional arsonists), musclemen or legbreakers, and enforcers. He is in a position to fence large amounts of stolen goods—he can truly "get it for you wholesale"—or to lend out various amounts of money at usurious interest—loansharking. He will act as a center for information (providing targets for professional burglars, for example), "license" criminal activities (for example, enable a high-stakes dice game to operate), and use his position to assist criminals in linking up for specialized operations (for example, finding a driver for a robbery or hijack team). He can provide firearms and autos and other items necessary for conventional criminal activity. Thus, despite their relatively small numbers, persons in organized crime can present a significant public threat—a single member can be at the center of, and act as a catalyst for, an extraordinary amount of criminal activity.

Criminal activities in his territory that are not under his patronage are "outlaw" operations whose participants act without his grace. If they are arrested, he will not intervene; if their activities conflict with those under his patronage, police raids or violence will result. When a member of the Genovese Family decided to deal with an independent bookmaker not under his patronage, he called upon a New York City Police Department detective (Manca and Cosgrove 1991: 129): "Later that day," the detective writes, "I drove down to Union Square. The bookie was so independent and small-time that he was running his own slips. I followed him into an apartment house, stuck a gun in his back, and forced him down to the basement. His knees were practically knocking. I grabbed this big manila envelope he was carrying, then handcuffed him to the boiler. He was begging me not to kill him. I emptied the envelope—money and slips fell out. There was about twelve hundred dollars. I scooped the money up, put it in my pocket. Then I picked up the betting slips and threw them in the boiler. The guy started to cry. I left him there, cuffed to the boiler."

When the Chicago Outfit crew headed by Rocky Infelise expanded into Lake County (just north of Cook County), gamblers were given a choice: pay street taxes, split the gambling business 50–50, turn it all over to the Outfit—or die. The body of one who failed to comply was found in the trunk of a car—"trunkin," as it is known in the Windy City, has been an Outfit favorite. Similar overtures were made to the proprietors of houses of prostitution and marginal businesses, such as bars with sex shows or adult bookstores, throughout Chicago and nearby suburbs. A number of those who resisted became murder victims.

Independent criminal operatives may be forced to pay tribute for "protection"—protection from violence that the organized crime member can inflict or cause to be inflicted. Professional criminals who are not necessarily part of organized crime will often pay financial tribute to an organized crime patron, indicating *rispetto*—respect—a concrete recognition of his power. This enables criminals to secure vital information and assistance and ensures that other criminals will not jeopardize their operations: *respect* demands recognition of the immunity belonging not only to the member but also to everything that he has to do with or to which, explicitly or implicitly, he has given a guarantee of security.

Vincent Siciliano (1970: 55) provides an example. He and his gang held up a card game that was under the patronage of the Genovese crime Family in New York—a "connected" game. And he was summoned: "When we got to the cafe and those big shots started laying down the law and telling us we knocked over one of their games, butter wouldn't melt in my mouth.

I told them I was careful to ask if the game has any connections, and the other guys agreed that nobody had any idea in the whole world that the game had any connections. The way we always put it (the way you still put it) is that we didn't know they were 'good people,' which is like saying the guy is an American or an official something. Part of some organization. Not an outlaw." Then they made Siciliano give back the money. When the married ex-cons Tom and Rosemarie began robbing Gambino Family social clubs, victims used their own investigative techniques. As Jerry Capeci (2003: 109), notes, although wiseguys "agree with many law enforcement officials about the necessity of the death penalty, they don't go along with things like jury trials." Tom and Rosemarie were in their car getting ready to do some Christmas shopping when each was shot in the head three times.

GLOBALIZATION OF ORGANIZED CRIME

"Recent changes in the global economy and in international political alignments have greatly benefited the criminal underworld" (Viano, Magallanes, and Bridel 2003: 3). The collapse of the Soviet Union was a pivotal historical event that intertwined with the rapid expansion of global markets—"money, goods and people have circulated with a rapidity and facility which were once unthinkable. . . . Whether in the developed or in the developing world, criminal organizations' scope of action and range of capabilities are undergoing a profound change" (Violante 2000: x). Furthermore, note Roy Godson and William Olson (1995: 19), the decline in political order and deteriorating economic circumstances have led to a growing underground economy that habituates people to working outside the legal framework. Easy access to arms, the massive flow of emigrants and refugees, and the normal difficulties involved in accomplishing meaningful international cooperation are working to the advantage of criminal organizations. And the "rise of better-organized, internationally based

criminal groups with vast financial resources is creating a new threat to the stability and security of international systems."

Ciudad del Este (CDE), "City of the East," of South America provides a microcosm of the nexus between organized crime and terrorism. This remote Paraguayan city is the center of a tri-border area that includes Brazil and Argentina where border controls barely exist—a free trade zone for contraband infested with criminals and terrorists. Originally a village, this rapidly expanding city of some 250,000 people was developed by the military dictator Julius Stroessner, who turned Paraguay into a haven for fugitives, including Nazi war criminals (Shelley et al. 2005). Today, organized crime groups of all types thrive in the tri-border area. It is a meeting place for the Yakuza (discussed in Chapter 9) as well as Colombian and other Latin American crime groups (discussed in Chapter 7) who pass illegal drugs through the area on their way to the ports of Brazil, Argentina, and Uruguay, and then into the United States and Europe. Chinese Triads such as the Fuk Ching, Big Circle Boys, and Flying Dragons (discussed in Chapter 9) are well established and believed to be the main force behind organized crime in the area (Shelley et al. 2005).

CDE is also a center of operations for several terrorist groups, including al-Qaeda, Hezbollah, Islamic Jihad, Gamaa Islamiya, and FARC (discussed in Chapter 7). Although local structures used by both terrorist and criminal organizations may overlap, cooperation is ad hoc. "There is no indication of any significant organizational overlap between criminal and terrorist groups" (Shelley et al. 2005: 61).

The Arab population, mostly Lebanese, has connections to Hezbollah, sending millions of dollars to that organization while automatic weapons are trafficked to the violent street gangs of Rio de Janeiro; stolen cars are available to anyone who wants them. Drugs and counterfeit consumer goods round out business portfolios. The area banks facilitate money laundering, although many make use of the *cambista* system: Money is dropped off with a *cambisto* who, for a service fee

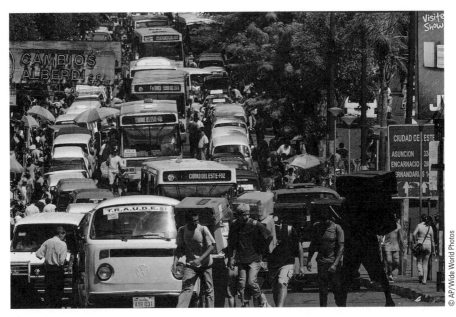

Crossing the Friendship Bridge into Ciudad del Este, "City of the East," Paraguay. *Ciudad del Este* provides a microcosm of the nexus between organized crime and terrorism. This remote city is the center of a tri-border area that includes Brazil and Argentina where border controls barely exist—a free trade zone for contraband infested with criminals and terrorists. Organized crime groups of all types thrive in the tri-border area, a meeting place for criminals who pass illegal drugs through the area on their way to the ports of Brazil, Argentina, and Uruguay, and then into the United States and Europe.

of 1 or 2 percent, arranges through his network for an equivalent amount of money to be picked up in another country (Samuels 2008).

Chapter 3 will show how Prohibition acted as a catalyst for the unprecedented mobilization of criminal organizations and the cooperative ventures of syndication. The international trade in liquor altered the heretofore local scope of most criminal organizations, whetting the appetite for further innovative opportunities and fueling the trade in heroin. The expanded capacity of contemporary criminal organizations derives from intensification of goods traditionally traded by organized crime, in particular, drugs, arms, and sex workers. In each case, the country of destination is different from that of its origins. Consignments transit across national boundaries and even oceans. As is the case with legitimate trade, arrangements need to be made that involve the use of banks, finance houses, customs formalities, and require ongoing relationships with criminal organizations of different countries. "These commercial necessities have created solid international relations between all the most dangerous criminal organizations" (Violante 2000: ix). In 1994, French intelligence monitored a meeting of representatives of the Gambino Family, Japanese *yakuza*, and Colombian, Russian, and Chinese crime bosses: "The apparent purpose of the meeting was to subdivide Western Europe for drugs, prostitution, smuggling and extortion rackets." United States officials believe that other meetings have since taken place on chartered yachts in the Mediterranean (Jamieson 2000: 193).

In Chapter 2, we will discuss theories that attempt to explain the existence of organized crime.

SUMMARY

- Although there is no generally accepted definition of *organized crime*, eight attributes help distinguish it from terrorists and groups of conventional criminals: (1) has no political goals, (2) hierarchical, (3) has a limited or exclusive membership, (4) constitutes a unique subculture, (5) perpetuates itself, (6) exhibits a willingness to use illegal violence and bribery, (7) monopolistic, and (8) governed by explicit rules and regulations.
- The criminality of persons in organized crime differs from that of conventional criminals because their organizational affiliation provides a form of credentialing and networking that facilitates cooperation between criminals that would not otherwise occur, which allows them to commit crimes of a different variety and on a larger scale than their less organized colleagues.

- Although organized crime and terrorism differ in their goals, with terrorism being inherently political and organized crime having more pecuniary goals, they frequently use the same tactics, their financial activities may overlap or intertwine, and at times their relationship becomes symbiotic.
- Contemporary organized crime can manifest two contrasting organizational models that represent two ends of a continuum: the *bureaucratic/corporate* and the *patron-client network*. Criminal groups, if they are to be defined as *organized*, can be located somewhere along this continuum.
- Criminal organizations, if they find it necessary to organize in a bureaucratic fashion, will typically manifest a compartmentalized version.
- The collapse of the Soviet Union has intertwined with the rapid expansion of global markets, providing greater opportunity for transnational organized crime.

REVIEW QUESTIONS

1. How does the criminality of persons in organized crime differ from that of conventional criminals?
2. What are the eight attributes of organized crime?
3. What are the attributes of a bureaucracy?
4. What are the advantages of compartmentalization?
5. How does the patron-client network model of organized crime differ from the bureaucratic/corporate model?
6. What is the role of a patron in organized crime?
7. How can a member of organized crime act as a catalyst for a great deal of conventional criminal activity?
8. How does an organizational affiliation enhance the ability of a criminal to engage in illegal activities?
9. In the American Mafia, how does being a "made guy" provide a form of franchise?
10. How does terrorism differ from organized crime? In what ways do they overlap?
11. What explains the globalization of organized crime?

© Darren McCollester/Getty Images

C H A P T E R

2

Explaining Organized Crime

Chapter 1 explored the issue of defining organized crime and presented the structures it can manifest, and Chapter 3 will examine its development. But what explains the existence of organized crime (OC)? That is the subject of this chapter. Organized crime has been subjected to only limited attempts at explanation, and this chapter will examine relevant theories in sociology and psychology. As sparse as the sociological literature is on organized crime, psychology provides even less, though some psychological theories offer insight. In this chapter we will draw from the two main streams of psychology, clinical and behavioral, to offer psychological explanations for organized crime.

THE SOCIOLOGY OF ORGANIZED CRIME

Although sociologists have offered a number of theories to help explain crime and criminal behavior, rarely have these been directed specifically at organized crime. Nevertheless, some sociological theories of crime and deviance provide insight into organized crime, and they will be examined in this chapter.

The Strain of Anomie

Building on a concept originated by the nineteenth-century French sociologist Émile Durkheim (1951), in 1938—during the Great Depression—Robert K. Merton set forth a social and cultural explanation for deviant behavior in the United States. To Merton, organized crime is a normal response to pressures exerted on certain persons by the social structure. He points to an American preoccupation with economic success—*pathological materialism*. During the 1830s, a visitor from France, Alexis de Tocqueville, wrote: "It is odd to watch with what feverish ardor the Americans pursue prosperity and how they are tormented by the shadowy suspicion that they may have not have chosen the shortest route to get it" (1966: 536). According to Merton, it is the goal that is emphasized, not the means, which are at best only a secondary consideration. "There may develop a disproportionate, at times, a virtually exclusive stress upon the value of specific goals, involving relatively slight concern with the institutionally appropriate modes of attaining these goals" (1938: 673).

This being the case, the only factors limiting goal achievement are technical, not moral or legal: "[E]mphasis on the goals of monetary success and material property leads to dominant concern with technological and social instruments designed to produce the desired result, inasmuch as institutional controls become of secondary importance. In such a situation, innovation [such as organized crime] flourishes as the range of means employed is broadened" (Merton 1938: 673). Thus, in American society, "the pressure of prestige-bearing success tends to eliminate the effective social constraint over means employed to this end. 'The-ends-justifies-the-means' doctrine becomes a guiding tenet for action when the cultural structure unduly exalts the end and the social organization unduly limits possible recourse to approved means" (1938: 681). The activities of earlier capitalists, the unscrupulous "Robber Barons" (discussed in Chapter 3), exemplify the spirit that Merton refers to as *innovation*. Taking advantage of every (legitimate and illegitimate) opportunity, these men became the embodiment of the great American success story. However, the opportunity for economic success is not equally distributed, and the immigrants who followed these men to America found many avenues from "rags to riches" significantly limited if not already closed.

Some immigrants recognized that the cards were stacked against them, and as a result, organized crime flourished. Writing several years before Merton, Louis Robinson (1933: 16) spoke of an American credo according to which "we dare not or at least will not condemn the criminal's goal, because it is also our goal. We want to keep the goal ourselves and damn the criminal for pursuing it in the only way he knows how."

> The methods which criminals use in attaining our common goal of wealth may, of course, differ from those which the non-criminal classes use. But this is to be expected. They are probably not in a position to employ our methods. We can think of a variety of reasons why a man without capital or without education or without industrial skill or without this or that advantage or handicapped by any one of several factors which anyone could easily name would be forced

to seek the common goal by means differing from those employed by another man better situated or endowed. In other words, he would *play the game differently*. (1933: 15–16; emphasis added)

Anomie results when numbers of people are confronted by the contradiction between goals and means and "become estranged from a society that promises them in principle what they are deprived of in reality" (Merton 1964: 218). Despite numerous success stories, "We know in this same society that proclaims the right, and even the duty, of lofty aspirations for all, men do not have equal access to the opportunity structure" (1964: 218). Yet those with ready access to success ("born with a silver spoon") *and* those who are at a distinct disadvantage are constantly exposed to the rewards of "fame and fortune" by the mass media. For some, particularly the disadvantaged, anomie is the result. Merton states there are five modes of individual adaptation to this phenomenon: conformity, ritualism, rebellion, retreatism, and innovation. We are concerned only with the last adaptation—*innovation*—since it includes organized criminal activity for those who would *play the game differently*.

British sociologists Ian Taylor, Paul Walton, and Jock Young (1973: 97) summarize the anomic condition in the United States: "The 'American Dream' urges all citizens to succeed whilst distributing the opportunity to succeed unequally: the result of this social and moral climate, inevitably, is innovation by the citizenry—the adoption of illegitimate means to pursue and obtain success." However, "routine" pedestrian criminal acts do not lead to any significant level of economic success. Innovation, then, is the adoption of sophisticated, well-planned, skilled, organized criminality.

Although *strain* can help explain why some persons from disadvantaged groups become involved in organized crime, it fails to provide a satisfying explanation for the continued existence of the American Mafia. In other words, even though poverty and limited economic opportunity can certainly impel one toward innovative activities, they do not explain why middle-class youngsters become involved in organized crime or why crimes by the wealthy and the powerful—for example, massive savings and loan industry fraud,[1] securities fraud, insider trading, collusive agreements—continue to be a problem in the United States. Perhaps the mind-set we are referring to as "wiseguy" transcends socioeconomic boundaries. In fact, organized criminal activity on a rather outrageous scale, for example, by Robber Barons, without necessarily being connected to conditions of *strain*, has been an important part of American history.

A question remains: Why do some persons suffering from anomie turn to criminal innovation, whereas others do not? Edwin Sutherland, the "father" of American criminology, provides an answer: *differential association*.

Differential Association

According to Sutherland (1973), all behavior—lawful and criminal—is learned. The principal part of learning occurs within intimate personal groups. What is learned depends on the intensity, frequency, and duration of the association. When these variables are sufficient and the associations are criminal, the actor learns the techniques of committing crime and the drives, attitudes, and rationalizations that add up to a favorable precondition to criminal behavior. The balance between noncriminal and criminal behaviors is tipped in favor of the latter.

Learning the techniques of sophisticated criminality requires the proper environment—ecological niches or *enclaves* where delinquent or criminal subcultures (discussed later) flourish and this education is available. In a capitalist society, socioeconomic differentials relegate some persons to an environment wherein they experience a compelling sense of strain—anomie—as well as differential association. In the environment where organized crime has traditionally thrived, strain is intense. Conditions of severe deprivation are coupled with readily available success models and

associations that are innovative, such as racketeers and drug dealers. This makes certain *enclaves* characterized by social disorganization and delinquent or criminal subcultures spawning grounds for organized crime:

> Various types of people tend to seek out others like themselves and live close together. Located within these distinctive clusters are specialized commercial enterprises and institutions that support the inhabitants' special ways of life. . . . Each distinctive group, along with its stores and institutions, occupies a geographic area that becomes intimately associated with the group. Through this linkage, areas acquire symbolic qualities that include their place names and social histories. Each place, both as a geographic entity and as a space with social meaning, also tends to be an object of residents' attachments and an important component of their identities. For example, people living in Little Italy or Chinatown think of themselves as Italian or Chinese, but their place of residence is also a prominent part of their self-concepts. . . . [The] enclave has some characteristics of a subculture, in which a group of people shares common traditions and values that are ordinarily maintained by a high rate of interaction within the group. (Abrahamson 1996: 1, 3)

Instead of conforming to conventional norms, some persons, through differential association, organize their behavior according to the norms of a delinquent or criminal group to which they belong or with which they identify. This is most likely to occur in environments characterized by relative social disorganization, where familial and communal controls are ineffective in exerting a conforming influence. In certain areas—enclaves with strong traditions of organized crime, be they in Chicago, Medellín, Odessa, or Sicily—young persons stand a greater chance of being exposed to criminal norms. In these areas persons exhibiting criminal norms are often well integrated into the community, and such areas are the breeding ground for

---

[1]See Tillman and Pontell (1995).

delinquent subcultures and entrants into organized crime (Kobrin 1966).

Subcultures and Social Disorganization

Culture refers to a source of patterning in human conduct: it is the sum of patterns of social relationships and shared meanings by which people give order, expression, and value to common experiences. The strength of a culture is determined by the degree of commitment of its members: culture is a valued heritage. A *subculture* "implies that there are value judgments or a social value system which is apart from a larger or central value system. From the viewpoint of this larger dominant culture, the values of the subculture set the latter apart and prevent total integration, occasionally causing open or covert conflicts" (Wolfgang and Ferracuti 1967: 99). "Subcultures are patterns of values, norms, and behavior which have become traditional among certain groups. These groups may be of many types, including occupational and ethnic groups, social classes, occupants of 'closed institutions' [for example, prisons and mental hospitals] and various age grades." They are "important frames of reference through which individuals and groups see the world and interpret it" (Short 1968: 11).

Central to the issue of culture versus subculture are *norms*, "group-held prescriptions for or prohibitions against certain conduct" (Wolfgang and Ferracuti 1967: 113). Norms are general rules about how to behave and expectations that are predictive of behavior. These rules and expectations are approved by the vast majority of a society, which provides rewards or punishments for conformity or violation. "The 'delinquent subculture' is characterized principally by conduct that reflects values antithetical to the surrounding culture" (1967: 110). Subcultural theory explains criminal behavior as learned; the subcultural delinquent has learned values that are deviant. Ideas about society lead to criminal behavior. A number of studies indicate that delinquent youths hold values that differ markedly from those of nondelinquents. Indeed, they may view their criminal behavior as

morally wrong, but this is not the controlling attitude. Being right or wrong in terms of the wider society is simply not a guidepost for behavior. Nonconventional behavior is admired—the ability to fight, to win at gambling (Elliott, Huizinga, and Ageton 1985).

The connection between subcultural deviance and organized crime was revealed in an interview with an experienced investigator:

> They saw the Outfit [Chicago organized crime] guys, and gave them deference. It's in the culture. They don't grow up to believe this is wrong; it's a perverted sense of values: Knockin' down an old lady to take her purse; killing the clerk at the store for a few bucks, that's wrong. But everything to do with organized crime is perfectly acceptable. They know it's illegal, but who cares. . . . There's one group, for example, who we first noticed in 1990, '91, who call themselves the "Boys in the 'hood." There are about fifty or sixty of them, many of whom are now associates of the street crews. We had some as young as sixteen, but usually eighteen, nineteen, and usually from Elmwood Park, Melrose Park, the Northwest Side of Chicago [a residential area with many Italian Americans, and police officers and firefighters]. They were doing any scam that the Outfit would let them do—major burglaries, jewelry thefts, drug sales, credit card fraud. Many of them are relatives of Outfit members. Many of them now—they're in their twenties— work for the Elmwood Park [Taylor Street] crew. (Scarmella 1998)

Clifford R. Shaw and Henry D. McKay, sociologists at the University of Chicago, used that city as a laboratory for their study of patterns of criminality during the 1920s and 1930s.[2] They found that certain clearly identifiable neighborhoods maintained a high level of criminality over many decades despite changes in ethnic composition.

---

[2]Despite the prominence of organized crime in Chicago during this period, the University of Chicago sociologists did not show much scholarly interest in the phenomenon (Reynolds 1995).

Thus, although one ethnic group replaced another, the rate of criminality remained constant. What was it about the environment of these neighborhoods that made them criminogenic?

According to Shaw and McKay (1972: 72), such neighborhoods are characterized by attitudes and values that are conducive to delinquency and crime, particularly organized crime:

> The presence of a large number of adult criminals in certain areas means that children there are in contact with crime as a career and with the criminal way of life, symbolized by OC. In this type of organization can be seen the delegation of authority, the division of labor, the specialization of function, and all the other characteristics common to well-organized business institutions wherever found. . . .
>
> The heavy concentration of delinquency in certain areas means that boys living in these areas are in contact not only with individuals who engage in proscribed activity but also with groups which sanction such behavior and exert pressure upon their members to conform to group standards. (1972: 174)

A disruption of the social order is associated with high rates of delinquency in a community, the result of a breakdown in mechanisms of social control. In many U.S. cities around the turn of the century, the social order was disrupted by the combined interactive effects of industrialization, immigration, and urbanization. Deviant traditions developed and competed with conventional norms; in some communities, deviant norms won out. Once established, these norms took root in areas that, according to Shaw and McKay, are characterized by attitudes and values that are conducive to delinquency and crime, thus creating a subculture of crime. The attitudes and values, as well as the techniques of organized criminality, are transmitted culturally. "Delinquent boys in these areas have contact not only with other delinquents who are their contemporaries but also with older offenders, who in turn had contact with delinquents preceding them, and so on back to the earliest history of the neighborhood. This contact means that the traditions of delinquency can be and are transmitted down through successive generations of boys, in much the same way that language and other social forms are transmitted" (1972: 174).

Back in the 1920s, John Landesco (1968) found that organized crime in Chicago could be explained by the prevalence of social disorganization in the wider society (during the period of Prohibition) and by the distinct social organization of urban slums from which members of organized crime emerge. "Once a set of cultural values is created and established—either because of economic factors or intellectual or moral transformations—they tend to become autonomous in their impact. From that point on, they can influence human relations independently of their original sources. And since they are, as a rule, accepted uncritically and through the most inadvertent process of socialization, they are regarded as normal and inevitable within each cultural system" (Saney 1986: 35).

In other words, the roots and culture of particular neighborhoods explain why gangsters come from clearly delineated areas "where the gang tradition is old" (Landesco 1968: 207) and where adolescents, through differential association, can absorb the attitudes and skills necessary to enter the world of adult organized crime. Indeed, in such neighborhoods, organized crime can provide a level of social control—limiting predatory crime, for example—that would otherwise be absent. At night, in an organized crime–dominated neighborhood in Brooklyn, a young woman did not realize she was being followed as she approached the door to her home. The young man following her did not realize that he was being watched. His attempt at a knifepoint robbery was foiled by several large men who quickly carried him up the stairs. An observer recalls: "I could make out the small roof wall on the front of the building—it was made of brick—and then I saw the guy launched right over it into the air. He hung there for just a second, flailing arms like a broken helicopter, and then he came down hard and splattered all over the street" (Pileggi 1990: 40). As ex-FBI agent Joe

Piston notes: "Neighborhoods that are dominated by wiseguys are considered to be under the protection of these wiseguys. There are far fewer robberies, rapes, or muggings in wiseguy neighborhoods than even the safest precincts of the city" (Pistone 2004: 76)

Inadequate familial socialization prevents some persons from conforming to the conventional norms of the wider society. Through differential association, some of these persons organize their behavior according to the norms of a delinquent or criminal subculture with which they identify or to which they belong. This is most likely to occur in environments characterized by relative social disorganization, where familial and communal controls are ineffective in exerting a conforming influence. In his classic study of Chicago street gangs originally published in 1927, Frederic Thrasher (1968: 270) notes: "Experience in a gang of the predatory type usually develops in the boy an attitude of indifference to law and order—one of the basic traits of the finished gangster." Thrasher (1968: 273) points out: "If the younger undirected gangs and clubs of the gang type, which serve as training schools for delinquency, do not succeed in turning out the finished criminal, they often develop a type of personality which may well foreshadow the gangster and the gunman." In the Chicago of the Prohibition era, there was no hard-and-fast dividing line between gangs of boys and youths, and adult criminal organizations (1968: 281): "They merge into each other by imperceptible gradations."

To survive, an organized crime group must have "an institutionalized process for inducting new members and inculcating them with the values and ways of behaving of the social system" (Cressey 1969: 263). Donald Cressey notes: "In some neighborhoods all three of the essential ingredients of an effective recruiting process are in operation: inspiring aspiration for membership, training for membership and selection for membership (1969: 236)." In his research, Gerald Suttles (1968) refers to areas from which members of organized crime have typically emerged as *defended neighborhoods*: recognized ecological niches whose inhabitants form cohesive groupings and seal themselves off

through the efforts of delinquent gangs, restrictive covenants, and a forbidding reputation. Such neighborhoods have traditionally provided the recruiting grounds that ensure the continuity of organized crime.

In such communities, the conventional and criminal value systems are highly integrated. Leaders of organized criminal enterprises "frequently maintain membership in such conventional institutions of their local communities as churches, fraternal and mutual benefit societies, and political parties" (Kobrin 1966: 156). Formal and informal political, economic, and religious ties provide both illegitimate and legitimate opportunities. These leaders are able to control violent and delinquent behavior in their domain—they are effective instruments of social control. "Everyone," particularly would-be miscreants, "knows" not to "mess around" in certain neighborhoods. And those who do not "know" have suffered serious consequences—selling drugs in one Chicago suburb, for example, resulted in mutilated corpses. In the Italian area of New York's Greenwich Village, "street corner boys" enforced the social order—made sure the streets were safe. And their self-appointed role was backed by the formidable reputation of the neighborhood's organized crime figures. For this protection, neighborhood residents reciprocated by providing "wiseguys" with a "safe haven" (Tricarico 1984).

Nicholas Pileggi (1985: 37–38) describes a defended neighborhood in Brooklyn:

In Brownsville–East New York wiseguys were more than accepted—they were protected. Even the legitimate members of the community—the merchants, teachers, phone repairmen, garbage collectors, bus depot dispatchers, housewives, and old-timers sunning themselves along the Conduit Drive—all seemed to keep an eye out to protect their local hoods. The majority of the residents, even those not directly related by birth or marriage to wiseguys, had certainly known the local rogues most of their lives. There was the nodding familiarity of neighborhood. In the area it was impossible to betray old friends, even those old friends who had grown up to be racketeers.

The extraordinary insularity of these old-world mob-controlled sections, whether Brownsville–East New York, the South Side of Chicago, or Federal Hill in Providence, Rhode Island, unquestionably helped to nurture the mob.

Recruitment into organized crime is made viable because "in the type of community under discussion boys may more or less realistically recognize the potentialities for personal progress in the local society through success in delinquency. In a general way, therefore, delinquent activity in these areas constitutes a training ground for the acquisition of skill in the use of violence, concealment of offense, evasion of detection and arrest, and the purchase of immunity from punishment" (Kobrin 1966: 156).

Robert Lombardo, a former organized crime investigator and ranking Cook County police official, points out that prospective members of organized crime "typically come from communities which share collective representations and moral sentiments which allow them to recognize the pursuit of a career in the underworld as a legitimate way of life" (1979: 18; 1994a). Young men from these areas dress in a certain style—"gangster chic"—and congregate in social clubs and night spots where they are able to associate with the men who have already been allowed entry into organized crime. They are ready and eager to show their mettle by accepting assignments from "goodfellas."

Even those who have moved to suburban locations—if they accept the "wiseguy" credo—gravitate back to the 'hood. In Chicago this phenomenon has been referred to as the "suburbanization of the mob"—young men who have known only middle-class living conditions becoming part of organized crime. Like the members of outlaw motorcycle clubs discussed in Chapter 11, these young men are attracted to a subcultural lifestyle but not necessarily by the potential financial rewards offered by organized crime. For example, Salvatore ("Solly D.") DeLaurentis

(b. 1938), who was raised in the Taylor Street neighborhood in Chicago, aspired to be a "gangster"—a term he uses to describe himself—since his earliest days. But his family moved out to suburban Lake County, and Solly D. found himself cut off from his career path: Lake County lacked the critical mass of older criminals and their young associates/wannabes. So DeLaurentis gradually made connections back in the old neighborhood and eventually became a member of the Infelice crew (discussed in Chapter 5) in charge of Lake County. (He is currently serving an 18-year sentence for a racketeering conviction.)

In Chicago, even senior members of the Outfit who reside in suburban locations frequent the restaurants, nightspots, and social clubs back in the 'hood. James D. ("Jimmy D.") Antonio, the ranking member of the Grand Avenue crew, resided in suburban Skokie. But until his death in 1993 from an auto accident, the 65-year-old operated a storefront social club in the Grand Avenue neighborhood, which even sponsored a boys' baseball team for neighborhood youths (O'Brien 1993). But many "mob neighborhoods" are changing. In one of them, a southwest Brooklyn area known as Bensonhurst whose main commercial strip is Bath Avenue, it is nearly impossible to find any trace of its mob past (Fernandez 2007).

According to Irving Spergel (1964), in such communities life in organized crime is considered acceptable and therefore a legitimate aspiration for young persons. Although these communities provide an appropriate learning environment for the acquisition of values and skills associated with the performance of criminal roles, integration into organized crime requires selection and tutelage in the process of acquiring recognition—and only a select few are given recognition by those who control admission. Entry into organized crime is characterized by *differential opportunity*.

Differential Opportunity

In agreement with Merton, Richard Cloward and Lloyd Ohlin (1960) note that American preoccupation with economic success, coupled with socioeconomic stratification, relegates many persons to an environment wherein they experience strain: "Many lower-class male adolescents experience extreme deprivation born of the certainty that their position in the economic structure is relatively fixed and immutable—a desperation made all the more poignant by their exposure to a cultural ideology in which failure to orient oneself upward is regarded as a moral defect and failure to become mobile as proof of it" (1960: 107).

Conditions of severe deprivation with extremely limited access to ladders of legitimate success result in collective adaptations in the form of delinquent subcultures. Cloward and Ohlin distinguish three types:

1. *Retreatist subculture*: Activities in which drug usage is the primary focus; the anomic condition leads the sufferer to reject the goal of economic success in favor of a more easily obtainable one— the "high."
2. *Conflict subculture*: Gang activities devoted to violence and destructive acting out as a way of gaining status. As with retreatists, the anomic condition leads to a rejection of economic success in favor of a more easily obtainable goal.
3. *Criminal/rackets subculture*: Gang activity devoted to utilitarian criminal pursuits, an adaptation that begins to approximate organized crime.

Anomie alone, note Cloward and Ohlin, is not sufficient to explain participation in organized crime: what is necessary is cultural transmission (Shaw and McKay) through differential association (Sutherland). However, Cloward and Ohlin point out that illegitimate opportunity for success, like legitimate opportunity, is not equally distributed throughout society (1960: 145): "Having decided that he 'can't make it legitimately,' he cannot simply choose from an array of illegitimate means, all equally available to him." In other words, access to criminal ladders of success is no more freely available than are noncriminal alternatives:

Only those neighborhoods in which crime flourishes as a stable, indigenous institution are fertile learning environments for the young. Because these environments afford integration of different age-levels of offender, selected young people are exposed to "differential association" through which tutelage is provided and criminal values and skills are acquired. To be prepared for the role may not, however, ensure that the individual will ever discharge it. One important limitation is that more youngsters are recruited into these patterns of differential association than the adult criminal structure can possibly absorb. Since there is a surplus of contenders for these elite positions, criteria and mechanisms of selection must be evolved. Hence a certain proportion of those who aspire may not be permitted to engage in the behavior for which they have prepared themselves. (Cloward and Ohlin 1960: 148)

The increasing scale and complexity of modern life has altered the social structure of urban communities. Greater social mobility has marked the end of many ethnically defined and defended neighborhoods. Racket subcultures vanish as residents became educated, find well-paying jobs, and move to the suburbs. But in some suburbs—think of where Tony Soprano, in the television show *The Sopranos*, lives—the tradition has moved with its adherents.

Although various types of conventional crime are open to everyone, "things are somewhat more complicated where organized crime in concerned" (Kleemans and de Poot 2008: 74). In organized crime, social relations are of greater importance, and illegal business relationships have to be built up: "Not everyone has suitable social ties and building up such relationships takes time and energy" (2008: 75). This is of particular importance in criminal activities that are transnational: smuggling drugs, arms, stolen vehicles, human trafficking for sexual exploitation, and money laundering. The very complexity of transnational organized crime may require going beyond one's own social circle. This is facilitated by the credentialing discussed in Chapter 1, and acquiring credentials requires affiliation with a known and respected (at least in criminal circles) criminal organization. In some (perhaps many) cases, however, persons with specific skills or occupations, such as those involving transportation and finance, may be drawn into a criminal organization through a serendipitous social relationship with an organized crime network—*social opportunity* (Kleemans and de Poot 2008). Such persons are relatively late starters who do not follow a career path from juvenile delinquency to adult crime.

In neighborhoods where the organized crime tradition continues, or among persons who have access to a requisite social network, why do young people who have the opportunity choose not to become contenders for positions in organized crime? *Social control theory* offers an explanation.

Social Control Theory

Social control refers to those processes by which the community influences its members toward conformance with established norms of behavior. Social control theorists argue that the relevant question is not, "Why do persons become involved in crime, organized or otherwise?" but rather, "Why do most persons conform to societal norms?" If, as control theorists generally assume, most persons are sufficiently motivated by the potential rewards to commit criminal acts, why do only a few make crime a career? According to social control theorists, "delinquent acts result when an individual's bond to society is weak or broken" (Hirschi 1969: 16). The strength of this bond is determined by external and internal restraints. In other words, external and internal restraints determine whether we move in the direction of crime or of law-abiding behavior.

External restraints include social disapproval linked to public shame and/or social ostracism and fear of punishment. In other words, people are typically deterred from criminal behavior by the possibility of being caught and the punishment that can result, ranging from public shame to imprisonment (and, in extreme cases, capital punishment). In neighborhoods or among subcultural groups with moral sentiments favorable to organized crime, such public shame/social ostracism is ineffective. Only the threat of imprisonment can offer a deterrent.

The strength of official deterrence—force of law—is measured according to two dimensions: risk versus reward. *Risk* involves the ability of the criminal justice system to detect, apprehend, and convict the offender. The amount of risk is weighed against the potential rewards. Both risk and reward, however, are relative to one's socioeconomic situation. In other words, the less one has to lose, the greater is the willingness to engage in risk. In the words of a Bob Dylan song (*Like a Rolling Stone*), "When you ain't got nothin', you got nothin' to lose." And the greater the reward, the greater is the willingness to engage in risk. This theory explains why persons in deprived economic circumstances would be more willing to engage in criminal behavior. However, the potential rewards and a perception of relatively low risk can also explain why persons in more advantaged economic circumstances would engage in remunerative criminal behavior such as corporate crime.

Internal restraints include what psychoanalytic theory refers to as the *superego* (discussed later): an unconscious, yet powerful, conscience-like mechanism that provides a sense of guilt. According to Sigmund Freud, conscience is not something that is a part of us from the very beginning of our lives. It is a controlling mechanism that develops out of the relationship with, and influence of, our parents. In the adult who experienced "healthy" parental relationships as a child, the superego takes the place of the controlling parental function. Dysfunction during early stages of childhood development, or parental influences that are not normative, result in an adult who is devoid of prosocial internal constraints; some refer to this as psycho- or sociopathology, or antisocial personality disorder (ASP), characterized by a combination of antisocial behavior and emotional detachment (discussed later).

Ethnic Succession

As will be discussed in subsequent chapters, during the decades following World War II, organized crime underwent considerable change. It became increasingly clear that in the United

States, organized crime was dominated mainly by Italians—the Irish, except for small pockets in New York and Boston, were no longer involved. And although the sons of Jewish immigrants played a vital role in organized crime, by the third generation, the Jews had moved out. Jackson Toby (1958: 548) explains:

Jews and Italians came to the United States in large numbers at about the same time—the turn of the century—and both settled in urban areas. There was, however, a very different attitude toward intellectual accomplishments in the two cultures. Jews from Eastern Europe regarded study as the most important activity for an adult male. The rabbi enjoyed great prestige because he was a scholar, a teacher, a logician. He advised the community on the application of the Written and Oral Law. Life in America gave a secular emphasis to the Jewish reverence for learning. Material success is a more important motive than salvation for American youngsters, Jewish as well as Christian, and secular education is better training for business and professional careers than Talmudic exegesis. Nevertheless, intellectual achievement continued to be valued by Jews—and to have measurable effects. Second-generation Jewish students did homework diligently, got high grades, went to college in disproportionate numbers, and scored high on intelligence tests. Two thousand years of preparation lay behind them.

Immigrants from southern Italy, on the other hand, tended to regard formal education either as a frill or as a source of dangerous ideas from which the minds of the young should be protected. They remembered Sicily, where a child who attended school regularly was a rarity. There, youngsters were needed . . . only to help on the farm. Equally important was the fact that hard-working peasants could not understand why their children should learn classical Italian (which they would not speak at home) or geography (when they would not travel in their lifetimes

more than a few miles from their birthplace). Sicilian parents suspected that education was an attempt on the part of Roman officials to subvert the authority of the family. In the United States, many southern Italian immigrants maintained the same attitudes. They resented compulsory school attendance laws and prodded their children to go to work and become economic assets as soon as possible. They encouraged neglect of schoolwork and even truancy. They did not realize that education has more importance in an urban-industrial society than in a semi-feudal one. With supportive motivation from home lacking, the second-generation Italian boys did not make the effort of Jewish contemporaries. Their teachers tried to stuff the curriculum into their heads in vain. Their lack of interest was reflected not only in low marks, retardation, truancy, and early school leaving; it even resulted in poor scores on intelligence tests. They accepted their parents' conception of the school as worthless and thereby lost their best opportunity for social ascent.

The pool of available candidates for membership in organized crime dwindled in Jewish communities. In Italian communities it remained adequate enough; the large-scale organizations needed to profit from Prohibition were no longer necessary. In Chicago, for example, during the height of Prohibition, Al Capone is reputed to have employed 700 gunmen for an organization that involved thousands of persons, while contemporary estimates of the size of the Chicago Outfit have ranged only as high as 130. The largest of the crime Families, the Genovese Family of New York, is estimated to have no more than 400 members. These core members, however, have associates, and the total number of criminal actors participating directly or indirectly in a crime group's enterprises is many times the size of the core membership at any given time.

Noting the small size of Italian American crime groups and the absence of armed retainers, Peter Reuter (1983: xi) has concluded: "My analysis suggests that the Mafia may be a paper tiger, rationally reaping the returns from its reputation while no longer maintaining the forces that generated the reputation." He theorizes that having established a dominant position, an unchallenged monopoly of force, the Mafia can depend on its fearsome reputation, an asset that can be substituted for personnel costs that would be incurred by maintaining armed forces. Reuter states that challenges to Mafia power in black and Hispanic communities have not "generated any effort by the Mafia to assert control through superior violence" (1983: 136; also 1995). Reuter theorizes that this may result from the lack of available force or simply from a cost-benefit analysis that militates against its use—excessive force attracts law enforcement attention and is bad for business in general.

Reuter notes, however, that challenges to the Mafia outside of black and Hispanic communities have not been noticeable. The structure of Italian American organized crime groups provides an explanation. As noted in Chapter 1, business activities are typically decentralized, often franchised, while violence is not. The Mafia is often "invisible"; that is, members usually avoid directly operating illegal enterprises such as gambling or marginal businesses such as "topless bars" or "strip joints." Instead, they often finance or "license" such enterprises, sometimes receiving payments for restricting entry or competition, sometimes providing no service—simple extortion. How would a competing group set out to deal with this operation? The most obvious method would be a direct attack on its members. But they do not reside, meet, or otherwise assemble in significant numbers, and they may be unknown to anyone except persons intimately involved in the local criminal underworld. The decentralized nature of the organization would render a frontal assault unproductive. While a number of members and associates could be killed here and there, the net effect would be analogous to punching an empty bag.

Any group with the temerity to undertake this challenge would require the resources necessary to sustain an "army in the field" for an indefinite period. Elderly members would probably head for condominiums in South Florida and Palm Springs, California, but remaining behind would be a cadre of assassins whose sole function would be to murder those mounting the challenge to the group's supremacy. They could be reinforced by a cadre of assassins from other groups. As Reuter (1983: 133) notes: "Large numbers of young men in major American cities are willing to accept paid employment as violence disputants." Rational criminals with martial skill would be inclined to side with an organization with proven staying power—the Mafia—rather than take a chance with a seemingly reckless new group.

As Nicholas Gage (1971a: 113) points out, *The Mafia Is Not an Equal Opportunity Employer*: "No door is more firmly locked to blacks than the one that leads to the halls of power in OC." He states that Irish, Jewish, and Italian mobsters have tended to recruit and promote from within their own ethnic groups, while cooperating with one another. Organized crime is no less stratified than the wider "legitimate" society, and the dominant groups in both have always been white. This leads to the issue of *ethnic succession* in organized crime.

Daniel Bell (1964) refers to crime as an American way of life, "A Queer Ladder of Social Mobility." He points out that the "jungle quality of the American business community, particularly at the turn of the century, was reflected in the mode of 'business' practiced by the coarse gangster elements, most of them from new immigrant families, who were 'getting ahead' just as Horatio Alger had urged" (1964: 116). Francis Ianni (1974) notes that this "queer ladder" had organized crime as the first few rungs:

> The Irish came first, and early in this century they dominated crime as well as big-city political machinations. As they came to control the political machinery of large cities they won wealth, power and respectability through subsequent control of construction, trucking, public utilities and the waterfront. By the 1920s and the period of prohibition and speculation in the money markets and real estate, the Irish were succeeded in OC

by the Jews, and Arnold Rothstein, Lepke Buchalter and Gurrah Shapiro dominated gambling and labor racketeering for over a decade. The Jews quickly moved into the world of business and the professions as more legitimate avenues to economic and social mobility. The Italians came next. . . . (1974: 13–14)

According to this thesis, each successive immigrant group experienced *strain* to which some members reacted by *innovating* in accord with a tradition that had been established by earlier American entrepreneurs—the "Robber Barons." Ethnic succession results when a group experiences success in crime, and legitimate opportunities thereby become more readily available. Strain subsides, and the group moves out of organized crime, creating an opportunity for innovation for the succeeding immigrant group. According to this thesis, persons involved in organized crime are not committed to a deviant subculture but are merely using available, albeit illegal, opportunity to achieve economic success. Letizia Paoli and Peter Reuter (2008) state that blocked opportunity and the "queer ladder" may also explain participation in organized crime by members of the immigrant community in Europe.

Ianni states that ethnic succession is continuing, that "the Italians are leaving or being pushed out of OC [and] they are being replaced by the next wave of migrants to the city: blacks and Puerto Ricans" (1974: 14). Although they might not have been obvious to Ianni when he was conducting his research in New York during the early 1970s, today we would have to add other ethnic groups: Cubans, Chinese, Colombians, Dominicans, Jamaicans, Mexicans, Nigerians, Russians, and outlaw motorcycle clubs. According to the ethnic succession thesis, involvement in organized crime is simply a rational response to economic conditions: Organized crime can be understood as a rational choice for responding to anomie.

Other theorists reject this one-dimensional view. Organized crime, they argue, provides important psychic rewards and meaningful social structures. Young Italian American males from middle-class circumstances continue to be drawn by the allure of the American Mafia—a romantization of the mob kept alive in certain neighborhoods—enclaves—and reinforced by media representations. Being "connected" brings prestige, and in the social environment inhabited by wiseguys—bars, restaurants, nightclubs—a privileged status is evident. The "wannabe" outlaw is socialized into an exciting world where he eagerly adopts the attitude, behavior pattern, and even the clothing styles exemplified by wiseguys.

"If the real wiseguys were half as bright as the popular culture wants them to be, they would have muscled Microsoft, and looted all the savings and loans before the amateurs got a chance" (television critic John Leonard 1996: 55).

An example was the rise of a notorious gang of Italian American hoodlums in the Pleasant Avenue section of Harlem, a six-block Mafia stronghold that runs from 114th Street to 120th Street, just east of First Avenue. Dubbed the Purple Gang, apparently after the murderous Detroit (Jewish) mob of Prohibition days, they were used as "muscle" and executioners in many gangland murders, and their reputation for violence made them very useful to the Mafia leadership. The Purple Gang has been involved in numerous rackets, particularly drug trafficking, which is facilitated by their contacts with young men of other ethnic backgrounds who have access to importation quantities of heroin and cocaine. In his study of some members of the Purple Gang, Peter Lupsha (1983) found that they tend to have been born between 1946 and 1951 and to be third-generation Italian Americans who are related by blood and marriage. Even though they come from the Pleasant Avenue neighborhood, most reside in the Bronx or suburban Westchester County. "They are now, like many New York suburbanite businessmen, commuters to the old neighborhood for work, money, and visiting rather than residents" (1983: 76). Many Purple Gang members have been "made"—inducted into membership in traditional organized crime Families in New York. Similar groups have been identified.

Journalist Mike McAlary (1998) has been following the exploits of a group of young Italian Americans known as the "Tanglewood Boys"—they used the Tanglewood Shopping Center in suburban Yonkers, New York, as a hangout. Six of the post-adolescent gangsters had fathers who were members of New York's organized crime Families. The Tanglewood Boys committed armed robberies and murders, some for personal reasons, others for reasons related to business.

In Queens, the "Giannini crew" consisted of young men who worked for three New York City crime Families—their hangout is the Caffe Giannini on Fresh Pond Road in Ridgewood. They began their criminal careers in the late 1980s as a violent street gang affiliated with an older set of men, the Ridgewood Boys, some of whom had ties to organized crime. Federal officials describe the group as a "farm team" for organized crime. In 2001, when one of the Giannini crew, age 28, pled guilty to racketeering, he described several murders as if they were trips to the dry cleaners (Feuer 2001). One of the crew members, whose father is serving a life sentence for his involvement in the "Pizza Connection" heroin case (discussed later), became a made guy in the Bonanno Family (Marzulli 2005a). Anthony ("Ace") Aiello was described by the Family boss as "Luca Brasi," a reference to the hulking and murderous enforcer in the *Godfather* novel and film. In 2005, Aiello, 28, was arrested in Syracuse while a fugitive following the 2004 murder of a mob associate (Marzulli and Lemire 2005). Another Queens crew of young "wannabes," dubbed the "Young Guns," reported to a Gambino Family *capo* and worked in New York and Florida. In addition to armored car and bank robberies, crew members were responsible for at least four murders (McPhee 2003).

In a recent visit to New York, an organized crime insider explained to the writer that although older wiseguys may try to hide organized crime affiliations from their offspring, the sons and daughters discover the truth during adolescence. He noted that without any encouragement—and even with discouragement—from their fathers, some of these young men take advantage of their fathers' reputations to form crews of organized crime aspirants. Why? They are attracted by the allure of organized crime, the wiseguy lifestyle.

Entry into organized crime, states Lupsha (1981: 22), is not based on blocked aspirations, that is, on anomie or strain. Rather, it "is a rational choice, rooted in one perverse aspect of our values; namely, that only 'suckers' work, and that in our society, one is at liberty to take 'suckers' and seek easy money." In fact, the term *wiseguy*, a description of a member of traditional organized crime, exemplifies such an attitude. Pileggi (1985: 20) presents Paul ("Paulie") Vario, a powerful *caporegime* in the Lucchese crime Family, as an example:

> Paulie was always asking me for stolen credit cards whenever he and his wife, Phyllis, were going out for the night. Paulie called stolen credit cards "Muldoons," and he always said that liquor tastes better on a Muldoon. The fact that a guy like Paul Vario, a *capo* in the Lucchese crime family, would even consider going out on a social occasion with his wife and run the risk of getting caught using a stolen credit card might surprise some people. But if you knew wiseguys you would know right away that the best part of the night for Paulie came from the fact that he was getting over on somebody.

With a great deal of insight, Pileggi (1985: 36) captures the wise guy attitude toward society: "They lived in an environment awash in crime, and those who did not partake were simply viewed as prey. To live otherwise was foolish. Anyone who stood waiting his turn on the American pay line was beneath contempt." According to this view, organized crime comprises a deviant subculture to which members have a commitment that is not mitigated by the absence of strain. As one Gambino crime Family member told a reporter: "We don't want to be part of your world. We don't want to belong to country clubs" (Brenner 1990: 181). Benjamin ("Lefty") Ruggiero of the Bonanno Family explained: "As a wiseguy you can lie, you can cheat, you can steal, you can kill people—*legitimately*. You can do any goddamn thing you want, and nobody can say anything about it. Who wouldn't want to be a wiseguy?" (Pistone 1987: 330). As former undercover FBI agent Joe Pistone (2004: 9) points out:

Wiseguys exist in a bizarre parallel universe, a world where avarice and corruption are the norm, and where the routines that most ordinary people hold dear—working good jobs, being with family, living an honest life—are seen as the curse of the weak and the stupid. Wiseguys resemble us in many ways, but make no mistake, they might as well be from another planet, so alien and abnormal are their thoughts and habits.

Ianni (1972) describes the "Lupollos," the Italian organized crime Family he studied, whose core members are all related by blood or marriage. In the fourth generation, "only four out of twenty-seven males are involved in the family business organization. The rest are doctors, lawyers, college teachers, or run their own businesses" (1972: 193). Ianni argued that ethnic succession continues (1974: 12): "We shall witness over the next decade the systematic development of what is now a scattered and loosely organized pattern of emerging black control in organized crime into the Black Mafia." Gus Tyler (1975: 178) did not find Ianni convincing, claiming that Ianni's evidence "consists of a pimp with a stable of seven hookers, a dope pusher, a fence who dabbles in loan sharking and gambling, a con man who gets phony insurance policies for gypsy cabs, and a numbers racketeer, etc." Tyler points out that, although these activities are "organized," they are not in a class with white organized crime either qualitatively or quantitatively. Indeed, early in his (1974) book, Ianni reports that the brother and partner of the aforementioned "dope pusher," actually a large-scale heroin dealer in Paterson, New Jersey, was found sans genitals—a "message" from the "White Mafia." A similar result obtained in Newark, New Jersey, when the Black Panthers attempted an incursion into a numbers operation that was under the patronage of the Lucchese Family (Raab 2005).

As for blacks and Latinos replacing Italians in organized crime, Lupsha (1981) argues that black and Latino groups have only succeeded in controlling markets that Italian American groups have discarded because of poor risk-to-profit ratios.

DeMeo's "Brooklyn Butcher Shop"

Killings typically took place in a Brooklyn apartment. When the victim arrived, he would be shot with a silencer-equipped gun, and a towel was wrapped around his head to stop the blood. He would then be stabbed in the heart to stop the blood from pumping, and the body would be placed in the shower to bleed him. He was then placed on a pool liner in the living room, dismembered, and wrapped in plastic bags that were placed in cardboard boxes and taken to a nearby dump (Capeci 2003).

Lupsha (1981: 22) questions the "ethnic succession" thesis. He argues that despite Ianni's (1972; 1974) limited findings, Italian organized crime figures who have gained economic status are not leaving organized crime and, in many instances, their progeny have followed them into organized crime. This view certainly has empirical support—there are dozens of contemporary American Mafia members whose children have followed them into "the life."

In New York, young men raised in comfortable middle-class circumstances have advanced into organized crime in a most violent way. Roy DeMeo of Brooklyn, for example, a second-generation American of Neapolitan heritage, became a loan shark while still in his teens. His uncle was a star prosecutor in the Brooklyn District Attorney's Office. But at age 32, to protect an extortion scheme run with his partner, a member of the Gambino Family, Roy committed his first murder—a solo job using a silencer-equipped pistol. He subsequently put together a crew of active criminals from the (middle-class) Canarsie section of Brooklyn. Their first murder victim, a car dealer who was testifying against them before a Brooklyn grand jury, was kidnapped, stabbed repeatedly, and dismembered. The medical examiner who handled the case, Dr. Dominick DiMaio, did not know that his cousin Roy DeMeo—his branch of the family spelled the name differently—was responsible for the murder. DeMeo was initiated into the Gambino Family, and his crew eventually killed and usually dismembered an estimated 200 persons; most of the bodies were never found. In fact, contrary to mob custom, Roy DeMeo added murder-for-hire to his repertoire and, against the edict of the Gambino Family boss, dealt in cocaine. One of DeMeo's leading assassins

was arrested and began providing evidence against the Gambino Family. Soon afterward, in 1983, at age 42, DeMeo was the victim of a volley of shots fired into his head at close range (Mustain and Capeci 1992; Capeci 2003).

A meeting between John Gotti, boss of the Gambino Family, and Vincent ("Chin") Gigante, boss of the Genovese Family, reveals their different attitudes toward offspring following them into organized crime. Gambino underboss Sam Gravano reports: "One thing I'll never forget from that meeting, was John telling Chin in sort of a proud way that his son, John Junior, had just been made. Chin said, 'Jeez, I'm sorry to hear that'" (Maas 1997: 239–40).[3] A journalist quotes Colombo Family *caporegime* Salvatore ("Big Sal"—350 pounds) Miciotta: "Only a real *gavone* [lowlife] wants for his kids what we got. . . . Idiots and wannabes are who's attracted to this life now" (Goldberg 1999: 27). The shrinking of Italian neighborhoods, notes Ronald Goldstock, former director of the New York State Organized Crime Task Force, "results in a lack of gangs, which means that there are no minor leagues to supply the majors" (Goldberg 1999: 71).

Though many young men appear to enjoy playing the wiseguy role—often outfitted with large pinkie rings, gold chains, and other symbols of gangster chic—many are neither bright

---

[3]In 2002, the son of Vincent Gigante was indicted for acting as intermediary for his father who was allegedly running the Genovese Family from prison. The following year, Andrew, at 46, was sentenced to two years in prison for extorting $90,000 from a businessman. His guilty plea also included a fine of $2 million. He was ordered by the court to desist from any future business activity at the New York City waterfront district (Marzulli 2003).

The New Wiseguys

"These 'men of honor' who once swore a blood oath to live and die by the gun, now do their swearing from the witness stand while their agents negotiate book deals and peddle movie rights. Now the only people making offers that can't be refused are the authorities who run the Witness Protection Program and the producers who run Hollywood" (Anastasia 1998: 23).

Also Not Rocket Scientists

He was called "Frankie the Beast" because of his skill in using a baseball bat on victims. This enforcer for the Colombo Family spotted the concealed video camera and turned to a very fearful Vinnie, the informant who had led him into an elaborate FBI sting: "Hey, looks like a great [security] system you got here, Vinnie." His *capo*, he explained, was looking for a security system for his home. Vinnie had one installed, *gratis* (Bonavolonta and Duffy 1996: 148).

Six-foot, 250-pound Jack Falcone gave Gregory DePalma a cell phone as a gift. What DePalma, a captain in the Gambino crime Family, didn't know was that Falcone was an FBI agent and the cell phone allowed the bureau to hear conversations even when it was not turned on (G. Smith 2005b).

nor tough.[4] As journalist George Anastasia notes, "they value form over substance" (1998: 25). The long neighborhood-based apprenticeships through which organized crime chooses the cream of the "wannabes" are history. Those accepted into membership are often not the tough, street-smart, stand-up kids of yesteryear, but rather social failures and potential informants quick to play "I've got a secret"—turn on their closest associates to avoid incarceration. Psychiatrists would point out that psychopaths and sociopaths have a weak sense of loyalty. Anthony ("Gaspipe") Casso recalls his first murder, committed at the behest of the Lucchese Family: "For me it was just business. I didn't know the guy. I'd never seen him before. He had to go. That's all I knew. That's all I needed to know" (Carlo 2008: 83). Faced with a long prison term, Casso, Luccchese Family underboss, became a government informant.

The testimony of two former acting bosses of the Lucchese Family, Alphonse ("Little Al") D'Arco, 71, and Joseph ("Little Joe") DeFede, 69,

resulted in the 2004 conviction of acting boss Louis ("Crossbay") Daidone, 57. D'Arco had previously testified against Vincent Gigante and Colombo boss Victor Arena. Michael ("Mikey Scars") DiLeonardo, a Gambino captain, testified against acting Family boss Peter Gotti, while Colombo captain Joseph ("Joe Campy") Campenella turned on members of his Family. Bonanno captain James ("Louie") Tartaglione, 55, taped conversations with acting Family boss Anthony ("Tony Green") Urso and acting underboss Joseph Cammarano. In one conversation, Urso spoke of killing the child of a cooperating witness (Marzulli 2004c). Frank ("Curly") Lino, 66, a long-time member of the Bonanno Family, became a witness not only against Gambino boss Peter Gotti, but also against his own son, Joseph, and several cousins. In 2004, a Colombo informant resulted in the 63-year-old pony-tailed Family boss receiving a 20-year sentence for murder. Bonanno Family underboss Salvatore ("Good Looking Sal") Vitale, at 56, became a cooperating witness against his brother-in-law, Family boss Joseph Massino. And in 2005, Massino, long regarded as the last of the old-time bosses—tough, vicious, and low profile—but facing a death penalty for murder, became

---

[4]Some, however, do have a college education. Two older "players," Thomas Gambino, son of boss Carlo Gambino and a *caporegime* in that crime Family, is a college graduate, as is Jack Tocco, boss of the Detroit crime Family.

an informant against members of his own crime Family.

Even in Chicago, where made-guys have not heretofore become informants, things are changing. In 2005, fourteen Outfit members and associates were indicted for racketeering and plotting at least eighteen murders—two are former Chicago police officers. The evidence includes recordings of conversations between Frank Calabrese, Sr., a notorious loan shark, and his son Frank, Jr., who was wearing a listening device while both were serving federal prison sentences. Another informant is Frank senior's brother Nick, also a made-guy in the Outfit (Warmbir, Herguth, and Main 2005). While the Detroit Family had been successful in avoiding informants, in 2000, Nove Tocco, at 52, the grandson of deceased Family boss Joe Zerilli and the nephew of underboss Anthony Zerilli, became the first member of the Detroit Mafia to become a government witness, testifying against his cousin, Family boss Jack W. Tocco.

The relationship between certain insular—*defended*—neighborhoods and organized crime also appears to be undergoing change. For example, the traditional symbiosis was violated by the young, newly initiated members of the Nicky Scarfo group in South Philadelphia who intimidated and abused neighborhood people who had once been cultivated with favors by the older criminals. In Bensonhurst, Brooklyn, young members of the Lucchese Family—perhaps hastily recruited because of the death and imprisonment of older members—set up a crack cocaine business that sold drugs to neighborhood youngsters (Kennedy 1996; Volkman 1998).

A development affecting ethnic succession in organized crime is the arrival of relatively large numbers of southern Italian immigrants into the New York metropolitan area during the 1960s—"Zips."

Zips The connection between the criminal organizations of southern Italy—Mafia, Camorra, 'Ndrangheta, Sacra Corona Unita—and the American Mafia are the *Zips*,[5] recent immigrants from the *Mezzogiorno*. Many are *mafiosi* fleeing intense pressure from Italian law enforcement and murderous factional conflicts between competing Mafia, Camorra, and 'Ndrangheta groups (discussed in Chapter 6). "Their entry to the United States was made particularly easy by the reversal of a restrictive immigration statute that had discriminated against southern and eastern Europeans" (PCOC 1986c: 53). Any number are related to members of traditional organized crime groups in New York. According to police sources in New York City, some of these Zips have been admitted to membership in American Mafia Families, and many more are operating in their own associations independent of, but in cooperation with, traditional crime groups. They have been particularly active in heroin trafficking. Using drug profits, Zips have opened strip malls containing bakeries, tobacco shops, cafes, newspaper stands, and limousine service storefronts. They are essentially reproducing the small-scale neighborhood life in which organized crime has traditionally felt most comfortable.

Among Italian American crime groups in the United States, there has been a demand for criminal labor, particularly in the highly rewarding but dangerous enterprise of drug trafficking. Southern Italy has provided a vast labor market for Italian American drug trafficking organizations. "In southern Italy, *mafia* and *camorra* groups can rely on a "reserve army" of individuals prepared to endanger their own—and other people's—lives in the execution of especially risky and violent tasks, because the problems of inner-city environment and youth unemployment are growing continually worse in the *Mezzogiorno*, so that the supply of criminal labour is continually increasing" (Arlacchi 1986: 194). In Naples and the surrounding Campania area, for example, the *Nuova Camorra Organizzata* of Raffaele Cutolo[6] recruited young boys, most under 14—the Italian penal code exempts them from punishment—to commit murders and deliver heroin. "For a child growing up in the slums of Naples, amid daily violence and where

---

[5]The term is an allusion to the immigrants' rapid speech in Italian dialect.

[6]While Raffaele was in prison, his sister Rosetta ran his crime Family, one of the most important in Naples (Stille 1995a).

© AP/Wide World Photos

Two Zips were with Bonanno crime Family underboss Carmine Galente in a Brooklyn restaurant when he was shot down in 1977. Baldo Amato and Cesare Bonventre, Zips and cousins of Joseph Bonanno, for whom the Family is named, helped set up Galente's murder on behalf of Family boss Phil Rastelli.

only the strong and cunning are admired, the Camorra bosses grow to idol stature" (Schmetzer 1985: 4).

Ties between traditional organized crime and the Zips were highlighted during the "Pizza Connection" case concluded in 1987. Former Sicilian Mafia boss Tommaso Buscetta was a prosecution witness in the trial of twenty-two defendants.[7] A Mafia group headed by Gaetano Badalamenti, then 64, an ousted *capomafioso* from Cinisi, Sicily, was found to have supplied heroin with a total value in excess of $1.6 billion to a group headed by Salvatore ("Totò") Catalano, then 46, a captain in the Bonanno crime Family of New York. Catalano[8] arrived in the United States from Sicily in 1961 and headed a crew of Zips in the Knickerbocker Avenue section of Brooklyn. The Sicilian defendants purchased morphine base in Turkey and processed it in Sicily. Pizza parlors in the United States owned by the defendants were used to facilitate the drug trafficking.

Two men implicated in the case were with Bonanno crime Family underboss Carmine Galente in a Brooklyn restaurant when he was shot down in 1977. Baldo Amato[9] (born in 1952) and Cesare Bonventre (born in 1951), both Zips and cousins of Joseph Bonanno, for whom the Family is named, helped set up Galente's murder on behalf of Family boss Phil Rastelli.[10] Sicilian-born Gerlando Sciascia, 65, a major heroin dealer

---

[7]For an exciting journalistic look at the "Pizza Connection" investigation, see Blumenthal (1988b); also Alexander (1988).

[8]Catalano is serving a 45-year federal sentence. Badalamenti, at 80, died in 1987 while serving a 45-year sentence.

[9]In 2006, Amato, 54, was sentenced to life imprisonment for two 1992 murders.

[10]In 1984, the body of Bonventre was found stuffed into two barrels in a Garfield, New Jersey, warehouse.

and Bonnano Family *caporegime* in charge of a crew of Zips, was shot at close range in 1999, and his body dumped on a Bronx street (Capeci 1999b). In 2006, the *New York Daily News* reported that the acting head of the Bonanno Family is Sicilian-born Sal ("The Ironworker") Montagna, age 35 (Marzulli 2006).

One of the important Zip drug organizations was led by several Sicilian cousins of Carlo Gambino and headquartered in Cherry Hill, New Jersey:

> Although related to the late crime boss Carlo Gambino of New York, the New Jersey Gambino drug operations are independent from the New York family. There are direct lines of communication and influence based on actual blood ties between the New Jersey Gambinos and other traditional organized crime families in New York. Gambino family members own significant interests in the pizza industry in South Jersey and parts of Pennsylvania. These businesses have been used for concealing illegal immigrants, for laundering money, and for storing drugs. They are known to have employed illegal aliens and other nonfamily members who were more experienced in drug trafficking to smuggle heroin into and transport it within the United States. (PSI 1983a: 134)

With permission from Philadelphia crime Family boss Angelo Bruno, several "Cherry Hill Gambinos" operated pizza shops, restaurants, and a disco in the City of Brotherly Love, including the brothers Giuseppe and Giovanni Gambino. Giovanni was a fugitive from an Italian conviction for heroin trafficking and a *caporegime* in the Gambino Family under John Gotti; Giuseppe is a soldier in that Family. A third brother, Rosario, is serving a 45-year sentence for heroin trafficking. In 1984, after a six-week trial, four Cherry Hill Gambinos were convicted in Newark federal court of marketing heroin in South Jersey. The 1993 the trial of Giuseppe and Giovanni Gambino and two of their associates resulted in a mistrial. They were convicted of bail jumping.

The Zips and their American counterparts "share similar customs, criminal philosophies and a common heritage. The prototype of the crime Family is identical in each system" (PCOC 1986c: 53). In criminal and law enforcement circles, however, their "Old World" ways have earned the Zips more fear and respect than their American counterparts. Just how many Zips are in the United States is not clear, but they are believed to be concentrated in the Northeast, particularly in the New York City area. Other groups are known to be located in Boston, Buffalo, Chicago, Philadelphia, Houston, and Dallas.

In recent years, however, the ranks of the American Mafia have been thinned by successful federal prosecutions using the Racketeer Influenced and Corrupt Organizations (RICO) statute (to be discussed in Chapter 15)—particularly the long, double-digit sentences typically handed down. Whether or not the Italian American community and the Zips will be able to provide sufficient replacements to keep the American Mafia viable in the years to come remains an open question. In the meantime, new criminal groups are emerging that may prove to be more powerful and difficult to combat than those of traditional organized crime. Gary Potter (1994) concludes that, historically, "ethnic succession" appears to be a dubious concept. Instead, he argues, new groups become part of organized crime, but they do not necessarily *replace* the older groups. This would appear to be the case with members of Italian American organized crime, whose strong subcultural orientations have resisted changes in their economic status. In later chapters we will examine these emerging criminal organizations.

Prohibition was the turning point that allowed Jews and Italians to ascend the crooked ladder provided by participation in organized crime. In the United States, culture conflict between earlier and later immigrants created a demand from the latter for goods and services outlawed by the former. This led to the creation of gambling syndicates and infamous criminal organizations of the Prohibition era. Today, alcohol and various forms of gambling are legally available in most areas of the country, but the outlawing of certain chemicals enjoyed by a large minority of the population provides continuing incentive and opportunity for criminal innovation. Though the Jews, largely in New York, were the next group to dominate organized crime, they quickly turned to business and the professions. Prohibition affected the Italian gangsters in a manner different from earlier immigrant groups. Before Prohibition, ethnic organized crime was restricted to the local community. Prohibition encouraged the creation of city- and regional-wide criminal organizations that allowed Italian gangsters to consolidate their power and keep it longer.

THE PSYCHOLOGY OF ORGANIZED CRIME

While sociological theories may help to identify societal variables that motivate involvement in organized crime, they fail to explain why only a small fraction of persons exposed to such variables actually become criminals. Why do people exposed to the same milieu react differently? Psychology, a discipline that focuses on the individual, provides some answers.

Clinical Psychology/Psychoanalytic Theory

Clinical psychology is based, to various extents, on psychoanalytic theory, a body of work fathered by Sigmund Freud (1856–1939). Over the years the theory has undergone change, although Freud's basic contribution, his exposition of the importance of phenomena of the unconscious in human behavior, remains. Personality is strongly influenced by determinants in the unconscious that develop early in life. Simply put, this concept argues that the most important determinants of our behavior are not available to our conscious thought (Cloninger 2004). These determinants evolve during early stages of psychological development.

A delicate balance is maintained by unconscious forces as a person experiences various sociocultural and biological aspects of existence. When the balance is upset, the psyche passes from the normal to the psychoneurotic or the psychotic (mental illness). The fact that a fine line exists between the normal and the neurotic and between the neurotic and the psychotic is basic to psychoanalytic theory. In fact, only a difference of degree separates the "normal" and the "abnormal." The degree to which there is a malfunctioning in psychic apparatus is the degree to which a person is "abnormal" or "sick," that is, socially dysfunctional.

Central to the psychoanalytic explanation for crime is the superego, a conscience-like mechanism whose function is to restrain the person from antisocial behavior. According to August Aichhorn (1963: 221), "the superego takes its form and content from identifications which result from the child's effort to emulate the parent. It is evolved not only because the parent loves the child, but also because the child fears the parent's demands." If the superego does not attain full strength, the person is more likely to act on primitive impulses, often of a violent nature. Persons with an *antisocial personality disorder* (ASP) have a poorly developed superego—they are psychopaths or sociopaths—who are restrained only by the fear of punishment that alone cannot exercise adequate control over antisocial impulses. Such persons suffer little or no guilt as a result of engaging in socially harmful behavior. They are characterized by a combination of antisocial behavior and emotional detachment (Black 1999) exemplified by a willingness to murder persons against whom they harbor no animosity. The nonfiction character portrayed by Joe Pesci in the movie *Goodfellas* exemplifies this type of personality, as does the DeMeo faction of the Gambino crime Family discussed earlier. In Mexico, several men wearing military garb burst into a bar in southwestern Mexico, brandishing machine guns, and spilled the contents of a heavy plastic bag: five bloody human heads freshly removed from their victims with a bowie knife while they were still alive. The killers were part of the enforcement branch of a Mexican drug cartel (McKinley 2006b).

"The most disturbing symptom of ASP is often aggression, expressed in shades from quiet intimidation to explosive violence. . . . His actions may be sudden and unpredictable, but more likely they are deliberate, purposeful, and designed for maximum impact" (Black 1999: 47). The psychopathic criminal is totally without conscience, capable of unspeakable acts, and shows no external signs of psychoses or neuroses. In his autobiography, Gambino crime Family underboss Sammy Gravano recalls his first murder—he shot a close friend in the back of the head on orders from the Colombo Family: "Am I supposed to feel remorse? Aren't I supposed to feel something? But I felt nothing like remorse. If anything, I felt good. Like high. Like powerful, maybe even superhuman. It's not that I was happy or proud of myself. Not that. I'm still not happy about that feeling. It's just that killing came so easy to me" (Maas 1997: 52).

While the writer was a New York State parole officer, his partner supervised a captain (*caporegime*) from the Brooklyn-based Colombo Family. Salvatore Albanese was built like a football linebacker with close-cropped hair; he was out of prison as the result of bureaucratic missteps by government officials. Sal had a reputation for being deliberate, purposeful, and quite violent. Although always polite and soft-spoken to my partner and me, in areas of Brooklyn where he was known, people frequently crossed the street when Sal approached lest they risk raising his ire by looking at him too intently. When violence broke out between two factions in the Colombo Family (discussed in Chapter 4), the group opposed to Sal's was too fearful of him to make any moves against their opponents. Instead, they lured him to a meeting by feigning a desire for peace—a meeting from which Sal never returned. Then all hell broke loose.

In sum, criminal behavior is related to the superego function, which is a result of an actor's relationship to parents (or parental figures) during early developmental years. Parental deprivation through absence, lack of affection, or inconsistent discipline—or parental influence that is deviant—stifles the proper development of the superego. Parental influence weakened by deprivation during childhood development will result in an adult unable to adequately control aggressive, hostile, or antisocial urges.

Behavioral Psychology/Learning Theory

Central to behavioral psychology is that all behavior is shaped by its consequences. Behavior is acquired through operant conditioning—a method of learning through rewards and punishments for behavior—that occurs through interaction with the environment. Through operant

Murderous Indifference

Sicilian *mafisoi* "do not usually feel any sense of guilt or sorrow when they kill somebody who is not a mafia member . . . since they do not consider the victim to be a human being and therefore do not view him as worthy of emotional involvement" (Paoli 2003: 84–85).

conditioning, an association is made between a behavior and a consequence for that behavior. If a person's "aggressive behavior has been rewarded, at least part of the time, no further explanation in terms of internal needs is necessary"; the person simply learns to behave aggressively (Nietzel et al. 2003: 47).

According to learning theory, antisocial behavior is the result of learning directly from others (for example, peers) or the failure to learn how to discriminate between competing norms, both lawful and unlawful, because of inappropriate reinforcement. When conforming behavior is not adequately reinforced, an actor can more easily be influenced by competing, albeit antisocial, sources of positive reinforcement (for example, money and excitement from criminal behavior). The environment inhabited by organized crime is awash with reinforcement for antisocial behavior.

While sociology helps explain why persons in certain environments would be motivated to get involved in organized crime, most people similarly situated do not become so involved. Perhaps, then, what is needed for such involvement is the right environment coupled with the relevant psychological elements.

SUMMARY

- Some theories of crime and deviance provide insight into organized crime.
- Anomie suggests a strain between societal expectations for success and limited opportunity that causes certain persons to innovate in the form of organized crime—a queer ladder of social mobility.
- According to differential association, all behavior—lawful and criminal—is learned in intimate personal groups, although learning the techniques of sophisticated criminality requires the proper environment.
- Subcultural theory explains criminal behavior as learned; the subcultural delinquent has learned values that are deviant in an environment characterized by social disorganization. In these defended neighborhoods, which have traditionally provided the recruiting grounds that ensure the continuity of organized crime, inhabitants form cohesive groupings, sealing themselves off through the efforts of delinquent gangs and a forbidding reputation.
- The theory of differential opportunity notes that illegitimate opportunity for success, like legitimate opportunity, is not equally distributed throughout society and access to criminal ladders of success are no more freely available than are noncriminal alternatives.
- According to social control theorists, delinquent acts result when an individual's bond to society is weak or broken and the strength of this bond is determined by external and internal restraints.
- As the only theory developed to explain the continued existence of organized crime, ethnic succession posits that organized crime provides a "queer ladder to success" for disadvantaged groups who eventually leave organized crime, making way for the next wave.
- Psychological theories, psychoanalytical and behavioral, help to explain why persons exposed to the same social and physical environment react differently, and the concept of superego helps explain antisocial and psychopathic behavior frequently found in organized crime wherever it is found.

REVIEW QUESTIONS

1. How does Robert Merton's theory of anomie explain organized crime?
2. What is the connection between differential association and organized crime?
3. How does social disorganization explain why organized crime is more likely in certain neighborhoods?
4. How does cultural transmission (Shaw and McKay) explain the continuity of organized crime in certain neighborhoods?
5. What do Cloward and Ohlin (differential opportunity) say about organized crime?
6. What qualities of the delinquent subculture correlate well with the prerequisites of organized crime?
7. What is meant by the "defended neighborhood"?
8. How does social control theory explain the emergence of organized crime?
9. What is the theory of ethnic succession?
10. Why did Italians remain in organized crime so long? What factors explain the exit of Italian Americans from organized crime?
11. How have the Zips affected the ethnic succession theory?
12. How does psychology explain the behavior of persons in organized crime?

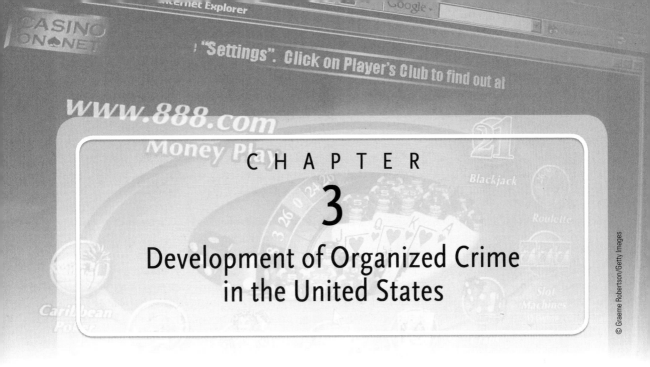

CHAPTER

3

Development of Organized Crime in the United States

This chapter presents a history of organized crime (OC) in the United States and its historical antecedents. The intertwining of urban machine politics and Prohibition provided Irish, Jewish, and Italian immigrants unparalleled opportunity to climb the queer ladder of social mobility. But it was the Robber Barons who helped enrich the fertile soil necessary for the growth of organized crime in the United States and whose spiritual legacy lives on in twenty-first-century corporate crime.

THE ROBBER BARONS

"Al Capone," notes Michael Woodiwiss (1987: 8), "was not the first ruthless entrepreneur to combine with thugs, gunmen, and government officials and carve out an illegal fortune. But the expression—'organised crime'—was not commonly used until the 1920s and the Prohibition era when academics and newspaper editors found it to be a convenient new label for an old phenomenon." While contemporary organized crime has its roots in Prohibition (1920–1933), unscrupulous American business

entrepreneurs, such as Astor, Carnegie, Vanderbilt, Drew, Gould, Sage, Rockefeller, Stanford, and Morgan, provided role models and created a climate conducive to its growth. These earlier generations of predatory Americans with English, Scottish, Scandinavian, and German ancestry paved the way for later generations of Irish, Jewish, and Italian criminals who, in turn, are being emulated by criminals of Asian, African, Hispanic, and Russian ancestry. Rampant—that is, uncontrolled—capitalism, a feature of nineteenth-century America, is now being experienced by the former Soviet Union, and it too has spawned extensive corruption and organized crime. In Chapter 10 we will examine Russian organized crime, whose development in many aspects (including a class of robber barons) appears to parallel that in the United States.

John Jacob Astor

John Jacob Astor (1763–1848) arrived from Germany penniless and died the richest man in America; in today's value he was worth $78 billion (Klepper et al. 1998). He was "the first great self-made millionaire whose career whetted the ambitions of a host of young Americans" (Rugoff 1989: 40). The Astor fortune was based on alcohol and fraud: Drunken Native Americans were systematically cheated by agents of Astor's American Fur Company. When the victims complained to the government, Astor's agents resorted to violence. When the Indians retaliated, troops were sent to quell the "Indian disorder." In addition to exploiting Native Americans, Astor succeeded in forcing his employees in the western wilderness to buy from company-owned stores at exorbitant prices. By the time they returned east, most employees were actually in debt to Astor (Myers 1936; Rugoff 1989).

Astor was able to monopolize the fur trade and "was never prosecuted for the numerous violations of both penal and civil law invariably committed at his direction and for his benefit. With the millions that rolled in, he was able to command the services of the foremost lawyers in warding off penalties of law, and also to have as his paid retainers some of the most noted and powerful politicians of the day" (Myers 1936: 103). For example, he paid Lewis Cass, then governor of the territory of Michigan, $35,000 for unexplained services. David Loth (1938: 104) notes that the money was well invested. Later, as secretary of war, "Cass was to hear, and dismiss, many charges of corruption, extortion, trespass and violence against the [American Fur] company and its representatives." The money gained through lawlessness and violence against Native Americans in the western fur trade was used for real estate speculation in New York, where easily corrupted officials helped Astor become America's greatest "slumlord," extracting money from poor immigrants for the privilege of living in the vilest of tenement housing. The Astor-inspired slums became a spawning ground for organized crime.

Cornelius Vanderbilt

Cornelius Vanderbilt (1794–1877) came from a small farming family on Staten Island (now part of New York City). He parlayed profits from a ferryboat venture into shipping and shipbuilding, and at age 47, the "Commodore" was a rich man. The government of Nicaragua had given his Accessory Transit Company a monopoly over transportation across the isthmus connecting the two great oceans. In 1853, while Vanderbilt was on a European vacation, two members of his board of directors, in accord with business practices of the day, usurped control of Accessory Transit. Vanderbilt retaliated by setting up a competing line and, by cutting prices, forced the two directors, C. K. Garrison and Charles Morgan, to withdraw. They retaliated by financing an insurrection in Nicaragua, where Accessory Transit was chartered. The revolutionary forces, led by an American adventurer, William Walker, achieved a great victory. Early in 1856, the Vanderbilt charter was canceled and Vanderbilt's property was confiscated.

Vanderbilt responded that summer by persuading the governments of Honduras, San Salvador, and Costa Rica to form an alliance against Nicaragua. Then, on Vanderbilt's orders, two American mercenaries led an invasion of Nicaragua. By the end of the first year the invasion force was progressing quite well; then the Nicaraguans counterattacked. Vanderbilt thwarted the offensive by persuading the State Department to send in the U.S Marines, who succeeded in deposing the revolutionary government, and Vanderbilt's charter was restored (Andrews 1941). Even Mario Puzzo's fictitious godfather did not use "muscle" on this scale.

Like many other successful businessmen of the era, Vanderbilt was a "war profiteer." During the Civil War he acted as an agent for the Union Army, securing unfit and rotting vessels for the transportation of federal troops at exorbitant prices. However, his primary interest was civilian transportation, and Vanderbilt moved from shipping to railroads. Striving for monopoly, he gained control of the Hudson River and Harlem lines and forced the competing New York Central to sell out. In 1866 he sought to complete his transportation stranglehold by taking over the Erie Railroad line, which was a direct competitor. Vanderbilt, however, was ambushed by the Erie Ring, comprising three of America's greatest pirate capitalists: Daniel Drew, James Fisk, and Jay Gould.

The Erie Ring

As part of a scheme to fleece Vanderbilt, the Erie Ring secretly authorized the issue of ten million new shares of Erie stock while Vanderbilt was busy buying up shares to gain control of the Erie Railroad. The more stock he purchased, the more stock was issued by the ring, which declared their actions in accord with the First Amendment— "freedom of the press." In 1868, after Vanderbilt realized he had bought more Erie stock than was known to exist and still did not control the line, an obliging New York Supreme Court judge, part of the notoriously corrupt "Tweed Ring," signed an injunction against further issue of Erie stock. The judge also ordered the ring to return to the treasury one-fourth of what they had already issued. "When Vanderbilt needed a court order in a hurry or a special bill or a joker in a franchise, he could rely on the 'Boss' [Tweed] to have it in stock" (Loth 1938: 196). "Boss" William M. Tweed was the head of Tammany Hall, an organization that dominated New York City politics and government for more than one hundred years (discussed later).

The judge's injunction drove up the price of Erie stock but did not stop the ring. They had "their judge" issue a counterinjunction, and chaos swept Wall Street. Trading in Erie stock was suspended by the stock exchange, but not before Vanderbilt had lost between $5 and $7 million (a significant sum in those days). He responded by having "his judge" issue contempt-of-court arrest warrants for the members of the ring.

The Erie Ring withdrew all its combined funds from New York banks, took all its securities and documents from safes, and crossed the Hudson River to Jersey City with its printing press—out of range of Boss Tweed. Arriving just ahead of pursuing sheriff's deputies, Gould, Drew, and Fisk set up headquarters in Taylor's Castle Hotel, dubbed "Fort Taylor." In Jersey City they were guarded by their own railroad police and cooperative city police officers. Cannons were mounted on piers to thwart any landings from New York, and the ring counterattacked by reducing fares to Buffalo, undercutting the hard-pressed Vanderbilt line.

Vanderbilt retaliated by ordering a band of thugs into New Jersey. The members of the Erie Ring fled to New York, where the field of battle shifted to the state capital in Albany.

In Albany the ring spread $1 million worth of "good will" in an effort to legalize its theft of the Erie from Vanderbilt. Jay Gould even "drew the 'Boss' away from the Commodore's New York Central by the present of a block of Erie stock, a directorship and a retainer of many thousands as counsel" (Loth 1938: 197). Vanderbilt joined the fray but soon grew tired of trying to satisfy state legislators' seemingly insatiable appetites for bribe money. The ring achieved a "legislative victory," and Vanderbilt sued for peace. In return for $4.5 million he relinquished his interest in the Erie, and the arrest warrants were quashed (Josephson 1962; Rugoff 1989).

Daniel Drew

The oldest member of the Erie Ring, Daniel Drew, was born in Carmel, New York, in 1797. An illiterate raised in poverty, Drew began his business career as a cattle drover, buying cattle on credit from New York farmers and driving them to market for sale. He often failed to pay his debts and was forced to move operations to Ohio, where he perfected the technique that resulted in the term *watered stock*. His cattle were kept thirsty by a liberal diet of salt and very little water. Before arrival at the drover's market, the cattle were allowed to quench their thirst, increasing their poundage accordingly. With money thus earned, Drew purchased a tavern and became a moneylender, a steamship owner, and a stockbroker. He gained notoriety by his comments on the advent of the Civil War: "Along with ordinary happenings, we fellows on Wall Street now have in addition the fortunes of war to speculate about, and that always makes great doings on the stock exchange. It's good fishing in troubled waters" (O'Connor 1962: 51).

Drew became treasurer and virtual dictator of the Erie Railroad. He would issue stock for new steel rails and other vital equipment and divert the money for his own speculative investments. As a result, the Erie's "schedules were fictional, its rolling stock ruinous, and its rails so weak and chipped as to invite derailment" (Swanberg 1959: 24). For his own enrichment, Drew ran what had been considered a technological marvel, the Erie Railroad, into the ground (Ackerman 1988). A typical Drew enterprise involved the Erie, which ran from Jersey City to Lake Erie. In 1866 the line was in financial trouble and borrowed $3.5 million from Drew. As collateral, he received 28,000 shares of unissued stock and $3 million in convertible bonds. The securities had been entrusted to him only as collateral; they were not to be sold. Drew converted the bonds into 30,000 shares of stock and, with Jim Fisk as his broker, began selling short—speculating that the price of the stock would go down. To ensure that this would happen, Drew dumped all 58,000 shares on the market and realized a profit of almost $3 million (at a time when most workers earned less than $25 a week and New York State legislators were paid $300 a year).

Drew, an ardent Methodist churchgoer, was responsible for the founding of the Drew Theological Seminary in New Jersey, now part of Drew University. As a pious fraud, notes Milton Rugoff (1989), Drew offered to endow the seminary with $250,000 but wound up giving the institution only the 7 percent interest on this amount. He founded a brokerage firm, but the panic of 1873 wiped out his fortune. Whereas Cornelius Vanderbilt died leaving an estate valued at $90 million (today's value: $95.9 billion) and a university named in his honor, Drew died a pauper in 1879 (Swanberg 1959).

James Fisk

James Fisk, Jr., was born in Vermont in 1834 to a family of English ancestry. He left home at age 15 to join the circus, returning a few years later to join his father as an itinerant peddler. His success at this trade led to a job as a salesman for Jordan, Marsh and Company of Boston. During the Civil War, Fisk acted as an agent for Marsh to the Union Army, lobbying congressmen and generals with lavish entertainment and liberal spending. This led to lucrative contracts for Marsh and advancement for the young Fisk. While other young men were dying by the thousands defending the Union, Fisk was making Marsh a fortune through a smuggling operation that moved southern cotton to the northern mills of Jordan Marsh. At the end of the war, a grateful Marsh presented Fisk with a bonus of $65,000. Fisk took his Civil War profits and used them to swindle buyers of Confederate bonds in Europe. After the fall of Richmond, he sold short to Englishmen who did not know that the Confederacy had collapsed.

Although he successfully avoided military service during the Civil War—when a man could get killed—in peacetime he and his fortune assumed command of a National Guard militia unit. "The Ninth New York," notes Richard O'Connor (1962: 116), "was up for sale; without transfusions of men and money it would have to be disbanded." The newly elected Colonel Fisk, in uniform and astride his horse, was at the head of his militiamen during the Orangemen parade of 1871. When the English loyalists were attacked by a mob of Irish Catholics, Fisk reacted by throwing away his sword and fleeing. Three of his militiamen died in the fighting, and the colonel prudently absented himself from their funeral.

Known as a bon vivant, Fisk was murdered in 1872 by the paramour of his favorite mistress, the actress Josie Mansfield. He left an estate valued at $1 million. Although his wife was reputed to be worth $2 million, in 1912 she died a poor woman living on an income of $50 a month from some rental property (Swanberg 1959).

Jay Gould

The third member of the Erie Ring, Jay Gould (1836–1892), was born in Roxbury, New York, the son of a poor farmer. The Golds (the original family name) had roots in America dating back to 1674, when the family first settled in Connecticut (Klein 1986). At age 16, having a neat hand and a good head for figures, the future member of the Erie Ring was working as a clerk for a village storekeeper. He discovered that his employer had negotiated to buy a piece of property for $2,000. Gould secured a loan from his father, purchased the land for $2,500, and sold it to his employer for

$4,000. Taking advantage of positions of trust was to become the basis for Gould's early financial success. At age 20, he took $5,000 he had accumulated and entered the leather market in New York.

Gould was befriended by a wealthy businessman who, impressed with the young man's ability, provided him with $120,000 to establish a large tannery in Pennsylvania. "Early in life," writes Maury Klein (1986: 43), "he revealed a talent for charming people." According to Matthew Josephson (1962), the company did well, but the owner in New York was receiving no profits—Gould was systematically diverting the funds for his own speculative investments. (Klein states, however, that there is no evidence to support this conclusion.) When the investor arrived in Pennsylvania, he found the books in disarray. Fearing for his investment, he offered to sell the company to Gould for only $60,000—money that Gould didn't have. Gould found other backers, paid off the original owner, and continued to divert funds for his own use until the new owner attempted to physically take back his property. Using hired thugs and idle workers, Gould resisted the effort until officers of the law finally ousted him (Josephson 1962). Klein states that Gould was blameless and that his financial backer used the hired thugs, Gould relying on the tannery's workers. However, notes Klein, "Jay came out of the episode in better financial shape than when he began it. The tannery may have lost money, but Jay did not" (1986: 60).

Gould entered the railroad business, first buying mortgage bonds of the Rutland and Washington Railroad. For 10 cents on the dollar Gould was able to gain controlling interest in this small, bankrupt line. He then hired men with managerial ability, improved the railroad's rolling stock, and consolidated it with other small lines whose stock he had also purchased. By complex stock manipulations, Gould was able to drive up the price of his holdings. He then purchased a controlling interest in the Cleveland and Pittsburgh Railroad, using profits from bond speculation, and manipulated the line's stock to an all-time high. Gould then sold it to the Pennsylvania Railroad Company (Myers 1936). His next great enterprise involved him as part of the Erie Ring in its battle with Cornelius Vanderbilt.

In 1869, the United States had an unfavorable balance of trade—a problem that has again gained widespread attention. To trade successfully, American importers had to pay European exporters in gold. Gould discovered that there was only about $15 million in gold in the New York market, and he plotted to corner that market. Gould already owned $7 million worth of gold, and using the Erie's resources and that of his backers, he could easily absorb the outstanding $15 million and drive the price of gold sky high. Only one ingredient of Gould's plan remained to be dealt with—President Ulysses S. Grant. The president had the power to release some of the $100 million in gold reserves, which the federal government did periodically in the interest of fostering trade and commerce. Gould attempted to influence the president through a financial relationship with Grant's brother-in-law. Gould also had stories placed in newspapers that the government was going to refrain from releasing any gold reserves. These activities, in addition to his and Jim Fisk's feverish buying, caused a "bull market," and the price of gold skyrocketed (Loth 1938).

Gould discovered, however, that Grant had not been influenced—the president would not permit the price of gold to rise freely. Gould began to sell off his gold. Suddenly, on September 24—known as "Black Friday"—the price of gold plummeted. Enraged mobs of investors sought to lynch Gould and Fisk, who were protected by their paid thugs from the Erie line. Gould, of course, made a handsome profit—$1 million—from the entire venture (Swanberg 1959; Rugoff 1989). In 1886 the Knights of Labor demanded a minimum wage of $9 a week. Gould responded with wholesale firings at one of his holdings and the union called a strike. Violence broke out, and with the help of private detectives and strikebreakers, Gould broke the strike and the union (Rugoff 1989).

When Gould died he left an estate whose value in today's dollars was $42.1 billion (Klepper et al. 1998). His progeny, however, fought costly legal battles over the estate and frequently mismanaged what they inherited. Nevertheless, the last surviving son, Howard, who died in 1959, left an estate of more than $62 million to twenty-eight relatives (O'Connor 1962). On

January 3, 1984, the *New York Times* reported that the jewelry collection of the late daughter-in-law of "railroad magnate Jay Gould" would be auctioned at Christie's on April 11. The widow of Jay Gould's youngest son had a jewelry collection insured for more than $100 million, in addition to an art collection of 120 works by van Gogh, Renoir, Monet, Degas, Goya, and others of like quality. The bulk of the estate went to the Gould Foundation to promote Franco-American friendship (Reif 1984). The Gould family also provided generous endowments to New York University, where Frank, Jay's youngest son, graduated in 1899. Several of the school's buildings bear the Gould name.

Russell Sage

Russell Sage (1816–1906) was born in Oneida County, New York. He worked in his brother's grocery store as a clerk, and in 1839 became a partner in a wholesale grocery business. In 1851 he engaged in the first of his major swindles, and the resulting legal action reached the U.S. Supreme Court. For seven years Sage held the office of alderman in the city of Troy and was treasurer of Rensselaer County in New York. Using his public positions and chicanery, he succeeded in getting the city of Troy to sell its Troy and Schenectady Railroad, which had been constructed at great public expense. Through intermediaries, Sage bought the line for a mere $200,000—$50,000 down and fourteen years to pay. He then arranged to sell the line to the New York Central Railroad for $1 million.

In 1853, Sage was elected to Congress, and during his terms enormous grants of land and financial subsidies were given to railroad corporations. When he left Congress after serving two terms, Sage was a major stockholder of the La Crosse and Milwaukee Railroad, which had received land grants from the state of Wisconsin worth more than $17 million at a cost of about $1 million in bribes. Sage eventually gained control of the line and swindled stockholders and creditors. Driven into bankruptcy, the line was turned over to the major bondholders, who were Sage front men. The line was then renamed and (on paper) reorganized, and the whole scam was repeated. Although the overplundered line was unsafe and inefficient, its owner became a multimillionaire. He was also involved with Jay Gould in a number of stock and railroad schemes.

Using his accumulated railroad wealth, Sage became one of America's greatest usurers, charging as much as 2 percent per day to hard-pressed businessmen. He survived an attempt on his life, though his clerk and the bomber died, and when he died quietly at home in 1906, he was worth in excess of $29 billion in today's dollars (Klepper et al. 1998). His widow and second wife devoted much of her husband's wealth to philanthropy, particularly Russell Sage College and the Russell Sage Foundation "for the improvement of social and living conditions in the United States." Through the efforts of the foundation, small-loan acts were passed to protect workers from the usurious practice known as "salary lending."

Leland Stanford

The railroading tradition of Vanderbilt, Drew, Fisk, Gould, and Sage was not reserved for the eastern portion of the United States. But in the West there was none of the cutthroat competition that pervaded the East. Leland Stanford was born in Watervliet, New York, in 1824. In 1852, after a fire destroyed his law office in Wisconsin, Stanford moved to California, where he became involved in Republican politics. Elected governor in 1861, Stanford approved four public grants totaling millions of dollars for the construction of a transcontinental railroad line—he was president of the Central Pacific Railroad. With three colleagues he formed the Pacific Association and used their combined assets, $200,000, prudently—but not to build a railroad: The money was "laid out in bribes to Congressmen or others with influence" in the nation's capitol. Loth (1938: 159) states: "The Central Pacific had thrown its $200,000 upon Congressional waters and lo! it had returned in the form of a land grant for 9,000,000 acres and a loan of Federal bonds for $24,000,000."

The Central Pacific would run from the ocean to as far as it could reach in a race east,

These late nineteenth-century cartoons reflect popular attitudes toward two of the most powerful and ruthless robber barons of the day. Railroad magnate Cornelius Vanderbilt (left) tightens his stranglehold on the American public, while oil monopolist John D. Rockefeller (right) balances the world in the palm of his hand.

with the Union Pacific racing west. The lines linked up in 1869. For every mile of track, the lines received a subsidy from the government. This did not satisfy Stanford and his associates. They intimidated local governments into providing millions of dollars by threatening to have the line bypass their communities. San Francisco, for example, provided $550,000 (Myers 1936; Josephson 1962). Nevertheless, Stanford was elected to the U.S. Senate by the legislature in 1885 and reelected in 1890. In 1885, he established Leland Stanford, Jr., University—now known as Stanford University—in memory of his son, who had died in 1884 at age 15. Stanford died in 1893 worth over $18 billion in today's dollars (Klepper et al. 1998).

John D. Rockefeller

John D. Rockefeller (1839–1937) was born in Richford, New York, the son of a vendor of "patent medicines" (which had no patent and frequently contained cocaine and opium). A studious, hardworking youngster, at age 16 he secured a job as a bookkeeper for a produce merchant. He saved his meager earnings and become a successful commodities broker, buying and selling grain and produce. During the Civil War, Rockefeller made a fortune selling grain to the military while avoiding conscription. In 1862, he invested in a technique to extract kerosene from crude oil and in 1865 sold his share in the produce business to devote all his time and money to oil. His remarkable success in the oil business was aided by the Vanderbilt-owned railroad, which shipped the Rockefeller oil at a discount. A portion of the shipping costs were rebated—"kickbacks"—allowing Rockefeller to undercut his competitors.

In 1870, Rockefeller and Henry Flagler incorporated the Standard Oil Company, and during the following year they conspired to control the entire oil industry in the United States. First they obtained the Pennsylvania charter of a defunct corporation that had been authorized to engage in a plethora of business activities—the South Improvement Company (SIC). Then, in collusion with railroad officials, they doubled shipping rates for competing oil companies. But the increase for the SIC was rebated. By 1872, Rockefeller was intimidating rival oil companies into selling out to SIC. An "oil war" resulted as independent oil dealers fought the SIC by refusing to sell their oil to the Rockefeller-controlled refineries. The oil boycott hurt the railroads, which rebelled against Rockefeller. The Pennsylvania legislature finally revoked the SIC charter (Lloyd 1963).

The great monopolist struck again, this time conspiring with refinery owners to gain control over the setting of railroad oil shipping rates. The owners of the fifteen strongest oil firms in the United States swore an oath of secrecy and became part of what became known as the Standard Oil conspiracy. In league with the railroads, they controlled the delivery of oil, forcing competitors to sell out to Standard or pay exorbitant shipping costs that would render them noncompetitive. Those who were stubborn enough to resist were harassed with price wars and, if that didn't work, dynamite. The Rockefeller trust—Standard Oil—extended its vertical control of the oil industry to include pipelines, oil terminals, and direct marketing. By 1876 Standard Oil controlled 80 percent of the oil production in the United States, and by 1878 Rockefeller dominated the entire industry.

In 1877, a great oil boom threatened to break the Standard Oil monopoly. Rockefeller fought the new independents by refusing them the use of railroads, pipelines, and storage facilities. The independents organized and fought back,

financing the construction of the Tidewater Pipe Line to break Rockefeller's control over railroad rates. They attacked Standard Oil in the courts, and Flagler and Rockefeller were indicted in Pennsylvania for conspiracy in restraint of trade.

Undaunted, Rockefeller built a rival pipeline, slashed prices, attacked Tidewater credit in the money market, and convinced "his judges" to enjoin the issue of Tidewater bonds. In the finest tradition of direct action, Standard Oil operatives plugged up Tidewater pipelines. Under siege, Tidewater finally capitulated and was bought out by the National Transit Company, which was owned by Standard Oil (Lloyd 1963). By 1890, the Rockefeller trust controlled about 90 percent of the petroleum production in the United States, a situation that led to the passage of the Sherman Anti-Trust Act that same year. Nevertheless, by 1913, Rockefeller was worth $189.6 billion in today's dollars (Klepper et al. 1998).

John D. Rockefeller died in 1937. His legacy lives on in the University of Chicago, Rockefeller University, and the Rockefeller Foundation. His descendants have served as governors of New York, Arkansas, and West Virginia, U.S. senator from West Virginia, and vice president of the United States.

Conclusion

What does all this add up to, what are we to conclude? First, we must understand that the United States, as the Eisenhower Commission[1] pointed out, is quite a violent country (see also Hofstadter and Wallace 1971). Important aspects of U.S. history have hinged on the use of violence, both figurative (for example, "financial piracy") and literal (for example, the use of gunmen, thugs, private police, law enforcement agents, the National Guard, and the military), to further *private* ends. And as Woodiwiss (2005) notes, this legacy continues: "Corporate violation of health and safety laws, consumer- and environmental-protection laws kills thousands prematurely each year. Corporate fraud in the mutual fund business and the

---

[1]National Advisory Commission on the Causes and Prevention of Violence (1969); see also Graham and Gurr (1969).

insurance business, in particular, as well as the tidal wave of corporate fraud in general, jeopardizes the funds that many Americans have been putting away to educate their children and sustain a reasonable standard of life in their retirement." While the United States is telling other nations and the United Nations how to control organized crime, "so much of its business activity can be defined as simple racketeering" (2005: 1). And the insatiable need for campaign financing in the age of television gives the magnates of corporate America an influence that may exceed that of their nineteenth-century brethren.

Lincoln Steffens noted in 1902 that the "spirit of graft and of lawlessness is the American spirit" (1957: 8). With the western frontier closed, with the wealth of the "Robber Barons" institutionalized and their progeny firmly in control of the economy, there was only modest opportunity for the poor but ambitious adventurers of our urban frontiers. Among these later immigrants—Irish, Jewish, Italian—some have sought to innovate, not on the grand scale of the Vanderbilts, the Goulds, and the Rockefellers, but in a manner more consistent with available opportunity. Many found this opportunity in the politics and vice of urban America beginning in the latter half of the nineteenth century.

IMMIGRATION AND URBAN POLITICS

Immigration into the United States, except for brief depressions, grew dramatically in the years from 1820 to 1850, particularly in urban areas. During those three decades, the population of cities in the East and West quadrupled—New York's population rose to half a million (Bennett 1988). Immigrants and their offspring comprised more than two-thirds of the population of the largest cities in the Northeast and more than three-quarters of the population of New York, Boston, and Chicago (Buenker 1973).

These urban immigrants found employment in the most dangerous, monotonous, and poorly paid industries; women and children often labored as well. They were forced into slum housing reserved for their own ethnic group. Their culture, customs, and religious beliefs and practices were subjected to virulent attack by Americans of earlier stock. "Beset by hostility and discrimination on virtually all sides, the immigrant gradually found that he possessed at least one commodity that some native Americans coveted: his vote" (Buenker 1973: 3). A new breed of broker—the political boss—emerged to channel these votes into a powerful entity known as the "machine."

The necessities of urban America required construction workers, street cleaners, police and firemen, and service workers of all kinds, thus providing the immigrant with his livelihood and the political boss with patronage (Hofstadter 1956). During the 1880s, for example, New York's Tammany Hall had more than 40,000 municipal jobs at its disposal (Erie 1988). "The immigrant, in short, looked to politics not for the realization of high principles but for concrete and personal gains, and he sought these gains through personal relationships. And the boss, particularly the Irish boss, who could see things from the immigrant's angle but could also manipulate the American environment, became a specialist in personal relations and personal loyalties" (Hofstadter 1956: 182).

Organized crime in America "is the product of an evolutionary process extending more than a century" (Tyler 1962: 89). The roots of organized crime can be found in the politics of urban America before Prohibition, in the exemplary patron-client network known as the political machine. The underpinnings of this phenomenon are found in immigrant America and in the role of the Irish.

The Irish

There are strong historical parallels between the repression suffered by Sicilian peasants (discussed in Chapter 6) and that endured by their Irish counterparts. In both cases, this helped shape their culture. Ireland fell under foreign domination in the twelfth century, although it was not until the latter half of the sixteenth century and the reign of Elizabeth I (1558–1603) that England tried to impose Protestantism on the largely Catholic Irish. England used the religious dispute to seize large tracts of the most fertile land in Ireland. Thousands of Protestant Lowland Scots (and to a lesser extent, English) were encouraged to settle in Northern Ireland, and they soon owned most of the land. In the south, Oliver Cromwell crushed an Irish rebellion in 1649 and parceled out two-thirds of the land to his soldiers and followers (Shannon 1989). Ireland was reduced to a "country of peasants who were constantly oppressed by excessive rents, taxes, and tithes, and for whom poverty was a general condition" (Levine 1966: 5). Before Queen Elizabeth's rule, people of the island identified themselves as followers of a particular local chieftain; afterward, they called themselves Irish.

Paradoxically, this environment of misery gave rise to a culture of hospitality and openhandedness. The Irish looked forward to opportunities for social gatherings—even events as sad as death which meant gathering for an "Irish wake." As in southern Italy, a certain attitude developed: Let outsiders, the government, and the world be damned (Shannon 1989). Finding no justice in the formal system of government imposed by the British, the Irish turned to informal mechanisms, bargaining and negotiating for favorable outcomes. The Irish resorted to secret and open organizations on local and national levels as part of their continuous efforts to deal with British oppression. When the franchise was extended to Ireland, the Irish were caught up in the corrupt politics fostered by the British, and they became a thoroughly politicized people (Levine 1966).

Two centuries of personal experience with Anglo-Saxon (British) Protestant government led to a disdain for law among the Irish and provided the knowledge and skill that enabled them to serve an important role in the rough-and-tumble politics of America's urban areas. "The Irish political personality was shaped by confrontation with British imperialism and colonialism. In their efforts to free themselves from anti-Catholic Penal Laws and to achieve national independence, the Irish learned to compete within the context of the Anglo-Saxon political system. They became particularly adroit in the techniques of mass agitation, political organization, confrontation, and liberal, democratic politics" (McCaffrey 1976: 8).

English policy reduced the Irish to abject poverty. "Unless an Irish labourer could get hold of a patch of land and grow potatoes on which to feed himself and his children, the family starved." When the Irish potato crop failed (1845–1847) because of a fungus, there was widespread famine that resulted in the deaths of about 1.5 million people (Woodham-Smith 1962: 32). The workhouses, supported by taxes on landowners, were overflowing and they encouraged and sponsored Irish immigration to the United States as a way of easing their tax burden (Wyman 1984).

Once in the United States, the Irish tended to settle in urban areas. Uneducated and often illiterate—the British had denied them educational opportunity—Irish immigrants secured employment as unskilled laborers (McCaffrey 1976). But, "Irish immigrants came to America with a live political tradition" (Shannon 1989: 15): They "were the world's greatest experts in the art of warfare without confrontation. They could make alliances without formal conferences, agreements, or treaties that would leave a record. They could act in concert without giving commands but with a clear understanding of who was in charge. These were the lessons they had learned while living under repression. It did not take very long to learn how to apply their underground tactics to a democracy" (Reedy 1991: 22).

Between 1840 and 1844, about a quarter of a million people from mostly Catholic districts in Ireland entered the United States (Bennett 1988). In a single decade, 1845–1854, almost 1.5 million Irish immigrants entered the United States, and from 1855 until the turn of the twentieth century three million more arrived. They constituted the first large-scale immigration to the United States of a group since the arrival of Anglo-Saxon Protestants in the 1600s and 1700s. And "although generally peasants in their homeland, most of the new arrivals lacked either the resources or the desire to resume agrarian life. Arriving at a time when available land was scarce and agriculture mechanized, most sought work as unskilled laborers in the burgeoning industrial metropolises" (Buenker 1973: 2); only 6 percent would become farmers (Erie 1988). "By 1870, while only about 10 percent of the country's twenty-nine million native-born whites lived in the big cities, 42 percent of the nation's 1.8 million Irish-born lived in the twenty-five cities with populations greater than 50,000" (Erie 1988: 25). By 1850, more than one-third of New York City's population was Irish (Shannon 1989).

In the United States the Irish found themselves restricted from upward mobility, which was reserved for middle-class Protestants. In response, Irish immigrants remained in close-knit neighborhoods, where they joined the Democratic Party as an outlet for social and economic advancement. However, "instead of using politics as an avenue to integration into the middle class, politics enveloped the Irish, and the Irish social structure became an integral part of the process of recruiting other Irishmen into both the party and government. As the Irish swarmed into city politics, political office was recognized as the career among them, and politics became the secular extension of their essentially religious identity" (Levine 1966: 5).

Irish Catholic immigrants distrusted the public education system, which was dominated by Protestants: "Most Irish took a dim view of the usefulness of education and left its destiny in the hands of the clergy" (Levine 1966: 87). Although Catholic parochial education promoted Irish solidarity, it did not encourage secular intellectual pursuits and higher education. "Before World War I, few Irish boys and girls went on to secondary schools and before World War II few of them enrolled in college" (McCaffrey 1976: 82).

Politics and government employment provided the most readily available road to social mobility. Irish success in politics coincided with a decrease in the substantial crime rate among Irish immigrants, that is, until Prohibition in 1920 suddenly offered a new fast track to economic—albeit crime-based—success. "The Irish, the most numerous and advanced section of the immigrant community, took over the political party (usually the Democratic Party) at the local level and converted it into virtually a parallel system of government" (Shannon 1989: 62). The Irish clan system welded the Irish into a community capable of acting in concert while disregarding the formal governmental and legal structure (Reedy 1991).

Irish success in politics was also advanced by their ability to speak English, knowledge of government, and the timing of their arrival in the United States. They were also "community-minded, gregarious by nature, fond of visiting and talking" (McCaffrey 1976: 65); "the Irish have, in fact, been a highly social people, gregarious above everything" (Woodham-Smith 1962: 266). The Irish were also "neutral outsiders in the traditional ethnic antipathies and hostilities which the Central and East European ethnic groups brought to America from their homelands. 'A Lithuanian won't vote for a Pole, and a Pole won't vote for a Lithuanian,' according to a Chicago politician. 'A German won't vote for either of them—but all three will vote for a 'Turkey,' an Irishman" (Rakove 1975: 33). And there was the Irish connection to the saloon, a refuge from overcrowded slum dwellings. "For many years the saloon was as important a link in the communications process of the Irish social structure as was the parish church" (Levine 1966: 119). "Irish politicians used Catholic solidarity as a voting base, saloons as political clubs" (McCaffrey 1976: 140).

THE SALOON AND THE MACHINE

Throughout much of urban America, the saloon was a center of neighborhood activity, an important social base for political activity, and saloonkeepers became political powers in many cities. "Part of the appeal of the saloon was due to the social services it provided. In saloons files of newspapers in several languages were available along with cigars, mailboxes for regular patrons, free pencils, paper, and mail services to those wishing to send letters, and information on employment. Saloons provided a warm fire in the winter, public toilets, bowling alleys, billiard tables, music, singing, dancing, constant conversation, charity and charge accounts, quiet corners for students, and special rooms for weddings, union meetings, or celebrations. No other institution provided such a variety of necessary services to the public" (Engelmann 1979: 4).

City government was fragmented and power was dispersed. The city was divided into wards or districts, which were both electoral and administrative units containing relatively small numbers of people. The police and police (lower) courts operated on the ward or district level (Haller 1990a). These wards or districts were divided into electoral precincts. In this environment saloonkeepers were in a position to influence their customers and their votes—they could deliver their precincts and thus control the wards or districts. It was only a slight exaggeration to jest that in New York the easiest way to break up a meeting of Tammany Hall leaders was to open the door and shout: "Your saloon's on fire."

The Constitution does not provide for or even make mention of political parties. Indeed, the Founders perceived the political party as an unnecessary, if not divisive, element in the democratic process. Because of this constitutional omission, political parties enjoyed the same degree of autonomy as any other voluntary association, despite the reality that a political party often determined the outcome of an election. Until the late 1880s, a political party was a private association and as such determined its method for nominating candidates. The methods used lacked state control; they were informal and often effectively disenfranchised the electorate.

Throughout most of the nineteenth century, each political party provided its own ballots and ballot boxes at the general election—previously, a voter stated his preference in a voice vote. Parties printed their own ballots, called "tickets," in different colors. Voters chose one and placed it in the ballot box under the careful eye of party workers. This system virtually precluded "split-ticket" voting and facilitated the buying of votes, because party workers could readily see which ballot a voter cast.[2] This system enabled ward politicians, often with the help of street-corner boys and gangs that proliferated in urban ghettos, to deliver lopsided votes that helped the machine to dominate a city. Politicians employed the gangs for legitimate

purposes such as distributing campaign literature, hanging posters, and canvassing for votes. Gang members were also used as "repeaters" (who voted early and often) and as sluggers, who attacked rival campaign workers and intimidated voters. "Elections were held at odd hours in odd places, including bars and brothels. Voters seldom were informed of their franchise, and there was frequent intimidation of voters whose loyalties were suspect" (Johnston 1982: 46). With a small following and a willingness to engage in "political hardball," machine politicians could easily win power. "Powerful ward chieftains were often rewarded with a share of the patronage commensurate with their district's share of the total party vote" (Erie 1988: 26).

The machine politician was usually a popular figure who, in the days before social welfare programs, provided important services to loyal constituents—jobs, food, and assistance in dealing with public agencies, including the police and the courts. All that he asked for in return were votes and a free hand to become wealthy in politics. To the impoverished and powerless ghetto dweller, this was a small price to pay for services that would otherwise not be available. And even when such services became available through government agencies during the Great Depression, the loss of self-respect that this entailed discouraged many from applying. On the other hand, the precinct captain "asks no questions, exacts no compliance with legal rules of eligibility and does not 'snoop' into private affairs" (Merton 1967: 128).

The very personal nature of the machine is highlighted by one day in the life of George Washington Plunkitt, a Tammany district leader at the turn of the twentieth century who died a wealthy man in 1924 at the age of 82 (Riordon 1963: 93):

- 2:00 A.M. Aroused from sleep by ringing on his doorbell; went to the door and found a bartender, who asked him to go to the police station and bail out a saloonkeeper who had been arrested for violating the excise law. Furnished bail and returned to bed at three o'clock.

---

[2]From 1888 to 1890, states began providing the ballots for general elections, placing party labels on these ballots. This made the ballot secret and gave formal recognition to political parties, but only the major political parties. Laws were enacted to restrict third-party access to the new ballot. The treatment of political parties as public entities provided legal justification for government control of the primary elections that followed: "By 1896 all states but one had statutory regulations for nominating candidates for elective office" (Epstein 1986: 166).

- 6:00 A.M. Awakened by fire engines passing his house. Hastened to the scene of the fire, according to the custom of the Tammany district leaders, to give assistance to the fire sufferers, if needed. Met several of his election district captains who are always under orders to look out for fires, which are considered great vote-getters. Found several tenants who had been burned out, took them to a hotel, supplied them with clothes, fed them, and arranged temporary quarters for them until they could rent and furnish new quarters.
- 8:30 A.M. Went to the police court to look after constituents. Found six "drunks." Secured the discharge of four by a timely word with the judge, and paid the fine of two.
- 9:00 A.M. Appeared in the Municipal Court. Directed one of his district captains to act as counsel for a widow against whom dispossess proceedings had been initiated and obtained an extension of time. Paid the rent of a poor family about to be dispossessed and gave them a dollar for food.
- 11:00 A.M. At home again. Found four men waiting for him. One had been discharged by the . . . for neglect of duty, and wanted the district leader to fix things. Another wanted a job. . . . The third sought a place on the Subway and the fourth . . . was looking for work. The district leader spent nearly three hours fixing things for the four men, and succeeded in each case.
- 3:00 P.M. Attended the funeral of an Italian. . . . Hurried back to make his appearance at the funeral of a Hebrew constituent . . . and later attended the Hebrew confirmation ceremonies in the synagogue.
- 7:00 P.M. Went to the district headquarters and presided over a meeting of election district captains. . . .
- 8:00 P.M. Went to a church fair. . . .
- 9:00 P.M. At the clubhouse again. . . . Listened to the complaints of a dozen pushcart peddlers who said they were persecuted by the police and assured them he would go to Police Headquarters. . . .
- 10:30 P.M. Attended a Hebrew wedding. . . . Had previously sent a handsome wedding present to the bride.
- 12:00 P.M. In bed.

And no job was too unpleasant or demeaning for Democratic machine alderman Charley Weber of Chicago, as newsman Len O'Connor (1984: 117) reports:

When he hung up the phone, Charley looked at me with sadness and said, "That woman's lived in the ward for more than twenty years and she's Republican. . . . Now she's got a dead rat in the alley behind her house—and she don't call no Republican to come over and take care of her dead rat; she calls the alderman."

"So what are you going to do, Charley?"

"What can I do?" he replied. "I got to go over there, like I said, and pick up her rat and find a good garbage can with a top on it and, well take care of it."

"With one phone call," I said, "you could get somebody to do this."

"You crazy?" he said. "It's a good chance, dealin' with the rat. This woman'll be peekin' out the kitchen window and see the alderman drive up in his Cadillac and get out and pick up her dead rat and drive away with it. She'll tell everybody."

Robert Merton points out that the "political machine does not regard the electorate as an amorphous, undifferentiated mass of voters. With keen sociological intuition, the machine recognizes that the voter is a person living in a specific neighborhood, with specific personal problems and personal wants. Public issues are abstract and remote; private problems are extremely concrete and immediate. It is not through the generalized appeal to large public concerns that the machine operates, but through the direct quasi-feudal relationships between local representatives of the machine and voters in their neighborhood" (1967: 128). "There is nothing satanic about the Chicago machine," notes one newsman. "The basis of its success has always been the machine's dedication to a policy of doing little favors for the people. If a humble householder is getting the runaround from City Hall when he complains about a crew from the Department of Streets and Sanitation smashing up his curbing, a ward committeeman who learns of this will instantly raise hell with "somebody downtown" and get the curb fixed. The widow who is struggling to make ends meet will get a food basket delivered from the ward office" (O'Connor 1984: 114).

The very personal nature of the machine was noted back in 1931: "In the midst of the current depression, an Irish alderman named Moriarity distributed unleavened bread [matzah] to hundreds of Jewish families in his district, so that they might keep the feast of Passover. This will not cost him any votes" (McConaughy 1931: 312). A Tammany district leader in Manhattan at the turn of the century understood the business of being a political leader: "His job was to see that politics in his district were run efficiently for the purpose for which primarily politics existed. That purpose was to look after the welfare of individuals who resided in the district.... Almost any family was likely to want something. Perhaps the father had died and there was not money enough for the funeral. Perhaps one of the boys had been arrested, justly or unjustly. Perhaps a man who had a job on the police force had been dropped or moved to an undesirable location. Perhaps laborers had to be placed in the street cleaning department, or a transfer effected for one of his constituents from one department to another, or an increase in salary negotiated" (Hapgood and Moskowitz 1927: 41).

And when challenged, the machine could fight back with "hardball" tenacity. Besides voter fraud, machines used repression to weaken their opponents. "Irish party bosses were famous for the ingenuity with which they systematically weakened labor and socialist parties. Machine-controlled bureaucrats and judges denied parade and meeting permits. The party's plug-uglies armed with brass knuckles waded into peaceful assemblies. Opposition leaders were frequently arrested on trumped-up charges. For insurgent Jews and Italians, the Irish machines specialized

in rigorous enforcement of Sunday closing laws and in punitive denial of business permits" (Erie 1988: 11). By 1890, most big-city Democratic machines were controlled by Irish bosses. In New York, Irish immigrant Richard Croker led the infamous Fourth Avenue Tunnel Gang and, in 1886, at age 44, Tammany Hall which commanded 90,000 precinct workers and 40,000 jobs (Stevenson 2006).

UNDERWORLD AND UPPERWORLD

The machine leader was a master at keeping his ward or district organized, a broker par excellence who was in a key position to perform services for both the captains of industry and the captains of vice. The machine leader mediated between unorganized urban masses, the underworld, and the upperworld. The machine could deliver franchises, access to underdeveloped land sites, government contracts, tax abatements, and other special considerations (Steffens 1931). Once entrenched, the Irish machine bosses quickly built alliances with older-stock business interests (Erie 1988).

In Chicago, corrupt and inefficient government was promoted by business interests: "All factions, Republican and Democratic, were the handmaidens of the business interests" (Gosnell 1977: 8). "Populous and efficient as the underworld is, it could not wield the influence it does if it were not for its financial and political alliance with the inhabitants of Chicago's upperworld.... The deal is that the underworld shall have a 'liberal government' and a 'wide open town' and its upperworld allies shall be permitted to plunder the public treasury and appropriate wealth belonging to the people" (Dobyns 1932: 8).

In most cities, particularly Chicago, Kansas City, New York, Philadelphia, Pittsburgh, and St. Louis, "the rough and tumble ward and city bosses allowed the private utilities and favor-seeking men of wealth as well as the purveyors of vice to exploit the great mass of citizens" (Douglas 1974: ix; also Steffens 1957). Merton (1967: 135) notes the irony: "The supporters of the political machine include both the 'respectable' business class elements who are, of course, opposed to the criminal or racketeer and the distinctly 'unrespectable' elements of the underworld."

"Just as the political machine performs services for 'legitimate' business, so it operates to perform not dissimilar services for 'illegitimate' business: vice, crime and rackets" (Merton 1967: 132). Actually, the relationship between the racketeer and the machine was symbiotic. "Not only are the contributions from the underworld interests an important item in the campaign funds of the dominant party, but the services of the underworld personnel are also significant. When word is passed down from the gangster chiefs, all proprietors of gambling houses and speak-easies, all burglars, pick-pockets, pimps, fences, and their like, are whipped into line. In themselves they constitute a large block of votes, and they frequently augment their value to the machine by corrupt election practices" (Gosnell 1977: 42). As I was reminded many times while living in Chicago in the late twentieth century, death did not preclude the deceased from casting a vote.

In Kansas City, Missouri, a professional criminal (Audett 1954: 120) writes that he received his orders from gangster chief John Lazia, who was an important part of the Pendergast political machine. He looked up vacant lots: "I looked them up, precinct by precinct, and turned them lists in to Mr. Pendergast—that's Tom Pendergast, the man who used to run Kansas City back in them days. When we got a precinct all surveyed out, we would give addresses to them vacant lots. Then we would take the addresses and assign them to people we could depend on—prostitutes, thieves, floaters, anybody we could get on the voting registration books. On election days we just hauled these people to the right places and they went in and voted—in the right places."

In return for "delivering the vote," the ward boss was rewarded with patronage and recognized as lord of his area in a system that resembled feudalism. He appointed, directly or indirectly, police officials in his area, so he was in a position to protect vice activity (gambling, prostitution, liquor-law violations), which he "licensed."

In Kansas City, James Pendergast began his political career as a saloonkeeper. He became a dominant power in the First Ward, and his ability to deliver the vote enabled him to provide police protection for organized gambling. The police acted on his behalf, forcing independent operators to join the gambling combine or get out of business. Between 1900 and 1902, Pendergast named 123 of the 173 policemen on the Kansas City force. The Pendergast machine, under brother Tom, received the support of the gang bosses, and they in return secured police protection (Dorsett 1968). This led to the Election Day outrage of 1934. Despite an estimated 50,000 to 100,000 fake registrations, the machine was taking no chances (Steinberg 1972: 307):

> In the streets that morning, long black limousines cruised slowly past voters on their way to the polls and created an atmosphere of fright, for none of the cars had license plates and their passengers looked like gangsters. One of the cars did more than cruise. When it rolled past the opposition's headquarters in downtown Kansas City, seven shots were fired through the big window, though miraculously no one inside the crowded office was hit by a bullet. Another car pulled up at the ninth ward center of the opposition, and its passengers rushed inside to beat several persons with blackjacks.

With repeat voters, the beating of opposition voters, guns and baseball bats at polling places, the Pendergast machine won an overwhelming victory; four persons were killed and dozens beaten.

In Chicago, "the police department generally, and the [38] district stations in particular, were parts of the Democratic political machine. The department was a source of patronage jobs, and alderman and ward committeemen controlled law enforcement in their districts. In effect, each alderman functioned as the mayor of a community, with the district captain acting as his chief of police. Alderman would choose their own captains and controlled promotions, assignments, and transfers of personnel" (Bopp 1977: 91).

In New York, "in each district of the city, saloon keepers, owners of houses of prostitution, grocers who wanted to obstruct sidewalks, builders

Upperworld

Vice Entrepreneurs/Gangs - - - - - - - - **Political Machine** - - - - - - - - - - - - -Police

Immigrants/Workers

The political machine organized and mobilized urban immigrants and workers into a political force through which it dominated city government. Control of government, in particular the police, enabled the machine to protect vice entrepreneurs and gang leaders who reciprocated with financial and voting support. Control of government enabled the machine to provide special favors to the captains of business and industry who reciprocated with financial support. Control of public and private sector jobs, and funds with which to provide social services, strengthened machine support among the urban masses.

who wanted to violate the building regulations of the City, paid tribute at election time to the district leaders, who turned the money over to the general campaign fund of Tammany Hall. The organization collected not only from those who wanted to violate the laws, but also from those who wanted to live peacefully without having the windows of their shops smashed by the district leader's gang, or without being unnecessarily molested by the police" (Werner 1928: 293–94; Lardner and Reppetto 2000). And the Tammany-controlled district attorney was no better than the police: The district attorney's office "was a dumping ground for machine loyalists who could be trusted not to upset any of these arrangements" (Steinberg 2003: 775).

In Chicago, Kansas City, New York, and elsewhere, gambling operators paid heavily for protection, with the understanding that an occasional police raid would have to be staged "for appearances." The raiding squads were careful not to damage furniture or equipment, and policemen obligingly guarded the resort while the gambling operators and their customers made a brief, perfunctory appearance before a friendly magistrate before returning to the gaming house to resume play (Commission on the Review of the National Policy Toward Gambling 1976). An extraordinary Kings County (Brooklyn) Grand Jury, which sat for four years (1938–1942) investigating police corruption in that borough, found bookmaking and policy operations flourishing. Furthermore, the police had "a tendency to make unfounded arrests in order to create a record of apparent efficient law enforcement," and they had a "practice of presenting the evidence in such a manner that a conviction cannot possibly result." An "examination of the plainclothes policemen who were assigned to gambling cases in Kings County during the period covered by this investigation revealed that in all except a few cases the assignment to plainclothes work on gambling violations was accompanied by a distinct change in financial status" (Supreme Court of the State of New York 1942: 5–6).

A special grand jury in Philadelphia in 1928 found that certain members of that city's police department received $2 million in bribes annually (Haller 1985b). The National Commission on Law Observance and Enforcement concluded (1931: 45): "Nearly all of the large cities suffer from an alliance between politicians and criminals. For example, Los Angeles was controlled by a few gamblers for a number of years. San Francisco suffered similarly some years ago and at one period in its history was so completely dominated by gamblers that three prominent gamblers who were in control of the politics of the city and who quarreled about the appointment of the police settled their quarrel by shaking dice to determine who would name the chief for the first two years, who for the second two years, and who for the third."

REFORM AND NATIVISM

In cities dominated by machine politics, the same ones that would spawn organized crime, a pattern of corruption-reform-corruption-reform was often interspersed with investigations and widely publicized hearings. It is important to recognize the political motivation, and the not-insignificant degree of hypocrisy, behind many of these exposés and reform efforts. In New York, investigations were often initiated by upstate, rural, Protestant Republican interests against downstate (New York City) urban, Catholic and Jewish Democrats. In 1894, for example, the New York State Senate appointed a special committee, five Republicans and two Democrats, headed by Senator Clarence Lexow of (heavily Republican) Rockland County, to investigate charges of vice and corruption leveled by the (Presbyterian) Reverend Charles H. Parkhurst. The hearings revealed a sordid tale of corruption. However, the recommendations of the committee, given its findings, were actually quite modest, because they were designed not to correct the problem but rather to enable Republicans to share in the rich patronage created by the Democratic machine (Fogelson 1977). The threat of investigation and public disclosure was often used to secure the support of city politicians for

legislation favored by rural or big business interests. Corruption was real and often rampant, but many of the efforts purporting to deal with it were just as corrupt—morally, if not legally.

Reform was typically fostered by business leaders for their own ends: "The machine leaders had to be paid to defeat legislation opposed by business interests: municipal ownership, labor legislation, adequate health regulations, better schools, new parks, decent housing, aid to the needy. . . . Businessmen in politics were eager without bribes to oppose anything that raised taxes or threatened private enterprise. They wanted to stop paying graft, but keep all the favors graft bought. They demonstrated that the perennial demand for business methods in government was as logical as a cry that penitentiaries ought to be run by criminals" (Loth 1938: 280).

In Chicago, dishonest, corrupt, and inefficient government was actually promoted by business interests: "All factions, Republican and Democratic, were the handmaidens of the business interests" (Gosnell 1977: 8). "Reform" was frequently a favorable label applied by newspapers to the efforts of two, sometimes overlapping, interest groups: businessmen and white, Anglo-Saxon Protestants, whose voting strength was in rural America. "Most immigrant voters realized instinctively that honesty, efficiency, and economy in government would do nothing to alleviate their condition and could severely cripple the system's ability to dispense favors" (Buenker 1973: 26).

Reformers were often part of the rampant *nativism* that at times intertwined with social Darwinism. Nativism helped tie urban dwellers—immigrants in general, Catholics (and often Jews) in particular—to the political machine. Attitudes of extreme religious prejudice have a long history in our country, dating back to the first colonists. Settlers came to the New World in search of religious freedom, but they sought only *their* religious freedom. Virulent anti-Catholicism was such an important part of Colonial America that in the seventeenth century, Mass could not be publicly celebrated anywhere in Colonial America except in Pennsylvania. In 1834, a mob of Protestant workmen in Charlestown, Massachusetts, ransacked and burned a convent, the first fruit of Catholic educational enterprise in New England (Bennett 1988). Samuel Morse (1791–1872), distinguished painter, inventor of the telegraph, and son of a prominent minister, wrote, "We are the dupes of our hospitality. The evil of immigration brings to these shores illiterate Roman Catholics, the tools of reckless and unprincipled politicians, the obedient instruments of their more knowing priestly leaders"[3] (quoted in Bennett 1988: 40). In contrast, the machine politician "cultivated the immigrant's ethnic pride by defending him against nativist attack, observing his customs, and concerning himself with conditions in the homeland" (Buenker 1973: 5). The most successful campaign waged by nativist interests involved prohibiting the beverages most favored by immigrants.

PROHIBITION

The acrimony between rural and urban America, between Protestants and Catholics, between Republicans and (non-Southern) Democrats, between "native" Americans and more recent immigrants, and between business and labor reached a pinnacle with the ratification of the Eighteenth Amendment in 1919. Efforts at limiting or prohibiting alcohol consumption, however, date back to the earliest days of our republic. Residents of the United States have traditionally consumed large quantities of alcoholic beverages. In 1785, Dr. Benjamin Rush, surgeon general of the Continental Army and a signer of the Declaration of Independence, wrote a pamphlet decrying the use of alcohol. The pamphlet helped fuel the move toward prohibition and inspired in 1808 the establishment of the first temperance society whose cause was supported by Protestant churches throughout the country (Hamm 1995).

The temperance movement made great progress everywhere in the country, often accompanying nativist sentiments that swept over the United States during the late 1840s and early 1850s. In 1869, the Prohibition Party attempted, with only

limited success, to make alcohol a national issue. In 1874, the Women's Christian Temperance Union (WCTU) was established, and in 1893 the Anti-Saloon League was organized. Around the turn of the twentieth century, both groups moved from efforts to change individual behavior to a campaign for national prohibition. The WCTU was handicapped because its members lacked the franchise—women could not vote. After a period of dormancy, the prohibition movement was revived in the years 1907–1919 (Humphries and Greenberg 1981). By 1910, the Anti-Saloon League had become one of the most effective political action groups in U.S. history. It had mobilized America's Protestant churches behind a single purpose: to enact national prohibition (Tindall 1988). In 1915, nativism and prohibitionism fueled the rebirth of the Ku Klux Klan, which spread into northern states and exerted a great deal of political influence, including control of state politics in Indiana (see Tucker 1991). During World War I, anti-German feelings, already strong, were made more intense because brewing and distilling were associated with German immigrants (Cashman 1981).

Prohibition was accomplished by the political efforts of an economically declining segment of the American middle class. "By effort and some good luck this class was able to impose its will on the majority of the population through rather dramatic changes in the law" (Chambliss 1973: 10). Andrew Sinclair (1962: 163) points out, "In fact, national prohibition was a measure passed by village America against urban America." We could add: much of Protestant America against Catholic (and, to a lesser extent, Jewish) America. "Thousands of Protestant churches held thanksgiving prayer meetings. To many of the people who attended, prohibition represented the triumph of America's towns and rural districts over the sinful cities" (Coffey 1975: 7; Gusfield 1963). Prohibition reflected not only revulsion at drunkenness and contempt for the drinking immigrant masses, but also represented an assault on the pleasures and amenities of city life (Bennett 1988).

Big business was also interested in Prohibition; alcohol contributed to industrial inefficiency, labor strife, and the saloon that served the interests

---

[3]Morse was also a strong defender of slavery.

of machine politics. Workmen's compensation laws also helped stimulate business support for temperance. Between 1911 and 1920, forty-one states had enacted workmen's compensation laws. "By making employers compensate workers for industrial accidents the law obligated them to campaign for safety through sobriety. In 1914 the National Safety Council adopted a resolution condemning alcohol as a cause of industrial accidents" (Cashman 1981: 6).

The Eighteenth Amendment to the Constitution was ratified in 1919 and ten months later, over a veto by President Woodrow Wilson, Congress passed the Volstead Act. The act strengthened the language of the amendment and defined all beverages containing more than 0.5 percent alcohol as intoxicating. Although prohibitionists believed that primary enforcement would come at the state and local level, the Volstead Act provided for federal enforcement and the Prohibition Bureau, an arm of the Treasury Department, was created. Local enforcement was unenthusiastic and inconsistent, and the Prohibition Bureau soon became notorious for employing agents on the basis of political patronage (Hamm 1995).[4] This patronage provision helped pass the act, and almost 18,000 federal jobs were exempted from Civil Service restrictions: "The clause had been passed by dry votes in Congress. The lobbyists who cracked the whip over the legislators later explained that Congress had insisted upon the exemption in return for passage of the Volstead Act" (Loth 1938: 346). The treasury agent who brought down Al Capone commented that the "most extraordinary collection of political hacks, hangers-on, and passing highwaymen got appointed as prohibition agents" (Irey and Slocum 1948: 5).

In addition to being inept and corrupt, Prohibition Bureau agents were a public menace: They ran up a record of being killed (by 1923, 30 had been murdered) and for killing hundreds of civilians, often innocent women and children. By 1930, the figure rose to 86 federal agents and 200

civilians killed. Prohibition agents set up illegal roadblocks and searched cars; drivers who protested were in danger of being shot. Agents who killed innocent civilians were rarely brought to justice—when they were indicted by local grand juries, the cases were simply transferred, and the agents escaped punishment (Woodiwiss 1988).

The bureau was viewed as a training school for bootleggers, because agents frequently left the service to join their wealthy adversaries. The Treasury Department was headed by the banking magnate Andrew Mellon (1855–1937), a man who had millions invested in the liquor trade before Prohibition and was not interested in enforcing the new law (Sinclair 1962). Neither were most local police agencies, and very little money was allocated to enforce the most sweeping criminal law ever enacted in the United States (Asbury 1950). Ten days after the Eighteenth Amendment went into effect, three Prohibition agents were indicted in Chicago for bribery and selling seized liquor to bootleggers. And it got worse. Prohibition agents escorted liquor trucks and helped smugglers unload cargoes: "On salaries averaging less than three thousand dollars a year, prohibition agents bought country homes, town houses, city and suburban real estate, speedboats, expensive automobiles, furs, and jewelry for their women, and fine horses; many reported to work in chauffeur-driven cars." One agent had been a worker on a garbage truck before being appointed: "He worked three months as an agent and then took a six-month leave so that he and his wife could tour Europe" (Irey and Slocum 1948: 6). It was not until 1930 that Prohibition Bureau agents were placed under civil service procedures (Gottschalk 2006).

Herbert Packer (1968: 263) reminds us that people do not necessarily respond to new criminal prohibitions by acquiescence. He points out that resistance can be fatal to the new norm; moreover, when this happens "the effect is not confined to the immediate proscription but makes itself felt in the attitude that people take toward legal proscriptions in general." Thus, primary resistance or opposition to a new law such as Prohibition can result, secondarily, in disregard for laws in general: *negative contagion*. During Prohibition, a "general

---

[4]In 1923, New York repealed a statute that had incorporated Prohibition into state law, thereby placing the burden of alcohol law enforcement on federal agents.

tolerance of the bootlegger and a disrespect for federal law were translated into a widespread contempt for the process and duties of democracy" (Sinclair 1962: 292). This was exemplified by the general lawlessness that reigned in Chicago:

> Banks all over Chicago were robbed in broad daylight by bandits who scorned to wear masks. Desk sergeants at police stations grew weary of recording holdups—from one hundred to two hundred were reported every night. Burglars marked out sections of the city as their own and embarked upon a course of systematic plundering, going from house to house night after night without hindrance. . . . Payroll robberies were a weekly occurrence and necessitated the introduction of armored cars and armed guards for the delivery of money from banks to business houses. Automobiles were stolen by the thousands. Motorists were forced to the curbs on busy streets and boldly robbed. Women who displayed jewelry in nightclubs or at the theater were followed and held up. Wealthy women seldom left their homes unless accompanied by armed escorts. (Asbury 1942: 339)

Every year until Prohibition was repealed, the murder rate rose, going from 6.8 per 100,000 persons in 1920 to 9.7 in 1933 (Chapman 1991).

In the ninety days preceding the date the Eighteenth Amendment became effective, $500,000 worth of bonded whiskey was stolen from government warehouses, and afterward it continued to disappear (Sinclair 1962). Less than one hour after Prohibition went into effect, six armed men stole $100,000 worth of whiskey from two Chicago boxcars. In February 1920, a case of whiskey purchased in Montreal for $10 could easily be sold in New York for $80 (Coffey 1975). In fact, the Canadians began making so much money from Prohibition that provinces with similar laws soon repealed them (Sinclair 1962). The heavily Catholic state of Rhode Island refused to ratify Prohibition and its 400 miles of coastline soon became awash with boats bringing in liquor from Canada. Newport, Rhode Island, is barely 200

nautical miles from Nova Scotia and Yarmouth where the Bronfman brothers, owners of the Seagram liquor empire, sold legal liquor at 65 cents a gallon to smugglers who resold it in the United States for $7 a gallon (Krajicek 2007).

A limited amount of beer and wine could be made under the Prohibition law for personal consumption and almost immediately, stores sprang up selling hops, yeast, malt, cornmeal, grains, copper tubing, crocks, kettles, jugs, bottle tops, and other equipment for home distilling and brewing. Within one week of the onset of Prohibition, portable stills were on sale throughout the country (Asbury 1950; Kavieff 2000). This legal loophole was soon exploited for commercial purposes by organized crime.

ORGANIZED CRIME

Until Prohibition, gangsters were merely errand boys for the politicians and the gamblers; they were at the bottom of a highly stratified social milieu. The gamblers were under the politicians, who were "kings" (Katcher 1959). Prohibition changed the relationship among the politicians, vice entrepreneurs, and gang leaders. Before 1920, the political boss acted as a patron for the vice entrepreneurs and gangs: He protected them from law enforcement, and they gave him financial and electoral support. The onset of Prohibition, however, unleashed an unsurpassed level of criminal violence, and violence is the specialty of the gangs. Physical protection from rival organizations and armed robbers was suddenly more important than was protection from law enforcement. Prohibition turned gangs into empires (Logan 1970). With Prohibition "pumping money into mob pockets, power shifted from men with votes to men with money and guns" (Pietrusza 2003: 302).

Although America had organized crime before Prohibition, it "was intimately associated with shabby local politics and corrupt police forces"; there was no organized crime activity "in the syndicate style" (King 1969: 23). The "Great Experiment" was a catalyst that caused organized crime, especially violent forms, to blossom into

Changes in the Social Order	
Pre-Prohibition	**Prohibition**
Machine Politicians	Gangs
Vice Entrepreneurs	Machine Politicians
Gangs	Vice Entrepreneurs

an important force in American society. Prohibition mobilized criminal elements in an unprecedented manner. Pre-Prohibition crime, insofar as it was organized, centered around corrupt political machines, vice entrepreneurs, and, at the bottom, gangs. The competitive violence of Prohibition turned the power structure upside down. It also led to a new level of criminal organization.

In order to be profitable, the liquor business, licit or illicit, demands large-scale organization. Raw material must be purchased and shipped to manufacturing sites. This requires trucks, drivers, mechanics, warehouses, and laborers. Manufacturing efficiency and profit are maximized by economies of scale. This requires large buildings where the whiskey, beer, or wine can be manufactured, bottled, and placed in cartons for storage and distribution to wholesale outlets or saloons and speakeasies. If the substances are to be smuggled, ships, boats, and their crews are required, as well as trucks, drivers, mechanics, laborers, and warehouses. And there is the obvious need to physically protect shipments through the employment of armed guards. "As illegal entrepreneurs," notes Mark Haller (1985a: 142), bootleggers "also had to learn to use legal institutions to service their illegal enterprises, they had to learn banking to handle their money, insurance to protect their ships, and the methods of incorporation to gain control of chemical and cosmetics companies from which they diverted industrial alcohol. They also dealt with varied legitimate companies to purchase trucks, boats, copper tubing, corn sugar, bottles, and labels." Businessmen who had previously been involved in the legal liquor industry did not remain in business during Prohibition; this left the field open to opportunistic amateurs, often violent young men who had heretofore been left behind in the race for economic success. Bootlegging "was

a relatively open field of endeavor and allowed ambitious young Italians and Jews (as well as some Poles and Irishmen) to catapult to quick success" (Haller 1974: 5).

Furthermore, Prohibition encouraged cooperation between gang leaders from various regions—*syndication*. Legal or illegal, the liquor business is international in scope. Smuggled rum and whiskey from Canada, the Caribbean, and Europe had to be moved across the Great Lakes or from the Atlantic onto beaches along the East Coast. Shipments then had to be trucked intra- and interstate to warehouses at distribution points. At each juncture the shipment required political and physical protection. Only the criminal organization dominant in the local area could provide such protection. Syndication arose out of these needs, and a number of meetings between important organized figures have been documented: "Meetings were held for a number of reasons—to settle disputes, choose successors for slain or deposed leaders, divide local or regional markets, or discuss production, supply, and distribution problems. Some gatherings consisted of Italian criminals and limited their discussions to problems of interest to them. Others involved only Jews or Irish or some other ethnic group; still others were formed of members of a variety [of] ethnic syndicates" (Nelli 1976: 212).

With the onset of the Great Depression (1929) and the subsequent repeal of Prohibition (1933), the financial base of organized crime narrowed considerably. Many players dropped out: Some went into legitimate enterprises or employment; others drifted into conventional criminality. Bootlegging, as noted earlier, required trucks, drivers, mechanics, garages, warehouses, bookkeepers, and lawyers—skills and assets that could be converted to noncriminal endeavors. For those who remained in the business, reorganization was necessary. "When prohibition ended in 1933, bootleggers were still young men—generally in their thirties— yet with wealth and nationwide contacts that had grown out of their bootlegging enterprises. In addition to their liquor interests, they already had substantial investments in restaurants, nightclubs, gambling, and other profitable businesses. In the 1930's and 1940's, then, they used their national contacts, diverse interests, and available capital to cooperate in a variety of entrepreneurial activities, legal and illegal" (Haller 1974: 5–6).

Some entrepreneurial bootleggers simply continued in the newly legitimate liquor trade. Sam Bronfman moved the main office of the Seagram Company from Canada to New York and paid $1.5 million in taxes that the United States said he owed on Prohibition-era shipments. Taking advantage of the start-up time American distillers needed to get back into business, Seagram flooded the country with Canadian whiskey (Allen 1998). His bootlegging confederate, Lewis Rosenstiel, continued to operate Schenley Distillers Company. The Reinfeld syndicate—Joe Reinfeld and New Jersey crime boss Longie Zwillman—became Renfield Importers. Joseph P. Kennedy, father of a future president, moved from bootlegging to head Somerset Importers (Fox 1989).

Just before the end of Prohibition, gang leaders began meeting throughout the United States in anticipation of the new era. In 1932, the Chicago Police Department detained a number of gangsters, including Paul Ricca of the Capone syndicate, Lucky Luciano, and Meyer Lansky of New York, for questioning. In 1934, the major leaders of organized crime in the East gathered at a New York hotel, with Johnny Torrio presiding. They came to an understanding: "Each boss remained czar in his own territory, his rackets unmolested, his local authority uncontested. In murder, no one—local or imported—could be killed in his territory without his approval. He would have the right to do the job himself or permit an outsider to come in-but only at his invitation. In fact, no lawlessness on an organized scale could take place in his domain without his sanction and entire consent, unless he was overruled by the board of governors." Now

each mob leader "had behind him not just his own hoods, but a powerful amalgamation of all hoods. Every gang chieftain was guaranteed against being interfered with in his own area—and against being killed by a rival mobster" (Turkus and Feder 1951: 99).

"A second meeting was called in Kansas City to hear from the Western executives. The Capone crowd from Chicago and the Kansas City mob liked the idea. Reports came from Cleveland and Detroit that the Mayfield Gang and the Purple Mob wanted in. Boston and Miami, New Orleans and Baltimore, St. Paul and St. Louis—all flocked to the confederacy of crime, until it was nationwide" (Turkus and Feder 1951: 99). Hank Messick (1967: 32) adds, "The country was divided into territories. Wars ended between regional groups, between religious groups, between national groups." There are several significant indications of this cooperation: the founding of modern Las Vegas (discussed in Chapter 12), labor racketeering on a national level (discussed in Chapter 14), and the establishment and joint ownership of illegal casinos by Irish, Jewish, and Italian criminals from New York, Detroit, and Chicago (Haller 1990a).

Beginning in 1950, organized crime drew the attention of Congress and became a political issue. James Jacobs and Elizabeth Mullin (2003: 293) state that "the largely successful war on organized crime has often been told as a story starring FBI investigators and federal prosecutors," and they argue that Congress has not been given sufficient credit for "bolstering support for and sometimes prodding the law enforcement agencies." Congress, in particular the United States Senate, has used the hearing process to expose organized crime and related activities such as corruption, providing the framework for statutes to deal with the problem.

THE KEFAUVER CRIME COMMITTEE

The importance of organized crime as a national political issue was recognized by Tennessee Senator Estes Kefauver in 1950. The five-term member of Congress had been elected to the Senate in 1948 despite vigorous opposition from the political machine headed by notorious "Boss" Ed Crump of Memphis. On January 5, 1950, Kefauver introduced a resolution "to investigate gambling and racketeering activities" by a special subcommittee. The crime committee was established by Senate resolution, but not without a fight. Bosses of big-city machines were concerned that an investigation might look into their activities. Further, the chairman of the Judiciary Committee, Pat McCarren of Nevada, was apparently worried about the impact of an investigation on his native state, so he held Kefauver's bill captive for several months. On April 6, 1950, Charles Binaggio, the gambling boss of Kansas City, Missouri, and one of his men were murdered in a Democratic Party clubhouse. This helped spur passage of the Kefauver legislation, and on May 10, 1950, the senator became chair of the Special Committee to Investigate Organized Crime in Interstate Commerce, launching the first major congressional investigation into the phenomenon (Moore 1974). This was made all the more dramatic by a new element in public hearings—television:

> One factor, television, was largely responsible for fixing the public consciousness upon this one investigation. . . . For the first time millions of Americans (some 20 million by one estimate) observed the periodic outbursts of drama and boredom which comprised a congressional hearing as it unfolded. Americans gaped as the denizens of other worlds—bookies, pimps, and gangland enforcers, crime bosses and their slippery lawyers—marched across their television screens. They watched and were impressed by the schoolmasterish Estes Kefauver, the dignified Tennessean who was the committee's first chairman, as he condemned criminals and the system of ineffective law enforcement, graft, and popular apathy which permitted them to thrive. (Wilson 1975: 353)

The first hearing was conducted on May 26, 1950. Before Kefauver's term as chair ended on May 1, 1951, the committee heard more than six hundred witnesses in fourteen cities. This whirlwind of activity led the committee to conclude:

> Crime is on a syndicated basis to a substantial extent in many cities. The two major crime syndicates in this country are the Accardo-Guzik-Fischetti syndicate, whose headquarters are Chicago; and the Costello-Adonis-Lansky syndicate based in New York. . . .
>
> There is a sinister criminal organization known as the Mafia operating throughout the country with ties in other nations in the opinion of the committee. The Mafia is the direct descendant of a criminal organization of the same name originating in the island of Sicily. In this country, the Mafia has also been known as the Black Hand and the Unione Siciliano [sic]. The membership of the Mafia today is not confined to persons of Sicilian origin. The Mafia is a loose-knit organization specializing in the sale and distribution of narcotics, the conduct of various gambling enterprises, prostitution, and other rackets based on extortion and violence. The Mafia is the binder which ties together the two major criminal syndicates as well as numerous other criminal groups throughout the country. (Kefauver 1951a: 1–2)

The committee reported that widespread corruption allowed the syndicates to flourish.

While the committee demonstrated extensive interstate contact and investments between gambling figures, notes Moore (1974: 101), "it failed to show extensive interstate control of gambling operations." He argues, however, that the committee's conclusions about gambling had intellectual sincerity based on substantial if not always convincing evidence. Such was not the case with its conclusions about the Mafia: "Inadequate evidence and the necessity to reach some conclusion rushed the Committee into fuzzy and ill-founded statements that brought the senators sensational headlines but left an ugly popular misunderstanding in the country" (1974: 114). The Mafia, according to Kefauver (1951b: 19), is "the shadowy international organization that lurks behind much of America's organized criminal activity," a conclusion for which he credits the Federal Bureau of Narcotics. In fact, the committee's final report contained a great deal of nonsense.

According to Dwight Smith (1974: 85), there is an American preoccupation with alien conspiracy. "One of the conditions required for an alien conspiracy theory is a set of 'facts' or assumptions that can be constructed into evidence supporting a conspiratorial explanation. Such 'facts' often make fascinating reading; they sell newspapers, books, and magazines." Smith argues that the conspiracy theory provided the Federal Bureau of Narcotics with an explanation for failure. "The notion of total suppression of illegal narcotics use through importation control was a self-proclaimed mission, and it had not been attained. How better to explain failure (and, incidentally, to prepare the ground for increased future budgets) than to argue that, dedicated though it might be, the bureau was hard pressed to overcome an alien, organized, conspiratorial force which, with evil intent and conspiratorial methods, had forced its way on an innocent public?" In this era of McCarthyism, the search for alien conspiracies proved to be good politics.

Moore (1974: 211) concludes that the committee's "most constructive work had been the documenting of widespread corruption at the local and state level and the exposing of attempts by law enforcement officials to conceal their malfeasance or ineptitude behind a maze of conflicting, overlapping jurisdictional boundaries." Unfortunately, notes Moore, committee preoccupation with ethnic conspiracies detracted from these findings and some of the committee's constructive policy recommendations. The committee tied organized crime and the Mafia inextricably, thereby equating Italians with organized crime.

THE McCLELLAN COMMITTEE

In 1956, the Senate Permanent Subcommittee on Investigations (PSI) began an inquiry into the Teamsters Union, an effort that met with union recalcitrance (see Chapter 14). The Senate responded by establishing the Select Committee on Improper Activities in the Labor or Management Field. The findings of the Select Committee led to the passage of the 1959 Labor-Management Reporting and Disclosure Act, usually called the Landrum-Griffin Act after its two sponsors. The Select Committee expired in 1960, but Senator John L. McClellan (D-AR) remained chair of the Permanent Subcommittee on Investigations (PSI). In 1963, the PSI held televised hearings on organized crime and introduced the public to its star witness, Joseph Valachi. Peter Maas (1968: 40) states that Senator McClellan visited Valachi privately at the District of Columbia jail just before the hearings began: "According to Valachi, the senator requested he skip any mention of Hot Springs, in McClellan's home state," which was notorious for its wide-open gambling operations.

Joseph Valachi

In 1962, Joseph Valachi was a 60-year-old convicted drug trafficker and member of the Genovese Family serving a federal sentence for drug trafficking. A fellow inmate accused him of being an informer for the Federal Bureau of Narcotics; because his accuser was also a member, a "made guy," the accusation was life-threatening. Valachi was subsequently approached by an inmate he thought was an enforcer for the Genovese Family. He attacked the inmate with a lead pipe—the wrong man, as it turned out—and beat him to death. In 1963, the gravel-voiced Valachi was in Washington, DC, appearing before the McClellan (PSI) Committee.

Valachi was inducted into the faction headed by Salvatore Maranzano during the "Castellammarese War" (discussed in Chapter 4), and had been a soldier for more than 30 years. The career criminal told of a secret society that insiders referred to as *Cosa Nostra*, replete with blood oaths and murders. He discussed the Castellammarese war, Luciano's murder of Joe "the boss" Masseria, Salvatore Maranzano, and the assassination of some forty other Mafia bosses (that never happened). Valachi outlined the structure of each crime Family and explained how they were linked together through a national commission—the "Supreme Court of Organized Crime." Once the television lights were turned on, notes Maas (1968: 41), senators bombarded Valachi with questions designed to score points with the voters back home. Nebraska Senator Carl Curtis, for example, asked about organized crime in Omaha: "After a moment's reflection, the barely literate Valachi carefully cupped his hand over his mouth, turned to a Justice Department official sitting next to him, and whispered something. Those viewing the scene could be forgiven for supposing that Senator Curtis had hit on a matter of some import that Valachi wanted to check before answering. He was in fact asking, 'Where the hell is Omaha?'"

Valachi was a low-echelon soldier whose first-hand knowledge of organized crime was limited to street-level experiences. Much of the information attributed to him is obviously well beyond his personal experience. Virgil Peterson notes that some of Valachi's testimony was extremely vague, confusing, and inconsistent. "Not infrequently, it would appear, he either withheld facts that should have been known to him or deliberately lied" (1983: 425). Nevertheless, this did not prevent his disclosures from becoming the core of a chapter on organized crime in the final report of the President's Commission on Law Enforcement and Administration of Justice.

PRESIDENT'S COMMISSION ON LAW ENFORCEMENT AND ADMINISTRATION OF JUSTICE

In 1964, Lyndon B. Johnson was serving the remainder of John F. Kennedy's term and seeking election as president. The Republicans had nominated Senator Barry M. Goldwater of Arizona, who launched what has come to be known as a "law-and-order" campaign: The Republicans attacked the Democratic administration for being "soft on crime." Johnson won a landslide victory, but the issue of "crime in the streets" lingered on. In order to blunt criticism (and, Richard Quinney [1974] argues, to divert attention from the Vietnam conflict), Johnson launched his own "war on crime."

On March 8, 1965, in a message to the Eighty-ninth Congress, "Crime, Its Prevalence and Measures of Prevention," President Johnson announced: "I am establishing the President's Commission on Law Enforcement and Administration of Justice. The commission will be composed of men and women of distinction who share my belief that we need to know far more about the prevention and control of crime." Nine different task forces were established, including the Task Force on Organized Crime, headed by Charles H. Rogovin, with Donald R. Cressey and Ralph Salerno serving as consultants. Cressey (1969) and Salerno (with Tompkins 1969) extended the influence of the President's Commission by writing books on organized crime. In its report to the commission, the Task Force on Organized Crime (1967: 6) stated: "Today the core of organized crime in the United States consists of 24 groups operating as criminal cartels in large cities across the Nation. Their membership is exclusively men of Italian descent, they are in frequent communications with each other, and their smooth functioning is insured by a national body of overseers. To date, only the Federal Bureau of Investigation has been able to document fully the national scope of these groups, and the FBI intelligence indicates that the organization as a whole has changed its name from the Mafia to Cosa Nostra." The last statement was obviously based on the revelations of Joseph Valachi.

The Task Force continued what the Kefauver Committee had begun, equating organized crime with Italians. The only new wrinkle was a name change (Messick 1973: 8): "La Cosa Nostra was created [by the FBI via Valachi] as a public image. This simple device of giving the Mafia a new name worked wonders. Hoover was taken off the limb where he had perched for so long, and citizens had a new menace to talk about with tales of blood oaths, contracts for murder, secret societies." Hank Messick (1967) argues that this picture was 30 years out of date. More important, however, were the policy implications.

The Task Force recommended a witness protection program, special federal grand juries, and legislation permitting electronic surveillance—recommendations that were enacted into law. The Task Force noted the inadequacy of budgetary allocations devoted to dealing with organized crime and the lack of coordination among agencies charged with combating organized crime activity. Accordingly, budgetary allocations were increased to deal with the "new" menace, and in 1967 federal organized crime strike forces were established in each city with a *Cosa Nostra* Family. In 1968, the Omnibus Crime Control and Safe Streets Act was enacted, providing law enforcement agencies with legal guidelines for electronic surveillance (discussed in Chapter 15). In 1970, Congress passed the Organized Crime Control Act, which contains the RICO provisions discussed in Chapter 15.

The Task Force concluded that the major income for organized crime is derived from gambling, with loansharking second. Little attention was given to other sources of income, in particular drug trafficking and labor racketeering. After the task force disbanded, the Permanent Subcommittee on Investigations remained the congressional committee most interested in organized crime, although it was eclipsed for several years by the President's Commission on Organized Crime. (In government, a committee is a legislative unit, while a commission is part of the executive branch.)

PRESIDENT'S COMMISSION ON ORGANIZED CRIME (PCOC)

The Reagan administration era was extraordinary with respect to organized crime. The man who welcomed the support of the International Brotherhood of Teamsters and who appointed its president, Jackie Presser (see Chapter 14), to his interim planning staff also issued Executive Order Number 12435 of July 28, 1983, creating the President's Commission on Organized Crime: "The Commission shall make a full and complete national and region-by-region analysis of organized crime; define the nature of traditional organized crime as well as emerging organized crime groups, the sources and amounts of organized crime's income, and the uses to which organized crime puts its income; develop in-depth information on the participants in

organized crime networks; and evaluate Federal laws pertinent to the effort to combat organized crime." The commission was charged with advising the president on "actions which can be taken to improve law enforcement efforts directed against organized crime, and make recommendations concerning appropriate administrative and legislative improvements in the administration of justice." The commission was given 33 months and $5 million to accomplish these formidable tasks.

Controversy and discord were a dominant characteristic of the commission (Shenon 1986). Irving R. Kaufman of the U.S. Court of Appeals for the Second Circuit (New York) was appointed as chair. Judge Kaufman's sole connection to efforts against organized crime consisted of presiding at the 1959 conspiracy and obstruction of justice trial of some of the men who were arrested at the infamous "Apalachin Crime Convention" in 1957 (discussed in Chapter 4). The first executive director resigned before the commission began its work, reportedly because of a disagreement with Judge Kaufman. After a second candidate for executive director was rejected by the Justice Department, James D. Harmon, Jr., was selected and served until the commission completed its work. During the first year there was a conflict with the Justice Department over the commission's independence and personnel. As a result, the commission was unable to fulfill its mandate to evaluate federal prosecutorial efforts. Finally, on July 17, 1984, the commission was given subpoena power.

Many important organized crime figures were subpoenaed. As expected, they invoked the Fifth Amendment or presented some novel arguments for their refusal to respond to commission questions. When he appeared on April 23, 1985, Teamster's Union president Jackie Presser invoked the Fifth Amendment in response to commission questions. One subpoenaed witness refused to testify after being granted immunity, and he was sentenced to one year of imprisonment by a federal judge in Miami—he was already serving a 62-year prison sentence for drug trafficking.

The seven public hearings held by the PCOC generated a great deal of media attention. They were denounced by some as mere publicity stunts, particularly when witnesses were produced wearing hoods to hide their identities. The commission highlighted the problem of money laundering, the continuing problem of labor racketeering, and drew attention to the problem of "mob lawyers." A staff study (PCOC 1985a: 3) "confirmed the existence of a small group of attorneys who have become integral parts of criminal conspiracies, using their status as sworn officers of the court to advance the criminal purposes of these criminal organizations. It is clear that traditional organized crime and narcotics traffickers depend upon and could not effectively operate without these attorneys."

While the commission revealed little that was new, it avoided an overemphasis on Italian American organized crime and, instead, reflecting changes in organized crime, presented information on Colombian cocaine cartels, and examined to a lesser degree other criminal organizations including outlaw motorcycle clubs. In fact, there was so little attention paid to the American Mafia that the commission failed to determine how many Mafia groups were actually operating in the United States—it used the number 24, which dates back to 1967 and the Task Force on Organized Crime.[5] The commission concluded that drug trafficking was the greatest moneymaker for organized crime. As opposed to its predecessor, the Task Force on Organized Crime, the President's Commission found existing laws generally adequate for dealing with organized crime, although it found significant deficiencies in carrying out the statutes. While the Task Force on Organized Crime had great political impact, the President's Commission created hardly a ripple—new legislation was not forthcoming, nor did new initiatives result. The policy that was in place before the commission was established remained in place.

_____

[5] So little information was gathered about the American Mafia that just before the commission was to disband, I was asked to provide extensive information on the state of Italian American organized crime and was given 30 days to research and respond.

SUMMARY

- Although the financial piracy of the Robber Barons, nativism, and the corrupt political machines of urban America were the contexts from which organized crime emerged, the actual trigger was Prohibition.
- Outlawing alcoholic beverages served as a catalyst for organizing crime in an unprecedented manner. Prohibition allowed coarse street criminals to become "beer barons" who ruled large swaths of urban America.
- The liquor business, which demands large-scale organization, encouraged cooperation between gang leaders from various regions—*syndication*. When Prohibition ended, these ties continued and facilitated gangster control of major national unions and the founding of modern Las Vegas.
- By the end of World War II, the Irish presence in organized crime was limited and the heyday of Jewish criminals was over. Italians and the American Mafia were now the dominant force.
- Congressional interest in organized crime in 1950 resulted in Kefauver Committee hearings during which crime bosses from throughout the country were subjected to televised questioning—most refused to answer. Committee preoccupation with ethnic conspiracies equated Italians with organized crime.
- In 1963, a successor committee chaired by Senator McClellan held televised hearings on organized crime and introduced the public to Joseph Valachi, whose revelations became part of the report of a presidential task force on organized crime that concluded organized crime in the United States consists of 24 groups of exclusively men of Italian descent.
- The Task Force continued what the Kefauver Committee had begun, equating organized crime with Italians. But its work resulted in the passage of the most important legislation to deal with organized crime: RICO.

REVIEW QUESTIONS

1. What are the characteristics of "political machines"?
2. What explains the success of the Irish in American machine politics?
3. What was the relationship between the saloon and the political machine?
4. What was the relationship between the machine and big business?
5. Why did business interests often support reform politics?
6. How did nativism generate support for the political machine?
7. What was the conflict between rural and urban America that helped fuel the Prohibition movement?
8. How did Prohibition change the relationship between political machines and the underworld?
9. How did Prohibition stimulate the development of organized crime?
10. How did Prohibition lead to criminal syndication?
11. How did the onset of the Great Depression affect organized crime?
12. How did organized crime change with the repeal of Prohibition?
13. What conclusions about organized crime were shared by the Kefauver Committee and the Task Force on Organized Crime?
14. How did the conclusions of the Task Force on Organized Crime differ from those of the President's Commission on Organized Crime?

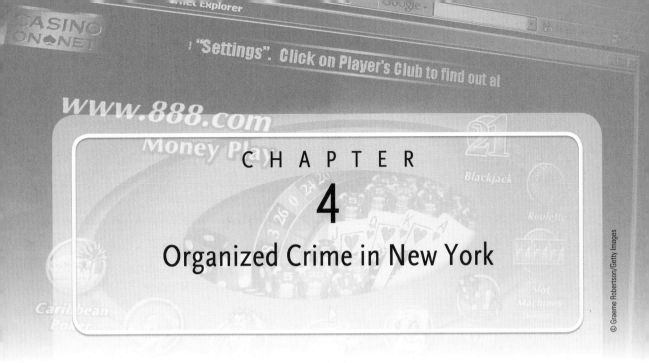

CHAPTER
4
Organized Crime in New York

The history of organized crime (OC) in the United States encompasses cities in every region of the country.[1] A lack of space and detailed (reliable) information prevents a historical review of all of them. Instead, we will examine the phenomenon in New York and, in Chapter 5, Chicago because organized crime elsewhere approximates that in New York and Chicago.

In order to understand the development of organized crime in New York, we need to examine a most unique political organization—the Society of Saint Tammany, usually referred to as Tammany Hall.

TAMMANY HALL

The Society of Saint Tammany, named for a legendary Delaware Indian chief, began in 1789 as a fraternal and patriotic society, with chapters in a number of states, and quickly emerged as a full-fledged political organization in New York.[2] The guiding genius behind Tammany's rise to power was Aaron Burr (Peterson 1983), who in 1800 became vice president of the United States.[3] In 1836, Tammany leader Martin Van Buren was elected the eighth president of the United States (Connable and Silberfarb 1967). Tammany eventually became synonymous with the Democratic Party of New York City.

In post–Revolutionary War New York, only landowners could vote, an obvious handicap to an organization striving for broad-based support. Tammany responded with "collective property" in which the title to a house might be held by a

[1]Boston, Massachusetts (see O'Neil and Lehr 1989; Lehr and O'Neil 2000); Buffalo, New York; Cleveland, Ohio (see Porrello 1995); Dallas, Texas; Denver, Colorado; Detroit, Michigan (see Kavieff 2000); Elizabeth, New Jersey; Kansas City, Missouri (see Hayde 2008); Los Angeles, California (see John L. Smith 1998); Miami, Florida; Milwaukee, Wisconsin; Minneapolis, Minnesota; Newark, New Jersey; New Orleans, Louisiana; Philadelphia (see Anastasia 1991), Pittsburgh, Pittston, Reading, and Scranton, Pennsylvania; Providence, Rhode Island (see Teresa and Renner 1973); Rochester, New York; St. Louis, Missouri (see Waugh 2007); San Francisco and San Jose, California; Springfield, Illinois; Tampa, Florida (see Deitche 2004); and Youngstown, Ohio.

[2]At the time, the city of New York meant Manhattan; it was not until January 1, 1898, that forty governments, including the separate cities of Brooklyn and New York (Manhattan), were consolidated, becoming America's largest city.

[3]In a duel in 1804, Burr killed former secretary of the treasury Alexander Hamilton.

number of persons, who would then be enfranchised as freeholders. Tammany established a system of district leaders and precinct captains in each assembly district and by 1838 had a reputation for dispensing favors and social services from funds extorted from vice entrepreneurs and a 6 percent kickback from all city employees. The tie-in between criminals and politicians was now firmly established.

During the latter half of the 1840s and early 1850s, large numbers of Irish immigrated to New York in order to escape famine and British repression. Despite nativist and anti-Catholic sentiment in Tammany, the Irish quickly rose to leadership positions and by the turn of the century clearly dominated "the Hall." The Irish immigrant spoke English and was quite at home in a saloon; his willingness to engage in fisticuffs made him a "natural" for the rough-and-tumble politics of that period. There was also an Irish genius for politics. "It is in close, warm, personal contact with local life that the Irish have excelled. That the Irish in New York have been almost altogether Democrats has been one element in making the character of the Democratic Party in that city" (Hapgood and Moskowitz 1927: 43). The Irishman, because of his stature and ability to speak English, also dominated the city's police force, which was in effect an adjunct of Tammany Hall.

The Tammany Police

In 1844, the New York State legislature authorized the creation of a police force for New York City patterned after the London Metropolitan Police of Sir Robert Peel (from which they get the nickname "Bobbies"). Whereas the London model centralized the police command, in New York the police in each of the city's wards were controlled by the alderman, who could hire and fire police officers. "Even after aldermanic appointment was formally discontinued, local politicians continued to exercise de facto control" (Reppetto 1978: 41). Positions on the police force were sought after: The policeman's salary, compared with that of a skilled laborer, was good, qualifications for the job

were almost nonexistent, discipline was lax, and opportunities for graft were extensive. "Cops who chose not to take graft had to immerse themselves in areas of policing where they did not need to deal with vice—quiet precincts or special units such as the homicide squad—and to ignore any corruption they saw. To be a squealer in a predominantly Irish police force was a fate worse than death" (Reppetto 1978: 75).

The police tended not only to be corrupt but also to be brutal toward the poor and the helpless, as the story of Alexander ("Clubber") Williams highlights. This vicious and corrupt officer, who rose to the high rank of inspector, told his recruits: "Boys, there's more justice in the end of this nightstick than there is in all of the courts of the land" (Logan 1970: 106). In two decades, he amassed 358 brutality complaints and was fined 244 times as a result (Krajick 2004).

The police received very little public support and were often subjected to abuse by Tammany-linked street gangs. To arrest a suspect the officer frequently had to physically subdue him or her: "A tradition of police brutality developed out of this disrespect. Officers sought to gain with their billy clubs the deference to their authority that was not freely given" (Walker 1980: 63). The police manhandled and brutalized prostitutes, miscreants, and members of the underclass in general. In return, they were abused by the Tammany politicians. Police brutality was a "delegated form of vigilantism" tolerated by the respectable middle-class citizenry, who perceived a need to control the "dangerous classes" (Walker 1980: 63). "Many a morning," noted reporter Lincoln Steffens at the turn of the twentieth century (1957: 207), "when I had nothing else to do, I stood and saw the police bring in and kick out their bandaged, bloody prisoners, not only strikers and foreigners, but thieves too, and others of the miserable, friendless, troublesome poor."

Tammany Hall protected the wealthy of uptown from the radical elements of downtown. In 1872, the Tammany police proved reliable in putting down a strike of some 70,000 workers (out of a city population of 1 million) who were demanding that employers comply with an 1870 state law requiring an eight-hour day. Police officers worked overtime without extra compensation to suppress the strikers. In 1874 club-swinging police officers broke up a peaceful demonstration called by organized labor in Tompkins Square because organized labor posed a threat not only to industrialists but also to the machine (Erie 1988).

During the years before World War I, the New York City Police Department was more or less a branch of Tammany; indeed, a fee of $250 to Tammany was required to secure a job as a policeman, and promotions were handled in a similar manner (Logan 1970). For $15,000, "Clubber" Williams affected a transfer to the midtown Manhattan area where lucrative graft was available from gambling establishments and brothels. Williams informed an inquiring newspaper reporter: "I've had nothin' but chuck steak for a long time, and now I'm going to get a little bit of the Tenderloin" (Connable and Silberfarb 1967: 215), as this section of Manhattan was known. When he was called to testify before a legislative committee investigating corruption in New York City (Lexow Committee), Williams acknowledged that he had more money and property than his salary could account for. And how did he manage this? Land speculation in Japan, he responded (Steffens 1958). Williams was eventually dismissed from the force by New York City Police Commissioner Theodore Roosevelt, a Republican appointed during a reform administration.

The Tammany Gangs

From the mid-1800s until World War I, old-style gangs were an important feature of the Tammany-criminal tie-in. By the 1920s, when they were disappearing, the *New York Times* could wax nostalgic about the "old breed" of gang with its twisted sense of valor, as compared with the current (1923) variety that operated with "the calculation and efficiency of an industrial tool for breaking strikes or wrecking factories" ("New Gang Methods Replace Those of Eastman's Days" 1923: 3).

The *Times* referred to the demise of the Shirt Tails, Dead Rabbits, Plug Uglies, Bowery Boys, Hudson Dusters, Cherry Hill Gang, Gophers, Five Points, and the notorious Whyos, whose name derived from the Gaelic meaning "noble few" (English 2005).

On election day, Tammany used these gangs as "repeaters" and "sluggers," which led the notorious, apelike Lower East Side Gang leader Monk Eastman (born Edward Osterman in Brooklyn in 1873 to German-Jewish parents) to utter: "Say, I cut some ice in this town. Why, I make half the big politicians" ("New Gang Methods . . ." 1923). Gangs were so useful on Election Day that the politicians made natural alliances with them: "To keep gang members in funds between elections, the politicians found jobs for them in the off-season months" (Logan 1970: 56). They worked as lookouts, steerers, and bouncers—resident thugs for the gambling houses and brothels under the patronage of Tammany.

One of the more infamous of the Tammany gangs was the Five Points, with an estimated 1,200 members led by Paul Kelly, an ex-pugilist of Neapolitan descent born Paolo Vaccarelli in 1877 (it was not unusual for prizefighters or criminals to assume Irish names). Five Points refers to a neighborhood portrayed in the movie *Gangs of New York* whose center was an intersection of three streets now located above City Hall and encompassing much of Chinatown. Before he left for Chicago, Al Capone was a member of the Five Points Gang (Kobler 1971), as was Lucky Luciano (Powell 2000). One of the highlights of New York gang history is the feud between Kelly and his Italian Five Points gang and the Jewish gang led by Monk Eastman over a small piece of Lower Manhattan real estate that each gang claimed as its "turf." Eastman dominated the Lower East Side and Kelly controlled an adjacent area from Broadway to the Bowery and from Fourteenth Street south to City Hall Park (Downey 2004). When their political patrons insisted that they cease the headline-generating bloodshed, Kelly and Eastman fought it out in a fracas that lasted two hours and ended in a draw when both combatants collapsed from exhaustion.

Eastman fell into disfavor with his Tammany patrons and was imprisoned for a 1904 robbery attempt. After his release in 1909, unable to reestablish himself as a gang leader, Monk enlisted under an alias and served with distinction in World War I. Later, he received a full pardon from Tammany Governor Alfred E. Smith for his outstanding military service. Eastman was shot to death by an old crony after a petty quarrel that followed a Christmas Eve drinking bout. The friend, a federal Prohibition agent, escaped with a three-to-ten-year sentence by claiming self-defense—he thought the unarmed Monk was reaching for a gun (Lee 1963). In the absence of Eastman, acrimony and violence between the gangs continued (Downey 2004).

Eastman's gang came under the leadership of Max ("Kid Twist") Zweibach until he was shot to death by one of Kelly's Five Pointers in 1908 and replaced by William ("Big Jack Zelig") Alberts, who became a labor racketeer in the city's garment industry. Zelig was murdered in 1912 and replaced by Benjamin ("Dopey Benny"—an adenoid condition gave him a sleepy look) Fein who fine-tuned labor racketeering on behalf of garment center unions: His men showed up on union picket lines with bats, blackjacks, and occasionally guns to thwart strikebreakers. When Fein became a government witness, one of his leading men, Austrian-born Jacob ("Little Augie") Orgenstein, took over and became "the last of the old-time labor racketeers, preferring quick payoffs from employers and unions to the more sophisticated infiltration of labor unions" (Kavieff 2006: 30).

Kelly eventually left the mayhem of lower Manhattan for Harlem, where he founded the Harlem Branch of the Paul Kelly Association. Like his Jewish opponents, Kelly entered the labor-management field, becoming a labor organizer and, with the help of some of his Five Pointers, a vice president of the International Longshoremen's Association (a union discussed in Chapter 14). Kelly died of pneumonia in 1936.

Gambling and house prostitution in Manhattan was "licensed" by the Five Points–born saloonkeeper and Tammany state senator, Timothy Sullivan,[4] with the support of the police chief. When a Tammany alderman opposed brothels in his heavily Irish district, Sullivan organized a primary election fight against him and sent in the Kelly and Eastman gangs to beat and intimidate his opponent's supporters, while the Tammany police remained passive. Sullivan's candidate won by a margin of three to one (Connable and Silberfarb 1967).

Charles Murphy, a former saloonkeeper, became the Tammany boss in 1902 and remained in that position until his death 22 years later, amassing a personal fortune of $2 million—$25 million in today's dollars (Van Devander 1944). Murphy changed Tammany operations: Open gambling and prostitution were ended, and total immunity for gangsters was withdrawn. Murphy also moved to cut down the power of the police who had occasionally challenged Tammany (Katcher 1959; Pietrusza 2003). Murphy "concluded that the use of the police as major graft collectors was an antiquated concept" (Logan 1970: 340). Modern organization was needed—a conduit between the politicians and the gamblers who, like the brothel owners, would be organized into a dues-paying trade association. That conduit was Arnold Rothstein who became the great go-between. "If politicians wanted something from gamblers and vice lords, they approached A. R. If the underworld sought protection from Tammany's judges and prosecutors and pliant police officers, it, too, approached Rothstein. He made things happen, quietly and without fuss" (Pietrusza 2003: 92). Organized crime was beginning to evolve and in New York its "Godfather" was Jewish.

---

[4]Sullivan, a former member of the notorious Whyos, is best remembered in New York as the author of the "Sullivan law," which prohibits the carrying of concealed firearms without a permit. This law was enacted to enable Tammany to better control the behavior of their street gang allies. If they got out of line, gang members could be frisked by the police for firearms that could always be "found" (planted). He also sponsored the legislation that made Columbus Day a legal holiday (Reppetto 2004).

JEWISH ORGANIZED CRIME

Under the czars, Jews were confined to life in the *stetls* of Russia's western territories—Latvia, Lithuania, eastern Poland, Ukraine, and Belarus—or a ghetto reserved for them in the cities of Minsk, Odessa, Vilnius, and Warsaw. The professions were closed to them and their choice of occupations was severely limited. Poverty and persecution fueled immigration, and during the first two decades of the twentieth century millions fled to the United States, where they settled in areas already characterized by rampant criminality. These areas served as the breeding ground for Jewish organized crime.

At the turn of the twentieth century, the Irish still constituted the dominant force in the dominant political organization, Tammany Hall. But in organizing gamblers and brothels[5] and in the emerging arena of labor-management conflict, Jews, toughened by the ethnic conflicts of urban America and endowed with a cohesion forged by centuries of anti-Semitism, began to gain a niche. By the second decade of the twentieth century, however, opportunities afforded by America released an entrepreneurial spirit that had been bottled up in the ghettos of Eastern Europe and gave free rein to the Jewish pursuit of education—the Jewish criminal was being pushed to the fringes of the past. Then came Prohibition and the fast-track opportunities presented brought the Jewish criminal to the fore: "During Prohibition, 50 percent of the nation's leading bootleggers were Jews, and Jewish gangs bossed the rackets in some of America's largest cities" (Rockaway 1993: 5). In New York, Jewish gangsters helped rationalize illicit activities and also provided a conduit between local crime personnel and Tammany. Among Jewish organized criminal operatives, Arnold Rothstein was the most important organizer and innovator.

Arnold ("The Brain") Rothstein at his office in 1928. If organized crime in New York can be said to have had a godfather, it was Rothstein, who was murdered that year.

Arnold Rothstein

The specter of Arnold Rothstein looms so large over organized crime in New York that it would not be much of an exaggeration to call him its "Godfather." Jenna Joselit (1983: 143–44) states:

> Rothstein transformed criminal activity from a haphazard, often spontaneous endeavor into one whose hallmarks—specialized expertise, administrative hierarchy, and organizational procedure—correspond to the classic sociological model of a bureaucracy. Thus, Rothstein's illegal business had a definite administrative structure based on specific skills; competence and not ethnic pedigree determined one's rank and, of course, one's position in his outfit.
>
> Rothstein's office . . . in the middle of the midtown business district, employed a staff comparable to that of any large (and legitimate) commercial firm, replete with

[5]For a historical examination of Jewish involvement in "white slavery," see Bristow (1982).

© Bettman/CORBIS

secretaries, bookkeepers, and legal counsel. . . . A decision to enter some new illegal venture tended to be based not on personal motives of revenge or power but on strictly commercial considerations: the amount of profit to be made and the length of time it would take to make it. Finally, by investing the money he earned through illegal channels into legal enterprises such as real estate and the theater, Rothstein made it difficult to ascertain where the illegal enterprise left off and the legitimate one began.

"A. R.," or "the Brain," as Damon Runyon called him, was born in New York in 1882, a member of Monk Eastman's gang, a protégé of State Senator Big Tim Sullivan, and served as the inspiration for Meyer Wolfsheim in F. Scott Fitzgerald's *The Great Gatsby* and for Nathan Detroit in Damon Runyon's *Guys and Dolls*. His father, an Orthodox Jew born of immigrant parents, was a respected and successful businessman. Arnold was also respected and quite successful, but his business comprised gambling, bootlegging, drug smuggling, and labor racketeering (Katcher 1959; English 2005). Rothstein is probably best remembered for his alleged involvement in the "Black Sox Scandal," the fixing of the 1919 World Series (Pietrusza 2003).

Rothstein also fenced stolen bonds and securities, and when Prohibition arrived he organized the importation of liquor from England and Canada. At the same time, diamonds and drugs, which took up very little space, were smuggled in on his whiskey ships, and he established an international heroin-smuggling network. His buyers overseas shipped the drugs into the United States, where they were distributed to criminal organizations in several states. On Rothstein's payroll were the son and son-in-law of the head of the Federal Bureau of Narcotics and the federal-agent-in-charge of the metropolitan New York district (Pietrusza 2003).

"Rothstein set new and historic standards in the development of organized crime in America" (Lacey 1991: 50). He played the role of broker, not only between Tammany and the gamblers but also between two of New York's political-crime factions, one Italian, one primarily Irish and Jewish. Rothstein was tied to both factions and did favors for both—furnishing pistol permits and bail bonds, fencing stolen merchandise, and financing illegal operations. In 1929, it was publicly revealed that Rothstein had loaned nearly $20,000 to a Bronx magistrate who had helped Tammany get out the Italian vote (Mann 1965).

One Sunday night in 1928, Arnold Rothstein was found staggering into the service entrance of the Park Central Hotel, where he resided. He had been shot once in the abdomen with a small-caliber gun. At age 46, Rothstein died after refusing to name the person who shot him, and the murder was never solved. It has been attributed to Rothstein's refusal to pay a gambling debt in excess of $300,000—he maintained that the card game was rigged ("Gamblers Hunted in Rothstein Attack" 1928). After his death, federal officials opened many of his safes and files. Papers found in his apartment linked Rothstein to what the U.S. attorney called the largest drug ring in the United States ("Unger Indicted in Drug Conspiracy" 1928; "$4,000,000 in Narcotics Seized Here, Traced to Rothstein Ring" 1928). Rothstein left a public estate appraised at $1,757,572 ($22 million in today's dollars)—his hidden assets, of course, are not known (S. Smith 1963).

Dutch Schultz

Arthur Flegenheimer—"Dutch Schultz"—provides an outstanding example of how the opportunities afforded by Prohibition turned street thugs into wealthy "beer barons." At the beginning of Prohibition, Schultz, a street tough, worked for a trucking company whose owner went into the beer business. In 1928, Schultz became a partner in a Bronx speakeasy. The partners soon bought trucks and garages and became major beer distributors, aided by a vicious crew of gunmen including Legs Diamond, the Weinberg brothers, Bo and George, and the Irish-born Coll brothers, Vincent ("Mad Dog") and Peter. Next, the partners began to expand into the territories of rival beer businesses. One unfortunate was kidnapped, severely beaten, hung by his thumbs, and eventually blinded—sending a message that was not lost on other recalcitrant beer distributors.

While Prohibition was in full swing, prominent gangsters did not pay attention to the numbers (illegal lottery), often referring to it derisively as "nigger pool" because many of its followers were African American. With Prohibition on the way out, however, Schultz began searching for new areas of profit. His attorney, who also represented some numbers operators, engineered Schultz's takeover of the business in Harlem from independent African American, Hispanic, and some white numbers bankers. Schultz was able to offer political protection from arrest and physical protection from robbers as well as financing—several operators had had a costly run of bad luck: "Harlem numbers were not consolidated into a syndicate that pooled resources and assets; it was fragmented and lacked big layoff bankers who could handle a large 'hit' (win)" (Schatzberg and Kelly 1996: 79). By 1932, a combination of superior financing, force, and political power enabled Schultz to reduce independent operators to being his employees, and he centralized policy operations in Harlem (Sann 1971; Schatzberg 1993). Schultz also moved into labor racketeering, and in 1934 the *New York Times* reported an alliance between officials of the restaurant workers union and the Schultz organization ("Gang Linked to Union Charged at Trial" 1934).

In 1931, the Coll brothers rebelled against Schultz and began killing off the Dutchman's drivers and payoff men: The "band of killers would wake the Schultz employees in their homes at the dead of night and kill them in their own bedrooms" (Berger 1935: 17). In a five-month period in 1931, seven Schultz men were murdered ("Schultz Aide Slain; 7th in Five Months" 1931). Schultz responded by placing a $50,000 contract on Coll and began to return the gunplay ("Woman, 2 Men, Slain as Gang Raids Home in Coll Feud" 1932). Vincent Coll received his

nickname, "Mad Dog," during this feud. Coll's men opened fire at a leader of the Schultz organization who was standing in the street near a group of playing children. He escaped injury, but a 5-year-old child was killed and four other children were wounded. Coll was arrested as one of the shooters, but his attorney disclosed that the witness to the shooting had a criminal record and a history of providing false testimony. Coll went free (O'Connor 1958).

Another important Prohibition figure soon played a role in the Schultz-Coll war. Owney Madden, born in England of Irish parents in 1892, began his career in crime as head of the Gophers, a notorious and widely feared gang that controlled an area of Manhattan's West Side appropriately called Hell's Kitchen. The gang's name was derived from their habit of holing up in basements and cellars (Sante 1991). Owney "The Killer" Madden earned his nickname after committing the first of his many murders at age 14 (English 2005). In 1912, he was surrounded and gunned down by eleven members of the Hudson Dusters gang—shot six times but survived. In less than a week, three of his assailants had been murdered (English 2005). In 1915, Madden was sentenced to Sing Sing Prison for ordering the murder of one of his rivals. In 1923, he was paroled and began to hijack liquor trucks, including those of Vincent ("Bill") Dwyer, a major bootlegger. Instead of responding violently, Dwyer, ever the rational businessman, chose to make Madden part of his organization (Peterson 1983). Madden also became a partner with George Jean ("Big Frenchy") de Mange, a bootlegger and speakeasy owner who saw the need for the services that Madden and his Hell's Kitchen stalwarts could provide (O'Connor 1958).

In need of money to help finance his campaign against Schultz, Coll kidnapped de Mange and demanded ransom from Madden, who turned over $35,000 for "Big Frenchy's" return. Coll then tried to extort money from Madden by threatening to kidnap him. The outraged Madden joined forces with Schultz in an all-out war against Coll. Madden and Schultz divided the city into zones and dispatched their gunmen to find the "Mad

Dog." In the interim, Madden[6] fled to Florida, and Schultz barricaded himself in a bordello surrounded by bodyguards. In the end, Coll's bodyguards "fingered" him for Schultz. In 1932, the "Mad Dog" stepped into a drugstore phone booth and made a call. While he was busy on the telephone his bodyguard discreetly left, and two men entered. One of the men carried a Thompson submachine gun. After ordering the customers to remain calm, he fired several bursts into the phone booth: Coll was almost cut in half by the barrage (O'Connor 1958).

With Coll out of the way, Schultz began to experience a new problem—the Internal Revenue Service. He went into hiding for 18 months. In 1934, he surrendered but subsequently succeeded in obtaining a change of venue based on his notoriety in New York City. The case was moved to Syracuse, New York, where a mistrial (hung jury) resulted. The retrial was moved to the small upstate community of Malone. Schultz traveled to Malone in advance of his trial, bought candy and flowers for the children he visited in the hospital, held a grand ball to which he invited the entire town, and generally endeared himself to the good people of Malone. They acquitted Schultz, a verdict that outraged the presiding judge (R. N. Smith 1982).

Schultz could not safely return to New York; the federal government had several counts of the original indictment held in abeyance and, to avoid possible double-jeopardy problems, indicted Schultz for a series of misdemeanors. In addition, New York State had a warrant outstanding for income-tax evasion; Schultz owed the state $36,937 in back taxes. It was understood that if Schultz could be arrested in New York City, the authorities would be able to set a prohibitive

bail and thus keep him in custody. Schultz traveled to New Jersey and surrendered to the federal charges; bail was set at an amount that enabled him to remain at liberty (Sann 1971). The Dutchman set up headquarters in a Newark tavern but faced threats from two sources: Thomas E. Dewey and Lucky Luciano.

Dewey, a special anti-rackets prosecutor, had successfully prosecuted Irving Wexler ("Waxey") Gordon,[7] a major bootlegger and former member of Monk Eastman's gang, and was now after Schultz. Luciano, a leader of the American Mafia, and his colleagues expected Schultz to be convicted and imprisoned as a result of his trials in Syracuse and Malone. They were planning to move in on his numbers and restaurant rackets, and his acquittal presented them with a serious setback. The independent and violent Schultz, for his part, became even more unpredictable, personally murdering two of his own men. The Dutchman was also threatening to kill Dewey, an idea that had been rejected by a commission of the other leading gangsters in New York; they were fearful of the "heat" that would result (R. N. Smith 1982).

On the evening of October 23, 1935, Dutch Schultz entered the Palace Chop House and Tavern in Newark, where he had established his headquarters "in exile." With him were his two bodyguards as well as the financial wizard of the Schultz organization. When Schultz went to the men's room, two Jewish gunmen suddenly entered the tavern and opened fire with handguns and a shotgun; the Schultz men were mortally wounded. One of the gunmen entered the men's room and shot the Dutchman, who died about 20 hours later.

Lepke Buchalter

As a leading member of the syndicate "ruling commission" in New York, Louis Buchalter—known as "the Judge"—"vetoed" the murder of Thomas E. Dewey (Turkus and Feder 1951), a decision he probably lived to regret. "Lepkeleh"

---

[6]As a result of his partnership with Bill Dwyer, Madden became a millionaire during Prohibition. He continued his operations until 1932, when he was arrested for parole violation and returned to prison. A year later he was paroled again and retired to Hot Springs, Arkansas, a town known for corrupt machine politics and illegal gambling. There, according to Stephen Fox (1989), he controlled the rackets, married, and lived out his days in comfort. In 1935, Lucky Luciano found temporary refuge from a New York indictment by hiding out in Hot Springs. On April 24, 1965, the front page of the *New York Times* reported that Madden, an "ex-gangster" who had given big contributions to charity, had died of emphysema.

[7]With Prohibition over, Gordon turned to drug trafficking and in 1951 received a 25-year sentence. He died in Alcatraz Prison in 1952.

(an affectionate Yiddish term for "Little Louis") was born on New York's Lower East Side in 1897 into a family of Russian immigrants. His father died when Lepke was 13 and his mother married a widower with children. Lepke had three brothers: One earned a PhD and became a rabbi and college professor; another became a pharmacist; and a third became a dentist. Lepke took a different route. He was arrested and imprisoned for burglary several times. After being released from Sing Sing Prison in 1922, he teamed up with Jacob ("Gurrah") Shapiro (born in Russia in 1896), and the two began working as strong-arms for labor-industrial racketeer Little Augie Orgenstein, discussed earlier.

In 1927, a labor dispute erupted in the painting trade, and the head of the painters' trade association gave Little Augie $50,000 to end the strike. Without consulting his lieutenants, Augie ordered the union to stop the walkout. The brother of one of Augie's top lieutenants, however, was a friend of a painter's union official who had asked that the mob remain neutral. Augie's men demanded that he return the $50,000 retainer, but instead Augie contracted with Legs Diamond for help in breaking the strike. "At 8:30 P.M., on October 15, 1927, Li'l Augie and his new associate were walking along a lower Manhattan street. A black sedan picked its way through the pushcarts. Behind the wheel was Lepke. Next to him, pistol in hand, sat Gurrah . . . [who] hit the sidewalk yelling, 'Move over Diamond!' Legs fell back instinctively against the building. Li'l Augie, transfixed, was killed. Diamond got a bullet through his shoulder—for butting in" (Turkus and Feder 1951: 336–37).

After taking over Little Augie's organization, Lepke and Gurrah revolutionized industrial racketeering. "Instead of using his sluggers and gunmen to terrorize labor unions during strike periods, Lepke worked them directly into the unions. By threat and by violence they controlled one local after another" (Berger 1944: 30). Manufacturers who hired Lepke to deal with the unions "soon found themselves wriggling helplessly in the grip of Lepke's smooth but deadly organization. He moved in on them as he had on the unions" (Berger 1944: 20). Until 1940, Lepke was the head

of an organization that extorted wealth from New York's garment, leather, baking, and trucking industries. He was driven out of the fur industry in 1933 by the fierce resistance of industry workers (Kavieff 2006).

Lepke's estimated income was between $5 million and $10 million annually—and this was during the Depression (Turkus and Feder 1951). "All through the Prohibition era, when other mobsters were splashing headily in alcoholic wealth and getting their names in headlines with a series of competitive killings that strewed urban and suburban landscapes with untidy corpses, Lepke went his quiet way" (Berger 1940: 30).

Special Prosecutor Dewey began to move against Buchalter and Shapiro, and by 1937 both were in hiding, leaving day-to-day operations to an aide. In an effort to eliminate all possible witnesses, Lepke ordered a murder rampage—the number of killings at his direction is estimated at between sixty and eighty (Berger 1944). Despite his deservedly violent reputation, Lepke was a shy, slender man of about five feet, seven inches. In contrast with many of his more flamboyant colleagues, Buchalter preferred to spend most of his nonworking time at home with his English wife and stepson, occasionally playing a round of golf or basking on the beach at Miami (Tully 1958).

The murder binge backfired; the reign of terror turned loyal Lepke men into terrified informers seeking police protection (Turkus and Feder 1951). Law enforcement pressure against organized crime intensified in an effort to "smoke" Lepke out of hiding, particularly after one of his gunmen mistakenly killed an innocent music publisher. There was also a $50,000 reward on his head. In 1939, according to a prearranged plan, Lepke surrendered to J. Edgar Hoover and columnist Walter Winchell. Buchalter had been misled into believing that a deal had been arranged with the authorities and that he would only have to stand trial for federal (drug) and not state (murder) charges. In 1935, Lepke apparently decided to diversify. He established an international drug ring that moved heroin from China into Marseilles and finally New York (Reppetto 2004). In 1940, Buchalter was convicted in federal court of antitrust and narcotics law violations and sentenced to 14 years. Gurrah Shapiro surrendered to federal authorities in 1938 and was tried and convicted for extortion in the bakery industry. He spent the rest of his life—he died in 1947 at age 50—in prison (Joselit 1983).

To Buchalter's dismay, he was subsequently turned over to New York authorities and prosecuted by Dewey for extortion, for which he received a sentence of 30-years-to-life. Then, in 1941, he was prosecuted for murder in Brooklyn. After a protracted legal battle, Buchalter was electrocuted in 1944. He has the dubious distinction of being the only major organized crime figure to be executed by the state.

Meyer Lansky and Benjamin Siegel

Lansky was born in either 1902 or 1904 in Byelorussia, one of the fifteen republics that became the Soviet Union. Meyer, his brother Jacob, and his sister were brought to the United States by their parents in 1911. Meyer attended school in Brownsville, Brooklyn, and on the Lower East Side, where he completed the eighth grade. At age 15, Meyer left school for a job as a tool and die maker. His first recorded arrest was in 1918. Until then, various popular sources report, Meyer was an honest and hardworking apprentice craftsman. In that year, he was arrested for assaulting Lucky Luciano with a crowbar. According to Messick (1973), Lansky was returning home from work, tools in his hand, when he came upon Luciano beating a woman in an alley while the young (age 12) Ben Siegel feebly attempted to stop him. Meyer and his crowbar succeeded. They were all arrested, and Lansky was fined $2 for disorderly conduct. The judge is reported to have stated to Siegel and Lansky: "You boys have bugs in your heads." Messick notes that Siegel not only kept the nickname but also lived up to it. No one, however, called Ben Siegel "Bugsy" to his face—a second time.

Lacey (1991) presents a different version of the first encounter between Lansky and Luciano. The young Sicilian, head of a gang that preyed on Jewish youth, encountered the physically unimpressive

Lansky. Surrounded and subjected to threats and demands for money, Lansky reportedly told the Sicilians to commit a physically impossible sex act. His pluck apparently provided the basis for a lifelong friendship.

Benjamin Siegel was born in 1906, and raised in the Williamsburg section of Brooklyn (just across the Williamsburg Bridge from the Lower East Side). He had four sisters and a brother, Maurice. Maurice became a respected Beverly Hills physician. Ben grew into a handsome and powerfully built young man who was quick to violence (Jennings 1967). The diminutive Lansky (five feet, four inches, 135 pounds) and his friend Ben Siegel were part of a gang of Jewish young men—Lansky the brains, Siegel the brawn.

In addition to his legitimate shop work, Lansky accepted assignments as a labor union strong-arm and protector of dice games, and he and Siegel organized their own games (Lacey 1991). As they grew successful, the duo surrounded themselves with *starkers* (Yiddish for "tough guys"). At the onset of Prohibition, they were primed to take advantage of the new opportunities that would present themselves, and they found one in the transportation business. Lansky became an automobile mechanic. His reputation and mechanical ability soon led to his servicing and "souping up" of stolen vehicles for use by bootleggers. Hauling whiskey, however, was a very risky business, and the "Bug and Meyer Gang" provided the *starkers* necessary to protect those valuable shipments from the likes of Legs Diamond.

In addition to transportation and bootlegging activities, Lansky and Siegel continued their gambling operations. This eventually attracted the attention of Italian crime boss Joe Masseria, whose men tried to "muscle in." At this point, Luciano, who was working for Masseria, intervened and reconciled the differences between the Jewish and Italian gangsters. Throughout his career, Luciano was able to act as an intermediary between Jewish and Italian gangsters, enabling him to gain important stature in organized crime. The two, often in partnership with Luciano, also initiated their own bootlegging business. By the end of Prohibition,

Lansky and Siegel were major powers in organized crime.

In 1936 or 1937, Siegel left New York for the West Coast, sent by eastern gang leaders who were interested in exploiting opportunities in California (Turkus and Feder 1951). Syndicate units in Cleveland, Chicago, and New York sent men to join the Siegel operation on the West Coast. One of them was the notorious ex-boxer Meyer ("Mickey") Cohen. Cohen, in his 1975 autobiography, confirms that he was sent to California by Lou Rothkopf, one of the leaders of the Cleveland syndicate. Cohen reports (1975: 35) that Jack Dragna (born in 1891 in Corleone, Sicily), crime boss in southern California, was not running things too well: "The organization had to pour money on to help Dragna at all times. So Benny came out here to get things moving good."[8]

Siegel got things moving: He organized a coalition of the crime bosses in California, with himself at the top and crime boss Jack Dragna as his top lieutenant. His thugs forced bookmakers in California and Arizona to subscribe to the syndicate-backed wire service (which reported racing results throughout the country). He muscled in on gambling operations throughout the state, set up a narcotics pipeline through Mexico, and organized prostitution from Seattle to San Diego. Siegel also established offshore gambling on ships anchored beyond the three-mile limit, gained control of the union that represented movie extras, and extorted money from the movie industry. He was the (hidden) owner of the California Metals Company in Los Angeles, which handled salvage metals during the Second World War (Reid and Demaris 1964).

Although he established himself in a host of rackets, Siegel is best remembered for his activities in Las Vegas. Beginning in 1946, with financial backing from Nevada-based gamblers and eastern gang leaders, Siegel built the first of the grand-style Las Vegas gambling casino hotels, the Flamingo. Upon opening, however, the not-quite-finished luxury hotel became a money loser because of a combination of bad luck, incompetent help, and a business downturn. Siegel reached out for more financing, but his activities apparently became more independent, which alienated him from Lansky and the other gang leaders. At midnight, June 20, 1947, Siegel was hit by a "fusillade of bullets fired through the living room of a Beverly Hills house [home of Virginia Hill] where he was staying" ("Siegel, Gangster, Is Slain on Coast" 1947: 1). Lacey (1991) states that Siegel's Las Vegas partners were behind his murder.[9] In any event, they took over the Flamingo upon Siegel's demise.

During the 1930s, Lansky was able to arrange with the Cuban dictator Fulgencio Batista for the syndicate to control gambling in Havana. This domination was interrupted by World War II and Batista's postwar exile in the United States. A coup in 1952 brought Batista back to power, and Lansky returned to Cuba. Until he assumed dominance in Havana gambling, the industry had been crippled by dishonesty and publicity about cheated tourists. Lansky put an end to this and turned the city into a gambling Mecca, until Fidel Castro booted both Batista and the syndicate out of Cuba (Lacey 1991). Lansky moved his gambling interests to the Bahamas and Haiti.

Despite his limited education, Lansky was known as a thinker and a reader—he belonged to the Book-of-the-Month Club—features of his personality that apparently brought kudos from his colleagues. His extensive gambling enterprises, many in partnership with Vincent ("Jimmy Blue Eyes") Alo, a boyhood friend from the Lower East Side and a partner of Lucky Luciano, reached from upstate New York to Fort Worth,

---

[8] By the end of World War II, Mickey Cohen was well established (and notorious) in suburban Los Angeles, where he ran a large gambling operation. Jack Dragna had a number of Cohen associates killed and also attempted to kill Cohen in a secret but unsuccessful attempt to take over his gambling operations (Demaris 1981). Dragna died in 1956, Cohen in 1976, both of natural causes. The Los Angeles crime Family has long been considered weak and ineffectual—sometimes referred to as the "Mickey Mouse Mafia." During the 1980s, one mob associate—a strong-arm from Boston—was insulted by the offer of membership in the Los Angeles Family headed by Peter John Milano (J. Smith 1998).

[9] Gus Greenbaum, Moe Sedway, Davie Berman, Morris Rosen, and Willie Alderman.

Texas. Alo, a captain in the Genovese crime Family, provided the muscle for Lansky's operations (Lacey 1991). Lansky became known as the premier "money mover" for organized crime, "washing" illegitimate funds and investing them in legitimate enterprises such as hotels and the jukebox business.

During World War II, Lansky registered for the Selective Service but was never called because he was above the draft age. In 1953, he served a brief jail term for running a gambling operation in Saratoga Springs, New York (just north of Albany). Afterward, Lansky moved to Florida and concentrated on investments in the southern part of that state. His operations were so lucrative that he is reputed to have kept a former bootlegger associate, living in Switzerland, as his full-time money manager (McFadden 1983). In 1970, fearing an indictment for income-tax evasion, Lansky fled to Israel, where he touched off a 26-month legal fight. Lansky claimed citizenship as a Jew under Israel's "Law of Return." He also reported that his efforts before the 1948 War of Independence resulted in badly needed munitions being smuggled out of East Coast ports to the Jewish underground in Palestine. The United States pressured Israel for his return, saying Lansky was a dangerous criminal. The case went to Israel's highest court, which in 1972 ruled that he was not entitled to citizenship because his past made him a "danger to public safety" (McFadden 1983).

When Lansky returned to Miami, he was immediately arrested and posted a cash bail of $250,000. He was ultimately cleared of, or ruled too ill to stand trial on, all the tax evasion, conspiracy, and Las Vegas "skimming" charges against him. Lansky spent his last years in seclusion in a Miami Beach condominium with his second wife. He died of cancer in 1983.[10]

---

[10]Lansky's first marriage in 1929 ended in a divorce in 1946. The couple had two sons and a daughter. One of Lansky's two sons, Paul, is a graduate of West Point and a pilot with a master's degree in engineering who served a tour in Vietnam (Lacey 1991).

INTERETHNIC COOPERATION: MURDER, INC.

The setting is the East New York–Brownsville section of Brooklyn, a Jewish neighborhood, and the adjoining Italian neighborhood of Ocean Hill. The story begins in the spring of 1930, when Abe ("Kid Twist"—from the twisted chocolate candy he favored) Reles, Martin ("Bugsy") Goldstein, and Herschel ("Pittsburgh Phil") Strauss decided to take over the neighborhood rackets dominated by the three Shapiro brothers, Irving, Meyer, and Willie. The boys from East New York–Brownsville secretly teamed up with a crew from Ocean Hill, all of whom had worked as strong-arms for the Shapiros. An attempt to kill the three brothers while they were checking the inventory at their brewery failed, and the Shapiros responded (Ross 2003).

In 1930, a member of the Reles group was killed, and Reles and Goldstein were wounded. Meyer Shapiro then abducted Reles's girlfriend, whom he beat and raped. The Reles group struck back. During 1930 and 1931, eighteen attempts were made on Meyer Shapiro's life—number nineteen was successful. Brother Irving's demise followed, and Willie was abducted, severely beaten, and buried alive. The Reles group took over gambling, loansharking, and prostitution in the East New York–Brownsville sections, and they soon became involved in labor racketeering. Their specialty, however, became murder. Joselit (1983: 153) stresses the level of intergroup cooperation, noting that the Jewish and Italian members of the group "worked side by side on a daily basis, physically molesting tardy borrowers and stubborn union leaders." Moreover, they took orders from Lepke Buchalter and Albert Anastasia (discussed later).

The "Boys from Brooklyn" were used as staff killers by the newly formed confederation of organized crime leaders that emerged from Prohibition. In addition to their various criminal enterprises, the "Boys" received a retainer to be "on call" whenever the occasion arose—and it arose often. In a 10-year period they murdered more than 80 persons in Brooklyn alone. They were so efficient that gang leaders from across the country made use of their services, and Paul Kavieff (2006) reports that the Boys from Brooklyn murdered about 1,000 persons nationally.

There were full-dress rehearsals; getaway routes were carefully checked. A "crash car" followed the stolen vehicle containing the actual killers in the event of a police pursuit. Guns were rendered untraceable, although ropes and ice picks were often the preferred weapons. One of the group's members describes the "contract system" (Berger 1940: 5): "The 'trooper' [killer] is merely directed to take a plane, car, or train to a certain place to meet 'a man.' The man 'fingers' [points out] the victim for the trooper, who kills him when it is convenient. The trooper then leaves town immediately, and when local hoodlums are questioned, their alibis are perfect."

In 1940, several of the "Boys" were indicted for the 1933 murder of a 19-year-old who had been "convicted" of talking to the authorities. Quite to the surprise of the Brooklyn district attorney's office, one of the group's members agreed to become a government witness. Reputedly the toughest of the "Boys," Abe Reles, upon being granted immunity from prosecution, began to disclose the sensational details of Murder, Inc. His information and subsequent testimony led to the conviction and electrocution of seven men. Before any case could be made against Albert Anastasia, Reles had an accident. On November 12, 1941, while under constant police guard, he fell out of the sixth-floor window of the Coney Island Half-Moon Hotel. His death remains officially unexplained.

T. J. English (2005) notes that in the early years of Prohibition, it would not be an exaggeration to say that Irish gangsters ran New York City. However, as the United States inched toward the Second World War, except for a few pockets in New York (the Westies) and Boston (discussed in Chapter 15), the Irish role in organized crime had ended and the Jewish role was beginning to wane. Restrictive immigration laws—the Johnson Act of 1921 and the Reed-Johnson Act of 1924—had cut off Jewish immigration, and the pool of available candidates for membership in criminal organizations was rapidly declining. By the end of the war, it was apparent that Italians had eclipsed the Jewish role in organized crime. As Thomas Reppetto (2004: xii) reports, Jewish (as well as Irish) gangs grew out of neighborhood bonds formed by young men involved in such conventional criminality as robbery and burglary. While Prohibition served to transform them into powerful groups, they continued to operate much as they had in their early violent days—their organizations were largely extensions of street gangs. When death or imprisonment removed their leaders, their organizations usually collapsed. "In contrast, despite their reputation for violence and ruthlessness, Italian leaders eschewed senseless mayhem in favor of more rational methods."

ITALIAN ORGANIZED CRIME

Between 1891 and 1920, 4 million Italians entered the United States, the overwhelming majority coming from the *Mezzogiorno*—the area south of Rome—in particular, Sicily, Naples, and its surrounding Campania area, and the province of Calabria (Gallo 1981). Every important Italian American organized crime figure has had cultural roots in the *Mezzogiorno* (discussed in Chapter 6). These poor immigrants encountered an economy shaped by the Astors, the Rockefellers, and the Vanderbilts, in which powerless people had little opportunity. Facing enormous social and economic hardship exacerbated by ethnic prejudice, they "found work in the city's construction crews, laboring as ditch diggers, hod carriers, and stone cutters. As long as they had strong arms, it did not matter if they could not speak English or operate a complex machine" (Gallo 1981: 44).

By early 1900, about 500,000 (mostly southern) Italians lived in New York City, in the most deprived social and economic circumstances. Italian immigration "made fortunes for speculators and landlords, but it also transformed the neighborhood into a kind of human ant heap in which suffering, crime, ignorance and filth were the dominant elements" (Petacco 1974: 16). The Italian immigrant provided the cheap labor vital to the expanding capitalism of that era. As with earlier generations of immigrants, a small number sought to succeed by bending and breaking both moral and legal codes. Being relative latecomers, they could not imitate the scions of earlier generations, the Robber Barons who had already, by "hook or crook," secured a place in society. Instead, they adapted their southern Italian culture to the American experience.

"Functional deficiencies of the official structure," notes Robert Merton (1967: 127), "generate an alternative (unofficial) structure to fulfill existing needs somewhat more effectively." Randall Collins (1975: 463) adds, "Where legitimate careers are blocked and resources available for careers in crime, individuals would be expected to move in that direction." Thus, Collins notes, the prominence of Italians in organized crime is related to the coincidence of several historical factors: "The arrival of large numbers of European immigrants from peasant backgrounds who demanded cultural services that the dominant Anglo-Protestant society made illegal; the availability of a patrimonial form of military organization that could be applied to protecting such services; and the relatively late arrival of the Italians in comparison with other ethnic groups (for example, the Irish) who had acquired control of legitimate channels of political and related economic mobility" (1975: 463).

"In order to beat rival organizations," notes Luigi Barzini (1965: 273), "criminals of Sicilian descent reproduced the kind of illegal groups they had belonged to in the old country and employed the same rules to make them invincible." Richard Gambino (1974: 304) concludes that, although southern Italian characteristics do not predispose people toward crime, "where the mode of life has been impressed onto OC it has made it difficult to combat effectively the criminal activity" (1974: 297).

Among these immigrants were *mafiosi* who established protection regimes in every American city that had a sizable Sicilian population, "feeding off the common laborer's honest toil and claiming to serve as a means of easing adjustment to American society" (Nelli 1976: 136). The Mafia "was imported by Sicilian immigrants, who reproduced it in the cities in which they settled, as a ritual brotherhood consisting of loosely linked but otherwise independent and uncoordinated 'families' organized hierarchically" (Hobsbawm 1969: 686). Mafia groups "served important social as well as financial functions. The group produced a sense of belonging and of security in numbers. This function was at least in part through the use of initiation ceremonies, passwords and rituals, and rules of conduct with which members must abide" (Nelli 1976: 138). "The fertile criminal soil of the United States," notes John Dickie (2004: 164), "was one of the rare environments into which the mafia's method could be transferred wholesale." Similar groups of Neapolitan origin, *camorra*, also operated, and by 1915, camorrista Giosue Gallucci dominated Harlem's Little Italy.[11] These groups of *mafiosi* and *camorristi* were also involved in the manufacture of low-cost, high-proof, untaxed alcohol, a business that prepared them well for Prohibition.

One of Francis Ianni's (1972: 57) informants describes a Mafia gang operating in Brooklyn in 1928: "All the old Sicilian 'moustaches' used to get together in the backroom of the club—it was a *fratallanze* [brotherhood] and they used to call it *Unione Siciliana*. They spent a lot of time talking about the old country, drinking wine and playing cards. But these were tough guys too, and they were alky cookers [bootleggers] and pretty much ran things in the neighborhood. They had all of the businesses locked up and they got a piece of everything that was sold."

The *Unione Siciliana* emerged in nineteenth-century New York as a lawful fraternal society designed to advance the interests of Sicilian immigrants. Branches were established wherever new colonies of Sicilians expanded. With Prohibition, gangsters began to infiltrate and pervert the association. With an expanding criminal front, *Unione* leaders became natural catalysts for any racketeers

---

[11]Gallucci was killed in 1915 in a feud with Ciro Terranova who took over control of Harlem and the deceased's lucrative artichoke monopoly, becoming known as the "Artichoke King" (Downey 2004).

seeking to widen their influence and profit potentials.[12] Membership included clannish old-world criminal types who stressed the maintenance of the cultural traditions of the Sicilian Mafia, and a younger Americanized faction anxious to increase operations through cooperative agreements even with non-Italians. "The *Unione* of the 1920s became the object of power struggles, with both orientations contending at local, regional, and national levels for more advantageous posts. This struggle terminated in 1931 in the Castellammarese war" (Inciardi 1975: 115).

CASTELLAMMARESE WAR

By 1930, there were two major Mafia factions in New York, one headed by Giuseppe ("Joe the Boss") Masseria operating out of the Little Italy of East Harlem, and the other by Salvatore Maranzano whose business office was in midtown Manhattan. Prohibition had enabled the Mafia gangs to break out of the bounds of "Little Italy" and operate in the wider society—booze-hungry Americans were not fussy about the source of their liquor. The struggle for domination of Italian American organized crime in New York became known as the Castellammarese war because Maranzano and many of his supporters came from the small Sicilian coastal town of Castellammare del Golfo. The Maranzano group consisted mainly of Sicilians, especially the "moustaches," Old World types, many of whom had fled from Mussolini's persecution of *mafiosi* (discussed in Chapter 6). After his own escape, Maranzano helped smuggle many of his compatriots into the United States, and these supported their *padrone*. The Masseria group had both Sicilian and non-Sicilian members, including Lucky Luciano and Gaetano Lucchese (Sicilians), Vito Genovese (Neapolitan), and Frank Costello (Calabrian). Through ties developed by Luciano, they were allied with non-Italians such as Meyer Lansky and Ben Siegel. As the war turned against Masseria—the Maranzano forces were reinforced by a continuing supply of Sicilian exiles—five of his leading men, led by Luciano, went over to the other side.[13] They failed to notify Joe the Boss.

On April 15, 1931, Masseria drove his steel-armored sedan, a massive car with plate glass an inch thick in all of its windows, to a garage near the Nuova Villa in the Coney Island section of Brooklyn. He then walked to the restaurant for a meal and a card game with Luciano. It was Masseria's last meal ("Racket Chief Slain by Gangster Gunfire" 1931). Luciano excused himself and went to the washroom: "Joe the Boss was shot as he sat at the table. As Masseria died, he still clutched the ace of diamonds, and that, in years to come, became a symbol of impending death to all good Mafia members" (Messick 1973: 54). The Castellammarese war was over.

It did not take long for Maranzano to irritate many of his followers, particularly the more Americanized gangsters such as Luciano. Joseph Bonanno, who was born in Castellammare del Golfo, was a staunch ally of Maranzano. In his autobiography Bonanno points out that the new Mafia boss was out of step with the times. "Maranzano was old-world Sicilian in temperament and style. But he didn't live in Sicily anymore. In New York he was advisor not only to Sicilians but to American Italians. Maranzano represented a style that often clashed with that of the Americanized men who surrounded him after the war. It was difficult, for example, for Maranzano even to communicate effectively with many of these men, for they only understood American street cant" (Bonnano 1983: 137–38).

On September 10, 1931, four men carrying pistols entered a suite at 230 Park Avenue, the Grand Central Building, in New York City. "One of them ordered the seven men and Miss Frances Samuels, a secretary, to line up against the wall. The others stalked into the private office of Salvatore Maranzano. There was a sound of voices raised in angry dispute; blows, struggling,

---

[12]In Italy, the Freemasons reportedly played a similar role: Mafia bosses and members became members to enhance their relationships with business and political leaders (della Porta and Vannucci 1999; Paoli 1999).

[13]Thomas Repetto (2004) claims that Masseria discovered Luciano's treachery.

and finally pistol shots, and the four men dashed out of the suite." Maranzano was found with "his body riddled with bullets and punctured with knife wounds" ("Gang Kills Suspect in Alien Smuggling" 1931: 1). The killers are believed to have been Jews (who Maranzano and his bodyguards would not recognize) sent by Lansky and Siegel at the behest of Luciano. Because the killers flashed badges, Maranzano and his bodyguards apparently believed them to be federal immigration agents who had visited him before as part of an investigation into the smuggling of Sicilians into the country. They attempted to kill him silently with knives, and when Maranzano fought furiously to save his life, they shot him.

In the aftermath of the Castellammarese war, five Italian American crime Families emerged, and they continue to maintain distinct identities.

At the center of the American Mafia Family patron-client network is the boss—the *paterfamilias*, who may be assisted by an underboss (*sottocapo*) and counselor/advisor (*consigliere*). The boss is the "patron's patron." In a structure that resembles a model of the universe, the boss is surrounded by clients, for example, captains (*capiregime*), to whom he acts as a patron. The captains are surrounded by members or soldiers (*soldati*), to whom they act as patrons. This crime unit is tied together in a network that includes nonmember associates who are clients of each of the members, including the boss and captains (see Figure 4.1). In the American Mafia, each of the bosses is connected (by kinship, friendship, mutual respect) to every other boss. This structure represents what Richard Scott (1981) refers to as a *natural system*: Members are not necessarily guided by their organization's goals, but they share a common interest in the survival of the system and engage in collective activities informally structured to secure this end. In organized crime as a natural system, the organized crime unit is more than an instrument for attaining defined goals; it is fundamentally a social group attempting to adapt and survive in a dangerous environment. In New York, the basic unit is the Family, or *borgata*. However, the actual name by which a group is known may vary. In New England, for example, it is the "Office," in Chicago, "The Outfit." Although any number of members may be related, the term *Family* does not imply kinship by blood or marriage. Each crime unit is composed of members and associates.

Membership

Each member of a Mafia Family, a "made guy," has been accorded a valuable franchise, a sense of entitlement that enables him to engage in a virtual smorgasbord of criminal activity with the knowledge that he will be supported and protected by the Family. Although an independent entrepreneur, he will share a portion (roughly 15 percent) of all profits from crime with his captain who in turn shares his earnings with the boss. In return, he will be protected by the Family from other criminals and has unlimited access to the network in which the Family is enmeshed. His reputation as a "made guy" serves to instill fear, a valuable resource in the otherwise anarchic world of criminals. Even when a made guy engages in legitimate business, he enjoys advantages: Unions may avoid pressing demands, security costs are minimized (dangerous to victimize a made guy), and competitors can be intimidated.

In criminal circles, the importance of membership is revealed by the numerous terms and phrases used to indicate membership status: "made guy" (the Sicilian Mafia refers to a newly initiated member as being "made into a man" [Paoli 2003]), "wiseguy," "button" or "receiving his button," "being straightened out," "goodfella," "amico," and "friend of ours." And there is an initiation ceremony. Testifying before a senate subcommittee ("Russian Organized Crime" 1996: 46), Anthony ("Gaspipe") Casso,[14] imprisoned former underboss of the Lucchese Family, stated:

> To become a "made" member, you would have to be sponsored by a captain of the family, who would bring you to the boss of the family and sponsor you to become a "made" member. They have a ceremony with the

---

[14] For a journalistic biography of Casso, see Carlo (2008).

FIGURE 4.1   *American Mafia Family*

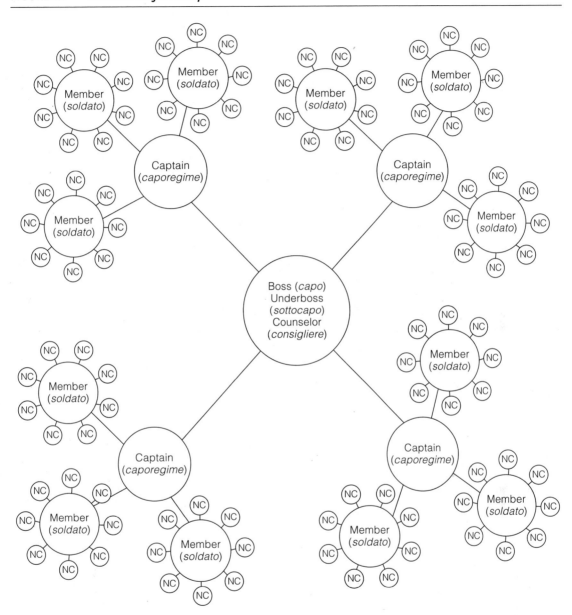

NC = Nonmember Client
The members act as patrons to nonmember clients.
Each unit is tied to other Families throughout the country by the Capo, whose sovereignty is recognized by the other bosses.

boss, the *consigliere*, and the underboss present at the time, and the captain who brings you in. They prick your trigger finger and make it bleed, and then they put a little piece of paper; they set it on fire and you burn it in your hand, and you repeat after them that you will never betray La Cosa Nostra, or you will burn like the paper is burning in your hand. And your life does not belong to you anymore; your life belongs to them.

In 1989, two electronic eavesdropping devices were placed in the basement ceiling of a house in Medford, Massachusetts, a Boston suburb. The bugs recorded the initiation of four men into the crime Family then headed by Raymond Patriarca, Jr., who presided at the ceremony.

[Patriarca] We're all here to bring in some new members into our Family and more than that, to start maybe a new beginning. Put all that's got started behind us. 'Cause they come into our Family to start a new thing with us. . . .

The prospects were introduced to the gathered Family members, and the *consigliere* asked each to individually take an oath in Italian/Sicilian (translated): "I want to enter into this organization to protect my family and to protect all of my friends. I swear not to divulge this secret and to obey with love and *omertá*." He was then assigned to a *caporegime*.

Each candidate was then asked which finger he shoots with, and that finger was pricked to draw blood. A holy card with the image of the Patriarca family saint was burned. The prospect was told that he was required to keep secrets and could not leave the Family unless he was dead. Some details of mob protocol and rules were explained: to introduce other members as "a friend of ours" and associates as "a friend of mine"; if ordered, to kill anyone who betrays the Family, even if he is your brother; to respect the female relatives of other members— under penalty of death; to memorize the chain of command; to keep your *caporegime* informed of your whereabouts; to remember that all crime Families in America are related; and to avoid kissing other members in public—too conspicuous.

Michael Franzese,[15] a captain in the Colombo Family, reports a two-stage process. First, he was formally proposed—taken by an old-time member to meet the Family boss, who explained the rules: "After the meeting, my name, along with those of the other potential inductees, was circulated around the other four families" (Franzese and Matera 1992: 124). Franzese was then assigned to a *caporegime* for a probationary period of nearly a year. In 1975 he was formally inducted in a ceremony similar to those already described.

Former NYPD detective Ralph Salerno (with Tompkins 1969) reports that recruitment into organized crime involves the careful study of neighborhood youngsters by those who control membership. A potential recruit must exhibit a recognition of the authority of the organization and a willingness to perform various criminal and noncriminal functions (usually minor at first) with skill and daring and without asking questions. Robert Woetzel (1963: 3) points out: "The standards of the teenage gang from which the potential criminals come are the same as those of an adult conspiracy": a code of loyalty and exclusive "turf" (territory). The gang boy may also have a criminal record and an antisocial attitude, which indicate that he is a "stand-up" kid, the proper credentials for a career in organized crime.

Raymond Martin, a former ranking officer with the NYPD, describes why recruitment is made easy in certain Italian neighborhoods in Brooklyn (1963: 61):

On so many street corners in Bath Beach, in so many luncheonettes and candy stores in Bensonhurst, boys see the mob-affiliated bookies operate. They meet the young toughs, the mob enforcers. They hear the tales of glory recounted—who robbed what, who worked over whom, which showgirl shared which gangster's bed, who got hit by whom, the techniques of the rackets and how easy it all is, how the money rolls in. What wonder is it that some boys look forward to

---

[15]Michael's father, John ("Sonny") Franzese, when he was arrested in 2008 at age 89 for racketeering, was identified as underboss of the Colombo Family.

being initiated into these practices with the eagerness of a college freshman hoping to be pledged by the smoothest fraternity on campus. With a little luck and guts, they feel, even they may someday belong to that splendid, high-living band, the mob.

The centrality of the neighborhood for providing a pool of organized crime aspirants cannot be overemphasized. In these areas, there is a "romanticization of the mob"—young "wannabes" copy the styles of their notorious idols and are eager to ingratiate themselves with made guys. As one recruit, raised in the organized crime neighborhood of Brooklyn's East New York–Brownsville section, recounts, "At the age of twelve my ambition was to be a gangster. To be a wiseguy. To me being a wiseguy was better than being president of the United States. It meant power among people who had no power. It meant perks in a working-class neighborhood that had no privileges. To be a wiseguy was to own the world. I dreamed of being a wiseguy the way other kids dreamed about being doctors or movie stars or firemen or ball players" (Pileggi 1985: 13).

An undercover FBI agent describes the day an associate was "made"—initiated as a member of the Bonanno crime Family (Pistone 1987: 64): "When he came back, he was ecstatic, as proud as a peacock. 'Getting made is the greatest thing that could ever happen to me,' he said. 'I've been looking forward to this day ever since I was a kid.' . . . That night we partied together for his celebration. But now everybody treated him with more respect. He was a made guy now." After completion of his initiation, Jimmy ("the Weasel") Fratianno "was so excited that he could feel his legs tremble." Becoming a member of the Los Angeles crime Family of Jack Dragna "made him a special person, an inheritor of enormous power. It was something he had wanted for as long as he could remember" (Demaris 1981: 3).

To be eligible for membership, a young man (there are no female members) must be of Italian descent. As Gambino Family underboss Sam Gravano states, "Years and years ago, you had to be Italian on both sides. Then it became that

you only had to be that on your father's side. Not your mother's. Because they say you are what your father is, you carry his name. Like John Gotti's wife is part Russian Jew. So his son, John Junior, got made, right? He's part Italian and part Russian Jew" (Maas 1997: 84). One source reports that this change in qualifications occurred in 1975 as a response to recruiting difficulties experienced by the New York Families (Volkman 1998).

The prospective member requires a sponsor and must have a long history of successful criminal activity or possess certain skills required by the group. They can be roughly divided between the "earners" and the "shooters." The earners have proven their mettle by financial success, while shooters, such as Jimmy Fratianno, possess the ability to execute persons in an efficient, impersonal, and dispassionate manner (Demaris 1981). However, every potential member is expected to participate in a murder—although not necessarily as the actual executioner. Such participation serves to more closely bind the person to the ongoing conspiracy that is organized crime, and it precludes government agents from becoming members. Peter Maas (1997: 46) points that even though committing a murder—making your bones—was not a prerequisite for induction into *Cosa Nostra*, more often than not, it would happen. "Murder was the linchpin of *Cosa Nostra*—for control, for discipline, to achieve and maintain power. For made members and associates, it was an everyday, accepted fact of life." Sam and Chuck Giancana (1992) state that in Chicago, a guy didn't necessarily have to kill someone to be made if he had powerful friends to protect him from such dirty work. There is also evidence that one can get credit for killing someone by assisting in the murder rather than carrying out the killing itself. An organized crime group is particularly interested in criminals who have proven to be moneymakers, "earners" who can increase the group's income. In 1988, the former underboss of the Cleveland Family testified before a congressional committee:

My name is Angelo Lonardo. I am 77 years old, and I am a member of the La Cosa Nostra. I am the former underboss of the

Cleveland organized family. I became a member of La Cosa Nostra in the late 1940's, but have been associated with the organization since the late 1920's. When I was "made" or became a member of La Cosa Nostra, I went through an initiation ceremony. I later learned that to be proposed for membership in La Cosa Nostra, you would have to have killed someone and stood up to the pressure of police scrutiny. Today, you do not have to kill to be a member, but just prove yourself worthy by keeping your mouth shut or by being a "stand-up" guy. However, if you are called upon to kill someone, you have to be prepared to do it.

In New York, each member is an independent operator, not an employee—he receives no salary from the group. Instead, the made guy or wiseguy has a form of "franchise": He is authorized by the group to make money by using the Family connections that come with membership, bolstered by the status (fear) that membership generates. Although part of a particular crew, he is an independent entrepreneur, violent and aggressive, constantly on the prowl for moneymaking opportunities. In a typical pattern, a made guy, a franchised member, will attract nonmembers who are eager to associate with him, to become "connected," because an associate enjoys some of the status and connections that the crime Family enjoys. In a discussion with an associate, a new member of the Colombo Family reported on his recent change in status: "Since I got made I got a million fuckin' worshippers hanging around" (Iannuzzi 1993: 172). The member-as-patron thus sits at the center of a network of nonmember clients that constitutes an action-based unit for coordinated criminal activities. If the member is able to generate considerable income, he gains greater status in the Family and can become a candidate for advancement to *caporegime*. If successful associates are Italian, they become candidates for membership.

According to FBI recordings released at the 1992 trial of John Gotti, in New York the "making" of prospective members requires passing the list around to other Families. But this is complicated by the very informality that characterizes organized crime—men are typically known only by their nicknames, which may not be precise enough to identify a particular person for such an important function as determining fitness for membership. In fact, just before a ceremony for the making of new members, Sam Gravano reported to *consigliere* Frank Locascio that "I don't have it right, Frank. I don't have their last names. I don't have the proper spellings. I ain't got the, the guys all down" (recorded January 4, 1990). At his 2005 sentencing hearing, Bonanno Family boss-turned-informant Joseph Massino was asked by a federal judge for the real names of people against whom he had testified. "I don't know their proper names," Massino replied.

Because of their acquisitive and violent nature, members of organized crime can easily come into conflict with members of the same or another organized crime unit. The more members a group has, the greater the likelihood of conflict—too many made guys in search of too few moneymaking opportunities. Under such circumstances, members are more likely to become involved in high-risk ventures that can be a threat to the safety of the group. This dynamic places natural limitations on membership. Furthermore, each new member is a potential threat to the security of the group—a potential informant—so new members are selected with caution and great care. A prospective member may have to serve the group for many years before achieving membership status. During the 2006 trial of John Gotti, Jr. (for ordering the beating of radio personality and head of the Guardian Angels Curtis Sliwa—he was not convicted), a member of the Gambino Family testified that there is a ceiling on how many members each of the five New York Families can initiate—someone has to die (Hartocollis 2006).

Membership, compared with some type of associate status, provides rewards associated with being an "insider." As one member told me, "A made guy is considered more honorable," meaning that there is a greater level of trust—and respect. Only members will be allowed to attend certain important meetings and be privy to important conversations and information, and information is an important basis of power. The basic mechanism for resolving disputes is arbitration—a *sitdown* or *table*—and a nonmember needs a member to represent him. A nonmember associate in a dispute with a made guy is at a distinct disadvantage—a disadvantage that can be life-threatening. This can become balanced if the associate is an "earner"—a source of substantial funds.

Considerable "psychic gain" accrues with membership. Within criminal and certain legitimate circles, being "made" conveys a great deal of prestige, if not fear. The President's Commission notes that although a soldier is the lowest-ranking member of the organization, "he is a considerable figure on the street, a man who commands respect and fear" (PCOC 1986c: 44). In testimony before the commission, a witness elaborated:

[Q:] How did you come to know that Greg Scarpa [soldier in the Colombo crime Family] is a "made" individual while someone in his crew is not "made"?

[A:] Conversation—you could just see the way that everybody answers to him; I mean, he has a club on 13th Avenue [in Brooklyn] and everyone comes up to him, and no one—they don't double park their car without getting his permission, so to say. In other words, no one does anything without getting his permission. So you could just see the respect he gets.

A number of otherwise legitimate persons are attracted by the mystique that surrounds organized crime. Popular sources report that many young women are attracted to organized crime figures and to the bars and nightclubs that are owned or frequented by them. For similar reasons young men may aspire to membership in organized crime—reasons that go beyond economic advantages—out of a desire to be part of the mystique reinforced by media representations such as *The Godfather* trilogy, *Goodfellas*, and *The Sopranos*.

There are also important disadvantages associated with membership. Law enforcement agencies take great interest in a criminal if they discover he is a made guy. Any insult or assault on a member requires that he kill the offender. He is also required to obey the orders of his boss, even if

this means participating in the murder of a complete stranger or perhaps a close friend or relative. But, of course, the member is protected by the boss, who will respond to any attack on one of his soldiers as a personal affront, a fundamental lack of respect, requiring mobilization of the group's resources for violence. It is the ready availability of private violence that makes the organized crime group a viable entity.

The continuation of the American Mafia depends on the ability of crime units to recruit new members, which, in turn, depends upon the availability of a pool of qualified applicants. For at least some crime groups, this is becoming more difficult. On January 4, 1990, John Gotti, boss of the Gambino Family, was recorded by the FBI decrying the paucity of qualified candidates for membership to *consigliere* Frank Locascio: "And where we gonna find them, these kinda guys? Frank, I'm not being a pessimist. It's gettin' tougher, not easier. We got everything that's any good. Look around, ask your son someday, forget who you are, what you are. Talk to your son like his age. Put yourself in his age bracket, and let him tell you what good kids in the neighborhood other than the kids that are with you. Or good kids in the neighborhood other than with him. You know what I'm trying to say? I told you a couple of weeks ago, we got the only few pockets of good kids left."

Crews

Members and associates are organized into crews, semi-independent units nominally headed by a *caporegime*, a *capodecina*, a street boss, or even a soldier. Crews generate finances, which they share with their crew chief, who shares it with the *caporegime* or with the boss. These crews have been described in a number of popular books on organized crime. FBI agent Joseph Pistone (1987: 51–52),[16] in his undercover role, describes the crew of a soldier in the Bonanno Family, whose "headquarters" was the back room of a store stocked with expensive clothing—stolen merchandise: "Although these

---

[16]Pistone's exploits became the subject of a book and movie, *Donnie Brasco*. The Bonanno Family captain who had permitted the agent's penetration was found murdered, his hands symbolically cut off.

were lower-echelon guys in the mob, they always had something going. They always had money. They were always turning things over. They always had swag around. . . . You name it, they stole it. Jilly's crew would hit warehouses, docks, trucks, houses. . . . There wasn't one hour of one day that went by when they weren't thinking and talking about what they were going to steal, who or what or where they were going to rob. . . . The mob was their job."

The crew headed by Paul Vario,[17] a *caporegime* in the Lucchese crime Family, used a drab, paint-flecked storefront cabstand and dispatch office in Brooklyn as its headquarters. Nicholas Pileggi (1985: 35) notes that the Vario crew did most of the strong-arm work for the Lucchese Family. "At the cabstand there were always young tough guys ready to go out and break a few heads whenever Paul gave the order and killers who were happy to take on the most violent of assignments." The persons in Vario's crew "had always been outlaws. They were the kids from the neighborhood who were always in trouble. As youngsters they were the ones invariably identified as toughs by the police and brought into the precinct for routine beatings, whenever some neighborhood store burglary or assault moved the station house cops into action."

The crew headed by John Gotti, a *caporegime* and later boss of the Gambino Family, was head-quartered at the Bergin Hunt and Fish Club, a (very) private storefront in the Ozone Park section of the New York City borough of Queens: "The Bergin men were good customers in the small cafes and stores operating on slim margins. Around his neighbors, Gotti acted like a gentleman; around him they acted as though he were a successful salesman. He began saluting the community with Fourth of July fireworks displays and barbecues; some residents began saluting him by alerting the club when men resembling undercover detectives were around" (Mustain and Capeci 1988: 112). The fireworks display was reportedly not appreciated by important wiseguys who considered it part of a pattern by Gotti of drawing unnecessary attention to organized crime.

---

[17]Vario, played by Paul Sorvino in the movie *Goodfellas*, died in prison while serving a 15-year sentence.

The Boss

Although he is at the center of the universe of an American Mafia unit, the boss does not have a complete overview of the decentralized activities of his members. In the past the boss was usually a senior citizen—it takes many years to gain the respect of members and the knowledge and connections needed by the group. It is a sign of weakness that many of the current *Cosa Nostra* bosses are relatively young, as well as volatile and violent. In 1996, for example, Liborio Bellomo, acting head of the Genovese crime Family, the largest in the United States, was indicted on racketeering charges in New York—at age 39 (Van Natta 1996).

Typically, the boss operates out of a fixed location: a restaurant, a private club, or his own business office. Raymond Patriarca, Sr., the New England crime boss who died of natural causes in 1984 at age 76, operated out of his vending-machine business, the National Cigarette Service, in the Federal Hill section of Providence, Rhode Island. Vincent Teresa (and Renner 1973: 95) states that the entire area around Patriarca's headquarters was an armed camp: "It was impossible to move through the area without being spotted and reported." Throughout the day, Patriarca received visitors, sometimes legitimate persons asking for a favor, usually to resolve a dispute, but more frequently "a parade of the faithful bearing tithes, cold cash for the middle drawer in the dirty back room of a cigarette vending-machine business in a run-down section of Providence. It could be the receipts from a wholly owned subsidiary or rent from a franchise. In a complex maze of interests, he completely controlled some markets, especially those involving gambling, loansharking, and pornography, and dabbled in others such as truck hijacking and drug trafficking in which free-lancers negotiated fees to do business" (O'Neill and Lehr 1989: 43).

The boss of the Genovese Family in New York operated out of an Italian restaurant in lower Manhattan, to which he was driven every day from his home in Long Island by a chauffeur-bodyguard. In the back of the restaurant was a table reserved for him. Persons having business with the boss would come in all day long and sit at the table for varying periods. Strangers were not welcome in the restaurant, which was located in the heart of an Italian neighborhood dominated by the Genovese Family. There was no place to park; all parking spaces were taken by members of the Family or their associates. Anyone walking in the area who was not recognized would be reported to the Family members at the restaurant. If a stranger entered the restaurant, he or she was told that a reservation was needed—but the restaurant refused to take reservations (Abadinsky 1983). Joseph Colombo, whose crime Family bears his name, operated out of a neighborhood real estate firm, Cantalup Realty Co., in the Bensonhurst section of Brooklyn. He was on the books as a licensed real estate salesman—the licensing test was fixed (Cantalupo and Renner 1990). Gambino Family boss John Gotti operated out of the Ravenite Social Club on Mulberry Street in Manhattan's Little Italy; every Wednesday, Gotti would hold court at a gathering of Family captains. To avoid being electronically surveilled, Gotti would discuss business on the street or in an apartment upstairs from the club; however, the apartment was bugged by the FBI (Coffey and Schmetterer 1991).

A boss has a number of men who report directly to him. They carry messages and perform assignments as necessary; they also physically protect the boss. In many crime groups, particularly those in New York, where five Families—and one from New Jersey—operate, most of the activities of Family members are not under the direct or indirect supervision of the boss. He often finds out about many of the activities of members only as the result of periodic briefings by the captains.

Crime boss Joseph Bonanno (with Lalli 1983: 157) describes how he operated as "Father" of his Family:

> Internal disagreements between Family members were solved at the grassroots level by group leaders or by the consigliere. A Family member's personal or business problems were usually handled in this manner, and the problem rarely had to be brought to my attention.

On the other hand, if a Family member wanted to go into business with a member of another Family, such an association would need the approval of the Fathers of the respective Families. A Family member's relations with non-Family members was his own affair.

> Other than meeting with other Fathers and meeting with group leaders within my Family on an ad hoc basis, being a Father took up relatively little of my time. Family matters were largely handled by the group leaders under me. Indeed, there were many Family members I never met. If I convened a Family meeting, I met only with the group leaders, who in turn passed the information to the people in their groups.

Peacekeeping, notes Bonanno, was his main responsibility as head of the Family. According to the PCOC (1985a), the Family boss is also responsible for making all important decisions on trial strategy when a Family member is the defendant. This responsibility is for protecting Family interests during the trial.

Crime boss Carlo Gambino would often conduct briefings in a moving car to reduce the possibility of surveillance. Very important or sensitive operations, such as those that could result in conflict with other crime Families or attract undue law enforcement attention, are cleared with the boss in advance. And, as noted earlier, in all but the smallest units, the boss will be assisted by an underboss (*sottocapo*) and a counselor/advisor (*consigliere*).

The boss, like many other members of a crime Family, has investments in illegitimate and legitimate enterprises, often in partnership with other members of his own or other crime groups or with nonmember associates. He receives a portion of the illegal earnings of all of the members of his Family. A soldier will share his earnings with his captain, who will pass on a portion to the boss. A captain will expect 15 percent of an ongoing business, such as loansharking or extortion, but more from a particular score, such as a hijacking. According to undercover FBI agent Joe Pistone (2004: 36), a greedy captain "will take fifty percent of whatever is waved under their noses" and he must provide the boss with whatever amount is requested. "All the captains of the family must make weekly payments to the boss, and the amount of these payments is completely at the whim and discretion of the boss." The captain has to produce that amount every week, and when "he falls short, the captain usually goes nuts and terrorizes his soldiers and demands they increase their payments to him."

Sitting in the back of his restaurant headquarters, the head of the Genovese Family would receive visitors who passed sealed envelopes filled with money to his bodyguard—their show of respect (Abadinsky 1983). As opposed to bureaucratic organizations, the money goes only in one direction—upward. When the boss gives someone money, it is for investments on which a substantial return is expected, or violence is guaranteed.

The boss demands absolute respect and total obedience. His working day is spent in exchanges with many people. With a word or two, a sentence, a shake of the head, a smile, or a gesture, he can set in motion a host of activities and operations involving dozens, if not hundreds, of persons. The boss is treated with a great deal of deference. People rise when he enters the room, and they never interrupt when he is speaking. If they are close, a kiss on the boss's check is considered an appropriate gesture of respect. If the boss rises, all rise. If the boss rises and embraces an individual, this is considered a great honor, often reserved only for other bosses.

The intensity of government surveillance and prosecution of organized crime during the last three decades has made the position of boss less desirable than in the past. As a result, filling the position may be difficult because those most qualified—men with good incomes and low profiles—may also be those who are most reluctant to undergo the law enforcement scrutiny that comes with the position. In such circumstances, the boss may be a relatively weak figure, with strength concentrated in the captains heading crews of earners.

The weakness of current Mafia Families is highlighted by the meteoric rise of Carmine Sessa, a killer who admitted to eleven murders. Inducted into the Colombo Family in 1987, three years later he was *consigliere*, and three years after that a government witness testifying against fellow Family members (Capeci 2003).

The Commission

All crime bosses are linked in a rather informal arrangement known as the "commission," but only the bosses of the most powerful groups—particularly those in New York, Chicago, Buffalo, and Philadelphia—are considered actual commission members. "The national commission regulates joint ventures between families, intervenes in family disputes, approves the initiation of new members, and controls relations between the U.S. and Sicilian branches of La Cosa Nostra" (PCOC 1986c: 37). The commission, reports Bonanno (with Lalli 1983: 159), can arbitrate disputes. Having no direct executive power, however, it has to depend on influence: "It had respect only insofar as its individual members had respect. More than anything else, the Commission was a forum."

In addition to the "national commission," which is a body that rarely, if ever, meets as a group,[18] the bosses of the New York Families constitute a commission that serves to arbitrate disputes and deal with joint ventures between their Families. In 1986, in what became known as the "Commission Case" (*United States v. Salerno*, 85 Cr. 139, SDNY, 1985), a number of New York bosses were convicted of conducting the affairs of "the commission of La Cosa Nostra" in a pattern of racketeering that violated the RICO statute (discussed in Chapter 15). The case revealed the role of the commission in New York:

- Regulate and facilitate relationships between the five Families
- Promote and facilitate joint ventures between Families

---

[18]According to Bill Bonanno (1999), until 1961, the national commission met regularly in odd years. He states that he was at a special commission meeting in 1962, which was called because of problems in the Profaci Family.

Rules of the American Mafia

- Always show respect to those who can command it.
- Report any failure to show respect to one's patron immediately.
- Violence must be used, even if only of a limited type, to ensure respect.
- Never ask for surnames. (Underboss Sam Gravano testified that there were many people in his crime Family whose last names he did not know.)
- Never resort to violence in a dispute with a member or associate of another Family.
- Never resort to, or even threaten, violence in a dispute with a member of your Family.
- Do not use the telephone except to arrange for a meeting place, preferably in code, from which you will then travel to a safe place to discuss business.
- Avoid mentioning specifics when discussing business—for example, names, dates, and places—beyond those absolutely necessary for understanding.
- Keep your mouth shut—anything you hear, anything you see, stays with you, in your head; do not talk about it.

- Do not ask unnecessary questions. The amount of information given to you is all you need to carry out your instructions.
- Never engage in homosexual activities.
- If your patron arranges for two parties to work together, he assumes responsibility for arbitrating any disputes between the parties.
- The boss can unilaterally direct violence, including murder, against any member of his Family, but he cannot engage in murder-for-hire, that is, make a profit from murder. (The murder need not be related to business: Paul Castellano ordered his son-in-law murdered, believing his philandering responsible for the boss's daughter's miscarriage.)
- The boss cannot use violence against a member or close associate of another Family without prior consultation with that Family's boss.
- The principal form of security in the American Mafia is an elaborate system of referral and vouching. Vouching for someone who turns out to be an informant or undercover officer entails the death penalty.

Sources: Abadinsky (1981a, 1983); Capeci (2003); Coffey and Schmetterer (1991); D. Jacobs (2002); transcripts from the 1992 trial of John Gotti.

- Resolve actual and potential disputes between Families
- Regulate the criminal activities of the Families
- Extend formal recognition to newly chosen Family bosses and resolve leadership disputes within Families
- Authorize the execution of Family members
- Approve of the initiation of new members into the Families

The power of approving the initiation of new members keeps Family size stable and prevents wholesale initiation, which would be likely in times of intra-Family conflict. During the struggle to lead the Colombo Family (1991–1993), for example, the commission would not permit either faction to initiate new members and thereby gain an advantage over its opposition.

Rules

Even though traditional organized crime does not have written rules, it has an elaborate set of norms that govern behavior. Francis Ianni (1972) argues that the rules of the American Mafia are actually standards of conduct based on the traditions of southern Italy, particularly the concept of family loyalty. However, my research (Abadinsky 1981a, 1983) indicates that the rules are not traditional but quite rational and sometimes counter to southern Italian tradition. For example, loyalty to the crime Family supersedes loyalty to one's own blood family. According to the rules, if required by the boss, a member must participate in the murder of a relative (usually by helping to "set him up"). When Vincent Siciliano (1970: 74) discovered who had killed his father, he swore vengeance but later found out that the hit had been "authorized," the killers carrying out Family orders. Finding one of the killers at a restaurant, Siciliano told him: "Look, I came here to talk to you. I want to apologize about the noise I was making." His father's murderer responded: "Hey, don't worry about it. I know how you felt about your father. I understand. There are no hard feelings, Vinnie." In Philadelphia, Frank ("Chickie") Narducci was killed on orders of Family boss Nicky Scarfo; yet his sons, Philip and Frank, Jr., continued to work as enforcers for Scarfo (Anastasia 1991). After John Gotti had *caporegime* Thomas Gambino's uncle, Paul Castellano, murdered, Gambino continued to report and show respect to Gotti, who became boss of the Gambino Family.

This is all contrary to the southern Italian credo *sangu de me sangu* ("blood of my blood"), which actually means *famiglia* (family) above all: *o tortu o gridu difenni i to* ("right or wrong, defend your own" kin). Actually, the rules of traditional organized crime have succeeded in preventing the emergence of a violent southern Italian tradition: vendetta, the irrational blood feud that is bad for business. Since the 1930s, there have been no "wars" between traditional organized crime groups, although there has been a great deal of intragroup violence.

ANALYSIS OF THE STRUCTURE

The structure of New York–style Mafia Families is only loosely coupled to its criminal activities. The structure is rather fluid, similar to that of the real estate development business: "A great deal of illegal activity within the illegal industries is not routine production and distribution carried on under the auspices of a specific firm, but instead the result of many ad hoc deals and projects" (Moore 1987: 54). The firms (crews) in the New York model are not consistently in one business but are intermittently in several. They are organized not as a "production line" but as a "job shop." Annelise Anderson (1979) found that the formal organizational structure of the Philadelphia crime Family was not the same as its economic structure. There was a relatively clear

hierarchy within the Family—boss, underboss, captains, soldiers—but its income-generating activities were based on several smaller operationally independent crews involved in gambling and loansharking. This structure, notes Ronald Goldstock (Stone 1992: 29), former director of the New York State Organized Task Force, is less like a corporation and more like a government: "In a corporation, people at the bottom carry out the policies and perform tasks assigned to them by the executives at the top. In the Mob, the people at the bottom are the entrepreneurs. They pass a percentage of their income upward as taxes in return for government-type services: resolution of disputes, allocation of territories, enforcement and corruption services." Anderson (1979: 46) argues that the most threatening aspect of this type of organized crime is the "group or organization's capacity for forming a quasi-government, giving it a competitive advantage."

LUCIANO/GENOVESE FAMILY

Born Salvatore Lucania in western Sicily, in 1897, Luciano arrived in New York with his parents early in 1907. The family settled on Manhattan's Lower East Side. He apparently did not like being called "Sally" and assumed the surname Charlie (Reppetto 2004). Although Luciano's conduct in school was satisfactory, his academic record was poor and made worse by chronic truancy. He left school when he was 14 and secured employment as a shipping boy in a hat factory owned by Jewish man. The young Luciano became a member of the Five Points Gang and a heroin user and seller. In 1916, he was found guilty of possessing narcotics and sent to a reformatory for six months (Nelli 1976; Powell 2000).

With the advent of Prohibition, Luciano emerged as a leader in the Masseria crime Family. During the Castellammarese war, he was kidnapped, badly beaten, and left for dead. His survival has often been cited (incorrectly) as the source of his nickname Lucky.[19] He had been

---

[19]Articles in the *New York Times* refer to Lucania as "Lucky" before this incident. The nickname is apparently derived from a shortening of Lucania to "Luc" and then "Lucky."

under the tutelage of Arnold Rothstein (discussed in Chapter 3), and with the deaths of Masseria and Maranzano, Luciano became the most important Italian organized crime figure in New York, a status he would enjoy until 1935. In that year, investigators for Thomas E. Dewey discovered an extensive prostitution network that, although independent at one time, had been subject to extortion by a member of the Luciano Family. In a single raid, Dewey's investigators arrested prostitutes, madams, and "bookers" (pimps). They were pressured and cajoled into testifying against Luciano, who protested that he had no knowledge of or involvement in the extortion activities. Dewey charged that acting on behalf of Luciano, two hundred bordellos and three thousand prostitutes were organized into a $12-million-a-year business. In fact, the witnesses tying Luciano to prostitution were not credible, and this enterprise was not even a good moneymaker for the syndicate (Powell 2000). "Dewey's argument seemed to be that Luciano was a prostitution overlord but even if he was not, he still was a menace to society" (Stolberg 1995: 128).

Luciano chose to take the stand in his own defense—a bad decision, as it turned out. Dewey was able to trap him in lies about his criminal record. In 1936, Luciano was found guilty of sixty-one counts of compulsory prostitution and sentenced to a term of 30 to 60 years in prison, despite an arguably weak case and a pervasive feeling that Luciano was actually convicted of being "notorious" (Powell 2000); Thomas Reppetto (2004), however, finds the evidence credible.

Luciano languished in Clinton State Prison at Dannemora, New York, while war raged in Europe and the Pacific. By 1942, German submarines operating in U.S. coastal waters had sunk 272 U.S. ships. It was suspected that information on American shipping was being leaked to the Germans by people employed in eastern ports.[20]

It was also suspected, incorrectly, that German submarines were receiving supplies from American fishing boats. The specter of sabotage was raised when the luxury liner *Normandie*, which had been refitted as a naval vessel, rolled over in flames while harbored in the Hudson River. (In fact, renamed the U.S.S. *Lafayette*, the *Normandie* was accidentally set ablaze by workers using acetylene torches.)

With the help of the Manhattan district attorney, naval intelligence officials met with Joseph ("Socks") Lanza, the vicious criminal "czar" of the Fulton Fish Market, who was under indictment for conspiracy and extortion.[21] Lanza agreed to help but noted that his influence was limited; he suggested the man to see was Lucky Luciano. Luciano was transferred to a prison closer to New York City to meet with naval intelligence officers. Through Meyer Lansky, the word went out. According to Rodney Campbell (1977), in addition to ordering port workers and fishermen to "keep alert," crime figures helped place intelligence operatives in key areas by supplying them with union cards and securing positions for them on the waterfront, on fishing boats, and in waterfront bars, restaurants, and hotels. Crime figures also provided another important service. At the request of naval officials, they prevented strikes and other forms of labor unrest that could interrupt wartime shipping. According to Ezio Costanzo (2007: 56), strikes and protests were curtailed through intimidation, firings, and, in some cases, murder. "Following the agreement between the Mafia and Naval intelligence, some thirty homicides that took place on the waterfront could almost certainly be attributed to the secret pact." There was no sabotage, and waterfront workers became careful about what they said lest they reveal the kind of goods that were being unloaded, loaded, and their destination.

Though Campbell provides documentation of Luciano's domestic role during the war, his data on Luciano's role in the invasion of Sicily are tenuous. According to Campbell, Luciano

---

[20]Coastal cities such as New York, Atlantic City, and Miami, fearing a loss of tourist trade, refused to enforce blackouts, creating a neon shooting gallery for German submarines: "The U-boats nightly lay in the wait on the seaward side of the shipping lanes and picked off their sharply silhouetted victims at will" (Kennedy 1999: 68).

[21]Socks Lanza is discussed in Chapter 14.

sent word to Sicilian *capimafiosi* to assist the Allied landing. However, *mafiosi* did not need encouragement from Luciano—their desire to rid the island of Mussolini's iron hand was incentive enough.

In 1945, Dewey, then governor of New York, received a petition for executive clemency on behalf of Luciano, citing his efforts during the war. The following year, Dewey announced that Luciano would be released from prison and deported to Italy. Luciano left the United States on February 9, 1946. Before the end of the year, however, he was in Havana holding court with the elite of New York's underworld. The following year, U.S. pressure on Cuba compelled Luciano to return to Italy, where he died of a heart attack in 1962.

Frank Costello

With Luciano in prison and then deported to Italy, leadership of his crime Family was assumed by Frank Costello. Christened Francesco Castiglia, Costello was born in Calabria in 1891. Like several other Italian criminals (and boxers), he affected an Irish surname, which was certainly no hindrance in New York, where the Irish dominated Tammany and Tammany dominated the city. In 1915, Costello served a 10-month sentence for carrying a concealed firearm. By 1923, he was a successful bootlegger working for Bill Dwyer, an ex-longshoreman turned rumrunner, who brought liquor from Canada across the Great Lakes in armored speedboats (Talese 1965). Costello moved into gambling and eventually became a successful (and legitimate) real estate dealer. Known as the "King of the Slots," Costello operated an extensive network of "one-armed bandits"[22] in New York City until Mayor Fiorello La Guardia went on a highly publicized campaign to rid the city of "that bum." Many sources report that Costello was then invited to bring his slot machines to New Orleans

by the political boss of Louisiana, Senator Huey P. Long—"The Kingfish."[23]

Costello was known for his political influence. In the 1940s, "Tammany's aging Irish chieftains turned to the Italian-controlled underworld for desperately needed funding." This "Mafia Plan" was not without risk: Costello and his colleagues "decided to install their own Italian district leaders in Tammany clubhouses" (Erie 1988: 122).

In 1951, Costello appeared before the Kefauver Committee (discussed in Chapter 3) and was exposed on national television as a major crime figure. However, only Costello's hands could be seen; his lawyer had insisted that Costello not be televised. The crime boss's evasive responses, coupled with a dramatic walkout, eventually led to an 18-month prison term for contempt of the Senate. In 1952, the government moved against him for income-tax evasion, for which in 1954 Costello received a sentence of five years' imprisonment. In 1956, his attorney proved that the conviction had been based on illegal wiretaps, and Costello was freed ("Frank Costello Dies of Coronary at 82" 1972: 21).

Costello routinely traveled without any bodyguards. In 1957, he had an appointment to meet a Family *caporegime* in charge of Greenwich Village. The restaurant meeting had been arranged by Vito Genovese, Family underboss, and Costello's movements were being monitored. A call was made to a pay phone where a double-parked car was waiting for word that Costello was on his way home. As Costello rushed to catch the elevator in his luxury apartment building, he ran by a large man wearing a fedora. The man yelled, "This is for you, Frank." As Costello turned, the man fired a revolver at Costello's face from a distance of six to ten feet. The bullet hit Costello in the head but caused only superficial damage. When questioned by authorities, Costello insisted he did

---

[22]The slot machines dispensed candy mints as well as tokens that were redeemable for money. "The purpose of this arrangement was to make it arguable before friendly judges that the one-armed bandits were actually vending machines" (Peterson 1983: 183).

[23]The Kingfish's biographer, T. Harry Williams (1969), questions Long's connection to Costello. Costello informed a federal grand jury that Senator Long had invited him into New Orleans to set up a thousand slot machines for a fee of $30 per machine. However, Williams argues that such a setup would require police protection in a city that in 1935 was controlled by Semmes Walmsley, a bitter enemy of the Kingfish.

not recognize his assailant, the easily recogniz-able Vincenzo ("Chin") Gigante, an ex-pugilist and Genovese gunman.[24] Several months later, in what is believed to have been a related inci-dent, Albert Anastasia, Costello's close ally and boss of the Mineo crime Family, was murdered. Costello retired, leaving Vito Genovese as boss of the Luciano Family (Katz 1973).

Vito Genovese

The man who allegedly ordered the bungled attempt on Costello's life was born near Naples in 1897. At age 15, he arrived in New York and lived with his family in the Little Italy section of downtown Manhattan. Beginning as a street thief, Genovese graduated to working as a collector for the Italian lottery and eventually became an asso-ciate of Lucky Luciano. When his first wife died of tuberculosis in 1931, Genovese announced his intention to marry Anna Petillo—but she was already married. Twelve days later, Mr. Petillo was strangled to death and Genovese married the widow Petillo. After 12 years of marriage, Anna Genovese sued him for support and denounced Vito in court as a racketeer with a huge income. The much-feared crime boss did nothing; report-edly Genovese was too much in love with her to have her killed (Gage 1972).

During the 1930s, Genovese was already a power in organized crime, making huge profits in narcotics. In 1934, however, he was involved in a bungled murder and forced to flee to Italy to avoid prosecution; he took $750,000 with him. In Italy he is reputed to have become a confidant of Benito Mussolini. In 1943, a stridently anti–Fascist Italian newspaper editor in New York was shot to death "gangland style." The contract for his murder has been linked to Genovese's friend-ship with Mussolini (Peterson 1983). Neverthe-less, during the American invasion, Genovese was able to gain the confidence of American mili-tary authorities, for whom he acted as an inter-preter. This position enabled him to become a

major black marketeer, until he was identified as an American fugitive and returned to the United States for trial. While awaiting trial, a key witness was poisoned while in protective custody and Genovese went free.

In 1959, Genovese, along with fourteen oth-ers, was convicted of conspiracy to violate narcotic laws. In 1969, while serving his 15-year sentence, Genovese died of a heart ailment. However, despite numerous changes in leadership, the group he headed is still referred to as the Genovese Fam-ily. Its operations extend into New Jersey, Con-necticut, parts of Massachusetts, and upstate New York.

MINEO/GAMBINO FAMILY

Al Mineo was a close ally of Joseph Masseria and also a victim of the Castellammarese war—he was murdered in 1930. After the death of Masseria, Frank Scalise, who had defected from the Mineo Family early in the war, was made boss of that Family. He became a close confidant of Maran-zano, and after Maranzano's death was replaced by Vincent Mangano. In 1951, after his brother Philip was murdered, Vincent Mangano disap-peared, presumably murdered at the direction of Family underboss Albert Anastasia, who then became Family boss.

Albert Anastasia

Albert Anastasia was born Umberto Anastasio in Tropea, Italy, in 1902. He entered the United States in 1919 and reportedly changed his name to save his family some embarrassment because of his 1921 arrest for murdering a fellow longshoreman (Freeman 1957). His brother, Anthony ("Tough Tony") Anastasio became the official ruler of the Brooklyn waterfront as head of Local 1814 of the International Longshoremen's Association (ILA). Albert became the unofficial ruler of these same docks. (A third brother, Salvatore, became a priest.) Albert was widely feared even among his associates and reportedly enjoyed the title "Executioner"

---

[24] In 1985, Gigante became boss of the crime Family; he died in prison in 2005.

(Berger 1957)—he issued the "contract hits" for Murder, Inc. (discussed earlier).

In 1923, Anastasia was sentenced to two years' imprisonment for possessing a firearm, although this did not prevent him from serving stateside in the U.S. Army during World War II. In 1955, he served a one-year sentence for income-tax evasion. In 1957, Anastasia, who lived in a home along the Palisades in Fort Lee, New Jersey, was in a chair at the Park Sheraton Hotel barbershop in midtown Manhattan.[25] Two men—reportedly Joey Gallo and Carmine Persico (discussed later)—walked in through the hotel lobby door. One walked up to Anastasia and fired a .38 into the back of his head while the second shooter fired a .32. Anastasia staggered out of the chair and crashed to the floor— the "Executioner" had been executed (Carlo 2008). Underboss Carlo Gambino, believed to have been in league with Vito Genovese, became boss of the crime Family.

Carlo Gambino

Born in Palermo in 1902, Gambino arrived in the United States (an illegal alien) in 1921 and never became a citizen. He resided in Brooklyn, assisted by numerous relatives who had arrived earlier. In turn, he helped his brothers when they arrived in the United States. His boyhood friend from Palermo, Gaetano Lucchese, was already in the United States and rising in the ranks of organized crime, first under Masseria and then, as a defector, under Maranzano. Gambino followed Lucchese into the Maranzano camp and after Maranzano's death moved into the ranks of the Mineo Family, eventually becoming a *caporegime* under Vincent Mangano. Gambino's son Thomas married Lucchese's daughter.

After Prohibition, Gambino continued in the bootlegging business and in 1939 received a 22-month sentence for conspiracy to defraud the United States of liquor taxes. Eight months later, the conviction was thrown out because evidence had been based on illegal wiretaps. World War II

made Gambino a millionaire; it also prevented him from being deported to Italy. Joseph Valachi testified before a Senate committee that Gambino "made over a million dollars from ration stamps during the war. The stamps came out of the O.P.A's [Office of Price Administration] offices. First Carlo's boys would steal them. Then, when the government started hiding them in banks, Carlo made contact and the O.P.A. men sold him the stamps" (Gage 1975: 26). "Wartime rationing of gasoline, meat, and groceries opened a nationwide black market that the American public patronized as eagerly as it had once bought bootleg booze" (Meskil 1973: 58).

When Anastasia became Family boss, he made Gambino the *sottocapo*. After Anastasia's murder in 1957, Carlo became boss. A strong family man, Gambino had one daughter and two sons who operated a trucking firm in the garment center. When Gambino became ill and his underboss, Aniello ("Neil") Dellacroce, was in prison for income-tax evasion, Gambino appointed his first cousin and brother-in-law, a powerful Brooklyn *caporegime*, ("Big") Paul Castellano, as acting boss (Maas 1997). When Gambino died of a heart attack in 1976, Castellano assumed control of the Family.

On December 16, 1985, Castellano and his underboss, Thomas Bilotti, were heading to a meeting at Spark's Steak House in midtown Manhattan:

> Three men in trench coats, tipped off to Castellano's expected arrival by a confidant-turned traitor named Frankie DeCicco, loitered in the urban shadows of the early Christmas-season dusk. Thomas Bilotti turned his boss's black Lincoln onto Forty-sixth Street, and parked it directly in front of a *No Parking* sign; the car had a Patrolmen's Benevolent Association sticker on the windshield. As the two victims emerged, the assassins approached them, producing semiautomatic weapons from under their coats and loosing a barrage of bullets at close range. Castellano and Bilotti were each shot six times in the head and

---

[25]In 1928, the Park Sheraton was known as the Park Central, the hotel where Arnold Rothstein was shot.

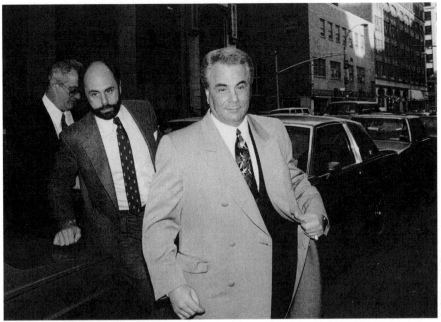

John Gotti, right, arrives at court on the morning of February 9, 1990. The jury continued to debate charges that Gotti ordered the assault on John F. Connor, former vice president of Carpenters Union Local 608. Attorney Gerald Schargel follows Gotti and his brother Peter Gotti, at left.

torso.... [O]ne of the killers then crouched over Castellano's body and delivered a *coup de grâce* through the skull. (O'Brien and Kurins 1991: 11)

At a meeting of Family captains called by the Family *consigliere*, John Gotti was "elected" boss (Gotti trial tapes).

John Gotti

Gotti was a career criminal whose media coverage eclipsed that of all previous crime figures. As with Al Capone, also a man of Neapolitan heritage, notoriety aided his downfall. Gotti was born in the South Bronx in 1940 and raised in the East New York–Brownsville section of Brooklyn, of Murder, Inc., fame, where he was a member of a neighborhood gang. Dropping out of high school at 16, Gotti began working for a soldier in the Gambino Family. Later he became part of the East New York crew headed by Carmine ("Charley Wagons") Fatico, a hijacker and Gambino *caporegime*.

Gotti, a strong-arm ex-convict (for a hijacking conviction), moved to Queens when Fatico set up headquarters at the Bergin Hunt and Fish Social Club, two storefronts in Ozone Park, a quiet working-class neighborhood. In 1973, in a poorly executed murder, Gotti and his close friend Angelo Ruggiero gunned down one of the kidnap-murderers (the head of an Irish gang from Hell's Kitchen) of Carlo Gambino's nephew. In a plea bargain, Gotti and Ruggiero received sentences with four-year maximums. Shortly after his release from prison in 1977, Gotti was inducted into the Gambino Family and became a confidant of underboss Dellacroce. When Fatico came under intense federal investigation and became inactive, Gotti, despite his lackluster performance as an "earner"— his wife once sued him for nonsupport—was placed in charge of the Fatico crew by Dellacroce.

When Carlo Gambino died in 1976, succession should have gone to Dellacroce. Instead, Dellacroce and Castellano met at a private home in Brooklyn and a deal was struck: Castellano would become boss and, to appease the Dellacroce faction, he would keep Dellacroce as underboss, just as Gambino had appointed Dellacroce underboss to placate Anastasia stalwarts. The loyal Dellacroce opposed any efforts to move against Castellano.

But the Family now had two factions, one headed by Castellano, the other by Dellacroce. The more sophisticated Castellano faction was immersed in labor and business racketeering, while the "thug 'n drug" Dellacroce group engaged in hijacking, extortion, loansharking, gambling, and, in violation of a Castellano edict, drugs. (In 1989, Gotti's brother Gene, then 42, was convicted of drug violations and sentenced to 50 years' imprisonment.) In fact, before he became Family boss, drugs were the primary source of Gotti's income. When Angelo Ruggiero was indicted for drug trafficking, Gotti feared that he and Ruggiero would be killed by Castellano—Castellano had copies of government surveillance tapes proving the crew's involvement in drugs. Soon afterward, in 1985, Gotti's mentor, Dellacroce, died of cancer at age 71. Castellano, awaiting trial, failed to attend the funeral and replaced Dellacroce with a loyal aide who lacked real stature—Thomas Bilotti, a vicious 45-year-old enforcer. Two weeks later, both were dead.

In 1990, Gotti was indicted for racketeering and murder. He had previously been acquitted at three separate trials in five years, earning him the sobriquet "the Teflon Don." Dexterity at avoiding conviction appears to have been aided by a several factors: competition between Justice Department officials (Dannen 1992a), a detective on the New York City Police Department's Intelligence Unit (Lubasch 1992d) who in 1993 pled guilty to selling secrets, and jury tampering—one juror was convicted of selling his vote. In 1992, Gotti was found guilty of forty-three federal charges, including six murders, one being that of Paul Castellano. Gotti was betrayed by his handpicked *consigliere* and (later) underboss Salvatore ("Sammy the Bull") Gravano and by his own careless (and intercepted) communications. Gravano's testimony also led to the conviction of thirty-six other organized crime figures. Gotti died in prison in 2002.

In 2008, eighty-seven members and associates of the Gambino Family were indicted by a federal grand jury for more than three decades of crime, including the murder of a New York State court officer who, while off-duty in 1975, had arrested a Gambino soldier for carrying a handgun. Those indicted included the acting boss, acting underboss who headed the Family's Sicilian faction, and the Family *consigliere*.

Despite the changes in leadership, the crime group is still referred to as the Gambino Family. Its operations extend into upstate New York, New Jersey, and parts of New England.

REINA/LUCCHESE FAMILY

Gaetano ("Tommy") Reina headed one of the five Families in New York City that "formed spontaneously as Sicilian immigrants settled there" (Bonanno and Lalli 1983: 84). Bonanno reports that because of the power of "Joe the Boss" Masseria, Reina had to be careful not to offend him "and generally toed the Masseria line" (1983: 85). At the start of the Castellammarese war, however, Reina began talking (privately) against Masseria, and it was reported to the boss—in 1930, Reina was killed by a blast from a sawed-off shotgun. According to Bonanno, Masseria backed one of his own supporters to head the Reina Family. However, Gaetano Gagliano formed a splinter group and was joined by Thomas Lucchese, who became the underboss of the newly formed Gagliano Family. Gagliano emerged on the side of the victorious Salvatore Maranzano. Gagliano's leadership of the crime Family lasted until his death in 1953, at which time Lucchese became boss.

Lucchese was born in Palermo, in 1900, and came to the United States in 1911. In 1919, he lost his right index finger in a machine-shop accident. A gang member, Lucchese's nickname, "Three-Finger Brown," was the result of a 1921 arrest for car theft—the policeman who fingerprinted Lucchese was a fan of Mordechai ("Three-Finger") Brown, a pitcher for the Chicago Cubs. He wrote that name down under the alias section of the fingerprint card. Despite the 1921 conviction, for which he served 13 months in prison, in 1943, Lucchese became a naturalized citizen (Reid and Demaris 1953; Volkman 1998).

Lucchese was active in gambling, particularly numbers and bookmaking, in Queens, New York. During the 1930s he dominated the kosher chicken industry in New York City, organizing a cartel that controlled prices and competition (Volkman 1998). "Police officials listed eight dress firms in New York City in which Lucchese was a part owner and he had similar holdings in Scranton, Pennsylvania." His firms in New York City were nonunion and "strangely free from labor troubles" (Peterson 1983: 403). Lucchese lived in a luxurious yellow-brick ranch house that he constructed in Lido Beach, Long Island. His son Robert is a graduate of the U.S. Air Force Academy and became an Air Force officer. His daughter Frances went to Vassar College and later married the son of Carlo Gambino. Lucchese died of natural causes in 1967, and leadership passed to 53-year-old Anthony ("Tony Ducks") Corallo.

"Tony Ducks" Corallo

Corallo controlled the private waste hauling industry on Long Island and had a stranglehold on much of the city's construction business through his control over the pouring of concrete. He received the nickname "Ducks" because of his ability to escape ("duck") assassinations and convictions. In 1968 this "ability" failed: He was sentenced to three years for trying to bribe both a New York State judge and a chief assistant U.S. attorney. The case he was trying to fix involved the head of Tammany Hall.

After his release from prison, the cautious Corallo ran operations from his Jaguar to avoid electronic surveillance, but to no avail—in 1983, the New York State Organized Crime Task Force planted a bug in the car. The "Jaguar Tapes" were a central piece of evidence in the "Commission Case" that led to the 1986 conviction of Corallo, Carmine Persico, boss of the Colombo Family, and Anthony Salerno, boss of the Genovese Family. Defendant Paul Castellano was murdered before the trial ended. In 2000, at 87, Corallo died while serving a life sentence in federal prison.

In recent years, the Lucchese Family has been plagued by betrayal, rebellion, and prosecution. Despite changes in leadership, this crime Family is still referred to as the Lucchese Family.

PROFACI/COLOMBO FAMILY

Joseph Profaci was born in Palermo in 1897. An ex-convict, he came to the United States in 1922, when Mussolini was chasing *mafiosi*. In the United States, Profaci never served a prison sentence, a remarkable feat for the man who had a crime Family named after him. He did, however, manage to owe the United States $1.5 million in income taxes. And he became the only mob boss to be arrested at organized crime conclaves both in Cleveland in 1928 and Apalachin, New York, in 1957 (discussed later).

Profaci owned at least twenty legitimate businesses, and as the "Olive Oil King," he was the largest single importer of Italian olive oil into the United States. In addition to his modest Brooklyn home, he owned a luxurious home in Miami Beach and a hunting lodge ("Profaci Dies of Cancer, Led Feuding Brooklyn Mob" 1962). His daughter Rosalie married Joseph Bonanno's son Salvatore ("Bill"), and another daughter is married to Jack Tocco, Detroit crime Family boss. His son Salvatore is a *caporegime* in the Colombo crime Family.

Although clean-shaven, Profaci was clearly a "moustache," faithful to Old World traditions. He was a devoted family man, devoid of any apparent extramarital interests. His profession notwithstanding, Profaci was a faithful churchgoer, a friend of the priest, and a large contributor to church charities. One of the churches in the Bensonhurst–Bath Beach section of Brooklyn, where he lived, had a statue adorned with a crown of jewels worth several thousand dollars. Some reports indicate that Profaci contributed the crown. In any event, a local thief decided to steal the crown—an outrage that Profaci ordered "corrected." Although the crown was returned, the culprit failed to restore three missing diamonds. His body was subsequently found, and lest the reason for his murder be misinterpreted, a set of rosary beads was wrapped around his neck (Martin 1963).

The Gallo Brothers

Profaci's traditionalism was viewed as despotic by some members of his crime Family. He apparently demanded a large percentage of all their illegal profits and placed "blood" and friendship above business: Relatives and old friends received larger shares of Family opportunities than did others in his ranks. In 1959, a numbers operator was murdered on orders from Profaci. The contract was carried out by Joseph ("Joe Jelly") Gioiello, a short, rotund, vicious killer, part of a Profaci crew headed by the Gallo brothers in Red Hook, Brooklyn. The Gallo brothers—Larry, Albert ("Kid Blast"), and ("Crazy") Joey—expected to receive a large share of the deceased victim's gambling operations. Instead, Profaci divided it up among friends and relatives. The Gallo crew fumed until February 1961. Then, in one 24-hour period, they abducted four of Profaci's closest associates, but the boss himself eluded capture. What transpired afterward would rival the Roman plots in the days of the Caesars.

Profaci agreed to be more generous with the Gallo crew. However, several Gallo men secretly went over to the Profaci side, and on August 20, 1961, they lured Larry Gallo to a lounge in Brooklyn. Early in the morning, before the lounge opened for business, Carmine ("Junior" or "the Snake") Persico[26] and Hughie ("Apples") McIntosh[27] placed a rope around Larry's neck and slowly began to squeeze the life out of him. A police sergeant came into the lounge only minutes before the victim would have expired—Gallo had already lost control of his bowels and bladder. The officer noticed Larry's feet sticking out from behind the bar, and he saw two men dash from the darkened room out a side door. His driver, a patrolman waiting outside, attempted to stop the two men and was shot in the face, suffering a wound in the right cheek. Larry survived the ordeal, his neck badly scarred.

Later that day "Joe Jelly" was "put to sleep with the fishes"—his coat was dumped in front of the Gallo's South Brooklyn headquarters wrapped around several fresh fish. The "war" was on, but it was a rather one-sided affair. At least twelve men were killed, mostly Gallo loyalists. The Gallo group "took to the mattresses"—they sought refuge in their Red Hook headquarters at 49–51 President Street, a block away from the Union Street 76th Police Precinct House. A special squad of New York City detectives headed by Raymond V. Martin (whose book on the subject was published in 1963) was assigned to maintain surveillance of the area. The police probably saved the Gallo crew from being completely wiped out by Profaci gunmen. During this period, the Gallos were responsible for saving several neighborhood youngsters from a building fire; they joked to television reporters that the police would probably arrest them for arson. In any event, the Gallo boys became neighborhood heroes, and the news media reported extensively on their exploits.

Gang wars are expensive. It is difficult to earn money if one is in hiding or spending most of his time seeking out the enemy while avoiding being killed.[28] The financial condition of the Gallos grew worse. In 1961, in an effort to replenish his dwindling income, Joey Gallo attempted to extort money from the owner of several bars. The victim refused to pay, so "Crazy Joey" performed his best "Richard Widmark," explaining to the businessman that he could meet with an "unfortunate accident." It was no accident that two detectives were in the bar, and Gallo received a lengthy prison sentence. In 1968 Larry Gallo died of cancer.

Joseph Colombo

In 1962, Profaci died of natural causes, and his place was taken by his brother-in-law, Joseph Magliocco. Magliocco died of natural causes at the end of 1963, and his place was taken by Joseph Colombo, Sr. In 1964, a truce was finally arranged

---

[26]In 1972, Persico became boss of the Colombo Family.

[27]In 1997, McIntosh, a longtime associate of Carmine Persico and a feared enforcer who wore a size 52 suit, died at age 70 while serving a sentence in federal prison.

[28]For an interesting discussion of the preparations that are necessary for a gang war, see Bill Bonanno's (1999) discussion of his own experience during the "Banana War" (discussed later).

with the Gallo faction. One condition of the truce was that several top Gallo men were "made," inducted as members of the Colombo Family (Salerno and Tompkins 1969). The Gallo crew was subsequently moved into the Genovese Family (Capeci 1999b).

While in prison, Crazy Joey continued to "raise hell." He so annoyed some of his fellow inmates in Attica that several of them threw him off a tier. Transferred to another prison, Joey befriended many black inmates, several of whom he recruited for his Brooklyn organization. In 1971, Gallo was released from prison, and the intrigue reached new heights.

There appears to be general agreement on how Joseph Colombo was chosen to succeed Magliocco as boss of the Profaci Family. A plot was afoot to kill two crime Family chieftains—Carlo Gambino and Thomas Lucchese—and Colombo informed Gambino of the plot. Some accounts say that the person who was supposed to affect the murders was Colombo, acting on behalf of Joseph Bonanno. One source (Salerno and Tompkins 1969) reports that Bonanno and Magliocco, underboss of the Profaci Family, were behind the plot. Another (Talese 1971) places responsibility on Magliocco. Joseph Bonanno (with Lalli 1983) and his son Bill Bonanno[29] (1999) deny any involvement. Instead they blame their jealous cousin, Buffalo crime boss Stefano Magaddino, for "disseminating the story that Joe Bonanno wanted to kill Gambino and Lucchese" (1983: 235). In any event, Magliocco died, and Joseph Colombo was chosen by the "commission" to head the Profaci Family (Bonanno and Lalli 1983).

In 1970, Colombo founded the Italian-American Civil Rights League and led in the daily picketing of the New York FBI headquarters, generating a great deal of media coverage. The league soon became a vehicle for protesting discrimination against and negative stereotyping of Italian Americans. Colombo and the league succeeded in having all references to the Mafia or *Cosa Nostra* deleted from the scripts of *The Godfather* and the television series *The FBI*. United States Attorney General John Mitchell and New York's Governor Nelson Rockefeller ordered their employees to refrain from using such references.

The league raised large sums of money through dues and testimonial dinners and held an "Annual Unity Day" rally, which in 1970 drew about 50,000 persons to Columbus Circle in Manhattan. Nicholas Gage (1972: 172) notes that the "rally conspicuously closed stores in neighborhoods controlled by the Mafia: New York's waterfront was virtually shut down . . . and almost every politician in the city joined" the 1970 celebration. There were articles in newspapers and magazines about Colombo and the league, and the boss began to portray himself as a civil rights leader who was simply misunderstood by the police.

Reports state that other crime Family bosses, particularly Carlo Gambino, did not look favorably on the activities of Colombo and the league, either because Colombo failed to share the financial fruits or because they resented the publicity—or both. At the second Annual Unity Day rally in 1971, only an estimated 10,000 persons attended. While reporters and news photographers crowded around the podium, a lone black man wearing a camera and apparently presenting himself as a newsman approached Colombo, pulled out a gun, and shot him in the head and neck. The gunman, 24-year-old Jerome Johnson, was immediately shot to death: "Johnson's killer escaped as professionally as he had carried out his mission, shooting Johnson 3 times even as police clustered around" (Gage 1972: 171). Colombo remained paralyzed until his death in 1978.

Interest focused on Johnson. He was never connected to organized crime, although he had a criminal record and was known as a violent person. Suspicion immediately centered on Joey Gallo, who had reason to dislike the Family boss and was known to have black criminals as associates. The day after Colombo was shot, the *New York Times* (Gage 1971b: 21) stated: "When Joseph Gallo was released in May from prison he was reported to have complained that the lot of his faction within the family had not improved much in his absence. He was also said to have questioned Colombo's involvement in the Italian-American Civil Rights League as drawing undue attention to the family."

---

[29]In 2008, Bill Bonanno, 75, died of natural causes at his home in Tucson, Arizona.

Nepotism, Mafia Style

Carmine Persico, who is in prison serving combined sentences of 100 years, attempted to engineer a shift in leadership to his son Alphonse ("Allie Boy"), who was expected to be released from prison shortly. In the meantime, Persico chose Victor J. Orena to be acting boss. Before Alphonse was released from prison, Orena let it be known that he would not step aside for the much younger Persico—taking orders from junior after being boss was apparently too much for Orena to accept.

Beginning in 1991, the two factions began shooting at each other's partisans. Persico loyalist Gregory Scarpa would drive past opponents' houses and "one night he surprised a rebel who stood on a ladder, with his back turned, hanging Christmas lights on his house. Scarpa rolled down his car window, stuck out his rifle, and picked the man off with three shots" (Dannen 1996: 68). In 1992, in Queens, New York, four men wearing masks jumped from a stolen van and opened fire at a car with shotguns and semiautomatic weapons. They killed the driver and wounded his two passengers. The victims were carpenter union officials associated with the Orena faction. Later that year, the then 58-year-old Orena was convicted in Brooklyn federal court of RICO violations and murder. He received a life sentence. Nine days later, Scarpa[31] was ambushed near his Brooklyn home, receiving wounds in the face and left eye. Two associates were also wounded in the attack (Raab 1992c). The violence ended in 1993, both sides recognizing the futility and danger inherent in continuing the war. The imprisoned Persico picked his cousin, Andrew T. Russo (born in 1934), to be acting boss (Raab 1995g), and the Colombo Family resumed initiating new members to replace those killed or imprisoned—twelve dead and more than fifty convicted of crimes related to the struggle. In 1998, Russo was convicted of federal charges and Allie Boy, at 45, once again emerged as acting boss of the Colombo Family. In 2002, he pleaded guilty to racketeering, loan-sharking, and money laundering, and in 2008, at age 53, he was convicted of murder.

With Colombo out of the way and acting boss Carmine Persico in prison, Gallo men began moving in on Colombo activities and completely took over the South Brooklyn waterfront (Goddard 1974). On April 7, 1972, Joey Gallo was celebrating his birthday with a late-night stop at Umberto's Clam House in Lower Manhattan, owned by a member of the Genovese Family and frequented by members of the Genovese and Colombo Families. With Joey's party were his new bride, her daughter, and his bodyguard. Three Colombo gunmen, who had apparently been quickly mobilized for the occasion, entered the restaurant and opened fire, killing Joey and wounding his bodyguard, who sought to return the fire (Diapoulos and Linakis 1976; Goddard 1974).

Despite the death of Joseph Colombo, the group he headed is still referred to as the Colombo Family.[30]

BONANNO FAMILY

We know more about Joseph ("Don Peppino") Bonanno than about most other crime figures because he was the subject of a biography by Gay Talese (1971), authored his own autobiography (with Segio Lalli 1983), and his son Bill published an autobiography in 1999. Bonanno states that his father, Salvatore ("Don Turridu"), was head of the Bonanno clan in Castellammare del Golfo and a "man of honor" (*mafioso*). Salvatore left Sicily for the United States with his wife and three-year-old son, Giuseppe, in 1908 to avoid prosecution (Bonanno does not say for what crime). In 1911, at the request of his brothers in Castellammare, Don Turridu returned home

---

[30]In 2007, Joseph Colombo's son Anthony pled guilty to extortion from a Manhattan construction firm and was sentenced to 18 months in federal prison.

[31]Scarpa, who was suffering from AIDS, the result of a blood transfusion in the wake of hernia surgery, pleaded guilty to murder and racketeering charges in 1993. He died in a prison hospital the following year. His bizarre role as an FBI informant is discussed in Chapter 15. Scarpa's son "Jr." is a made guy.

Apalachin Crime Conference

In November 1957, a New York state police sergeant became suspicious of the activities at the home of Joseph M. Barbara, Sr., boss of the Northeastern Pennsylvania crime Family. Barbara was from Castellammare del Golfo and had become the wealthy owner of a soda pop distributing business and a bottling plant outside Endicott, New York. His estate in Apalachin was about six miles away. While investigating a bad check case at a hotel in the area, the sergeant discovered Barbara's son making room reservations. He later noted a number of expensive automobiles with out-of-state license plates parked at the Barbara estate. There was nothing the officer "could legally do about Barbara's visitors, but by Saturday, November 14, 1957, with what he figured to be as many as seventy guests assembled," he could no longer stifle his curiosity. "He organized what few deputies he had and conducted a raid on Barbara's house, one merely, as he explained later, 'to see if anything criminal was going on or if Barbara's guests were wanted on any outstanding warrants'" (Brashler 1977: 144). "Within minutes dozens of well-dressed men ran out of the house and across the fields in all directions" (Salerno and Tompkins 1969: 298). Using roadblocks and reinforcements, the police reportedly took sixty-three men into custody, although this figure is disputed. Joseph Bonanno was reported to have been at the meeting, and his driver's license was confiscated. However, he claims to have been elsewhere, attending a private meeting in a nearby motel.

The men were summoned to the sergeant's office where they "gave their names and addresses, took off their shoes, emptied their pockets as troopers searched and watched" (Sondern 1959: 36). Those arrested included Joseph Profaci, Carlo Gambino, Paul Castellano, Vito Genovese, the Philadelphia crime boss and his underboss, and Russell Bufalino.[32]

In 1959, Bonanno and twenty-six other leading organized crime figures, after refusing to answer questions as to the purpose of the meeting in Apalachin, were indicted for conspiracy and obstruction of justice. Bonanno's case was separated from the others when he suffered a heart attack. After a three-week trial, a jury found twenty defendants guilty of conspiracy. The verdict, however, was overturned in 1960 by the U.S. Court of Appeals; the court concluded that the people at the Barbara estate had been taken into custody, detained, and searched without probable cause that a crime had or was being committed: "[I]n America we still respect the dignity of the individual, and even an unsavory character is not to be imprisoned except on definite proof of specific crime" (*United States v. Bufalino et al.*, 285 F.2d 408, 1960).

with his wife and child. He died there in 1915 of a heart attack.

Joseph Bonanno states that he was attending the nautical preparatory school when Mussolini came to power. He claims that his anti-Fascist activities forced him to leave, and he entered the United States in 1924. Bonanno quickly found help and refuge among friends and family from Castellammare. His cousin Stefano Magaddino was already a criminal power in Buffalo, New York, and Bonanno eventually became involved in bootlegging with the Castellammare clan in Brooklyn under Salvatore Maranzano. During the Masseria-Maranzano conflict, Bonanno became an aide to Maranzano and was seen as a leader of the Castellammare group arrayed against Joe the Boss. After Maranzano's murder, a meeting of Family members was held, and Bonanno was elected "Father" (a term he uses for "boss") of what became known as the Bonanno Family. Bonanno successfully parlayed income received as boss of his own Family into legitimate enterprises such as garment and cheese manufacturing.

[32]Russell Bufalino, who was born in Sicily in 1903, became Joseph Barbara's underboss. When Barbara died in 1959, Bufalino became boss of the Northeastern Pennsylvania Family.

In 1959, a federal grand jury indicted him for conspiracy to obstruct justice in the aftermath of the (in)famous meeting of crime bosses in Apalachin, New York, in 1957. In that year, events such as the attempt on the life of Frank Costello and the murder of Albert Anastasia sparked a top-level conference at Apalachin, New York.

In 1963 came the alleged plot against Gambino and Lucchese, and Bonanno sought, and was denied, Canadian citizenship. In February 1964, while Bonanno was still in Canada, at a meeting of crime Family captains his son Bill was chosen *consigliere*. The elevation of the young Bonanno was opposed from within and without the Bonanno Family. This act, coupled with the plot against Gambino and Lucchese, resulted in a "summons" for Joseph Bonanno to appear before the commission, of which he was one of the nine members; Bonanno declined. On October 21, 1964, Bonanno and his attorney were standing in front of a luxury apartment house in Manhattan, where they had sought shelter from the rain. Bonanno describes what followed (with Lalli 1983: 260): "Two men grabbed me from behind by each arm and immediately forced me toward the nearby street corner. . . . "Come on, Joe, my boss wants you. . . . As they rushed toward the corner, I heard Maloney [Bonanno's attorney] shouting after us. He was saying something about my being his client and they couldn't take me away like that. A pistol shot pinged the sidewalk. Maloney retreated."

Bonanno reports that he was kidnapped by two of his cousins, the son and brother of Stefano Magaddino, and held in a rural farmhouse for more than six weeks. Federal officials called it a hoax, an effort by Bonanno to avoid appearing before a grand jury investigating organized crime. Bonanno states that following his release, he remained in hiding in his Tucson home for more than a year. In the meantime, a revolt broke out within the Bonanno Family led by *caporegime* Gasper DiGregorio, Bill Bonanno's godfather and best man at the wedding of Fay and Joseph Bonanno.

On January 28, 1966, in an effort to reestablish unity, Bill Bonanno and several Family members loyal to his father went to Troutman Street in Brooklyn to meet with DiGregorio. The unity meeting turned out to be an ambush, and the young Bonanno narrowly escaped in an exchange of gunfire. On May 18, 1966, Joseph Bonanno reappeared and the revolt (dubbed the "Banana war") raged on. DiGregorio eventually withdrew, and the commission turned the Family over to an acting boss. Joseph Bonanno retired to his Tucson home, leaving a three-man committee to fill the leadership until the "loyalists" could select a new boss.

In 1979, a federal grand jury indicted Bonanno and a commodities dealer for obstructing justice. During the 14-week nonjury trial in 1980, the prosecutor maintained that Bonanno and his codefendant worked together to keep the records of several businesses from the grand jury. The FBI collected evidence by tapping Bonanno's telephone and retrieving his garbage for four years. The defense objected to the introduction of notes in Sicilian fished out of Bonanno's garbage, contending that their translation into English was in doubt because there are no English equivalents to many of the terms used. Nevertheless, Bonanno was found guilty and sentenced to a term of one year. He entered the federal prison at Terminal Island at the end of 1983.

Despite Bonanno's retirement, the crime Family he headed is still referred to as the Bonanno Family, something Bonanno decried: "It is improper for people to still refer to this Family as the Bonanno Family. It stopped being the Bonanno Family when I retired. In Sicily, a Family is sometimes likened to a *cosca*—an artichoke. The Family members are like the artichoke leaves and the Father is like the central stem on which they all hang. Remove the central stem and all you have is a lot of separate leaves. When I left New York to retire, all the separate leaves had to find themselves another stem" (Bonanno and Lalli 1983: 292). On May 12, 2002, Bonanno died at age 97.

The Bonanno Family is the only one of the five New York Mafia groups to have a crew operating in Montreal, Canada, where it has ties to the Hell's Angels (Lamothe and Humphries 2006). In the twenty-first century, the Family has been weakened by more than a dozen members who have become informants including Joseph Massino, the only boss of the five Families to become a government witness (DeStefano 2006).

THE FIVE FAMILIES

The New York Families have been subjected to successful prosecution aided by a breakdown in discipline and loyalty. There have been dozens of made-guy turncoats, many ranking members. By 2004, the heads of all five Families were incarcerated.

Their weakened condition may be encouraging challenges from other crime groups. While Albanian criminal groups have operated for decades without serious conflict with the American Mafia, that may be changing. In Astoria, Queens, for example, an Albanian group, the Rudaj Organization or "The Corporation," operating out of a small Albanian café on Morris Avenue in the Bronx, successfully challenged Greek associates of several crime Families for control of the neighborhood's gambling operations. Alex ("Allie Boy") Rudaj had worked for years as an enforcer for Bronx-based Gambino Family soldier ("Skinny") Phil Loscalzo. After Loscalzo's death, Rudaj recruited several dozen mostly Greek and Albanian associates for "The Corporation." They committed numerous crimes in the Bronx, Westchester County, and Astoria, Queens, including racketeering offenses, murder conspiracy, extortion, and loansharking; they also operated a network of illegal gambling parlors and a bookmaking operation. Feared for their level of violence, they are reported to have successfully and violently thwarted a challenge by the Gambino Family. One member of the group was overheard being lauded for "his courage" in strangling an old man with a shoelace until his eyes were popping out of his head. In 2004, Rudaj, at age 37, and twenty-six members of The Corporation were indicted. In 2006, Rudaj and six others were convicted of racketeering, and Rudaj was sentenced to 27 years in federal prison (Fahim 2006; Hartocollis 2005; G. Smith 2004a, 2004b; Zambito 2005a). The Albanian connection to crime groups in Southern Italy is discussed in Chapter 6.

SUMMARY

- During the last decade of the nineteenth and the first two decades of the twentieth centuries, millions of Italians from poverty-wracked southern Italy arrived in America's urban areas.
- Limited education and widespread prejudice consigned these Italians to "Little Italys" where they reproduced Italian village life that included secret organizations of Mafia, Camorra, and 'Ndranghetta.
- Organized along patron-client lines, Prohibition offered these criminal groups, at times in partnership with Jewish and Irish criminals, unparalleled opportunity as they moved beyond their ghettoes and into the world of organized crime.
- During the early 1930s, conflict between the two major Mafia factions in New York—the Castellamarase war—led to the emergence of the "Five Families" that, in a much weakened form, continue to operate in the New York metropolitan area.

REVIEW QUESTIONS

1. What was the relationship between Tammany Hall and the development of organized crime?
2. Why was Arnold Rothstein so important for the development of organized crime?
3. What were the roles of Meyer Lansky and Bugsy Siegel in organized crime?
4. What led to the murder of Dutch Schultz?
5. How did Lepke Buchalter differ from most Prohibition gang leaders?

6. How did organized crime in New York change after the repeal of Prohibition?
7. How does Murder, Inc., provide an example of interethnic cooperation in organized crime?
8. What are the responsibilities assigned to each of the ranks of an American Mafia Family?
9. Why is the concept of "membership" important in the American Mafia?
10. What are the advantages and disadvantages of membership?
11. What are the basic qualifications for *Cosa Nostra* membership?
12. What is a "crew?"
13. How did his broker role allow Lucky Luciano to become so important in organized crime?
14. What was the *Unione Siciliana* and what was its role in organized crime?
15. What was the Castellammarese war?

CHAPTER

5

Organized Crime in Chicago[1]

Organized crime (OC) in the Windy City—a nickname that refers to its politicians, not its weather—differs from that in New York City by degree. The connection between politics and the dominant criminal organization has been extraordinary both for its intensity and longevity. Chicago has also been remarkable for the extent to which persons of various ethnicity have been integrated into the dominant criminal organization, now known as "The Outfit."

When Chicago was incorporated as a town in 1833, it was little more than an Indian trading post. Immigration, usually by steamship, increased with the breaking of ground for the Lake Michigan–Illinois River Canal in 1836. By 1855, Chicago was the terminus of ten railroad trunk lines and eleven branch lines and was the country's greatest meat-packing center and grain port (Asbury 1942). The boom naturally attracted adventurers, gamblers, pimps, prostitutes, and other undesirables.

The Civil War brought further prosperity to Chicago, but it also brought thousands of soldiers and the gambling establishments and brothels that were patronized by large numbers of unattached young men on military leave. At this time, Chicago became known as "the wickedest city in the United States" (Asbury 1942: 6). But not until Mike McDonald became established could vice in Chicago be said to be truly *organized*.

MIKE MCDONALD

The origins of organized crime in Chicago can be traced to the mayoralty election of 1873, in which Mike McDonald backed the victorious candidate for mayor (Nelli 1969). "McDonald, the gambling boss of Chicago, demonstrated that under effective leadership the gamblers, liquor interests, and brothel keepers could be welded into a formidable political power" (Peterson 1963: 31). The election pitted reformers who insisted on the enforcement of Sunday closing "blue laws" against a party, organized by McDonald, whose ranks were swelled by Irish and German immigrants (Flinn 1973). Until McDonald, gambling had been rather unorganized

---

[1]Unless otherwise cited, information on the Chicago Outfit is from court documents in *United States v. Carlisi*, 92 Cr. 1064 (1990); *United States v. Damico et al.*, 94 Cr. 723 (1994); *United States v. Infelise et al.*, 90 Cr. 87 (1990); *United States v. LaMantia*, 93 Cr. 523 (1996); *United States v. Rainone et al.*, 91 Cr. 727 (1992); *United States v. Calabrese et al.*, 2 Cr. 1050 (2006).

in Chicago, and so were politics. When his candidate won the election, "McDonald had Chicago in his back pocket" (Sawyers 1988: 10). From then until his death in 1907, McDonald controlled mayors, congressmen, and senators. His newspaper, the *Globe*, often influenced the outcome of elections, and he also owned the elevated railroad line in Chicago (Wendt and Kogan 1974). Any gambler who wanted to operate outside of the red-light districts had to see Mike to arrange to pay over a large proportion of his income for division among the police, various city officials, and the members of McDonald's syndicate. As a close friend and chief advisor of mayors, and as a leader of the Cook County Democratic organization, McDonald was the boss of Chicago (Asbury 1942).

Reform hit Chicago in 1893 at a time when a rich and powerful McDonald had lost interest in maintaining his vast political-gambling empire. His political mantle was picked up by Michael ("Hinky Dink") Kenna and John ("Bathhouse") Coughlin; gambling went to Mont Tennes (Asbury 1942; Sawyers 1988).

"HINKY DINK" AND "THE BATH"

McDonald's saloon-headquarters was located in the Levee District of Chicago's notorious First Ward. With his backing, a "Mutt and Jeff" team became the political "Lords of the Levee": John ("Bathhouse") Coughlin, a powerfully built six-footer, and Michael ("Hinky Dink") Kenna, a diminutive organizational genius. Born in the First Ward to Irish immigrant parents in 1860, Coughlin began his political career as a rubber in the exclusive Palmer Baths, where he met wealthy and powerful politicians and businessmen. These contacts helped him when he opened his own bathhouse and soon other bathhouses. Among his customers were important politicians, and the Bath (a nickname he enjoyed) became a Democratic precinct captain and president of the First Ward Democratic Club.

In 1892, Coughlin was elected alderman from the First Ward, one of thirty-five city wards. The First Ward, in addition to the Levee, contained the city's central business district, "the Loop" (so-called because of the elevated train line circling the area). The city council that Coughlin joined was literally selling out the city of Chicago. The "boodles," schemes through which city privileges were sold, made the $3-a-meeting alderman's position quite lucrative.

Kenna was born in the First Ward in 1858 and became a successful saloonkeeper (despite being a teetotaler) and, of course, a politician. He worked hard in First Ward Democratic politics as a saloon-based precinct captain and eventually became friendly with the Bath. With Kenna as the mastermind, the two men organized the vice entrepreneurs of the First Ward, established a legal fund, and forged an alliance with the mayor. Eventually they "found themselves in possession of a thriving little syndicate" (Wendt and Kogan 1974: 81).

After the mayor was murdered by a disgruntled job seeker, the Bath and Hinky Dink provided his successor with the margin of victory. When a depression swept the country in the winter of 1893, Kenna provided care for 8,000 homeless and destitute men, who did not forget this kindness. They registered in the First Ward and were brought back for each election. Coughlin and Kenna were also assisted by the police of the ward and the Quincy Street Boys, who included some of the toughest and most feared hoodlums of the First Ward. Actually, notes John Landesco, in 1929, the use of street gangs in politics became widespread in Chicago (1968: 184–85): "The young of the immigrant group, beginning with the child at play in the street, were assimilated uncritically into all of the traditions of the neighborhoods in which they lived. Street gangs were their heritage, conflict between races and nationalities often made them necessary—conflict and assimilation went on together. The politician paid close attention to them, nurturing them with favors and using them for his own purposes. Gang history always emphasizes this political nurture. Gangs often became political clubs."

The ability of Coughlin and Kenna to deliver the vote was key to their power. Majorities in the

First Ward were so overwhelming that they could affect city, county, and even state elections. And as their power grew, it became necessary to be "licensed" by Kenna and Coughlin to do business in the First Ward. In 1897, they skillfully engineered the Democratic nomination for Carter Henry Harrison, son of the murdered mayor. In the First Ward they delivered a vote of five to one, and Kenna was elected to the city council. However, Harrison eventually allied himself with reformers and moved against the Levee, which cost him the vital support of the First Ward and led to the 1915 election of Republican William Hale ("Big Bill") Thompson.

"BIG BILL" THOMPSON

Thompson's victory in 1915 was based on his demagogic appeals. In German and Irish neighborhoods he attacked the British; in German-hating Polish neighborhoods he attacked the Germans; and when addressing Protestant audiences he warned that a vote for his Catholic opponent was a vote for the pope. He promised the reformers strict enforcement of the gambling laws, and he promised the gamblers an open town. Thompson received strong support in the black wards, and many Harrison Democrats deserted the party to support the Republican.

"During the last few months of Mayor Harrison's final term Chicago was probably as free from organized vice as at any time in its history" (Asbury 1942: 309). With the election of Thompson, "the spoils system swept over the city like a noxious blight, and city hall became a symbol for corruption and incompetence" (Merriam 1929: 22). "Within six months he had violated every campaign promise but one. He did keep Chicago wide open" (Kobler 1971: 57). Despite these excesses, Big Bill was reelected in 1919. In 1923, with Prohibition in full swing, and despite the support of Al Capone, Thompson was defeated by reformers. In 1927, running on a pledge to let the liquor flow again in Chicago, Thompson was swept back into office for a third term. In 1931, Thompson was defeated by Anton J. Cermak, the founder of what

has since been called the "Cook County Democratic Machine."

Mont Tennes inherited much of the gambling empire left by Mike McDonald. Writing in 1929, John Landesco stated (1968: 45): "The complete life history of one man, were it known in every detail, would disclose practically all there is to know about syndicated gambling as a phase of organized crime in Chicago in the last quarter century. That man is *Mont Tennes.*" Anyone wanting to enter the gambling business had to apply to the Tennes ring. He controlled the wire service and paid politicians and the police; gamblers who paid Tennes received race results immediately and protection from police raids (Landesco 1968).

With the advent of Prohibition, the level of violence in organized crime increased dramatically. In the end, Tennes became an associate of the Capone organization. He withdrew from this "shotgun marriage" and retired about 1927, a millionaire (Smith 1962). Tennes died of a heart attack in 1941 (Pietrusza 2003).

FROM COLOSIMO TO TORRIO TO CAPONE

Like Tennes, Coughlin and Kenna soon felt the power of gangsterism in the First Ward. With Thompson in charge of city hall, the power of the Bath and Hinky Dink was reduced considerably. Political-police protection now had to be negotiated directly from "the hall"—individual Democratic aldermen had little or no influence with Big Bill. One of their precinct captains, a man who had aided Coughlin and Kenna in capturing the growing Italian vote of the First Ward, began to assert control over the Levee.

James ("Big Jim" or "Diamond Jim") Colosimo was 10 years old when his father brought him to the United States from Calabria, Italy. He spent all but three years of the rest of his life in the Levee, the waterfront district of Chicago. Beginning as a newsboy and bootblack, by the time he was 18, Colosimo was an accomplished pickpocket and pimp. In the late 1890s, after several close brushes with the law, he obtained a job as a street cleaner and by 1902 had been promoted to foreman. Known as the "white wings" because of their white uniforms, sweepers were organized by Colosimo into a social and athletic club that later became a labor union. Kenna appointed Colosimo a precinct captain in return for delivering the votes of his club, a position that brought with it virtual immunity from arrest (Asbury 1942).

In 1902, Colosimo married a brothel keeper and began to manage her business. In 1903, he helped organize a gang of "white slavers," an operation that brought girls, often as young as 14, from many American and European cities—turnover was good for business (Asbury 1942). Most were willing entrants to the business of house prostitution, but others were lured by false promises of domestic employment or some other duplicity, such as promises of marriage. Once in Chicago, the recruiters turned the girls over to specialists, who would drug, rape, and humiliate the girls for days. After being thus "broken in," they were sold as chattel to brothel keepers, who would restrict their contacts with the outside world.[2] Colosimo opened several brothels and a string of gambling houses. He also owned the nationally famous restaurant, Colosimo's Café, which attracted luminaries from society, opera, and the theater (Nelli 1969). He was the "first Italian-American gangster to cross over from the underworld to the fringes of respectability" (Repetto 2004: 56). "By the middle of 1915, Colosimo was the acknowledged overlord of prostitution on the South Side, and because of his political power was almost as important in other sections of the city" (Asbury 1942: 314).

Colosimo flaunted his success: "He wore a diamond ring on every finger, diamond studs gleamed on his shirt front, a huge diamond horseshoe was pinned to his vest, diamond links joined the cuffs, and his belt and suspender buckles were set with diamonds" (Asbury 1942: 312). All this attracted attention, some of it unwelcome. In 1909, Colosimo, like many other successful Italians, became the target of Black Hand[3] extortion threats. In response, he brought Johnny Torrio to Chicago. Some sources refer to Torrio as Colosimo's nephew, whereas others report that he was a distant cousin of Colosimo's wife, Victoria.

Torrio was born near Naples in 1882, and his parents settled on New York's Lower East Side. Using brains rather than brawn, Torrio became the leader of the James Street Boys, which was allied with Paul Kelly's Five Points gang. He later moved operations to Brooklyn and entered into a partnership with Frankie (Ioele or Uale) Yale, a member of the Five Points gang who became a notorious gang leader in Coney Island. Though Torrio, a happily married man, did not smoke, drink, or consort with women, he was the right man for the job. Shortly after arriving in Chicago, Torrio lured three Black Handers into an ambush, where gunmen shot them to death. His Chicago career was underway (McPhaul 1970; Schoenberg 1992). Torrio's usefulness extended to overseeing brothels and gambling operations for Colosimo. Eventually, Colosimo left Torrio in charge of his operations.

Back in New York, Frankie Yale hired a heavy-fisted member of the Five Points gang to deal with obstreperous customers in his saloon. On one occasion, however, the young bouncer made an offensive remark to a young girl in the saloon, which led to a four-inch scar courtesy of her irate brother and his pocketknife. The young Five Pointer was prone to be overexuberant in carrying out his responsibilities—a suspect in two murders, his third victim was on the critical list when Yale thought it best that Alphonse ("Scarface") Capone leave New York. Al Capone arrived in Chicago at a fortuitous time, 1919, the year before Prohibition went into effect. Although Capone first worked as a bouncer, Torrio began to give him important responsibilities (McPhaul 1970). Then came Prohibition.

---

[2]The activities of white slavers led to the enactment of the Mann Act in 1910, making it a federal crime to transport females interstate for "immoral purposes."

[3]*La Mano Negro*, or Black Hand, consisted of individuals or small gangs of extortionists preying on Italian immigrants who had achieved a level of financial success. Victims would receive a crude letter or note demanding money and signed with a skull or black-inked hand (Lombardo 2002a, 2004).

PROHIBITION

With the coming of Prohibition, "the personnel of organized vice took the lead in the systematic organization of this new and profitable field of exploitation. All the experience gained by years of struggle against reformers and concealed agreements with politicians was brought into service in the organizing and distribution of beer and whiskey" (Landesco 1968: 43). Colosimo, however, was fearful of federal enforcement efforts and wanted to stay away from bootlegging (McPhaul 1970). Torrio and Capone chafed at this reluctance; not only would it deny access to untold wealth, but it would also enable competing racketeers to grow rich and powerful. On May 11, 1920, Diamond Jim was found in the vestibule of Colosimo's Cafe—he had been shot to death. "After Colosimo's death, John Torrio succeeded to the First Ward based Italian 'syndicate' throne, which he occupied until his retirement in 1925. An able and effective leader, Torrio excelled as a master strategist and organizer and quickly built up an empire which far exceeded that of his predecessor in wealth, power, and influence" (Nelli 1969: 386).

As an organizer and administrator of underworld affairs, Torrio is unsurpassed in the annals of American crime. Like Arnold Rothstein in New York (see Chapter 4), he conducted his criminal enterprises as if they were legitimate businesses. "In the morning he kissed his wife good-by and motored to his magnificently furnished offices on the second floor of the Four Deuces [saloon/gambling house/brothel]. There he bought and sold women, conferred with the managers of his brothels and gambling dens, issued instructions to his rumrunners and bootleggers, arranged for the corruption of police and city officials, and sent his gun squads out to slaughter rival gangsters who might be interfering with his schemes." His workday over, "Torrio returned to his Michigan Avenue apartment and, except on rare occasions when he attended the theater or a concert, spent the evening at home in slippers and smoking jacket, playing cards with his wife or listening to phonograph records" (Asbury 1942: 320–21).

As in New York, Prohibition enabled men who had been street thugs to become crime overlords. Outside of the First Ward, various gangs ruled over sections of Chicago, where they pushed aside the local aldermen and parlayed crime and politics into wealth and power. On the North Side, the gang headed by Dion O'Banion controlled the 42nd and 43rd Wards. O'Banion controlled the Irish vote much as Colosimo controlled the Italian vote in the First Ward. Despite his sordid background, including several shootings in public view, in 1924, a banquet was held in O'Banion's honor by the Cook County Democratic organization. It seems that O'Banion had decided to swing his support to the Republicans because the reform-minded Democratic mayor was insisting that laws against many of O'Banion's activities be enforced. Democratic officials made speeches in his honor and even presented O'Banion with a platinum watch—to no avail. O'Banion and the votes of his wards went to the Republicans. O'Banion was a regular churchgoer and loved flowers. This led him to purchase a florist shop and become gangland's favorite florist (Asbury 1942; Landesco 1968). He would soon clash with the Torrio-Capone organization.

THE TORRIO-CAPONE ORGANIZATION

Late in the summer of 1920, Torrio held long conferences with the major gang leaders in Cook County and persuaded them to abandon predatory crime in favor of Prohibition-related activities. To facilitate operations, the city and county were divided into spheres of influence. In each, an allied gang chieftain was supreme, with subchiefs working under his direction. "A few of these leaders themselves owned and operated breweries and distilleries, but in the main they received their supplies from Torrio and were principally concerned with selling, making deliveries, protecting shipments, terrorizing saloonkeepers who refused to buy from the syndicate, and furnishing gunmen for punitive expeditions against hijackers and independents who attempted to encroach upon Torrio territory" (Asbury 1942: 324–25).

Torrio also moved to extend the suburbanization of his business and by 1923 had expanded beer and bordello operations well beyond his South Side stronghold into towns west and southwest of Chicago. He toured the Cook County suburbs, and when a location was decided upon, the neighborhood people were canvassed. If they were agreeable, Torrio agents would provide rewards: a new car, a house redecorated or painted, a new furnace, mortgage payments. The local authorities were then approached and terms negotiated (Allsop 1968). Most of this was accomplished peacefully—but then there was Cicero.

When You Smell Gunpowder, You're in Cicero

Adjacent to Chicago's Far West Side is the suburban city of Cicero (current population about 55,000). In 1923, reform hit Chicago and the mayoralty went to Democrat William Dever. He ordered the police to move against the rampant vice in Chicago, but corruption was too deeply ingrained to be easily pushed aside. However, with the Democrats in control of Chicago, the Republicans were fearful of a reform wave that would loosen their control of the suburban areas of Cook County. As a result, a local Republican leader made a deal with Al Capone while Torrio was on vacation in Italy. In return for helping the Republicans maintain control in Cicero, Torrio would be given a free hand in that city (Allsop 1968).

In the election of April 1924, the Capone brothers, Al and Frank, led a group of two hundred Chicago thugs into Cicero. They intimidated, beat, and even killed Democrats who sought to oppose the Republican candidates. Some outraged Cicero officials responded by having a county judge deputize seventy volunteer Chicago police officers, who entered Cicero and engaged the Capone gangsters. In one incident, Chicago police saw the Capone brothers, Charlie Fischetti (a Capone cousin), and a Capone gunman standing by the polls with guns in their hands ushering voters inside. In the ensuing exchange of gunfire, during which the police were probably mistaken for rival gunmen, Frank

Capone was killed (Schoenberg 1992). Despite this, the Capone candidate was overwhelmingly reelected mayor of Cicero (Kobler 1971).

Capone moved his headquarters from Chicago to Cicero, where he took over the Hawthorne Inn with a little help from his friends—they opened fire at the owner "while shopping housewives and local tradesmen threw themselves behind cars and into doorways in the horizontal position that was becoming an identifiable posture of Cicero citizens" (Allsop 1968: 62–63). At the Hawthorne Inn, Capone ruled with an iron hand. When the Cicero mayor failed to carry out one of his orders, Capone went to city hall, where he personally knocked "his honor" down the steps and kicked him repeatedly as a policeman strolled by (Allsop 1968). Corruption problems in Cicero continued into the twenty-first century.

THE CHICAGO WARS

The election of a reform mayor in Chicago had unanticipated consequences. It created an unstable situation and encouraged competitive moves by various ganglords. When Thompson lost to Dever in 1923, the system of protection broke down, and in the ensuing confusion Chicago became a battleground. The most significant feud was between the Torrio-Capone syndicate and the forces headed by Dion O'Banion.

In 1924, the North Side O'Banion forces began to feud with the fearsome South Side Genna brothers and O'Banion hijacked a load of Genna liquor. The Gennas bristled, but Torrio restrained them and attempted to negotiate a peaceful settlement. In that same year, O'Banion swindled Torrio and Capone out of $500,000, selling them his share in a brewery he knew was going to be raided by the police. This indicated that Torrio had lost control of the police under Mayor Dever. Emboldened by the lack of a response from Torrio, and apparently mistaking caution for fear, O'Banion went around boasting about how he had "taken" Torrio: "To hell with them Sicilians" was a phrase O'Banion gunmen quoted when they told the story in underworld circles (Asbury 1942). This was a serious violation of respect and the response was inevitable.

On November 10, 1924, Mike Genna and two Sicilian immigrants who worked for the Gennas entered the O'Banion flower shop on the Near North Side. O'Banion was busy preparing flower arrangements for the funeral of Mike Merlo, president of the *Unione Siciliana*, who had died of natural causes a few days earlier. What the florist didn't know was that Merlo had been exerting his influence to keep the Gennas and Torrio from moving against O'Banion. Merlo abhorred violence and got along very well with O'Banion—but now he was dead (Kobler 1971). "Hello, boys, you want Merlo's flowers?" a porter told the police he heard O'Banion say to the three men. Torrio had placed an order for $10,000 worth of assorted flowers, and Capone had ordered $8,000 worth of roses. While shaking O'Banion's hand, Mike Genna suddenly jerked him forward and seized his arms. Before he could wriggle free and reach for any of the three guns he always carried, O'Banion was hit by five bullets. A sixth, the coup de grâce, was fired into his head after he fell to the floor. The war that followed took many lives and ended on St. Valentine's Day, 1929 (Allsop 1968; Asbury 1942; Kobler 1971).

The O'Banion forces, under the leadership of Earl Wajciechowski, a Pole better known as "Hymie Weiss," struck back. Torrio left Chicago one step ahead of Weiss gunmen and early in 1925, Capone's car was raked with machine-gun fire. His driver was wounded, but Capone and his bodyguards were not hit. Capone began traveling in a specially built armored Cadillac limousine. Later that year, twelve days after his return to Chicago, Torrio was critically wounded while shopping with his wife. In the fall of 1925, he went to Italy for a visit, leaving his organization to Capone (Landesco 1968). As far as is known, Johnny Torrio never returned to Chicago.[4]

Weiss gunmen made a dozen attempts to kill Capone, and they nearly succeeded in 1926. The street in front of Capone's Cicero headquarters was filled with a lunch-hour crowd, and Capone was eating at a restaurant next door when "eleven automobiles filled with Weiss gangsters drove slowly past the Hawthorne Inn and began firing machine-guns, automatic pistols, and shotguns. After the roar of the attack had subsided, bullet holes were found in thirty-five automobiles parked at the curb. Inside the hotel, woodwork and doors had been splintered, windows shattered, plaster ripped from walls, and furniture wrecked in the office and lobby." Capone, however, was uninjured, although one of his bodyguards was hit in the shoulder, and a woman sitting with her infant son was struck thirty times. Capone paid the physicians who saved her sight (Asbury 1942: 358–59).

Soon afterward, two gunmen armed with submachine guns, who had been waiting for three days, opened fire on Hymie Weiss and his four companions as they approached their headquarters above the O'Banion flower shop. Weiss was hit ten times. He and one of his companions died; the others survived. Weiss, at age 28, reportedly left an estate worth $1.3 million (Allsop 1968).

Gang wars are "bad for business," so in 1926, in the middle of the mayhem and murder, a truce was called. Weiss was dead by that time, and the O'Banion forces were led by George ("Bugs") Moran. The assembled gang chieftains divided up the city and the county, with the largest shares going to the Capone organization and Moran gang.

In 1928, Capone clashed with Frankie Yale. Capone had discovered that Yale—his one-time Brooklyn boss and the person responsible for protecting Capone's liquor shipments as they were trucked west to Chicago—was actually behind a series of hijackings (Kobler 1971). A black sedan

---

[4]Torrio emerged as part of organized crime in New York, where he apparently received some type of senior advisory status. He worked in partnership with a number of leading New York organized crime figures, including Dutch Schultz, with whom he was a partner in the bail bond business, and Frank Costello (Peterson 1983). He later received a two-and-a-half-year sentence for income tax evasion (Irey and Slocum 1948). Some sources (for example, Messick 1967, Turkus and Feder 1951) credit Torrio with inspiring the formation of a national crime syndicate in 1934. Torrio suffered a heart attack while in a barber's chair in Brooklyn and died on April 16, 1957. His death went unnoticed by the media until May 8, when the *New York Times* ran a story: "Johnny Torrio, Ex-Public Enemy 1, Dies; Made Al Capone Boss of the Underworld." Torrio was described as a real estate dealer at the time of his death.

followed Yale's new Lincoln as it moved down a Brooklyn street. As the sedan drew near, shots were fired, and Yale sped off with the sedan in pursuit. The end came with a devastating blast of gunfire that filled Yale's head with bullets and buckshot ("Gangster Shot in Daylight Attack" 1928). He was 35 years old.

During the first few months of 1929, while a peace agreement was in effect (at least in theory), Bugs Moran had been hijacking Capone's liquor, owned jointly by Capone and the (predominantly Jewish) Purple Gang of Detroit. Capone gave orders and went off to enjoy the Florida sun at his palatial fourteen-room estate on Miami's Palm Island. On February 14, St. Valentine's Day, Capone entertained more than one hundred guests on Palm Island: gangsters, politicians, sports writers, and show-business personalities. They all enjoyed a hearty buffet and an endless supply of champagne (Galvan 1982).

Meanwhile, back in Chicago, six of Bugs Moran's men, and an optometrist who liked to associate with gangsters, were waiting at a North Side warehouse to unload a shipment of hijacked liquor from Detroit. A Cadillac touring car with a large gong on the running board, similar to those used by detectives, stopped outside, and five men, two wearing police uniforms, entered the warehouse. Once inside, they lined up the seven men against the warehouse wall and systematically executed them with Tommy guns. One of the victims lived nearly three hours with fourteen bullets in him but refused to tell the police who was responsible for the shooting. Bugs Moran was not in the warehouse at the time, even though the "St. Valentine's Day Massacre" had been arranged in his honor. He arrived late, and seeing the "police car," left. It was later learned that the killers thought Moran was among the victims; lookouts had mistaken one of the seven for the gang's leader (Koziol and Estep 1983). The killers were never caught; it was suspected that they were brought in from Detroit or St. Louis where Capone had ties with "Eagan's Rats" (Kavieff 2000). The affair was apparently arranged by South Side hit man and Capone bodyguard James DeMora, who some

sources refer to as Vincenzco Gibaldi, but who is better known as "Machine-Gun Jack McGurn."[5] For a long time it was generally believed that *real* policemen were the actual killers (Kobler 1971).[6]

Although the wrath of Bugs Moran continued, his gang withered. The man who handled brothels and "immoral cabarets" for Moran was gunned down in 1930. Less than three months later, Moran's partner and president of the *Unione Siciliana*, Joe Aiello, met the same fate. Moran left Chicago and eventually returned to more conventional crime. In 1946, he was sent to prison for robbing a tavern employee of $10,000 near Dayton, Ohio. After 10 years, Moran was released from prison, and a few day later was arrested for bank robbery. On February 26, 1957, the *New York Times* reported that Moran died while serving his sentence in the federal penitentiary in Leavenworth, Kansas ("Bugs Moran Dies in Federal Prison" 1957).

AL CAPONE'S CHICAGO

In May of 1929, after attending a national crime conclave in Atlantic City, Capone decided to go to jail to avoid the wrath of the Bugs Moran gang and any number of Sicilians who had vowed to kill him to avenge the vicious beating deaths of three of their countrymen, whom Capone suspected of disloyalty. He arranged to be arrested by a friendly detective in Philadelphia on a firearms violation. Although the maximum sentence was one year, Capone anticipated a sentence of about ninety days, enough time to let things cool down in Chicago. His arrest, however, generated a great

---

[5]The Moran gang had twice tried to kill McGurn, and on one occasion he was seriously wounded. Believed responsible for killing at least twenty-two people, McGurn used to place a nickel in the hands of his victims. He was responsible for the 1927 attack on comedian Joe E. Lewis, during which his vocal cords were slashed and his tongue lacerated. Lewis, then a nightclub singer, had left McGurn's club for employment at another speakeasy. The Lewis story was told in the Frank Sinatra motion picture *The Joker Is Wild*. Seven years after the massacre, on the eve of Valentine's Day, McGurn was machine-gunned to death in a Chicago bowling alley. The two killers left a comic Valentine card next to his ruined body.

[6]The old garage at 2122 North Clark Street was demolished in 1967.

deal of media attention, and the judge imposed the maximum sentence, twelve months; he was released from his comfortably furnished cell in 1930, two months early, for "good behavior." Although he continued to live with his family in a modest red-brick, two-flat house at 7244 South Prairie Avenue, the former saloon bouncer from Brooklyn was now the most powerful person in Chicago, thanks to Prohibition.

The Depression severely reduced the income of the Capone organization. New areas of profit were sought by the chieftains of organized crime who had grown wealthy in gambling and bootlegging. Until 1929, business and labor racketeering was only a sideline for most top gangsters such as Capone. However, as liquor sales fell off with the onset of the Depression, gang leaders were faced with a restless army of young and violent men whom they were committed to paying anywhere from $100 to $500 per week (Seidman 1938). Capone also recognized by 1928 that Prohibition would probably last only a few more years; new sources of income would be needed.

During Prohibition, numerous forms of racketeering flourished in Chicago: The small businesses of the city were generally marginal and intensely competitive. To avoid cutthroat competition, businessmen formed associations to make and enforce regulations illegally limiting competition. "Many of the associations were controlled, or even organized by, racketeers who levied dues upon association members and controlled the treasuries; they then used a system of fines and violence to insure that all businessmen in the trade joined the association and abided by the regulations" designed to keep prices uniform and high (Haller 1971–72: 225–26).

The Capone organization moved into racketeering on a grand scale and took over many rackets then prevalent in Chicago. In 1928, the Cook County state's attorney listed ninety-one Chicago unions and business associations under gangster control, and these gradually came under the control of the Capone organization—the gangsters who controlled racketeering in Chicago proved no match for the Capone forces (Kobler 1971;

Seidman 1938). It was the same in other cities. In Detroit, for example, the Purple Gang took over labor racketeering through a reign of terror. The Capone organization "controlled a score of labor unions, most of them officered by ex-convicts, and as many protective associations. To build up this phase of the Capone syndicate operations, and to hold in line the businesses already conquered, bands of gunmen and sluggers hijacked and destroyed truckloads of merchandise, bombed stores and manufacturing plants or wrecked them with axes and crowbars, put acid into laundry vats, poured corrosives onto clothing hanging in cleaning and dyeing shops, blackjacked workers and employers, and killed when necessary to enforce their demands or break down opposition" (Asbury 1942: 366–67).

Capone's Downfall

The Depression severely reduced the income of the Capone organization, and a special team of federal investigators, headed by Eliot Ness and dubbed "the Untouchables," began to move against Capone distilleries, breweries, and liquor shipments. The most important event for Capone, however, was a 1927 U.S. Supreme Court decision (*United States v. Sullivan*, 274 U.S. 259) that upheld the Internal Revenue Service's contention that even *unlawful* income was subject to income taxes, the Fifth Amendment guarantee against self-incrimination notwithstanding. The tax evasion case against Capone was initiated in 1929 by the Special Intelligence Unit of the Treasury Department, a low-key agency that avoided publicity. A nearsighted special agent who never carried a firearm was put in charge of the investigation. He brought Capone down with a pencil.

Capone stood trial for having a net income of $1,038,654 during the years 1924 to 1929 for which he failed to pay income tax. In 1931, he was found guilty of income-tax evasion and received sentences totaling 11 years. In 1932, his appeals exhausted, Capone entered the federal prison in Atlanta. He was transferred to Alcatraz in 1934, where he was found to be suffering from syphilis. For several years Capone refused treatment. Early in 1938 he began showing symptoms of paresis and was transferred out of Alcatraz. Capone was released in 1939, his sentence shortened for good behavior, and by then he was suffering from an advanced case of syphilis. He headed for his winter home on Palm Island, Florida, and, after living years as an invalid, died in 1947 of pneumonia following a stroke.

THE OUTFIT EMERGES

The Capone organization "can best be described *not* as a hierarchy directed by Al Capone but rather as a senior partnership involving four men, who in turn entered into a variety of partnerships to run specific enterprises." These four—Al Capone, his brother Ralph, Al's boyhood friend Frank Nitti, and Jake Guzik, Capone's accounting wizard—each received one-sixth of the income that they derived from their various enterprises. The rest was for the maintenance of their central headquarters with its personnel—mostly clerks and gunmen. "The senior partners, in turn, invested money and, when possible, provided political protection for an expanding and diverse group of enterprises" (Haller 1974: 11).

When Prohibition ended, Capone was in prison and the country was several years into the Great Depression. These changes affected organized crime in Chicago. At the height of his power, Capone is reputed to have had 700 gunmen under his control (Palsey 1971). This expensive army was no longer necessary; the Capone syndicate, consolidated under what became known as the Outfit, had an unchallenged monopoly on organized crime in Chicago, maintained with minimal force and a great deal of political influence.

The city's First Ward remained at the center of the Outfit's political influence, which reached into towns and villages of suburban Cook County. Frank Nitti ran the Outfit with the help of Capone's brothers Ralph and Matt, Capone cousins Charlie and Rocco Fischetti, Paul de Lucia (better known as Paul "the Waiter" Ricca),

Anthony ("Joe Batters") Accardo, Jake Guzik, and Welshman Murray Humphreys. The Chicago Crime Commission points out that the Outfit "has been somewhat unique in its willingness to deal with and, indeed, grant considerable responsibility to non-Italians." For many years, Humphreys,[7] was the Outfit's chief political fixer and troubleshooter, and he was succeeded by Gus ("The Greek") Alex ("Spotlight" 1981).

Nitti was born in Sicily in 1889 and brought to the United States at 2 years of age. Known as "The Enforcer" for his role in dealing with internal discipline and external enemies of the Capone organization, Nitti began his career as a barber fencing stolen goods on the side. He had been a boyhood friend of Capone and a fellow member of New York's Five Points gang—he followed Capone to Chicago (Napoli 2004). Although physically unimposing, he had Capone's confidence and became his second in command (Schoenberg 1992). In 1943, Nitti, who had been in poor health, feared prosecution for a nationwide extortion scheme involving the motion picture industry (Demaris 1969), discussed later. On the day an indictment was handed down by a New York grand jury, Nitti committed suicide with a .32 revolver (Koziol and Baumann 1987).

With Nitti's death, Paul Ricca, born in Naples in 1897, became head of the Outfit. A noted political fixer, Ricca arrived in New York in 1920, fleeing prosecution for murder, and eventually settled in Chicago. There he secured employment with "Diamond Joe" Esposito, a major bootlegger and political power. He also worked in Esposito's restaurant, earning the nickname "Paul the Waiter." Ricca left Esposito to manage a theater in Little Italy and was hired by Capone to manage his World Playhouse Corporation. This theater background provided the knowledge he needed to engineer the Browne-Bioff extortion scheme—a scheme that reveals how Prohibition acted as a powerful catalyst for the nation's gang leaders to form a syndicate for cooperative ventures.

---

[7]For a journalistic biography of Murray Humphreys, see Morgan (1985).

The Browne-Bioff Episode

Willie Bioff was a Chicago racketeer who specialized in shakedowns of kosher butchers. He went into partnership with George Browne, a local official of the International Alliance of Theatrical Stage Employees (IATSE), whose members also included motion picture projectionists and other movie theater employees. The two began extorting money from theater chains under the threat of "labor trouble." With Prohibition ending, the Outfit was searching for new areas of profit, and Frank Nitti soon "muscled in" on the scheme, first as a 50 percent and eventually as a 75 percent partner. In 1932, Browne unsuccessfully ran for the presidency of the international union. Then, in 1934, Nitti arranged for Browne to gain the support of major east coast gangsters, Lucky Luciano and Lepke Buchalter in New York, and Longie Zwillman of New Jersey, and Browne was elected president of the IATSE (Nelli 1976). The convention that elected Browne was pervaded with "such an atmosphere of intimidation that opposition wilted" (Johnson 1972: 329).

Browne appointed Bioff to a union position, and the two increased their extortion activities, this time on a nationwide scale. They were able to extort money from Hollywood film studios such as RKO and Twentieth Century-Fox under the threat of closing down theaters throughout the country (Johnson 1972). The scheme ended in 1941, when the brother of the Twentieth Century-Fox chairman of the board was indicted for income-tax evasion. In exchange for leniency, he disclosed the activities of Bioff and Browne. Bioff was eventually sentenced to ten years, Browne to eight. As a result of their cooperation, important members of the Outfit, including Ricca, were convicted.[8] Three years later, all were paroled in a scandal that rocked the administration of President Harry Truman.

When Ricca was imprisoned for his role in the theater scheme, Tony Accardo emerged as

leader of the Outfit. One of six children, Accardo was born in Chicago in 1906 to Sicilian parents. His father was a shoemaker. Raised in the tough Grand Avenue neighborhood, an Italian area on Chicago's Near West Side, the future crime boss dropped out of school at age 14. He subsequently became a member of the Circus Cafe gang (named after the site of its headquarters), a truck driver in the bootleg trade, and an enforcer and bodyguard for Al Capone who gave him the nickname "Joe Batters" (or "J.B.") for his ability to wield a bat (Roemer 1995). Though his arrest record dates back to 1922, and although he had been arrested about thirty times and was a suspect in at least two murders, Accardo could boast that he had never spent a night in jail. In 1955, the Internal Revenue Service (IRS) expressed dissatisfaction with his tax returns: Since 1940, Accardo had reported more than 43 percent of his income as coming from "gambling and miscellaneous sources." The IRS considered this too vague, and prosecution was initiated for income-tax violations. He was eventually convicted and sentenced to six years' imprisonment, but the conviction was reversed on appeal.

In 1955, fearing further federal prosecution as head of the Outfit, Accardo and his aging partner, Paul Ricca, looked for someone to take over the day-to-day operations of the Outfit. They turned to Sam Giancana (Brashler 1977; Peterson 1962).

SAM GIANCANA

Christened Momo Salvatore, Sam Giancana was born in Chicago, in 1908, to Sicilian immigrants and raised in the notorious "Patch" of the Taylor Street neighborhood. Abused as a child, Giancana dropped out of school at age 14. Living mostly in the streets, he became a member of the "42 Gang"—a group that even other criminals of that day viewed as "crazy." They specialized in truck hijacking and auto theft, becoming notorious for their level of violence (Brashler 1977; Giancana and Giancana 1992; Landesco 1933). Fellow members of the 42s would also gain prominence in the Outfit. Although the gang was

---

[8]In 1955, living under an assumed name, Bioff left his Phoenix home and entered his pickup truck. A moment later, Bioff and the truck went up in a tremendous explosion—a dynamite bomb had been wired to the starter.

periodically involved in politics and union organizing as "muscle," their primary activity centered around conventional and often reckless criminality. Deaths, via the police or rival criminals, and imprisonment eventually brought an end to the 42s (Brashler 1977).

As an adolescent, Mooney (Giancana's nickname) served as a gunman for Al Capone. Arrested dozens of times and indicted on several occasions for felonies, not a single case reached the trial stage—"friendly" judges are the explanation. In one murder indictment, the prosecution witness was murdered before the trial. In 1929, however, Giancana's "luck" finally ran out, and he received a one-to-five-year sentence for burglary. Drafted by the army in 1943, Giancana was rejected for being a "constitutional psychopath" with an "inadequate personality and strong antisocial trends" (Demaris 1969: 8; Giancana and Giancana 1992).

Giancana's specialty for the 42s was being a "wheelman"—driving a getaway car. This eventually earned him a position as chauffeur for "Machine Gun" Jack McGurn and later Paul Ricca. His Outfit connection, however, was no advantage in rural Garden Prairie, where Giancana was convicted of bootlegging in 1939. (The Outfit continued in the alcohol business after Prohibition, selling backwoods-still whiskey bottled as imported or quality domestic brands to saloonkeepers eager to improve their profits.) Giancana served three years in the federal prison at Terre Haute, Indiana, where he met Eddie Jones, a wealthy black numbers operator. Jones and his brothers were major gambling and political figures in the city's African American areas (Chepsiuk 2007). Jones, who had pled guilty to income-tax evasion in 1939, told Giancana about the large amount of money he and his brother George had made in this enterprise, which had been dismissed by leading white gangsters as "penny-ante." Since Prohibition, blacks had dominated the numbers business in Chicago (Haller 1990b). When Giancana was released from prison in 1942, Jones financed his entry into the jukebox and vending machine business and became his partner in a variety of gambling enterprises centered in the African American areas of the city's South Side.

Giancana repaid his benefactor by advising Ricca and Accardo of the lucrative black numbers operation and requesting permission to take it over using his crew of 42s (Brashler 1977). After Jones's release from Terre Haute in 1946, he was kidnapped and held for ransom in Giancana's new suburban home in Oak Park. After his family made a payment of $100,000, Jones was released and fled to Mexico with his brother, leaving Teddy Roe in charge of the business. Roe proved to be a tougher opponent than Jones and did quite well for six years—his income tax returns indicating an income of more than $1 million a year—but he was feeling heat from Giancana. After a campaign of intimidation, murder, beatings, and bombings, Roe became the last holdout from Giancana's takeover of the South Side numbers racket. Aiding Giancana's efforts were the police, who raided Roe's policy wheels. In 1951, Roe successfully fended off a kidnapping attempt, killing one assailant and wounding a second, but in 1952, he was ambushed and cut down by a shotgun blast. Sam Giancana had become a principal player in Chicago organized crime. Money from the numbers enabled Giancana to branch out into other enterprises, and his organizational skills and murderous crew allowed him to prosper. In 1955, Giancana was in charge of the Outfit's day-to-day operations (Brashler 1977; Giancana and Giancana 1992; Roemer 1995).

Giancana lived a high-profile social life, something that had become anathema to the now-modernized leaders of organized crime. He had a widely publicized romance with Phyllis McGuire (of the singing McGuire sisters) and a public friendship with Frank Sinatra. He even shared a girlfriend with President John F. Kennedy. Giancana generated a great deal of publicity when he secured an injunction against the FBI's intensive surveillance of his activities. In 1965, he was imprisoned for a year for contempt, refusing to testify before a federal grand jury after being granted immunity from prosecution (Peterson 1969). Following his release, Giancana sought refuge in Mexico. His daughter states that her father was forced into exile by Ricca and Accardo (Giancana and Renner 1985). Giancana remained in Mexico until 1974, when Mexican immigration agents dragged him to a waiting car, drove him 150 miles, and pushed him across the border into the waiting arms of FBI agents. He was then brought to Chicago for grand jury investigations.

The organization was running smoothly without Giancana—Accardo[9] had apparently resumed active control—and Giancana's subsequent return to Chicago was apparently not welcomed by the Outfit leadership. In 1975, Giancana was shot to death at close range in his suburban Chicago home by someone he apparently knew and obviously trusted. Even in death, controversy about Giancana continued. It was disclosed that in 1960, the Central Intelligence Agency had contacted John Roselli, a Giancana lieutenant, to secure syndicate help in assassinating Fidel Castro. Syndicate leaders had reason to dislike Castro, and they had contacts in Cuba and with exiles in South Florida. The plot apparently never materialized; in 1976, Roselli's body was found in an oil drum floating in Miami's Biscayne Bay.

In 1986, top leaders of the Outfit were convicted of skimming $2 million from gambling casinos in Las Vegas—portrayed in the 1995 motion picture by Martin Scorsese, *Casino*—except Accardo, who had assumed senior and semiretired status. A key witness at the trial was Angelo Lonardo, the head of organized crime in Cleveland.

Joseph ("Joe Nagal") Ferriola assumed leadership. This former Outfit enforcer is alleged to have permitted members to involve themselves in drug trafficking, something that had heretofore been off limits. Ferriola died of natural causes in 1989, and leadership was assumed by Sam Carlisi (born in 1921) and John ("No-Nose"[10]) DiFronzo (born in 1928). In 1993, DiFronzo was found guilty of attempting to infiltrate an Indian reservation gambling operation in California for illegal purposes and sentenced to 37 months. That same year, Carlisi

and seven members of his crew were convicted of racketeering and related charges. Carlisi, at age 74, was sentenced to 12 years; he died of natural causes in 1997. DiFronzo successfully appealed his conviction and was released in 1994.

OUTFIT STREET CREWS

New York has five separate crime Families, but the Chicago Outfit has traditionally been organized on the basis of separate street crews, each associated with a particular geographic area. There is evidence of criminal specialization among the various street crews, although it appears currently that various forms of gambling are a primary activity of each. Many of these criminal specializations are related to ecological aspects of each area. For example, the North Side contains Rush Street, Chicago's adult nightclub entertainment district, and the North Side/Rush Street crew is noted for its vice operations: prostitution, pornography, and liquor law violations. The 26th Street area contains a large number of railroad yards and associated shipping and trucking terminals, providing an opportunity for cargo theft and truck hijacking. Chicago Heights, located on the southern edge of the Chicago metropolitan area, has a reputation for automobile theft and chop shop operations, which became a major business for the Chicago Heights crew. This specialization did not prevent members of other crews from cartage theft: In 2001, the Chicago police uncovered an elaborate fencing operation whose source was goods stolen by members of the Grand Street and Elmwood Park crews from semitrailers parked in railway freight yards (Ferkenhoff and Vogell 2001).

Chicagoans refer to their neighborhoods in terms of South Side, North Side, and West Side (East Side is not used in Chicago), so we need to explain their meaning. The city has base lines with Madison Street, which runs east and west, and State Street, which runs north and south, intersecting at the zero point. Everything north of Madison is the North Side; everything west of State Street is the West Side. Buildings are numbered with increases or decreases of one hundred, roughly equivalent

---

[9]Tony Accardo died of natural causes in 1992.

[10]As a young man, DiFronzo was a "smash and grab" thief—smash the window, and grab the fur coat. On one occasion, before he could strip the mannequin and get back into his car, a jagged piece of glass took off part of his nose, which doctors were subsequently able to reattach.

to one city block. To provide greater specificity, locations may be given additional identifiers such as "Far" and "Near," for example, the Near North Side is closer to the South Side and the Far North Side is closer to the northern suburbs than to the zero point.

Taylor Street Crew

The preeminent street crew associated with the Taylor Street neighborhood is contained within the Near West Side community area of Chicago. Poverty and overcrowding led to the establishment of Chicago's first settlement house by Jane Addams in 1889, and Mother Cabrini, the first and only American saint of the Catholic Church, also labored among the poor in this area until her death in 1917. The police precinct encompassing the area was referred to as the "Bloody Maxwell" district because of frequent gunfights between police and criminals (Longstreet 1973). Several urban renewal projects affected the area, including the Chicago campus of the University of Illinois in 1961. As they improved their lot, or were displaced by these massive urban renewal efforts, the early immigrants moved from the Near West Side to other growing areas of the city. By the end of World War II, except for the Italian enclave along Taylor Street, the Near West Side was made up largely of African Americans who had recently emigrated from rural areas of the South.

The Taylor Street neighborhood served as the model for Gerald Suttles's (1968) original conceptualization of the *defended neighborhood* (discussed in Chapter 2), and the defended neighborhood concept accurately describes Chicago's inner-city racket neighborhoods. The Taylor Street neighborhood was also the setting for Solomon Kobrin's (1966) study of status criteria among street-corner groups. In describing the Taylor Street neighborhood, Kobrin writes that a firmly established integration of legitimate and illegitimate elements has existed in the community for some time. This integration of deviant and conventional lifestyles manifested itself in a locally acknowledged alliance between the political leadership and the leadership of the Outfit.

Taylor Street's direct connection to the Outfit can be traced to the 1920s and the 42 Gang. Many members of the 42s were recruited during the 1920s by "Machine-Gun" Jack McGurn who grew up in the neighborhood (Brashler 1977). Remnants of the 42s made up the core of what eventually became known as the Taylor Street crew. As already noted, gang member Sam Giancana rose through the ranks to head organized crime in Chicago.

Despite its history and formidable reputation, the neighborhood has changed because of the presence of the University of Illinois and rising property values brought on by the neighborhood's proximity to Chicago's central business district. However, perhaps out of feelings of nostalgia, Outfit wiseguys can still be found dining, meeting, and socializing in Taylor Street restaurants. Demographic changes have resulted in many Taylor Street stalwarts moving out to the western suburbs, and the crew identified with Taylor Street is sometimes referred to as the Cicero, Melrose Park, or Elmwood Park crew.

Rocco ("Rocky") Infelise Until his death in 1989, Joe Ferriola of Cicero was street boss of the Taylor Street crew of about twenty persons and head of the Outfit. He was replaced as street boss by his top assistant, Rocco Ernest Infelise (born 1922), a paratroop combat veteran with an expensive home in upscale suburban River Forest and a vacation residence in Fort Lauderdale, Florida. Infelise paid $1,000 a month to the police chief of Forest Park to allow high-stakes dice games in the Chicago suburb. A major bookmaker for his crew, the Republican Party boss and town assessor of Cicero acted as a fixer and provided warnings of police raids. In 1993, a year after Frank ("Baldy") Maltese pleaded guilty to gambling conspiracy charges, his wife was elected Cicero town president.

On orders from Ferriola, the Infelise crew participated in a massive effort to extort money from independent bookmakers and other gambling entrepreneurs in the Chicagoland area. Bookmakers were given a choice: pay street taxes, make an Outfit representative a fifty-fifty partner, go out of business, or be "trunked" (placing murder victims in car trunks has been an Outfit favorite). Operators of other types of gambling businesses (card rooms, for example) were ordered to pay a specific amount in taxes—or else. When the Infelise crew expanded into Lake County (just north of Cook County), they encountered recalcitrant gamblers; the body of one was subsequently found in a car trunk. In Lake County, similar overtures were made to the proprietors of houses of prostitution and marginal businesses, such as bars with sex shows or adult bookstores.

The crew included enforcers such as Harry ("The Hook") Aleman, William ("Butch") Petrocelli, and Gerald Scarpelli—experts at intimidation. Aleman (born in 1939 to a Mexican father and Italian mother) is Ferriola's nephew and is believed responsible for at least eighteen homicides. His looks—5 feet, 8 inches, and 145 pounds—belie a fearsome reputation, and the mob hit man fancies himself an artist; his canvases usually depict outdoor scenes. After high school, Aleman attended art school in Chicago. In 1997, in a historic trial, he was convicted of the 1972 murder of a Teamsters Union steward. Aleman had been tried for the same murder in 1977 and acquitted after a bench trial. It was subsequently revealed that the judge, since deceased, had taken a $10,000 bribe to fix the case. The appellate courts ruled that the special circumstances of this case did not violate the constitutional protection against double jeopardy (because there had never been jeopardy in the first trial). Aleman was sentenced to 100–300 years' imprisonment (Cooley 2004; Possley and Kogan 2001).

The 5-foot, 9-inch, 220-pound Petrocelli grew up on Taylor Street. An older brother became a Chicago police sergeant, but Butch became a juice loan collector. He was known to sit across the table from a recalcitrant street tax victim, staring intently and in total silence. That was usually sufficient to gain compliance. "Those who somehow missed Butch's silent message, became corpses" (Brashler 1981: 152). He traveled all over the country, becoming a prime suspect in many gangland murders. In 1981, when he failed to turn over $100,000 collected for the family of imprisoned Harry Aleman, Petrocelli was found dead in the back seat of his car: His mouth and body were bound with duct tape, his eyes and testicles melted away with a blowtorch, and he died of asphyxiation (Cooley 2004).

Scarpelli was born in New York in 1938 and raised on Chicago's West Side. Arrested seventeen times since 1960, he served prison sentences for armed robbery and counterfeiting. In 1989, while in federal custody, and after providing information to the FBI, Scarpelli committed suicide (Federal Bureau of Investigation 1988).

A typical ploy used by the trio involved associates making bets with unaffiliated bookmakers. If the bets were profitable, they would be collected; when a string of losses occurred, they would fail to pay. The bookmaker involved would demand a meeting and usually show up with one or more intimidating colleagues. They would find themselves face-to-face with Chicago's "fearsome threesome." With roles thus reversed, the unfortunate bookmaker would be ordered to pay a fixed amount in back taxes and to pay weekly street taxes.[11]

Crew members appear to enjoy their work. In a 1989 tape-recorded conversation, Infelise's second-in-command told William Jahoda, who was secretly cooperating with the government, about how much he enjoyed his work and the technique of putting on a turban: "I'm so busy. But I enjoy it. I enjoy my work. I wish I didn't have that sentence threatening over me all the time, but that's what it is. . . . Told him [potential competitor trying to engage in loansharking in Lake County], 'I'll put a turban on his head.' You break a guy's head, they got to wrap it." As a ranking intelligence officer told the author: "To a large extent they enjoy what they're doing; it's a game."

In the spring of 1975, an independent bookmaker and former Chicago police officer was told by members of the Taylor Street crew that he would have to pay street taxes. Harry Aleman became his business partner—a "forced marriage"—and directed the bookmaker to contact other gamblers on the North Side to tell

---

[11]A Los Angeles crime Family *caporegime* used a similar approach to extort bookmakers in that city: "His men bet into bookmakers across the city. When they won, they would collect. When they lost, they would stiff the bookies and remind them who they were dealing with and what right did they have to operate in this town?" (J. Smith 1998: 190).

them to pay street taxes; one was A.R. The ex-cop told the bookmaker that he represented "Harry," who on behalf of the Outfit was demanding 50 percent of his business. Unfortunately for A.R., he was not from Chicago and knew little about the Outfit. He responded: "Go fuck yourself and tell them guys to fuck themselves." After being told of his response, Aleman directed the bookmaker to try again. He did, with the same response. Subsequently, A.R. found out who "Harry" was and changed his attitude. But it was too late. An example was necessary and Aleman told his "partner" to stay far away from A.R.

On the evening of October 31, 1975, A.R., 34, entered a restaurant on the Far West Side and asked the cashier if anyone had been looking for him. When the response was negative, he ordered dinner. Shortly afterward, two men wearing ski masks entered the restaurant, one carrying a .30 carbine, and the other a short-barreled shotgun. When the men approached, A.R. tried to rise but was pushed back into the booth. One masked man raised his carbine and fired four rounds into his chest. Blood spurted out, and the second masked man placed his shotgun against the bookmaker's head and fired two shots. Both men pointed their guns at patrons as they calmly exited the restaurant and entered a car, later found abandoned. Aleman's thumbprint was discovered on a warranty book in the car's glove compartment—dangerous does not necessarily mean smart. As part of an agreement, in 1978 Aleman pled guilty to home invasions in Indiana and Illinois and received an 11-year sentence; he was released in 1989. A.R.'s murder convinced most bookmakers and other gamblers to capitulate to Outfit demands, although there were exceptions.

In 1982, a bookmaker was lured to an illegal gambling casino in the suburb of Libertyville, where he was attacked and beaten to death. In 1984, the man in charge of the crew's Lake County activities demanded $6,000 a month in street taxes from successful bookmaker Hal Smith, declaring "Or you're 'trunk music,'" alluding to the sound of flesh decomposing in the trunk of a car. Smith made a counteroffer: $3,500. Rocky Infelise was informed, and the counteroffer was obviously rejected.

Jahoda, a successful bookmaker associated with the Taylor Street crew, told Infelise he knew Smith and arranged to meet him at Jahoda's suburban home. Before the meeting, Smith's demise was rehearsed. Jahoda met Smith in a suburban tavern where they had a drink. Jahoda told Smith that he had a couple of girls back at his house. When the two pulled into Jahoda's garage, Jahoda told Smith to go into the house while he checked the mail. Through the window Jahoda saw Smith walk into the kitchen when suddenly a man appeared behind the victim. When Jahoda entered the house, Smith was lying on the kitchen floor with his back against a cabinet. Infelise later told Jahoda that Smith had pulled a gun, but it had been taken away from him by one of Infelise's men. Smith's decomposing body was discovered in the trunk of his car. He had been severely beaten around the face and upper torso, and there were thirteen incision-like marks around his neck; he had finally been strangled to death.

The Taylor Street crew also ran illegal gambling operations such as the Rouse House casino in suburban Libertyville, which offered dice and card games. As a natural extension of their gambling activities, the crew was heavily involved in loansharking. But Infelise also had significant expenses, aiding incarcerated members with legal fees and paying them part of the crew's profits. In a 1989 recording, Infelise complained that he was giving away $35,000 a month "for guys that are away, and the coppers. . . . We got seven guys away, [who] get $2,000 a month."

In 1992, Infelise and several members of his crew were found guilty of racketeering and murder conspiracy. The conviction was largely the result of testimony from Jahoda who became an informant. At his sentencing hearing, Infelise castigated the judge and made a veiled threat against Jahoda, who was in the witness protection program. Infelice was sentenced to 63 years.

Grand Avenue Crew

Grand Avenue is located within the West Town community area of Chicago. Anthony Accardo was born in 1906 on W. Grand Avenue and his

Outfit members Paul Schiro (left), Frank Calabrese, Sr. (center), and Joseph ("Joey the Clown") Lombardo have been implicated in more than a dozen murders.

involvement with Capone is commonly believed to have been the beginning of the Grand Avenue street crew. The headquarters of the *Unione Siciliana* was located within the Grand Avenue neighborhood, and Accardo was at one time the president of the organization.

The 1982 imprisonment of Grand Avenue boss Joseph Lombardo left the crew leaderless and without direction, causing a decline in their activities. Before his imprisonment, Lombardo and the Outfit played a role in the Grand Avenue community. A Chicago police officer familiar with the Grand Avenue crew reports that Lombardo would hold meetings in an old funeral parlor on Grand Avenue. "There, the old men came and told Joe their problems. If an old Italian told Joe that someone was speeding up and down his street and he was afraid kids would get run over, Joe would send someone to threaten the driver. The police couldn't do that, but the 'moustaches' can. It ain't right but the people got service that way." Lombardo was released from prison in 1995 and returned to the Grand Avenue neighborhood. He had been imprisoned as a result of his involvement with Allen Dorfman (discussed in Chapter 14). In 2005, the federal government indicted fourteen Outfit members, including Lombardo, for racketeering and

murder. Before he could be taken into custody, the 77-year-old eluded authorities and remained at large for nine months; he was arrested while sitting in a parked car in the Chicago suburb of Elmwood Park.

Tony Spilotro   One of the most infamous members of the Grand Avenue crew, Tony Spilotro (whose activities have been portrayed in the book and motion picture *Casino*) was the son of Italian immigrants, small restaurant owners. Born in 1938, he grew up in the Grand Avenue neighborhood. An older brother became an Air Force captain and a dental surgeon, but Tony dropped out of high school in his sophomore year. He associated with other dropouts, formed a gang, and earned a police record for various crimes. Although of small stature, Tony was widely feared because of his ferocity. This reputation earned him a spot with Chicago's most notorious loan shark, Sam ("Mad Sam") DeStefano, a former 42 Gang member. This sadistic and violent individual killed his own brother for using drugs and was dubbed the "Marquis de Sade" of the Chicago Outfit. He was murdered in 1973 (see Kidner 1976 for a discussion of DeStefano). At age 27, Tony took over his business, becoming the youngest loanshark in the Chicago Outfit.

Spilotro also carried out executions for the Outfit leadership. His most infamous, the "M & M murders," involved two young criminals who killed an Outfit-connected man in the off-limits suburb of Elmwood Park. One had his head placed in a vise that Spilotro turned until an eye popped out and he revealed his partner's name (Corbitt with Giancana 2003).

In 1964, Spilotro was sent to Miami, Florida, to assist Frank ("Lefty") Rosenthal, who was running gambling operations for the Outfit. In 1969, he was back in Chicago overseeing gambling operations and gaining a high profile because of his murderous activities. Two years later, apparently to let things cool off, Tony went to Las Vegas. There, Rosenthal was in charge of the Stardust Casino Hotel where enormous sums were being skimmed off on behalf of organized crime bosses throughout the country. Spilotro brought with him a group of enforcers from the Windy City, and soon the tortured bodies of murder victims—wayward loansharks and cheating employees of mob-controlled hotels—began turning up. He extorted street taxes from local criminals and opened a jewelry store, which served as his headquarters. When his "Hole-in-the-Wall Gang" of burglars began looting homes, the store served as a fencing outlet (Griffin and Cullotta 2007).

In 1979, Spilotro's name was added to the *Black Book* of persons banned from casino hotels. In 1981, several members of the Hole-in-the-Wall Gang were arrested while engaged in a major burglary. One, believing he had been betrayed, became a witness against Spilotro in an old Chicago murder case. Spilotro was acquitted, but he had become infamous in Las Vegas, and his high profile disturbed the Outfit leadership whose chief concern was maintaining their share of the "skim." He killed people without mob permission, bombed a mob associate, and in a serious violation of mob etiquette, Tony was having an affair with Rosenthal's wife. In 1983, Outfit leaders and Spilotro were indicted for conspiracy related to the Las Vegas skimming. Spilotro claimed ill health—he had a coronary bypass—and his case was severed from that of the other defendants who were eventually convicted.

According to trial testimony, in 1986, Outfit boss Joey ("Doves") Aiuppa held a meeting with Outfit leaders who were preparing to go to prison—he wanted Spilotro killed. After Outfit executioners failed to kill him in Las Vegas, Tony was called back for a meeting in Chicago. His body and that of his younger brother Michael were discovered buried in an Indiana cornfield—they had been beaten and strangled (Griffin and Cullotta 2007; Pileggi 1995; Roemer 1994; and newspaper articles from Chicago and Las Vegas).

26th Street Crew

The 26th Street neighborhood is contained within the Armour Square community area of Chicago, named after the Armour Institute of Technology, the original name of the Illinois Institute of Technology. Armour Square is truly an interstitial space in that it is a one-half mile wide strip of land bordered by a railroad yard and the Chicago River on the north and raised embankments of railroad tracks on two of the remaining sides. Just west of the neighborhood is the town of Cicero.

The neighborhood was the site of Al Capone's headquarters, the Lexington Hotel, and the 26th Street crew is considered a direct descendant of the original Colosimo-Torrio-Capone syndicate, because many of the people who worked for Colosimo and later Torrio and Capone lived there. Much of the area has been replaced by an interstate roadway and public housing, reducing the size of the Italian enclave. Nevertheless, it is probably the strongest street crew neighborhood in metropolitan Chicago. Unlike Taylor Street, there have been no major urban renewal efforts in this Italian community; the homes are well cared for and the neighborhood is stable. As reported by one organized crime investigator: "While guys from other neighborhoods have moved out, people from 26th Street have remained in the neighborhood. They have such a base there. All of their people are right there. . . . Yeah, that neighborhood has been like time-frozen. It's like you go back to the [19]60s; it is still there. They still have the social club there." The presence of crime syndicate members in the 26th Street community is recognized by both community residents and government agencies.

The original boss of 26th Street was Bruno ("The Bomber") Roti, whose son became the chief deputy sheriff for Cook County in the 1980s; another son became alderman of the First Ward and was later convicted of corruption. When The Bomber gave up his position, he was replaced by an assistant who died in 1983 and was succeeded by Angelo ("The Hook"—from which he hung his torture victims) LaPietra. In 1987, LaPietra was convicted in the Las Vegas skimming case—the government placed a court-authorized bug in the storefront headquarters of the 26th Street crew. (He died of natural causes in 1999, a year after being released from prison.) The crew has extensive involvement in gambling and loansharking.

North Side Crew

The North Side racket area is located within the Near North Side community that includes the city's "Gold Coast" and downtown entertainment area. By the turn of the century, a portion of the Near North Side was already referred to as the "Gold Coast" because of the large number of luxurious homes that were built along the lakefront. The turn of the twentieth century also brought large numbers of Italians, particularly Sicilians, to the area, eventually replacing earlier immigrant groups. The "dark people," as they were called, soon dominated the area.

The natural clash between the well-to-do families of the eastern part and the immigrant families of the western portion of the Near North Side resulted in a central area that became progressively less desirable as a residential district. As a result, many of the wealthier families and businesses moved from the area. During the 1920s, many of the residential hotels and large homes that were left behind were transformed into boarding houses to make them profitable. These rooming houses brought a large transient element to the area as well as a population of lower economic status. Soon, the once fashionable district became a center for dance halls, nightclubs, prostitution, and other forms of illegal activity and the beginning of the Clark Street and later Rush Street vice district in Chicago.

The North Side was the focus of Harvey Zorbaugh's classic community study *The Gold Coast and the Slum* (1929: 198), which described the North Side "as a community in the process of disintegration where church, school, family, and government have ceased to have any influence on community life." Existence there, he stated, "was without the law and without the mores of the larger society," a classic case of social disorganization. William Whyte (1961) challenged these findings, noting that portions of the North Side, particularly the Italian settlement, were highly organized. Citing one of the leaders of the Chicago Area Project Near North Area Program, Whyte argued that even though the area was characterized by congested population, poor housing, and low family income, people there lived in family groupings and built up elaborate social networks reminiscent of Italian village life.

The connection between the North Side community and the Chicago Outfit can be traced to Prohibition, Al Capone, and the *Unione Siciliana*. In 1929, Capone's handpicked successor to the leadership of the *Unione* was murdered by the Aiello brothers allied with Bugs Moran. Capone responded by sending a cohort of men led by Frank Nitti into the area. They systematically bombed Aiello-Moran alky stills and speakeasies all over the North Side. The blasting continued until the St. Valentine's Day massacre of 1929 ended the Aiello-Moran axis forever and left the Capone syndicate firmly in control of Chicago's Near North Side.

Just as they had done in the Taylor Street area, the Capone organization turned to local Italian street toughs in the North Side community to find recruits for their criminal organization. Once the Capone organization had taken control of bootlegging activities on the North Side, it was a simple matter for them to dominate other vice activities.

The North Side was known as a "honky-tonk town," as saloons, cabarets, and rialtos marked every block on Clark Street from Grand Avenue to Division Street. Today there is nothing left of the Clark Street rialto, though neighboring Rush Street contains numerous restaurants and upscale liquor establishments, and further north into the Forty-third and Forty-fourth Wards are numerous night spots featuring blues and jazz, for which Chicago is famous. The North Side racket community no longer exists. Most of the members of the original Sicilian community moved away when the neighborhood was torn down between 1941 and 1962, during successive stages of the construction of the Cabrini-Green housing complex. Many North Side Italian emigrants resettled in the suburb of Melrose Park.

Lottery king Ken ("Tokyo Joe") Eto, born in 1920 of Japanese ancestry, paid thousands of dollars a month in street taxes to the North Side crew to remain in business. In 1983, he was convicted of operating an illegal lottery business that grossed nearly $6 million between May 4, 1980, and August 20, 1980. Facing imprisonment, he met with the crew's street boss, Vincent Solano, who was also head of Laborers Union Local 1. Eto assured Solano that he could be trusted to be a "stand-up guy," but the street boss was apparently unconvinced. In 1983, Tokyo Joe was taken for a ride by two men, one a Cook County deputy sheriff, shot three times in the back of the head, and left for dead. But Eto survived. Later that year, the bodies of Eto's would-be assassins were found in the trunk of a car with multiple stab wounds— being "trunked" was apparently the Outfit's penalty for botching a murder. Eto went into the federal witness protection program. The North Side crew made headlines in Chicago during the 1990s, because of the activities of Lenny Patrick.

Lenny Patrick Leonard Patrick was born in England (or possibly in Chicago to English parents, Jews who had somehow acquired Irish surnames) in 1913. He grew up in the Jewish community on Chicago's West Side, where he became a legend for his easy use of violence and strong defense of the neighborhood. His criminal record includes a seven-year sentence for a 1933 Indiana bank robbery. He has admitted committing two murders and ordering four others, all during the 1930s and 1940s. He has been closely associated with Gus Alex, a major Outfit power and political fixer, for decades. With a crew of vicious enforcers, Patrick was responsible for gambling and loansharking operations on the North Side and northern

suburbs. He also controlled several legitimate industrial laundering companies that rented towels, linens, and uniforms.

According to court records, the Patrick group extorted money from seven legitimate businesses: In each case, members of his crew approached the owners of the businesses and demanded payments of between $50,000 and $500,000. To back up their demands, they used threats and violence, routinely threatening to kill not only the primary victim but also family members. Patrick's group extorted street taxes from bookmakers and other gambling operators and engaged in loansharking at rates as high as 260 percent annually; those who were slow to repay were routinely beaten.

In 1992, after being accused of extortion from numerous legitimate firms and gambling operators, Patrick pled guilty and agreed to become a government witness. Gus Alex and the crew's primary enforcer were found guilty of extortion. Alex, at age 76, was sentenced to 15 years. Patrick's contribution to the success of the federal government, however, is dubious. According to court records: "While Patrick purported to cooperate with the government beginning on November 6, 1989, his cooperation was at best halfhearted, and he continued at the same time to participate in the conspiracy and to hide his participation from the FBI."

THE OUTFIT TODAY

Chicago differs from New York in that the Outfit has always been a cooperative venture with other groups, although the Italians have been dominant. There has been an absence of independent entrepreneurs, and important decisions are made at the executive level. In a truly hierarchical organization, the decision to move into a new business or new territory is determined at the top; and so, for example, when the Outfit decided to get into the lucrative video poker machine business, an important question had to be answered: Should distribution be controlled centrally, or should each crew be allowed to distribute in its own territory? The boss, apparently in consultation with his advisors, decided on decentralization (Herion 1998).

The Outfit is led by a boss who at various times has actually been akin to a chief executive officer responsible to one or more persons constituting an informal board of directors. This was the case during the leadership of Sam Giancana, who reported to Tony Accardo and Paul Ricca. Ricca died in 1973, and until his death 20 years later, Accardo served as something analogous to a powerful president who appoints the prime minister. Assisted by a committee of older and influential members who assume some type of senior status, the boss controls three area bosses. Each area boss has responsibility for a particular part of "Chicagoland"—Cook County and the surrounding collar counties area. He oversees the activities of street bosses who direct the day-to-day activities of crew members.

Each of the crews is associated with a particular geographic area, although these areas have undergone change over the years. In addition, there are subgroups nominally attached to crews. Thus, major gambling operations are the responsibility of a specialty crew whose members report to the Outfit hierarchy, rather than a street boss. Further complicating the picture is the custom of referring to a crew by the name of its current street boss (for example, the "Carlisi street crew" or the "Ferriola street crew") or the primary residence of the street boss (for example, the "Cicero crew") by federal officials, the Chicago Crime Commission, and even Outfit members themselves. Members of the various crews are not necessarily familiar with members of the other crews.

Each street crew, for the most part, acts independently of the other crews, and each street boss, assisted by (two or more) lieutenants, is responsible for supervising the activities of his crew. The head of the Outfit settles disputes between the crews and is responsible for relations with those outside the organization such as corrupt public officials and organized crime groups in other cities. A street boss may also be involved in activities, such as labor racketeering, on an "industry" rather than a territorial basis. For example, Vincent Solano was boss of the North Side as well as president of Local 1 of the Laborers Union.

In Chicago, made guys are supervisors, and the people they supervise (associates) begin working for $500 a week in an entry-level position; an investigator (O'Rourke 1997) compared this to starting out as a ballplayer in the minor leagues. Salaries are kept on a par across crews, apparently to avoid competition or jealousy. Associates are assigned to activities for which they are equipped: Someone with numbers skills would, for example, work as a clerk for a bookmaker; someone with a tough-guy reputation would be assigned to collections. The clerk can earn additional income by recruiting customers and will even be allowed to have his own betters for whom he is responsible. If he becomes very successful, he will be allowed to start a bookmaking business of his own. The collector for a loan shark can earn half of the vigorish (interest) of loans he has arranged. There is little crossover; clerks, for example, would not be used as collectors or vice versa. There are also special people "kept on the shelf," provided with money-making opportunities to have them available for "heavy work"—murder (Moriarity 1998).

Outfit employment is not exhausting work, often requiring only a few hours a day. A worker may also hold a legitimate job, for example, employment with the city Streets and Sanitation Department or (in the past) the county sheriff. Indeed, Outfit employment is often geared to keeping people busy so they remain tied to the Outfit—for some, crime may not pay (a great deal), but the hours are great! A successful bookmaker who also ran nightly gaming rooms (which were fixed—loaded dice, marked cards, magnetized roulette wheels) was asked why he did not give up the more time-intensive bookmaking for the time-limited and lucrative gaming rooms: "What would I do all day?" (Herion 1998; Moriarity 1998). "Some of the mob's worst hit men and goon enforcers were on the public payroll. Usually they did not even show up to punch in" (Cooley 2004: 113).

But every Outfit guy is on call. "It's worse than the FBI or the military. If they get a call at three in the morning: 'Go see Howard and collect some money; give him a whack or break his legs,' they can't say 'I'm tired.' They've got to do it." And they can be called to a meeting at any time: "Refusing to go to a meeting is a killing offense. It's the way they test loyalty. They call him in—call him in for 'a cigar,' where they get their ass chewed out by the boss. It's an easy way to set someone up for a murder. If you don't show up you got a problem; if you do show up . . . " (O'Rourke 1997).

Outfit Membership

Each crew is composed of made guys and associates who are said to be "connected" or "Outfit guys." The street boss and his lieutenants, if they are of Italian heritage, are made guys. Everyone else connected to the crew is an associate (although they are commonly referred to as "members" of a crew). There is some disagreement about the various terms used to describe positions within the Outfit. According to virtually all sources, the Outfit does not use terms common to the New York Families, such as *consigliere*, *caporegime*, or *Cosa Nostra*. And there is little evidence of an initiation ceremony involving oaths of secrecy and obedience, the drawing of blood, and the burning of a saint's portrait. To the extent that there is a ceremony, it appears to be more like a luncheon at which the person is introduced by the boss as a made guy. "In Chicago, according to informants, they do not go through an old-country style initiation and they kind of laugh at that. If you talk to guys actually going out bombing places, collecting the tax, threatening people, someone like that is going to laugh and say 'We don't do that in Chicago.' You become a made guy by being nominated by your boss because you have a history of making lots of money, a good earner. It's unclear if, like in the old days, you actually have to participate in a murder. Obviously, if you participated in a hit, either as the killer or getaway driver, you've made your bones and that helps your reputation" (O'Rourke 1997).

There is some evidence, however, that the traditional ceremony was used by some crews in the past. In court testimony, a government informant related that the Taylor Street crew under Rocky Infelise made people "the old way," and testimony in the "Family Secrets" trial (discussed later) revealed an induction ceremony for the 26th Street crew with cut fingers and the burning of a saint's picture. Such persons may have gone through two ceremonies: one with the Outfit boss, and another with his street boss.

In any event, there are definite distinctions between being a made guy and being an associate. In the Chicago Outfit, made guys hold supervisory (or senior advisory) status; everyone else is a worker, with a few important exceptions. Persons who have proven their value to the Outfit have sometimes been given important responsibilities even in the absence of Italian heritage, for example, Gus Alex (Greek), Murray Humphreys (Welsh), and Lenny Patrick (Jewish). Being "made" also conveys important status: "Being a made guy grants certain rights and privileges that nobody else gets. You get a cut of the pie. You can order other people to do things. You get to work in a closed circle and you profit from it more so than everybody else. When you are a made guy, you are a guy that gets the money. All the rest of those guys get just a little shred. But there aren't that many made guys" (O'Rourke 1997). And there is considerable "psychic gain." Within criminal and certain legitimate circles, being "made" conveys a great deal of prestige, if not fear.

The requirement of being Italian has helped to prevent infiltration of the organization. It has also ensured that members of the Outfit share the same values. Many of the Southern Italian and Sicilian immigrants who were attracted to organized crime subscribed to the code of *omerta´* and had lived under a Mafia dominated social order, both of which facilitated their participation in organized crime. Today, the requirement of being Italian accomplishes a similar goal. Though the average recruit today has never been exposed to the Mafia, many have been raised in neighborhoods where the Outfit is part of the social structure, ensuring that potential recruits have been exposed to values supportive of organized crime.

Many Italian Americans, however, wiseguys among them, reside in suburbs where the critical core of street corner boys no longer exists. The traditional storefront social clubs are rare; often they are places where elderly Italians—Outfit guys among them—gather to talk, tell tales of the old days, and play cards or dominos. But certain traditions supportive of organized crime, such as cultural deviance (discussed in Chapter 2), continue to exist among some families even in the suburbs: "Their time frame is short and dishonesty is something that someone else has defined. They don't see anything wrong, when they need a suit for the kid, when someone graduates from high school, they go down the street to see 'Louie' and take care of it. If someone gets into trouble, they know who to go to, who the fixer is" (Risley 1998).

Italian American young men are being raised in more comfortable surroundings than their predecessor's ghetto experiences. A few—the Outfit does not require many replacements for its considerably streamlined operations—may still fantasize about being part of the "mob," being a wiseguy. If they have a connected relative, or perhaps a neighbor with whom they are close, they may be given an opportunity to be a clerk or a collector. Though many members of the Outfit are related by blood and marriage, the sons of Outfit members are rarely found in the ranks of Chicago organized crime.[12] As lawyers and accountants, they are sometimes found working for the same union locals traditionally associated with the Outfit, or they may be defense attorneys in Outfit cases. And until recently, the Chicago Outfit had been free of the made-guy-turned-informant syndrome affecting crime Families in New York.

The size of the Outfit today is markedly smaller than the version once ruled by Al Capone. Estimates of membership range from as low as 30 to as high as 130, revealing that it is still hard to determine who is and who is not a "member." Best current estimates are about 50 made guys. Nevertheless, outside of predominantly black and Hispanic neighborhoods, the Outfit has been able to maintain hegemony over gambling and related activities in an area ranging from southern Wisconsin to northern Indiana. They have been able to do this in recent years using considerably less violence. Perhaps this is to be expected from the nature of Outfit leaders who haven't "come up from the streets" and who seem to prefer competitive business strategies rather than intimidation.

The Outfit's political base in the First Ward has been destroyed. From the 1870s to 1990, Chicago's First Ward remained a seemingly untouchable political link to organized crime. That changed in 1990, when indictments were announced against First Ward politicians and gangsters, most of whom were subsequently found guilty. The First Ward case was developed by the FBI through the use of a corrupt lawyer acting as a mole and the placing of an electronic bug in a restaurant frequented by First Ward politicians (Cooley and Levin 2004). In 1992, Mayor Richard J. Daley put an end to the long and sordid political reign of the First Ward. In redrawing aldermanic districts, the Loop—the central business district—and the Michigan Avenue shopping area were placed in the Forty-second Ward, and a new First Ward was created from parts of neighboring wards to ensure the election of a Latino alderman.

In the past, aspiring Outfit members cut their teeth on theft, particularly from interstate truck and train shipments; today, gambling and its related activities—taking bets, collecting receipts, servicing video poker machines—is the route to membership. Gambling is crucial to the Outfit; it provides considerable income and gives members something to do (they have considerable leisure time) while networking and socializing. The Outfit continues to be involved in the red light districts that appear in certain suburbs; and through control of unions, the Outfit is able to provide favored businessmen with a competitive edge, for example, by investing union funds. A number of Chicago union locals whose officers in the past were Outfit members or associates now have the sons and grandsons of these officials holding the same positions (Herguth 2004).

The most significant convictions involving members of the Chicago Outfit in the last few years have involved persons on the "heavy" side, that is, those associated with violence. As a result, it appears the Outfit leadership has made a decision to stay away from business operations most likely to require violence. In recent years, there have been few murders related to organized crime—one in 1999 and another in 2001 involved the demise of two men with violent reputations who had been involved in loansharking. The thug side of the Outfit, however, led to the most important federal case in decades, dubbed "Operation Family Secrets."

[12]One notable exception is the son of deceased Outfit boss Joe Ferriola.

Family Secrets

The success of the Chicago Outfit in avoiding having made guys become informants ended in a most spectacular way—the ultimate betrayal of son against father, brother against brother. Frank Calabrese, an Outfit loan shark with a particularly violent reputation, was raised in the Outfit neighborhood surrounding the intersection of Grand Avenue and Ogden Street on Chicago's South Side. Expelled from school for fighting, he eventually went to work for Angelo LaPietra (discussed earlier), and as Angelo rose in the Outfit, so did Frank. Nick Calabrese, Frank's younger brother, graduated from high school and served honorably in the Navy, but nevertheless became an important part of his brother's crew. Frank's son, Frank Calabese, Jr., who also participated in some of his father's activities, secretly provided information to law enforcement. In 2004, after being confronted by the FBI with evidence of his role in a murder, Nick Calabrese agreed to become a witness against his older brother. In 2007, Nick pleaded guilty to planning or carrying out fourteen murders, including those of the Spilotro brothers discussed earlier. Frank, Jr.'s cooperation with the government included recording incriminating conversations with his father who was incarcerated at the time.

The disclosures resulting from Operation Family Secrets led to the indictment of fourteen persons (*United States v. Calabrese et al.*, 2 Cr. 1050, 2006), including ranking members of the Outfit and two former police officers accused of providing confidential information to Frank Calabrese. In 2007, five defendants, including Frank Calabrese, were found guilty after a jury trial.

SUMMARY

- In Chicago, organized crime in the form of the Torrio-Capone organization emerged from Prohibition during which gangsters supplanted machine politicians as the city's centers of power.
- The Torrio-Capone organization eventually eclipsed its rivals and, after Prohibition was repealed, emerged as the Outfit whose street crews continue to dominate organized crime in the Chicagoland area.
- More hierarchically structured than Mafia Families in New York, the Outfit in recent years has shied away from violence.
- The success in avoiding made guys becoming informants ended in the Family Secrets case that led to the conviction of major Outfit figures.

REVIEW QUESTIONS

1. In Chicago, what was the connection between corrupt politicians, vice entrepreneurs, and big business?
2. What was the importance of the First Ward in the development of organized crime in Chicago?
3. How and when did the influence of the First Ward end?
4. What was the effect of Prohibition on Chicago politics, politicians, and vice entrepreneurs?
5. What effect did the election of a reform mayor have in Chicago during Prohibition?
6. How did the onset of the Depression and the end of Prohibition affect organized crime?
7. What happened to the Capone organization after the imprisonment and subsequent death of Al Capone?
8. How does the Chicago Outfit differ from New York's Mafia Families?
9. What is so unusual about the "Family Secrets" case?

CHAPTER
6
Italian Organized Crime and the Albanian Connection

In this chapter we begin our examination of organized crime (OC) on the global scene, sometimes referred to as transnational organized crime. Our focus will be on criminal organizations that have affected, or have the potential to affect, the United States. We will begin our examination of four of these criminal organizations—*Mafia*, *Camorra*, *'Ndrangheta*, and the *Sacra Corona Unita* (with its Albanian connection)—which have their roots in southern Italy, the *Mezzogiorno*.

THE *MEZZOGIORNO*

The southern Italian experience, which dates back more than a thousand years, led to the development of a culture that stresses the variables necessary for survival in a hostile environment. "To be respected in traditional southern Italian societies," notes Letizia Paoli (1999: 19), "meant to be entitled to the deference of others that came from the ability to use violence." The southern Italian developed an ideal of manliness, *omertá*, that includes noncooperation with authorities, self-control in the face of adversity, and the *vendetta*—"*blood washes blood*"—"which dictated that any offense or

slight to the *famiglia* (family) had to be avenged, no matter what the consequences or how long it took. Neither government nor church was to be trusted. The only basis of loyalty was *famiglia*—"blood of my blood" (*sangu de me sangu*). "The *famiglia* was composed of all of one's blood relatives, including those relatives Americans would consider very distant cousins, aunts, and uncles, an extended clan whose genealogy was traced through paternity. The clan was supplemented through an important custom known as *comparático* or *comparaggio* (godparenthood), through which carefully selected outsiders became, to an important (but incomplete) extent, members of the family" (Gambino 1974: 3).

The family patriarch, the *capo di famiglia*, arbitrated all ambiguous situations. The family was organized hierarchically: "One had absolute responsibilities to family superiors and absolute rights to be demanded from subordinates in the hierarchy" (Gambino 1974: 4). "The family, first source of power, had to be made prosperous, respected, and feared with antlike tenacity; it was enlarged (like dynasties of old) by suitable marriages, strengthened by alliances with families of equal status, by negotiated submission to more powerful ones, or by establishing domination over weaker ones. In the *famiglia,* physical aggression was rewarded and the strongest member of the domestic group assumed the dominant status" (Barzini 1977: 36).

The *Mezzogiorno,* literally *midday,* but a nickname for southern Italy (Paoli 2003), never enjoyed a Renaissance, remaining mired in feudalism and dependant on agriculture; a legacy of political, social, and economic repression; and exploitation (Putnam 1993). A succession of foreign rulers ended in 1860 with a revolution against (Spanish) Bourbon rule that eventually united Italy. For the people of the *Mezzogiorno,* however, little changed. Instead of foreign repression, the *contadini* (peasants) were repressed by other Italians: "The political foundation of the new Italian state was an alliance between the northern industrial bourgeoisie and the southern landed aristocracy" (Chubb 1982: 16). The *Mezzogiorno,* with a population of about 20.8 million persons (out of a population of 59 million), continues to lag far behind northern Italy (and the rest of western Europe) in economic development. The rate of unemployment—12 percent—is roughly three times that of the north (Naravane 2008). About half of all murders committed in Italy take place in the *Mezzogriorno*—Campania, Puglia, Calabria, and Sicily—although the population of these four southern regions accounts for less than 30 percent of all Italians (Maffei and Betsos 2007).

Vast government spending in the *Mezzogiorno,* often on useless building projects that provide patronage opportunities, became a vehicle for Mafia infiltration. "By corruption and physical intimidation, Mafia-controlled firms took their share of public contracts, either directly or through subcontracts and dummy companies."

This approach has aided the spread of the Mafia phenomenon beyond its traditional areas "to towns and provinces that had once been free of organized crime. In many areas, democracy as we know it ceased to exist" (Stille 1993: 63). And the *mafioso* adds nothing of value to his environment: "Even in Medellín of the cocaine barons [discussed in Chapter 7], the Escobar clan and the Gavirias wanted an ultra-modern airport, a futuristic elevated metro system, and first-class hospitals. But in Cosa Nostra's Sicily, in the *'Ndrangheta's* Calabria, in the Camorra's Naples, yesterday's ragamuffins turned into today's gang bosses exploit without putting anything back in except the frills and fancies of fly-by-night consumerism" (Siebert 1996: 81)—and garbage.

Campania has become northern Italy's garbage dump where waste management firms controlled by the Camorra (Neapolitan mafia discussed later) arrange for the shipping of garbage, often toxic, from northern Italy and other European Union countries to illegal dump sites throughout the province. Campania has become so flooded with illegal exogenous trash that provincial waste must be shipped to Germany for disposal at great cost to local industry (Saviano 2007). Furthermore, fear of organized crime discourages business investment, and "although the Mafia's grip on Sicily has been visibly diminished, the island still suffers under the weight of poverty and unemployment" (Hundley 1998c: 5). Gangsterism also increases the cost of credit—4 percent more than in northern Italy—that serves the business interests of Mafia loan sharks (Bohlen 1997). At the end of 2007, Italy's largest cement company announced that it was closing its Sicilian operations rather than give in to Mafia demands for protection money.

The south "was brought into the Italian nation dragging its feet as the new government issued edict after edict that affected the southerners adversely" (Mangione and Morreale 1992: xv). This history led to the development of three different types of criminal organization. "The volatile urban criminality of the Neapolitan Camorra was very different from the old rural mafia's activities in the Sicilian hinterland, and the Calabrian *'Ndrangheta* was another thing again. But in each case a parasitic criminal class had inserted itself in the interstices between rulers and the ruled, exploiting both" (Robb 1996: 37). The Mafia—whose members refer to it as *Cosa Nostra*—and the *'Ndrangheta* "were an outgrowth of a section of the middle class which had been licensed to use violence by the ruling classes of the day and were founded on codes of honour, secrecy and silence." The Camorra was "an association of the poorest classes for whom crime was a means of survival and was neither secretive nor elitist." A fourth criminal organization, *Sacra Corona Unita*, is more recent, its expansion dating back to the 1970s because of "a desire by the other three criminal groups, at different times and for different motives, to have a consolidated criminal base on [the Italian] Apulia's long southeastern seaboard" (Jamieson 2000: 11).

THE SICILIAN MAFIA

The largest island in the Mediterranean Sea, Sicily lies almost at its center. As such, it was a bitterly fought over prize colonized by commercial powers: Greeks, Romans, Arabs, the Normans, and, during the Napoleonic Wars, the British. In the twelfth century, rule passed to a German dynasty, then to the French, the Austrians, and, finally, Spain under the Bourbons. "Until the nineteenth century, aristocratic families controlled Sicilian life more or less independently of whatever conqueror happened to be ruling at any given time" (Orlando 2001: 10). In 1860, Italy was freed of foreign rule and united by Giuseppe Garibaldi (1807–1882), but for the exploited Sicilians, little changed. Although his success was via Sicily and the *Mezzogiorno*, Garibaldi handed over all of his territorial gains to the king of Piedmont. Instead of foreigners, Sicily was ruled by Vittorio Emmanuel II of the House of Savoy, a monarch from northern Italy.

The new Italian state was unable to establish a monopoly over the use of force in Sicily and, instead, violence became democratized as a "whole range of men seized the opportunity to shoot and stab their way into the developing economy. . . . Officials complained that what they called these 'sects' or 'parties'—sometimes they were merely extended families with guns—were making many areas of Sicily ungovernable" (Dickie 2004: 58). Unwilling or unable to impose law and order, the government in Rome turned a blind eye through successive regimes as Mafia clans maintained a uniquely Sicilian form of order—brutal, at times protecting the property of the landed elite, at other times protecting outlaws (Schneider et al. 2005).

The government in Rome (the Italian capital had briefly been in Turin—home of the House of Savoy—and Florence) imposed a tax policy on the island that had the "overall effect of taking money out of Sicilian agriculture for investment in the north" (Finley, Smith, and Duggan 1987: 186). Landowners escaped heavy taxation, which fell disproportionately on the peasants (Catanzaro 1992). Eventually the aristocracy collapsed and the administration of their lands fell to middlemen called *gabelloti*, managers who had already gained the reputation of *uomi inteso*—"strong men" (Orlando 2001). The *gabelloto* ruled over the estate—*latifondo*—with brute force, protecting it from bandits, peasant organizations, and unions. He was assisted by *famiglia*, *amici* (friends), and *campieri* (lawfully armed mounted guards). The *campieri* were hired because they were *uomini di rispettu*, "men of respect," meaning they were quick to use violence and people feared them. An important—that is, widely feared—*campiere* could become a *gabelloto*. The *gabelloto* did not usually perform his overseer's functions in person—often he did not even show up on the estate that had been entrusted to his custody. "He simply allowed his name to be mentioned, with the declaration that the estate was under his protection" (Catanzaro 1992: 28). John Dickie (2004: 133) writes that "*Gabelloti* were such pivotal figures in Sicily's violent economy that it was often assumed that being a *mafioso* and being a *gabelloti* were the same thing. It is more accurate to say that joining the Mafia enabled a *gabelloto* to do his job better."

The *gabelloto* was a patron to his peasants who labored on the *latifondo*; he controlled access to scarce resources, in particular farming land, and he acted as a mediator between official power and government and the peasantry, a position he maintained by the exercise of force. In league with the landlords, he fought land reform, labor unions, and revolution (Servadio 1976). Peasants revolted in many parts of the *Mezzogiorno*, and an 1866 uprising in Palermo required an expeditionary force to quell it. "Such events soldered the alliance between the Mafia and aristocracy even more firmly" (Jamieson 2000: 12).

Headed by a *capomafioso*, each group of *mafiosi* is organized into a *cosca* (the plural is *cosche*) associated with a particular *mandamento* or district. "The mafia was outlaw, but tolerated, secret but recognizable, criminal but upholding of order. It protected and ripped off the owners of the great estates, protected and ripped off the sharecroppers who worked the estates, and ripped off the peasants who slaved on them" (Robb 1996: 48). *Mafiosi* also exploited the landowners who were forced to hire them, stealing as much as they could until the property could be purchased for an artificially low price. "Men with commercial or political ambitions

in Sicily were faced with two alternatives: either to arm themselves; or more likely, to buy protection from a specialist in violence, a *mafioso*" (Dickie 2004: 59).

Explanations of the term *mafia* come from Sicilian historical and literary works that link its root and meaning to elements prevailing within Sicilian culture: "The word *mafia* is apparently Sicilian-Arabic derived from terms meaning to protect and to act as guardian; a friend or companion; to defend; and preservation, power, integrity, strength, and a condition that designates the remedy of damage and ill." In sum, *mafia* means "protection against the arrogance of the powerful, remedy to any damage, sturdiness of body, strength and serenity of spirit, and the best and most exquisite part of life" (Inciardi 1975: 112–13).

Luigi Barzini (1965: 253) separates *mafia* as a state of mind from Mafia as an illegal secret organization. The former (*mafia*) is shared by all Sicilians, the honest and the criminal: that "they must aid each other, side with their friends, and fight the common enemies even when the friends are wrong and the enemies are right; each must defend his dignity at all costs and never allow the smallest slight to go unavenged; they must keep secrets and beware of official authorities and laws." The anti-Mafia Sicilian author Leonardo Sciascia notes the dichotomy: "When I denounce the *mafia*, at the same time I suffer, since in me, as in any Sicilian, there are still present and vibrant the residues of feeling *mafioso*. So by struggling against the *mafia* I also struggle against myself" (quoted in Siebert 1996: 57).

Barzini points out that the two (Mafia and *mafia*) are closely related, that Mafia could not flourish without *mafia*, which represents a general attitude toward the state: "A *mafioso* did not invoke State or law in his private quarrels, but made himself respected and safe by winning a reputation for toughness and courage, and settled his differences by fighting. He recognized no obligation except those of the code of honor or *omertá* (manliness), whose chief article forbade giving information to the public authorities" (Hobsbawm 1976: 92). As a nineteenth-century observer notes, the *mafioso* dresses modestly; his manner of speech is the same. When confronted with a greater power, he "makes himself seem naïve, stupidly attentive to what you are saying. He endures insults and slaps with patience. Then, the same evening, he shoots you" (Giuseppe Alongi quoted in Dickie 2004: 85). Or, he will wait patiently for months or for years for an opportunity to avenge humiliation and thereby makes himself unconquerable.

Because kinship can strengthen cohesion, sons, brothers, nephews, and other relatives are frequently admitted to *cosca* membership. In Mafia families it is almost obligatory for boys to consider a criminal career. But there is also a matter of talent. If a *mafioso's* son lacks the *fegato* (guts), he is allowed to go his own way (Schneider et al. 2005). Familial ties, however, can conflict with members' obligation of obedience to the *capomafioso*. "So Mafiosi are sometimes forced to show in dramatic fashion where their loyalty ultimately lies"; they are offered a choice: Kill a relative or die with him (Dickie 2004: 80). Some *cosche* have rules against too many relatives (Schneider et al. 2005).

In southern Italy an ethos of mistrust and suspicion pervades personal and business relationships—a dilemma the *mafioso* can overcome by offering himself as a guarantor (Putnam 1993). In Mafia areas the issue is never who is "right" and who is "wrong." Instead, "preference tended to be given to whichever party proved victorious in the end, irrespective of the original conflict" (Arlacchi 1986: 13). Thus, in Mafia areas, at bottom nothing could really be unjust, and honor "was connected less with justice than with domination and physical strength": a Hobbesian world ruled by the credo "might is right." The *mafioso* brought order, albeit in a conservative if not reactionary form, and dispensed primitive justice in a lawless society. *Mafiosi* were frequently not only tolerated by their communities but "respected to the point where they could parade as standard bearers of a more equitable system of justice than that provided by the state" (Finley, Smith, and Duggan 1987: 157).

Every *mafioso* demands *rispetto*, indeed, is referred to as a *uomo di rispetto*—a man worthy of respect. American *mafioso* Bill Bonanno (1999: xiii) points out that this "respect has nothing to do with affection or even with a show of good manners. It is

an acknowledgement of power" that Cesare Mori notes requires a concrete recognition of the prerogative of immunity belonging to the *mafioso*, not only in his person, but also in everything that he had to do with or that he was pleased to take under his protection. Thus, "evildoers had to leave the *mafioso* severely alone, and all the persons or things to which, explicitly or implicitly, he had given a guarantee of security." As a man of respect, "the *mafioso* is in a position to provide protection where the state is unwilling or unable; to provide arbitration services superior to those available from local judges, especially to the poor person who cannot afford a lawyer, or for those whose justice is of a social, not a legal, nature—the pregnant daughter whose seducer refuses to marry." The *mafioso*, and in particular the *capomafioso*, can put it all right, and his services are speedy and final (Mori 1933: 69).

These "services" are the essence of *mafia*—the *mafioso* is a provider of protection broadly defined. For legitimate entrepreneurs he provides insurance against otherwise untrustworthy suppliers or customers and will limit competition by restricting market entry. He acts as a guarantor so that persons who do not trust one another can transact business with a significant degree of confidence; this refers to legitimate entrepreneurs and, most particularly, the illegitimate, who cannot turn to the police or courts to remedy their grievances.[1] A *mafioso* engaged in a legitimate business enjoys advantages over other businessmen: Potential competitors are likely to be deterred, and criminals will give his enterprise a wide berth (Gambetta 1993).[2]

"The constitutional state and elected parliament that accompanied Sicily's union with Italy provided a crucial step in the rise to power of the Mafia—Sicily's special kind of middle class" (Servadio 1976: 17). "With an electorate of little more than 1 percent, the landlords and their friends

---

[1] In later chapters we will see instances of the crucial "service" role played by members of American organized crime in the private waste-hauling and construction industries, as well as in New York's major wholesale fish market.

[2] Inspiring fear without a direct threat is a valuable asset, one that was used quite successfully by the Gambino brothers in New York's garment center, discussed in Chapter 14.

and employees [*mafiosi*] were often the only voters. If there was any doubt about the result of an election, intimidation was usually effective" (Finley, Smith, and Duggan 1987: 183). In 1912, universal male suffrage was introduced and because of its ability to control elections, the Mafia was courted by political powers in Rome. The "Mafia became the only electoral force that counted in Sicily and the government was realistic in acceptance of the fact" (Lewis 1964: 41). The situation remained unchanged until the rise of Benito Mussolini and the Fascist state.

MUSSOLINI AND THE MAFIA

Mussolini's rise to power in the 1920s had important implications for both the Sicilian and American Mafia. Although the south resisted fascism, "once it became clear that the Fascists would obtain a major share in national power, the entire south became Fascist almost overnight" (Chubb 1982: 25). "The mafia had always known how to cozy up to those in power" (Robb 1996: 48). The impact of the Mafia can be seen by comparing the elections of 1922, when no Fascist was elected to Parliament from Sicily, with the elections of 1924, when thirty-eight Fascists were elected out of the fifty-seven representatives from Sicily (Servadio 1976).

Mussolini, known as *Il Duce*, visited Sicily in 1924 and was introduced to Ciccio Cuccia, a *capomafioso* who was also a local mayor. Don Ciccio[3] accompanied *Il Duce* on a tour and, after seeing the large number of police officers guarding him, is reputed to have said: "You're with me, so there's nothing to worry about" (Lewis 1964). To Don Ciccio, the large police escort indicated a lack of *rispetto*. When Mussolini declined to discharge the police contingent, the *capomafioso* arranged for the town piazza to be empty when *Il Duce* made his speech: "When Mussolini began his harangue he found himself addressing a group of about

20 village idiots, one-legged beggars, bootblacks, and lottery-ticket sellers specially picked by Don Ciccio to form an audience" (Lewis 1964: 72).

A totalitarian regime does not tolerate pockets of authority that are not under its control, and Mussolini quickly moved to destroy the Mafia. Elections were abolished in 1925, depriving the Mafia of its major instrument of alliance with government and an important basis for its immunity from criminal justice. The other important basis was intimidation. However, "Fascist courts trying criminal cases in which members of the Mafia were implicated found it just as impossible to obtain convictions as it had been for the democratic courts of old" (Lewis 1964: 68). Mussolini responded by investing Prefect Cesare Mori of Lombardy, a career police officer, with emergency police powers and sending him after the Mafia. (Christopher Duggan [1989] stresses general lawlessness in western Sicily and a request by a delegation of war veterans as the bases for Mussolini's intervention.)

Mori assembled a small army of agents and set about the task of purging the island of *mafiosi*. "Under the jurisdiction of Prefect Mori, repression became savage. Many *mafiosi* were sent to prison, killed or tortured, but also many left-wingers were called '*mafiosi*' for the occasion, and were disposed of.... In many cases the landowners provided Mori with information against the *mafiosi* they had so far employed, who had been their means to safeguard their interests against the peasantry. This was logical because they saw that the regime would provide a better and cheaper substitute" (Servadio 1976: 74). Thus, the Fascists replaced the Mafia as intermediaries and maintainers of Sicilian law and order.

Mori swooped down on villages and with the free application of torture reminiscent of the Inquisition arrested 11,000 persons, not all of them *mafiosi* (Dickie 2004). He arrested such powerful *capomafiosi* as Don Vito Casio-Ferro and Don Ciccio Cuccia. *Gabelloti* were required to swear an oath of allegiance to the government, and in 1928, Mori declared that the Mafia had been destroyed. However, the reality was otherwise, and the Mafia began to reassert itself by 1941.

---

[3]The appellation *Don* is an honorific title used in Sicily to refer to clergymen, government officials, and important *mafiosi*. It derives from the Latin *dominus*, "lord," and is used with the person's first given name.

Many Mafia bosses assumed important positions within the regime, and the Fascists failed to significantly transform social and economic conditions upon which the Mafia depended. When Mori began to investigate the connection between the Mafia and high-level Fascists, he was forced into retirement (Orlando 2001). "It was no surprise that the Mafia rapidly reemerged as soon as fascism fell" (Chubb 1982: 27). Many *mafiosi* awaited "liberation," which came in the form of the Allied landing in 1943. The campaign against the Mafia did succeed in driving some important *mafiosi* out of Sicily. They traveled to the United States at an opportune time, during the Prohibition era, and took up important positions in a newly emerging form of organized crime. The end of World War II led to a Mafia Renaissance out of which the *Nuovo Mafia*—a "new" Mafia—emerged.

NUOVO MAFIA/COSA NOSTRA

World War II had negative consequences for southern Italy, blocking the northward migration of excess labor (Catanzaro 1992). The end of the war brought a Mafia renaissance in Sicily as a vacuum in local leadership was filled by former *capomafiosi*: "Not only were they respected local figures, but as victims of Mori's operation against the mafia they were also in a good position to pose as antifascists" (Finley, Smith, and Duggan 1987: 214). Many *mafiosi* became town mayors under the Allied military government, and they violently thwarted the efforts of trade unionists, socialists, communists, and land reformers (Catanzaro 1992; Costanzo 2007; Robb 1996). A brief flirtation with Separatism—seceding from the mainland in favor of affiliation with the United States—was discarded in 1946 when the government in Rome announced Sicilian autonomy. In return, the most important *capomafioso*, Calògero Vizzini ("Don Calò"), the illiterate son of a peasant father, pledged support for the Christian Democratic Party (CDP) that would hold power in Italy for almost five decades. In return, *capomafiosi* were frequently accorded places of honor in the party, and "it was not uncommon for prominent politicians to appear as honored guests at the christenings, weddings, and funerals of major Mafia figures. In Sicily, being known as a friend of a *mafioso* was not a sign of shame but of power" (Stille 1995a: 20); it advertised the solidarity of the alliance between official power and the informal power of the Mafia (Dickie 2004).

Born in 1877, Don Calò was imprisoned by Mussolini. Vizzini spent only a few days in prison before being released through the intervention of a young Fascist he had befriended. Vizzini was now a *gabelloto* and mayor of Villalba, and he "would hold court each morning in the small plaza of Villalba. People would approach him for favours, such as help with a bank loan or assistance with a court case—indeed anything in which 'authority' could be useful" (Duggan 1989: 67). As an "anti-Fascist," he possessed a special business license from the Allied military government. This allowed him to head up a flourishing black market in olive oil. In this endeavor Vizzini worked with American expatriate Vito Genovese (Lewis 1964).

When Don Calò died of natural causes in 1954, he left an estate reputed to be worth several million dollars (Pantaleone 1966). He was the last of the old-style *capomafiosi*, characterized by modesty in both speech and dress: "The old Mafia chief was a rural animal, holding sway over the countryside, dressed in shirt-sleeves and baggy pants: a multimillionaire who chose to look like a peasant" (Servadio 1974: 21). Actually, notes Pino Arlacchi (1986), the behavior of the old *mafioso* had power—*rispetto*—as its primary goal. The modern *mafioso*, however, is a materialist for whom power is simply a means to achieve wealth; and he exudes conspicuous consumption. The new *mafioso* is not bound by the traditions of the rural *cosca*. He dresses like a successful businessman, sometimes a bit flashy, like the American gangster whose pattern he seems to have adopted—cross-fertilization. The New Mafia—called *Cosa Nostra* by its members—has a distinctly American tint, the result of American gangsters being deported to Sicily, "where they immediately assumed leading positions in the Mafia hierarchy of the island" (Lewis 1964: 273).

Initially, *Cosa Nostra* resorted to robbery and kidnapping to accumulate the capital necessary to be a player in legal endeavors such as the construction industry and in the illicit heroin and cocaine marketplaces. Drug money changed the functioning and mode of organization of the Mafia in which luxury and extravagant consumerism has become the norm (Siebert 1996). The New Mafia has also continued the *pizzo*, protection money extorted from large and small businesses (Cowell 1992b). But financial considerations reportedly play a secondary role in this enterprise, being primarily a Mafia way of maintaining territorial domination (Stille 1993): "While managing millions and operating on a grand scale, he [a *mafioso*] does not slacken his hold over the corner butcher's shop. Not so much for the sake of money perhaps, as to demonstrate the permanence of his power" (Siebert 1996: 123).

Agrarian reform broke up the landed estates and did away with the traditional *capomafioso* who lived off agricultural profits, theft of cattle, control over water supplies, and peasant labor. "The new Mafia was making deals in luxury hotels, in the offices of multinational corporations, and the well-appointed studies of politicians" (Costanzo 2007: 139). The contrast between the "Two Mafias" is evidenced by a conflict between the *capomafiosi* of Corleone in the immediate postwar years. Michele Navarra was a medical doctor and (despite his education) a representative of the Old Mafia. Luciano Leggio (which the police misspelled Liggio), born in 1925, represented the New Mafia. At the age of 19, Leggio became the youngest *gabelloto* in the history of Sicily (his predecessor was murdered). Navarra was the inspector of health for the area, and head of the town's only hospital (his predecessor was also mysteriously murdered). In the tradition of Don Calò, he was a political power who served as chairman of the local branch of the Christian Democratic Party. The doctor also trafficked in stolen beef. Leggio was his most violent assistant. Leggio and an associate hanged a trade unionist who was a threat to Navarra's power, and the murder was witnessed by a shepherd boy. In a state of shock after telling his story, the boy fainted and was taken to the hospital. There, an injection from the "good doctor" ended the boy's life (Servadio 1976). Navarra was convicted of the murder. Although he was sentenced to five years' exile in Calabria, he returned home after a few months (Robb 1996).

With his followers, Leggio began to develop activities of his own. However, the Leggio group "had nothing in common with the organization presided over by Don Calò but its iron laws of secrecy and the vendetta" (Lewis 1964: 123). Leggio chose to control the supply of meat to the Palermo market rather than raising livestock. He drove out all of the tenant farmers on the estate under his protection, burning down their houses, and replaced them with day laborers. He recruited gunmen, and anybody who crossed him was summarily shot. From 1953 to 1958 there were 153 recorded Mafia murders in the Corleone area (Servadio 1976). According to one source (Mangione 1985: 147), Leggio was connected to organized crime in the United States and "had been a key contact man working closely with Joseph Profaci of the American Mafia."

The Old Mafia benefited from feudal conditions, living off control of the land, and cheap labor. When a dam was proposed for the town of Corleone to harness the river water flowing to the ocean, Dr. Navarra vetoed it because he made money from the water pumped from artesian wells. *Cosa Nostra*, oriented toward capitalistic change, recognized the profits that could be earned from control over building projects, although this dam has yet to be built. Navarra and his followers were living in the nineteenth century, but Leggio was a man of the times. With Navarra in control, nothing would change, and the New Mafia recognized this reality (Lewis 1964). In 1958, fifteen of Leggio's men ambushed Dr. Navarra's car; 210 bullets were found in his body. One by one, the remaining followers of Navarra were murdered and Leggio became the undisputed *capomafioso* of the Corleonesi *cosca* (Servadio 1976).

During the 1960s, the emerging *cosche* engaged in a bitter struggle for dominance. The struggle between Mafia clans led to an emigration of *mafiosi* similar to that experienced during the reign of Mussolini. This proved to be quite beneficial as these overseas *mafiosi* provided the links for greater international operations. The Mafia connection to the cocaine trade is largely a result of this diaspora (Williams 1995a, 1995b).

In 1967, the Mafia war led to the trial of 114 *mafiosi*, and Leggio emerged as the most powerful *capomafioso* (Shawcross and Young 1987). In 1974, Leggio was convicted of the murder of Dr. Navarra and sentenced to life imprisonment; he died in prison in 1993. Leggio's right-hand man, Salvatore (Totò) Riina, became head of the Corleone *cosca*. A short, stocky man, the son of poor farmers with only a elementary school education, Riina is known as *La Belva*—"The Beast"—for ordering mass killings and personally participating in some of them. He built a secret army by initiating men without informing other Mafia leaders (Dickie 2004). Riina formed private alliances with rising members of many *cosche*, planted his own men in others, and then with a reign of terror came to dominate the Mafia—at a cost of nearly one thousand lives (Robb 1996; Stille 1993, 1995a). "Rather than wage a street war like the previous Mafia conflict of the 1960s, Riina worked to peel away supporters from his rivals' forces, letting them see the inevitability of the Corleonesi" (Orlando 2001: 67). Many members of his *cosca* are close relatives, including his son and nephew.

After being tried in absentia and sentenced to life imprisonment for murder and drug trafficking, Riina became the most wanted man in Italy. He was able to avoid authorities for more than 23 years, partly because photographs of him were out of date. While living as a fugitive, Riina married the sister of a powerful *mafioso* in a ceremony performed by a Mafia priest (who was eventually defrocked), honeymooned in Venice, sired four children, and continued to oversee the activities of his Mafia clan (Robb 1996).

One of the victims of Riina's campaign to centralize and control the Mafia was *capomafioso* Tommaso Buscetta, who lost ten relatives, including two sons, a brother, a nephew, a son-in-law, and two brothers-in-law. In 1995, another Buscetta relative, his 45-year-old nephew, was murdered in Palermo (Bohlen 1995a). In 1983,

Buscetta, who had escaped to Brazil, was arrested on an international warrant. He attempted to commit suicide with a strychnine pill. When he recovered, Buscetta agreed to cooperate with American and Italian authorities.[4] In 1987, with the help of Buscetta and other informants, the Italian government convicted almost 600 *mafiosi* in the largest mass trial (706 defendants—referred to as the maxitrial) of its kind ever held in Italy (Paoli 2003). Paralleling events in the United States, a breakdown in the Mafia code of silence caused hundreds of *mafiosi* (*pentiti*) to cooperate with the government.

POLITICS AND THE MAFIA

Mafia voting strength is based on the circle of family and friends that each *mafioso* can deliver—as many as forty to fifty votes (Arlacchi 1993). In Sicily, at least 500,000 persons (out of a population of 5 million) are directly tied to the Mafia (Cowell 1992f). The Mafia is able to control votes because in the environment in which it operates there is always fear of reprisals. Intimidation, surveillance of polling places, and sometimes rigged elections guarantee an outcome favorable to Mafia candidates. But frequently outright intimidation is unnecessary. In the absence of political enthusiasm and voter passion, a cynical view prevails. Instead of signifying a preference among competing political ideas, the vote simply indicates support for a clientelistic group. The leveling of political traditions and an absence ideology among the political parties leads voters almost naturally, without any forcing, to respect the "marching orders" given by the Mafia (della Porta and Vannucci 1999). In 2008, the governor of Sicily was sentenced to five years' imprisonment for providing a Mafia boss with confidential information—while being tried he was reelected.

In 1987, angry over the government's maxitrial, the fugitive *capo di tutti capi* Totò Riina ordered a switch in votes: The Christian Democrats increased their strength throughout the

---

[4]Buscetta died of cancer in 2000.

Economic Determinism

"A state relegated to purely economic functions has not only failed to produce a culture of legality, but has favored the culture of partiality, of doing favors for a friend, of trading interests, of ignoring the law—of promoting Mafia-type crime. In effect, the State in certain regions of Southern Italy is merely perceived as an economic entity, solely concerned with assistance and patron-client matters. All the institutions have been utterly relegated and no authority, even of a moral nature, attaches to them" (Argentine 1993: 21). Similar arguments could be made about the former Soviet Union discussed in Chapter 10.

Governing Italy

It is said that Italy's curse is to be the home of three world powers: the Italian government, the Catholic Church, and the Mafia, of which the government is the feeblest (Bohlen 1995d). This is reflected in the collecting of taxes. "While the economy of Italy has changed dramatically since the end of World War II, from an agriculturally based economy into an industrial state ranking as the world's sixth-largest market economy, Italy has an underground economy worth some 27 percent of its gross domestic product not subject to taxation" (Maffei and Betsos 2007: 462).

American versus Italian Mafia

"The American Mafia is a parasitic phenomenon operating at the margins of society. The Mafia of southern Italy plays a central role in almost every phase of economic and political life" (Stille 1993: 63).

---

rest of Italy, but in Palermo only Mafia-backed candidates won (Robb 1996). In 1992, the Mafia murdered the Sicilian head of the Christian Democratic Party in a Palermo suburb; it was his job to keep peace between the party and the Mafia. "This was the Mafia's way of announcing that it was 'renegotiating' its arrangement with the Prime Minister" (Cowell 1992f; Kramer 1992: 112). It appears that Totò Riina remained furious at the Christian Democrats for not intervening in the Mafia maxitrial (della Porta and Vannucci 1999).

Since the end of World War II, the CDP had ruled Italy, and "the party's bedrock . . . was the *mezzogiorno* and especially the *friends* in Sicily" (Robb 1996: 22). By 1993, increasing scandal and the collapse of European communism finally led to the demise of the CDP, which, despite its corruption[5] and ties to the Mafia, had been the only viable alternative to the Communist Party[6] (Stille 1993). The most powerful Christian Democrat in Sicily was Salvo Lima, the former *mafioso* mayor of Palermo who later became a deputy minister in Rome and a member of the European parliament. When Lima entered a restaurant in Palermo, people fell silent and kissed his hand. However, when scandal drove the Christian Democrats from power, Lima was no longer of use to the *friends*—he was gunned down by a man riding on the back of a motorbike (Robb 1996).

---

[5]For an examination of political corruption in Italy, see della Porta and Vannucci (1999) and Orlando (2001).

[6]In 1991, the Italian Communist Party, the most powerful in Europe, reorganized itself as the Democratic Party of the Left, social democrats seeking mainstream support (Burnett and Mantovani 1998).

THE STRUCTURE OF THE MAFIA

At the center of the Mafia is the *padrino* or *capomafioso*, around whom other *mafiosi* gather, forming a *cosca*. The word *cosca* refers to the leaves of an artichoke, the *capomafioso* being the globe's heart. The structure consists of a network of two-man, that is, patron-client, relationships based on kinship, patronage, and friendship (Catanzaro 1992). The typical *cosca* rarely has more than fifteen or twenty members, and at the center are four or five blood relatives (Arlacchi 1986). The *cosca* is devoid of any rigid organization; it is simply *gli amici degli amici*—"friends of friends." The members are *gli uomini qualificati* ("qualified men"). Flexibility prevents the *cosca* from becoming bureaucratic: "The need continually to broaden the scope of the networks of social relationships reinforced the impossibility of creating stable organizational structures" (Catanzaro 1992: 40). The *mafioso* succeeds because he commands a *partito*, a network of relationships whereby he is able to act as an intermediary—a broker—providing services, which include votes and violence for the holders of institutionalized power. All he requests in return is immunity to carry out his activities (Hess 1973). He serves as a guarantor for price rigging and collusive bidding on building projects: "Any businessman who defects from the collusive agreement or refuses to take part in it, exposes himself to violent retaliation from a Mafia protector" (della Porta and Vannucci 1999: 229).

Standardized rituals around the Mafia developed in the 1870s (Hobsbawm 1976). The initiation ceremony is similar to that used by American Mafia Families discussed in Chapter 4 (Schneider et al. 2005). *Carabinieri* (national paramilitary police) reports from the early Mussolini era reveal that the "Mafia had already become a secret organization, structured in the form of clans or *cosche* and divided by sector or activity and geographical area" (Jamieson 2000: 14). Once initiated into the *cosca*, the *mafioso* became a *compadre*, a practice based on the custom of *comparático* (fictional kinship or godparenthood). A ceremony of affiliation creates ritual ties of brotherhood among the members of a *cosca*. Once initiated each becomes a brother to all other members with whom they share an obligation of mutual aid without limits and without measure. Thanks to the trust and solidarity created by fraternization, it becomes possible to pursue the personal interests of the members through collective action (Paoli 2001). When the *cosca* initiates a novice, he assumes an identity as a "man of honor" and subordinates all previous allegiances, even blood ties (Paoli 2003).

The remnants of preunification power in western Sicily[7]—*gabelloti*, *campieri*, and in some instances clergymen—formed the *cosche* (plural of *cosca*). Each village has its own *cosca*, larger ones have more, and collectively they are the Mafia. Barzini (1965) delineates four levels of organization that constitute the Mafia. The first, the *famiglia*, constitutes the nucleus. Some families, he notes, have belonged to the *societá degli amici* for generations, each *padrino* bequeathing the family to his eldest son. The second level consists of a group of several families who come together to form a *cosca*; one family and its *padrino* are recognized as supreme. In the third level, the *cosca* establishes working relationships with other *cosche*, respecting territories and boundaries. The fourth level is achieved when *cosche* join in an alliance called *consorteria*, in which one *cosca* is recognized as supreme and its leader is the leader of the *consorteria*—*capo di tutti capi*, the boss of all bosses. "This happens spontaneously . . . when the *cosche* realize that one of them is more powerful, has more men, more friends, more money, more high-ranking protectors. . . . All the *consorterie* in Sicily . . . form the *onerata societá*, a solidarity that unites all *mafiosi*; they know they owe all possible support to any *amico degli amici* who needs it . . . even if they have never heard of him, provided he is introduced by a mutual *amico*" (Barzini 1965: 272).

The New Mafia has a membership in excess of 5,000, each with his own network—a circle of dozens of relatives, friends, associates, and employees—divided into about 180 *cosche* (de Gennaro 1995; Jamieson 2000; Stille 1993). Each

---

[7]The eastern half of the island did not have a Mafia Family until 1925 (Arlacchi 1993). According to Paoli (2003), a fully developed *cosca* did not develop there until the 1970s.

cosca is held together by a core of blood relatives and encompasses a membership of twenty-five to thirty persons (Argentine 1993; Arlacchi 1986). The *cosche* form alliances that are sealed through marriage: "Such is the strategic significance of marriages for the structure of the criminal organization and the arrangement of alliances between the different cells, that by following the trail of weddings, christenings and confirmations, the judges [in the 1986–1987 Mafia maxitrial] managed to gather information about internal changes within the organization" (Siebert 1996: 29).

Capomafioso-turned-informer Buscetta describes the *cosca* as hierarchical, with elected leaders[8] and precise decision-making processes. Each *cosca* takes its name from the territory under its control, and is composed of *uomini d'onore* ("men of honor") in numbers varying from ten to one hundred. They are organized into groups of ten (*decina*) headed by a *capodecina*. Above the *capidecina* is the *capofamiglia* who has a deputy and a few advisors. Three or more families with adjoining territories are represented by *capimandamenti* who are members of the *cupola* or commission. This central directorate of the Mafia is headed by a commission *capo* who oversees the activities of the organization on a provincial level. More recent reports (for example, Jamieson 2000) indicate that the Mafia has become less hierarchical and more impermeable with small, tightly structured cells that, like those of Colombian organizations (discussed in Chapter 7), have a membership that is unknown to all but a few persons. There is greater internal secrecy and selectivity in recruitment, an increased tendency to favor family members to reduce the likelihood of informants, a strategy long-favored by the *'Ndrangheta*. In contrast with crime Families in the United States, many Mafia and *'Ndrangheta* chieftains provide their members with salaries, and there is a common fund to deal with legal expenses to support the families of imprisoned members (Paoli 2003).

According to a *capomafioso* turned *pentiti* (repentant—an informer), "men of honor become such in large part through heredity, but not in the same way as the aristocracy, where the father leaves his title to his son. In the *mafia* it's more complicated. There's observation, a study of the best young men by the oldest ones. The most senior *mafiosi*—friends of the father, relatives of the mother—watch the young ones, some of whom come to stand out from the others. . . . When one of them distinguishes himself because he's clever, determined, and ruthless, he is cultivated, encouraged by adult men of honor who teach and guide him, and if he follows them they start to let him do a few things" (quoted in Arlacchi 1993: 21).

Despite its weakened condition, the pool of Mafia prospects remains strong, the result of an unemployment rate approaching 60 percent among the young of Sicily (Stanley 1998). But since the capture of Riina, the Mafia operates with a much lower public profile, and new initiates are from families with long-established Mafia histories (Dickie 2004).

DECLINE OF THE MAFIA

As the political role of *mafiosi* changed, so too did their ability to act as brokers between peasant and officialdom. The *mafioso* was no longer *un uomo di*

---

[8]Catanzaro (1992) discounts the "electoral procedure" because it is not used to decide between two or more contenders, but simply to confirm the single contender for leadership.

rispetto but simply an urban gangster in the American tradition, that is, a predatory criminal without popular roots or popular backing. The New Mafia reflects the emerging *Mezzogiorno*. The south is changing; modernization, fed by government-sponsored public works, is slowly encroaching on feudal ways. Above all, the mark of respect has more to do with one's wealth than with one's name or reputation. It was power, not wealth, that the traditional *mafioso* pursued: "The possession of wealth, regarded by the traditional *mafioso* as one among the proofs and results of a man's capacity to make himself respected, becomes, in the 1960s and 1970s, meritorious in itself." Family wealth, not family honor, is a reason for violence: "Wealth, in a word, becomes intrinsically honourable and confers honour on its possessors" (Arlacchi 1986: 60).

Since 1971, the *Nuovo Mafia* has assassinated investigative, judicial, and political officials, something that was anathema to the old Mafia: "Offenses against symbols of authority were foreign to the methods of a Mafia that, considering itself an authority and surrogate for the state, wanted to preserve and respect certain values" (Kamm 1982b: E3). Indeed, "the *mafioso* customarily collaborated with the justice system. In fact, he would often appear before those who accused him of illicit activities as an honest citizen who helped bring the true outlaws to justice, claiming it was to his credit that order reigned in his community" (Catanzaro 1992: 24). As the Mafia was reduced to a marginal role in society, many *mafiosi* reacted in a manner similar to other marginalized persons. They pursued wealth as the only way back to honor and power, and Mafia violence as a result of economic competition polluted the Sicilian political system (Arlacchi 1986; Catanzaro 1992). Across southern Italy, the government dissolved dozens of town councils because of their corrupt relationships with Mafia, Camorra, and *'Ndrangheta* clans (Jamieson 2000).

Following the assassinations of government officials, the New Mafia lost the support of important elements of Italian society. In 1982, Salvatore Cardinal Pappalardo, the Sicilian-born archbishop of Palermo, led Sicilian priests "in a vocal campaign against the Mafia, reversing decades of church indifference toward and even tolerance of local dons"[9] (Withers 1982: 5). Later that year, while on a visit to the island of Sicily, Pope John Paul II issued an attack on the Mafia. And since 1983, Palermo has elected and reelected an anti-Mafia mayor. In 1993, the Mafia struck back at its critics in the Church: A 56-year-old priest who spoke out against the Mafia was shot to death in front of his rectory in a Palermo slum[10] (Orlando 2001). And as part of its campaign of terror, the Mafia bombed two of Rome's most venerable churches, in addition to other bombings in Rome, Milan, and Florence that killed ten people and left dozens injured (Bohlen 1996c). In 1993, the Mafia bombed the world-famous Uffizi gallery in Florence, killing five persons and causing extensive damage (Bohlen 1995c).

In 1992, the prosecutor who helped gather evidence for the Mafia maxitrial, Judge Giovanni Falcone, was killed, along with his wife and three bodyguards, when a half-ton of TNT was detonated by remote control on a road near Palermo.[11] The killers obviously had inside information about Falcone's movements. His murder led to an anti-Mafia demonstration by about 40,000 persons in Palermo, a remarkable occurrence for that city (Cowell 1992a). But it did not prevent the Mafia from striking again. Later that year, Paolo Borsellino, Falcone's replacement as Palermo's chief public prosecutor and head of a new anti-Mafia superagency, was killed along with five police bodyguards; 175 pounds of a Czech-made plastic explosive placed under a car was detonated while Borsellino was walking outside an apartment building where his mother and sister resided (Cowell 1992d).

The government responded by dispatching 7,000 troops to Sicily in a highly publicized anti-Mafia campaign, and Palermo reelected a crusading anti-Mafia mayor (Hundley 1998a). The

---

[9]At times the Church-Mafia relationship was symbiotic, and some clergy were *mafiosi* (see, for example, Gambetta 1993: 48–52).

[10]In 1994, a priest who had spoken out against the Camorra was killed by two gunmen in his church north of Naples (Cowell 1994).

[11]For an examination of his anti-Mafia activities and the events surrounding Judge Falcone's assassination, see Stille (1995a). For an analysis of anti-Mafia activities in Italy, see Jamieson (2000).

soldiers were withdrawn in 1998: Italy, which had recently been admitted to the European monetary union, wanted to shed the image of a nation that needs a peacekeeping force occupying its own territory (Stanley 1998). The day after troops were withdrawn, the police arrested scores of *mafiosi*, including twenty members of the Corleone *cosca*, whose boss was already in custody (Associated Press 1998a). And there have been dramatic results: Murders in Palermo, which averaged 130 to 140 annually, fell to fewer than ten in 1997 (Hundley 1998a). As a sign of the Mafia's weakness, in 1999, the president of Italy led an anti-Mafia demonstration in the notorious city of Corleone on a day dedicated to victims of the Mafia (Reuters 1999).

The violence that gained Don Totò Riina his nickname also drove *mafiosi* seeking protection from "the Beast" to the authorities (Cowell 1992e, 1993a). In 1992, Italy enacted a witness protection law. The cooperation of *mafiosi* is believed to

be behind the capture of the 62-year-old Riina, arrested in his car on a Palermo street at the beginning of 1993. He and his driver were unarmed. Later that year, Riina was ordered imprisoned for life by a Palermo court, and officials confiscated about $300 million worth of his property (Dickie 2004). Like Palermo, his home city of Corleone elected an anti-Mafia mayor. Officials arrested other leading *mafiosi*, including the boss of eastern Sicily, Riina's heir apparent, who had been a fugitive for 11 years; the heads of the Camorra and 'Ndrangheta and hundreds of their followers were also arrested. As a result, a sharp decrease in Mafia killings has been recorded in Palermo and the rest of Sicily (Maffei and Betsos 2007).

Riina was replaced as the "boss of bosses" by Bernardo Provenzano, known as "The Tractor," a fugitive who had eluded authorities for more than 40 years (Horowitz 2005). Despite only a third-grade education, he is reputed to have ironed out

In 2007, a policewoman looks at dozens of photos of alleged members of a Mafia syndicate arrested in an anti-Mafia round-up called "Occidente" (West) in Palermo, the capital city of Sicily, Italy.

© AP/Wide World Photos

internal rivalries among Mafia bosses to more efficiently divide up illegal bidding for public-works contracts (Isrealy 2004; Povoledo 2006). Provenzano, 73, was apprehended on a farm near Corleone in 2006 and replaced by another fugitive, Salvatore Lo Piccolo. On November 5, 2007, Lo Piccolo, 65, was arrested at a Mafia meeting just outside of Palermo; he had been on the run from a life sentence for murder since 1993. Also arrested was his son Sandro, 32, also a fugitive from a life sentence since 1998. Symbolically, the arrests took place on Italy's national day of mourning for Mafia victims (Povoledo 2007).

Excesses at home, the vigorous government response, and the increasing number of inform-ers have weakened the Mafia. This fact and the emerging role of women in the *Mezzogiorno* have led to the rise of women to prominent positions in organized crime, most notably in Naples but also in the Sicilian Mafia where they have replaced their imprisoned husbands (Hundley 1998c; Stanley 2001).[12]

THE NEAPOLITAN CAMORRA[13]

Whereas the Mafia began as more of an idea than an organization and evolved along cultural lines in western Sicily, the Camorra was deliberately structured as a criminal society. The term *Camorra* is believed to have derived from the Castilian *kamora*, meaning "contestation," and to have been imported into Naples during the years of Spanish domination (Serao 1911a). Ernest Serao reports that the forbears of the Neapolitan Camorra were the Spanish brigands of the Sierras known as the *gamuri* (1911a: 723): "Not a passer-by nor a vehicle escaped their watchful eye and their fierce claws, so that traveling or going from one place to another on business was impossible for anyone without sharing with the ferocious watchers of

the Sierras either the money he had with him or the profits of the business that had taken him on his journey."

Although there are several versions of how the term *Camorra* came into being (Walston 1986), it seems clear that the Camorra as an organization developed in Spanish prisons during the Bour-bon rule of the Two Sicilies (the *Mezzogiorno*) early in the nineteenth century. The members of this criminal society eventually moved their control of the prisons into Naples proper. They were "rather tightly, centrally, and hierarchically organized" (Hobsbawm 1959: 55). The Camorra "was organized as openly and carefully as a pub-lic school system, or an efficient political machine in one of our own cities. Naples was divided into twelve districts, and each of these into a number of sub-districts. Although burglary and other remu-nerative felonies were not neglected, extortion was the principal industry; and the assassination of an inconvenient person could be purchased by any-one with the price. In the case of a friend in need, a murder could be arranged without any charge—a simple gesture of affection" (McConaughy 1931: 244).

One English diplomat in Naples during the 1860s observed:

> There was no class, high or low, that did not have its representatives among the mem-bers of the Society that was a vast organized association for the extortion of blackmail in every conceivable shape and form. Officials, officers of the King's Household, the police and others were affiliated with the most des-perate of the criminal classes in carrying out the depredations, and none was too high or too low to escape them. If a petition was to be presented to the Sovereign or to a Min-ister, it had to be paid for; at every gate of the town Camorristi were stationed to exact a toll on each cart or donkey load brought to market by the peasants; and on going into a hackney carrosel [sic] in the street, I have seen one of the band run up and get his fee from the driver. No one thought of refus-ing to pay, for the consequences of a refusal

---

[12]For a discussion of the role of women in the Mafia and '*Ndrangheta*, see Siebert (1996).

[13]Saviano (2007) points out that modern Neapolitans in general, and *camorristi* in particular, do not use the term *Camorra* but instead refer to clans as the System, as in "I belong to the *Secondigliano* System."

were too well known, anyone rash enough to demur being apt to be found soon after mysteriously stabbed by some unknown individual, whom the police were careful never to discover. (quoted in Hibbert 1966: 181–82)

The Camorra was "more efficiently organized than the police, and set up a parallel system of law in the typical southern Italian style" (Ianni 1972: 22). In contrast with the Mafia, the Camorra was highly organized and disciplined (Serao 1911a: 724):

There is a *capóntrine*—a sectional head—and a *capo in testa*, or local head-in-chief of the Camorra, a kind of president of the confederation of all the twelve sections into which Naples is divided and which are presided over by the *capíntrini*. The lowest or entry level of the Camorra is the *picciuotto*, which requires an act of daring, often simply a bloody deed, including very dreadful crimes committed against very peaceful and quiet people. The *picciuotto* has no share in the social dividend. If he wishes to live on other people's money, he must do the best he can by stealing, cheating, or swindling whom he can, giving, however, to his superiors of the Camorra proper *shruffo* or proportionate percentage. (Serao 1911b: 781)

Below the *picciuotti* were specialized associates of the Camorra, such as the *batista*—a person who could plan burglaries because of his access to the homes of wealthy persons. The Camorra had its own authorized fences, usually dealers in second-hand goods, who arranged for the auction of stolen articles.

The Camorra welcomed Garibaldi and his "Red Shirts" in 1860, and after his success its power increased. Upon the proclamation of the constitution in 1860, *camorristi* were freed from the prisons in Naples, and the new prefect used the Camorra to maintain order: The Camorra constituted not only the *de facto* but also the legally constituted police power in Naples (Walston 1986). Devoid of a political ideology, the Camorra continued to act as mercenaries in the various struggles for

power (Behan 1996). At the peak of their power, from 1880 until 1900 (Gambino 1974), "if they so decided, there would not be, in some regions, a single vote cast for a candidate for the Chamber of Deputies who was opposed to their man" (Ianni 1974: 246).

The Camorra also differed from the Mafia in the style of dress and comportment of their members. Though even a *capomafioso* exuded an air of modesty in both dress and manner of speaking, the *camorrista* was a flamboyant actor whose manner of walking and style of dress clearly marked him as a member of the *societá*. In the United States, the public profile of important Italian American organized crime figures with a Neapolitan heritage have tended toward Camorra, while their Sicilian counterparts have usually been more subdued. Al Capone, for example, and, in more recent years, John Gotti, former boss of the Gambino crime Family, are both of Neapolitan heritage.

In 1912, in the "Cuocolo Case," a key witness allowed the Carabinieri to prosecute the entire Camorra hierarchy (Walston 1986). Given its highly formal structure, this was devastating to continuity. The old Camorra did not survive Mussolini because, like the Mafia, it required weak government control (Ianni 1972). One source (McConaughy 1931: 248) writes that members of the Camorra welcomed the Fascists as they had Garibaldi; after that there was not a Camorra: "They are all Fascists, and everything they do is legal." Fascism ended Camorra influence in the city of Naples; the few remaining members were incorporated into the Fascist power structure, and Camorra gangs in the countryside were used by the Fascists to intimidate antigovernment peasants (Behan 1996).

Although there are still criminals operating in Naples identified as being part of the Camorra, Francis Ianni (1972) argues that they have no direct links to the criminal society of the past. Vincenzo Ruggiero (1993: 143) reports that the last boss of the traditional Camorra died of natural causes in 1989 "after having acted for years as an informal 'justice of the peace' in one of the most crowded areas of the city. He settled disputes and, it is said, helped the poor." In an interview shortly before his death, "he mourned an end of an era—that of the men of honour who succored the people—and condemned the present, dominated by cruel, greedy and unscrupulous individuals."

Indeed, postwar Naples has been plagued with violence attributed to these "unscrupulous individuals." Suspected but not convicted, Sicilian *mafiosi* were forced into "internal exile"—*soggiorno obbligato*—obliged to live in Naples. In collusion with local criminals, they began to expand illegal opportunity. In the countryside Camorra gangs began to emerge as soon as the Allied forces withdrew. They asserted control over agriculture and cattle markets. Slowly, they began to move into the urban areas of Naples to further their control over these markets, dictating prices and acting as brokers between sellers and buyers. These gangs subsequently moved into and expanded upon the Naples contraband industry—from cigarettes to drugs. An estimated three-quarters of the cigarettes sold in Naples, where about one-third of the inhabitants are unemployed, originate in the black market[14]—Italy has very high cigarette taxes. In 1997, more than two dozen murders were blamed on a feud between two Camorra groups (Mazzarella and Contini clans) for control of the contraband cigarette business (Hundley 1997). At the end of 2007, Edoardo Contini, 52, boss of the Contini clan, was arrested on the outskirts of Naples; he had been a fugitive since 2000.

When government reconstruction programs were initiated in the Campania region, much like their Mafia "brothers" in Sicily, Camorra members soon found a new source of income, and their ability to provide jobs gained them political influence (Behan 1996). The earlier versions of Camorra were not directly involved in politics, but during the 1980s the new Camorra began to penetrate the local political scene, and some members hold local elected offices. In Campania, dozens of town counsels have been dissolved because of Camorra influence (de Gennaro 1995).

Government redevelopment was a failure—a testament to political patronage and corruption. This was repeated when an earthquake devastated Naples in 1980, claiming almost 3,000 lives and leaving 300,000 homeless. A huge program of reconstruction was effectively hijacked by corrupt politicians, government bureaucrats, and the Camorra, which diversified its wealth from drug trafficking by moving into the construction industry. The Camorra's ability to intimidate workers thwarted union pressures and ensured lower costs, allowing Camorra firms a competitive advantage (Behan 1996). Camorra clans traffic in arms which they secure in countries of the former Soviet Union and sell to groups that have the cash, their ideology notwithstanding: from leftist guerillas in Peru, to Somali warlords, to Catalonian ETA separatists. There is also gambling, and extortion from illegitimate and legitimate enterprises.

In addition to their lucrative drug wholesaling, the *Secondigliano Alliance* (*Secondigliano* is a Neapolitan suburb), a collection of some of the most ruthless Camorra clans, controls clothing manufacturing in a business zone on the outskirts of Naples. "Everything that is impossible to do elsewhere because of the inflexibility of contracts, laws, and copyrights is feasible here" where clan factories "produce garments and accessories identical to those of the principal Italian fashion houses" (Saviano 2007: 38, 39). They own entire retail chains that dominate the international clothing market while also distributing to outlet stores. Slightly inferior products go to African street venders and market stalls. The Alliance branched out into electronics, importing high-quality products from China and adding fake labels for international distribution (Saviano 2007). The Camorra has had remarkable business success in the manufacture of counterfeit designer clothing and consumer electronics and influence extends into the United States where members are reportedly trafficking in these products (California Department of Justice 2007). While trafficking drugs in the United

---

[14]In 1994, when the government threatened a crackdown on this practice, hundreds of street vendors for whom the contraband is their only source of income, took to the streets in demonstrations (Tagliabue 1994). The largest American tobacco companies have been accused of cooperating with smugglers, and in 1998, an RJR Nabisco subsidiary pled guilty to federal criminal charges stemming from a scheme to smuggle cigarettes into Canada through an upstate New York Indian reservation (Bonner and Drew 1997; Drew 1998). The illicit trade in cigarettes, often a tax-avoidance scheme, has been integral part of the business portfolio of terrorist groups (Shelley and Melzer 2008).

States can result in long prison sentences, trafficking in counterfeit goods is low risk with minimal penalties.

Camorra clans form alliances, enterprises mixing legitimate business, such as construction, with illegitimate, such as drug and arms trafficking. Profits from one are invested in the other, and vice versa, but even legitimate business often has a criminal dimension. Camorra firms underbid competitors by cutting corners, for example, using cement to hide waste and exposing workers to toxic dust, substandard scaffolding, bogus insurance, and long hours of toil for substandard wages (Saviano 2007). Campania has been turned into a massive illegal trash dumping ground for the Camorra, threatening the buffalo milk mozzarella—an Italian delicacy—industry which has flourished in the Naples area since ancient times (Fisher and Pinto 2008).

A growing population and rampant poverty led to the development of new Camorra gangs that operated for many years without direct conflict with their older and more established brethren who often had Sicilian Mafia ties. A "New Camorra Organization," *Nuova Camorra Organizzata* (NCO), was organized by the leader of one of the important Camorra groups, Raffaele Cutolo. Born in 1941, Cutolo had been running his group while serving a 24-year sentence for murder and extortion. Consistent with the Camorra's historical origins, Cutolo did much of his recruiting among the violent young men in Neapolitan prisons. "Cutolo protected these kids in jail, looked after their families outside and guaranteed a job on release. In return he got an oath of loyalty to the Nuova Camorra Organizzata" based on eighteenth-century Camorra rituals (Robb 1996: 165).

Naples was divided into zones by the older established Camorra groups, but Cutolo shattered the arrangement—and the peace—by attempting to bring all Camorra groups under his NCO. In 1980 and 1981, there were 380 murders attributed to the "Camorra war." Cutolo's opponents formed their own *Nuovo Famiglia* and received help from their Sicilian Mafia allies (Robb 1996). In the end, the NCO attempted takeover failed, and Cutolo was moved to a maximum-security prison on an island near Sardinia. With Cutolo and his NCO no longer a threat, both the NCO and the *Nuovo Famiglia* fell apart into competing and often feuding Camorra groups (Argentine 1993; Behan 1996; Robb 1996).

Structure of the Camorra

Compared with its predecessors, the modern Camorra "has a 'fragmented' and widespread structure, made up of a number of gangs [more than 100] which easily band together and then split up, sometimes peacefully, but more often after bloody wars" (de Gennaro 1995: 36). At the center of a typical Camorra group is a boss whose group is known by his surname, such as the *Alfieri* headed by Carmine Alfieri[15] in Nola. A high turnover has resulted in members and leaders who are younger than those of other southern Italian criminal groups, and the modern Camorra is less structured and less family based than the Mafia is. There is a general absence of rituals, although the NCO used a century-old ceremony to initiate members. Estimated Camorra membership is about 7,000. One of the most important Camorra groups headed by the Nuvoletta brothers had important links to the powerful *capomafioso* Luciano Leggio discussed earlier and is the only clan outside of Sicily that sits on the *cupola*, the Mafia's supreme council (Saviano 2007). The family of imprisoned *camorristi* is entitled to a monthly allowance.

Territorial control is reputedly essential to Camorra clans. Although extortion from legitimate businesses provides a relatively low return for the effort and risk involved, it is a way of asserting domination over a geographic area; it also provides an opportunity for those on the lower rungs to prove themselves and thereby move up in Camorra ranks. Roberto Saviano (2007: 51) states, however, that it is only the "begger clans," inept

---

[15]Alfieri was known as first among equals and able to maintain discipline and territorial integrity among the more than 100 Camorra clans. In 1992, he was arrested and subsequently became a government informer. This led to a breakdown of Camorra order and an upsurge in feuds and murders (Hundley 1997).

Camorra Justice

Less than twenty-four hours after Paolo Di Lauro, a clan boss of the *Secondigliano Alliance*, was arrested, the body of the man suspected of betraying him was found in a trash dump—only his lips were still intact: "His body was riddled with holes and encrusted with blood. They had tied him up and tortured him with a spiked bat—slowly for hours. Each blow cut new holes, piercing his flesh and breaking his bones as the nails sunk in were then yanked out. They had cut off his ears, cropped his tongue, gouged out his eyes with a screwdriver—all while he was still alive, awake, conscious" (Saviano 2007: 130).

at more lucrative business and desperate to survive, who practice monthly extortions. Camorra groups dominate illegal gambling and usury within their territorial hegemony, although some of their gambling operations reach northern cities such as Rome, Florence, and Milan. Territorial control extends to local politics and is enhanced by the Camorra's ability to provide employment where unemployment rates are consistently high. "Unlike Sicilian Mafia groups, the Camorra clans don't need the politicians; it's the politicians who need the System," its constituents and financial wealth (Saviano 2007: 47).

Despite their business acumen, like the Sicilian Mafia of recent past, Camorra leaders have engaged in violent struggles that have taken the lives of dozens of people (Arie 2004; Fisher 2005). At the end of 2004, a feud between loyalists and secessionists of a major *Secondigliano Alliance* clan claimed more than twenty-five lives in a little more than a month (Fisher 2004; Horowitz 2004; "Naples Police in Huge Mafia Sweep" 2004). The clans maintain military wings comprised of salaried retainers and many of the killings are perpetrated by young men—twelve to seventeen—enlisted by the military branch of the clans; they are often the sons or brothers of clan affiliates or from families without steady income: "A whole army of them" (Saviano 2007: 105). Even clergy are not spared. In 1994, when Father Giuseppe Diana dared speak out publicly against the Camorra, the 36-year-old priest was gunned down in his church on March 19th, on the feast of San Giuseppe. And like Sicilian *mafiosi*, dozens of *camorristi* have become *pentiti*—government informants. As of 2008, there were 236 confessing *mafiosi*, 271 *camorristi*, 86 from the *Sacra Corona Unita*, and 100 from the *'Ngrangheta* (Crisanti 2008).

THE *'NDRANGHETA*

The province of Calabria is located in the far south of the Italian "boot." It encompasses about 6,000 square miles of which more than 90 percent is hills or mountains. Italy's poorest province, Calabria has a population in excess of two million people; the capital city, Reggio di Calabria, is home to about 200,000. Lacking the charm of historical sites and world-class art, tourism is almost nonexistent. Much of the housing stock was built illegally by criminal groups, the fearsome *Onerate Societá* ("Honored Society") or *'Ndrangheta* ("Brotherhood"), which in the early twentieth century established groups in Canada and Australia (Nicaso and Lamothe 2005; Paoli 2003).

In Calabria, the term *'ndrangheta*, "society of men of honor," is used to indicate a high degree of heroism and virtue as embodied in the *'ndranghetisti*, men who are governed by *omertá* (Arlacchi 1986; Paoli 1994, 2003). The word *'ndrangheta* derives from the Greek *andra gateo*,[16] meaning to behave like an *able* man. There is a Mafia-type hierarchy in each *andrine or 'ndrina*—equivalent to a *cosca*—and members take a blood oath (Argentine 1993). Paoli (2003: 46) reports that *'ndrangheta* families, often called *locali* in Calabria, "have developed a complex system of ranks and power positions

---

[16]The Greek derivation may be from the word *andragaqos*, "brave man" (Paoli 1994).

that clearly differentiates them from the biological families of their members."

Originally several bands that grew out of government repression, *'Ndrangheta* gained popular support because of its political stance against the central government. "In 1861, the new Italian government sent troops to police Calabria. The old economic order had collapsed under the strains of national unification, and the number of gangs had increased. Because of the government's deliberate policy of favoring the North over the South of Italy in its programs of economic development, and because of its ignorant and arrogant insensitivity to the customs of the South, the Calabrians soon grew to hate the new government in the North. They naturally turned to the gangs" (Gambino 1974: 289).

These gangs mixed political insurrection with banditry and were supported and romanticized by the repressed peasantry. But *'Ndrangheta* had no positive program; its sense of social justice was basically destructive: "In such circumstances to assert power, any power, is itself a triumph. Killing and torture is the most primitive and personal assertion of ultimate power, and the weaker the rebel feels himself to be at bottom, the greater, we may suppose, the temptation to assert it" (Hobsbawm 1959: 56). Antonio Nicaso and Lee Lamothe (2005: 10) state that Calabria was a place where government interest or involvement was minimal and, therefore, "it was only natural that strong men—as in Sicily—emerge to effectively control citizen's activities."

The *'Ndrangheta*, sometimes referred to as the "Calabrian Mafia," consists of 85 (Paoli 1994) to 144 (Snedden and Visser 1994) or 160 (de Gennaro 1995) *andrine*, some exceeding 200 members, with a combined membership of 5,000 to 6,000. Each group—*'ndrina*—exerts influence over a well-defined geographic area generally corresponding to a town or village, although the *'Ndrangheta* now operates in cities of northern Italy and throughout much of Europe, wherever Calabresi have settled. They are particularly strong in Canada and Australia (Nicaso and Lamothe 2005; Paoli 1994). In the larger areas like Reggio, where two or more *'ndrina* could be located, criminal functions will be divided either by "turf" or by function. For example, one may control extortion while another will control drugs (Snedden and Visser 1994). The *'Ndrangheta* also collaborates with Sicilian and Neapolitan counterparts. Unlike these groups, however, *'Ndrangheta* clans are based on blood ties, allowing for a high degree of internal cohesion which protects against informants. A chief with a large number of sons and men linked by direct kinship has more power in the criminal world, and members are less likely to betray one another (Paoli 2003). *Omertá* remains strong, and there are few cooperating witnesses of Calabrian origin (Bohlen 1996b; de Gennaro 1995). Their violence is reminiscent of the cruel Colombian practice (see Chapter 7) of *no dejar la semilla* (don't leave the seed): Known as *fida*, all members, including women and children, of a victim's family are killed (Snedden and Visser 1994).

At its core, a *'ndrina* is composed of one or two biological families and their network of artificial kinships. "In order to strengthen the cohesion of the inner nucleus, the practice of intermarriage between first cousins is strongly encouraged and marriages are also used to cement alliances with other groups in the immediate neighborhood" (Paoli 1994: 215). Loyalty is further promoted through the use of initiation ceremonies similar to those of the American Mafia, and *Malavita*, songs performed at important occasions such as the induction of a new member: "For over 100 years members of the Calabrian Mafia has [sic] developed and sung Malavita songs among themselves" (Strauss 2002: B1). These songs have now been recorded and are available on CDs throughout Europe (Ali 2002; Strauss 2002). 'Ndrangheta women frequently play important roles, maintaining family traditions and running family enterprises.

Like its Sicilian counterparts, 'Ndrangheta has a commission that recognizes territorial hegemony and mediates disputes in an effort to reduce the high level of violence for which Calabresi are noted. 'Ndrangheta bosses from as far as Canada and Australia—"the 'Ndrangheta has had a remarkable ability to establish branches abroad" (Varese 2006: 42)—regularly attend annual meetings at the Calabrian Sanctuary of Our Lady in Polsi, an indication that the *'ndrine* around the world perceive themselves as being part of the same collective entity. In 1999, the Carabinieri captured the man reputed to be the most powerful 'Ndrangheta boss; Giuseppe Piromalli was convicted of murder in absentia and had been a fugitive since 1993. He was arrested inside a secret apartment, which was located in what appeared to be an uninhabited old hut, but which contained highly sophisticated "James Bond" type electronic equipment (Reuters 1999). In 2007, a feud between two 'Ndrangheta clans spread to Germany where six Calabresi were murdered with shots to the head outside of a Duisburg pizzeria (Landler and Fisher 2007).

The organization exhibits its criminal skills mainly in kidnapping, vast-scale international arms and drug trafficking, extortion from almost all profit-making activities, and control of public contracts (de Gennaro 1995). Extortion inhibits legitimate investment and plays a significant role in the backwardness of the region. During the 1980s, ransom kidnappings provided capital for entry into large-scale drug trafficking. The most notorious was the 1970s abduction of John Paul Getty III, heir to the Getty oil fortune. Almost $3 million was paid for his return, but only after one of the youngster's ears was severed. The ear and a photo of the victim were sent to the family (Nicaso and Lamothe 2005). Many of these kidnappings were collaborative efforts between 'Ndrangheta, Camorra, and Mafia groups (Siebert 1996). Ready access to the sea makes drug, as well as arms and cigarette, smuggling, relatively easy. Drug profits led to the purchase of large tracts of land and the opening of legitimate businesses, such as supermarkets, although not necessarily in Calabria (Paoli 1994). The growing of cannabis has become part of their portfolio, and marijuana plantations have been discovered in western Calabria (Snedden and Visser 1994). Like the Mafia, the 'Ndrangheta has been active in provincial politics, but unlike the Mafia, until 2005 the 'Ndrangheta avoided direct confrontations with the Italian state. In that year, they assassinated the vice president of the regional council (Capé 2005).

SACRA CORONA UNITA AND THE ALBANIAN CONNECTION

The Puglia (Apulia) region at the heel of the Italian boot forms an elongated peninsula on the Adriatic and Ionian Seas. The *Sacra Corona Unita* (SCU), Sacred United Crown, evolved in the region already noted for Camorra and 'Ndrangheta activities. As the name suggests, the SCU uses a great deal of Roman Catholic imagery as part of its rituals. But despite these religious trappings, the SCU originated as a criminal organization. At the end of the 1970s and early 1980s, local criminal gangs began patterning themselves on their elder Mafia and Camorra colleagues, eventually coalescing into the SAC. The origins of the SAC are traced to Giuseppe Rogoli who, while a prisoner serving a life sentence for murder, reportedly established the organization as a ritual brotherhood on Christmas day 1983 at least in part as a response to the expansionist plans of Camorra leader Raffaele Cutolo discussed earlier (Varese 2006).

The SCU is organized horizontally with a series of about forty-five autonomous clans accountable to the common interests of the organization (Hess et al. 1999: 387). Total membership is estimated at about 2,000, and women often play important roles in its business operations. The SCU has close ties to the Balkans, particularly Albania, located just across the Strait of Otranto from Puglia. During World War II, Albania was occupied by Mussolini's Italy.

Organized crime in the largely rural countries of the Balkans has its roots in the traditional clan structure based familial ties for protection and mutual assistance. Dating back to the fifteenth century, clan relationships operate under the *kanun*, or code, which values loyalty and *besa*, or secrecy. Each clan established itself in specific territories and controlled all activities in that territory. Protection of activities and interests often led to violence between the clans. The elements inherent in the structure of the clans provided the perfect backbone for what is considered modern-day Balkan organized crime exemplified by that emanating from Albania where the sway of the *kanun* remains strong, continuing a tradition of blood feuds (Bilefsky 2008).

Albanian Connection

Since 1992, ethnic Albanian organized crime groups have profited greatly from instability and war in the Balkans to become the fastest growing ethnic criminal presence in Europe, with operations reaching as far as Australia and the United States (LaVerle et al. 2003).

Albania, a primarily Muslim nation with a population of about 3.5 million, is slightly smaller than Maryland. Albania declared its independence from the Ottoman Empire in 1912. The country was conquered by Italy in 1939, but Communist partisans took over in 1944. Albania allied itself first with the Soviet Union (until 1960), and then with China (to 1978). Europe's poorest country and noted for corruption (Simpson 2002), Albania is a mostly mountainous country with small plains along its long coastline on the Adriatic Sea. Albania is distinguished by its strong sense of familial and clan ties, and the country's criminal groups (*fis*) have much in common with their southern Italian colleagues, including the concepts of *omertá* and *famiglia*. Albanian tradition includes absolute loyalty to the extended family and clan, known as *fare*, and the notion of *bessa* requires total respect for verbal promises (Nicaso and Lamothe 2005). Albanian influence in the *Mezzogiorno* dates back to the migration of Albanians driven from their country by the Ottoman invasion in the fifteenth century. Known as *arbresheri*, many settled in Calabria and Sicily where they quickly integrated with the existing culture of southern Italy (Bequai 1979).

Once the most isolated country in Europe, Albania became a haven for local and foreign criminal groups after the collapse of its Stalinist regime in the early 1990s. "During the communist years, the Fifteen Families—fifteen *fis*—had controlled organized criminal activities in Albania, primarily through smuggling and corruption. But with the collapse of the communist government and the military, the Fifteen Families were in essence the only groups that didn't descend into anarchy and chaos" (Nicaso and Lamothe 2005: 187). Albanians suffered a classical form of anomie: "A social disorganization of the entire society ensued. Organized social life, as it used to be under communism, was now outdated; yet the new societal behavior was not yet in place" (Gjoni 2004: 2). From the firm hand of Stalinesque communism to unbridled freedom—anarchy—criminal groups quickly filled the power vacuum. Most of these groups are small and flexible—less than a half-dozen members—and the death or incarceration of a leader will often cause the members to disperse and join other groups. A few are larger—fifteen to twenty members—and have a more hierarchical structure resembling that of the Sicilian Mafia. Even when these groups operate on a transnational basis, they prefer to reside in Albania where they benefit from a weak and corrupt justice system (Gjoni 2004).

The opening of the country's borders and political disarray have allowed Albania to become a primary alternative to traditional Balkan smuggling routes through the former Yugoslavia that were disrupted by the breakout of ethnic fighting in the early 1990s. Taking advantage of a weak central government and a great deal of political chaos, SCU clans were quick to establish a presence in Albania, linking up with local criminal groups.

In 1997, Albania erupted into nationwide riots over failed pyramid schemes that bankrupted most families. Thousands of citizens stormed police stations and looted one million guns. The ensuing chaos fed Albania's criminal gangs. They were already expanding across the continent while at home the corrupt regime of President Sali Berisha permitted drug trafficking to flourish.

Massive migration of Albanians abroad during the 1990s and the drastic increase of the Albanian Diaspora in the USA, Canada, and Europe, provided a perfect cover for Albanian criminals who brought with them a strong sense of extended family: "Many Albanian men can still identify relatives of the seventh to tenth degree and expect to be able to rely on them if they need support in either licit or illicit businesses" (Paoli and Reuter 2008: 25). Similar to the culture of the *Mezzogiorno*, "family interests and values are put first and pursued even at the expense of the interests of the larger collectivities and in defiance of state rules (Paoli and Reuter 2008: 26).

Albanian crime groups are very violent. Their major source of income is derived from trafficking in economic migrants, women, children, drugs, contraband, weapons, and automobiles. "Albania is an origin and transit country and the criminal elements take advantage of the instability, corruption and lack of organization and resources of the Albanian law enforcement entities. Illicit funds are being laundered back into Albania from abroad to purchase and develop choice properties suspiciously acquired during the privatization program" (Gjoni 2004: 15). Illegal arms trafficking has been fed by an estimated 550,000 military weapons, nearly 1 billion rounds of ammunition, and 16 million explosive devices that were removed from military stockpiles during the rioting of 1997—only 200,000 of the weapons have been recovered in the government's guns-for-money swap program. Albanian criminal organizations are believed to have gained possession of a large share of the unaccounted-for arsenal (LaVerle et al. 2003).

In neighboring Yugoslavia, ethnic Albanian crime Families were looking to widen their drug, prostitution, and weapons smuggling rings. Some dispatched lieutenants to countries such as Italy, Germany, and Slovakia. Their criminal endeavors eventually intersected with activities of the Kosovo Liberation Army (KLA), whose guerrillas since 1998 have fought for independence for Kosovo's 1.8 million ethnic Albanians. In this struggle against Serbian anti-Albanian policies, Kosovo's Albanians developed a strong ethnic conscience, a sense of collective identity that facilitated their ability to engage in organized crime. It also encouraged links between Albanian-organized Albanian crime, Albanian ideals, politics, military activities, and terrorism. Albanian drug lords established elsewhere in Europe supported the independence cause (LaVerle et al. 2003). In 2008, Kosovo, despite Serbian and Russian opposition, declared its independence from Serbia.

Being a rather recent phenomenon not as strong as the Mafia or Camorra, SCU leaders apparently decided to join forces rather than run the risk of a conflict with Albanian groups who are known to be extremely violent. As a result, in certain areas of Italy, the market for cannabis, prostitution, and the smuggling of illegal immigrants is run mainly by Albanians. "As the Albanian gangs continue to proliferate, the SCU has been there to support them in joint venture opportunities such as the trade of weapons and drugs" (Hess et al. 1999: 390). The SCU is behind the smuggling of thousands of Albanians into Italy, including Albanian women sold into prostitution. Macedonia, which borders on Albania, has become a major center of the European sex trade (Gall 2001).

A crackdown in Sicily led hundreds of *mafiosi* to relocate to the Albanian coastal town of Vlorë, and their Albanian counterparts are found throughout Italy (Cilluffo and Salmoiraghi 1999). Albanian criminals frequently reside in Calabria, indicating ties to the *'Ndranghetta*, and in 1999, police in the coastal Albanian city of Durrës, with Italian assistance, arrested one of the godfathers of the SCU. With its strategic position on the Adriatic, the SCU is able to provide smuggling services to the Mafia, Camorra, and *'Ndranghetta*. They routinely use Albania's long and now virtually unguarded coastline as a staging area for smuggling drugs—Southwest Asian heroin, hashish, and, to a lesser extent, cocaine—arms, and other contraband across the Adriatic Sea to Italy. There are also ties between the SCU, Colombian cartels, Russian, and Southeast and Southwest Asian criminal groups.

Albanian criminals are also involved in the traffic of illegal immigrants to western Europe—not only Albanians, but also Kurds, Chinese, and people from the Indian subcontinent. Albanian groups are mainly responsible for the crossing of the Adriatic Sea from the Albanian coast to Italy. From Italy, illegal immigrants are transported by allied criminal groups such as the SCU. Besides being a source of income, immigration is important in creating networks in foreign countries, bridgeheads for the Albanian Mafia abroad. Reports indicate that some of the people admitted into western Europe or North America as refugees during the Kosovo conflict had been carefully chosen by the Albanian Mafia to stay in the host country and act as a future liaison for the criminal networks (Hess et al. 1999; National Security Council and Interpol information).

Now that we have examined the criminal organizations of Italy and Albania, in the next chapter we will cross the Atlantic to Latin America.

SUMMARY

- The *Mafia, Camorra, 'Ndrangheta,* and the *Sacra Corona Unita* (with its Albanian connection) developed along cultural lines in southern Italy, the *Mezzogiorno,* an area of poverty and repression characterized by an ideal of manliness, *omertá,* that includes noncooperation with authorities and the *vendetta,* where the only basis of loyalty and trust is *famiglia.*
- In Sicily, *mafiosi* are organized into a *cosca* associated with a particular district in which they provide a parallel government while acting as brokers between peasants, landowners, and government. Because of an ethos of mistrust and suspicion, businessmen use a *mafioso* to serve as a guarantor instead of contracts.
- Mussolini's crackdown on the Mafia drove many of them to the United States at an opportune time—during Prohibition.
- After World War II, a new Mafia emerged divorced from the traditions of the old rural *cosca* and resembling American gangsterism. The new Mafia murdered public officials and outraged the public.
- Murderous struggles for power weakened the Mafia whose ranks became filled with informants.
- In the Naples area, the Camorra, a criminal society that emerged from Spanish prisons, actually ruled the city at one time. Camorra groups engaged in a murderous struggle for dominance in the early 1980s and at the beginning of the twenty-first century.
- The Camorra has a fragmented structure made up of more than 100 gangs that easily band together and then split up, sometimes peacefully, but more often after bloody wars.
- There are now important Camorra links with the Sicilian Mafia. The Camorra has had remarkable business success in construction,

drugs, the manufacture of counterfeit designer clothing, and illegal trash dumping.

- The province of Calabria, located in the far south of the Italian "boot," is home to Mafia-style organizations collectively called the *'Ndranghetta*. Each exerts influence over a well-defined geographic area generally corresponding to a town or village.
- The *'Ndranghetta* collaborate with Mafia and Camorra groups, and all three are involved in extortion and drug trafficking.
- At the end of the 1970s, local criminal gangs in the Puglia region began patterning themselves on their elder Mafia and Camorra colleagues, eventually coalescing into the *Sacra Corona Unita*, which uses a great deal of Roman Catholic imagery as part of its rituals.
- Often in collaboration with Albanian crime groups—who emerged as important players in drug, arms, and human trafficking—as well as the other criminal societies of the *Mezzogiorno*, the *Sacra Corona Unita* is involved in smuggling illegal immigrants and in weapons and drug trafficking.

REVIEW QUESTIONS

1. What is the parallel between Prohibition and the expanded capacity of contemporary criminal organizations?
2. How is the development of the Mafia related to absentee ownership of estates in Sicily?
3. How did Mussolini affect the Mafia and the Camorra?
4. What led to the reawakening of Mafia power at the end of World War II?
5. How does the "new Mafia" differ from the "old Mafia"?
6. How do the Mafia, Camorra, and *'Ndrangheta* differ?
7. What is the relationship between the *Sacra Corona Unita* and Albanian crime groups?
8. What led to the international expansion of Albanian organized crime?

CHAPTER

7

Latin American Organized Crime

A common element that characterizes most of the criminal organizations examined in this and subsequent chapters is extensive—sometimes exclusive—involvement in drug trafficking. "Narcotics and drug traffic have the same pattern of relationship which surrounded alcohol and bootlegging during the prohibition era" (Ianni 1974: 320). If anything positive can be said for the drug business, it is that trafficking is *an equal opportunity employer* (Durk and Silverman 1976).

As noted in Chapter 1, a criminal organization can exhibit a formal structure while its economic activities may actually involve small firms or partnerships among members and include nonmember associates. This is often the case with outlaw motorcycle clubs and the American Mafia. In contrast, income-producing activities of many Latino organized crime groups are integrated into a bureaucratic structure—it is their sole raison d'être—devoid of subcultural traditions that distinguish the Sicilian Mafia and outlaw motorcycle clubs.

In the United States, most Latino organized crime groups import their criminal organizations along with the drugs they sell.[1] Most prominent among them are groups based in Colombia and Mexico.

COLOMBIA

Control of most of the world's cocaine industry remains in the hands of Colombian organizations. Colombia is the only South American country with both Pacific and Caribbean coastlines. The high Andes divide the country into four ranges,

---

[1] This is not to say that Latinos are not involved in other areas of organized crime. Raymond ("Spanish Raymond") Marquez, a Puerto Rican, was a (perhaps *the*) major numbers operator in Harlem. In 1997, he announced his retirement, but a year later, at 68, Marquez was arrested with twenty-four others and charged with handling more than $6 million in bets annually. A resident of Great Neck, New York, Marquez, suffering from a number of ailments, pled guilty and was sentenced to five years' probation. He was represented by his son, attorney R. David Marquez. José Miguel ("El Padrino") Battle, a Cuban veteran of the Bay of Pigs fiasco, for decades controlled numbers operations in parts of Florida, New York City, and New Jersey. In failing health, in 2006, he pled guilty to federal racketeering charges and died the following year at age 77. That same year, his son, José Battle, Jr., 54, was sentenced to 15 years for his role in heading "The Corporation," as the Battle organization is known.

with most of Colombia's 45 million persons concentrated in green valleys and mountain basins that lie between the Andes ranges; travel between populated areas is difficult (Buckman 2004).

Colombia has been torn by political strife, with three civil wars during the nineteenth century, and two in the twentieth—in 1902 and 1948. In 1948, the popular leftist mayor of Bogotá was assassinated in the street before thousands of his supporters. The assassin was immediately lynched. Three days of rioting ensued, setting the stage for a civil war. *La Violencia*, as the 1948–1958 civil war between wealthy landowners and poor *campesinos* is known, cost the lives of about 300,000 persons (Griswold 2005; Riding 1987a). Most deaths were typically not the result of conflict between armed forces, but were atrocities and vengeance killings. The war officially ended when the Liberals and the Conservatives formed the National Front, but Marxist insurgencies and right-wing paramilitaries continue to threaten the stability of the central government. *La Violencia* "debased the incipient development of judicial and police apparatuses, as well as the moral foundations of political action" (Palacios 2007: 138).

In Colombia, drug traffickers exemplify a lack of belief in the legitimacy of the country's political and economic institutions. When citizens doubt the fairness of their country's political and economic institutions, even if they do not themselves violate the law, they become more accepting of its violation by others (Villarreal 2002). "Breaking the law—any law—is justified, and not just for the usual economic reasons that criminals favor. For traffickers, the law, law-enforcement officials, U.S. drug operatives, and drug-control organizations all represent the traditional elite, international imperialism, or other international competitive economic interests, none of which has any historical moral standing in their eyes. Therefore, moralistic arguments about restraining violent behavior do not capture these people's attention . . . [and] allows traffickers to garner enthusiastic support in some areas" (Tullis 1995: 66).

Murder is frequent and the methods often sadistic, such as the *corte de corbata*—the infamous "Colombian necktie"—in which the throat is cut longitudinally and the tongue pulled through to hang like a tie. Another practice, *no dejar la semilla* ("don't leave the seed"), includes the castration of male victims and the execution of women and children (Wolfgang and Ferracuti 1967): "In Colombia, it wasn't enough to hurt or even kill your enemy; there was a ritual to be observed." Rape had to be performed before family members. "And before you killed a man, you first made him beg, scream, and gag . . . or first you killed those he most loved before his eyes. To amplify fear, victims were horribly mutilated and left on display. . . . Children were killed not by accident but slowly, with pleasure" (Bowden 2001: 14).

"At the root of Colombia's easy violence is an extraordinary indifference toward death" (Romoli 1941: 37). The homicide rate is eight times higher than that of the United States. Murder is the leading cause of death for Colombian males aged 15 to 44 (Schemo 1997a). The country has the highest child murder rates in the world—street children kill each other, and hundreds are murdered by vigilante groups as part of their campaign of "social cleansing" (Luft 1995a; Palacios 2007).

In this sociopolitical atmosphere, bandits have roamed freely, engaging in a combination of brigandage, terrorism, and revolution. In the northern cities of Barranquilla and Santa Marta and in the La Guajira peninsula, which juts out into the Caribbean, smuggling (*contrabandista*) groups have operated for decades. Bandits, *contrabandistas*, and Guajiran Indians, often backed and financed by businessmen in Bogotá, emerged as crime Families, or a *narcomafia*. Members are often related by blood, marriage, or *compadrazgo* (fictional kinship), and in many important respects the core groups resemble those of the Sicilian Mafia except that Colombian groups are sometimes headed by women. When President Richard Nixon declared a "war on drugs" in 1972, the United States succeeded in shutting down the flow of marijuana from Mexico. Encouraged by drug entrepreneurs from the United States, four years after Nixon's success on the Mexican border, marijuana was being widely cultivated in Barranquilla, Santa Marta, and La Guajira for the U.S. market (Paternostro 2007).

In a country where drug barons act as a state within a state, dozens of well-armed paramilitary groups "ply their murderous trade in the cities and countryside, sometimes selling themselves to the highest bidder as outmanned and intimidated judges and government officials feel helpless to stop them" (de Lama 1988a: 5; also Duzán 1994). These paramilitaries are sometimes allied with— sometimes fighting against—the drug traffickers, and they receive financial backing from wealthy landowners. Indeed, paramilitary leaders have become wealthy landowners themselves by making the rightful owners an offer that cannot be safely refused. The land is then registered in the names of third parties (Forero 2004f).

THE CUBAN-COLOMBIAN CONNECTION

When Fidel Castro overthrew the corrupt dictatorial regime of Fulgencio Batista early in 1959, he expelled American gangsters who operated gambling casinos in Havana. Many of their Cuban associates fled to the United States, along with *narcotraficantes* who had distributed cocaine in Cuba. They settled primarily in the New York, New Jersey, and Miami areas and began to look for new sources of income. Many Cubans who fled with, or soon after, the Batista loyalists were organized and trained by the Central Intelligence Agency (CIA) in an effort to dislodge Castro. After the Bay of Pigs debacle in 1961, members of the CIA-organized Cuban exile army were supposed to disband and go into lawful businesses. However, as Donald Goddard (1978: 44) points out, "They had no lawful business." Elements of these exile groups (they often overlapped) began to enter the cocaine business. At first they imported only enough cocaine to satisfy members of their own community, but by the mid-1960s the market had expanded way beyond the Cuban community, and so they began to import the substance in greater quantities.

Until the early 1970s, the importation of marijuana and cocaine into the United States was largely a Cuban operation, although the suppliers were Colombians. During the latter half of the 1960s, Colombians began emigrating to the United States in numbers sufficient to establish communities in Miami, Chicago, Los Angeles, and New York. Many were illegal immigrants who entered the United States through the Bahamas carrying false documents such as phony Puerto Rican birth certificates and forged immigration papers of high quality.

The Colombian traffickers became highly organized both in the United States and at home and by 1973, independent foreign nationals could no longer "deal drugs" in Colombia. In 1976, the Colombians became dissatisfied with their Cuban agents in the United States, who were reportedly making most of the profits and shortchanging the Colombians. Enforcers, often young men from Colombia's version of the "Wild West," La Guajira, or from Barrio Antioquia, the slums of Medellín, were sent in and systematically executed Cubans in Miami and New York. By 1978, Cubans remaining in the cocaine business had become subordinate to the Colombians. Then the cocaine wars between rival Colombians began, bringing terror to South Florida.

COLOMBIAN DRUG TRAFFICKING

The Colombians have been able to control the cocaine market for a number of reasons. The President's Commission on Organized Crime (1986a: 78–79) notes, "Colombia is well-positioned both to receive coca from Peru and Bolivia and to export the processed drug to the United States by air or by sea" (see Figure 7.1). And "the country's vast central forests effectively conceal clandestine processing laboratories and air strips, which facilitate the traffic." The Colombians "have a momentum by benefit of their early involvement in the cocaine trade." "In 1968, in an attempt to bolster its domestic economic performance, Colombia proudly established the Institute of Advanced Chemical Research in Bogatá, which started to train top-class chemists, who were later to find lucrative work in the employ of the Medellín and Cali cartels" (Glenny 2008: 245).

FIGURE 7.1   *Map of Northern Latin America, Colombia*

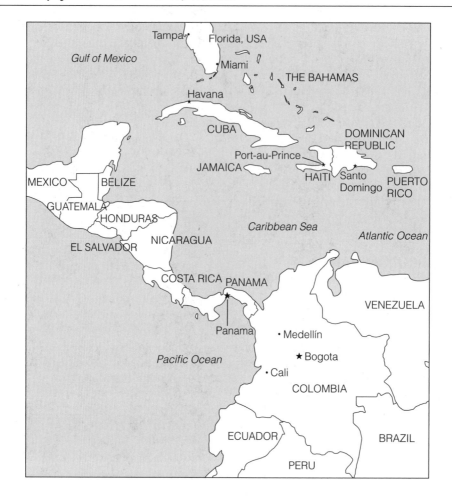

And, "there is a Colombian reputation for violence that serves to maintain discipline and intimidate would-be competitors" (PCOC 1986a: 78–79). The propensity to use violence led to domination of potential Bolivian and Peruvian rivals in the cocaine business. It permitted Colombian cartels to face down attempts at intimidation by other criminal organizations. On several occasions, the Sicilian Mafia tried to acquire the monopoly of the European cocaine market, challenging the Colombians with the threat to kill their independent couriers. That Colombian cocaine couriers continue to pour into Italy "is good enough proof of the fact that the Mafia received a negative answer to its demands" (Rey and Savona 1993: 75). During the 1990s, ties between the Cali cartel and Italian Mafia Families were revealed (Chepesiuk 2003).[2]

The economic modernization of Colombia failed to bring about a corresponding respect for government. Delegitimization of government and *La Violencia* "left legacies which have worked to permit, if not encourage, the development

_____

[2]For an insider's look at the relationship between the Medellín cartel and the Sicilian Mafia, see Gately and Fernandez (1994).

of the cocaine industry" (Thoumi 1995: 84). Delegitimization spurred the development of smuggling, particularly export of products out of Colombia and into Venezuela and Ecuador—cattle, emeralds, coffee—that provided experience in the contraband trade and money laundering. The drug trade "melded with a preexisting illegal trade in emeralds" (Palacios 2007: 197). Aside from their disdain for Colombian institutions and their long criminal records, Colombian traffickers share other characteristics. "They appear to be great believers in fate and providence and seem unmoved by normal considerations of personal danger. It is a perspective unaltered by normal law-enforcement efforts and one that makes dealing with or trying to control them such a dangerous enterprise" (Tullis 1995: 67). Speculative capitalism, focus on very high short-term profits—a feature of Colombia's financial elite—provided the resources for development of a cocaine industry (Thoumi 1995).

Colombia is a relatively large country, and many regions have only a weak federal presence. "While Colombian authorities built suburbs and major highways between cities, they ignored vast sections of the country; much of rural Colombia is isolated by hilly, trackless terrain" (Duzán 1994: 63). During the 1960s, the government encouraged Colombians to move into the remote southern province of Caquetá. There, farmers used slash and burn tactics to clear the land and plant subsistence crops. But an absence of adequate roads delayed marketing until the 1980s when the drug cartels persuaded them to grow coca. In the 1990s, when international pressure caused a reduction in coca planting in Bolivia and Peru, Colombian coca provided a readily available alternative (Villalón 2004) and Colombian coca accounted for about 80 percent of the cocaine reaching the United States (Marquis and Forero 2004).

In the south, there are three steep Andean ranges that run the length of Colombia, and impenetrable jungle. Government presence is concentrated in the cities of the Andean mountains and is essentially nonexistent in southern Colombia and marine outlets that provide access to both the Caribbean Sea and the Pacific Ocean. "The government didn't lose control of this half of Colombia; it never had

it" (Robinson 1998a: 39). The vacuum left by the central government has proved ideal for coca cultivation and cocaine manufacture because it left areas where only local officials had to be bribed, a cheaper and less risky action (Thoumi 1995). With the collapse of the Medellín and Cali cartels (discussed later), Marxist guerilla forces saw an opportunity.

The Politics of Dope

Drug money entered Colombia freely through an "ask no questions" attitude of the central bank and through unregulated currency exchanges. This movement of money was stimulated by periodic tax amnesties, and money was laundered though the purchase of rural and urban real estate and contraband imports—some of it "ended up in the increasingly costly campaigns of Colombian politicians" (Palacious 2007: 198).

In remote jungle areas where coca is cultivated, powerful Marxist guerilla forces protect the crops and levy taxes on the drug business. They have been effective against Colombia's mostly poorly trained and motivated conscript military (Robinson 1998b). And members of the Colombian military, often those trained by the United States, have been involved in widespread human rights abuses that often generate support for the rebels and drug traffickers (Schemo and Golden 1998). Attempts to eradicate the crop have encountered stiff opposition from the subsistence farmers, for whom coca is an economic lifeline ("Anti-Drug Efforts Encounter Resistance in Colombia" 1995).

At the end of 1998, in an effort to advance peace negotiations with Revolutionary Armed Forces of Colombia (FARC) guerillas, the Colombian government evacuated its security forces from a swath of central Colombia the size of Switzerland. There, FARC acts as a "labor organizer in the coca fields, keeping the price of a bushel up while taking a hefty percentage from the farmers" (Howe 2000: 38). In FARC controlled areas, the economy is built on coca, and coca paste often serves as the local currency. Paper currency is in short supply, so "it is not unusual for people to be paid for their work in coca. They, in turn, pay for the necessities with the paste, which is soft and powdery like flour" (Forero 2001h: Sec. 4: 12). The traffickers buy the paste, process it into cocaine, and ship it by the ton to the United States, while FARC taxes the trade. "To prevent narcotraffickers from ripping off farmers, the rebels set a minimum price for a kilo of coca paste. They also tax the traffickers for protection of smuggling routes, the use of clandestine runways, the importation of cocaine-processing chemicals, and the export of every kilo of refined cocaine shipped from the region" (Semple 2001a: 61). According to the Drug Enforcement Administration (Mulvey 2008), FARC is organized hierarchically with a 7-member secretariat and a 27-member central general staff, or *Estado Mayor*. At the bottom of the hierarchy are 77 distinct military units—called fronts—organized by their geographical location. Clusters of fronts form 7 blocs, each led by a bloc commander. Government successes against and defections from FARC have considerably weakened the organization whose membership is estimated to be less than 10,000 (Romero 2008e). In 2008, hundreds of thousands of Colombians demonstrated and marched in cities throughout the country to show their outrage at the kidnappings carried out by FARC.

Contesting FARC and other leftist militias are right-wing paramilitaries that often receive assistance from wealthy landowners, ranchers, and the Colombian military. They are part of a loose-knit coalition, United Self-Defense Forces of Colombia (AUC)—about 13,000 strong—fighting Marxist guerillas for control of poppy- and coca-producing regions. Ranchers who had been under siege from the guerillas helped transform this small group of outlaws into a formidable army (Forero 2001d). The major banana importer, Chiquita Brands, was fined $25 million by the United States for making payments to the AUC. The paramilitaries control several northern states that contain major drug trafficking routes, and they are aligned with one of the country's most notorious drug cartels, the Norte del Valle group (Forero 2004a, 2004b, 2004d, 2004e). One of the paramilitaries consists of about 8,000 uniformed, well-trained, and well-armed men who regularly do battle against leftist guerrillas. Their methods are characterized by their nickname, "The Headcutters." Victims—anyone

© AP/Wide World Photos

FARC commander who was asked to give his towel to a Colombian museum. Colombian peasants traditionally carry a towel to wipe sweat.

believed collaborating with leftists—are frequently kidnapped and usually found decapitated.

Operating out of the foothills of the Sierra Nevadas is another paramilitary group, *Los Chamizos* (Charred Tree), who routinely kill suspected leftists, including university professors, student activists, and trade unionists (Forero 2001f). Between 1985 and 2008, more than 2,500 union members were killed because of their involvement in the labor movement. The paramilitaries are believed responsible (Romero 2008a). *Los Chamizos* are reputed to control a drug syndicate that exports more than $1 billion worth of cocaine to the United States and Europe, but is not adverse to other means of raising money. In 1995, they kidnapped a wealthy local businessman and demanded a $1 million ransom. After the money was delivered, the victim was shot and his body carved up with chain saws. Three years later, they abducted the victim's widow and demanded a ransom of

$5 million. After the money was delivered, she met the same fate as her husband.[3]

The militias have proven more effective against the guerillas than government forces, and this has endeared them to elements of the population at risk. The militias have reinforced this support by building roads and schools in the areas from which they have driven the guerillas (Forero 2001d). "Through its infiltration of Colombian institutions, including the security forces, regional governments and even Congress, the group has a level of power that even the most notorious drug trafficker, the late Pablo Escobar [discussed later], never had" (Forero 2004f).

In exchange for not being prosecuted, beginning in 2003, paramilitary leaders agreed to disarm, and many turned to politics to maintain power. They have elected governors and mayors across northern Colombia by bribing, murdering, or intimidating opposing candidates and boast of having influence over one-third of the Colombian congress (Forero 2005d). In some areas, their candidates succeed by winning more than 90 percent of the votes or run unopposed. The militias are also being reshaped into criminal networks that traffic in cocaine, smuggle cheap subsidized petrol from Venezuela, extort from businesses, and loot local governments (Forero 2006). Some have adopted exotic names—Black Eagles (*Aguilas Negras*) and New Generation Organization (*Organización Nueva Generación*—ONG). While there is no consensus on what the new groups actually are and to what extent they continue the AUC, and although all are involved in criminal activity, organization and modus operandi vary

from region to region. Some are headed by paramilitaries who did not demobilize, while others are commanded by former mid-ranking AUC leaders who took up arms again; still others are the armed wing of drug-trafficking organizations that have existed for years, or even combinations of all these. Some, such as the ONG, continue the tradition of wearing military-style uniforms, while others, such as the Black Eagles, prefer civilian garb (*Colombia's New Armed Groups* 2007).

Colombian Drug Trafficking Organizations

The term *cartel* identifies a criminal network whose structure resembles that of a holding company: a collection of flexible groups with senior managers responsible for coordinating cartel operations (Glenny 2008). The cartels are compartmentalized (see Figure 7.2) to control each intermediate step required in processing and exporting cocaine. Each contains various sections with a separate function, such as manufacturing, transportation, distribution, finance, and security. This bureaucratic structure not only promotes greater efficiency, but it also protects the organization: "Few members of one section are aware of the others involved, and the loss of one member or even a whole section does not threaten the stability of the entire organization" (PCOC 1984c: 562). In fact, at the lower levels of organization there are many workers who move between one organization and another and are often unaware of which organization they are working for at any given time. At the highest levels, members are well insulated from the physical operations of their organizations. "The money generated by the wholesale cocaine

---

[3]Kidnapping is a major source of funds for both right- and left-wing groups, as well as common criminals in Colombia.

transaction is maintained for the organization by financial experts familiar with international banking and investing drug profits, and for assuring that a portion of the drug profit is returned to Colombia for reinvestment in the organization's cocaine enterprise. The cartel's own financial experts are supported by a complement of bankers, lawyers and other professionals in the United States, who play a crucial role in facilitating these transactions" (PCOC 1986a: 82).

In the United States, cocaine cartel representatives act as brokers to coordinate deliveries, usually 100 kilos at a time, to the various drug networks, franchising others, particularly Dominican organizations (discussed later) and, to a lesser

degree, Jamaican posses (discussed in Chapter 8), to distribute drugs. Colombian cocaine networks are informally structured and operate in a fluid, transactional manner. Often, a network will develop solely to distribute a single shipment of cocaine. The network may operate from six months to one year and then dissolve. Although structurally independent of the cartels, these distribution networks are symbiotic and in regular contact with their cartel sources. "While the main organizers are hand-picked by the Colombian traffickers, individual members of the same network seldom know one another and usually deal with one another only on a single occasion. Each drug transaction is conducted separately and each

FIGURE 7.2 *Compartmentalized Colombian Drug Organization*

Colombian headquarters: The drug lord oversees operations through designates who are responsible for regional directors. He will also have a staff responsible for Colombian operations including production, transportation, distribution, finances, and enforcement. Each of his employees is given a code number a record of which is kept at headquarters.

Regional director: Responsible for overall operations of the several cells within a region, the regional director reports via cell phone, fax, or e-mail to a designate in Colombia. They have discretion in the day-to-day operations, but ultimate authority rests with the leadership in Colombia.

Cell: Compartmentalization involves cells of ten or more members, each operating independently—members of one cell typically do not know members of other cells. Upper echelon and management levels of these cells are normally comprised of family members or long-time close associates who can be trusted because their family members remain in Colombia as hostages to the cell members' good behavior. Operating within a geographic area, each cell specializes in a particular facet of the drug business, such as transport, storage, wholesale distribution, or money laundering. The head of each cell reports directly to a regional director.

Source: Based on Chepesiuk (2003); Constantine (1999); and Ledwith (2000).

part of the network is compartmentalized. Inventories are stored in hidden locations. After raids or arrests, the cartels conduct internal investigations to assure that their employees were loyal, security measures were followed, and lessons were learned to improve the operation" (Comptroller General 1989: 14).

The sheer volume of Colombian drug transactions makes them vulnerable to sophisticated law enforcement efforts. "While most drug traffickers conduct financial transactions in cash, the volume of business conducted by the Colombian traffickers requires sophisticated record-keeping to track expenses and sales. Modern methods of monitoring inventories and deliveries are used; advanced communication centers arrange for the arrival of smuggled drugs, their distribution, the movement of cash proceeds, and other logistical matters. Distributors are instructed to keep accurate records, and many use facsimile machines to keep track of sales and to relay information to Colombia" (Comptroller General 1989: 19). However, infiltrating a Colombian group is near impossible. A prospective wholesale buyer must establish his bona fides at an audience with top management in Colombia. "If he is approved, he is not required to pay cash up front. He will send the cartel payment after he resells the drugs to middlemen. The wholesale buyer must put up collateral, cash, or deeds to real property, as insurance if he is caught. He must also provide human collateral in the form of his family in Colombia, who will pay with their lives if he ever turns informer" (Shannon 1991: 32). The most notorious of the Colombian cartels are those of Medellín and Cali.

Medellín

Medellín, an Andean industrial and tourist city of about three million people in the province of Antioquia, has a culture of violence that "makes its streets among the most dangerous on earth" (Griswold 2005: 82). It is the home of some of Colombia's most notorious drug traffickers. Antioquia and neighboring provinces bore the brunt of the civil war violence of 1948–1958. Long before cocaine emerged as an important commodity,

Medellín had a longstanding reputation for smuggling and a school for pickpockets. It is known as a place where assassins are trained in such techniques as the *asesino de la moto*: a passenger on a motorbike uses an automatic weapon—usually a .45 caliber machine pistol. The murder rate in Medellín is nearly nine times that of New York City. The city served as the headquarters for drug trafficking organizations known in Colombia as *Los Grandes Mafiosos* and in the United States as the Medellín Cartel, whose founders include Pablo Escobar, the Ochoa clan, and Carlos Lehder-Rivas.

Lehder-Rivas was indicted in 1981 by a Jacksonville, Florida, federal grand jury for drug trafficking and income tax evasion, and in 1983 the United States requested his extradition. Lehder-Rivas went underground, emerging back in Medellín denouncing the United States for imperialism and threatened to join forces with the Marxist revolutionary group known as M-19. In a 1987 shootout, Lehder-Rivas was arrested by Colombian authorities and extradited to the United States. The following year he was convicted of shipping 3.3 tons of cocaine to Florida and Georgia in 1979 and 1980 and sentenced to life without parole. In 1991, he appeared as a U.S. government witness in the trial of General Manuel Noriega, who, he stated, provided enormous help—and sometimes double-crossed—the cartel. Lehder-Rivas alleged that Noriega had sold the cartel an arsenal of Uzi submachine guns as well as photographs and addresses of DEA agents but had also seized their cocaine and, after being praised by the DEA, sold it back to the traffickers (Rohter 1991).

Ochoa Family The class and social backgrounds of the Ochoa clan differs from that of their Medellín colleagues. The *paterfamilias* of the Ochoa clan, Fabio Ochoa Restrepo, owns a country estate with herds of cattle and horses, *La Finca de la Loma* ("The Ranch on the Hill") in Medellín. Nearby is a bullring in which he has invested; his family business is inextricably tied to bullfighting. Don Fabio, as he is known locally, heads a wealthy and close-knit clan of old-line cattle breeders and landowners. They claim to have descended from the second wave of settlers to Colombia from the

Basque region of Spain who founded Medellín in 1616. These Spaniards enslaved and annihilated the native Indians they found.

During the early 1970s, Fabio Ochoa experienced financial difficulties that forced him to sell off some horses in Venezuela. At the time, his middle son, Jorge Ochoa (Vasquez), lived in Miami, where he headed an import-export firm that imported cocaine for Jorge's uncle, Fabio Restrepo Ochoa. A narrow escape from the DEA caused Jorge to flee to Medellín, where he informed his father, Don Fabio, of the demand for cocaine in the United States (Eddy, Sabogal, and Walden 1988). Fabio Restrepo Ochoa was mysteriously murdered in Miami shortly after his nephew returned to Colombia (Gugliotta and Leen 1989).

Jorge Ochoa, born in 1949, owns large tracts of land in Medellín, where he raises horses for bullfighting. He also owns a horse-breeding farm near Bogotá and a bullfighting arena near Cartagena. He was a frequent traveler to Panama, where his assets are in secret accounts, to Brazil, where he has important investments, and to Spain. In 1984, Jorge Ochoa and his associate Rodriguez Orejuela, of the Cali cartel, were arrested while living under assumed names in Spain; they were reportedly setting up a Colombian cocaine network in Europe. After two years in a Spanish prison awaiting extradition to the United States, they were instead extradited to Colombia. Meanwhile, Spain emerged as a major consumer and transshipment point for cocaine—as in the United States, cocaine operatives were able to mix with their law-abiding compatriots who in Spain number about one-quarter million persons (Paoli and Reuter 2008).

In Colombia, Jorge Ochoa was convicted of illegally importing bulls—it turned out that they had hoof-and-mouth disease and had to be destroyed. Although serious drug charges and a U.S. extradition request were outstanding, Ochoa was released pending appeal. Even though the judge who released Ochoa lost his job, he remains alive and is rumored to be quite wealthy. The Colombian extradition treaty with the United States was subsequently declared unconstitutional.

In response to the release of Jorge Ochoa, the U.S. Customs Service increased inspections of all cargo, passenger luggage, and passengers arriving from Colombia. Reprisals, however, have caused strong feelings of nationalism and generated anti-U.S. sentiment that is exploited by Colombian left-wing political groups, who often denounce the United States as "imperialistic." Colombian officials chide the United States for not providing enough material support for Colombian efforts against the *narcotraficantes* and for not doing enough about the demand for cocaine in the United States.

In 1981, Lehder-Rivas was kidnapped. He escaped, but not before being wounded by the Marxist revolutionary group M-19 (Gugliotta and Leen 1989). That same month M-19 kidnapped Jorge Ochoa's 28-year-old sister, Marta Nieves, from the campus of the University of Antioquia in Medellín and demanded a ransom of $1 million. In response, the Ochoa family called a meeting of traffickers—223 attended. Leaflets later announced that each had contributed to a common fund to establish a special enforcement section, *Muertes a Secuestradores* ("Death to the Kidnappers"—MAS), for the "immediate execution of all those involved in kidnappings." The leaflet warned that those who escaped would simply leave their families and friends liable for retribution. Soon afterward, dozens of persons believed connected to M-19 were tortured and murdered (Kerr 1988c): "Ten M-19 guerrillas were kidnapped and tortured, and two of them—who were on the Colombian army's 'most wanted' list—were handed over to the military commanders amidst widespread publicity. In Medellín, MAS invaded homes and shot suspected guerrillas—but also trade unionists, old ladies, young children, horses, pigs, and chickens. Mere sympathizers of M-19 were abducted from the university, tortured, and, if they were lucky, sent home in their underwear." After a few weeks of this Marta Nieves was released unharmed[4] (Eddy, Sabogal, and Walden 1988: 289). MAS surpassed its

---

[4]In 1990, M-19 disarmed its fighters and formed a political party whose leader was appointed the Colombian minister of health. A small group of members, however, returned to insurgency.

original purpose and proved capable of protecting trafficker's lands, eventually morphing into the paramilitaries discussed earlier.

During the 1980s, conflict between leftist guerrillas and the *narcotraficantes* intensified as the drug barons purchased huge tracts of land, an estimated 2.5 million fertile acres, and emerged as a powerful political force in the countryside, where they are backed by private armies of gunmen (Riding 1987b). Families displaced by this upheaval drifted into coca and poppy cultivation (Schemo 1998b). For the traffickers, a Marxist government would bring an end to their lucrative business, if not their lives. In fact, guerilla activity, particularly extortion, left many cattlemen eager to sell their ranches, often to the *narcotraficantes*, who are the most willing buyers and whose private armies are able to keep the guerrillas at bay (Weisman 1989). The rancher-traffickers invested their resources in organized peasant bands that were turned into fighting units. A U.S. congressional committee revealed that the private armies had been trained by British and Israeli mercenaries under the guise of helping Colombian ranchers fend off leftist guerrillas.

Jorge Ochoa responded to a government offer of amnesty for major traffickers. He surrendered, confessed, and was sentenced to eight years. In 1996, after serving five and one-half years, the Ochoa brothers, Jorge, Fabio Ochoa Sanchez, and David, were released from prison for "good behavior." They were whisked away in a bulletproof Mercedes Benz, rich men who own farms and other valuable properties. The United States protested their release, and in 1999, Fabio Ochoa Sanchez (b. 1957) was one of thirty-one persons arrested in Colombia for drug trafficking and money laundering. In 2001, Colombia's Supreme Court ordered him extradited to the United States where he was convicted of drug conspiracy in Miami and in 2004 sentenced to 30 years' imprisonment.

Pablo Escobar The most notorious member of the cartel was born in 1949; his father was a farmer, his mother a schoolteacher. Pablo Escobar (Gaviria) received a high school education but was too poor to attend college. He embarked upon a career in petty crime, later rising to bodyguard-enforcer for an electronics smuggler. By 1976, Escobar headed a small group of "mules" who transported raw coca paste and base from the south into Colombia, where it was processed into cocaine. In that year he was arrested with five other men and charged with attempted bribery—they had attempted to smuggle a thirty-nine-pound shipment of cocaine inside a spare tire. After three months, the case was dropped on a technicality. The records of the case subsequently disappeared and the two officers who had arrested Escobar were murdered.

As the market for cocaine in the United States increased dramatically, Escobar invested much of his profits in a fleet of planes. He was now able to deal directly with source countries (Peru and Bolivia) for his coca paste and coca base and to ship the finished cocaine directly to the United States. As his wealth grew, his lifestyle changed accordingly. Escobar purchased several large ranches, houses, and apartments in and around Medellín, and he invested in legitimate businesses. In 1980, he purchased a Miami Beach mansion and the following year, the King's Harbor Apartments in Plantation, north of Miami, for more than $8 million.

In 1982, Escobar was elected as an alternate Colombian representative in Envigado, a *barrio* outside Medellín. There he cultivated a Robin Hood image, building 500 small houses for slum squatters, which is still known as Barrio Pablo Escobar, and financing the construction of eighty soccer fields for the young men. His newspaper, *Medellín Cívico*, was a public relations piece that promoted Escobar as an up-from-the-slums statesman. As a representative he enjoyed immunity from arrest, until this was removed by the government of Colombia and a warrant was issued for his arrest for having smuggled an assortment of African wildlife into the country for his own personal zoo (Eddy, Sabogal, and Walden 1988; Gugliotta and Leen 1989). Escobar shared a trait with Al Capone and John Gotti—he enjoyed being in the public spotlight, even hiring publicists to advance his image (Bowden 2001).

Marco Palacios (2007) reports that the Medellín bosses offered to abandon the drug business, deposit all of their funds in Colombian banks, dismantle their drug laboratories, and with official oversight sell the chemical and transportation businesses that supported the cocaine trade. In return, they wanted elimination of the extradition treaty with the United States. When their offer was not accepted, Escobar declared an all-out war. Ron Chepesiuk (2003: 62) notes, Escobar and his cartel colleagues never realized their political ambitions: "When the Colombian state bureaucracy began to breathe down their necks in the mid-1980s, they dropped out of mainstream politics and turned to the terrorist's way of doing business."

In 1984, the minister of justice responsible for a major seizure of Medellín cocaine labs was murdered, creating a public backlash against the Medellín cartel. This was followed by the murder of more than thirty judges who had been considering extradition requests from the United States for cartel members. In a communiqué from the "Extradictables" printed in Colombian newspapers, Escobar warned anyone who supported extradition to the United States. With his high public profile, Escobar bore the brunt of a campaign to bring cartel members to justice. In an effort to mollify the police, he tipped them off to the whereabouts of Lehder-Rivas (Bowden 2001). But the pressure continued, and Escobar's carefully crafted public persona was abandoned for a more instinctive reaction: He orchestrated a campaign of increasing terror. In 1989, his men executed the favored candidate for president of Colombia because he had pledged to bring the *narcotraficantes* to justice. Three months later, in an effort to kill his victim's successor, Escobar had a bomb planted on an Avianca airliner—110 passengers died when the plane was blown out of the sky.

In response to the intensive police campaign to apprehend him, Escobar offered a bounty of $4,200 for each police officer killed. In the following month, forty-two police officers were murdered, and in 1990, some 250 more were murdered (Brooke 1990). The police responded by killing dozens of major traffickers and their enforcers as well as many innocent civilians (Marx 1991).

Escobar operatives were tortured with electric shocks and thrown out of police helicopters (Bowden 2001).

In 1990, Escobar began hinting that he would surrender and, in an effort to dictate the terms, went on a bombing campaign that terrified the public. His men kidnapped ten journalists—two were eventually killed (see Márquez [1997] for an intimate look at these kidnappings). In 1991, ten hours after the constitutional assembly voted to ban extraditions, Pablo Escobar, at 41, surrendered to authorities. He was accompanied by a popular television priest who had helped negotiate the surrender and placed in a specially built jail overlooking his hometown of Envigado. In Envigado, Escobar assisted in the construction of a hospital and sports stadium and endeared himself to the people with jobs and lavish gifts.

The jail was a converted mountaintop ranch with many amenities—jacuzzi, waterbed, bar, wood-burning fireplace, sophisticated electronic equipment that included a computer with a modem, 60-inch television set, and cellular telephone. The guards were assigned by Envigado's mayor, and several aides to Escobar also surrendered to provide him with companionship and security while he awaited further legal action. He also enjoyed female companionship. On July 22, 1992, the Colombian government attempted to transfer Escobar to a more secure prison, a site where he would (in theory, at least) be unable to continue overseeing the drug trade. The result was a furious gunfight during which Escobar and nine of his aides escaped.

After his escape, the police began tracking and killing his men; Escobar responded by killing more police officers. Early in 1993, bombs began destroying property linked to Escobar and the bodies of his associates began turning up in Bogatá and Medellín—the work of two extended families whose members, former Escobar associates, had been killed by the drug lord. They called themselves *Los PEPES*, an acronym in Spanish for "People Persecuted by Pablo Escobar." Information targeting the victims of *Los PEPES* reportedly came from Colombian law enforcement who were privy to the results of high-tech monitoring by American operatives in Colombia—monitoring that eventually led to Escobar himself (Bowden 2001; Brooke 1993). On December 2, 1993, the drug lord was killed in a rooftop shootout with police and soldiers while "attempting to escape"—Escobar probably realized there was no chance he would be taken alive. The fugitive was making a cellular call to his family when his whereabouts were determined by the use of telephone tracking equipment contributed by the United States (Brooke 1992a, 1992b; Christian 1992; Treaster 1991c; for a detailed look at the hunt for Escobar, see Bowden [2001]).

Of course, this being organized crime, the death of Escobar did not end the operations of his organization. Diego Fernando ("Don Berna") Murillo-Bejarano, 47, referred to as the "Exterminator" because of his wanton cruelty, a former Escobar henchman who became a leader of *Los PEPES*, took over his drug empire. Until his surrender in 2005, as a paramilitary leader, Murillo controlled a large expanse of Colombia's northwestern cattle country (Rashbaum and Forero 2005). With the exception of the considerably weakened "Don Berna" organization, no single group, or even confederation, has emerged to replace the Medellín cartel (*Colombia's New Armed Groups* 2007). In 2008, Murillo-Bejarano was extradited from Colombia to the United States along with thirteen other paramilitary leaders (Romero 2008c, 2008d). Later that year he pled guilty to conspiring to import multi-ton quantities of cocaine into the United States.

Cali Cartel

The drug boom inspired a competing cartel in Cali, a city of 1.5 million persons located about 250 miles south of Medellín. Cali is second only to Spain in the number of Spanish language books it publishes each year, and advanced printing technology has also made the city a center of counterfeiting, mostly of U.S. currency (Brooke 1991b). The Cali cartel refers to a loose alliance of five major trafficking groups with preeminence shared by the kinship/crime families of Gilberto Rodriguez Orejuela ("the Chess

Player"), born in 1939, his brother Miguel, born in 1943, and José Santacruz Londono ("Don Chepe") (*Intelligence Bulletin Colombia* 1995). The brothers grew up in a poor Cali barrio. Gilberto never finished high school and his brother allegedly purchased a college degree (Chepesiuk 2003). As teenagers, both were widely feared and became involved in criminal activities with their boyhood friend José Santacruz Londono. They reportedly used $75,000 from kidnappings to finance entry into the drug business in the 1970s. While Pablo Escobar was a typical gold-chain, fancy-car gangster who enjoyed a flamboyant lifestyle, members of the Cali cartel were low key and manipulative: "Buy Colombia, rather than terrorize it became their guiding philosophy" (Chepesiuk 2003: 68).

The Orejuelas owned banks, a national chain of drugstores—which could import cocaine precursor chemicals—and supermarkets, television stations, and a leading soccer team. Gilberto's seven children have been educated at U.S. and European universities (Moody 1991). Santacruz Londono was trained as an engineer. When he was refused membership in a local club, he had a replica built in an exclusive suburban neighborhood (Brooke 1991a). Members of the Cali cartel favored bribery over violence—cartel members were taped talking about millions of dollars in contributions to the successful presidential bid of Ernesto Samper.[5] In 1995, Londono was indicted in the United States and subsequently arrested in Colombia, only to slip out of a maximum-security prison in 1996. Two months later he was killed in a shootout with police.

Cartel members took a percentage of the profits from shipments by smaller organizations and, in return, provided transportation, distribution, and enforcement services. Despite their reputation for preferring diplomacy, enforcement services could be quite violent—suspected informants were

---

[5]In 1996, the Clinton administration revoked Samper's entry visa to visit the United States. Several officials of the Samper campaign team have been sentenced to imprisonment for taking money from the drug traffickers. In 1998, the man who had accused Samper of accepting drug money, Andrés Pastrana, was elected president—he defeated the candidate who had defended Samper.

immersed in barrels of acid. The cartel's chief of enforcement, known as "the Scorpion," launched a year-long reign of terror against unionists and guerilla sympathizers who threatened his way of life as newly landed gentry[6]—in 1991, 107 persons were tortured and killed, most dismembered with chain saws (Brooke 1995a).

Organized in a patriarchal manner, the Cali cartel stressed discipline and loyalty. Leaders operated compartmentalized organizations (see Figure 7.2) so that the loss of any one section does not destroy the enterprise. In Cali, there was a chief executive officer whose executives were responsible for acquisition, production, transportation, sales, finance, and enforcement (Shannon 1991). There were also dozens of overseas branches.

Cali operations in the United States were headquartered in the Elmhurst-Jackson Heights area of Queens, New York, home to more than 30,000 Colombians, a section known as "Little Colombia" because of the numerous ethnic restaurants and businesses owned by Colombians.[7] Close to La Guardia Airport and within easy distance of Kennedy Airport, the neighborhood provides cover and financial outlets for the group's activities. A walk through the neighborhood reveals an excess of travel agencies and wire services that facilitate the movement of drug money to Colombia. Cocaine was sold wholesale through the use of cells, each headed by a manager. Each cell operated with little or no knowledge of other cells, and cell managers reported to a regional manager who oversaw distribution and the maintenance of storage and commercial facilities. Regional managers attended periodic business meetings in Cali. If an employee attracted law enforcement attention, he would be transferred to another city. Employees received regular bonuses and vacations and had instructions to maintain low profiles in the United States. The cartel retained a team of lawyers and private investigators. But the shear scope of operations required constant phone communications that made the organization vulnerable to law enforcement (Chepesiuk 2003).

In 1991, the Orejuela brothers and forty-two others were indicted in the United States for allegedly laundering $65 million a year in drug profits from Miami, New York, and Los Angeles. In 1995, Gilberto was apprehended in a secret compartment at a luxurious house in Cali and Miguel was arrested two months later. The brothers confessed to drug trafficking and agreed to turn over $2.1 billion in assets in order to secure leniency; in 1997, Miguel and Gilberto received sentences of 9 and 10 years, respectively. At the end of 2004, Gilberto Rodriguez Orejuelo was extradited to the United States, followed by his brother Miguel, where in 2006 they were sentenced to 30 years in prison.

But when it comes to the drug business, some things do not change. In 2006, in a town fifteen miles south of Cali, a team of ten uniformed soldiers from the Colombian Special Forces moved toward a rural psychiatric facility that was reportedly being used as a center for drug trafficking. Without warning, the team was ambushed by twenty-eight gunmen who, despite shouts from the soldiers for mercy, continued firing until all were dead. Investigations later determined that the gunmen were members of the Twenty-third Mountain Brigade of the Colombian Army (Glenny 2008).

Evolution of the Colombian Drug Business

The Medellín and Cali cartels were vertically integrated to maintain control over cocaine through the entire chain from manufacturing to wholesale distribution. While it worked, the profits were astronomical. But as with any vertically integrated organization, a broken link can be devastating. The successors to these major cartels learned this lesson. A multiplicity of smaller organizations—*cartelitos* ("baby cartels")—is filling the vacuum, and they maintain lower profiles in Colombia and the United States than their Medellín and Cali

---

[6]Drug traffickers have become Colombia's largest landowners.

[7]In 1992, a Colombian journalist who had written articles about the Cali cartel, was shot to death in Jackson Heights. The gunman, wearing a hooded sweater, walked calmly into a restaurant and fired two shots from a 9mm pistol into the brain of Manual de Dios Unanue. The gunman, 16 years old at the time, was subsequently convicted and sentenced to life imprisonment.

The Norte Valle Cartel (NVC)

The NVC employs hundreds of individuals who work in various "offices," or "crews," including: "drug offices" responsible for the manufacture, transportation, and export of multi-ton loads of cocaine from Colombia to Mexico, and ultimately to the United States; "money laundering offices," which employ dozens of money launderers, money couriers, accountants, and individuals who operate multimillion-dollar *coletas*, or money stash houses; "corruption offices" responsible for bribes to the police and other public officials in exchange for information about law enforcement actions against members of the cartel; and the "offices of the *sicarios*" employing dozens of gunmen who carry out murders, tortures, kidnappings, and violent collections of drug debts ("Cocaine Cartel Leader to Face Charges in the United States 2008).

cartel predecessors. Although the fragmentation reduces efficiency, combating this multiplicity requires even more personnel and greater intelligence gathering efforts (Chepesiuk 2003). Independent traffickers who worked in the shadows of the major cartels have joined forces and the cycle continues.

In the absence of powerful drug lords, the drug trade has become more decentralized. Power has swiftly passed to experienced traffickers who are now seizing opportunities to increase their own share of the drug trade (Romero 2008e). These enterprising traffickers come primarily from two areas: the Norte Valle del Cauca region, of which Cali is the capital city, located on Colombia's southeast coast; and the Caribbean North Coast. The DEA anticipates that Colombia-based cocaine trafficking organizations will remain the dominant players in the international cocaine trade well into the twenty-first century. They continue to control the supply of cocaine at its source, have a firm grip on Caribbean smuggling routes, and dominate the wholesale cocaine markets in the eastern United States and in Europe. They are also aggressively increasing their share of the U.S. heroin market.

Colombian entry into heroin is based on demographics. During the 1980s, the popularity of cocaine began to fade among urban professionals, and "cokeheads" tend to burn out after five years. With this dwindling consumer base, the Colombians expanded into Europe but with only limited success—heroin was the hard drug of choice

and that market was dominated by Pakistani and Turkish groups. So the Colombians diversified, importing poppy seeds, equipment, and expertise from Southwest Asia (Golden Crescent). By 1999, Colombians had become major heroin wholesalers, often selling cocaine and heroin to wholesalers as part of a package deal. Colombian market advantages include geographic proximity to the United States and established distribution networks. They required their Dominican cells in the United States to take a couple of kilos of heroin for every 100 kilos of cocaine to give out free samples to customers—and the strategy worked, creating an entirely new client base for heroin. The purity level of their heroin permits it to be prepared for smoking,[8] ridding the product of its dirty needles and HIV reputation (Brzezinski 2002). Smoking is a less efficient way of ingesting than intravenous use because a lot of the drug literally goes up in smoke. Therefore, only when it is relatively cheap and therefore plentiful will smoking heroin predominate.

The dismantling of the Cali cartel also created opportunities for their Mexican colleagues who began forging direct links with cocaine sources in Bolivia and Peru. In their weakened state, Colombians now have to compete with Mexican organizations for the U.S. market.

---

[8]Heroin is either heroin salt or heroin base. Heroin salt dissolves readily in water, so it is easy to inject or sniff. Heroin base is easy to smoke but needs to be mixed with an acid like vitamin C in order to dissolve.

Corruption in Mexico

For more than a decade, "American officials have been haunted by the spectacle of Mexican officials' being linked to illicit activities soon after they are embraced in Washington" (Golden 1999a: 10). When Carlos Salinas became president in 1988, his brother Rául was given a low-profile government post from which he reportedly played a central role in protecting the flow of drugs from Mexico into the United States. This enabled him to deposit more than $130 million in Swiss bank accounts (Golden 1998c, 1998d). In 1999, Rául Salinas was sentenced to 50 years for masterminding the assassination of a rival politician. In 1998, it was revealed that an elite Mexican drug enforcement unit trained by the FBI and the DEA had been compromised by members with ties to drug traffickers (Golden 1998b). At the end of 2005, the successor agency established to fight drug trafficking organizations, known by its Spanish acronym *AFI*, was the subject of scandals:

More than 450 of its approximately 7,000 officers had been indicted (McKinley 2005d).

The lack of trust in Mexican law enforcement has resulted in the families of victims of ransom kidnappings failing to inform the authorities. This lack of trust is influenced by a confirmed fear that it is the police who often carry out the kidnappings. In 2008, the 14-year-old son of a wealthy businessman was kidnapped by men dressed as federal police officers who tortured—all of his teeth were pulled out—and killed his driver and bodyguard. The boy's body was later found despite the family having paid a ransom reportedly in excess of $50 million (Lacey and Betancourt 2008).

Mexico has become one of the most dangerous places to practice journalism, outside of Iraq. Drug dealers and corrupt police officers regularly kill those who write about them . . . (McKinley 2006a: 6).

MEXICO

Mexico is a nation of about 100 million persons, 75 percent of whom live in urban areas; despite an abundance of natural resources, poverty is widespread. Independence from Spanish rule in 1821 was followed by a series of revolutions, rigged elections, and general turmoil. There was a war with the United States in 1848 and a French invasion and occupation from 1863 to 1867. In still another violent overthrow, Porfirio Diaz came to power in 1876 and ruled Mexico for thirty-five years. The revolution that ousted Diaz left turmoil and widespread violence in its wake. In 1929, political stability was achieved by the emergence of a dominant political party known as the PRI (rhymes with *free*)—*Partido Revolucionario Institucional*.

In the Mexican culture, "people are not treated alike; strangers, those outside the circle of family and close friends, are not wholly to be trusted. One is much safer giving one's confidence only to friends of long-standing or family members. Thus,

as in Southern Italy [see Chapter 6], societal focus is on the interests of the immediate and extended family, not the wider interests of a more impersonal societal good" (Shelley 2001). This effect is visible in Mexican political life where each political leader has his intimate circle of contacts, relatives and friends from childhood "whom he protects and appoints to key positions as he moves up the career hierarchy. These *camarillas*, or cliques of friends, are in some ways the basic unit of Mexican politics" (Needler 1995: 51). Patron-client relationships, political patronage, and endemic corruption provide the backdrop against which Mexican organized crime is to be understood.

For decades after its founding, the PRI "was a tool of successive presidents using authoritarian methods to insure one-party rule" (Dillon 1999b: 1). The police forces—federal, state, and local—that evolved out of this atmosphere were deployed not to protect but to control the population. Furthermore, police officers have been poorly paid, and it was understood that they could supplement their pittance with bribes as long as they remained loyal to the government (Dillon 1996f). Using tactics reminiscent of the political machines discussed in Chapter 3, the PRI ruled Mexico for more than seventy years without any strong opposition, during which corruption became endemic (Shelley 2001). The PRI governed through the use political patrons known as *caciques* whose power derived from their connection to the national party structure. In return for party loyalty, these bosses were able to operate with a great deal of immunity, securing resources for followers, withholding them from and threatening violence against opponents (Villarreal 2002).

With the assistance of foreign advisors, many of whom also advised the former Soviet Union in the same process, Mexico embarked on an ambitious program of privatization in the 1990s. As in Russia, this was done in the absence of a free and vigorous press in a system that lacked grounding in the rule of law. The lack of sufficient safeguards accompanying this economic transformation led to the acquisition of valuable assets—banks, communications, food sectors—by families whose source of capital was gambling and drugs, "thereby facilitating the infiltration of organized crime into the larger Mexican economy" (Shelley 2001: 218).

In 1997, an emerging opposition party that has been critical of PRI-inspired corruption won control of the lower house of congress. In 1999, in an effort to change its image, the PRI voted to hold a national primary to select its presidential candidates; previously, the sitting president was allowed to choose his successor. In 2000, in a major political upset, the PRI candidate for president was defeated by Vincente Fox of the National Action Party. However, the pace of political change has not been uniform. Many parts of the country, particularly rural areas, are still governed by PRI bosses, and by 2005, the PRI was making a remarkable political comeback (G. Thompson 2005b; Villarreal 2002).

As noted in Chapter 5, during the Capone era, the election of a reform mayor in Chicago shattered stable but corrupt relationships between politicians, the police, and the city's Prohibition-era gangs. This led to the onset of the "Chicago Wars" as gang lords struggled for supremacy. Similarly, the defeat of the PRI in Mexico ruptured a longtime implicit arrangement between *narcotraficantes* and the PRI-controlled government. With the government no longer acting as an arbitrator, an unparalleled level of violence has erupted as drug lords struggle for supremacy (Bussey 2008).

Despite political changes, Mexico remains in an economic crisis, crime has skyrocketed, and the criminal justice system is in an advanced stage of deterioration. Corruption extends into the banking system: In 1998, in the culmination of a three-year sting operation, U.S. authorities arrested more than 130 people in the largest drug laundering case in American history. They included twenty-two bankers from twelve of Mexico's largest banking institutions—who had been lured into the United States—charged with laundering drug profits for the Cali cartel of Colombia (discussed earlier) and the Juárez cartel (discussed later) of Mexico; $35 million, two tons of cocaine, and four tons of marijuana were seized as part of the operation (Van Natta 1998).

MEXICAN DRUG TRAFFICKING

The popular culture of Mexico is infused with songs, *corridos* (ballads), and *narco-corridos* glamorizing drug trafficking. Major *narcotraficantes* are celebrated, along with their subculture of violence (Edberg 2001). Many songs contain references to an outlaw code of behavior, and their music videos depict violence including torture and the murder of police officers (Dillon 1999a). In the "if you play with fire" category, more than a dozen performers have also been the victims of the violence they extol, often tortured before they are murdered (McKinley 2007c).

In the early 1990s, Mexican criminal organizations struck a deal with the Colombians whose cocaine they were moving from Mexico into the United States on a contract basis: For every two kilograms of smuggled cocaine, the Mexicans would keep one kilogram as payment in kind (O'Brien and Greenburg 1996; Wren 1996). The deal was brokered by Sandra Ávila Beltrán, a beauty born in 1960 and known as Queen of the Pacific who is part of the Sinaloa cartel (discussed later). She is the niece of Miguel Ángel Félix Gallardo, an imprisoned major trafficker. Married twice, both of her husbands were police-commanders-turned-traffickers and both were murdered. In 2007, Beltrán was arrested by Mexican authorities along with her lover, Juan Diego Espinoza Ramírez ("El Tigre"), part of the Colombian Norte del Valle cartel (McKinley 2007a).

Mexican traffickers attempted to convert Peruvian coca paste into cocaine, but the product had the odor of kerosene so the effort was abandoned in favor of dealing with Colombians (McMahon 1995). Both sides benefited from the arrangement. Colombians had an abundance of cocaine, and Mexicans had a distribution network in the United States that they had been using for heroin. This arrangement was aided by the North American Free Trade Act (NAFTA), which further opened the already porous borders with Mexico (see Figure 7.3). The benefits to the Mexican traffickers were significant: In 1998, for example, officials in Chicago seized 2,800 pounds of cocaine and $5 million at a West Side produce company being used to store drugs from Mexico (O'Connor 1998). There was also a dramatic increase in payments to public officials to protect the Mexican traffickers' lucrative business (Golden 1997a). As a consequence, Mexican traffickers control a substantial proportion of wholesale cocaine distribution throughout the western and midwestern United States. They also provide money laundering services for Colombian clients, and direct delivery to wholesale-level customers on behalf of the major Colombian-based cocaine groups (Marshall 2001).

FIGURE 7.3   *Map of Mexico and U.S. border*

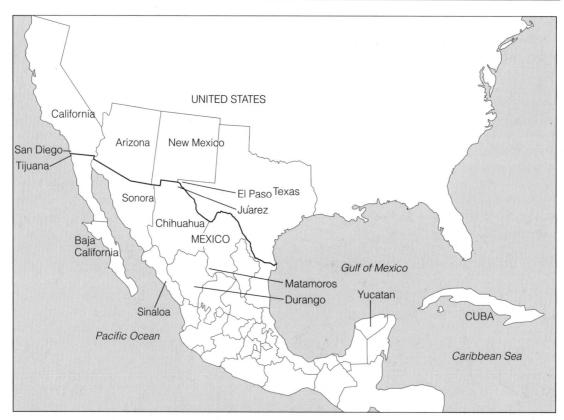

Source: Based on Ledwith (2000) and Constantine (1999b).

In 1998, there was a resurgence of heavy smuggling from the Bahamas and a corresponding drop off on the southwest border, an indication of Colombian concern that Mexicans are becoming their competitors in the cocaine business. Indeed, in 1997, twenty-nine persons working for the Juárez cartel were arrested as they competed with Colombians over drug distribution in the northeastern United States (Navarro 1998; Wren 1997). With the weakening of the major Colombian cartels, particularly the one centered in Cali, Mexicans have formed direct links to coca leaf farmers and processing laboratories in Bolivia and Peru (P. Smith 1999).

The relationship with the Colombians also led to structural changes, with some Mexican drug groups modeling their organizations along Colombian lines—compartmentalized units operating independently of each other but controlled hierarchically (see Figure 7.2 earlier in this chapter). The leading syndicates "are highly and efficiently organized. Often led by family members at the top, they involve hundreds of individuals with specialized roles—from security chiefs to hired guns to marketing agents, accountants, financial consultants, and money-laundering specialists. They make regular use of sophisticated technology, counter-surveillance methods, and state-of-the-art communications devices" (P. Smith 1999: 198). Financial rewards and intimidation help maintain strong internal discipline. Although they may be big businesses, Mexican drug organizations remain family-run operations with a corresponding high degree of personal trust (P. Smith 1999).

Mexican heroin smuggled into the United States is transported to metropolitan areas in the western and southwestern states with sizable Latino populations. Mexican heroin is also transported to primary markets in Chicago, Denver, and St. Louis. Attempts to find markets for black tar heroin[9] in East Coast cities, such as Boston and Atlanta, failed (Marshall 2001). On the Mexican side of the border across from Laredo, Texas, Nuevo Laredo, a city of more than 300,000, has been turned into a "Little Baghdad" by warring drug organizations—the Gulf cartel versus the Sinaloa cartel (discussed later)—attempting to control this critical distribution center. Victims have included journalists and police officers (G. Thompson 2005a). Assassins are often adolescents, and some are U.S. citizens, trained by instructors from the Mexican military in the employ of the cartels. In 2005, hours after being sworn in, a businessman who had volunteered to become Nuevo Laredo's police chief—no one else wanted the job—was assassinated by men firing assault rifles from an SUV. The federal government responded by sending in the military (Jordon and Sullivan 2005). Later that year, federal authorities arrested fifteen Laredo police officers for abducting people on orders from the Gulf cartel (Iliff 2005). In 2008, gunmen killed the head of the federal organized crime division, and two weeks later the chief of the federal police. Mexican authorities subsequently charged six men with links to the Sinaloa cartel including the man who hired the shooter, a federal police officer (McKinley 2008f, 2008g).

Superior organization and an extensive drug portfolio enabled Mexican cartels to diversify, dividing operations into heroin, cocaine, marijuana, and methamphetamine units. Mexican involvement with methamphetamine apparently began

---

[9]As opposed to the white heroin from Southwest and Southeast Asia, the less pure Mexican product has a dark color (discussed in Chapter 13).

when the Hell's Angels turned to them in order to avoid the hazards posed by drug's manufacture: It is explosive, the chemicals are caustic, inhalation can be fatal, and the strong odor can alert law enforcement. Mexican national trafficking organizations now dominate wholesale methamphetamine trafficking, using large-scale laboratories based in Mexico and the western and southwestern United States. Outlaw motorcycle clubs are still active in methamphetamine production, but do not produce the large quantities distributed by Mexican groups (Marshall 2001). Mexican-based methamphetamine trafficking organizations have ready access to the necessary precursor chemicals on the international market. These chemicals have fewer controls in Mexico than in the United States (Keefe 2001a).

Amezcuas (Colima) Cartel

Methamphetamine provides Mexican organizations with an opportunity for profit that does not have to be shared with others, as cocaine does for the Colombians. And the profits are substantial, usually a tenfold return on an investment (Arax and Gorman 1995). Although they started out as an alien smuggling ring in 1988, the Amezcua-Contreras brothers shifted to methamphetamine trafficking in the early 1990s. Among other properties, the brothers own drugstores in Tijuana that were used to facilitate the importation of precursor chemicals to manufacture methamphetamines. These chemicals are shipped to gangs in California who operate methamphetamine labs (Constantine 1999a).

In less than ten years, their cartel grew from a low-level cocaine trafficking group to the most prolific methamphetamine and precursor chemical trafficking organization in North America (Dillon 1998a; Labaton 1997). While working with Colombian organizations in the cocaine trade, the Amezcuas learned the lessons of marketing and structuring the drug trade as an international business. They also learned from the mistakes made by other organizations, avoiding violent clashes for territory and markets. By 1992, the Amezcuas had established their own international chemical contacts in Switzerland, India, Germany, and the Czech Republic. With their drugstores fronting for the business, they were able to exploit the legitimate international chemical trade. Being manufacturers as well as distributors, they kept 100 percent of all profits, providing the freedom to expand their trade and territory. Success and longevity of the organization has been promoted by the group's insular structure. The brothers recruited relatives and long-time friends, who then recruited a second tier of operatives to engage in the dangerous cooking of methamphetamine, as well as the risky activity of smuggling either chemicals or methamphetamine into the United States (DEA press release, June 2, 1998).

Despite their precautions, in 1994, a shipping agent in Frankfurt, Germany, made a decision that would eventually bring down the Amezcua brothers. They had arranged for a shipment of 120 barrels to Mexico City and had left explicit instructions to steer the load clear of U.S. ports. But the flight to Mexico City was overbooked and beyond its allowable cargo weight. Contrary to the shipper's wishes, the agent sent the load on a Lufthansa flight that landed in Dallas.

There, the shipment immediately raised suspicions, and U.S. Customs agents noticed that the labels had been altered. They pried open the barrel lids and found 3.4 metric tons of pure ephedrine powder, a methamphetamine precursor, enough to cook up more than 41 million doses of methamphetamine. For the first time, federal investigators had evidence they could use to trace precisely who was supplying ephedrine to the Amezcuas. Four months later, customs agents in Dallas seized another 2.4 tons of ephedrine. In October, Dutch authorities in Amsterdam stopped a 6.9-ton shipment of ephedrine that was bound for Guadalajara (Suo 2004). In 1998, Luis and José were arrested by Mexican authorities. They were transported to the same prison that holds their brother Adan (arrested in 1997). The Amezcuas brothers were under indictment in the United States but Mexico refused an extradition request. In 2004, José de Jesús Amezcua-Contreras was sentenced to more than 50 years by a Mexican court for trafficking in ephedrine; his brother Adan received a sentence of 22 years (Associated Press 2004a). Day-to-day operations of the cartel are believed to be run by two sisters of the imprisoned brothers, aided by male members of the family.

Herrera Family

For many years trafficking in Mexican heroin was dominated by the Herrera Family whose operations began shortly after World War II. From their first laboratory in Mexico, the Herreras shipped heroin to relatives who had moved to Chicago. Actually a cartel of six interrelated family groupings, the Herrera Family has been headed by the sometimes-imprisoned Jaime ("Don Jaime") Herrera-Nevarez (born 1924 or 1927), a former Mexican state Judicial Police officer. (The Judicial Police are similar to the Canadian Royal Mounted Police in jurisdiction.) Headquartered in Durango, a city of about 200,000 in the state of Durango (with a population of about one million), the organization is estimated to have around five thousand members, about two thousand of whom are related by blood or marriage.

Because key members are tied by blood, marriage, or fictional kinship (godparenthood), the group has proven to be very difficult to infiltrate on both sides of the border. In the United States the Family operates out of Chicago where Mexican heroin and marijuana is wholesaled to groups in New York, Philadelphia, Boston, Detroit, and Louisville. Organizational management is maintained by some two dozen executive-level directors and a vast array of field representatives in a number of American cities. The network is held together through the Herrera organization's U.S. headquarters in Chicago and through communications and trips back to the organization's headquarters in Durango. Don Jaime lives the life of a *padrone*, giving to the poor, befriending the rich, and playing godfather at weddings and baptisms. "In the village of Santiago Papasquiaro, where many of the opium farmers lived, the clan built the water system, installed streetlights, and created a town square. Three hospitals benefited from the clan's philanthropy" (Shannon 1988: 59). The Herreras did not buy off the power structure in Durango—they *are* the power structure.

By the 1980s, the Herrera Family had established cocaine contacts throughout Latin America. In fact, Colombians have now married into the Herrera Family. In 1985, federal Judicial Police arrested Don Jaime's son for cocaine trafficking. His case was subsequently transferred from Mexico City to Durango, where he was ordered released by a local judge for lack of evidence. In that same year, 135 persons comprising eight separate Herrera-related distribution rings were indicted in Chicago. By 1987, the Herrera Family was reeling under a continuing federal investigation in the Chicago area that resulted in more than eighty convictions, and dozens more became fugitives. By the end of 1988, however, those who had been convicted and those who were fugitives had been replaced. Herrera Family operations in cocaine surged, and intelligence gathered from two heroin laboratory seizures that occurred in the state of Durango "indicates that the members of the Herrera family continue to be active in the Mexican heroin trade" (Library of Congress 2003: 17).

But other organizations were coming to the fore. By 1995, it became apparent that Mexican drug trafficking was dominated by about a half-dozen *padrones* (bosses), leaders of cartels, who were sometimes allied, sometimes in competition, and sometimes in violent conflict, although gun battles had been infrequent. They are often referred to by their geographic location, such as the "Gulf cartel." Even though they operate out of discrete sites in Mexico, their stature "comes not from controlling territory so much as from the international scope of their contacts and their ability to operate across Mexico with Government protection" (Golden 1995b: 8). Thus, the leader of the infamous Juárez cartel in the state of Chihuahua, Amado Carrillo-Fuentes, resided in Culiacán, in the neighboring state of Sinaloa, which is actually the home of another cartel by that name. The absence of a strong sense of territoriality means the Mexican drug organizations are best described as *enterprise syndicates*. As such, two of the most important, the Carrillo-Fuentes organization of Juárez and the Arellano-Félix family of Tijuana, "have worked with Russian organized crime partners" (Curtis, Gibbs, and Miró 2004: 15; Library of Congress 2003).

Sinaloa Cartel

Sinaloa is a northwestern Pacific coast agricultural state that, with U.S. encouragement, grew poppies for morphine during World War II. Drug dealers are legendary in the state where they are memorialized in ballads. In 1989, the entire police department of Culiacán, a city of 700,000 and the capital of Sinaloa, was taken into custody by the Mexican army. Also arrested was the assistant director of the antinarcotics program in Sinaloa, who confessed to receiving $23,000 a month to keep an infamous drug boss informed of police activities against him (Rohter 1989b).

In 1993, Joaquín Guzmán Loera, known as "El Chapo" or "Shorty,"—he is 5 feet 6 inches—was arrested for murder and cocaine trafficking. He was sentenced to 20 years, but his Sinaloa cartel remained intact and continued to smuggle tons of cocaine each month into the United States. Indeed, they built a 1,500-foot concrete-reinforced, air-conditioned tunnel between Tijuana and Otay Mesa, a community within the City of San Diego that is one of the busiest commercial land border crossings in the United States.

In 2001, Guzmán escaped from Mexico's toughest prison—two guards for each inmate, isolated cells, and sophisticated video surveillance. A few years earlier, Guzmán's colleague, Palma Salazar, was arrested and 34 police officers, his private protection force, went to jail with him. Guzmán is wanted in the United States and his escape occurred a day after Mexico's Supreme Court ruled that he could be extradited to the United States (Weiner 2001a). In 2005, a close Guzmán ally, head of a Guatemala-based drug organization, escaped from a Mexico City prison. Otto Roberto Herrera Garcia had been one of Central America's most wanted men, and the United States had offered a $2 million reward for his capture (C. Marshall 2005).

In an effort to control most of the drug business in Mexico, Guzmán rebuilt his organization and allied himself with former foes to war on the competing cartels; he was aided by government successes against the Gulf and Tijuana cartels (McKinley 2005a; Thompson and McKinley 2005). Shortly after his escape from prison, Guzmán dispatched the light-skinned, blue-eyed Edgar Valdez Villarreal, known as "La Barbie," with a unit of well-trained gunmen to Nuevo Laredo where they violently challenged the Gulf cartel. Assisting him were agents of Mexico's equivalent of the FBI, while the Gulf cartel was aided by the city's police force (Thompson 2005c). Early in 2005, Mexican authorities found twelve bodies along a major highway in northern Sinaloa State, victims of a machine-gun battle between the cartels (McKinley 2005c).

Guzmán has several planes and at least one helicopter at his disposal. In his hometown of Badiraguato, he is both feared and respected—musicians make up ballads about him. Farmers and cattlemen in the area make a good living growing poppies and tip him off to raids. Indeed, drugs are such an important source of local income that politicians steer clear of conflicts with the traffickers—they also fear assassination (McKinley 2005a). In 2004, the DEA offered a reward of $5 million for Guzmán's capture.

Gulf Cartel

Juan Garcia Abrego was born in 1944 into a notorious smuggling family—his uncle is Juan N. Guerra, the legendary "godfather" of crime in Matamoros, Mexico (Dillon 1996b). Abrego eventually emerged as a leader of the Gulf cartel, controlling drug trafficking throughout northeastern Mexico and along the Gulf of Mexico. The chubby, curly-haired drug czar called "the Doll" or "Dollface" by his subordinates, borrowed organizing techniques from the Cali cartel, including compartmentalizing his organization into cells (Dillon 1996d, 1996g). He is reputed to have pioneered the Mexican role in cocaine trafficking and in over a decade built an empire estimated to be worth $15 billion (Eskridge 1998). Rather than pay cash for moving Cali cartel cocaine into the United States, Abrego decided to take cocaine as payment in kind. "He would guarantee delivery anywhere in the United States for 50 percent of the load. He would assume all risks" (Lupsha 1995: 90). "Instead of being paid $2,000 to move a kilo [2.2 pounds] of cocaine, Garcia Abrego allegedly would turn it into $16,000 or more by selling the drug in Houston, Dallas, or New York, his three main markets" (McMahon 1996: 4). Abrego paid

millions of dollars in bribes and headed a private army—whose members included law enforcement officers—that slaughtered dozens of people (Dillon 1996e; McMahon 1996). In 1996, it was disclosed that the deputy attorney general in charge of Mexico's federal Judicial Police counternarcotics program had accumulated $9 million by protecting Abrego's organization (Dillon 1996c). In 2008, the mayor of Matamoros was arrested in California and charged with smuggling cocaine into the United States.

Abrego was indicted in the United States in 1990, and in 1996 he was arrested in Monterrey by Mexican authorities. He was quickly flown to the United States where a reward of $2 million had been offered for his capture and where he received eleven life terms for drug smuggling. Although Mexico refuses to extradite its citizens for drug charges, Abrego holds U.S. citizenship and was technically expelled from Mexico. About sixty members of Abrego's organization are already serving time in U.S. prisons, which increased the power of competing cartels in the Mexican cities of Juárez and Tijuana (Katel 1996). At the time of his arrest, Abrego's power was waning: His Cali suppliers had cut him off because of the notoriety he had attracted and his most influential government protectors were out of office—he became a victim of Mexico's need to show progress in dealing with drug trafficking (Dillon 1996a). The primary witness against Abrego was a Mexican American FBI agent who, by pretending to be corrupt, had infiltrated his organization.

In the employ of the Gulf cartel is an assassination unit of former Mexican special forces trained in the United States and known as Los Zetas, named after the radio call name of their original leader who was killed in 2002. In 2004, the unit's chief was captured after a gunfight with Mexican agents who found a cache of military-grade automatic weapons and grenades (McKinley 2004a). That same year, a well-organized jailbreak freed five suspected cartel gunman who were being held on murder charges (Reuters 2004a). In 2005, it was reported that the Zetas were operating in Texas, both along the border and further north into San Antonio and Houston where they are believed to be responsible for dozens of murders (Associated Press 2005d).

Their leader, Heriberto Lazcano, 29, known as "El Verdugo," The Executioner, " is reported to have fed victims to the lions and tigers he keeps on his ranches. Lazcano was part of an elite special forces unit sent to combat drug trafficking on the eastern border that, instead, began working for Gulf cartel in the late 1990s. In place of their military pay of $700 a month, they are paid $15,000 a month. Their military discipline, training, arsenal, and wiretap capability make them a formidable organization that has expanded into ransom kidnapping and extortion from businesses (Padgett 2005). In 2008, Mexican federal agents arrested six Zetas who were guarding suitcases stuffed with $6 million in cash (McKinley 2008c).

Cartel militarization and the Mexican government's military response—beginning in 2007, thousands of troops sent into border towns—have resulted in fierce gun battles. Gunmen have refused to surrender and have ambushed soldiers and police officers. They have corrupted local police departments and assassinated honest police commanders. In 2008, after a violent gun battle with soldiers and police officers in Rio Bravo, Mexican authorities arrested three U.S. citizens, gunmen working for the Gulf cartel who had been recruited from across the border (McKinley 2008h). A few days later in Tijuana, government forces fought a three-hour battle with gunmen who used heavy machine guns and rocket-propelled grenades (McKinley 2008d, 2008e).

Tijuana Cartel

A city of more than one million persons just across the border from San Diego, Tijuana is the home of the Arellano-Félix family, seven brothers and four sisters. Noted for their level of violence—brother Ramón is a suspect in more than sixty murders—they literally shot their way into control of drug smuggling along the Mexico-California border (Preston and Pyes 1997). But they have not overlooked bribery: In 1998, two members of an elite Mexican drug enforcement unit working undercover were arrested by federal and state police acting on behalf of the Tijuana drug cartel (Dillon 1998d). Mexican police are reputed to have supplied the cartel with a steady flow of stolen vehicles, and members of the military have arranged for the purchase of assault weapons and machine guns. Using brokers, the brothers provide money to politicians and struggling business people (Golden 2000b).

Like their Colombian counterparts, the Tijuana cartel has intimidated and murdered journalists who have reported on their activities, and victims also include law enforcement officers (Dillon 1997; DEA "Fact Sheet" n.d.). In 2000, Arellano-Félix gunmen tortured and murdered three Mexican drug agents, one of whom was an expert on the Arellanos and their chief pursuer. The three were returning to Tijuana from San Diego, where they were living for security reasons. They were intercepted shortly after crossing the border and before they could retrieve their weapons—there is a dispute between Mexico and the United States about whether agents of one country working in the other can carry weapons (de la Garza 2000; Golden 2000a). On the U.S. side of the border, the cartel employs California street gang members to carry out murders (de la Garza 1997b).

In 1999, ten men believed to be overseeing operations for the Tijuana cartel in southern California were arrested. They were in possession of 1,100 pounds of cocaine and four pounds of heroin; one of those arrested also had $100,000 in cash in his home (A. O'Connor 1999). In addition to heroin and cocaine, the cartel deals in methamphetamine and marijuana. In 2000, DEA agents arrested more than eighty persons in the United States who were involved with selling 117 tons of Tijuana cartel marijuana to Jamaican traffickers. Among those arrested were employees of the FedEx parcel service who arranged to ship the drugs from California to the East Coast (Sniffen 2000).

The Tijuana cartel is allied with the Sonora cartel, and they have been feuding with the Carrillo-Fuentes/Juárez cartel. In 1998, Arellano-Félix gunmen entered a suburb of the city of Ensenada in Baja California, 60 miles south of California. Reportedly high on alcohol and cocaine, they rounded up and shot to death at least nineteen men, women, and children from three families with ties to the Tijuana cartel. The primary target was the head of a group that specialized in guiding drug planes to desert airstrips (Dillon 1998e; Eskridge 1998; Golden 1998c; Sandoval 1998).

"The Arrellano-Félix family, headed by Benjamin, evolved into one of Mexico's most powerful criminal drug enterprises for smuggling multi-ton quantities of drugs yearly" (Constantine 1999b: 8). While Benjamin managed the multimillion-dollar business, his brother Ramón headed security-related operations. Ramón's functions included recruitment of enforcers and killers from the streets of San Diego and Tijuana. In 2000, Ramón and Benjamin were indicted by a federal grand jury, and the U.S. Department of State offered a $2 million reward for their capture. In 2002, Ramón Arellano-Félix, 37, carrying a gold-plated handgun and fake federal police identification, was reportedly killed in a shootout with police. Before a positive identification could be made, his body was claimed by two unidentified persons and cremated. Benjamin was arrested shortly afterward and received a five-year sentence for arms possession. He was subsequently sentenced to 22 years for cocaine trafficking. In 2006, one of the last remaining brothers, Francisco Javier, was captured by the U.S. Coast Guard while deep-sea fishing off Baja, California. The following year, he pled guilty to running a criminal enterprise and received a life sentence. In 2008, one of the Arellano-Félix brothers, Francisco Raphael, 58, was released from a U.S. prison. He had been extradited from Mexico after serving a prison sentence, but was not successfully prosecuted in the United States.

In 2002, U.S. authorities arrested twenty-two suspected members of the Arellano-Félix organization in Minnesota, Colorado, California, and South Dakota (Weiner 2002). By the end of 2002, Mexican authorities had arrested more than 2,000 members of the organization, allowing a competing group headed by Ismael ("Mayo") Zambada Garcia, who lives on a ranch in Sinaloa, to improve their position in Tijuana (Thompson 2004). In 2003, Mexican and U.S. authorities arrested 240 members of Zambada's organization and seized 13 tons of cocaine and $8.3 million in cash (Lichtblau 2003a). In 2008, the last remaining Arellano-Felix brother not in custody or dead, Eduardo, was captured by Mexican federal police after a three-hour shootout in Tijuana ("Mexico Seizes Top Drugs Suspect" 2008).

Imprisoned leaders of the Gulf and Tijuana cartels have been able to continue running their organizations from prison. In 2005, the Mexican government sent in 750 troops and federal police to seize control of a maximum-security prison in which the leaders of the two cartels, who had joined forces in prison, were housed. It was alleged that they had bribed and intimidated guards so that it was necessary for the federal authorities to reassert control over the prison (McKinley 2005b).

Juárez Cartel

Ciudad Juárez, in the state of Chihuahua, is just across the Rio Grande from El Paso, Texas, and has a population of 1.5 million. The city is racked with poverty and lacks a sewage treatment facility but is home to one of Mexico's richest drug cartels. The Juárez cartel is the result of a mid-1980s consolidation of various drug rings accomplished by Rafael Aguilar Guajardo, a notoriously corrupt commander of a local unit of the federal Judicial Police, and his brother Rafael Muñoz Talavera. A 1989 raid on a Los Angeles warehouse uncovered 21 tons of cocaine that was traced to Muñoz

Talavera. After considerable U.S. pressure, Mexican authorities arrested Muñoz and he was held for trial. In 1993, Guajardo was murdered on orders of Amado Carrillo-Fuentes who took charge of the organization (Puente and de la Garza 1999).

The son of a mechanic from the state of Sinaloa, Carrillo-Fuentes proved to be gifted with organizational skills. The nephew of one of Mexico's drug trafficking pioneers, he started his career in the early 1980s as a drug mule for his uncle and built his own organization in the late 1980s, developing important ties to the Herrera Family (discussed earlier) and the Cali cartel. He spent lavishly to gain protection from government at all levels. By 1993, Carrillo-Fuentes and his brothers were in control of the Juárez cartel and the owner of a fleet of Boeing 727s, from which he derived his nickname "Lord of the Skies" (Brant 1997b). Estimates of his wealth reached $25 billion, and the head of Mexico's anti-drug agency was on his payroll—police and military forces were used on his behalf in efforts against rival drug organizations, in particular, the Tijuana cartel (Dillon and Pyes 1997a; Golden 1998a). Responsible for as many as 400 drug-related murders, Carrillo-Fuentes, nevertheless, contributed heavily to the church (de la Garza 1997a). In 1997, at age 41 or 42—neither his birth date nor his face is known to the police—Amado Carrillo-Fuentes died of heart failure after undergoing eight hours of plastic surgery at a posh maternity hospital in Mexico City (Brant 1997a).

In 1996, Muñoz Talavera was cleared of the charges against him—extensive bribery was later revealed as the reason—and launched a violent campaign to regain control of the Juárez cartel from the Carrillo-Fuentes brothers. In the struggle dozens of people died. In 1997, Muñoz gunmen sprayed a popular Juárez restaurant, killing a top Carrillo-Fuentes lieutenant and five bystanders. Several months later, in 1998, when he was age 46, Muñoz's body was discovered in Juárez, bound and with several bullet wounds (Dillon 1998c; de la Garza 1998). In 2004, Rodolfo Carrillo Fuentes, 29, Amado's brother, was killed by gunmen using automatic weapons and driving an armored SUV (Reuters 2004b).

The Carrillo-Fuentes organization continues to flourish, reputedly under the leadership of brother Alcides Ramón Magaña, a former Judicial Police commander and bodyguard for Amado Carrillo-Fuentes. Magaña moved the operations eastward along the Gulf coast and into the Yucatán Peninsula. Nicknamed "El Metro," Magaña had quick success in Quintana Roo state, home of Cancun, a popular vacation spot. In very little time he took what had been Colombian traffickers' territory and made it his own. In the process he reputedly bought the state's governor, who disappeared a few days before leaving office in 1999 and has not been seen since.

The Juárez organization "maintains drug transportation and distribution cells in U.S. cities such as Los Angeles, Houston, Chicago and New York from which it distributes cocaine to Nashville, Miami, Detroit, Raleigh, Houston, Newark, Philadelphia, San Antonio, Tulsa, and Los Angeles, cities where it is sold to domestic organizations The scope of the cartel was revealed by "Operation Impunity," a two-year U.S. federal investigation culminating in 1999 with the arrest of 93 persons and the seizure of more than $19 million in U.S. currency; another $7 million in assets was seized, as well as more than 27,000 pounds of cocaine and more than 4,800 pounds of marijuana ("Press Release" 1999). At the end of 2005, Mexican authorities claimed that the cartel was actually under the control of Ricardo Garcia Urquiza, known as "El Doctor" because he is a physician. In any event, in that year Dr. Urquiza was arrested by Mexican agents ("Cartel Leader Captured" 2005).

Ciudad Juárez continues to be the scene of an incredible level of violence. In the first three months of 2008, more than 210 were murdered, many of them gunmen from elsewhere in the employ of Sinaloa cartel which is contesting the Juárez cartel for control of the shipment of drugs through the city (McKinley 2008b).

Sonora Cartel

The state of Sonora borders Arizona and is ideal for facilitating drug trafficking: It is a sprawling region—Mexico's second largest state in size—of cattle ranches, desert landing strips, and isolated roads that lead north to the border (Dillon and Pyes 1997b). The Sonora cartel was founded by Miguel Ángel Félix-Gallardo, imprisoned since 1989 for the 1985 torture-murder of a U.S. DEA agent. Though wanted by both the Mexican and American governments, Gallardo was able to remain at large for more than a decade. He is a second cousin of the Arellano brothers (Golden 2000b).

The Sonora cartel is now run by the Caro-Quintero brothers, Rafael, Miguel, and Genaro. Like Felix-Gallardo, Rafael Caro-Quintero is imprisoned for his role in the murder of the aforementioned DEA agent. Miguel, who heads the organization, was indicted in the United States and arrested in Mexico in 1992, but the charges against him in Mexico were dismissed under questionable circumstances. Although his organization specializes in cultivation, production, and distribution of marijuana, like the other major drug organizations, it is polydrug in nature, transporting and distributing cocaine and amphetamine. Since 1992, Miguel has operated freely throughout northwestern Mexico, and runs his drug smuggling activities from the city of Caborca in Sonora (Constantine 1999a 1999b). In 1999, the Mexican Supreme Court ruled that if he is arrested by Mexican authorities, Miguel could be extradited to the United States, and in 2001, Mexican authorities arrested him for extradition. Later that year, the Mexican Supreme Court ruled that Mexican citizens could not be extradited to the United States if they faced either the death penalty or life imprisonment.

In addition to drug trafficking, Mexican criminals are involved in extensive alien smuggling, particularly young girls and women to work in brothels, especially those catering to migrant workers (Shelley 2001). These smuggling groups, though highly efficient, are typically less hierarchical and can be characterized more as loose networks of associates. They include local agents who recruit people interested in illegal immigration and who bring them together for departure, travel processors who arrange for identification and any necessary travel documents, and international brokers who facilitate passage along the way and make arrangements for arrival at final destinations. Because illegal aliens are typically handed from smuggler to smuggler during parts of their journey, it is difficult to target and disrupt the networks (Library of Congress 2003).

DOMINICANS

The Dominican Republic, with a population of 8.8 million, occupies about two-thirds of the Caribbean island of Hispaniola, which it shares with Haiti (see Figure 7.4). The Dominican Republic is a major transit country for cocaine moving to the United States and serves drug smugglers as both a command-and-control center and transshipment point. Increasing amounts of designer drugs, especially "ecstasy," are being moved through the Dominican Republic from Europe to the United States and Puerto Rico.

The movement of drugs is aided by the existence of structured and integrated criminal organizations of Dominicans, Puerto Ricans, and Colombians that operate in Santo Domingo as well as in New York, Boston, Providence, and other cities. The Colombians are generally in charge of control and supply in the Caribbean

Ecstasy

Ecstasy, the common name for MDMA (3, 4-MethyleneDioxyMethAmphetamine), is a synthetic drug possessing stimulant and hallucinogenic properties. Ecstasy (or "X-TC") proved popular among white professionals—earning its nickname as a "yuppie drug"—and persons who consider themselves part of the New Age spiritual movement. It is reported to be popular on college campuses in the United States and at dance parties or raves. MDMA is usually ingested orally in tablet or capsule form. It is also available as a powder and is sometimes snorted and occasionally smoked but rarely injected (Abadinsky 2008).

---

and begin the first phase of the transport. Later, Dominicans become the primary transporters (U.S. Department of State 2001). Dominicans have also imported MDMA ("ecstasy") directly from the Netherlands (Weiser 2002).

Although the Dominican Republic is not as depressed as Haiti, in the mid-1960s political unrest and economic upheavals caused many residents to seek their fortunes by going north. Violence often attends elections in the Dominican Republic. In New York City, there are about 575,000 Dominicans, many of whom have illegally entered the United States. They are among the poorest New Yorkers, with a poverty rate of 32 percent compared with the city total of 19 percent (Archibold 2004). Some of these immigrants, legal and illegal, have entered the drug trade. Known as Dominican-Yorks, the traffickers keep a low profile in the United States, returning their profits to cities in the Dominican Republic such as San Francisco de Macorís, conspicuous for its wealth in a country where the per capita income is less than $1,000 a year.

The center of the Dominican wholesale trade in crack is the uptown Manhattan neighborhood of Washington Heights. In recent years, some leaders have slipped out of New York and are running operations from their homeland where corruption is endemic among airport officials and law enforcement. Until 1998, the Dominican Republic refused to extradite its citizens for crimes committed in the United States. In that year, two notorious traffickers were sent to New York where they were wanted for drug trafficking and murder.

Dominicans have demonstrated the necessary talent for moving large amounts of heroin and crack cocaine at the wholesale and street level. They purchase directly from Asian and Colombian importers, sharing a common language and entrepreneurial values with the latter.

FIGURE 7.4   *Map of Hispaniola and the Eastern U.S. coastline*

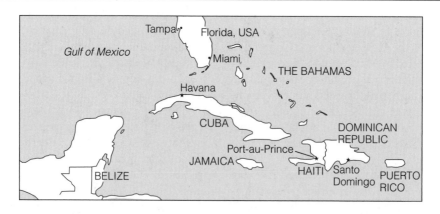

Dominicans have apparently applied their well-known skills as tradesmen and merchants to become New York City's top traffickers and have captured markets in Pennsylvania (Pennsylvania Crime Commission 1990). They also control a significant portion of the cocaine trafficking in New England (DEA 1991a). Dominicans generally provide top-quality uncut drugs at competitive prices, avoiding the common practice of diluting the product as it passes through the distribution chain. Often operating out of grocery stores, bars, and restaurants in Latino neighborhoods, they employ a variety of marketing gimmicks to move their product. In Philadelphia they sold heroin packets with lottery tickets attached that a winner could use to claim an additional twelve packets (Pennsylvania Crime Commission 1990).

The structure of Dominican drug trafficking organizations is based on familial or regional loyalties.

The organizations are *vertically integrated*, with the family maintaining control over several consecutive stages of the operation. They obtain uncut heroin and cocaine from Colombian and Chinese sources on the supply end in New York and then distribute the drug to street-level dealers who may be Dominican, Black, Puerto Rican, white, or someone of other ethnic origins. Activities of the group are directed by the leader through a number of "lieutenants," who may include brothers, sisters, cousins, and friends from home. Lower level workers—largely Dominican nationals, and often illegal aliens—will travel a circuit taking them between New York City and various communities in eastern and central Pennsylvania (and sometimes New Jersey), performing various specialized tasks as they are directed, serving as couriers, security for stash houses, cutters and packagers, lookouts, street dealers, and enforcers. Women often serve as "mules" or couriers, carrying kilo packages on their persons. When riding public transportation, these women may appear to be unaccompanied. Actually they are being shadowed by a group member who can provide protection if needed. (Pennsylvania Crime Commission 1990: 267–68, edited)

Dominicans developed a reputation as reliable dealers who promptly pay their suppliers and avoid violence to muscle in on others or maintain exclusive control of a particular market. Instead, they usually compete on efficiency and pricing, allowing them to avoid high-profile violence (Pennsylvania Crime Commission 1990). However, although "early Dominican gangs were known for keen marketing techniques . . . their successors in the 1990s mark out their territories" and use violence to maintain hegemony (Kleinknecht 1996: 260–61). Indeed, several Dominican groups have become noted for their excessive violence, both to maintain internal discipline and to deal with competitors. In one instance, "The Company," a Brooklyn-based Dominican gang, even lured a police officer to his death (Wren 1998b).

Dominicans have come to dominate the middle echelon between the Colombians and the street dealers of cocaine and heroin in the New York City area and into New England (Rohter and Krauss 1998a; Wren 1998b). In part, this is a result of Colombian dissatisfaction with their Mexican counterparts. By 1995, major Colombian organizations had established themselves in the Dominican Republic to coordinate activities with their Dominican partners. "While the bulk of Colombian cocaine and heroin continues to move through Mexico, the Colombian traffickers have in the last few years come full circle, returning to the Caribbean as a base of operations." And the influence of drug money on the island has been pervasive: "Office buildings, hotels and shopping centers are springing up in Santo Domingo, Santiago, and San Francisco de Macoris—often in the gaudy style that some describe as narcodeco" (Rohter and Krauss 1998b: 6). Police corruption is widespread and often coordinated with law enforcement counterparts in Colombia.

The Dominicans and their Colombian partners have made Haiti, which (along with the Dominican Republic) lies roughly between Colombia and Florida, the fastest growing transit point for cocaine being shipped to the United States. Haiti has proven attractive to the traffickers because it is the poorest country in the hemisphere, making it relatively cheap to find criminal labor and bribe officials. The police had to be created from scratch after the old force was abolished in the wake of the American troop landing in 1994; they have limited training and resources and have become notoriously corrupt. Light aircraft land with their drug cargoes on Route 9 in Port-au-Prince where Haitian national police block traffic and help with offloading and ground transport. Smugglers then leave Haitian ports in speedboats laden with drugs without interference from the understaffed coast guard (Polgreen and Weiner 2004; Sisk 2004).

MARA SALVATRUCHA (MS-13 OR LOS MARA)

In Salvadoran slang, *mara* means posse, and *salvatrucha* means "street-tough Salvadoran," although some sources (for example, Martel 2006) state that the name derives from a Spanish term for fire ants. El Salvador is one of the poorest countries in Latin America with almost half its population living in poverty. A civil war that began in 1980 left more than 70,000 people dead and displaced a fifth of the population.

Around 1988 or 1989, a small number of the roughly 300,000 Salvadorans living in Los Angeles formed MS-13. Several years later, the United States adopted a get-tough policy and began deporting thousands of Central Americans, including members of MS-13 who suddenly found themselves in the midst of a civil war. The gang spread among demobilized soldiers from the *Farabundo Marti Front for National Liberation* (FMNL), a leftist guerrilla organization trained in the use of firearms, explosives, and booby traps. In response, El Salvador cracked down on MS-13, and after being stranded in a country they did not know, the MS-13 deportees made their way back to the United States; they were accompanied by their battle-hardened brethren from the FMNL. The recycling continues, and there are an estimated 6,000 to 10,000 members in the United States—many of whom have been previously arrested and deported (Campo-Flores 2005; Quirk 2008).

MS-13 members have international connections with members maintaining constant contact with counterparts in El Salvador. To the dismay of U.S. authorities, these alliances provide MS-13 members with access to military arms and the wherewithal to traffic them to this country. Their experience with illegal immigration has led MS-13 to control many of the "coyote services" that bring aliens from Central America into the United States.

MS-13 operates in small groups known as *cliques* whose members range in age from 11 to 40 and whose leadership consists of one or two individuals known as *veteranos*. These are usually older members who have the overall responsibility of organizing meetings, directing criminal activity, regulating behavior, and maintaining cohesion among members. The number of members in each *clique* varies. While MS-13 operates in at least 42 states and the District of Columbia, with between 6,000 and 10,000 members, according to the FBI there is no official national leadership structure.

Individuals seeking membership in MS-13 are subject to various forms of initiation including beatings. Some candidates are "jumped in," a ritual that consists of a candidate being beaten by gang members for a period of thirteen seconds. In some *cliques*, participation in felonious activity may be required. There have also been instances where individuals have been required to assault a police officer in order to gain full membership. To signify allegiance, once accepted into the organization, members are expected to receive a tattoo (New Jersey Commission of Investigation 2004). Indeed, most *Los Mara* members are easily recognized by the tattoos on their heads, necks, and arms bearing the group's symbols: "MS," "13," and "18," in addition to dice, crossbones, and daggers, the colors blue and white, and hand signs: the thumb holding the two middle fingers pressed to the palm (Brzezinski 2004).

Although MS-13 was originally a self-defense group against local Mexican gangs—Salvadorans speak Spanish differently from Mexicans—today, there are Mexicans in leadership positions. *Los Mara* quickly developed a reputation for being extremely violent, and "members have committed violent offenses at appalling levels—dismembering bodies, terrifying drive-by shootings in broad daylight, and, in a few cases, hacking entire families to death" (Vaquera and Bailey 2004: 6). While *Los Mara* is reputed to be highly organized and disciplined with a vertical command structure in El Salvador, this is presently absent in the United States (Campos-Flores 2005).

Rounding out their criminal repertoire, *Los Mara* members traffic in methamphetamine, and their range of activities includes large-scale theft, chop shops, and extortion. They have developed important ties to Mexican and Colombian drug cartels. Because many are illegal immigrants to the United States, the U.S. Bureau of Immigration and Customs Enforcement (ICE) has been a leading agency in efforts against the MS-13 (LeDuff 2005). Other law enforcement agencies have been critical of ICE for arresting and deporting *Los Mara* members who have been under intense investigation before they can be charged with new crimes because deported gang members often return to the United States, and the recycling continues.

In response to the threat posed by the group, the FBI has created an MS-13 National Gang Task Force. In 2008, seven members of MS-13, including three leaders, pleaded guilty to RICO (discussed in Chapter 15) racketeering conspiracy charges arising out of the group's activities in Tennessee. Among those pleading guilty was Ericka ("Shorty") Cortez who was sentenced to 46 months of imprisonment for her role in a murder conspiracy. One of the group's leaders in Tennessee was sentenced to 45 years and a codefendant to life in prison. That same year in neighboring North Carolina, twenty-six MS-13 members

were indicted for murder and racketeering (U.S. Department of Justice press releases).

As part of an investigation by U.S. Immigration and Customs Enforcement (ICE) that ended in 2008, ICE agents set up an undercover storefront in Richmond, California, disguised as an export warehouse. From that location, an undercover officer, posing as a corrupt car exporter, purchased sixteen stolen vehicles. The investigation led to the seizure of more than twenty weapons, including three high-powered assault rifles, two machine pistols, and three shotguns. One of those shotguns was equipped with a high-capacity "magazine drum," allowing the weapon to be loaded with more than twenty rounds of ammunition at a time. In addition, agents involved in the case made nine separate narcotics seizures involving cocaine and methamphetamine (U.S. Department of Justice press release October 23, 2008).

THE MEXICAN MAFIA

Prison-based gangs have been gaining prominence as organized criminal groups, most notably the Mexican Mafia. Found in at least nine state prison systems and reputed to be the most powerful of the prison organized crime groups, the Mexican Mafia (also known as *la M*—pronounced *la em-aay*) comprises primarily Mexican American convicts and ex-convicts from the barrios of East Los Angeles. Like many other prison gangs, as well as their street counterparts, the Mexican Mafia has a "blood-in-blood-out" credo: Murder or the drawing of blood is a prerequisite for membership, and those seeking to resign will be killed.

Its origins are traced to the Deuel Vocational Institute in Tracy, California, where, in 1957, thirteen young Mexican Americans from the Maravilla area of East Los Angeles began the Mexican Mafia as a self-protection group. The number 13 has additional significance for *la M*, since *M* is the thirteenth letter of the alphabet. They soon "began to control such illicit activities as homosexual prostitution, gambling, and narcotics. They called themselves the Mexican Mafia out of admiration for *La Cosa Nostra*" (PCOC 1986: 73).

Aryan Brotherhood

Allied with the Mexican Mafia, the Aryan Brotherhood was founded in 1964 by white inmates at San Quentin in opposition to a black prison gang, the Black Guerilla Family. The Aryan Brotherhood soon became infamous for their level of violence, extraordinary even by prison standards. By 1975, the gang had spread into most of California's prisons with members sporting a green shamrock on their hands. Once dismissed as a fringe white supremacist gang, its members have now taken control of large parts of America's maximum-security prisons in California, Illinois, Texas, and Kansas. Also known as AB and the Brand, the Aryan Brotherhood established a hierarchical structure and asserted control over various prison rackets including gambling—debtors pay up by having a relative or friend send an untraceable money order to a designated member on the outside. In an effort to thwart their power, prison officials have transferred many identified members to supermax prisons. While the leadership is serving life sentences, released members maintain gang ties and represent a community threat (Grann 2004). In 2006, three AB leaders received life terms for what prosecutors called decades of terrorizing some of the nation's most dangerous prisons.

Attempts by the Department of Corrections to diminish gang power by transferring members to other institutions only helped spread their influence. Vigorous recruiting occurs among the most violent Mexican American inmates, particularly those housed in adjustment centers for the most dangerous and incorrigible. In 1967, Mexican Mafia reliance on wholesale violence increased, and in that year members attacked the first Mexican American outside their group. This attack on an inmate from rural northern California led to the formation of a second Mexican American gang, *La Nuestra Familia*, with whom the Mexican Mafia has been feuding ever since. The gang is anti-black and has aligned itself with the Aryan Brotherhood, an extremely violent prison-based white supremacist gang.

By the mid-1960s the Mexican Mafia had assumed control over prison heroin trafficking and numerous other inmate activities. In 1966, it started to move its operations outside the prison, and it reputedly organized Hispanic gangs into a confederation to confront black Los Angeles gangs for control of the drug trade (Mydans 1995). The gang, which has a membership of about 400, has direct ties with Mexican trafficking organizations and asserts control over drug trafficking by Hispanic street gangs, collecting "street taxes" in exchange for the privilege of staying in business and protection against encroachment by other gangs. In 1998, twelve members of the Mexican Mafia were convicted in a federal court in California of Racketeering and Corrupt Organizations (RICO) statute (discussed in Chapter 15) violations: directing a terror campaign from their prison cells to control drug trafficking by street gangs (Associated Press 1998b).

In the next chapter, we will examine black organized crime, as well as domestic African American and foreign-based criminal organizations.

SUMMARY

- The primary, almost exclusive, business of Latino organized crime is drugs. The drug cartels of Colombia, a country with a history and culture of violence, are the major distributors of cocaine and more recently heroin.
- Beset by Marxist insurgencies and right-wing paramilitaries who control large segments of the countryside, the police and military have had limited success in reducing the amount of drugs leaving Colombia.
- Even though the Colombian government has succeeded in dismantling the two most

infamous organizations, the Medellín and Cali cartels, smaller groups that have organized along bureaucratic/compartmentalized lines continue to be a formidable presence in Colombia.

- Mexico has a history of one-party domination intertwined with corruption, particularly in the underpaid law enforcement sector. Drug groups are bureaucratically organized, but in a Mexican fashion built around familial relationships.

- As opposed to organized crime groups that expend resources to defend territorial hegemony, Mexican organizations usually focus on enterprise that, nevertheless, often brings them into violent conflict with competing groups. Originating as heroin distributors, links with Colombian cartels led them to expand into cocaine.

- The dismantling of the major Colombian cartels has enabled the Mexicans to deal directly with Bolivian and Peruvian sources for cocaine. Better organization and an extensive drug portfolio have enabled Mexican cartels to diversify, dividing operations into heroin, cocaine, marijuana, and now methamphetamine units.

- Rounding out the portfolio of Mexican criminal organizations is involvement in the smuggling of immigrants, particularly young girls and women, to work in brothels, especially those catering to migrant workers.

- The Dominican Republic serves as a transshipment point for drugs, and Dominican criminals in the United States purchase directly from Asian and Colombian importers, sharing a common language and entrepreneurial values with the latter.

- Dominicans apply their well-known skills as tradesmen and merchants; generally provide top-quality, uncut drugs at competitive prices; and prefer to compete without violence.

- *Mara Salvatrucha*, which originated in El Salvador, has been a strong presence in Hispanic neighborhoods and has moved into more rural parts of the United States following the migration of Latino workers. With an estimated 8,000 to 10,000 members active in more than thirty states, M-13 has thousands of additional members in El Salvador, Honduras, and Guatemala.

- M-13 has elaborate initiation ceremonies and tattoos, and although reputed to be highly organized and disciplined with a vertical command structure in El Salvador, this is currently absent in the United States.

- *Los Mara* members traffic in methamphetamine and a range of other activities including large-scale theft, chop shops, and extortion. They have developed important ties to Mexican and Colombian drug cartels.

- Prison-based gangs have been gaining prominence as organized criminal groups, most notably the Mexican Mafia, which has been allied with the Aryan Brotherhood. Members released from prison remain in the gang, trafficking in drugs and extorting money from weaker dealers.

REVIEW QUESTIONS

1. What is the relationship between Cuban exiles, Colombians, and cocaine trafficking?
2. What variables account for the Colombian success in the cocaine business?
3. Why has it been so difficult for Colombia to eradicate its cocaine trafficking organizations?
4. Why has it been difficult for the United States to respond to the Colombian cocaine trafficking organizations?
5. What is the relationship between cocaine trafficking and politics in Colombia?
6. What are the characteristics of Mexican organized crime?

7. What it is the relationship between Colombian and Mexican criminal organizations?
8. How has the political climate of Mexico aided in the development of criminal organizations?
9. What are the unique characteristics of Dominican criminal organizations?
10. What is the relationship between the Dominicans and the Colombians?
11. What is the Mexican Mafia?
12. What is *Mara Salvatrucha* (or MS-13 or *Los Mara*)?
13. How does M-13 differ from other street gangs?

C H A P T E R
8
Black Organized Crime

Black is an imprecise term that includes many diverse groups, domestic and international, and "black organized crime" encompasses a variety of criminal groups that may in fact share only their race.[1] But race is an organizing variable much as religious background serves as a common denominator for Jewish criminals, and a shared cultural heritage serves the same purpose for the American Mafia. This chapter will examine African American, West African, and Jamaican organized crime.

African American criminal groups are using the drug trade much as their Irish, Jewish, and Italian predecessors did bootlegging. Black criminal groups in the United States, however, lack the incubation provided by the corrupt urban political machines and ineffective federal law enforcement of previous centuries. Black opportunity in organized crime (OC) has roughly paralleled opportunity in the wider legitimate community.

Important black criminal entrepreneurs were operating in the United States in the early decades of the twentieth century. In Chicago, African American entrepreneurs were successful in controlling extensive gambling operations in the city's "black belt," where they delivered votes and funds to the Republican mayor of Chicago, "Big Bill" Thompson. In 1927, after Thompson had been out of office for four years, black voters helped sweep him back into city hall. In the election of 1931, Thompson lost to what became known as the Chicago Democratic machine that dominated the city until almost end of the twentieth century. Like their white counterparts, black political-criminal leadership switched their allegiance and became part of the Democratic machine (Lombardo 2002b).

African American criminals dominated the numbers (illegal lottery) racket in cities such as New York, Philadelphia, and Chicago until they were overpowered by violent white gangsters such as Dutch Schultz (New York) and Sam Giancana (Chicago) who had superior police/political connections (Lombardo 2002b; Schatzberg 1994). Until his death of natural causes in 1968, Ellsworth ("Bumpy") Johnson headed an organization that ruled over the black Harlem underworld in New York in an alliance with the Genovese crime Family. The civil rights/"black power" movements of the 1960s eventually made it impossible for white

---

[1]*Race* is also an imprecise term, but discussion of the topic is beyond the scope of this book.

criminals to operate with the freedom necessary to continue dominating indigenous black criminal organizations.

A variety of black criminal groups exist throughout the United States; some are home-grown, such as Chicago's Gangster Disciples, while others, such as Jamaican posses, are imported. Important black criminal organizations have been active in the heroin business in New York, Detroit, Chicago, Philadelphia, and Washington, DC. Although blacks have traditionally been locked out of many activities associated with organized crime (labor racketeering and loansharking, for example) by prejudice, *dope is an equal opportunity employer*. African American criminal groups made important strides in the heroin business when the Vietnam War exposed many black soldiers to the heroin markets of the Golden Triangle—previously, black groups were dependent on American Mafia Families for their heroin. As a result of their over-seas experience, black organizations were able to bypass the American Mafia and buy directly from suppliers in Thailand. A pioneer in this endeavor was Frank Lucas and his "Country Boys."

FRANK LUCAS

The activities of Frank Lucas were popularized in the 2007 motion picture *American Gangster* starring Denzel Washington and Russell Crowe. Born to a large sharecropper's family who would later become part of his drug ring, in 1946, Lucas arrived in Harlem from North Carolina as a teen-ager with a serious criminal history. Lucas con-tinued his criminal activities as an armed robber until he found work with Bumpy Johnson as a col-lector in the numbers business; he also picked up Mafia heroin packages from "Pleasant Avenue."[2] In 1951, Johnson received a 15-year sentence for drug trafficking. Released after four years, in 1968, Bumpy was awaiting trial on another drug

Frank Lucas, the man that Denzel Washington portrayed in "American Gangster," is shown in New York in 2007.

charge when he died of a heart attack. Johnson had introduced Lucas to the drug business and after Bumpy's death, he had an inspiration, a way to bypass the Genovese ("French") connection—Johnson decided to go to Southeast Asia. "Because the war was on, and people were talking about GIs getting strung out over there, I knew if the shit is good enough to string out GIs, then I can make myself a killing" (quoted in Jacobson 2000: 41).

In the early 1970s, the famed "French Con-nection" was coming apart, and although he had never been to the Far East, the brazen, street-wise Lucas, traveling alone, quickly made contact with sources of heroin. A former Army sergeant, a North Carolina "homeboy" married to a Lucas cousin, was running a bar in Bangkok; together they organized a "military-homeboy" organization. They brought in a country carpenter from North Carolina who constructed copies of government coffins, but with false bottoms to hold six to eight kilos of heroin. Military personnel were bribed and the Southeast Asian connection was complete (Jacobson 2000). Ron Chepesiuk and Anthony Gonzalez interviewed the aforementioned Army

---

[2]Manhattan's Harlem neighborhood is informally divided into black, Latino, and Italian sections. The Italian section, known by its major street—Pleasant Avenue, has been a stronghold of the Genovese crime Family.

sergeant—Leslie ("Ike") Atkinson—in federal prison where he was completing a 31-year sentence and present a different version of the Lucas story: It was Atkinson, familiar with the military, who set up the drug-smuggling operation with a group of partners dubbed the "Black Masonic" club. And it was Atkinson who helped the barely literate Lucas get a visa through the Thai embassy in Washington and who agreed to allow Lucas to run the U.S. end of the enterprise. Atkinson told Ron Chepesiuk and Anthony Gonzalez that drugs were never shipped in coffins.

In a typical operation, a Lucas importer's agent left Kennedy Airport for Thailand carrying $600,000 in brand new $50s and $100s. In Bangkok, he would check into a hotel and telephone the overseas source's agent. The caller offered a password and was given instructions about where to deliver the money. At the money drop, the Lucas agent was informed of the shipping arrangements by an Asian. Shortly afterward, 150 kilos of heroin with a 1974 retail value of more than $50 million was smuggled into Georgia in the footlocker and trunks of a soldier returning to Fort Gordon. "The heroin is transported into New York by automobile with two back-up vehicles fore and aft. In New York, it is secreted in one of the apartments rented throughout the city for this purpose. Lucas then arranges for the cutting and distribution" (Langlais 1978: 14).

The stateside Country Boys organization was restricted to blood relatives and friends from rural North Carolina who actively trafficked the Lucas "Blue Magic" brand of heroin on Harlem's 116th Street while two Lucas brothers, Shorty and Larry, operated in northern New Jersey and the Bronx, New York. Frank Lucas also supplied rings in Chicago, North Carolina, and Los Angeles (Langlais 1978). Lucas quickly became a multimillionaire with a Cayman Islands bank account, office buildings in Detroit, apartments in Miami and Los Angeles, a string of gas stations and dry cleaning shops, and a several-thousand acre spread in North Carolina with 300 head of Black Angus cattle.

Like other major criminals before and after, Lucas had a fatal flaw. He enjoyed the public spotlight, and his high-profile drug-kingpin lifestyle—a Rolls Royce, flashy diamond jewelry, a chinchilla coat, retinue of bodyguards, women, and associates—eventually attracted law enforcement scrutiny (and apparently the ire of the Genovese Family): In 1975, a New York Police Department/Drug Enforcement Administration (DEA) task force (acting on a tip from "Pleasant Avenue" sources) staged a surprise raid on Lucas's Teaneck, New Jersey residence. They recovered more than half a million dollars in small bills and keys to safe deposits in the Cayman Islands. In 1975, Lucas was convicted of drug violations, and although sentenced to a federal 40-year term, he was subsequently released in 1983; he had provided the government with valuable information—the man who fashioned himself "Superfly" had become "Supersnitch" (Chepesiuk and Gonzalez 2007; Jacobson 2000). In 1984, Lucas was convicted again, this time for arranging to sell one ounce of heroin, and sentenced to seven years.

NICKY BARNES

Another high-profile criminal would suffer the same fate as Frank Lucas. Leroy Antonio ("Nicky") Barnes was born in New York's Harlem in 1933. In 1977, he posed in a color photo for the front page of the *New York Times* magazine that declared him "Mister Untouchable" because he had beaten government charges thirteen times—witnesses against Barnes disappeared or were found murdered. President Jimmy Carter was outraged and ordered the Justice Department to make Barnes a priority.

Barnes cultivated a public image: He donated turkeys to homeless shelters and toys to children at Christmas and sponsored a Harlem basketball team. In the nightspots he frequented, the superbly dressed heroin trafficker, his business notwithstanding, would enter like a movie star and be treated accordingly by adoring fans (Chepesiuk 2007).

A street-level drug dealer working for Dominicans, in 1959 Barnes was convicted and sent to New York's Green Haven Correctional Facility, a maximum-security prison located in Stormville.

There, Barnes met Matthew Madonna, a drug dealer and member of the Lucchese Family; they discussed how best to run the drug business. Paroled in 1962, three years later, Barnes was back in Green Haven for possessing $500,000 worth of heroin. There he met Joe ("Crazy Joey") Gallo (discussed in Chapter 4), a member of the Colombo Family who aided him in finding an attorney who succeeded in overturning Barnes's conviction.

From Madonna, Barnes got the idea of establishing a council of major traffickers in Harlem. Failing in his first attempt in 1969, with Madonna's Pleasant Avenue connection providing heroin, Barnes set up a council that consisted of seven lieutenants, each of whom controlled a dozen mid-level distributors, who in turn supplied about forty street-level dealers. Like the American Mafia, council members took an oath of brotherhood, pooled their resources, and allocated territories. In a typical operation, a Madonna confederate would park a car whose steel-reinforced trunk was loaded with plastic-wrapped kilos of heroin. The confederate would slip the key to Madonna who would hand it off to Barnes at a prearranged location. Barnes in turn would slip the key and the car's make and location to a confederate. Payments were handled in the same manner—an exchange of keys to a car whose trunk was filled with hundreds of thousands of dollars (Barnes and Folsom 2007). The council eventually distributed heroin throughout New York State, in Pennsylvania and Canada, and as far west as Arizona (Chepesiuk 2007).

Each kilo of heroin was cut—diluted—by an assembly line of women who worked naked—a precaution against purloining any of the precious powder—throughout the night. With a quarter spoon they scooped the heroin and added mannitol (a colorless, crystalline sugar) and quinine before placing the mix in a glassine envelope, the kind used by stamp collectors; the envelopes were sealed with black tape. In this manner, a kilo of almost pure heroin could be converted into eight to ten kilos. From there, sacks of individual packets of heroin would be moved to middlemen. A shipment of 200 kilos of heroin cost the council $5 million and earned them $20 million in 1973 dollars (Barnes and Folsom 2007).

But his life as Mr. Untouchable was relatively brief. In 1976, Barnes's supplier, Matthew Madonna, was arrested by federal agents during a key handoff, and the following year Mr. Untouchable was convicted by the first federal trial to use an anonymous jury and sentenced to life imprisonment. In 1981, he discovered that while members of the council were not supporting his legal efforts, they were making a very public display of cavorting with both his wife and his girlfriend—the DEA had sent him photographic proof. Barnes became a government informant leading to the conviction of fifty dealers and their associates. He was never offered an early release for his cooperation and languished in prison for 15 years until released into the Witness Protection Program in 1998 at age 64 (Barnes and Folsom 2007; Chepesiuk 2007).

GANGSTER DISCIPLES[3]

Frank Lucas could use his rural North Carolina ties to build a personalistic organization, but other African American criminals usually resort to a bureaucratic model. Francis Ianni (1974: 158) notes that for African American criminals, "prisons and the prison experience form the most important locus for establishing the social relationships that form the basis for partnerships in organized crime." During the 1970s, in the Stateville (Illinois) Correctional Facility, a maximum-security prison, thirty black inmates from Chicago formed the Royal Family, patterning themselves after popular renditions of Mario Puzo's *Godfather*. They formed close ties with the Chicago Outfit, acting as "muscle" and contract executioners in Chicago and elsewhere (Brodt 1981a, 1981b). The bureaucratic model was adopted by Chicago's best-known African American crime group, the Gangster Disciples.

The occupational opportunity structure of the United States has changed dramatically,

---

[3]Unless otherwise cited, this section is based on information from Bey (1995), Lehmann and McNamee (1995), Martin (1996), Martin and O'Connor (1996a, 1996b), O'Brien, O'Connor, and Papajohn (1995), O'Connor (1996b, 1996c), Papajohn and Dell'Angela (1995), and a variety of public and private sources.

characterized by a significant reduction in the number of good-paying jobs available to low-skilled workers. As such, the structural sources of mobility available to earlier immigrant groups have narrowed considerably. The deindustrialization of American society means that major cities are different places today than they were during the times of major European immigration. Advances in transportation and communication, industrial technology, and the global economy have transformed cities from centers of production and distribution to centers of administration, finance, and the exchange of information. In this environment, the blue-collar jobs that once provided a means of social mobility have vanished or moved to the Third World.

The congruent processes of social and spatial mobility that allowed earlier disadvantaged inner-city residents to succeed in society do not apply to large numbers of African Americans today. As a result, we have witnessed the formation of an urban underclass composed of men and women who are excluded from participation in mainstream occupations. This structural entrapment denies people a method of maturing out of crime and has fueled the development of supergangs such as Chicago's Gangster Disciples (Robert M. Lombardo, personal correspondence).

The Gangster Disciples (GD) was formed as the result of a merger of two South Side gangs, one headed by Larry Hoover (Supreme Gangsters) and the other by "King" David Barksdale (Black Disciples). The primary symbol of the GDs is a six-pointed "star of David" and crossed pitchforks; more elaborate versions include a heart.

In 1973, Hoover, born in Jackson, Mississippi, in 1950, was convicted of planning and ordering the murder of a man who had held up a GD drug house. Hoover has been incarcerated ever since, serving a 150-year sentence. After Barksdale's death from kidney failure in 1974, and despite his imprisonment, leadership was assumed by Hoover who was able to merge the Disciples into his organization now called the Gangster Disciples. With plenty of time on his hands, the incarcerated Larry Hoover developed a corporate-type structure for his organization (Figure 8.1).

While dabbling in community activities and local politics, the GDs have remained active in selling cocaine and heroin throughout Chicago, a number of suburban areas, and in several states including Wisconsin, Indiana, Missouri, Oklahoma, and Georgia. They also extort money from other drug dealers for the right to sell in areas in which the GDs assert control. Independent dealers who have achieved a level of success are typically approached by GD representatives and told to choose from three alternatives: (1) join the Gangster Disciples; (2) stop selling drugs; or (3) die.

Lower-ranking members who actually sell the drugs at the retail level keep most of the profit they make—they do not necessarily share it with higher-ranking members or the organization as a whole. Instead, the hierarchy makes considerable income from wholesaling drugs to these members. The GDs have been able to pool drug profits, street taxes, and membership dues to establish and operate legitimate businesses including apartment buildings, sometimes for the purpose of money laundering and to serve as centers for illegal operations. As noted several times earlier, a criminal organization can exhibit a formal structure while its economic activities may actually involve small firms or partnerships among members and include nonmember associates—the formal structure is not necessarily the same as the economic structure. However, the Gangster Disciples' size—about 6,000 members[4]—requires a corporate-style structure.

Indeed, the size of the GDs requires a level of bureaucracy rarely seen in organized crime, making the organization vulnerable to prosecution. A list is kept of all persons dealing drugs in GD territory so they can be forced to pay street taxes—one day's profit per week. In a 1995 raid on a GD front group—Save the Children Promotions, Inc.—federal agents found detailed records including an organizational chart, a list of GD officers and their rank, a list of opposing gang leaders, the gang's pledge of allegiance, and its "laws"—sixteen that

---

[4]According to one report (McCormick 1999), the GDs have 50,000 members in thirty-five states.

FIGURE 8.1   *Gangster Disciples*

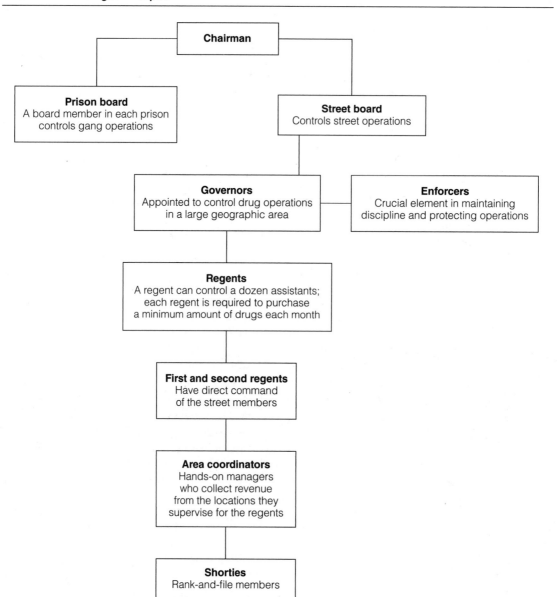

each member must memorize (Decker, Bynum, and Weisel 1998).

Inside prison, "legal coordinators" and "education ministers" indoctrinate new members with GD propaganda and assist fellow inmates in their appeals. Imprisoned members are instructed to complete their high school education and learn rudimentary principles of law from law books available in prison. They are directed to strengthen their bodies in prison weight rooms.

There has been extensive political involvement by the Gangster Disciples, at least in part to aid in the parole release efforts of their imprisoned leader. Under the name of 21st Century VOTE, GDs engaged in voter registration drives and have supported unsuccessful candidates for the city council. Support for Hoover's parole came from a former Chicago mayor and several state and local elected officials interested in the support of 21st Century VOTE. Most of these officials expressed dismay—if not remorse—when in 1995, Hoover and thirty-eight GDs were named in an indictment charging 149 counts of criminal conduct involving their drug trafficking operations. Authorities devised a prison visitor's pass with a hidden transmitter, and Hoover was recorded passing orders to lieutenants who visited him at the Vienna (Illinois) Correctional Center. One of those indicted was a Chicago police officer who had been assigned to the Gang Crimes Unit—she received a twelve-and-one-half-year prison sentence. Also convicted was a 30-year-old member of the "street board" (see Figure 8.1) who in 2000 was sentenced to 100 years (O'Connor 2000).

During the GD trials it was revealed that the offices of 21st Century VOTE served as a drop-off site for street taxes collected by gang members. In 1997, Hoover and Gregory Shell, GD leader on the street, were convicted of forty counts of drug trafficking (O'Connor 1997). Shell was sentenced to life imprisonment in 1998; Hoover was given six additional life sentences. Later that year, Darryl ("Pops") Johnson, then 33, who ranked second below Hoover, was sentenced to death for his role in the murder of two GD members who were suspected of being informants—Johnson rewarded the executioners with new cars. In 1999, three GD

officers who had vied for gang leadership were sentenced to life imprisonment for supervising a multimillion-dollar cocaine operation (O'Connor 1999). Following his additional convictions, Hoover was transferred to a federal supermax prison in Colorado.

As a result of the imprisonment or indictment of virtually its entire hierarchy and the conviction of about one hundred members and associates, the gang is having difficulties maintaining discipline and thwarting encroachments by rival groups. Street taxes often go unpaid or uncollected, and since the 1995 indictments, several members have been killed by other GD members or rival gangs selling drugs where the GDs once claimed hegemony. In 1997, the 19-year-old who ran a drug territory on the South Side was recorded exhorting his juvenile drug sellers to carry firearms at their drug spots—he received a 24-year federal prison sentence. That same year, the government taped a meeting at which a leading GD board member exhorted members to join in a "war" to retake territory lost to rivals since the federal crackdown, in particular, to deal with the Black P. Stone Nation, now known as the El Rukns, that had once been Chicago's premier African American gang. The GDs had been warring with the Black P. Stone Nation on and off for decades. In 2002, thirty-four members and associates of the GDs were indicted by a federal grand jury for using Chicago public housing projects as drug bazaars. Devoid of the tight discipline of Larry Hoover, the GDs have splintered into dozens of different factions.

EL RUKNS/BLACK P. STONE NATION

Chicago's El Rukns was founded by Jeff Fort who was born in Mississippi in 1947. Fort was brought to Chicago by his mother in 1955, and they eventually settled on South Blackstone Avenue in the poverty-stricken Woodlawn neighborhood. Slightly built, Fort left school after the fourth grade but nevertheless emerged as leader of Woodlawn's notorious Blackstone Rangers, named after the intersection of Sixty-fifth Street and Blackstone Avenue. He would grow into a physically imposing adult—from lifting weights in prison—with a beard and braids, often sporting fur coats and a Chinese coolie-type triangular hat.

With Fort at its head, the Blackstone Rangers fought a long and bloody gang war with a rival group. In 1965, the charismatic leader organized a coalition of twenty-one gangs into the Black P. Stone Nation governed by a commission of gang leaders known as the "main 21," with Fort as the head. From an initial membership of about 200, in three years it was in the thousands. As opposed to the exclusiveness of American Mafia membership, the Blackstone Rangers actively recruited and there are indications of violence being used against those who declined a membership invitation. Under Fort's direction they moved from extorting money from pimps to businesses in Woodlawn that catered to upscale clientele in Hyde Park (Chepesiuk 2007).

In 1969, referring to the Black P. Stone Nation as a community group, President Richard Nixon invited Fort to his inauguration. Through the efforts of some white clergymen and community activists who were seeking to channel gang violence into more constructive pursuits, the Black P. Stone Nation was given a federal grant of $1 million from the Office of Economic Opportunity for an elaborate grassroots learning program. Mayor Richard M. Daley was outraged, and in 1968 and 1969 the grant was the subject of a U.S. Senate investigation. In response to a subpoena, Fort appeared before the Senate Permanent Subcommittee on Investigations, introduced himself, and then walked out. In 1972, he was imprisoned for contempt of Congress and embezzlement of $7,500 in federal funds (Glab 1997).

While in prison, Fort had an epiphany and founded the El Rukns, a "Moorish" religious organization, and dubbed himself Prince Malik. After serving two years of a five-year sentence, Fort was paroled and his organization began to dominate large areas of the black community. He purchased a home in Milwaukee for his wife and children but spent most of his time in Chicago's South Side riding in a chauffeured limousine with several bodyguards. He granted no interviews and rarely spoke to anyone who was not part of his

organization, which Fort had restructured into a corporate-style entity with hand-picked generals at the top and with significantly reduced numbers of rank–and-file members (from several thousand to several hundred) for greater control. They converted a once-elegant theater at 3949 S. Drexel into a heavily fortified headquarters, the Grand Major Temple of America. Their application for tax-exempt status as a religious organization, however, was denied (Chepesiuk 2007).

In line with a longstanding Chicago tradition, the El Rukns established the Young Grassroots Independent Voters, and in the 1983 mayoral race, the Cook County Democratic organization paid them $10,000 to campaign in black wards and serve as poll watchers for Mayor Jane M. Byrne. In 1984, the Reverend Jesse Jackson publicly praised them for their role in a voter registration drive on behalf of his presidential campaign (Shipp 1985).

The El Rukns established their own real estate company and invested in apartment buildings; there were plans for restaurants and construction companies when, in 1983, Fort was indicted for participation in a cocaine conspiracy. Before his trial could begin, Fort pled guilty and was sentenced to 13 years' imprisonment. In 1987, Fort and four members of the El Rukns were convicted of plotting terrorist acts on behalf of Moammar Gadhafi of Libya; Fort was sentenced to 80 years. In 1988, Fort and three other El Rukns were convicted of the 1981 murder of a rival gang member who had failed to heed the El Rukn warning to share the proceeds of his drug dealings. With Fort in prison, the gang's headquarters were forfeited and destroyed, and a series of indictments and convictions followed. In 1989, sixty-five El Rukns were indicted, and by 1991, nineteen had been convicted of drug- and murder-related offenses. In 1992, numerous El Rukn generals who had held the highest rank under Fort, all in their thirties and forties, received long prison sentences. In 1993, serious charges of prosecutorial misconduct resulted in the convictions of many El Rukn defendants being thrown out and new trials ordered. Many already-convicted members were subsequently resentenced to significantly reduced terms.

Remaining El Rukns assumed their former name, the Black P. Stone Nation, and one faction ("Motown"), under the leadership of Jeff Fort's son, Watketa ("The Prince") Valenzuela, is estimated to have up to two thousand members, holding sway in the Motown section of Chicago's South Side. The "Mos," as they call each other, wear their hair in elaborate braids similar to those worn by the imprisoned Jeff Fort. In 1996, the young "Prince" and four other gang leaders were arrested and charged with running a major crack-cocaine network (Martin and O'Connor 1996a, 1996b). In 1997, Watketa, at 26, received a 30-year sentence.

OTHER DOMESTIC AFRICAN AMERICAN CRIMINAL ORGANIZATIONS

Jerome Skolnick and his colleagues (1990) distinguish between two gang types. *Cultural gangs* are strongly grounded in a neighborhood identity, and members may be involved in crime, including drug trafficking. *Entrepreneurial gangs* are organized for the express purpose of distributing drugs. The first type is maintained by loyalty to the gang and the neighborhood; the second is based on continuing economic opportunity. In the cultural gang, involvement in drug use and dealing can serve as membership requirements; stature in the group may be linked to success in the drug trade. Unlike the entrepreneurial gangs, these groups define themselves in terms of brotherhood, are highly protective of their turf, and engage in nonutilitarian violence with other gangs. Although the cultural gang is not organized expressly to sell drugs, "the gang organization facilitates that activity" (1990: 7). However, the low level of cohesiveness, loose organization, high member turnover, and unstable leadership typical of most street gangs militates against their being effective drug entrepreneurs (Klein, Maxson, and Cunningham 1991).

A variety of black street gangs have been expanding their operations and drug markets interstate, in particular the Crips and the Bloods of Los Angeles. The Crips, whose membership is reputed to be more than 10,000, have moved into Seattle and other large cities in the West and Midwest, as well as into smaller cities throughout California. Along with the Bloods, a smaller gang, members of the Crips have been slowly moving east, establishing drug distribution networks in Baltimore and Washington, DC.

Bloods and Crips are heavily armed and quick to use violence. The DEA (1988: 11) points out, however, that outside of Los Angeles, the Crips are "splinter groups composed of former gang members, ranging in age from their low to upper 20s, who utilize the gang names as a means of identifying their organization. These subgroups are independent entities, often operating in competition with one another"—they are extremely violent. "Neither gang is rigidly hierarchical. Both are broken up into loosely affiliated neighborhood groups called 'sets,' each with 30 to 100 members. Many gang members initially left Southern California to evade police. Others simply expanded the reach of crack by setting up branch operations in places where they visited friends or family members and discovered that the market was ripe" (Witkin 1991: 51). In 1992, it was reported that the Crips, or perhaps older former members of the gang, had developed direct ties with the Medellín cartel ("FBI Says Los Angeles Gang Has Drug Cartel Ties" 1992).

In many areas of the country, particularly in New York and Los Angeles, the relatively stable neighborhood criminal organizations that have dominated the heroin and cocaine trade have found new competitors: youthful crack dealers. Because it requires only a small investment to enter the trade, street gangs or groups of friends and relatives have entered the market, often touching off an explosive level of competitive violence that frequently involves the use of high-powered handguns and automatic weapons. Some have established direct connections to major Colombian traffickers.

Originating in 1968, Philadelphia's Black Mafia (BM) involved the coming together of fourteen extortionists and hold-up men in their late twenties and early thirties who preyed mostly on illegal entrepreneurs. A reputation for extreme violence soon gave them an air of invulnerability—victims and witnesses refused to testify. Fearing a war with the far more numerous Black Muslims, the BM entered into an agreement, becoming the extortion arm of the Black Muslims. A particularly gruesome series of robberies and executions gave the group a high profile, and in 1973, "affiliates" traveled to Washington, DC, where at the home of basketball star Kareem Abdul-Jabbar (formerly Lew Alcinda), they slaughtered seven persons, including five children, as part of a Black Muslim dispute with Hanafi Muslims. A split in the Black Muslim movement during the 1970s weakened the BM which no longer enjoyed the religious cover. But the single-most important factor in the gang's downfall was the result of moving away from extortion and, instead, specializing in drug dealing, for which prosecution did not require civilian witnesses. And successful prosecutions for drug trafficking meant the hierarchical structure was no longer being observed, so by the 1980s the BM disintegrated into a collection of criminals (Griffin 2003).

A number of other African American criminal groups operate in urban areas throughout the country, for example, the Junior Black Mafia of Philadelphia and the Vice Lords of Chicago, but they have a limited degree of organization and longevity. Whether or not they will emerge as a "black Mafia" is a question to be answered in the future. In comparison with the American Mafia, African American criminal groups have an inherent weakness: Confinement to the inner city thwarts the development of symbiotic community relationships that promote the survival of indigenous crime organizations. American Mafia Families have traditionally generated "goodwill" by providing certain community services, and by keeping the more predatory kinds of crime (such as drugs, prostitution, and robbery) out of their own neighborhoods even while organizing it elsewhere in the city. African American numbers operators (discussed earlier) cultivated considerable goodwill, but drug operators prey almost exclusively on their own people and thereby generate organized opposition from within their own communities (Pennsylvania Crime Commission 1990). Furthermore, new laws, particularly the Racketeer and

Corrupt Organizations (RICO) statute (discussed in Chapter 15), and effective law enforcement militate against the development and expansion of upstart criminals into self-perpetuating criminal organizations.

AFRICAN ORGANIZED CRIME

Several variables have made West Africa attractive for the development of criminal organizations including wide inequalities in wealth, unchecked population growth, and the associated rapid and uncontrolled urbanization. As we have seen in the United States during an earlier era, in West Africa organized crime provides an option for individuals seeking to break out of poverty. The region suffers from chronic armed conflict, extremely high rates of poverty, porous border security, and governmental inefficiency and corruption. These conditions promote the growth of armed insurgent groups; extensive narcotics trafficking networks centered in Nigeria; trafficking in women and children originating in many countries of the region; misallocation of natural resources such as timber, precious metals, and diamonds; and an enormous arms trafficking industry that is supplied from Eastern Europe and the former Soviet Union (LaVerle et al. 2003) "The very structure of many West and Central African economies, based on exploitation of natural resources (mining or single-crop, export-oriented agriculture), coupled with a patrimonial conception of the state within which national natural and financial resources belong to the individual(s) in power also contribute to the creation of an environment where a disregard for existing laws and the use of institutional prerogatives for private goals is considered not only justified, but an indicator of power" (Mazzitelli 2006: 1072). This has facilitated the growth of local and transnational criminal networks.

The structure of African criminal organizations is not that of the Sicilian Mafia (discussed in Chapter 6) or the Japanese *yakuza* (discussed in Chapter 9), but more closely akin to that of Russian organized crime in the United States (discussed in Chapter 10): project-based cells organized by

Guinea-Bissau

In Africa, in addition to drug trafficking, criminal organizations traffic in human beings, small arms, light weapons, and natural resources; they also illegally dump toxic waste. One of the countries most affected is Guinea-Bissau, which is emerging from decades of conflict. While most people live in poverty, some are tremendously wealthy because cocaine and illegal drugs are swamping the country's tiny export economy. The value of the cocaine transiting through Guinea-Bissau exceeds the entire national income. Law enforcement is woefully inadequate, and Guinea-Bissau risks becoming a "narcostate." Even when arrested, international drug traffickers are seldom sentenced—the country does not have a single prison (United Nations Office on Drugs and Crime 2008a).

kinship along ethnic or clan lines which complete an operation and disperse to regroup at a later date for another transaction. Groups may use religious rituals to further solidarity while each member brings a particular skill to the enterprise.

Criminal organizations in West Africa (Figure 8.2) use techniques similar to those of legitimate traders and business people typical of a lineage-based society. As the volume of business grows, an entrepreneur who succeeds in making money in a particular field invites one or more junior relatives or other dependents to join him in the business. They become apprentices to the original entrepreneur. If further additional personnel are required, they are recruited via personal acquaintances or relatives for a specific task, but not otherwise retained in permanent employment. It is common for junior associates to swear an oath of secrecy on a traditional oracle that implies death for its violation. This mode of operation creates strong associations between specific families, lineages, or ethnic groups, while those taking the greatest risks, actually transporting drugs, for example, have no permanent connection and are typically hired by a person using a pseudonym. Should this person be arrested, he or she can provide little that would endanger the enterprise (United Nations Office on Drugs and Crime 2005).

While trafficking in persons for cheap labor is the work of small networks, employing ships for this purpose requires significant investment and extensive transnational contacts, often involving different organizations in a cooperative venture: an organized crime enterprise. Those enterprises aimed at the commercial sex market are typically run by well-developed criminal networks. A recruiter and transporter of a woman to Europe spends approximately $2,000 to bribe appropriate officials, procure travel documents and safe houses, and transport the woman to a madam, who pays approximately $12,000 for the victim (Mazzitelli 2006).

Although drug trafficking remains by far the most lucrative transnational criminal activity, criminal networks have diversified their portfolios in order to reduce risk and to make it more difficult for law enforcement agencies to trace them: trafficking in people and smuggling of migrants, stolen vehicles, natural resources, firearms, counterfeiting and intellectual piracy, and cybercrime. These activities are accompanied by money laundering and corruption.

As a result of stepped-up enforcement against drugs entering Europe through Spain and the Netherlands, West Africa has become more attractive to smugglers. "The geographical position of West Africa, combined with a permissive working environment—corruption and inadequate law enforcement—makes the region an ideal staging post from South America to cocaine markets in Europe" (United Nations Office on Drugs and Crime 2007: 6). Latin American cocaine moves into West Africa's long Atlantic coast where it is rerouted for European markets by Nigerian and Ghanaian networks who are paid for their logistical services or who purchase the drugs directly. Heroin from the Golden Crescent and Golden Triangle (discussed in Chapter 13) enters West

FIGURE 8.2 *West Africa*

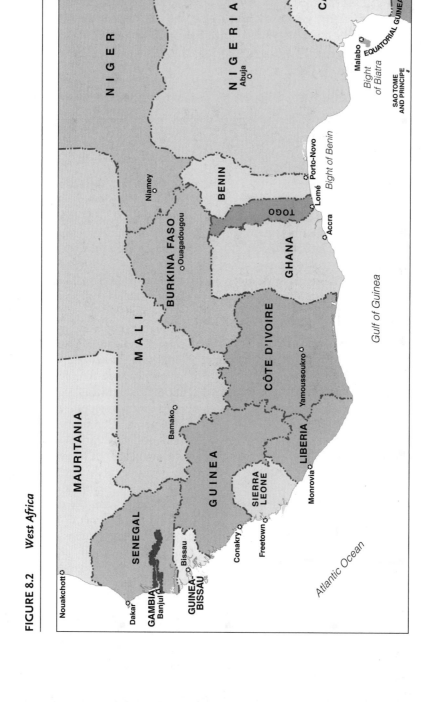

Africa to be re-exported to Europe and, to a lesser extent, the United States. Some of these drugs also enter the domestic market.

Cocaine is usually shipped to West Africa on fishing boats and freighters concealed in areas built especially for that purpose in the frame of the boat, such as a modified oil tank. These concealment areas make it very difficult to detect the drug without specific intelligence as to its location (United Nations Office on Drugs and Crime 2007a). Larger vessels may be used as mother ships from which small boats bring the drugs ashore. Drug smugglings routes are also used to move counterfeit and pirated items.

Antonio Maria Costa, Executive Director of the United Nations Office on Drugs and Crime, points out (2007: 1):

> With growing demand for cocaine in Europe, and improved security along traditional trafficking routes, criminals are now using West Africa as a hub for their illicit trade. Countries like Guinea Bissau are off most people's radar screens. They are poor, weak, and yet not so unstable as to attract attention. This makes them a perfect cover for criminal groups. As a result, in the past few years, the amount of cocaine moving from South America via West Africa to Europe has risen dramatically. In some cases, like Guinea Bissau, the value of the cocaine trafficked through the country may be greater than the entire national income.

With their low risk/high return business, drug traffickers can afford satellite phones, move around in fast boats and expensive cars, transfer money and information discreetly and buy protection. The mismatched police, who have low salaries that are seldom paid, lack phones, computers, and even electricity, have almost no ships for patrol. (United Nations Office on Drugs and Crime 2007b: 1)

NIGERIANS

About twice the size of California, Nigeria is Africa's most populous country: 100 million persons divided into 250 ethnic groups with a labor force employed primarily in agriculture. The country has an Atlantic coastline and a major port in its commercial center, the city of Lagos (Abujain).

This former West African British colony, where the official language is English, was granted full independence in 1960, but has been marked by civil wars and coups. In 1999, military rule ended and a civilian government was elected. Nevertheless, there has been a great deal of unrest and violence, the result of northern states attempting to enforce Islamic law (*Sharia*) and southern ethnic groups demanding more autonomy and control of natural resources. Through wanton violence, Muslim and Christian militias have created Muslim- or Christian-only enclaves (Sengupta 2004).

Inefficiency and decades of corruption continue to hamper this oil-rich country—Nigeria is the sixth largest oil producer in the world but the per capita income is about $1,000 a year. The military dictator who ruled Nigeria from 1993 to 1998 stole at least $3 billion which he deposited in foreign bank accounts (Polgreen 2005). The Nigerian police are poorly organized and financed, and carry the baggage of British rule during which the police served as an instrument of colonialism.

This climate proved fertile for the creation of crime syndicates that are active in drug trafficking as well as an array of sophisticated economic crimes such as bank, credit card, and insurance fraud. Nigerian criminal syndicates have centered in Lagos; many of them have global networks and operate with virtual impunity in an environment of pervasive corruption. Their organizational structures are quite flexible and fluid, cell-like syndicates that break apart and reform in other criminal initiatives with interchangeable members: "A noticeable trait that's fairly consistent is formation of small groups along tribal or family ties" (Nicaso and Lamothe 2005: 239).

Nigerian drug trafficking organizations have established links with heroin sources in the Golden Triangle and the Golden Crescent (discussed in Chapter 13). An extensive transnational network of narcotics traffickers extends out from Nigeria, which has become the West African center for drugs and money laundering. That network extends into neighboring countries and as far as Kyrgyzstan and South America. Nigerian groups have established ties with criminal groups in the United States, Europe, South America, Asia, and South Africa. A significant proportion of heroin arriving in the United States from Asia passes through Nigeria, and Nigerian agents in South America move cocaine to points in Europe, North America, and South Africa (LaVerle et al. 2003).

Nigerian drug networks are able to coexist with the more hierarchical, mafia-style operators who may dominate particular aspects of the drug trade, such as the powerful Colombian groups that may deal in very large quantities of cocaine. Nigerian networks are likely to deal generally in smaller quantities, thus not posing a major commercial threat to rival "mafias," while providing valuable smuggling services to major criminal operatives. While successful Nigerian syndicates import smaller quantities, they enjoy an exceptional range of contacts and an impressive flexibility of organization that enable them to exploit market niches that the more powerful organizations cannot always reach. "It is by these means that Nigerian drug traders have managed to gain a major stake in what is, literally, the world's most cutthroat market, yet without themselves using violence" (United Nations Office on Drugs and Crime 2005: 22).

Nigerian narcotics traffickers also are involved in counterfeiting documents, trafficking in migrants, and financial fraud; and financial fraud sometimes turns violent—more than a dozen foreign businesspeople caught up in Nigerian fraud have been murdered in several countries. Nigerian criminal cells target banks and financial institutions through credit card, check, student loan, and mortgage frauds; insurance companies through fraudulent claims for automobile accidents, personal injuries, and life insurance; and government entitlement programs through false or appropriated identifications. Nigerian criminals infiltrate major companies by applying for employment as security guards and cleaning personnel, positions giving them access to records during periods of minimal presence of company employees. Stolen data becomes the basis for securing false documents.

The most notorious of the Nigerian operations is the advance fee scam—referred to as 419s after a section of the Nigerian Criminal Code—in which thousands of unsolicited letters, faxes, and e-mails based on fraudulent representations are sent to people worldwide with the promise of great profits for an upfront cash investment. Simple investment schemes are set forth with promises of easy money, elaborate assurances, and extraordinarily low risk. They provide detailed instructions for establishing linked bank accounts and exchange of authorization letters and account numbers giving the appearance of legitimacy, and then require various transaction fees before any money can be released. Operators may portray themselves as former heads of state or government ministers with vast fortunes requiring a foreign partner for laundering purposes. Victims of Nigerian fraud schemes may be strung along for months or years paying transactions fees and taxes before realizing they are being conned (*Nigerian Advance Fee Fraud* 1997; United Nations Office on Drugs and Crime 2005).

Nigeria is a historical trading crossroads both on the African continent and along maritime routes between East and West. Accordingly, the international criminal operations of Nigerian syndicates are the legacy of a history of moving capital and commodities on a global scale. Nigerian involvement in international drug trafficking is remarkable, since the country is not contiguous to any major drug producer or consumer state (Williams 1995b). Although Nigeria produces no precursor chemicals or drugs that have a significant impact on the United States, the country is a major trafficking hub and the base for criminal organizations responsible for a significant amount of heroin used in the United States.

Nigerian sea and airports are rife with corruption, and borders are porous to criminals. As a result, Nigeria has become a major transshipment center for Golden Crescent heroin, and cocaine primarily from Brazil. In addition to drugs, these organizations are involved in collateral activities such as money laundering and document, immigration, and financial fraud (*International Narcotics Control Strategy Report 1999* 2000).

Organized along familial and tribal lines, high-level traffickers seldom deal with outsiders (NNICC 1998). In the capital of Lagos, multimillionaire drug barons rule vast organizations, at the bottom of which are drug couriers who take most of the actual risks. False birth certificates and passports are easy to obtain, and Nigerian couriers based in Lagos travel to Pakistan to obtain heroin or to Brazil to obtain cocaine, and then continue on commercial flights to their final destinations; or they return to Nigeria to repackage the drugs into smaller amounts for smuggling throughout the world. Nigerian students or poor residents of Lagos are used as mules; they receive a few thousand dollars a trip for bringing in 100 grams, usually by swallowing drug-filled condoms. Some Nigeria-based traffickers conduct "training schools" that teach couriers how to avoid the suspicions of customs officials. Traffickers often place many couriers on the same flight. This tactic, known as "shotgunning," overwhelms customs officials when the flight arrives. Even if most of the couriers on the flight are caught, a number will inevitably get through during the confusion. The markups in heroin trafficking are so high

that if only a small percentage of the product gets through, the traffickers will still reap huge profits. But as a result of increasing law enforcement pressure, Nigeria-based traffickers are beginning to switch from courier shipments to the use of express mail packages. In 1997, Nigerian organizations began using express mail services with shipments routed through European countries. Drugs can be mailed anonymously to fictitious persons or mail drops that decrease the risk and cost associated with couriers (DEA information).

Customs officials use X-rays of the digestive tract to discover the drugs. In 1991, a Nigerian-Chicago connection was uncovered that used the Philippines as a transshipment point. Asian women transported heroin from Bangkok to Manila, where Caucasian American women received the drugs for transportation to the United States. This elaborate setup was designed to reduce the suspicion that would accompany Asian women flying from Thailand to the United States. Couriers carried between 4.5 and 6.5 pounds of heroin and were paid $20,000 plus expenses (Schmetzer 1991a).

In 1996, thirty-six persons in three countries were arrested for being part of a Nigerian drug ring that had been in business for fifteen years. The group's leader, known as "the Policeman" for his ability to impose discipline, was living in Bangkok. While members operated out of London, Amsterdam, Pakistan, New York, and Detroit, most of those arrested were in Chicago where the group was headquartered at an African women's boutique in the Edgewater neighborhood on the city's North Side. Orders were placed by telephone and delivered to Chicago by female couriers who usually traveled with children from Bangkok, taking circuitous routes through Europe, Guatemala, and finally Mexico, before reaching the United States (Martin and O'Brien 1996; O'Brien 1996).

According to the DEA, Nigerians dominate the shipment of Southeast Asia heroin into the United States and Latin American cocaine into Europe (Dellios 1998). Nigerian wholesalers have developed close ties to street gangs in a number of urban areas, especially those with established Nigerian communities, particularly Chicago (NNICC 1998). But the Nigerian traffickers in the United States are finding it difficult to compete with Colombians who, with their own direct source of heroin, have been lowering their prices to capture a greater market share.

In recognition of the problem of Nigerian crime groups, the U.S. Department of Justice established a Nigerian Crime Initiative that coordinates the federal investigations of Nigerian criminal enterprises by using joint task forces in six major U.S. cities.

JAMAICAN ORGANIZED CRIME

Jamaica is a picturesque Caribbean island south of Cuba and slightly smaller than Connecticut, with a population of 2.8 million persons—2 to 3 million more live abroad—and a high murder rate: more than 1,550 murders in 2007. (In comparison, New York City, with two-and-one-half times the population, had fewer than 500 murders in 2007.) With 638 miles of coastline and over a hundred unmonitored airstrips, Jamaica is a major transit point for cocaine entering the United States and the largest producer and exporter of marijuana in the Caribbean (U.S. Department of State 2005).

Jamaica received its independence from Great Britain in 1962—the official language is English—but the island remained plagued by widespread poverty, particularly problematic in the capital city of Kingston. In the poorest sections of the city, criminals—known as *rankings*—are organized into gangs (*posses*) that have traditionally been supported and protected by the residents among whom they foster a Robin Hood image.

In a situation reminiscent of ties between big city political machines and gangs in the United States (discussed in Chapter 3), those at the top of the rankings' food chain have strong political affiliations with one of Jamaica's two major parties, the People's National Party (PNP) and the Jamaica Labour Party (JLP). Both use these gangs to intimidate and attack opponents. In Jamaica, a parliamentary democracy based on the British model, a politician's political survival depends entirely on his or her ability to win repeatedly in his local constituency. One sure method of ensuring

repeated victories is to create a garrison constituency: "a pocket of housing erected with public funds, with carefully screened residents who will constitute the unbeatable core of the politician's voters" (Patterson 2001: 21). Public housing projects were built for the partisans of each political party and their affiliated posses.

In addition to the name, posses developed their style and gunslinger ethos from American action movies, particularly the Westerns popular in Kingston. When they lost their favored position with their political party patrons, the posses began trafficking in homegrown marijuana and imported cocaine. Profits from drug trafficking further unraveled political ties, and party leaders, menaced by an outlaw underworld they could no longer control, turned the Jamaican police loose to imprison or execute their former allies. Like Mussolini's campaign against the Mafia (discussed in Chapter 6), this drove posse members to the United States at an opportune time: Colombians were looking for street-level dealers to sell a new product, crack cocaine. Jamaicans quickly acclimated to the United States where their language skills were an asset—the patois of Jamaica is a distinctly accented English. The posses also "brought with them a killer enthusiasm honed by years of warfare with one another and the police, and when they came onto America's mean streets, they were afraid of no one" (Gunst 1996: xv).

In the aftermath of the bloody 1980 election for president, more Kingston criminals began leaving the island for the United States, "transforming their island gang alliances into mainland drug posses" (Gunst 1996: xiv). By 1984, the Shower posse, with close ties to the JLP, had moved its base of operations to south Florida, followed by the rival Spanglers, affiliated with the PNP. Their Jamaica-based antipathy was transferred to the United States, a rivalry that led to many murders.

In the mid-1980s, Jamaican posses shifted from marijuana to cocaine and became heavily involved in the exploding crack cocaine trade. Jamaica became an important transshipment point for Colombian cocaine bound for the United States (Jones 2002). This was the source of much of the cocaine hydrochloride that the posses used to convert into and distribute crack cocaine. During the crack cocaine era, the posses gained a reputation as one of the most violent, sadistic group of criminals that ever operated in the United States. The Shower posse's chief enforcer would hold captive family members of those who owed the group money and repeatedly rape and sodomize the females until the debt was paid (Cardwell 2001). In one six-month period in the late 1980s, posse members were involved in 744 murders. Some of their victims were boiled alive; others were dismembered, with body parts shipped back to their families in Jamaica (DEA information).

Posse members are fascinated with firearms, particularly high-caliber weapons, and prefer to always be armed. Therefore, they avoid the use of commercial airplanes. Their favorite weapons include the Uzi and Mac-11, and a variety of high-quality semiautomatic handguns. The Jamaican's typical method of operations includes multiple shots with multiple weapons in a crowded public place. The most notorious, the 5,000-member Shower posse, reportedly got its name for engaging in frenzied shootouts—*showering* gunfire (Witkin 1991).

Jamaican posses differ from other trafficking groups in that their members are importers, wholesalers, and distributors. They maintain control over the product from acquisition of the cocaine powder close to the source; through cutting, manufacture, and distribution; to street sales. Therefore, their profit margin is higher than that of traffickers who use middlemen. "A posse that controls 50 crack houses in one city can make $9 million a month. Other major importers of illegal narcotics, such as the Colombians and Cubans, are usually only wholesalers. They will turn profit on only one sale. The Jamaicans, on the other hand, never exchange any money until the narcotics are sold at the street level by members of the organization. The money is then funneled back up to the leaders" (McGuire 1988: 22).

At the national level, posses have one or more top leaders, sometimes called "generals." The first region of the country in which a posse operates may evolve into a "headquarters" or base of operations from which the subsequent expansion of operations is directed. From the headquarters, posse leaders may send "captains" or "lieutenants" to establish operations in new regions. They are responsible for recruiting supervisors to manage workers, frequently illegal aliens smuggled from Jamaica into the United States (Pennsylvania Crime Commission 1990).

Street-level operations are carried out by managers, couriers, sellers, lookouts, and steerers, most of whom are African Americans (*Crack Cocaine* 1994). In 1990, federal agents arrested seventeen members of the Gulleymen—named after a neighborhood in Kingston, Jamaica—a posse that controlled crack houses in Brooklyn and Dallas and has been linked to at least thirty murders. As part of their business operations, the Gulleymen sold franchises to street-level dealers, providing them with crack and protection (McKinley 1990).

The demise of major posses, such as the Shower posse, was largely a result of their predilection for violence, which helped undermine loyalty: "Loyalty was a scarce commodity within the posse ranks. And when the dons resorted to violence to discipline their troops, some of the soldiers started going to the police with information. . . . Once the cops were able to flip one or two gang members it was only a matter of time before they could rope the don" (Gunst 1996: 140). Although the Shower posse disbanded, by the mid-1990s, those that remained active apparently abandoned many of the brutal practices that were their trademark and dropped the posse stigma, referring to themselves as "crews." Many also dropped out of the crack cocaine trade and returned to marijuana. They reasoned that a conviction for selling crack would mean serious time in prison, whereas a conviction for selling small amounts of marijuana generally results only in the payment of a fine.

The source of supply for some ethnic Jamaican gangs has shifted, as well. Instead of acquiring marijuana from their counterparts in Jamaica, some groups have begun to purchase marijuana from Mexico-based criminal organizations in the Southwest Border area and then transport it back to eastern U.S. cities. The Mexicans are also able to provide cocaine and heroin (DEA information). In 2005, authorities arrested nineteen members of the Harlem-based Two Mile Posse (named after an area of Jamaica) for trafficking in marijuana and carrying out at least four murders. The group, which maintained a base in Tucson and a distribution hub in Houston, purchased marijuana from Mexico for about $500 a pound and sold it whole-sale for about $1,100 a pound (J. Lee 2005).

The tradition of gang-related violence continues in Jamaica, and in 2001 more than two dozen persons were killed when the police entered Tivoli Gardens—a stronghold of the opposition JLP—to confiscate firearms. Cynics note that when the bullets fly in Jamaica, it means an election is coming. The gangs "have their own source of funds, the sale of drugs, but the parties still provide political cover for gang support at polling time" (Borger 2001: 6).

Jamaican criminal groups have proven quite troublesome in the United Kingdom (UK) where they are referred to as "Yardies." To Jamaicans a Yardie is someone who comes from Jamaica or "Yard"—as in backyard. A crackdown in Jamaica has led to an increase in Jamaican emigration and in England "Yardie" activity—they have been linked to more than twenty killings in London in 2000. The Yardie phenomenon in the UK was first noted in the late 1980s and linked to crack cocaine. The rise of crack cocaine is mirrored by that of Yardie members who are linked to drug and arms dealing, as well as robbery. Their lifestyle in England has been synonymous with violence—impulse shootings and gangland-style executions are used to sort out internal squabbles. There is no central control or brotherhood structure, so Yardies have few affiliations or loyalties. Gangs are very loose-knit and often fall out with each other, sometimes violently.

Although firearms are more difficult to acquire in England than in the United States, the Yardies have been using the "spray and pray" technique against adversaries, discharging a Mach 10 sub-machine gun that can fire 1,200 rounds a minute on full automatic. The Yardies have also spawned many imitators among Black British youth ("Police Tackle London's Yardies" 1999; Tendler 2000; "Who Are the Yardies?" 1999). In contrast with their counterparts elsewhere, here there seems to be a minimum of organization among Yardie gangs.

Increasing violence in Jamaica in 2001 led to an additional exodus of gang members, driven out by police and soldiers. They have been entering England with false passports and continuing their lethal feuds. As a result, London Metropolitan police officers were sent to the island to train their Jamaican counterparts and exchange intelligence.

SUMMARY

- Black opportunity in organized crime has roughly paralleled opportunity in the wider legitimate community. Important black criminal entrepreneurs were operating in the early decades of the twentieth century, but they were hampered by prejudice.
- Contemporary black organized crime is quite diverse and includes domestic and transnational groups. There are homegrown supergangs such as Chicago's Gangster Disciples (GD) and their adversaries the El Rukns, as well as Bloods and Crips.
- The size of the GD requires a bureaucratic structure that makes them vulnerable to law enforcement, whereas the Bloods and Crips have no overarching organization.
- Criminal organizations have emerged in West Africa where they are involved in drug trafficking as well as a diversified portfolio that includes trafficking in persons and firearms.
- Operating across borders if not continents are Nigerian groups that specialize in a host of fraudulent schemes such as the "advance fee scam," falsifying documents, and drug trafficking.
- Jamaican posses have important political ties back home and a reputation for extreme violence in the United States. Like domestic African American groups, they are almost exclusively drug traffickers.

REVIEW QUESTIONS

1. What led to the success of black criminal groups of the 1960s in the heroin trade?
2. Why are most black criminal organizations primarily, if not exclusively, involved in drug trafficking?
3. How was the organization of Frank Lucas structured?
4. How did Nicky Barnes decide to structure his heroin trafficking organization?
5. What helped lead to the downfall of Frank Lucas?
6. What helped lead to the downfall of Nicky Barnes?
7. Why do the Gangster Disciples exhibit a bureaucratic type of structure?
8. What is so extraordinary about the Nigerian success in drug trafficking?
9. What is the connection between Jamaican politics and the posses?
10. What factors militate against the development and expansion of upstart criminals into self-perpetuating criminal organizations?

C H A P T E R
9
Asian Organized Crime

Asian is a rather imprecise term that can include many diverse groups. In the United States, for example, Asian communities are made up of thirty-four distinct ethnic groups, including Chinese, which itself has several different groups such as Cantonese and Mandarin (Song 1996). In Asia, there has always been a symbiosis between the law and organized crime (OC) that "helps the authorities police more unpredictable, disorganised crime to keep the streets safe" (Lintner 2002: 10). A number of unrelated Asian groups are involved in organized crime. Some, such as the *yakuza*, are more of a problem in Japan, although there has been expansion overseas. Others, such as the Triads, have been an international problem for many years.

YAKUZA

Most Americans have heard of the Mafia, Lucky Luciano, Al Capone, and their "soldiers"—but what about the Yamaguchi-gumi, Kazuo Taoka, Hideomi Oda, and their *yakuza*? The Yamaguchi-gumi (*gumi* means "group") is a criminal organization that dominates the industrialized, densely populated region extending from Kyoto through Osaka to Kobe, as well as Tokyo and most other major centers in Japan. The Yamaguchi-gumi is the largest *boryokudan* ("violent groups"), organizations that constitute Japanese organized crime. These organizations have been in existence for about 300 years and have their roots in the Tokugawa period (1600–1867), when Japan united under a central system of government. With the end of Japanese feudalism, *samurai* (knights) lost their role in life, and many roamed the countryside as freelance mercenaries (Rome 1975). The *yakuza*—masterless *samurai*, unscrupulous itinerant peddlers, professional gamblers, and common criminals—eventually formed structured groups, *boryokudan*. Under the leadership of their *kumi-cho* (boss), they are able to exert control over sections of Japan's urban areas. By adhering to rules of conduct that preclude violence against the police and innocent civilians, *yakuza* syndicates have been able to operate openly, with high-profile headquarters. *Yakuza* "crime control" is believed to be at least partly responsible for Japan's low crime rate.

The term *yakuza* "is derived from an old card game . . . whose object was to draw three cards adding up as close as possible to 19 without exceeding it," similar to our game of "21" or blackjack. "*Ya-ku-za* represents the Japanese words for 8, 9, 3, which total 20, a useless number. Basically, *yakuza* means 'good for nothing'" (Haberman 1985: 6). Like many of their American counterparts, the *yakuza* "were born into poverty and graduated from juvenile delinquency into organized crime" (Kirk 1976: 93). The Al Capone of Japan, Kazuo Taoka, was, like Capone, born into a poor family. He began his criminal career as a bouncer in Kobe, much as Capone filled this capacity in Brooklyn before going to Chicago. Taoka, like Capone, played a major role in the mob conflicts of the day, and both men rose to prominence because of their penchant for violence and talent for organization. When Taoka, 68, died of a heart attack in 1981, his funeral was attended by more than 1,200 *yakuza*. "Taoka's friendships and contacts extended to the highest levels of government, with two former prime ministers . . . among his friends. That kind of relationship reflected not only Taoka's personal success but also historic ties between gangsters and prominent government figures" (Kirk 1981: 17).

Similar ties were forged by Susumu Ishii, boss of Japan's third-largest crime group, the Tokyo-based Inagawa-kai. Before he died of natural causes in 1991, Ishii was involved with the world's largest brokerage houses, from whom he received $2.3 billion in loans and loan guarantees (Kaplan 1998). He had invested heavily in real estate and stocks: His portfolio was estimated to be worth more than $1 billion. Four thousand persons attended his funeral. In 1992, it was revealed that one of the most powerful political figures in Japan, a high-ranking governing (Liberal Democrat) party official, had business and political ties to Ishii; the politician's parliamentary colleague is, in fact, a former *yakuza* member (Sanger 1992; Sterngold 1992c). Executives of Japan's most profitable retailer paid gangsters (*sokaiya*) to ensure that the firm's stockholder meetings would not be disturbed—this is a standard, albeit now illegal, practice in Japan. A police raid on the offices of the Mitsubishi Motors found evidence of a continuing relationship between *sokaiya* and the company (Lev 1997).

Yakuza Structure

The *boryokudans* "form closed societies in their individual groups, but the groups are interlinked through a widespread underworld syndicate" (Takahashi and Becker 1985: 3). *Yakuza* syndicates in a particular area often form a confederation for intergroup conflict resolution (Hill 2003).

> *Boryokudans* distinguish between members (*kumiin*) and associates (*jun-kumiin*) who have not been initiated into the secrets of the organization by way of an elaborate *sake* ceremony, and are therefore at the bottom of the *yakuza* world. Rising in the ranks [of this pyramid-shaped organization] depends on the amount of money sent up to superiors in the organization, and one's share of profits is in order of rank, with the boss [*kumi-cho*] getting about half. There are a variety of ranks and titles in the various *yakuza* groups [*saiko-kanbu*, senior executives, one of whom may act as an underboss; *kanbu*, executives; *kumiin*, soldiers; *jun-kosei-in*, trainees]; these establish the status and power hierarchy and the order of authority within the family group. On occasion when a follower reaches a certain status in the hierarchy [usually a senior executive], he is given permission to train his own followers and become a small boss [while still remaining a senior executive]. He announces the name of his own family and, in accordance with his prestige, he is permitted to call himself either the boss of "a branch of the family" or boss of "a whole family." (Iwai 1986: 216–17)

Decisions that affect the organization as a whole are made by the boss and his senior executives, while routine day-to-day decision making is decentralized. *Yakuza* discipline and obedience is exemplified by the requirement that a low-ranking member can be called upon to take the place of a boss who has been implicated in a crime, even if this means a prison sentence. His family will be supported during this incarceration (Seymour 1996). Peter Hill (2003) reports, however, that because too many *yakuza* were underreporting their income, during the 1970s payments passed on to the boss became a fixed amount.

Initiation into a *boryokudan* involves an elaborate ceremony: At the front of a banquet hall is a simple wooden altar laden with *sake* and food, offerings to the gods of Shinto. Behind the altar are banners with the names of the sun goddess, the patron god of warriors, and another associated with the imperial household. Recruits dressed in kimonos sip *sake* and are given their regalia, a sword, a map of the group's turf, seals, and some swathes of cotton. There is a short address by the boss, and the new members accompany kimono-clad women for some less formal drinking (Lintner 2002).

World War II served to delineate *yakuza* groups, a situation that closely parallels that of the "old" and *Nuovo Mafia* in Sicily (Chapter 6). After Japan's defeat, the new *yakuza* that emerged was populated by unemployed returning combat veterans and was far more violent and materialistic than their prewar predecessors. Abandoning many *yakuza* traditions, they emulated American gangsters in dress, often using firearms obtained from American GIs in place of a traditional *samurai* sword. The "new *yakuza*" entered a burgeoning black market that included trafficking in amphetamines whose use had been promoted by the military and among industrial workers during the war to boost productivity.

Beginning in the 1950s, Japan experienced remarkable economic growth to which these postwar "economic mobsters" responded with expansive international connections that extended to Hong Kong, Southeast Asia, Russian Asia, Australia, and Latin American countries with large numbers of Japanese immigrants (French 2001; Hill 2003; Lintner 2002). Economic growth fostered development of an entertainment industry that included gambling and commercial sex—*yakuza* business—and the need for construction and waterfront labor whose supplies were controlled by *yakuza* firms. *Boryokudan* membership burgeoned, reaching a peak in 1963 of more than 180,000 members; so did competitive violence (Hill 2003).

Present-day *yakuza* view themselves as modern *samurai* and maintain exotic rituals, including

extensive tattooing that often covers their bodies from necks to ankles, and clipped fingers that have been self-amputated with a short sword in a ritual—*yubizume*—that serves as a sign of contrition for mistakes. The amputated top of the smallest digit is placed in a small bottle filled with alcohol with the person's name written on it; it is sent to whomever one is asking for forgiveness, typically a boss. Though not obligatory, the tattooing indicates the ability to withstand pain and commitment to the *yakuza* life. *Yakuza* members, in addition to tattoos and clipped fingers, display other "trademarks" such as dark glasses and flashy suits (Milhaupt and West 2000).

Resignation or expulsion is accomplished with a *homojo* or "red letter" to all members of the *boryokudan*, which signals that the person is no longer a member (PCOC 1984b). Tattooing

Yakuza view themselves as modern samurai and maintain exotic rituals, including extensive tattooing that often covers their bodies from neck to ankles, and clipped fingers that have been self-amputated with a short sword in a ritual that serves as a sign of contrition for mistakes.

was originally used by authorities to make it easier to recognize outlaws and has become a tradition among the modern outlaws of the *yakuza* (Lintner 2002). Expulsion is considered a more serious punishment than *yubizume*: former *yakuza* are not permitted to practice any illegal trade under penalties that include death; to do so as unaffiliated criminals would also make them quite vulnerable. Yet prior *yakuza* membership means they are virtually unemployable in the legitimate sector. After a period of time, expelled members who have conducted themselves honorably may be given an opportunity to rejoin (Hill 2003; Milhaupt and West 2000).

The self-image of the *yakuza* stands in contrast to that of their American counterparts. The Yamaguchi-gumi, for example, is listed in the telephone book and publishes a membership newsletter, and its headquarters are clearly marked for all to see. Group members typically wear lapel pins that designate their *boryokudan*. The logo of the Yamaguchi-gumi, for example, a golden diamond-shaped design, appears on their headquarters building in Kobe, on lapel pins, and on members' business cards. Movies that portray *yakuza* as noble gangsters are popular in Japan, and the *yakuza* are influential in the Japanese movie industry. In 1981, when Masahisa Takenaka was installed as the head of the Yamaguchi-gumi, the event was seen on national television. His funeral in 1985 was also telecast—Takenaka was gunned down by rival members of his *boryokudan*. When a rival for leadership seceded from the clan, he announced it at a news conference at one of Kobe's leading restaurants (Haberman 1985). With eighteen top lieutenants, he formed the 3,000-member Ichiwa-kai.

In 1999, Tokutaro Takayama, then 71, godfather of the Aizu Kotetsu-kai *boryokudan*, was interviewed by reporters at his private office just outside of Kyoto, surrounded by surveillance cameras and bodyguards with missing pinkies. He decried the state of *yakuza* in present-day Japan: "Today, they don't care about obligations, traditions, respect and dignity. There are no rules anymore" (Jordon and Sullivan 1999). Similar sentiments could be uttered by the elders of America's organized crime Families. Takayama's view is supported by the 2007 slaying of the mayor of Nagasaki by a member of a local branch of the Yamaguchi-gumi who confessed to the police. Police were unable to determine a reason for the murder (Fackler 2007).

Emerging out of the new postwar order, the 22,000-strong Yamaguchi-gumi, headed by Nobura Yamaguchi who died in 1946, was the most powerful of the *boryokudan*. Yamaguchi was succeeded by Kazuo Taoka and then Yoshinori Watanabe (b. 1941) who established a structure along feudal lines headed by a supreme boss (*kumicho*) aided by his senior advisor (*saiko komon*), with chief lieutenants assigned to head the various groups affiliated with the Yamaguchi-gumi. Watanabe's home in Kobe, a city about 275 miles southwest of Tokyo, also serves as the group's headquarters. The heavily guarded residence takes up a full city block in an upscale neighborhood. Steel doors are illuminated with floodlights and monitored by video cameras; bodyguards are quick to challenge unknown visitors. Watanabe is reputed to get $1 million a month in tithes from his top aides and has been moving the group into areas of legitimate business such as construction (Agence France-Presse 1997; Kristof 1995c; Talmadge 1999). "Not since the days of Kazuo Taoka has there been a *yakuza* boss as powerful as Wantanabe" (Lintner 2002: 175). Late in

2004, Watanabe, believed to be in poor health, announced his retirement and was replaced by his second-in-command.

About 60 percent of the estimated 85,000 *yakuza*[1] are affiliated with one of three groups: the Yamaguchi-gumi, Sumiyoshi-Kai, and Inagawa-Kai. *Yakuza* share similar backgrounds. In sharp contrast to Russian organized crime and reminiscent of the early days of American organized crime, *yakuza* are typically lower working class, high school dropouts, with one or two parents of Korean or Chinese extraction—marginalized persons with a history of juvenile delinquency (Seymour 1996). An estimated 75 percent of the Yamaguchi-gumi are ethnic Koreans or *burakumin*, descendants of outcasts—Japanese "untouchables"—who have been subjected to generations of discrimination because their families are associated with "dirty" occupations: butchers, tanners, and grave diggers (Kristof 1995a). In Japan, organized crime is an equal opportunity employer.

Recruitment is accomplished by "talent scouts" who scour hangouts most likely to attract young delinquents, who are given pocket money and employed in various errands as they are drawn into their mentor's circle. Due to increased involvement in white-collar crime, *yakuza* also welcome persons with financial and computer skills. Each recruit has a mentor, and *yakuza* apprenticeships range from six months to three years during which the apprentice lives in the house of the boss or other ranking member, performing housekeeping and other chores while learning *yakuza* protocol; learning includes being hit for committing an error (Hill 2003).

In contrast to most organized crime groups (see attributes of organized crime in Chapter 1), the *yakuza* have a distinct ideological orientation—ultra-nationalistic, conservative on matters of foreign policy, and vigorously anti-communist. This has endeared them to many right-wing politicians, and *yakuza* are intimately involved in the politics of Japan. The relatively low rate of street crime in Japan is often ascribed to a symbiotic, love/hate relationship between the *yakuza* and the police

(Hill 2003; Kaplan and Dubro 1986). The police share the political views of the *yakuza* and historically have done little against them—police raids are often publicity stunts. The *yakuza* reciprocate by keeping disorganized crime under control. In 1995, when leaders of the Pacific Rim countries met in Osaka, the Yamaguchi-gumi, like others concerned with the city's image, explained through a spokesman: "All members of our group want to do our part for our country. So we agreed to exercise self-control over our businesses" (Kristof 1995b: 6).

The *yakuza* are also concerned about their public image: When famed Japanese film director Juzo Itami (*Tampopo; A Taxing Woman*) portrayed them in an unflattering manner in film, he became the victim of a knife attack by assailants who slashed his neck and face (Goozner 1992; Sterngold 1992b). In 1995, when a devastating earthquake hit Kobe and killed 5,500 people, the relief efforts established by the Yamaguchi-gumi proved superior to those of the government. This was seen as a way of blunting the high-profile police campaign against the group (Sterngold 1995). The earthquake also provided a vehicle for Yamaguchi-gumi controlled construction firms to increase their wealth; they threatened rivals so that they did not submit lower bids and collected "greetings fees" as insurance against construction site disruptions (Kristof 1995c).

An internal rebellion by the Ichiwa-kai against the Yamaguchi-gumi resulted in a great deal of violence, and it caused headlines in Hawaii. Though Yamaguchi-gumi loyalists had numerical superiority, the Ichiwa-kai had seized most of the organization's arsenal. Desperate for firepower, Masashi Takenaka (brother of the slain leader and his replacement as head of the Yamaguchi-gumi) and two of his ranking officers attempted to exchange large quantities of amphetamines for military arms in Honolulu, but they were caught in a Drug Enforcement Administration (DEA) undercover sting. A DEA agent told Takenaka that the weapons would be delivered to Japan aboard a U.S. Air Force plane to avoid scrutiny by Japanese authorities—Japan has strict gun-control laws (Yates 1985). By the end of 1988, the war had left twenty-five dead and seventy

---

[1]This represents a significant drop in members since the peak years.

injured and had led to a significant increase in Yamaguchi-gumi membership. According to Japanese law enforcement officials, tough police crackdowns "may have worked to the syndicate's benefit, putting many smaller gangs out of business or forcing them to seek Yamaguchi-gumi protection" (Talmadge 1988: 4). An anti-*yakuza* law enacted in 1992 designates the seven major *yakuza* syndicates as dangerous entities whose members have diminished legal rights. *Yakuza* have held public demonstrations against these laws (Seymour 1996).

The Yamaguchi-gumi was able to lure back many defectors, and other Ichiwa-kai members found it difficult to operate without the established reputation of the Yamaguchi-gumi. Hill (2007: 50) points out that this exemplifies the need for an organized crime group to have a "brand image." The remnants of the Ichiwa-kai eventually disbanded.

Yakuza Business

Yakuza groups control most organized criminal activity in Japan, including gun trafficking, drug smuggling, alien smuggling, prostitution, illegal gambling, extortion, and white-collar crime through infiltration of legitimate businesses (French 2001; Kaplan 1998; National Police Agency of Japan 1996; Sims 2000a; Talmadge 1999). At one time the *yakuza* were largely local crime rings that controlled neighborhood card games and brothels. "As Japan grew into the world's second-largest economy, the *yakuza*, too, grew increasingly sophisticated and business-minded. A handful of super syndicates expanded nationwide, gaining political access and influence over the entertainment and construction industries" (Kaplan 1998: 46). They are widely reputed to control Japan's busy ports (Sanger 1997) and, in cooperation with violent Chinese "snakehead" groups, traffic in amphetamines smuggled in from the People's Republic (Jordon and Sullivan 1999). Japan has a serious drug problem, particularly the abuse of amphetamines, which the *yakuza* also produce in clandestine laboratories in Japan, the Philippines, and Korea. In 1994, a *yakuza*

subgroup boss pleaded guilty in Hawaii federal court to importing and distributing methamphetamine and was given an 11-year sentence. At times, the *yakuza* have been big news in Hawaii because of their involvement in methamphetamine trafficking, gambling, and prostitution on the islands. More recently they have been linked to the importation of cocaine, which is growing in popularity in Japan.

In 1994, it was revealed that the *yakuza* have close financial ties to the banking industry, which provided funds for the gangsters to invest in real estate. When property values deteriorated as a result of a market downturn, financial institutions found themselves holding many bad loans; efforts to collect proved dangerous—one banker was shot to death, and fire-bombings and cut telephone lines became frequent. In 1997, a securities executive was slashed to death as he walked home (Hirsch and Takayama 1997; Kaplan 1998; Sterngold 1994; WuDunn 1996). Banks in Japan frequently designate certain employees to deal with the *yakuza*, and the *yakuza* have played havoc with efforts to clean up the banking mess that is the heart of the Japanese economic downturn. Fear is widespread, making it difficult for banks to collect bad loans. American companies buying distressed Japanese firms often have written clauses that nullify contracts if they discover *yakuza* involvement (Jordan and Sullivan 1999).

The *yakuza* are also at the center of an international trade in sexual slavery: females, often children, bought and sold throughout Third World countries. *Yakuza* helped popularize the Southeast Asian "sex tours" (*Kisaeng* parties) favored by Japanese businessmen. These women and children also serve in the *yakuza*-dominated sex entertainment centers of Tokyo.

Rounding out *yakuza* criminal activities are extortion from both legitimate and illegitimate entrepreneurs, intimidation, and the evicting of people from their homes on behalf of real estate developers—Japanese law makes it virtually impossible to evict tenants (Milhaupt and West 2000). Automobile accident victims will sometimes hire *yakuza* to retrieve damage payments on a contingency basis (Weisman 1991). Japan has relatively few lawyers and "Japanese courts are notoriously slow and indifferent to the complaints of individuals. Essentially, the *yakuza* have taken on the role of lawyers-cum-negotiators" (Seymour 1996: 202). Similarly, most Japanese bankruptcies are handled informally by *yakuza*-backed "adjusters," and the police are reluctant to intervene in what they consider civil matters. Bankers sometimes dispatch *yakuza* to bankrupted businesses to confiscate property ahead of unsecured creditors (Hirsch and Takayama 1997; Kaplan 1998).

Police crackdowns on *yakuza* business interests and a downturn in the Japanese economy has affected organized crime. When the easy money was plentiful, *yakuza* "stuck closely to their own turf and honored hierarchy as if it were life itself. Things were so simple, in fact, that using a little muscle often meant little more than, say, depositing a dead cat on the doorstep of a landlord being pressured into selling a coveted property" (French 2001: 4). With business expense accounts slashed, *yakuza*-controlled bars and nightclubs began hurting, and the gangsters have become more competitive and more violent (Talmadge 1999). Members are having a more difficult time paying monthly honorariums to their leaders, and discipline has lapsed. Public bombings and shootings—traditionally an anathema to the image-conscious *yakuza*—have become more frequent (Sims 2000a, 2000b). In 1997, the Yamaguchi-gumi second-in-command was shot to death at a Kobe hotel by four gunmen (Agence France-Press 1997). In 2001, at a Sumiyoshi-kai funeral in Tokyo, two men laying white chrysanthemums on the altar suddenly pulled out handguns and killed two of the *boryokudan* bosses. Two days later, another ranking member of the Sumiyoshi-kai was shot to death in the doorway of his flat (Whymant 2001).

And the *yakuza* have not been without competition. In some areas, such as Tokyo's Kabukicho entertainment district, gambling and prostitution are controlled by snakeheads, who are considered more ruthless than their *yakuza* counterparts (Kristof 1999) and who often use guns smuggled in from the People's Republic. They are particularly active in the smuggling of Chinese immigrants into Japan and the United States (Chin, Zhang, and Kelly 1998; Huston 2001; Lintner 2002).[2]

TRIADS, TONGS, AND ASIAN GANGS

Secret societies have a long history in China, some dating back to the beginning of the Common Era (Chin 1990; Fong 1981). An important part of these societies are the Triads and their American offshoots—tongs and Chinatown gangs. Before we can understand the qualities of these groups, we need to explore the unique cultural dynamics of Chinese society in which loyalty to family and friends is a moral imperative (Liu et al. 1998).

Any member of the Chinese community is part of a latent organization because of the existence of *guanxi*, a phenomenon that parallels *partito*, discussed in Chapter 6: "Chinese are born into a hierarchically organized society in which they never see themselves or others as free individuals, but as bound to others in an ever expanding web of social relations bearing mutual obligate bonds of varying strength." The Chinese *guanxi* "embraces many concepts, some familiar to Westerners, such as connections, networks, and patron-client relations." They are built upon "a series of dyadic relationships, some that are naturally present and others which must be acquired, cultivated, and maintained" (W. Myers 1995: 3).

The Chinese concept of *qinqing* parallels that of the southern Italian *famiglia*. Family, the primary and most important group to a Chinese individual, "serves as the crucible for formation of the ideals of harmonious social relations and the model for social interaction. It is an association composed of parental and filial bonds carrying the strongest obligations of mutual reciprocity (*qinqing*)." Family resources "are pooled and shared according to apparent or expressed need. Each member is obligated to contribute to the family as able and the family is obligated to provide each member

---

[2]"People who leave China illegally are often called 'human snakes'; thus those who lead them across the borders are called snakeheads" (*Characteristics of Chinese Human Smugglers* 2004: 1). A U.S. Department of Justice research effort failed to find a connection between Chinese organized crime groups and human smuggling (*Characteristics . . .* 2004).

with the resources for living" (W. Myers 1995: 4). Pooling of familial resources has advanced the business interests of overseas Chinese in the many communities they have settled.

In this cultural setting, notes Willard Myers (1995), law is marginalized, relegated to a position well below mediative mechanisms within a particularistic social order of human relationships. Like *famiglia* and *partito*, these cultural manifestations, although not ipso facto criminal, facilitate criminal organization. Of particular interest are persons of Cantonese and Fukienese heritage,[3] who as immigrants throughout the world were subjected to pernicious discrimination to which they responded by relying on cultural attributes that provided great advantages in business, both legal and illegal. And *guanxi* is global, providing a dynamic for international business, both legal and illegal. The Triad phenomenon is a natural extension of these cultural attributes.

Triads

Despite its enormous population, China has only about 150 surnames representing different clans that often have their own mutual-aid associations. In times of unrest, many people with different surnames formed brotherhoods for protection, using secret oaths and rituals to substitute for familial ties. These secret societies practiced armed robbery, ransom kidnapping, and piracy. In 1821, the principal of an Anglo-Chinese college wrote the first systematic account of these secret societies that he called "Triads" (Lintner 2002). A political dimension was added when the Quing (or Ch'ing) dynasty, established by the conquering Manchus (from Manchuria) in 1644, attempted to wipe out the Triads (Fong 1981).

The term *triad* refers to the Chinese societies' common mystical symbol: an equilateral triangle representing the three basic Chinese concepts of heaven, earth, and man. Triad members are assigned numbers based on their position. For example, enforcers or "Red Poles" are assigned number 426; an ordinary member is a 49; a leader or "Hill Chief" is 489. Based on ancient occult numerology, assigned numbers always begin with a 4 (Booth 1990). These groups, based in Hong Kong and Taiwan, engage in highly ritualized dress and behavior—secret hand signs, passwords, and blood oaths are used in elaborate initiation ceremonies. The initiation ceremony includes the recital of the Triads' 36 oaths, each of which ends with the death penalty for its violation. For example: "If I am arrested after committing an offense, I must accept my punishment and not try to place blame on my sworn brothers. If I do so, I will be killed by five thunderbolts" (Carter 1991a). The ceremony may take six or seven hours (Booth 1990).

In contrast, Johnny Kon, the man who would later emerge as head of the powerful Big Circle (discussed later), recalls his initiation into the Green Gang (Triad) in a Bangkok hotel room in 1969. Instead of an elaborate ceremony, in the presence of his Green Gang mentor, Kon handed a cup of tea and an envelope with $108 to a ranking member, stating in Shanghai dialect: "If you accept me, I'll be very happy." The man placed the envelope in his jacket and responded: "Never tell secrets. Never betray anyone. If ever your brothers need help, never refuse them." "Thank you master," Johnny responded, and they adjourned to a celebratory meal at a Chinese restaurant. His subsequent admission into another (Red Gang) Triad, however, in addition to the ceremonial $108, was replete with 36 oaths, the decapitation of a live chicken, and the drawing of blood from his finger (J. Sack 2001). In any event, membership requires a sponsor who is a ranking official of the Triad.

Fenton Bresler, testifying before the President's Commission on Organized Crime (PCOC 1984b: 42–43), points out that each triad has its own triangular flag and territory. "If I want to become a new Triad head, I have to ask the original guy back in Hong Kong or Taiwan to give me a flag which means I can bring it over and that means this is my territory. . . . It authorizes for me to go to the new town and organize my branch." Although each Triad affiliate boss is theoretically

---

[3]Competition between members of these two groups, in both licit and illicit spheres, has led to violence in a number of American cities (W. Myers 1995).

independent, that is, has his own flag, he is really only semi-independent. Spiritually he is linked with the old country.

Martin Booth presents the typical structure of a Triad lodge. Each has a hierarchy that determines its activities (1990: 33–35, edited):

The leader is called the Shan Chu, and there is a deputy leader, the Fu Shan Chu. Below them come the Heung Chu, or Incense Master, and the Fin Fung, or Vanguard. These two officers administer the lodge rituals and have the power to invest, initiate, and order retribution against the members. Beneath them are a number of departmental heads responsible for the everyday running of the society and of any subbranches, each of the latter having an internal structure similar to that of the main lodge except for the Incense Master and Vanguard. These are only found in principal lodges and their presence is a sign that a lodge has reached maturity and achieved power in its own right. Subbranches are controlled by a leader, the Chu Chi, and his deputy, the Fu Chu Chi. Some lodges also have a treasurer, but this is comparatively rare. All Triad officers are appointed for fixed periods and are elected by lodge members. Initiate members are required to pay an entrance fee. They must also obtain a sponsor, to whom further fee is payable—often far in excess of the entrance fee. This is a private arrangement and is only reached after the initiate's credentials have been thoroughly checked by the Incense Master and the Vanguard. A sponsor must also be found, and paid for, when a member seeks promotion within the lodge. All monies earned by an individual society, from whatever source, are deposited in the central lodge fund. Embezzlement is not uncommon and has caused major rifts in some societies, sometimes leading to violence.

Within each society there are four ranks of officials. The first is the Hung Kwan, or Red Pole, who is a fighter and is responsible for discipline. The Paz Tsz Sin is also known as the White Paper Fan and occupies a position similar to the *consigliere* in the Mafia. The Cho-Hai or Messenger is a liaison officer who acts as a go-between in lodge affairs and as a representative in its dealings with the outside world or with other lodges.

The Quing dynasty ended in 1911 with the success of Dr. Sun Yat-sen (1866–1925). His successor, General Chiang Kai-shek, possibly a Triad member himself, imposed a military regime with help from the secret societies, in particular, the Green Gang (*Qing Bang*), a Triad that Bertil Lintner (2002: 54) refers to as China's first modern secret society. Mao Zedong and his Communist revolution, often aided by Triads, ousted Chiang from the Mainland and, in 1952, moved to obliterate the secret societies that were seen as competitors to the Communist Party. Among the victims was the Green Gang that had virtually ruled the city of Shanghai. Triad members who fled to Taiwan with Chiang Kai-shek were tightly controlled by the Kuomintang, his Nationalist Party, and were unable to expand their criminal operations on the island (Chin 1990). Driven out of the mainland and into Hong Kong, the leaderless "Greens" survived in small pockets and their power was eclipsed by the 14K.

The 14K was founded in 1947 by a Kuomintang general who fled with hundreds of his followers to Hong Kong after the Communist victory. The Triad has branches throughout the world, but they are not connected to each other through an overarching hierarchy (Lintner 2002). According to Yiu Kong Chu (2005), the 14K is less organized than most other Triads, with subgroups forming separate societies. Reputed to have as many as 30,000 members in Hong Kong (the former colony has a population of 5.6 million), and about 10,000 in Taiwan, in the nearby former Portuguese colony of Macau (population over 500,000), 45-year-old Wan Kuok-koi ("Broken Tooth Koi") headed the local 14K. When the colony was under the Portuguese, he directed a violent conflict to control the lucrative gambling business that accounts for more than 40 percent of the enclave's economy. Wan financed a film on his exploits and in a promotional interview promised to wipe out an opposition group. Less tolerant than their Portuguese predecessors, the People's Republic imprisoned Wan Kuok-koi in 1999 (Sly 1999).

Although most Triad societies are based in Hong Kong, Taiwan, or Macau, their influence spans international boundaries with members located in virtually every country that has a sizable Chinese community. Triads, which collectively have an estimated worldwide membership that exceeds 100,000, are fluid associations of ethnic Chinese criminals and quasi-legitimate businessmen involved in an array of criminal enterprises. Most of the approximately fifty Hong Kong Triads have evolved into loose-knit groups operating and cooperating with each other on the basis of personal introductions and mutual interests. While they are traditional secret societies, Triads are best described as loose cartels made up of independent groups that "adopt a similar organizational structure and ritual to bind their members together" (Chu 2005: 5). Triad leaders do not dictate to members what criminal activities they should pursue, and generally do not receive monetary benefits unless they are directly involved with the actual criminal enterprise. As in American Mafia Families and outlaw motorcycle clubs, Triads have an associational hierarchy that does not exert vertically integrated control over the members' criminal enterprises. Instead, leaders "devote their time to advancing the influence of the organization for the benefit of themselves and their members. When control is exercised it is to mediate a dispute or ensure the loyalty of a member." Furthermore, "triad members are not solely dedicated to criminal pursuits and are found in virtually every occupation and profession" (W. Myers 1995: 12). At the international level in drug trafficking, Chinese syndicates, whose members do not necessarily belong to a Triad, will come together for a particular enterprise and then reconfigure at a subsequent time for a new venture (Hopton 1996).

The major Triads like 14K, Sun Yee On, and United Bamboo, based in Taiwan, have autonomous branches extending worldwide that help to facilitate transnational criminal activities. In the 1990s, Hong Kong Triads strengthened their presence and relationships in Western countries by making investments in legitimate businesses as a hedge against the political, economic, and law enforcement uncertainties in the wake of Hong Kong's reversion to China in 1997. The 14K and Sun Yee On have made substantial property investments in Canada, and the 14K is reportedly the fastest-growing Triad in Canada. But, contrary to expectations, there has not been a mass Triad migration to Western countries; instead, they have increasingly entered the booming Chinese market (Chu 2005).

United Bamboo was established in Taiwan in 1956 and maintains strong ties to the Kuomintang Party. Although it was reputed to have only about one hundred members as late as 1970, the organization's size and sophistication have since increased notably (Huston 2001). The reputed leader of the United Bamboo is a wanted man in Taiwan who served several prison terms in the United States for drug trafficking. Nevertheless, he resides in Shenzhen, China, just north of Hong Kong. His activities might be anathema to officials in Taiwan and even in Beijing and Shenzhen, but his ties to Taiwan and to potential dealmakers and smugglers abroad make him a potential ally to the rich and influential. His politics—reunification of Taiwan with China—make him an attractive ally to Beijing. His presence in China highlights the ties between organized crime figures and the Communist Party (Pomfret 2001). Through the use of Triad members, Communist China "has extended its influence of North America's ethnic Chinese communities," and the "Donorgate" scandal of 1996 revealed that Beijing was using underworld figures to funnel money to a presidential candidate in the United States (Lintner 2002: 369).

At the top of the hierarchy of United Bamboo in Taiwan is an Ultimate Leader, an Ultimate Enforcer, an Ultimate Superintendent who oversees members and their activities, and an Ultimate Executive who operates organization businesses. There are reportedly more than sixty Taiwan branches, each with a Branch Leader, Deputy Branch Leader, and "brothers" or members. Some branches have other positions such as enforcer, communications officer, war officer, and internal regulator. There are neither specific requirements nor initiation ceremonies for membership. One becomes a member after hanging out and being introduced into the branch by a friend. Members of United Bamboo are heavily armed and engage in a plethora of business activities including extortion, debt collection, gambling, prostitution, trafficking in persons, and pirated movies. With a burgeoning of the economy, they branched out into construction and bid rigging (National Central Police University 2005).

It is not unusual for different Triads to work together where there is a specific opportunity for mutual profit. Hong Kong police, however, maintain that there is no international Triad network or centralized control over cross-border activities, such as drug trafficking or alien smuggling, between China and Hong Kong. Police state that most cooperation in such criminal enterprises is more ad hoc. That is, criminal groups from mainland China, typified by the Big Circle (*Dai Huen Jai*) and the Fuk Ching, have cells operating in countries around the world that cooperate with one another on an ad hoc basis to conduct far-reaching criminal schemes. These criminal cells typically operate autonomously with no known central authority controlling them. Cell leaders use their extensive connections to arrange complex criminal operations that require a high degree of organization and planning. Coordinated efforts of members in various countries enable them to carry out international drug trafficking, arms trafficking, alien smuggling operations, as well as a variety of more sophisticated financial fraud crimes. Most smuggling organizations such as the Fuk Ching are based in China's southwestern Fukien province whose residents have a history of overseas travel. The province's coast and harbors provide easy access to shipping (Huston 2001).

The Big Circle (Society or Brotherhood) has its origins in Communist China's Red Guard, Mao's personal militia established to enforce the "Great Cultural Revolution." When the Revolution was called off three years later, many of the paramilitary Red Guards fled to Hong Kong, but maintained camaraderie as the Big Circle—from their red armbands—and engaged in well-planned robberies, particularly of jewelry stores. As a result of their relationship with a leading Triad member in Hong Kong, the major bosses of Big Circle were initiated into the Society of Tranquil Happiness (Triad) and, in a short time, became one of the most active Asian criminal organizations in the world. Thus, although Big Circle is not itself a Triad, many of its members belong to Triads "in the typical pattern of overlapping membership among Chinese groups" (Curtis, Gibbs, and Miró 2004: 10).

By the early 1990s, the Big Circle had established criminal cells in Canada, the United States, and Europe that are highly sophisticated in their use of technology to thwart law enforcement. Known primarily for the manufacture and distribution of counterfeit credit cards and other documents, this group has also been involved in drug trafficking, extortion, prostitution, and gaming offenses (Huston 2001; National Security Council and Criminal Intelligence Service of Canada information; Sack 2001).

A report prepared by the U.S. Library of Congress (Federal Research Division 2002) points out that even when they are part of a specific organization, Big Circle members usually operate in small cells or partnerships that are often dissolved at the completion of a particular goal. In other words, Big Circle cells exhibit structural fluidity and flexibility, and it is not unusual for members and associates to conduct "numerous dissimilar criminal activities, often with different groups simultaneously, be they ethnically homogeneous or heterogeneous." Instead of an overarching pyramid, "Asian OC groups are organized more as autonomous mini-pyramids, with small cells and mini-bosses dictating the actions of only their particular cell" (Federal Research Division 2002: 4). Cells located in different countries provide important networking capabilities, contacts they can trust and do business with on a transnational level.

The drug trafficking Triads expanded their operations during the Vietnam War, when thousands of GIs were attracted to the potent heroin of Southeast Asia. When the Americans withdrew from Vietnam, Triads followed the market and internationalized their drug operations. Many soldiers were stationed in Europe, so a major Triad marketplace developed there, with operations headquartered in Amsterdam. Many of the younger members are involved in the martial arts and martial arts schools are often controlled by Triads. In British Hong Kong, membership in a Triad was a criminal offense. In the Hong Kong controlled by the People's Republic, there have been reports of ties between Triads and members of the Communist Party, and Triads have moved beyond Hong Kong into several mainland cities (Lintner 2002; Sheridan 1997).

Triads have been producing martial arts action ("chop socky") movies that, despite requiring little capital investment, are extremely popular in Asia (Dannen 1995: 31–32): "The only thing that matters is the cast. Indeed, many Hong Kong films are shot without a script. Anyone—literally anyone— who can persuade a popular performer or two to appear in his movie can make the movie with little or no investment." Triad persuasion techniques frequently "compensate for their ignorance of film technique."

Tongs

Chinese were originally brought into the United States after 1848 to work in the gold fields, particularly in those aspects of mining that were most dangerous because few white men were willing to engage in blasting shafts, placing beams, and laying track lines in the gold mines. Chinese immigrants also helped build the western railroad lines at pay few whites would accept—"coolie wages." After their work was completed, the Chinese were often banned from the rural counties and by the 1860s were clustering in cities on the Pacific coast where they established Chinatowns.

The first significant piece of prohibitionary drug legislation in the United States was enacted by the city of San Francisco. The primary event that precipitated the campaign against the Chinese "was the sudden onset of economic depression, high unemployment levels, and the disintegration of working-class standards of living" (Helmer 1975: 32). Depressed economic conditions and xenophobia led one western state after another to follow San Francisco's lead and enact anti-Chinese legislation (Bonnie and Whitebread 1970). Anti-Chinese efforts were supported and advanced by Samuel Gompers (1850–1924) as part of his effort to establish the American Federation of Labor. Chinese served as scapegoats for organized labor that depicted the "yellow devils" as undercutting wages and breaking strikes. In 1882, the Chinese Exclusion Act banned the entry of Chinese laborers into the United States. (It was not until 1943, when the United States was allied with China in a war against Japan, that citizenship rights were extended to Chinese immigrants and China was permitted an annual immigration of 105 persons.)

Chinese became the targets of abuse and random violence and found refuge in urban areas where they established "Chinatowns" and formed mutual aid societies and tongs. "*Tong* is an Anglicization of the Mandarin word *tang*. This in turn translates as 'hall' or 'lodge,' but it usually refers to the organization itself, not the building it might meet in" (Huston 2001: 46). Tongs were first established in San Francisco in the 1850s as benevolent societies (Chin, Kelly, and Fagan 1994). Some Chinese immigrants, like Sicilian immigrants who had been *mafiosi*, were Triad members at home. In the United States they engaged in organized criminal activities, particularly opium trafficking, prostitution, gambling, and extortion. In a pattern similar to that of the *Unione Siciliana* discussed in Chapter 4, many of these men joined tongs that have been able to transcend the worlds of legitimate business and crime. Because tong members' primary loyalty is to each other, if a member is involved in criminal activity, "the others are pledged not to turn him into the police" (Huston 2001: 60). At the turn of the century, "fighting tongs," patterned after Triads, controlled large-scale vice operations—gambling and prostitution—in urban areas with significant Chinese populations (Lintner 2002).

While most tongs were business, fraternal, or political in character, the "fighting tongs" licensed illegal businesses and were part of a tight-knit nationwide alliance. A purely local dispute between fighting tongs, therefore, "could and often did precipitate a fight between affiliates in every U.S. Chinatown" (Light 1977: 472). During the last decade of the nineteenth century and the first two decades of the twentieth, tong wars occurred on the East and West Coasts. In New York in 1909, a "tong war" between the On Leong ("Peaceful Dragon") and Hip Sing ("Prosperous Union") claimed an estimated 350 lives (Sante 1991). As the importance of gambling and house prostitution in Chinatowns declined following World War I, vice entrepreneurs discovered the profitability of tourist enterprises, and restaurants replaced the brothels and gambling halls. Nevertheless, the struggle between the On Leong and Hip Sing to control vice operations in New York's Chinatown continued into the 1930s. Contemporary tongs such as the Hip Sing and the On Leong have dropped the term from their names because of its association with "tong wars" (Chin 1990).

Nevertheless, these tongs continue to be associated with illegal gambling. In 1988, for example, federal agents raided the Chicago headquarters of the On Leong, where they found evidence of extensive commercial gambling, including more than $320,000 in cash and records indicating extortion from local Chinese merchants. A 1990 indictment accused the Chicago On Leong and affiliates in New York and Houston of being a key part of a gambling operation that netted $11.5 million. Gambling, in particular *Pai Gow*, an ancient Chinese domino game, was available from 9:30 A.M. to 7:00 P.M., seven days a week, at the On Leong Chicago headquarters, which was subsequently forfeited to the government. In 1994, Chicago On Leong officers were found guilty of running gambling operations, making payoffs to the police, and paying street taxes to the Outfit.[4] They also bribed a state judge to fix a murder case involving three members of a New York Chinese gang brought to Chicago to kill a troublemaker (Hayner 1990; O'Connor 1994a, 1994b).

Peter Huston (2001: 62) points out, "Important tong members have a network of social contacts throughout the country that often provide them with considerable help in carrying out complex criminal schemes or avoiding justice."

Asian Gangs

Many contemporary tongs are national in scope, particularly the Hip Sing, On Leong, and Tsung Tsin, and some are connected to Chinatown gangs such as the Ghost Shadows and the Flying Dragons in New York, Chicago, Boston, and San Francisco. Dating back to the 1960s, these gangs consist of American-born Chinese (ABCs) whose self-declared mission was to fend off attacks by non-Asian outsiders. At the same time, new immigration laws resulted in a large influx of youths from Hong Kong. Some of these FOBs (fresh off the boat) became alienated from school, found little economic opportunity, were beyond

---

[4]In 1991, a former national On Leong president from Pittsburgh testified that at his request the Pittsburgh crime Family arranged a deal with the Chicago Outfit to permit the On Leong to operate a gambling casino in that city. The On Leong paid $12,000 per month to the Outfit's 26th Street crew—Chinatown is in their territory—$4,000 of which was given to the Pittsburgh Family (O'Connor 1996c).

family control, and began to form their own gangs (Kelly, Chin, and Fagan 1993; D. Lee 2003). The result was an upsurge of violent street crime in communities that heretofore had been relatively crime free—"the gangs transformed themselves completely from self-help groups to predatory groups" (Chin, Zhang, and Kelly 1998: 131). "They terrorized the community by demanding food and money from businesses and robbed illegal gambling establishments. When the youth gangs began to 'shake down' merchants and gamblers who were themselves tong members, the tongs decided to hire the gangs as their street soldiers to protect themselves" (Chin, Zhang, and Kelly 1998: 131). "Wherever large sums of money exchanged hands, the gangs sought a slice of the action. Counterfeit handbags did not originate with the gangs, but they soon began getting a cut. Massage parlors and prostitution rings offered another revenue stream. By the mid-80s, 'China White' [heroin] was added to the list" (Lee 2003: CY 16). The gangs served as the final leg of a heroin distribution network that started in the Golden Triangle (discussed in Chapter 13).

Youths involved in these gangs were sometimes as young as 13, although established gang leaders—often martial arts masters—were normally in their thirties. Each gang typically had twenty to fifty members. As opposed to outlaw motorcycle clubs (discussed in Chapter 11) and Mafia groups, Chinese street gangs made great efforts to attract potential members and sometimes coerced others into joining. "Sometimes the *dai lo* [street boss] stages an incident in which he appears to be rescuing an innocent teenager from a gang beating, earning the victim's gratitude and admiration. This is followed by gifts and exposure to attractive women and the promise that no one will ever dare to bother the victim again if he joins the gang. He will have instant respect on the streets" (Kleinknecht 1996: 97). "Once a youth decides to join the gang, he goes through an initiation ceremony that is a simplified version of the Chinese secret societies' recruiting rituals. The youth takes his oaths, burns yellow paper, and drinks wine mixed with blood in front of the gang leaders and the altar of General Kwan, a heroic

figure of the Triad subculture" (Chin 1990: 124). Members often dress in black outfits and sport exotic tattoos—dragons, serpents, tigers, and eagles. The gang becomes a substitute for the member's family. "They are not youth gangs in the usual sense but, rather, a young form of organized crime" (Dannen 1992b: 77).

Although not all Asian gangs have a tong connection, some have formed around a tong member, typically a martial arts master who helps train the members (Chin 1990), and they may be used by the tongs to provide security for gambling operations: "The On Leong Merchants Association uses the services of the Ghost Shadows street gang; the Hip Sing tong is allied with the Flying Dragons; and the Tsung Tsin Association is connected to a gang called the 'Tung On Boys'" (Pennsylvania Crime Commission 1988: 22). In some instances Chinatown gangs have become inseparable from certain tongs, linked through certain tong members and gang leaders. If a tong needs help from its affiliated gang, the message will be conveyed to the *Dai Dai Lo* ("Big Brother") by the *Ah Kung* ("Grandpa"). A *Dai Dai Lo* may also be an officer of the affiliated tong. Likewise, the highest leaders of the gangs have served as officers of the affiliated adult organizations (Chin, Kelly, and Fagan 1994).

A 1995 federal indictment revealed that New York's Chinatown, the largest Chinese community in the United States, was divided into fiefdoms under the domination of tongs aided by their affiliated gangs: the Tsung Tsin and Tung On tongs with the Tung On Boys[5]; the On Leong tong with the Ghost Shadows; and the Hip Sing tong with the Flying Dragons. Through this arrangement protection money was collected from virtually every Chinatown business, legal or illegal; the latter included 24-hour-a-day gambling dens. In addition to the tong leaders, two Chinese American police officers were indicted

---

[5]In 1995, Clifford Wong, the head of the Tung On tong, was found guilty of murder and sentenced to life imprisonment. He had ordered the Tung On Boys to assault the Ghost Shadows in retaliation for the murder of a Tung On Boys member. The attack left a 17-year-old honor student with no gang affiliations dead ("Chinatown's New Enforcer" 1995).

for providing information about police investigations and planned raids on gambling houses and brothels; they also engineered raids on competing casinos (English 1995a; Faison 1995a, 1995b; Frantz and Toy 1995; Fried 1995; Kleinfield 1995; Sexton 1995).

In San Francisco, a researcher (Joe 1992: 10) found that a majority of Chinese/Vietnamese street gang members in the nine groups she studied knew little or nothing about the tongs and Triads. Ties that existed between the two groups were based on associations between individuals, not organizations—that is, gang members connected to particular tong members. Another researcher (Toy 1992: 655) points out that certain tongs have needed gang members "to ensure the smooth operation of the gambling houses; they needed guards, escorts for gamblers with large sums of money, lookouts for police raids, and especially people to collect gambling debts." The tongs "do not have direct control of gangs nor are the arrangements permanent. Tong members often use certain respectable gang leaders as liaisons between the tong and the gangs in order to carry out specific criminal activities. More often than not, the average gang member is not aware of the particulars of this connection" (1992: 656).

Although these gangs draw upon the traditions of the Triads, particularly the ceremonial aspects of initiation, they have many members who are Vietnamese (of Chinese ancestry); the latter are apparently favored because of their reputed ability with firearms. There are also mixed gangs of Vietnamese and Chinese-Vietnamese (*Viet Ching*, ethnic Chinese born in Vietnam), who are usually heavily armed. They operate mainly in California but also reach into Vietnamese and Chinese communities

in other locales. One such gang was founded by a member of (New York) Chinatown's Flying Dragons, David Thai, who was born in Saigon in 1956 and arrived in the United States in 1976.

As a Vietnamese, Thai was consigned to a smaller unit known as the Vietnamese Flying Dragons. Dissatisfied with his lesser status among Chinese criminals, Thai attracted adolescents who were recent immigrants from Vietnam, offering them a place to live and employment, slowly forming his own gang, which became known as the Canal Boys—their headquarters was on Chinatown's Canal Street. They asserted their territoriality by extorting money from the local Canal Street merchants.

In 1989, Thai formed a confederation of Vietnamese gangs in the New York City metropolitan area and adopted the name Born to Kill (BTK), a slogan that often appeared on the helmets of American GIs. Thai was the leader, *Anh hai*, and the constituent gangs were headed by a *dai low*. Each BTK member signed a paper agreeing to abide by the group's rules, which included a vow of secrecy and a requirement to clear all planned criminal activity with his *dai low*. Members were tattooed with the initials BTK, a coffin, and three candles, signifying that they do not fear death (English 1995a; Lorch 1990).[6]

Because they were viewed as interlopers and left out of the criminal power structure in Chinatown, there was nothing to restrain the BTK who victimized massage parlors, bars, and tong gambling dens. In broad daylight and in front of

---

[6]The BTK gang had many non-Vietnamese associates, some of whom were non-Asians, who participated in their robberies. The leadership and core members, however, were all Vietnamese.

numerous witnesses, two Flying Dragons who had insulted David Thai were shot to death. BTK members subsequently killed two Ghost Shadows at their hangout and, on orders from David Thai, a BTK member blew up a police van in front of an NYPD precinct house (English 1995a). The ultimate insult, however, was Thai's 1990 refusal to meet with Chinatown's "godfather," the venerable Benny Ong,[7] leader of the Hip Sing tong. This loss of face brought swift retribution—Thai's closest associate was gunned down, and at the funeral gunmen sprayed automatic fire at the mourners. Shortly afterward, three BTK members were slain execution style. This did not stop the BTK from committing a string of armed robberies in New England, the South, Canada, and anywhere else Asian businesses could be victimized. In Georgia they seriously wounded a jewelry store owner who had resisted. The arrest of a BTK member involved in the Georgia robbery led to an extensive interagency investigation and the successful prosecutions of the gang's leadership (English 1995a).

The Vietnamese avoid the territoriality that characterizes other similar crime groups, a lesson they learned from the Vietcong, who routinely changed their unit designations to confuse American intelligence (Okada 1992). In California, Vietnamese gangs, whose members often sport round, deep cigarette burns or blue dragons tattooed on their forearms, have been active in the armed robbery of computer chips, which are often smuggled to the Far East only to wind up back in computers lawfully imported into the United States (Webster 1994).

Founded in 1987, the Green Dragons, a Chinese gang based in Queens, New York, were enemies of the BTK. The group was made up mostly of recent immigrants from Fukien province on China's southeastern coast. Their leader was ambushed in 1989 by rivals and subsequently returned to China. Day-to-day leadership was assumed by Taiwan-born Chen I. Chung, who was barely out of his teens. The Green Dragons had a clearly defined hierarchy that exacted complete obedience from subordinates. An order to kill would be carried out even in the absence of an explanation. Without any ties to the tongs, and with only about two dozen members, the Green Dragons successfully moved the extortion practices of Chinatown into Queens. They were a particularly vicious group of criminals, murdering rivals and innocents alike. A joint NYPD-FBI investigation using wiretaps led to arrests of the gang leadership in 1990. They were prosecuted at the same time and in the same federal courthouse in Brooklyn as the Born to Kill defendants. On another floor, John Gotti was being tried; his trial garnered the media attention. Like Gotti, Chung and six of his Green Dragons received life without parole (Dannen 1992b; English 1995b).

As with almost all organized criminal groups before the onset of Prohibition, Asian criminal organizations have typically exploited only their own countrymen and were therefore able to avoid serious law enforcement efforts. In more recent years, however, the extensive heroin networks of Chinese organizations have drawn intensive

---

[7]Benny Ong died of natural causes at age 87 in 1994.

investigative efforts, particularly by the DEA. In 1989, for example, Johnny ("Onionhead") Eng, head of the Flying Dragons, was arrested in Hong Kong and extradited to the United States for masterminding the importation of 400 pounds of heroin. At the end of 1992, Eng was convicted in Brooklyn federal court, and in 1993 he was sentenced to 24 years in prison and fined $3.5 million. The efforts of the DEA, however, have been hampered by a lack of Chinese-speaking agents. In New York, Chinese organizations—not necessarily tied to Triads or tongs—sell their highly potent Southeast Asian "China White" directly to wholesalers from black and Latino groups.

Chinese crime groups are involved in smuggling illegal aliens for employment in garment-manufacturing sweatshops, particularly in New York and California. The aliens are treated as indentured servants—forced to work at below minimum wages to pay back their benefactors for getting them into the United States. Women are sometimes forced into brothels. In 1993, as a result of the seizure of a steamer with almost three hundred Chinese aboard, it was revealed that the Fuk Ching gang is a major player in the smuggling of illegal aliens. The leader of the Fuk Ching, Guo Liang Chi ("Ah Kay"), 27, often relayed orders to New York by telephone from his fortress-like headquarters in China's Fujian province. He was eventually arrested in Hong Kong as a fugitive from a murder charge in the United States (Faison 1993; Treaster 1993b).

In 1996, in a scenario reminiscent of recent traditional crime Family betrayals, the four top leaders of the Ghost Shadows became government witnesses, all but demolishing the gang. The Racketeer and Corrupt Organizations (RICO) statute (discussed in Chapter 15) prosecutions eventually decimated every Chinatown gang and the top leadership of the tongs (D. Lee 2003).

Meanwhile, gambling and heroin, the economic lifeblood of the gangs, began to dry up. Atlantic City casinos offered major entertainment and cheap bus rides; the Colombians offered cheaper heroin. In a manner reminiscent of the Irish and the Jews, the once readily available cohort of potential members also began to dry up, the result of education and legitimate opportunity (Lee 2003).

In the next chapter, we will examine Russian organized crime.

SUMMARY

- The term *Asian* encompasses many unrelated groups, and Asian organized crime includes *yakuza*, Triads, and tongs with their affiliated gangs.
- With elaborate tattoos and clipped fingers, *yakuza* have a long history in Japan and view themselves as more *samurai* than criminal. They help "police" entertainment districts, keeping the level of street crime very low.
- With business cards and clearly marked headquarters, *yakuza* differ from other organized crime groups in that they are ideological. Their right-wing views endear them to some in politics and law enforcement.
- *Yakuza* activities include gun trafficking, drug smuggling, alien smuggling, prostitution, illegal gambling, extortion, and white-collar crime through infiltration of legitimate businesses. As with organized crime groups in Italy and Russia, *yakuza* also offer a shadow system of justice.
- Most Triad societies are based in Hong Kong, Taiwan, or Macao; their influence spans international boundaries with members located in virtually every country that has a sizable Chinese community.
- As in Italian American crime Families and outlaw motorcycle clubs, Triads have an associational hierarchy that does not exert vertically integrated control over the members' criminal enterprises.
- Triads located in different countries provide important networking capabilities, contacts they can trust and do business with on a transnational level.
- American offshoots of Triads, tongs are often national in scope, particularly the Hip Sing, On Leong, and Tsung Tsin, and some are connected to Chinatown gangs such as the Ghost Shadows and the Flying Dragons in New York, Chicago, Boston, and San Francisco.

REVIEW QUESTIONS

1. Who are the *yakuza*, and how are they organized?
2. How do the *yakuza* differ from the American Mafia?
3. What are the varied business activities of the *yakuza*?
4. What are Triads, and how do they operate?
5. What is the relationship between the Triads and tongs?
6. What is the relationship between tongs and Chinese street gangs?
7. Why have the Triads had a great deal of success in international heroin trafficking?
8. How are the tongs similar to the *Unione Siciliana*?

CHAPTER
10
Russian Organized Crime[1]

In contrast to the criminal organizations discussed in Chapters 3, 4, and 5, emerging groups are flourishing in the United States in the absence of the corrupt political machines that provided a protective incubator for the Irish, Jewish, and Italian criminal organizations of an earlier era. Unlike these earlier groups, which in their infancy tended to be local in their operations and ambitions, emerging organized crime often has a great range of influence and action on an international level. This is exemplified by Russian organized crime.

"In the decade since the collapse of the Soviet Union, the world has become the target of a new global crime threat from criminal organizations and criminal activities that have poured forth over the borders of Russia and other former Soviet republics such as Ukraine" (Finckenauer and Voronin 2001: 1). Unlike the farmers and unskilled laborers who comprised the majority of earlier immigrations to the United States, "Russian émigrés are generally urban in origin, well-educated, and industrially and technologically skilled."

Despite a language barrier, although many have learned some English in Soviet-era schools, "they have marketable skills and have not been closed off from the legitimate ladders of upward mobility." Thus, "Russian-émigré crime in this country did not grow out of the same cultural alienation and economic disparity experienced by other immigrant groups." Furthermore, "Russian criminals did not begin their criminal careers as members of adolescent street gangs in ethnic ghettos," as did most of the criminals discussed in Chapters 4 and 5 (P. Williams 1997: 9–10). Russia (see Figure 10.1) has universal military service, and Russian criminals, therefore, typically possess martial skills.

THE ROOTS OF RUSSIAN ORGANIZED CRIME

With a landmass that stretches from Europe to Asia, 6.5-million square miles, and a population of more than 140 million, "Russian" does not necessarily reflect the ethnicity or nationality of many identified as part of organized crime. Thus, even though they may speak Russian—often a language imposed on conquered non-Russian peoples

[1]As Joseph Serio (2008) points out, statistics about the number of Russian criminal organizations and their size are devoid of empirical value; they will not be cited in this chapter.

FIGURE 10.1   *Map of Russia*

(Serio 2008)—and come from regions that have been dominated by Russia, many ethnic and groups and nationalities "do not regard themselves nor do Russians regard them as Russians" (Finckenauer and Waring 1999: 132). Therefore, *Russian organized crime* (ROC) encompasses any ethnic or national group—such as Armenian, Chechen, Georgian, Jewish, Latvian, Lithuanian, Tatar, Ukranian—from the territory of the former Soviet Union. Some also include Albanians (discussed in Chapter 6). Some prefer the term *Eurasian*.

In the Soviet Union, "organized crime" did not imply a Mafia-style organization, but was simply "a basic system of relationships and access among various sectors of society with the [Communist] Party in the dominant role and the traditional criminal world playing a relatively minor part" (Serio 2008: 19). In the successor states of the former Soviet Union, where law enforcement resources have been inadequate to deal with the menace, additional elements have elbowed their way into the world of organized crime. Many poorly paid officers are on gang payrolls, whereas others have left the service to work for the gangs full time (Gallagher 1992b; Hockstader 1995). "Parliamentary bodies are riddled with de facto criminal syndicate representatives, who diligently block or water down any significant anti-crime legislation" (Voronin 1997: 57). And although Chicagoans refer to politics as a "blood sport," it is less of a metaphor in the former Soviet Union (FSU) where elected and appointed officials are frequently the targets of hired killers (Wines 2002).

In Italy the word *Mafia* signifies discreet criminal organizations with strict hierarchical structures, but "in Russia it has come to mean much more. Here it embraces the noxious blend of crime, politics and business that has engulfed Russia since the lifting of Communist control" (Bohlen 1999: WK 6). Although there is no universally accepted definition of organized crime in Russia—in major part because Russian law (like U.S. law) provides no definition (Finckenauer and Voronin 2001)—some researchers have distinguished three levels (Foglesong and Solomon 2001):

1. *Gruppirovki*: Mainly gangs of extortionists, thieves, swindlers, and narcotics traffickers who exhibit a rudimentary and episodic structure.
2. *Prestupnaia organizatsiia*: This middle level involves relatively large formations with connections to authorities at the regional level.
3. *Soobshchestvo*: The highest level has influence extending to multiple regions of the country, often with international ties.

The breeding and training ground for Russian organized crime was established during the Communist era, and it is against this background that we must understand the variety of Russian organized crime. Citizens of the former Soviet Union were deprived of a work ethic—"We pretend to work, they pretend to pay us"—and schemed to survive. For the average Russian, the consequence of honesty was deprivation (Rosner 1995: vii). "In Russia, governments both under the rule of the Tzars and that of the Communist state represented totalitarianism in one form or another where individual freedom was suppressed. As such, like the invading foreigners of Sicily, the internal government system of Russia has made the Russian, like the Sicilian, distrustful of government" (Albini et al. 1995: 222). And like Sicily, the common method of social interaction, lawful and unlawful, is the patron-client relationship. And even though there is corruption in all countries, "in Russia, corruption is common in all organs of power and establishments" (Gilinsky 2004: 62), and this condition has roots that extend back to at least the sixteenth century (Serio 2008).

In many of the former Soviet republics, in the absence of western-style civil society, clans, which had operated for centuries, "took the situation into their own hands creating a system based more or less on their own strength" (Ceccarelli 2007: 22). The clans are informal organizations whose members share a set of behaviors and expectations. Members are united by kinship and friendship ties

and conform to unwritten group rules, norms, and practices. Ranging in size from 2,000 to 20,000, clans are governed by an elder's council and/or senior members. Clans may join in an alliance to expand their networks and influence enabling them to effectively compete with state apparatus. They may also compete with each other for influence, a situation that can lead to bloody civil wars. The clans have a close relationship with transnational organized crime groups, not only because they control territory, but also because the main aim of the clan is to provide assets and goods for members in any way possible, legal or illegal. Local criminal groups and drug mafias are also linked to the clans and transnational organized crime (Ceccarelli 2007).

The sudden onset of a market economy gave rise to unrestrained aspirations—the classic condition Émile Durkheim referred to as anomie (discussed in Chapter 2). Although written in 1897, Durkheim's concept of anomie fits the situation of present-day Russia: "The collapse of the previous system brought in fundamental changes in social and political order which shaped the personal lives of individuals in the most profound way. Several years of market reforms which changed the nature of the country's economy also brought with them hyperinflation, a sharp rise in unemployment and an overall drop in the standard of living" (Frisby 1998: 27). In 1991, the Soviet Union broke into fifteen independent states, with Russia dominant. Russia is struggling to establish a modern market economy and achieve strong economic growth. The economy initially contracted despite the country's wealth of natural resources, its well-educated population, and its diverse—although increasingly dilapidated—industrial base. Concomitantly, rapid social transformation resulting from market reforms created fantastic wealth for the few *nouveau riche*. Ironically, most of those who had power under Communism not only retained their material status, but frequently improved it considerably. Under Vladimir Putin, a former intelligence agency chief, Russia has experienced a lowering of civil liberties, and opposition political candidates have not been allowed to compete in national elections (Chivers 2008).

With the collapse of the Soviet Union, the nomenklatura (Communist elite) merged with the criminal underworld to take advantage of political and economic opportunity. Expanding illegal business activities to gain maximum profit in minimum time, however, is potentially dangerous, and the new pirate capitalists formed criminal organizations. "Thus, as strange as it might seem," notes Viktor Dryomin (2003: 57), "the communist ideology was easily replaced by a criminal one and the former party leaders eagerly entered into cooperation with the criminal world." While under communism managers of state-owned manufacturing diverted goods for sale outside of government control—a shadow economy—economic reforms enacted before the collapse of the Soviet Union provided managers, in collusion with local officials, unprecedented opportunity to purchase their firms. Among those who they turned to for the necessary capital were criminals (Foglesong and Solomon, Jr. 2001). In the late 1980s, with *Perestroika* (liberalizing of the economy) in bloom, the connection between the shadow (for example, black market) economy and criminal organizations was solidified, and various criminal organizations began to scramble for greater power and wealth.

Historically, Russia remained estranged from the European Enlightenment ideal of the rule of law, and this did not change with the advent of the Soviet Union (Shelley 2001). People in the FSU do not necessarily equate violating the law with criminality. People in the West are accustomed to fairly clear standards for judging who is guilty (even if these are not always or evenly applied). In the FSU, however, the standards applied to decide who is criminal are not as clear and are often situational and particularistic: "As under communism, the legal prosecution of an alleged perpetrator may depend on factors in the political-economic domain—such as the accuser's political and economic affiliations and current positioning and economic goals—and the political and economic affiliations and current positioning of the alleged perpetrator." Thus, the law "expresses less a system of shared ideals than a mechanism for exercising power in social relations," a mechanism that

"can be used as a weapon by one group against another" (Wedel 2001: 48).

Since the collapse of communism, the legal system has failed to keep pace with dramatic social and economic changes, and law enforcement institutions have become fragmented. Lacking coordination, they have been unable to cope with the sheer volume of work in processing mountains of information. The turnover of investigative staff has been high and technological provision low. Absent professionalism, morale declined and corruption increased rapidly. People, particularly vulnerable businessmen, began relying on the suddenly increasing private protection services, a large number of which operate without proper registration or licenses. Many resorted to taking justice into their own hands, often with assistance from the criminal fraternity. As a result, a kind of "shadow justice" appeared, dominated by criminals (Frisby 1998). The line between the private security forces and organized crime is often very narrow or nonexistent. With their high-level security training and knowledge of advanced military tactics and weapon systems, Russian military officers are in demand to organize and lead private security forces. Former special forces personnel are in particular demand (Center for Strategic and International Studies 1997).

Wars broke out as criminals struggled to claim state enterprises and property, leading to informal agreements that defined territories and functional boundaries. In industries owned or extorted by criminals, the result was higher prices passed on to consumers by industry-wide cartels. Criminals were now deeply entrenched in the Russian economy (Tomass 1998). Nascent capitalism, a relaxation of the totalitarian law enforcement apparatus, and liberalization of travel provided a fertile environment for these criminals schooled in a system rife with corruption and an underground economy.

During the Soviet era, three tiers of organized crime developed: "The first tier was high-level government and party bureaucrats; the second was shadow economy operators who produced goods off the books; and the third was professional criminals" (Finckenauer and Waring 2001: 3).

James Finckenauer and Yuri Voronin (2001) note the importance of economic deprivation, a shared ethnicity, culture, and language, as the building blocks for the "queer ladder of upward mobility" (discussed in Chapter 2) represented by organized crime. In the FSU, however—except in the Caucasus (Armenia, Chechnya, Georgia) and Central Asia (Uzbekistan)—the basis for criminal organization was driven solely by mutual participation in criminal activities, a connection that was economic, rather than ethnic or familial. Thus, the traditional elements that promote trust among participants in a criminal conspiracy were absent. In their place, these criminals were bound together by a rigid code of behavior that characterizes the *vory v zakone*.

THE *VORY*

While the former Soviet Union did not have organized crime in the pattern of the American racketeer, it did have an extensive professional underworld with roots that date back to the end of the seventeenth and beginning of the eighteenth century when gangs of itinerant petty criminals began to form a criminal hierarchy called by law enforcement the *vory v zakone*, "thieves with a code of honor." In the tradition of the Neapolitan Camorra, the *vory* thrived among hard-core prison camp inmates. With the growth of a revolutionary movement in Russia, the Czar consigned large numbers of educated political dissidents to prison camps where they replaced the older criminal leadership and established a *vory* code that forbade adherence to a conventional lifestyle. The *vory* conspiratorial code forbade any involvement in politics or collaboration with the state. Alexander Yarmysh (2001) considers this an extension of the "peasant commune mentality" according to which involvement with official authorities is forbidden— the state being viewed as hostile and oppressive. As Stalin's Gulags[2] began to fill up with political enemies, an even more rigid *vory* code of behavior

evolved, and during World War II the leadership began establishing an interregional corporate-type structure (Cheloukhine 2008). During World War II, the *vory* split into two factions; one (patriots) supported efforts to defeat the invading Nazis, whereas the other (traditionalists) remained aloof. By 1953, the patriots had been driven out of the "thieves' world" for their disloyalty to its traditions (Chalidze 1977; Friedman 2000). Eventually, the *vory* "changed its law to permit the scabs back in and to accept involvement with the authorities" (Schulte-Bockholt 2006: 164).

By the 1980s, a new generation of *vory* who prize greater violence came to the fore, and this is reflected by a repertoire of crime that includes debt collection, contract enforcement, contract killings, and providing protection broadly defined to business (Cheloukhine 2008). In a situation that parallels the split in post–World War II Sicily between the old and new Mafia (discussed in Chapter 6), a new (*novye*) *vory v zakone* began to appear in the late 1980s. "Contrary to the old thieves, the new *vory* appeared to organize and operate on a grander scale and took advantage of an opportunity to make a large sum of money quickly even if in violation of the thieves' traditions" (Serio 2008: 166). Steeped in ritual and custom with a rigid code of honor, the old *vory* was eclipsed by one whose ideals were more economically driven (Rawlinson 1997). Contemporary members are less likely to have served a prison term and often forgo the telltale tattooing.

Structure of the *Vory*

Emblazoned with tattoos, including giant eagles with razor-sharp talons on their chests, the *vory* developed a coded language decipherable only by other members of the criminal fraternity. *Vory* members often sported elaborate tattoos that reveal their status in the organization's hierarchy and even their criminal specialty. The title *vor* is bestowed at special initiation ceremonies during which the novice (*malyutka*) pledges fealty and is given a new name—a rechristening. *Vory* membership requires three sponsors and a ceremony with an oath of allegiance to abide by eighteen

---

[2]GULAG is an acronym for the Russian prison service and a term used to identify penal colonies (Cheloukhine 2008).

rules, the breaking of which is punishable by death. In particular, the rules require the *vor* to forsake all relatives, help other *vor*, never work (at legitimate employment), and never insult or raise a hand against another *vor* (unless sanctioned by a *vory* court). Prospects have to be free of involvement with conventional aspects of society, such as regular employment, paying taxes, or military service (Frisby 1998; Varese 2001). As does the Sicilian Mafia, *vory* embrace a principle of brotherhood and superiority according to which they have a right to live at the expense of others and to confiscate the property of those deemed inferior (Yarmysh 2001).

Vory organizations are conspiratorial and hierarchical. They include representatives of the administration of various enterprises who, during the Soviet era, were often party members with high positions who lived double lives. Organized into tight networks, "from their cells, crime bosses planned and organized their operations across the country . . . [while] lieutenants, often called *brodyagi* (vagabonds), conducted formal dealings with the outside" (Handelman 1995: 209). The criminal society has a form of insurance: "*obshchak*—derived from members' contributions and fines for violating the thieves' code, that is used to bribe officials inside and outside of prison, to provide amenities to imprisoned members and to help support their families. After leaving prison, members are expected to repay the *obshchak*" (Finckenauer and Waring 1999: 107).

The *vory* is exclusively male; females, even wives, lack status. Indeed, attachment to a spouse is seen as a weakness—undermining loyalty to the *vory*—as is faithfulness. A wife is not permitted to socialize outside of the thieves' world, and she is never permitted to leave. Paternal bonds lack emotional attachment, and it is assumed that the children of a *vory* member will follow him into the fraternity, although this often does not happen (Varese 2001).

Under communism, managers of state-owned enterprises became unofficial entrepreneurs. To meet the quotas set by the regime, they established informal networks to ensure the provision of supplies from other state-owned enterprises. There was rationing and price controls and, as a consequence, a divergence between market values and administrative controls. This led to the development of an underground economy whereby commodities were diverted to informal markets where they could be sold at higher prices. Managers reserved their most valuable goods for the *vory* who paid premium prices that the managers did not report and, subsequently, embezzled. Managers were unwilling to provide scarce goods to ordinary citizens, exacerbating existing shortages. The *vory*, taking advantage of the managers' inability to turn to law enforcement for protection, extorted money from their erstwhile partners in the black market. Subsequent privatization and legalization of joint ownership meant that state enterprises were handed over to corrupt managers and their *vory* partners through worker buyouts. The strategic use of intimidation and violence then allowed criminals to infiltrate the banking industry. All this occurred at a time when the law enforcement apparatus was considerably weakened. The law enforcers, employees of state justice and security agencies, acted informally as private enforcers or resigned and joined private protection companies. Many became partners with violent entrepreneurs in the racketeer gangs (Volkov 2000).

Each vory group is headed by a *vor v zakonye* who is recognized by all others as the authority in his territory. A *vor v zakonye* is chosen at a meeting of members and requires the recommendation of at least two other bosses—the more recommendations, the more prestige. By 1992, the most powerful bosses had reportedly divided the country into twelve regions where they interact with bureaucrats and industrial managers. Dressed in leather coats and driving flashy cars, they eat openly with government officials in restaurants they often control (Handelman 1995).

In a pattern that parallels that of the Chicago Outfit (Chapter 5), "the *vory* ritual now marks the entry of powerful crew leaders into the 'governing body' of the biggest criminal groups in Moscow"; that is, being "made" indicates a management position reserved for the leaders, rather than being a requirement for each group member (Varese 2001: 177).

New criminal groups devoid of the traditions of the *vory* have also emerged, and their leaders—*avtoritet* (authority)—in the competitive spirit of capitalism have challenged the *vory*.

THE RUSSIAN *MAFIYA*

Some observers report two levels of Russian organized crime. The first is inhabited by street thugs, basically low-level muscle who extort payoffs from small businesses for "protection" (Voronin 1997). The second level is more reminiscent of the Robber Barons than of Al Capone, where organized crime and government are symbiotic, criminals and bureaucrats forming a network "that is highly organized, stratified, meticulous in planning, highly efficient in execution and well disciplined" (Serio 1992a: 130; also Serio 2008; Stanley 1994). In most countries, organized crime thrives primarily through the provision of goods and services that happen to be illegal. In the former Soviet Union, by contrast, "organized crime flourishes well beyond these areas—it wields power over all the economy" (Voronin 1997: 55–56). In the important Asian port city of Vladivostok, 6,000 miles from Moscow, the criminal underworld merges with local government and a shadow economy whose benefactors can be seen driving luxury automobiles and sailing yachts (Spector 1995; Witt 1994). This shadow economy is pervasive throughout the country, a result of onerous taxes and licensing requirements imposed by the central government (Hockstader 1995).

Some Russian organized crime groups—the Russian *Mafiya*—emerged from the pastime of many Russian young men: participation in sports clubs and fitness centers. In the Soviet Union, sports were a major priority of the state because they expressed its might and socialized its youth. But in different circumstances, sports, especially fighting sports and martial arts, can supply all that is needed to create a racketeer gang: fighting skills, willpower, discipline, and team spirit. When the state withdrew sponsorship, the constraints of a rule-governed nonviolent competition also ended, and this was enough to launch a dangerous process whereby sportsmen started to look for an alternative career. Powerful gangs emerged from the gyms and sports clubs of the former Soviet Union. In Moscow and its suburbs, at the city markets, the first flowering of free trade and private entrepreneurship, the former sportsmen discovered a way for their physical assets to be turned into cash—offering protection for a regular fee. The market and the gym were at the origin of a peculiar local capitalism: Small business provided the economic base for new gangs supplying protection (Volkov 2000).

The *Mafiya* and the *vory* extort (offer *krysha*—literally a "roof" that provides protection) from both legitimate and illegitimate entrepreneurs. "*Mafiozy* approach businesses directly, visiting in groups of three or four. One of them speaks in a friendly manner, warning the directors that they must pay" 15 to 20 percent of their company's gross earnings "or suffer violence at the hands of unnamed gangs. If the *mafiozy* operate under the guise of a security agency, they may insist that the director sign a contract" (Tayler 2001: 38). Businesses refusing to pay, something rare, are subjected to a campaign that begins with verbal threats and escalates to bullets, bombs, and the torture of family members (Tayler 2001). These groups can also provide services such as restraining competition: "If competition with lower prices or better goods appear on the scene, fires, theft, murder, and other bedlam can be arranged" (Tayler 2001: 38). Russian organized crime groups have excelled at restraining trade and controlling pricing in a variety of arenas, including airport taxis and farmers' markets. Businessmen do not necessarily wait for the inevitable "visit." Instead, they may seek out the most effective "roof"—able to provide protection from competing Russian organized crime groups and predatory criminals (Varese 2001).

In the manner of southern Italy, organized crime bosses provide a viable alternative to a formal justice system that is ineffective, if not corrupt. Instead of hiring lawyers to settle contract disputes, Russians engage *Mafiya* bosses. Businessmen keep them on retainer to avoid shakedowns or to ensure that they have representation in the event of a business dispute (Gallagher 1995b; Witt 1996). In a country where contract law and a tradition of property rights are weak, the Russian wiseguy, like his Sicilian *mafioso* counterpart, acts as a guarantor so that persons who do not trust one another can transact business with a significant degree of confidence. "The introduction of private property in Russia has led to a demand for protection which the state has been unable to meet—and that organized crime is meeting instead" (Williams 1997: 6). A meeting between *Mafyia* bosses to resolve a business dispute is the *strelka* at which both sides are often accompanied by an armed retinue (Glenny 2008).

Russian organized crime also provides services to banks experiencing problems collecting debts. Resorting to the courts for such service is time-consuming and runs the risk that the debtor will declare bankruptcy (Varese 2001). Note the transition made by the *uralmashevskaya*—whose name derives from a district in the industrialized Urals Mountain city of Ekaterinburg—from gang to "financial-industrial enterprise." Formed around young toughs from the local sports clubs, they produced illegal alcohol and provided *krysha* to area businesses. Assets from these activities were invested in businesses experiencing a need for cash. As their enterprises expanded, the *uralmashevskaya* began to conflict with a similarly ambitious *vory*. Violence broke out in 1992 and 1993, and the *vory* were outmatched by their more ruthless opponents who were better disciplined and schooled in the use of force. After eliminating their rivals, the *uralmashevskaya* expanded their business interests and entered the political arena, financing candidates and having members run for elected office. They completed their transition by establishing institutionalized relations with the regional government (Volkov 2000).

In a scenario that parallels that of American organized crime after the repeal of Prohibition and the onset of the Great Depression, Russian criminals have ready access to investment capital in a society where sources of financing are scarce. "Even apparently legitimate entrepreneurs find it difficult to muster the necessary capital for new enterprises and all too frequently must borrow funds from mobsters at extortionate rates of interest" (Voronin 1997: 56). And many criminals have "displayed a surprising knowledge and expertise in the workings of the market" that is rare in post-Soviet society (Rawlinson 1997: 46).

And they have proven to be very violent: Machine-gun fire, car bombs, public assassinations, and onlookers who remember nothing have become common (Bohlen 1993; Spector 1994). As a result of the disintegration of the Soviet military and the breakdown in arms control at weapons plants, high-quality automatic weapons are available throughout the country (Hersh 1994; Hockstader 1995). Members of the military constitute an important element in Russian organized crime: "[P]oorly paid, badly housed, and demoralized, Russian military forces at home and abroad are deeply immersed in criminal activities conducted for personal and group profit. Smuggling crimes of all types (particularly drug and arms trafficking), the massive diversion of equipment and materials, illegal business ventures, and coercion and criminal violence, all fall under the umbrella of military organized crime" (Turbiville 1995: 63; also Gordon 1996). And there are close links with organized crime groups outside the military.

An undetermined number of banks have fallen under the effective control or ownership of organized crime groups who use them to launder and embezzle money. Bank records provide information for selecting businesses from whom to extort protection money (Bohlen 1994). The Russian banking system is grossly unregulated, which facilitates money laundering, not only for Russian criminals in the United States but also for Colombian cartels and Mafia *cosche* (Friedman 1996). The Russians provide money laundering services for the Colombians, while the latter provide cocaine for distribution among the elite of the former Soviet Union ("Russian Organized Crime" 1996; hereafter "ROC" 1996).

Moving into more risky spheres of criminal behavior, such as bank fraud and drug trafficking, these new groups command wealth beyond the dreams of the old *vory* (Handelman 1995). Russian gangsters have been involved in the production and sale of methadone and similar synthetic narcotics, such as trimethyl phentanyl, often called 3MF. Even when they are not directly involved in trafficking, Russian organized crime groups provide protection to drug trafficking networks bringing in Afghan heroin destined primarily for European markets. Transportation is typically split into phases: One group moves the cargo from Afghanistan to Tajikistan where it is sold to a wholesale buyer. The consignment is then loaded on trucks and concealed among legitimate cargo, such as fruits and vegetables. Once the consignment has reached the Russian border, it is reloaded onto different trucks and the manifests are altered to disguise the origin of the goods or produce. Guarding the border is a limited number of law enforcement agents and an unlimited opportunity for corruption. "Major heroin trafficking routes from Central Asia lead to Moscow, St. Petersburg, Saratov, Yekaterinburg, as well as the other large cities of Volga Region and Siberia. These locations are not only destination points but also serve as a transshipment point for further shipments to other destinations in Russia and in Europe" (United Nations Office on Drugs and Crime 2008b: 16)

There is also extensive trafficking in military weapons, which frequently wind up in areas of ethnic conflict, discussed in Chapter 12. There is fear that this could extend to nuclear devices, and the FSU has had more than two dozen reported nuclear trafficking incidents between 2001 and 2005[3] (Zaitseva 2007). Although these developments suggest a potential danger, there is an absence of compelling evidence of a solid nexus among weapons of mass destruction related trafficking, terrorism, and organized crime in the former Soviet Union (Ouagrham-Gormley 2007).

Ransom kidnappings are also part of the repertoire. Some of the gangs in the Russian *mafiya* are local, but "others span the entire former Soviet Union, and more and more are establishing links abroad" (Elliott 1992: 52). There have been reports (such as Friedman 1996) of meetings between Russian and Sicilian mobsters in Europe, and documented connections between Colombian drug traffickers and Russian criminals in the south Florida area (Navarro 1997).

---

[3]In 1995, it was revealed that 4.4 tons of beryllium—a critical element for building nuclear warheads—141 kilograms of which was radioactive, seized by police in Lithuania was from an experimental reactor in Russia (Zimmermann and Cooperman 1995). That same year, Chechen separatists buried a vial of low-level radioactive cesium in a Moscow park, apparently as a scare tactic ("Editorial" 1995).

One of the more nefarious activities associated with Russian organized crime is trafficking in women for the sex industry (discussed in Chapter 12). During the Soviet era, borders were tightly controlled and movement limited. "Therefore, human trafficking, or transporting people across borders for financial gain did not occur before 1991" (Glonti 2003: 71). When the Soviet Union collapsed, notes George Glonti (2003: 71), authorities were completely unprepared for the massive migration that ensued. "New criminal structures created expanding transnational networks for prostitution and exporting young people abroad for various forms of labour exploitation."

Women in the FSU often face chronic unemployment, forcing them to look abroad for employment, making them vulnerable to exploitation. The road leading to the sex industry typically originates with a newspaper ad or an unexpected meeting on the street, a proposition to work abroad as maid, secretary, showgirl, nanny, or waitress. The victims are often well educated and answer advertisements for positions in service industries for which they are overqualified—such is the state of the Russian economy and job market. Women are usually trafficked in Europe—Belgium, the Netherlands, Poland, and Switzerland—and Asia—China, Japan, and Thailand (Stocckers 2000).

Criminals can supply their victims with services such as fraudulent travel documents, transportation, guided border crossings, accommodations, and job brokering. Upon their arrival in a foreign destination, the women are informed that the job no longer exists, but they are still indebted to the agent for the trip, which usually costs them between $5,000 and $20,000. Women who refuse to cooperate are subjected to physical and sexual abuse; sometimes they are murdered. One victim who refused to have sex with potential customers was taken into a country field, and while other women were forced to watch, her throat was cut. Having lived in a society ruled by an oppressive government, Russian émigrés tend to be inherently distrustful of government and reluctant to speak with or seek assistance from law enforcement (Zalisko 2001).

The most powerful of the criminal groups is the Moscow-based *Solntsevo* (or *Solntsevskaya brigada* or *Solntsevskaya Bratva*—Solntevo Brotherhood), reputed to have thousands of members active in several countries. The organization, which takes its name from a Moscow suburb, is both hierarchical and flexible. At the top of the hierarchy is a supreme council consisting of twelve people who are the leaders of individual crews, who meet regularly to discuss matters of importance to the organization. The council manages a joint fund (*obshchak*) to which all brigades allocate money on a regular basis (Varese 2001). In another example of the value of a bad reputation, the *Solntsevo* are said to have "rented out" their notoriety to less formidable criminal groups—for a fee, they could represent themselves as *Solnetsevo* (Serio 2008).

Sergei Mikhailov, boss of the *Solntsevskaya* who is in his forties, held Russian, Israeli, and Costa Rican passports—he had legitimate business interests in these countries, as well as Hungary and Belgium. Decades ago, Mikhailov was employed as a waiter in a Moscow hotel. In 1984, he was imprisoned for collecting insurance on his motorcycle that he had fraudulently reported stolen. Prison contacts helped lay the groundwork for a flourishing criminal career (Bohlen 1999). In 1998, he was accused of illegally buying property in Switzerland where he lived with his wife and children in a village outside of Geneva. He had Swiss bank accounts totaling $2 million (Kaban 1998). At the end of 1998, Mikhailov was acquitted by a Swiss court: "If he were an Italian being tried in Italy, he might well have been found guilty under a 1982 law that makes 'mafia association' a criminal offense" (Bohlen 1999: WK 5).

CHECHENS

Members of various ethnic groups have also moved into *mafiya* activity. Organized around feudal clan and tribal relationships, literally "crime families," these groups are well suited to take advantage of dislocations in post-Soviet society. One of these groups originated in the Central Asian region of the Caucasus Mountains due north of the Georgian Republic. Largely Muslim, historically hostile to Moscow, and legendary warriors, the Chechens were subjected to massive deportations in 1944 by Stalin, who falsely accused them of collaborating with the Nazis during World War II; they returned to the region in 1957. Known for strong family loyalties and a sense of personal honor, Chechens, like Sicilians, are governed by the concept of *omertá—adat* requires vengeance to uphold family honor (Gallagher 1995a; "History of Antagonism" 1994). And the Russian attitude toward Chechens parallels that of northern Italians toward Sicilians.[4]

In 1991, Chechen leaders declared their independence and quickly became locked in violent conflict with the Russian military. Independence leader Dzhokar Dudayev is reported to have turned Chechnya into "Chicago of the twenties." "Chechen mafiosi engaged in some of the most

spectacular criminal scams Russia has ever known. With Dudayev's police looking the other way (or, more likely, cooperating at every turn), Grozny [the capital] became a center of illegal trade. The city's airport served as a hub for unsanctioned flights hauling contraband and outlaws. . . . The flights—from the Middle East, Turkey, central Asia, and elsewhere—brought in huge amounts of narcotics and 'duty free' goods, and a succession of bandits in hiding. Mafiosi were also in the habit of robbing cargo trains travelling through Chechen territory" (Remnick 1995: 53). After two wars, one from 1994 to 1996 and a second that began in 1999, Russian forces were successful in thwarting the independence movement and installing a pro-Moscow regime. Fighting continues, but it is sporadic and on a small scale (Kramer 2008a).

Vast supplies of arms were left in Chechnya by the Russian military; arms trafficking and counterfeiting of currency and financial documents are important parts of the Chechen crime portfolio. Chechen crime groups operate in many areas of the former Soviet Union, including Moscow. "The group is more structured than most. Most important for them is the strict hierarchical arrangement of their clan relationships. It is a closed organization, recruiting only from among their own people. Chechens actively recruit juveniles from the Chechen regions where unemployment is high. This ensures a degree of 'purity' in the membership, making it difficult for law enforcement agencies lacking personnel that speak Chechen to infiltrate the group. . . . Each group has a clear structure: leader, senior advisors, soldiers, and associated members" (Serio 1992b: 5). Chechens are the only criminal group that does not respect the territoriality of the *vory* (Cheloukhine 2008).

Organized crime is a business. Exhibiting the value of a bad reputation, Chechen crime groups guard their reputation for violence; any group claiming a Chechen connection that fails to carry out its threats—devaluing the brand—is likely to be "visited" by the genuine article (Glenny 2008). Protection rackets, enforcing restraint of trade agreements, and narcotics and weapons trafficking are all part of the Chechen crime repertoire. The Chechen reputation for being both violent and

---

[4]For a discussion of Chechnya and the conflict with Russia, see Gall and de Waal (1998) and Lieven (1998).

fearless is often sufficient to cow an opponent—but sometimes not: In 1993, a group of well-armed gangsters drove to a building across the Moscow River from the Kremlin to extort money from a local businessman. They were met by the businessman's protectors, Chechens, who opened fire, killing the gangster boss and four of his men (LeVine, McKay, and Lebedeva 1993). Members of Chechen groups have been found throughout Eastern and Western Europe and have sent members to New York to set up operations. Some have entered the United States for contract crimes—murder, extortion, fraud—after which they return home before authorities can detect and apprehend them.

RUSSIAN ORGANIZED CRIME IN THE UNITED STATES

A new wave of emigration, business travel, and tourism quickly exported organized crime to other countries (Cheloukhine 2008). Russian criminals enter the United States with backgrounds for excelling in organized criminal activity without moving through the more traditional routes that typically include street gang delinquency and apprenticeship under adult criminals. "Unlike their ethnic predecessors in crime, Russian émigrés do not have to go through any developmental or learning process to break into the criminal world in this country. They are able to begin operating almost immediately upon their arrival" (Tri-State Joint Soviet-Émigré Organized Crime Project 1997: 185). They typically have military experience and many are college-educated. "Many of today's foremost Russian mobsters have Ph.D.'s

in mathematics, engineering, or physics, helping them to acquire an expertise in advanced encryption and computer technology" (Friedman 2000: xviii).

These criminals have established themselves in a number of U.S. cities where Russian immigrants have settled—Boston, Chicago, Cleveland, Dallas, Miami, New York, Philadelphia, Portland, San Francisco, and Seattle. Although known by their fellow Russians as the *organizatsiya* (the organization), the actual degree of organization appears limited. What has not been limited is the exploitation of the Russian émigré community. In Brighton Beach, a major Russian émigré community in Brooklyn, Jewish criminals from the former Soviet Union, working in small "brigades," systematically extorted money from legitimate businesses (Friedman 2000).

Robert Friedman (2000) argues that in the United States, Russian criminals are well organized and pose a threat more serious than that of Italian American criminal organizations. Unfortunately, he provides virtually no information on the structure of the Russian groups, although he reveals that they are in awe of their Italian American counterparts. Friedman also uses terms such as *member* and *cartel* when referring to Russian organized crime but provides no explanation of their meaning. The Tri-State (New York–New Jersey–Pennsylvania) Joint Soviet-Émigré Organized Crime Project (1997) concludes that Russian criminals in the United States have neither the critical mass nor the criminal sophistication to create a major local or regional threat, much less a national or international one. They appear to be organized on an enterprise basis and not in a hierarchical manner.

Russian crime groups in the United States are typically fluid, and membership is transient, comprising five to twenty persons. Their pattern has been compared with that of the Zips discussed in Chapter 2 (Finckenauer and Waring 1999; Mitchell 1992). Loosely structured, without formal hierarchy, groups are usually formed on the basis of regional backgrounds or built around a particular enterprise. One group may comprise mainly immigrants from Kiev, whereas another may consist mainly of Georgians. Or a group may organize to extort money from local merchants or to operate a gasoline tax evasion scheme. Many group members are professional criminals; after their experience of criminal life in the Soviet Union, where police were feared and treatment of lawbreakers harsh, they view the United States as a haven.

The Tri-State Joint Soviet Émigré Organized Crime Project (1997; hereafter, Tri-State) states that the Russian émigré criminals in the United States typically mistrust each other. There is generally little or no personal loyalty based on common ethnic or cultural backgrounds, even though some of the criminals knew each other in the former Soviet Union. And betrayals have been frequent: Russian criminals, despite a background of hardship, have been quick to become informants to avoid the long sentences that are part of the Racketeer and Corrupt Organizations (RICO) statute, discussed in Chapter 15. This has reportedly impeded the development of larger, more structured organizations (Berkeley 2002a).

The Russian émigré criminal network structure is usually an ad hoc team of specialists teamed for specific criminal enterprises. They form opportunistic partnerships that are sometimes based on referrals by other Russian criminals. After the criminal objective is attained, the specialists may split up or may move together to other criminal ventures. There are also professional criminals with a propensity for violence who form small criminal groups to commit extortion or engage in drug trafficking. These groups often center around one or more dominant individuals and the composition of the group is subject to frequent changes. Colombo Family captain Michael Franzese, who worked closely with Russian crime

groups, states: "I did not find the Russian criminals to be a very structured group in comparison to the Italian La Cosa Nostra. They were very clannish, however, and the most financially successful Russian was looked up to by his comrades as their leader or boss. The boss was given a lot of courtesy and respect and in return provided the members of his group with opportunities to work for him and make money" ("ROC" 1996: 39). They engage in extortion, insurance fraud,[5] Medicaid scams,[6] securities-related fraud,[7] con games, identity theft, counterfeiting, tax fraud, and narcotics trafficking.

"One way to contrast La Cosa Nostra and Russian-émigré criminal organizations is to view the former as having a structure—a distinct, definable crime family—that is supported by criminal activities. The structure is continuous, and crime is used to carry out its objectives and maintain its strength and vitality. Russians, however, create floating structures on an as-needed basis to enable them to carry out particular crimes. The criminal opportunities come first, and the necessary structure to take advantage of those opportunities follows" (Tri-State 1997: 24).

Fuel Oil Scam

An example of the types of activities in which Russian criminals are involved in the United States, and their relations with the American Mafia, is the fuel oil scam. Michael Franzese, born in 1951, son of the infamous underboss of the Colombo Family, John ("Sonny") Franzese, testified before a congressional committee ("ROC" 1996) on how the scheme transpired.

In 1987, a major Italian American independent gasoline wholesaler approached Franzese for protection: He was involved in a massive tax evasion scheme and was being extorted by some mob figures. In return for his help, Franzese became a partner in the business. Later, Russian

---

[5]See, for example, Healy (2003).

[6]See, for example, Finkelstein (1998).

[7]See, for example, Eaton (1997).

gasoline dealers using the same scheme approached Franzese for help collecting some debts. Through his contacts, Franzese also helped them hold and obtain the wholesale licenses needed to keep their business in operation. In both cases, the tax evasion scheme was similar: Using a "daisy chain with a vanishing point," gasoline was transferred on paper from one bogus company to another. Taxes are due when the fuel is finally sold to retailers, but the last company receiving the gasoline existed only on paper, as revenue investigators discovered. By the time auditors and investigators would unravel the series of transactions to determine the tax liability, the "burn" company had disappeared without a trace of records or assets. The taxes were skimmed when the fuel was actually sold at discount prices to dealers (Van Duyne and Block 1995).

The wholesalers need to be able to purchase fuel tax free, and this requires an IRS excise tax Certification of Exemption. The certifications were obtained by buying out registered companies or falsifying documents of legitimate companies. In response to these schemes, in 1993, Congress moved the point of taxation on gasoline from the wholesale distributor to the distribution terminal. Unable to divert the excise tax, the Russians moved to a new scam. Using numerous dummy firms, they purchased home heating (diesel) oil, which is tax free. The diesel oil was then transferred through fake companies and sold as diesel fuel, which is subject to federal excise taxes, and they pocketed the tax money. Franzese recalls, "It was not unusual for me to receive $9 million in cash per week in paper bags" from the combined operation ("ROC" 1996: 38), estimated to have cost the government $140 million (Levy 1995). Legislation enacted in 1994 requires that only fuel dyed red—diesel fuel is typically yellow or green—can be tax exempt and can only be used for off-road purposes such as home heating or in tractors. The dyed fuel is easily spotted by IRS inspectors or state tax agents who check truck stops or set up road checkpoints. The Russians responded by purchasing fuel in low tax states and shipping it to high tax states that can produce a 12 percent advantage.

As a result of this successful collaboration, Franzese was involved in numerous lucrative deals with Russian criminals involving loansharking and insurance and securities fraud.

Anthony Casso, who later become involved with the fuel scam on behalf of the Lucchese Family—eventually four crime Families became involved, each working with different Russian groups—notes that the unstructured Russians needed the organizational experience of the Italians: "It is putting it together, because like Marat [Balagula, one of the key Russians], he owned a couple of hundred gas stations. So when we put the cartel together, now no one else was going to go into his stations to sell gas a little cheaper, just sell the gas, and they start fighting amongst themselves again. So we held peace, and, you know, protection goes more than one way" ("ROC" 1996: 48). The Lucchese Family also took care of a problem Balagula was having with the violent boss of a Russian gang—they shot him to death as he left a Brighton Beach restaurant. The FBI and IRS set up their own petroleum company to compete with the "bootleggers." The response by organized crime figures to this competition led to the breaking up of the petroleum cartel.[8]

In 2000, an investigation in the ports of Newark and Elizabeth, New Jersey, revealed a massive smuggling operation orchestrated by Russian criminals. At the behest of Russian criminals in the United States, a number of American distilleries were disguising millions of gallons of their product—192-proof grain alcohol—by adding dye and shipping it in giant containers marked windshield wiper fluid, cologne, mouthwash, and cleaning solvent. Once in Russia, using a formula provided by the distillers, the dye was removed, the alcohol diluted with water, and vodka flavoring added. The product was then distributed by

---

[8]In 1986, Michael Franzese pleaded guilty to the massive fuel tax fraud and received a 10-year sentence. He was released in 1989 and ordered to pay the government back more than $14 million—which was never paid. That year, under a grant of immunity, he admitted that he was a member of the Colombo Family. Franzese produced low-budget movies and wrote a book in which he portrayed himself as the "yuppie Don." In 1991, he received a four-year sentence for violation of probation.

Russia-based criminal organizations, evading millions of dollars in import duty and taxes. The smuggling was encouraged by high Russian tariffs designed to protect domestic alcohol production (Rashbaum 2000a).

Vory in the United States

Vory members are given special status—*respect*—in the Russian American underworld. In 1991, Vyacheslav Kirillovich (*Yaponchik*—"Little Jap") Ivankov, a high-ranking *vor v zakonye* with the *Solntsevskaya* (discussed earlier), was released early (political influence/bribery is suspected) from serving a 14-year prison sentence for robbery, aggravated assault, and extortion. After his release, he went on a campaign of extortion, often torturing victims, and was responsible for ordering many killings, including those of journalists and police officers. His murderous campaign against Moscow's powerful Chechen crime groups further raised Ivankov's profile to a liability: The *vor*

leadership's "Circle of Brothers" banished him to America (Friedman 2000).

Shortly after his arrival at JFK airport, Ivankov was given a suitcase with $1.5 million by an Armenian *vor*. He established his headquarters in Brighton Beach and recruited Russian combat veterans with a $20,000 a month retainer. They were sent out to extort money from legitimate businesses worldwide and to assassinate his rivals. Fear permeated the Russian émigré community, and its major criminal operatives were soon allied with Ivankov—or they were dead (Friedman 2000).

Ivankov's reign as the reputed leading Russian crime boss in the United States did not last long: In 1995, he was arrested for Hobbs Act (see Chapter 15) violations, attempting to extort millions of dollars from two immigrant businessman—both embezzlers—who had been kidnapped at gunpoint from a Manhattan hotel (Dubocq and Garcia 1997; L. Myers 1995). Ivankov become personally involved in the plot and was recorded

Vyachelav ("Little Jap") Ivankov, a top-ranking *vory*, being escorted by FBI agents from the agency's New York headquarters.

on a wiretap giving instructions on how it was to be carried out; he also threatened the two businessmen who, unbeknown to him, were cooperating with the FBI. While in custody awaiting trial, Ivankov so alienated his codefendants that two of them became cooperating witnesses against him (Friedman 2000). The following year, Ivankov and three codefendants were convicted of extortion; he received a nine-year sentence (Finckenauer and Waring 1999). Ivankov was released from the federal prison at Allenwood, Pennsylvania, in 2007 and immediately taken into custody by U.S. Immigration and Customs agents who placed him on a chartered flight to Russia where he is wanted for the murder of two Turkish men in Moscow.

One of Ivankov's business partners, Semion Mogilevich, is a Ukrainian-born Jew with a college degree in economics. Originally part of a Moscow crime group during the Soviet era, Mogilevich made his first fortune by defrauding fellow Jews who were fleeing to the United States. Holding Israeli and Hungarian citizenship—his wife is Hungarian—Mogilevich heads an organization of about 250 persons, many of whom are relatives, whose operations transcend national boundaries. In the Czech Republic, they have tortured and murdered businessmen who resisted their extortion efforts; at Moscow's international airport, they control smuggling; in Hungary, Mogilevich owns nightclubs and a major portion of the Hungarian arms industry; and in the United States, his operatives have been involved in money laundering and contract murders—supplying weapons and spiriting the killers out of the country after their assignment is complete (Friedman 2000). According to Friedman (2000: 239), Mogilevich built a "highly structured criminal organization in the mode of a 'classic' American Mafia family" with a clearly defined chain of command, specialization, and division of labor. While he may have indeed built such an organization, as noted in Chapters 1 and 4, the bureaucratic attributes Friedman describes are not the mode of a "classic American Mafia family."

In 1999, it was revealed that Mogilevich, who is an undesirable prohibited from entering the United States, set up a magnet manufacturing and importing company in suburban Philadelphia.

YBM Magnex had a blue-ribbon board of directors and was audited by two prominent American accounting firms. Before YBM pled guilty to securities fraud, Mogilevich and his associates had made millions of dollars from selling inflated shares of the company's stock (Bonner 1999). He was subsequently linked to a major money laundering operation in which billions of dollars were channeled through the Bank of New York. Some of the money from the account reportedly went to pay contract killers and some went to drug barons (Bonner and O'Brien 1999). Wanted by the FBI, in 2008, Mogilevich, 61, was arrested in Russia on unrelated charges of tax evasion (Kramer 2008b).

Many of the criminals, *vor* and non-*vor*, are Jews. Unlike Jewish immigrant groups that made up organized crime in the past (discussed in Chapters 3 and 4), the Russians are relatively well educated and adept at exploiting weaknesses in American society. Jewish émigrés—many from the Ukrainian seaport of Odessa, noted for its criminal subculture—have settled in the Brighton Beach section of Brooklyn ("Little Odessa"), and the New York police department has been handicapped in dealing with the protection rackets and loansharking activities in the community by a lack of Russian-speaking officers.

In the next chapter, we will examine a uniquely American phenomenon that has become part of transnational organized crime, outlaw motorcycle clubs.

SUMMARY

- Because of the lack of a reliable legal system, in the former Soviet Union, vulnerable businessmen rely on "shadow justice" provided by criminal groups, including the *vory v zakone*, "thieves with a code of honor," which developed among hard-core prison camp inmates and organized into tight networks that operate across the country.
- *Vory* members are given special status—*respect*—in the Russian American underworld.
- Powerful gangs emerged from the gyms and sports clubs of the former Soviet Union, and

former military personnel are well represented in Russian organized crime.

- In the manner of southern Italy, organized crime bosses provide a viable alternative to a formal justice system that is ineffective, if not corrupt.
- Members of various ethnic groups have also moved into *mafiya* activity, and the Chechens are the most feared.
- Unlike the farmers and unskilled laborers who composed most of earlier immigrations to the United States, Russians are generally urban in origin, well educated, and industrially and technologically skilled.
- Despite a language barrier (although many learned some English in Soviet-era schools),

Russians in the United States have marketable skills and have not been closed off from the legitimate ladders of upward mobility. Skilled in behavior needed for living in a particularly corrupt system, they have proved to be able and willing to engage in the type of violence that typifies organized crime in general (Raab 1994b), although they prefer financial accommodations to violence—they are essentially ruthless businessmen rather than gangsters.

- Although some Russians maintain links with groups in the former Soviet Union, in the United States, they tend to be enterprise groups devoid of any permanent hierarchy.

REVIEW QUESTIONS

1. Why do Russian criminals come to the United States well prepared for a life in organized crime?
2. What are the problems experienced by Russia that promote organized crime?
3. What are the different groups that make up Russian organized crime?
4. What types of activities are engaged in by Russian organized crime in the former Soviet Union?
5. What is the *vory*?
6. What are the similarities between the Russian organized crime and the Sicilian Mafia?
7. What are the similarities between the old and new *vory* and the old and new Sicilian Mafia?
8. What is the structure of Russian organized crime groups in the United States?
9. How do members of Russian organized crime groups in the United States differ from members of previous immigrant groups?
10. How does organized crime in Russia differ from that in the United States?
11. What have been the criminal activities of Russian crime groups in the United States?
12. What can we predict about the future of Russian organized crime in the United States?

CHAPTER

11

International Outlaw Motorcycle Clubs[1]

The outlaw motorcycle club is a uniquely American derivation, although several of these clubs have chapters throughout the world. The outlaw club phenomenon dates from the years after World War II, when many combat veterans, particularly those residing in California, sought new outlets for feelings of hostility and alienation. Some found release in riding motorcycles—military surplus motorcycles were plentiful—and in associating with others in motorcycle clubs. These clubs became a means of continued quasi-military camaraderie. At the same time, the motorcycle became a symbol of freedom from social responsibilities and restraints. Soon these new groups became a nuisance, if not a threat, to local communities in southern California.

Shortly after World War II, a group of California veterans formed a motorcycle club and called themselves the POBOBs, an acronym for "Pissed Off Bastards of Bloomington," a small southern California town in San Bernadino County whose current population is about 20,000.

By some accounts, the POBOBs were dedicated to mocking social values and conventional society through acts of vandalism and general lawlessness. Over the Independence Day weekend of 1947, following the arrest of a POBOB member for fighting in the small central California town of Hollister, a reported 750 motorcyclists descended on the small community and demanded his release. When local authorities refused, the cyclists literally tore up the town, a scene later depicted in the 1954 Marlon Brando film *The Wild One*. The movie, based on a *Harper's* magazine story and originally titled *The Cyclists Raid*, also featured Lee Marvin and actual bikers—it helped fuel the outlaw biker phenomenon (Briley 1997).

Hunter Thompson (1966) reports a different version of this incident, which he states grew out of a July Fourth celebration that included motorcycle races sanctioned by the American Motorcycle Association (AMA). About 3,000 cyclists participated, some became unruly, and the seven-man police force was unable to handle the ensuing disorder. The cyclists were easily controlled when additional officers arrived, and the actual riot was timid compared with the film version. Daniel Wolf (1991: 4) states that about 500 unaffiliated bikers

[1]The source of information not otherwise cited in this chapter is from court documents and related trial discovery materials in the United States and Canada and interviews with law enforcement personnel.

249

The Outlaw Credo

"Outlaw bikers view themselves as nothing less than frontier heroes, living out the 'freedom ethic' that they feel the rest of society has largely abandoned. They acknowledge that they are antisocial, but only to the extent that they seek to gain their own unique experiences and express their individuality through their motorcycles. Their 'hogs' become personal charms against the regimented world of the 'citizen.' They view their club as collective leverage that they can use against an establishment that threatens to crush those who find conventional society inhibiting and destructive of individual character" (Wolf 1991: 9).

disrupted the AMA-sponsored event "by drinking and racing in the streets of the host town of Hollister. The ineffective efforts of a numerically insufficient seven-man police force, in conjunction with the sometimes provocative vigilante tactics of indignant local residents, caused the motorcyclists to coalesce as a mob." Bikers rode motorcycles into bars and broke windows with beer bottles. This unruly behavior ended thirty-six hours later after the arrival of additional police. At the center of much of the mayhem was "Wino" Willie Forkner of the Boozefighters Motorcycle Club, who died of natural causes at age 76, shortly before he could lead a fiftieth anniversary outlaw biker rally in Hollister (Associated Press 1997; Hayes 2005).

The Hollister incident gave rise to an important outlaw biker tradition—the annual July Fourth run; another traditional run occurs over the Labor Day weekend. In 1997, Hollister played host to the fiftieth anniversary of the incident that brought the small town—population about 35,000—fame, and it is now the site of an annual Independence Day rally that attracts about 100,000 bikers (Singer 2002). Bikers, outlaw and otherwise, also rally every August in the Black Hills of South Dakota at the "Sturgis Rally and Races." The ten-day event, which began in 1938 with less than two dozen bikers, now draws in excess of 200,000 persons to this town of 5,500. It provides the outlaw clubs an opportunity to "profile," the biker equivalent of cruising. The obvious potential for violence requires an active presence of shotgun-wielding state police officers (Hamilton 1998).

The term *outlaw* was first used by the sheriff of Riverside to distinguish southern California bikers such as the POBOBs from those motorcycle enthusiasts affiliated with the mainstream AMA. The lifestyles and traditions of the outlaw biker are promoted by a handful of magazines catering to both the hardcore outlaw subculture and the "wannabe" outlaw. Biker magazines "make it possible for a man to construct a biker identity and develop a sense of loyalty to that image without having met another biker" (Wolf 1991: 37).

HELL'S ANGELS EMERGE

In 1948, in the Fontana area of San Bernardino County, dedicated outlaws from the POBOBs formed a new group and adopted a name favored by fighter pilots and bomber crews in the world wars—Hell's Angels. The club's logo, a grinning, winged death's head wearing a leather aviator's helmet, originally appeared on the fuselage of the 358th Bomber Squadron (Veno 2003). The chapter name was shortened to "Berdoo" to fit on the bottom of the rocker on the back of their jackets (Lavigne 1987). The Hell's[2] Angels became the first outlaw club to have a formal organizational structure with a constitution and bylaws (Veno 2003).

In 1957, a 19-year-old former infantry veteran joined the Hell's Angels. Ralph Hubert ("Sonny") Barger, Jr., had dropped out of the tenth grade to join the army; he completed basic training and advanced infantry training before being discharged

---

[2]When it appears on their logo, the possessive is omitted and it is written *Hells*.

for being too young. The five-foot, ten-inch, 145-pound novice quickly rose in the biker ranks to become president of the club. He moved its headquarters to Oakland (the "mother club"). In 1967, Barger appeared in a film with Jack Nicholson, *Hell's Angels on Wheels*, which did not win an Academy Award but added greatly to the outlaw motorcycle club mystique.

There were three Hell's Angels chapters, all in California, and a fourth had been established in (of all places) Auckland, New Zealand (Lavigne 1987). By 1965, police harassment of the Hell's Angels in California had thinned their ranks to fewer than 100 members; the original Berdoo chapter was reduced to only a handful of diehards (Thompson 1966). Yves Lavigne (1987) reports that police harassment and legal fees left the club on the brink of extinction. However, the Hell's Angels had been exposed to the drug subculture through a tenuous relationship with the counterculture movement— "hippies" and "flower children." Needing money to survive, they turned to a one-shot deal involving the sale of methamphetamine—"speed." The outlaw bikers eventually broke with the counterculture

over the Vietnam War—the former military veterans were rabid hawks. But the easy money they had found in drugs eventually moved the Hell's Angels beyond the biker subculture and into organized crime.

Until 1965, the Hell's Angels were virtually unknown outside California. In that year, the state's attorney general unwittingly helped them score a publicity coup. In his annual report, he exaggerated their violent activities, and the California correspondent for the *New York Times* hyped the report for readers of "All the News That's Fit to Print." The result was a spate of articles on the Hell's Angels in the national media, including *Time*, *Newsweek*, and the *Saturday Evening Post*. These articles led to radio and television appearances by club members, whose outrageous dress made for good "visuals." The exposure fueled interest in the Hell's Angels and the outlaw biker phenomenon, helping to swell their ranks. At the time, Thompson states that most of the Angels were lawfully employed, and the publicity caused many of them to lose their jobs. In 1966, the Hell's Angels were still confined to California (and New Zealand), but massive publicity and the Vietnam War soon changed this.

During the late 1960s and early 1970s, interest and membership in outlaw motorcycle clubs swelled because of the return of disgruntled veterans from the Vietnam War (Lavigne 1987). In some instances, entire outlaw motorcycle clubs were issued charters as Hell's Angels, a "patchover." The club "expanded rapidly in the 1980s, patching over motorcycle clubs in countries all over the world" and "systematically set out to eliminate competitors through violence and intimidation" (Lavigne 1996: 50). Sonny Barger explains the patchover process: "When we award charters in new states, it's always done by national vote. When a prospective club lets us know they want to become Hell's Angels, we'll check them out to see if they're standup people. We'll send officers out to meet with them, and in return they'll send guys out to meet with us. We might invite them to a run or two, and likewise we'll send some of our guys to party with them. At some point—time varies—we'll vote on whether they can become prospects. Eventually we'll vote on their membership status. The same process that lets in individuals applies to entire new chapters as well" (2000: 35). The organization is international in scope, with more than 2,000 members in about eighty-five chapters in fifteen countries. They also have "Nomad" chapters whose members have no fixed location, but serve as shock troops reinforcing chapters in conflict with other biker clubs.

In 1973, Barger was convicted and imprisoned for the possession and sale of heroin, marijuana, and other drugs. He was released in 1977, but other indictments against Barger and the Hell's Angels soon followed. The biker subculture had changed: "Some Hell's Angels made big money in the drug business, and suddenly they had something to lose, something to protect. Their bank accounts came first and the brotherhood second. When a member threatened their income, they beat or killed him. The Hell's Angels Motorcycle Club was no longer an organization that sheltered social misfits. It became an enclave for some of the underworld's most cunning drug manufacturers and dealers" (Lavigne 1996: 34). But the drug business breeds informants. In 1985, more than 100 Hell's Angels across the United States were arrested in a major federal effort against the club's drug trafficking. And dozens more are serving sentences for drug trafficking in the United States and Canada.

The development of the POBOBs from an outlaw motorcycle club (OMC) to a criminal organization was a model for other groups who wanted to emulate the Hell's Angels. According to Allen ("Rod") McMillan (personal correspondence), an expert on OMCs, these groups moved through four stages:

1. The club shows rebellious and anti-social activity that is random and nonutilitarian.
2. A police response causes less committed members to drop out; members of weaker clubs either disperse or join stronger clubs.
3. The remaining clubs are better able to exercise discipline and control over their membership, particularly control over violence, which now changes from random and nonutilitarian to instrumental. The basic element shared by all members of outlaw motorcycle clubs is a penchant for violence; violence thus pervades the world of outlaw bikers. Rationally used, violence may be for the purpose of maintaining organizational discipline or defending hegemony.

4. The leadership uses organizational skills and intimidation in utilitarian criminal pursuits, and the group becomes a fully committed criminal organization.

"Members of the outlaw motorcycle gangs refer to themselves as 'one percenters' in reference to an estimate advanced some years ago by the American Motorcycle Association that outlaw motorcyclists comprised less than one percent of the motorcycling population. Outlaw gangs immediately seized on the figure as a reflection of their belief that they are rebels, operating outside society's laws and mores" (PCOC 1986c: 61). James Quinn and D. Shane Koch (2003: 286) note, "Much 1%er behavior is linked to their desire to uphold this image because it provides them with a 'marketable commodity' in both legal (e.g., concert security, barroom bouncer) and illegal (e.g., loansharking) spheres of economic endeavor." From the fun-loving and hell-raising clubs of the immediate post–World War II era, a number of outlaw motorcycle clubs have developed into self-perpetuating, highly structured, disciplined organizations whose major source of income is from criminal activity. But not all of the hundreds of outlaw motorcycle clubs are sophisticated criminal organizations. While there is a wide array of outlaw motorcycle clubs in various countries, for example, the Mongols (Mexico and United States) and the Gypsy Jokers (Australia and United States), and an abundance in the United States that includes the Breed, the Iron Horsemen, Pagans, and the Vagos, only three have chapters that span the globe: (1) Hell's Angels, (2) Outlaws, and (3) Bandidos.

THE INTERNATIONAL "BIG THREE"

Hell's Angels chapters are centered in California and the East Coast; the mother club is in Oakland.[3] The Outlaws trace their origins to McCook, Illinois, a Chicago suburb that despite its small resident population—less than 300—is home to heavy industry. The Outlaws Motorcycle Club was founded in 1935, but the club grew in the postwar years, changing its name to the Chicago Outlaws and moving to that city in 1950. In 1954, the club adopted its skull and crossed pistons logo. Outlaw chapters are scattered throughout the Midwest, Northeast, and several southern states; they are particularly strong in Florida. The mother club moved from Chicago to Detroit in 1984.

In 1965, in the fishing village of San Leon, Texas, a group of ex-military dock workers got together after work and weekends to party. The next summer, ex-marine Donald Chambers organized the group into a club and adopted the name Bandidos, from the popular Frito Bandito commercial that used the "Frito Bandito" cartoon character who raises hell to sell potato chips. However, the organization's mascot, known as the "Fat Mexican," was given a machete and a gun. In 1968, the Bandidos moved to Corpus Christi, Texas, and

---

[3]A struggle between the Berdoo Chapter and Barger's Oakland chapter resulted in the mother club shifting to northern California (Lavigne 1996).

then to Houston, Texas, which is regarded as the mother chapter. Also called the Bandido Nation, the club has about 170 chapters in fourteen countries, including about 90 in the United States, concentrated in Texas, Louisiana, Mississippi, Arkansas, New Mexico, Colorado, South Dakota, and Washington State. United States membership is estimated at 2,400 bikers.

The Outlaws and the Bandidos are considered affiliated clubs, and they list each other as links on their websites. When the Bandidos wanted to establish a chapter in Oklahoma in the late 1990s, they sought and received permission from the Outlaws who already had Oklahoma chapters (Winterhalder 2005). Both clubs are united in their animosity toward the Hell's Angels and are allied in a struggle against the Hell's Angels with whom the Outlaws have been feuding since 1974 (Barker 2005). This conflict has had international ramifications, such as the war between the Hell's Angels and Bandidos in Scandinavia. With support from the California mother club, the Hell's Angels organized in Denmark during the 1980s but were challenged by a local group that the Angels almost wiped out—thirteen were shot and stabbed to death before the group disbanded in 1986. Remnants joined a new club that eventually became a chapter of the Bandidos, renewing conflict with the Hell's Angels, which in 1994 resulted more killings. During 1996, the conflict became even more violent, with the use of stolen and former Soviet block military weapons—high-caliber machine guns, hand grenades, and antitank missiles—in Denmark, Sweden, and Finland. That year, the Copenhagen Hell's Angels hosted a party for bikers from the Nordic countries at their headquarters, five buildings surrounded by a 10-foot wooden fence. An antitank grenade fired at the compound from the roof of a nearby building killed two and wounded nineteen, some seriously. Later

that year, a jury in Copenhagen found two Hell's Angels members guilty of murdering the leader of the Bandidos in an airport ambush. In 1997, the Norwegian headquarters of the Bandidos was obliterated by an explosion, killing a passerby and injuring four people, none of whom were bikers. Later, a rocket-propelled grenade was fired into a Danish jail in a failed attempt to kill an imprisoned Bandido leader. That same year, carloads of Hell's Angels drove into a Bandido stronghold in a small resort town near Copenhagen and opened fire with machine pistols, killing one Bandido and wounding three more. More than a dozen people had been killed before a truce was called and a very public handshake took place between outlaw club leaders on European TV (Paradis 2002). The peace deal had been brokered by Hell's Angels and Bandido leaders in the United States and resulted in the two clubs dividing up territory in Scandanavia (Sher and Marsden 2006).

In 1997, when the Hell's Angels opened their newest chapter in Stockholm, about 300 members from several countries gathered to celebrate: They were greeted by 300 police officers, who put a cordon around their new headquarters, searched all who entered the area, and even arrested one member for failing to wear a helmet (Ibrahim 1997). The authorities in Denmark have passed new laws that bar the bikers from having clubhouses in populated areas, and have asked for assistance from the United States for a problem they see as originating in the states (Associated Press 1996; "Biker Club House" 1997; "Bomb Kills 1 . . ." 1997; Kinzer 1996a; Moseley 1997; Reuters 1996).

In 1994, a similar situation arose in Illinois, where a local motorcycle club, Hell's Henchmen, was slated to become a chapter of the Hell's Angels, a patchover, giving the international club an important presence in the Midwest. The Henchmen are headquartered in Rockford, twenty-five miles away from the Outlaws' headquarters in Janesville, Wisconsin; the Outlaws also have a clubhouse in nearby Chicago. The Outlaws expressed their outrage: A bomb went off in front of the residence of the Henchmen's president, and six hours later another destroyed the Henchmen's Chicago clubhouse (Thomas 1994a). Later, the Henchmen's president was gunned down at his Rockford residence. In response, 300 Hell's Angels in full colors rode into Rockford for the funeral and a posthumous induction. The Outlaws answered with more bombings and shootings; in 1995, a Hell's Angels member was shot to death while sitting in his car near the Chicago trucking company for which he worked (Thomas 1994b; Martinez 1995). In 1997, seventeen members of the Outlaws from Wisconsin, Indiana, and Illinois were indicted for these and other acts of violence—listening devices had been planted in several clubhouses

Hundreds of bikers head to the cemetery Saturday, May 4, 2002, in Stockton, California, for the burial of Stockton motorcycle shop owner and Hell's Angel member Robert Emmett.

and the home of one Outlaw who is said to have orchestrated several murders and bombings. One of those arrested became a government witness and the violence stopped (Starks 1999). In 2000, the former head of the South Side Chicago Outlaw chapter was found guilty of racketeering acts that included the 1995 murder of a Hell's Angels member (Daley 2000).

Canada: A Special Case

The Hell's Angels first displayed their colors in Canada at the end of 1977, when the Popeyes, who had been warring for two years with the Satan's Choice and the Devil's Disciples over drug turf, became the Angels' Montreal Chapter. As Hell's Angels (HA), they immediately began to fight with the Outlaws Motorcycle Club.

With about three dozen members, in 1983, the Quebec HA expanded into British Columbia, and they patched over the Thirteenth Tribe club in Halifax. By the time the Montreal chapter celebrated its twenty-fifth anniversary in 2002, the Canadian Hell's Angels were connected to stockbrokers, bankers, and lawyers. They were particularly wealthy in British Columbia where club members owned such businesses as cell phone stores, stripper agencies, and porn sites on the Internet, and displayed a keen interest in stock-market fraud (Edwards and Auger 2004). The HA remain the largest and most powerful outlaw motorcycle club in Canada with chapters across the country comprising more than 500 members. Paul Cherry (2005: 21) notes changes in the club fostered by their newfound drug wealth: "The new generation of Hell's Angels was, for the most part, clean-cut men who took good care of themselves and worked out constantly. Gone was the beer gut associated with the image of a debauched biker who rides his Harley-Davidson for hours on end." In fact, Cherry reports, some of the younger members look pretty awkward on their massive machines that they are required to ride in accord with HA international rules.

During the 1980s, in Montreal, the HA defeated the Outlaws who were driven from the city, and the Angels negotiated affiliations with several local motorcycle clubs—collectively referred to as *Les Hells*. In 1985, five members of the HA Laval chapter were invited to the clubhouse of the Sherbrooke chapter where they were gunned down—their bodies were found in the St. Lawrence River in weighted-down sleeping bags—the HA way of maintaining organizational discipline and a response to the Laval chapter's reckless behavior, which included using cocaine that was intended to be sold.

In 1994, when negotiations between the HA and a powerful local club of drug dealers—the Rock Machine—broke down, a particularly violent struggle for control of drug trafficking broke out. Soon, heretofore independent dealers were told by each group that they could only buy drugs from that group or its affiliates, a directive enforced by violence (Paradis 2002). In opposition to the HA, a number of independent groups and former Outlaws joined with the Rock Machine and became known as the Alliance (Langton 2006).

When the conflict with the Hell's Angels ended in defeat, the Bandidos agreed to patchover five chapters of the Rock Machine who became the first Bandidos chapters in Canada. A Rock Machine member recalls the process: "Before becoming full Bandidos, our club would have to go through an initiation. First we would be a hangaround club for six months, and then promoted to prospect level as probationary Bandidos. After a year of that, we could be full Bandidos" (Paradis 2002: 155). A ranking member of the Bandidos states: "A Hangaround club is an existing club that wants to join the larger motorcycle club. Being accepted as a Hangaround club puts everyone in the biker world on notice. . . . In the Bandido world, after at least one year, the Bandidos vote as to whether all members of the smaller club are worthy to wear the Bandidos patch. If yes, they become Bandidos Probationary members" (Winterhalder 2005: 1). In 2001, violence again flared up between the Rock Machine (now Bandidos) and the Hell's Angels. In 2003, the Quebec Bandidos agreed to disband, and the Hell's Angels agreed that those who quit the club would be guaranteed safety while others were free to transfer to Bandido chapters in Ontario (Winterhalder 2005).

In 2006, eight members of the Canadian Bandidos were murdered and their bullet-ridden bodies found inside four vehicles in a farmer's field in Ontario. Four of their fellow Bandidos members (and one woman) were charged in connection with the killings in what police described as an internal cleansing, rather than an effort by the Hell's Angels to eliminate the competition. The Ontario Bandidos next attempted to expand into Alberta and then Manitoba, but the Alberta Bandidos quickly flipped and were absorbed by the Hell's Angels. In 2007, the Bandidos attempted to establish themselves in Calgary; soon afterward four Bandidos were severely beaten by six to eight Hell's Angels and the effort ended.

In 1994, Walter Stadnick,[4] a former Canadian national president of the HA and its most influential member, formed the Nomads Chapter made up of veteran Canadian members who would not be part of any chapter but, instead, became a freewheeling unit devoid of a clubhouse with unofficial oversight authority over all chapters (Langton 2006). Maurice ("Mom") Boucher, the charismatic president of the Nomads Chapter, subsequently negotiated an alliance with the Montreal-based Bonanno Family crew headed by Vito Rizzuto. Together they centralized the distribution and fixed the wholesale price of cocaine at $50,000 a kilo (2.2 pounds) throughout the province (Lamothe and Humprheys 2006). Boucher's Nomads bought cocaine directly from Colombia's Miguel Ángel and Víctor Manuel Mejía-Múnera, known as "the Mejía twins,"[5] and distributed the drugs to HA chapters, local allied clubs, and affiliated dealers throughout Quebec. Those who failed to maintain the set price, even if they were HA members, were murdered (Langton 2006).

Records seized by the police reveal that at the end of 2000, the net assets of the Hell's Angels operation was in excess of $15 million. Ten percent of the profits from each drug sale were deducted for a fund supporting club activities, in particular, the purchase of weapons. The conflict with the Rock Machine/Bandidos ended in 2001—Rizzuto[6] reportedly told Boucher that the violence, particularly the indiscriminate use of explosives, was bad for business—but not before it had claimed more than 150 lives, including that of an 11-year-old killed in an explosion and two randomly selected correction officers murdered by the HA (Lamothe and Humprheys 2006). The murders were ordered by Boucher in an effort to terrorize the criminal justice community in Montreal much as the Medellín cartel had done in Colombia (Langton 2006). In 2004, these murders led to the conviction of Boucher and a life sentence. Nevertheless, drug dealers in Quebec continued to pay a commission to the Hell's Angels (Seguin 2005).

The violence in Quebec can be understood by an examination of the profits flowing from control of the drug market. In 2000, police discovered an HA "bank"—apartments with counting machines and computers maintained to receive, record, and disperse funds. The sales for a 39-day period amounted to more than 18 million Canadian dollars. In raids on three apartments, the police found $5.6 million in Canadian and U.S. currency. The investigation also revealed that each member of the Nomads Chapter was receiving a fixed salary of $5,000 a week (Cherry 2005).

In 2005, based on a relatively new Canadian law (s. 467, *Criminal Code of Canada*) similar to the U.S. RICO statute (discussed in Chapter 15), an Ontario Superior Court judge declared the Hell's Angels a "criminal organization" (*R. v. Lindsay and Bonner* No. 022474). That decision has encouraged prosecutors to use the statute to move against HA chapters throughout Canada, and in at least one case against the Outlaws Motorcycle Club as well.

---

[4]In 2004, at age 51, Stadnick, at one time the most powerful Hell's Angel in Canada, was sentenced to 20 years in prison for drug trafficking, murder conspiracy, and gangsterism.

[5]The "Twins" worked for the Cali cartel and then became affiliated with the right-wing paramilitary United Self-Defense Forces of Colombia. The United States offered a reward of $5 million for information leading to the capture of Miguel Ángel.

[6]In 2007, Rizzuto was sentenced to 10 years after pleading guilty to participating in the 1981 murder of three Bonanno Family captains—depicted in the movie *Donnie Brasco*—during a struggle for control of that crime Family.

STRUCTURE

Consistent with their founders' background as military veterans, the Hell's Angels and outlaw clubs that have copied them exhibit a bureaucratic structure (see Figure 11.1). Each has a written constitution and bylaws. Although there are some minor variations, the Outlaws and Bandidos each have a mother club that serves as the international headquarters. The Bandidos' mother club consists of a president and four regional vice presidents. The national president ("el presidente") has final authority over all club activities. The Outlaws have a similar structure: The United States is divided into four regions; each has a regional president who reports to the mother club, which is ruled by the national president. Their responsibilities include making decisions on all problems that the local chapters are unable to resolve and seeing to it that each chapter generates income, from which the regional head receives a portion.

The Hell's Angels, reports Lavigne (1987), do not have a national president or national officers to give the club direction. Instead, in the United States the club is divided into East Coast and West Coast factions, with Omaha, Nebraska, as the dividing line. "East Coast Officers' Meetings (ECOMS) and West Coast Officers' Meetings (WCOMS) are held every three months in different chapters' areas. The faction officers and the president or vice-president from every chapter in the faction discuss only club business at the quarterly meetings: how to financially assist a chapter; should a new chapter be admitted; how individual chapters perform; how many new patches should be ordered; should the club issue a press release on the latest arrests of members. Drug deals and other crimes are not discussed" (Lavigne 1987: 66). The East Coast and West Coast factions also hold a meeting before their annual "USA Run," which each faction hosts in alternate years. The host faction president presides, and criminal activities are not discussed. In addition, special presidents' meetings may occasionally be called as needed (Barger 2000).

Any problems that involve a national outlaw club as a whole will usually be submitted to the mother club. The national secretary-treasurer is responsible for the club's finances, makes revisions in the club bylaws, and records and maintains the minutes and other club records. The national enforcer answers directly to the national president or to the mother club and may act as the president's bodyguard. In addition, he handles all

FIGURE 11.1   *National Organizational Structure of Outlaw Motorcycle Clubs*

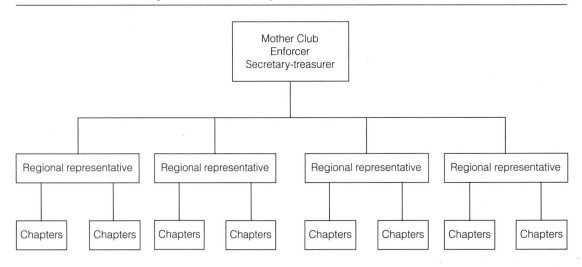

special situations involving violations of club rules. There are some standard functional positions. Each of the three clubs has a national enforcement unit. Hell's Angels enforcers are adorned with Nazi storm trooper-like lightning bolts tattooed underneath the words "Filthy Few," the Outlaws have their "SS Death Squad," and the Bandidos have their "Nomad Chapter." Barger (2000) states that Hell's Angels no longer sport any Nazi symbols because they are banned in Germany; thus, their German chapter cannot wear them. Outlaw clubs also have at least one member responsible for "security/intelligence." He often travels under a variety of names, does not wear his colors, and is rarely if ever seen near the clubhouse (David 1988: 17). He "compiles photographs, descriptions, addresses, phone numbers, personal and financial information, vehicle descriptions, not only on rival gang members, but on police officers, reporters, lawyers, judges, public officials and witnesses. Dossiers include names and addresses of relatives, girlfriends and boyfriends. Many of the newer members of the various outlaw motorcycle gangs have learned their intelligence skills in the military, where they also acquired the talent to use weapons and make bombs" (David 1988: 17).

FIGURE 11.2 *Chapter Organizational Structure of Outlaw Motorcycle Clubs*

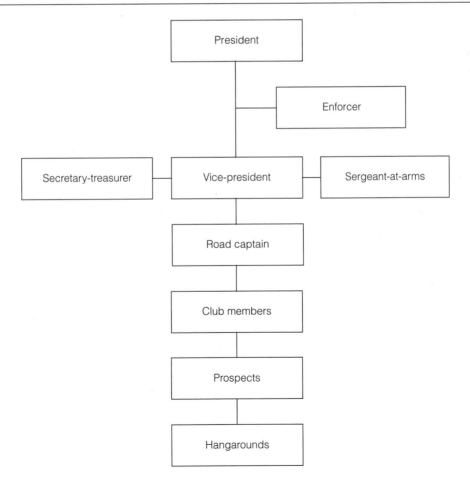

Each "Big Three" chapter has a president, vice president, secretary-treasurer, enforcer, and sergeant-at-arms (see Figure 11.2). The sergeant-at-arms is usually the toughest member and may also serve as an enforcer and executioner. There is also the road captain, who fulfills the role of logistician and security chief for club-sponsored "runs" or motorcycle outings. The road captain maps out routes; arranges for refueling, food, and maintenance stops en route; and establishes "strong points" along the route to protect the main body from police harassment or rival motorcycle clubs. Outlaw motorcycle clubs have several mandatory runs each year, and all members not otherwise incapacitated—hospitalized or imprisoned—must participate with motorcycles and full colors.

"Colors" are the official club insignia. A member typically wears colors on the back of a denim jacket with the sleeves cut off or, in colder climes, a leather jacket. The insignia consists of three separate sections, or "rockers." The top rocker carries the club name, the center rocker displays the club emblem, and the bottom rocker designates the club location or territory. Colors may also be worn as a tattoo—mandatory for Hell's Angels. A member is allowed to have only one club patch, the loss of which can bring sanctions, including expulsion from the club. Also sewed or pinned on the jacket are other "authorized" patches, which are usually quite offensive to conventional society—for example, swastikas, 666 (sign of Satan), FTW ("Fuck the World"), and 1%. Consistent with a military orientation, various offenses can result in the "pulling of patches." The clubs practice precision riding, and club runs are accomplished in a military-style formation (see Figure 11.3).

Outlaw clubs limit chapter membership to about twenty-five, which helps maintain a strong bond between members and facilitates the decision-making process. "Once a club chapter reaches twenty-five, a new chapter will generally be created" (Veno 2003: 89). Each chapter is composed of at least six "full-patch" members, as well as "strikers" or "prospects" who spend from one month to one year (striking period) on probationary status, and "hangarounds," who are permitted to associate with members in an effort to achieve striker status. Each prospect requires a sponsoring member who is responsible for the probationary member. "Gang members do extensive background checks on prospective members, often using female associates who have been placed in positions with public utilities, government services, and law enforcement agencies to assist them" (PCOC 1986c: 65). In the Hell's Angels, having been employed, or even having sought employment, in law enforcement precludes consideration for membership. If membership slips below six, the chapter may be dissolved, its members moving to become part of another chapter, or other chapters. Or members from nearby chapters may be sent to keep the chapter viable. Club officers are chosen by secret ballot and candidates are usually experienced members. To become a full-patch member of the HA, a candidate must be at least 21 years of age. Patches are owned by Hell's Angels, Inc., and not the individual members.

Prospects must be nominated by a member and receive a unanimous vote for acceptance into provisional status. They carry out menial jobs at the clubhouse and for other members. Barger (2000) states that there has never been an initiation rite in the Hell's Angels. When a man is admitted to membership, he is allowed to wear the club's colors—the proudest possession of any outlaw club member and clearly parallel to being "made" in the American Mafia. The death's head emblem of the Hell's Angels is copyrighted, although violations rarely result in litigation—the Hell's Angels prefer to *settle out of court* (Lavigne 1987). In fact, the club vigorously defends the copyrighted death's head icon and the term *Hell's Angels Motorcycle Club*, emblems that are never permitted to be used for pecuniary purposes such as on clothing for sale to the public. Minutes of Hell's Angels chapters are filled with discussions of copyright issues.

A member's death's head tattoo must be crossed out if he leaves the group. A Hell's Angels member who retires under "honorable" circumstances is permitted to keep the tattoo by adding the date of his separation from the club. While

FIGURE 11.3   *Riding Formation of an Outlaw Motorcycle Club*

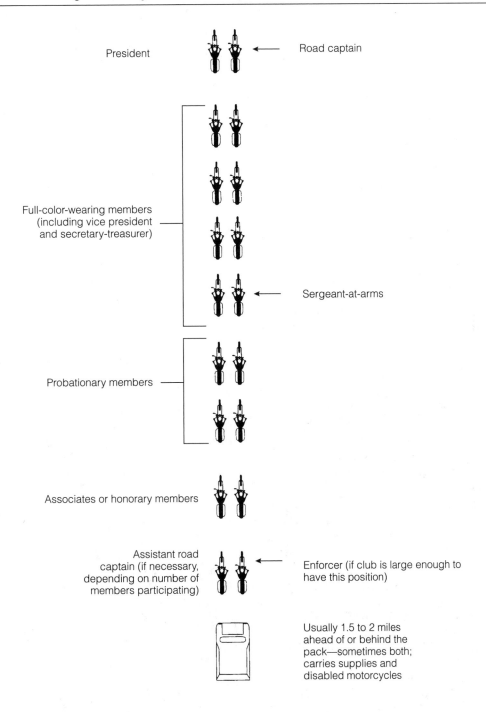

President

Road captain

Full-color-wearing members
(including vice president
and secretary-treasurer)

Sergeant-at-arms

Probationary members

Associates or honorary members

Assistant road
captain (if necessary,
depending on number of
members participating)

Enforcer (if club is large enough to
have this position)

Usually 1.5 to 2 miles
ahead of or behind the
pack—sometimes both;
carries supplies and
disabled motorcycles

most outlaw biker chapters have headquarters,[7] the Bandidos meet instead in members' homes, which, like clubhouses, are usually heavily fortified and guarded by attack dogs.

The Big Three also have support or puppet clubs—a type of farm team—that support their interests and are generally subservient, carrying out orders from the dominant partner. In Canada, for example, members of the Rockers, a Hell's Angels puppet club, serve as bodyguards for ranking full-patch members of the master club. Members of a puppet club who have proven themselves can be elevated to prospect and full-patch members, and there can be a patchover by which an entire club becomes a chapter, bypassing the customary waiting period imposed on prospective members. This occurs when a Big Three club wants to establish chapters in certain areas and/or in order to strengthen their position in a struggle with another club.

Outlaw motorcycle clubs usually exhibit racist attitudes, and in the United States no known black males hold membership in the Big Three. There are predominantly black clubs with some white members, and the Hell's Angels has Jewish members. Arthur Veno (2003) states, however, that he knows of a few black members of the Hell's Angels, and they also have Polynesians, Native Americans, and Hispanics. Women associated with a club are treated as nothing more than playthings—objects to be used, traded, and sold. "Old ladies" are the wives or steady girlfriends of club members. Sexual and other demands for their services can be made only by their husbands or boyfriends. "Mamas" and "sheep" belong to the club at large and are expected to consent to the sexual whims of any club member. While women are not permitted to wear club colors, they may wear denim jackets with the inscription "Property of . . . " (with the club's name embroidered on it). Women often carry the clubs's weapons and engage in prostitution or drug trafficking. Because of the freewheeling image of the outlaw clubs, teenage girls are often attracted to them. The girls are frequently gang raped, which bikers refer to as "training" or "pulling a train." Girls may also be photographed for blackmail purposes or transported to other states for employment in sex-oriented establishments, such as go-go bars and club-owned massage parlors.

OUTLAW BUSINESS

Outlaw motorcycle clubs "provide a context for individuals with a high propensity for illegal activity to unite long enough to operate enterprises of varying degrees of sophistication" (Quinn and Koch 2003: 281). They are involved in distributing firearms, explosives, stolen motorcycles, and motorcycle parts; providing exotic dancers and prostitutes for various sex-oriented establishments; and trafficking in lysergic acid diethylamide (LSD, a hallucinogen), phencyclidine (PCP, a hallucinogen), cocaine, and methamphetamine. They have been particularly successful in exerting control over the methamphetamine market. George Wethern (with Vincent Colnett 1978), a former ranking member of the Hell's Angels in Oakland, states that because of their reputation for violence and anti-establishment attitudes, the Hell's Angels are perfect middlemen for drug dealers. The wholesalers sell to the Angels, who then act as distributors for street-level operators. Any number of members also manufacture methamphetamine. Using violence, they are able to restrict market entry and monopolize the trade in various parts of the United States and Canada (Droban 2007). Other outlaw clubs have done the same. As Veno (2003: 166) notes, "Violence is central to club life."

Although most bikers operate along the lines of short-term hedonism, some profits have been invested in a vast array of legitimate businesses, often for profit and sometimes as fronts for illegal activities. The outlaw clubs have a reliable pipeline of members and chapters for the flow of illicit goods, and the members are highly mobile—they can find support and safety in any city that has a club chapter.

---

[7]In 1999, the New York chapter of Hell's Angels received $450,000 (plus the cost of legal fees) from the city of New York to settle a lawsuit arising out of a police raid on their Manhattan headquarters at 77 East Third Street (Weiser 1999a).

According to the President's Commission, if an outlaw motorcycle club has a discernible weakness, it is that members are easily identified by their colors. "However, there are growing reports that members are abandoning their outlaw image, wearing business suits and driving luxury cars; in essence, becoming an outlaw motorcycle gang without motorcycles. If so, that would complete the evolution that has been under way for more than twenty years, a period during which the Hell's Angels developed from a collection of rowdy rebels into a genuine OC group" (PCOC 1986: 65). In fact, the leadership of these outlaw clubs has become more conventional in appearance, leaving the more overtly subcultural dimensions to underlings.

Members of outlaw clubs have reportedly been involved in activities with traditional organized crime, providing muscle, firearms, bombs, or drugs. In 2008, a ranking member of the Chicago Outlaws was charged with the bombing of a vending machine company that was competing with the Chicago Outfit. But, as opposed to the American Mafia, as well as Russian, Southern Italian, and Japanese organized crime, outlaw motorcycle clubs have not been known to provide enforcement services for restraint of trade agreements among otherwise legitimate businessmen (discussed in Chapter 14) or representation and arbitration services for legitimate and illegitimate entrepreneurs.

ANALYSIS OF THE STRUCTURE

As we have seen, the outlaw motorcycle club exhibits a number of characteristics that are bureaucratic. Given the military background of the founders and many members of the outlaw biker subculture, this is to be expected. There is a rather elaborate hierarchy, specialization, advancement based on skill, and extensive rules and regulations that are in written form (see Figure 11.4). There is general uniformity in style of dress, colors, and motorcycles—mostly large Harley-Davidsons. The secretary-treasurer records the minutes of meetings and collects and maintains dues. Each member contributes weekly dues to his chapter, and the chapter pays into the national treasury. The Hell's Angels also maintain a multimillion-dollar fund to which members and chapters are occasionally asked to contribute. The fund goes for legal expenses and to help support the families of imprisoned members.

A criminal organization can exhibit a formal structure even though its economic activities may actually involve small firms or partnerships among members and include nonmember associates. This is often the case with outlaw motorcycle clubs. Each full-patch member of the Big Three is reputed to have about ten associates and his own network of friends. For business purposes, each member is at the center of an action group that, although tied to every other member through the structure of the club, operates independently or in partnership. In other words, the formal structure of the motorcycle club is not necessarily the same as its economic structure. Although there is a relatively clear hierarchy within each of the three outlaw clubs, income-generating illegal activities involve several smaller, operationally independent units. But members can call upon the muscle of the club in the event of conflict, making them formidable entrepreneurs. Indeed, it is the club

FIGURE 11.4 *Hell's Angels California Bylaws*

1. All patches will be the same on the back, nothing will show on the back except the HELLS ANGELS patch. City patch is optional for each chapter. 1 patch and 1 membership card per member. Member may keep original patch if made into a banner. Prospects will wear California rocker on back and prospect patch left from where top of pocket is on a Levi jacket.
   FINE: $100 for breaking above by-law.
2. No hypes. No use of Heroin in any form. Anyone using a needle for any reason other than having a doctor use it on you will be considered a hype.
   FINE: Automatic kick-out from club.
3. No explosives of any kind will be thrown into the fire where there is one or more HELLS ANGELS in this area.
   FINE: Ass-whipping and/or subject to California President's decision.
4. Guns on CA runs will not be displayed after 6 PM. They will be fired from dawn until 6 PM in a predetermined area only. Rule does not apply to anyone with a gun in a shoulder holster or belt that is seen by another member if it is not being shot or displayed.
   FINE: $100 for breaking above by-law.
5. Brothers shall not fight with each other with weapons; when any HELLS ANGELS fights another HELLS ANGELS, it is one on one; prospects same as members. If members are from different chapters, fine goes to CA Treasurer.
   FINE: $100 for breaking above by-law or possible loss of patch.
6. No narcotics burns. When making deals, persons get what they are promised or the deal is called off.
   FINE: Automatic kick-out from club.
7. All HELLS ANGELS fines will be paid within 30 days. Fines will be paid to that chapter's treasurer to be held for the next CA run.
8. One vote per chapter at CA officer's meetings. For CA 2 no votes instead of a majority to kill a new charter and a charter goes below 6 they must freeze or dissolve on the decision of CA Officers' Meeting.
9. If kicked out, must stay out 1 year then back to original chapter. HELLS ANGEL tattoo will have an in-date and out-date when the member quits. If kicked out HELLS ANGELS tattoo will be completely covered with a 1/2 X through the tattoo.
10. Runs are on the holidays; 3 mandatory runs are Memorial Day, July 4th, and Labor Day.
11. No leave period except hospital, medical or jail.

affiliation that enables members to safely conduct illegal business. Without the affiliation, they would be vulnerable to predatory criminals or rip-offs. An aura of distrust pervades wholesale drug transactions insofar as they transpire in a Hobbesian world ruled by the credo "might makes right." An outlaw club affiliation provides insurance against otherwise untrustworthy suppliers or customers or other criminals who would prey on illegitimate entrepreneurs. This allows persons who do not trust one another, who cannot turn to the police or courts to remedy a grievance, to transact business with a significant degree of confidence that the "no drug burns" rule of the Hell's Angels facilitates.

As Lavigne (1996: 246) notes: "The Hell's Angels are truthful when they say they are not a criminal organization. Rather, they are an organization of criminals. They go out of their way to maintain a barrier between the Hell's Angels as a club and the Hell's Angels as a business. Criminal matters are discussed among members of many cliques within the gang." Thus, though the outlaw motorcycle club is clearly bureaucratic, its illegal business activities are not. American Mafia groups are *criminal organizations*—their raison dêtre is the business of crime—whereas outlaw motorcycle clubs exist to promote a subcultural biker lifestyle. The American Mafia attracts and selects hard-core criminals. Outlaw biker clubs attract tough, violent young men who were not necessarily in the business of crime before joining a club, and the clubs place a firewall between the organization and the criminal activities of its members. This helps to insulate the group as an organization from the Racketeer Influenced and Corrupt Organizations (RICO) prosecutions (discussed in Chapter 15). "Bikers see their personal welfare as contingent upon the club's power and generally assure it some distance from their criminal enterprise" (Quinn and Koch 2003: 300). Each chapter enjoys considerable autonomy, and the flexibility this promotes renders it difficult to link members' criminal activities "to the group's formal leadership and keeps the relationship between the club and the actions of its members, chapters, and so forth murky" (Quinn and Koch 2003: 289). Nevertheless, the autonomous local chapters "must live up to the requirements of the club's national charter and maintain the group's power, persona, and reputation" (2003: 291).

Being a member of one of the Big Three enables *credentialing*. The Hell's Angels exemplify the "value of a bad reputation" that enables members to operate in a world of criminal anarchy. As portrayed in popular media (for example, Wethern and Colnet 1978; Lavigne 1996) and a book by Barger, the club is made up of violent and dangerous persons, a "brotherhood of men who will fight and die for each other no matter what the cause" (Barger 2000: 67); men of violence living by the credo "One on all, all on one," which "means that when you fight one Hell's Angel, you fight us all" (Barger 2000: 39). While a legitimate organization will fire, expel, or otherwise act against members whose behavior is socially unacceptable if not criminal, in the Hell's Angels, "We stick up for our own, right or wrong" (Barger 2000: 40).

SUMMARY

- Outlaw motorcycle clubs, a uniquely American derivation, date from the years after World War II when many combat veterans sought new outlets for feelings of hostility and alienation.
- A relatively unimportant incident in Holister, California, in 1947, led to a great deal of publicity and interest in the outlaw biker phenomenon and the establishment of the Hell's Angels.
- A brief relationship with the counterculture movement of the 1960s led the club into the drug business in which their fearsome reputation proved to be a valuable asset.
- Outlaw clubs that copied the Hell's Angels also adopted their quasi-military structure.
- The other two international clubs, the Outlaws and Bandidos, have been battling the Hell's Angels for years, and all three clubs attract violent men who enjoy the biker subculture.
- Although these clubs exhibit a bureaucratic style of organization, they maintain a firewall between the club and the illegal business activities of their members.
- Nevertheless, being a member provides a form of *credentialing* that facilitates the member's criminal endeavors.

REVIEW QUESTIONS

1. What led to the development of the original outlaw motorcycle clubs?
2. What explains the rather bureaucratic structure adopted by outlaw motorcycle clubs?
3. In the organizational structure of outlaw motorcycle clubs, what are the functions of the mother club?
4. What are the similarities and differences between the American Mafia and outlaw motorcycle clubs?
5. How does the structure of outlaw motorcycle clubs and the American Mafia differ with respect to their illegal business operations?
6. How does membership in a "Big Three" club facilitate illegal business activities?
7. With respect to outlaw motorcycle clubs, how do they provide *credentialing*?

CHAPTER

12

Gambling, Loansharking, Theft, Fencing, Sex, and Trafficking in Persons and Arms

The business of organized crime has been described as providing goods and services that happen to be illegal. According to the Task Force on Organized Crime (1967: 1) "the core of organized crime activity is the supplying of illegal goods and services—gambling, loansharking, narcotics, and other forms of vice—to countless numbers of citizen customers." Translating morality into a statute backed by legal sanctions does not provide for greater morality; it merely widens the scope of the law and creates both temptation and opportunity for a particular set of social actors (Packer 1968). As in any business, the better organized are usually the more successful, and organized crime is basically a business enterprise. However, the business of organized crime often includes activities that are neither "goods" nor "services" but are clearly parasitic. As will be discussed below, the connection between organized crime and illegal business can take one of three forms:

1. *Parasitic*: members of a criminal organization extort money from illegal entrepreneurs under a threat of violence

2. *Reciprocal*: members of a criminal organization require legitimate or illegal entrepreneurs to pay a fixed or percentage amount but in return provide services such as restricting market entry, debt collection, and arbitration

3. *Entrepreneurship*: a member of a criminal organization provides an illegal good such as drugs or a service such as enforcement of restraint of trade agreements

Some organized crime groups such as American, Sicilian, Russian, and Japanese "mafias" provide enforcement services for restraint of trade agreements among otherwise legitimate businessmen (discussed in Chapter 14) and representation and arbitration services for both legitimate and illegitimate entrepreneurs.

GOODS AND SERVICES OR EXTORTION?

Thomas Schelling (1971) states that organized crime has a relationship with the purveyors of illegal goods and services that is extortionate: *The business* of organized crime is extortion, and those criminals who provide goods and services are its victims. Thus, Schelling points out, a bookmaker operating in an area dominated by an organized crime unit will be required to pay for the "privilege" of doing business—or suffer from violence (or perhaps a raid by corrupt police). The organized crime unit merely "licenses" the business—in New York known as a "gambling package"—and the bookmaker or other criminal purchases a "license" through the payment of "street taxes" to avoid being beaten or killed (or subjected to police harassment). Edward Hegarty, former special agent in charge of the Chicago office of the FBI, pointed out that although persons in organized crime do not get involved in the theft of automobiles, they extort money from those who do: "Many of the murders which have been committed in the Chicago area in recent years arose from automobile theft and chop shop activity. Generally these murders resulted from a failure, inability, or cheating by lower level organized crime figures on their La Cosa Nostra superiors. They were cheating on the street tax which is imposed on criminal cartels of the lower strength, the lower power base, that you have in and around the Chicago area" (Permanent Subcommittee on Investigations 1983b: 33–34).

During the 1970s, the Outfit began "taking over" (collecting regular street taxes) from the owners of chop shops around Chicago and into Lake County, Indiana. About fourteen of those who resisted were killed (O'Brien 1988). A 1990 federal indictment revealed the Outfit's response when their hegemony over gambling was challenged: Three men from the street crew of Sam Carlisi forced their way into a Chicago apartment at gunpoint, taking money and jewelry from the persons running a high-stakes card game. There were threats of physical harm and a demand for $2,000 from each. The operators agreed to turn over 50 percent of the game's profits to Carlisi, who subsequently became the head of the Outfit. Games in suburban Cicero were similarly raided because the operators had not been paying street taxes. As noted in Chapter 5, unaffiliated gambling entrepreneurs in the Chicagoland area were routinely given the choice of paying street taxes

or being "trunked." Robert Cooley (2004: 14) provides an example involving Harry Aleman, a much-feared Outfit enforcer: "You wouldn't know that Harry was a killer until you looked into his eyes and saw his stone-cold evil stare." At his restaurant, Cooley once watched Harry stare daggers at a Jewish bookmaker because he wasn't paying street taxes. Two weeks later the bookmaker was the victim of a shotgun blast in a pizza parlor.

In Thunder Bay, a city in the western Canadian province of British Columbia, the Hell's Angels Motorcycle Club (HA) required drug traffickers who sold non-HA drugs to pay a tax: $100 an ounce for cocaine, $200 a pound for marijuana. The club would also provide debt collection services for a 50 percent commission.

The boundary between providing a good or a service and being parasitic is not clearly delineated. For example, while professional gamblers may be required to pay street taxes to operate in a particular area, in return the organized crime group may limit market entry—competition—and provide collection and/or arbitration services that are vital in such enterprises. In Chapter 9 it was noted that Chinese and Vietnamese gangs typically engage in extortion from legitimate Asian businesses. But the gangs affiliated with tongs also provide protection and collection services for tong-operated gambling establishments. Jonathan Rubinstein and Peter Reuter (1978a: 64) note a distinctive service provided by the American Mafia—arbitration: "In an economy without conventional written contracts, there is obviously room for frequent disagreements. These are hard to resolve. Many bookmakers make payments to 'wise-guys' to ensure that when disputes arise they have effective representation." As noted in Chapter 1, organized crime may operate as a shadow government, providing policing and judicial services to a vast underworld, thereby increasing efficiency and coordination in an otherwise anarchic—Hobbesian—environment. The historical effectiveness of the American Mafia is grounded in its power to provide illegal services to its own members and, for a price, to other racketeers and legitimate businessmen. "Among the more valuable services are mediation of disputes with other criminals, criminal enterprises, and ventures; allocating turf to Cosa Nostra and other criminal groups; fending off incursions by others into these territories; providing financing, muscle, or a corrupt contact wherever necessary to the success of a criminal venture" (New York State Organized Crime Task Force 1988: 73).

The concept of *rispetto* permits a made guy to act as an arbitrator. If, at the request of an aggrieved party, an *uomo di rispetto* is asked for assistance, he can summon the accused to a "sitdown" or "table," an informal hearing over which he presides. Robin Moore (Moore and Fuca 1977: 64) points out that "anyone in the community, mob-connected or not, who had a legitimate complaint against someone else was entitled to ask for a Table hearing" and "any ranking Mafioso or man of respect could be prevailed upon to preside at a Table." To refuse to appear or to disregard a decision made at a table would indicate disrespect with attendant life-threatening consequences. In Chicago, crime boss Joey ("the Clown") Lombardo reveled in his role as an arbitrator for all types of neighborhood disputes. As noted by Reuter (1983) and Abadinsky (1983), the arbitrator receives a fee for this service when the disputants are criminals.

A successful bookmaker in New York told me that he always kept a wiseguy on the payroll at a cost of several hundred dollars a week. This was insurance—it prevented other criminals from placing bets and then refusing to pay, using their status as made guys to protect them. It also kept other criminals from trying to "shake down" the bookmaker. The wise guy can also assist in the collecting of debts. The amount he keeps as a "commission" varies, but it can be as high as 50 to 100 percent. In northwestern Indiana, Ken ("Tokyo Joe") Eto, the lottery kingpin, paid thousands of dollars a month in street taxes to the Outfit in order to remain in business. In 2005, thirty-six persons in Queens, New York, were indicted for operating a multimillion-dollar bookmaking ring that paid a monthly tribute to a captain in the Bonanno crime Family in exchange for his "blessing" (Cimino 2005).

The Mafia needs victims who cannot easily hide, states Schelling (1971: 648), persons with fixed places of business. "Even if one can find and recognize an embezzler or jewel thief, one would have a hard time going shares with him, because the embezzler can fool the extortionist if he can fool the firm he embezzles from, and the jewel thief needn't put his best prizes on display." Schelling underestimates wiseguys who spend a great deal of time on the prowl for information and opportunity. Bartenders, fences, prostitutes, and a host of legitimate and illegitimate persons are often eager to provide the wiseguy with information to be on his "good side." They may owe him favors or money or may simply seek to ingratiate themselves for any number of reasons. Salvatore ("Sally Crash") Panico of the Genovese crime Family found out about upscale brothels operating in Manhattan by perusing sex-oriented publications in which the owners usually advertised. Each location was then visited by Panico and his men. Guns, threats, and robbery soon brought the brothel into line. The scheme ended when Panico appeared on closed-circuit television threatening an FBI agent who was playing the role of bordello manager (Post 1981).

Albert Seedman (1974: 70–74), former chief of detectives in New York City, taped a conversation between "Woody," who had swindled $500,000 from Mays Department Store in Brooklyn, and Carmine ("the Snake") Persico, an enforcer for the Profaci Family and subsequently boss of the Colombo Family. In this edited conversation, Woody wants to know why he is being "asked" to pay a rather large share of the money he had stolen to Persico, who had played no part in the scheme:

Persico: When you get a job with the telephone company, or maybe even Mays Department Store, they take something out of every paycheck for taxes, right?

Woody: Right.

Persico: Now why, you may ask, does the government have the right to make you pay taxes? The answer to that question, Woody, is that you pay taxes for the right to live and work and make money at a legit business. Well, it's the exact same situation—you did a crooked job in Brooklyn [in the territory of the Profaci crime Family]. You worked hard and earned a lot of money. Now you have to pay your taxes just like in the straight world. Why? Because *we* let you do it. We're the government.

The jewel thief deals in expensive merchandise, and he needs a fence who can provide large sums of cash on very short notice. Some jewel thieves fence their jewels the same night they are stolen (Abadinsky 1983). A fence connected to organized crime can be relied upon to have, or to be able to raise, large amounts of cash on short notice. Dealing with a "connected" fence also provides insurance for the thief. It guarantees that he will not be "ripped off" by other criminals (because this would indicate a lack of *rispetto* and raise the ire of the crime unit). Thus, dealing with *Cosa Nostra* can provide an umbrella of protection to independent criminals who might otherwise be at risk from other criminals. Marilyn Walsh (1977) notes that although fencing is basically a sideline for the organized crime entrepreneur, the organized crime connection "is particularly helpful to the vulnerable good burglar who needs a somewhat amorphous affiliation with the criminal superstructure to protect him from some of its less genteel elements" (1977: 132). She provides an example:

Greg and his three associates had successfully executed a residence burglary, netting a substantial amount of expensive jewelry, one item in particular being an $8,000 bracelet watch. A few days after the theft the following series of events evolved.

A local enforcer in the area decided he wanted the bracelet. Determining who had stolen it, he and two associates proceeded to the apartment of the youngest of the thieves involved and took him "for a ride," explaining that the thieves and the bracelet would be expected to appear the following day at a private club in the city so that he might bargain for the purchase of the bracelet. When the thief returned from his ride, he called Greg and explained the situation. Smelling a shakedown, Greg got in touch with the

bodyguard of one of the big syndicate men in the city. He offered to sell the bracelet to the latter individual at an extremely low price and asked for help. It was given.

The next morning only the bodyguard and Greg made the appointment at the private club. On entering it was obvious that Greg's evaluation of the situation had been accurate. There sat the enforcer with nearly ten others waiting for the burglars. The appearance of the bodyguard startled them. This latter individual said only three words, "Joe's getting it," and the whole charade was over. (1977: 108–109)

Because of the extensive network that characterizes the American Mafia, a connection can provide a professional criminal, such as Chicago's Frank Hohimer, with invaluable information (1975: xvii–xviii): "The outfit knows them all: Palm Springs, Beverly Hills, Shaker Heights. . . . You name the state and the Mob will give you not only the names of the millionaires and their addresses, but how many people are in the house, a list of their valuables, and where they keep them and when they wear them. . . . Their information is precise, there is no guess work. It comes from insurance executives, jewelry salesmen, auctioneers of estates. The same guy who sold you the diamond may be on the corner pay phone before you get home."

Information of value to conventional criminals operating in and around Kennedy Airport in New York comes from cargo handlers and persons holding similar positions. In one instance, a cargo supervisor in debt to organized crime–connected gamblers provided information to a Lucchese Family crew that led to the largest cash robbery in U.S. history—$6 million from Lufthansa Airlines: "He had methodically worked out the details: how many men would be needed, the best time for the heist, how to bypass the elaborate security and alarm system" (Pileggi 1985: 203).

For Vincent Teresa (Teresa and Renner 1973), an associate of the New England crime Family of Raymond Patriarca, what started out as a "service" ended up as an extortion scheme.

Joseph Barboza, a vicious ex-fighter, was an unaffiliated criminal operating in Massachusetts with his own band of thugs. One evening they were at the Ebbtide, a legitimate nightclub in the Boston suburb of Revere, where they beat up the owners and threatened to return and kill everybody. The owners went to Teresa for help. Teresa went to Patriarca's underboss, Henry Tameleo, who agreed to help—for a price. Acting on Tameleo's behalf, Teresa found Barboza: "Henry Tameleo wants to see you." When Barboza hesitated, Teresa explained the alternatives: "You want to come, fine. You don't want to come, you don't have to, but he'll send someone else to see you" (Teresa and Renner 1973: 123). After being "called in," Barboza agreed not to bother the Ebbtide—it was now a "protected" club. This gave Teresa an idea: "We sent Barboza and his animals to more than twenty nightclubs. They would go into these places and tear the joints apart. . . . These people would come running to us to complain about Barboza, to ask for protection" (1973: 123–24).

Sometimes the approach is less subtle but more lethal: In 1987, Gambino Family member Michael ("Mike Rizzi") Rizzitello, operating out of Los Angeles, decided "to pay a visit to Mustang topless bar owner Bill Carroll. Rizzi had met Carroll while in prison in 1970 and had been attempting to acquire a piece of the club for months. He had warned Carroll repeatedly to come up with part of the $150,000 the Mustang generated each month. Carroll refused. 'This is for not letting us eat,' Rizzitello said as he pumped three bullets into Carroll's head" (J. Smith 1998: 203).

When it comes to "goods and services," then, the picture is mixed. Many of those who provide gambling and other goods and services such as loansharking have a relationship with organized crime that is forced upon them. Others find the organized crime connection useful to their enterprise, and sometimes the made guy is a bookmaker, numbers operator, or (more frequently) a loan shark.

To understand the business of organized crime, we need to consider the degree to which a crime group's business activities are integrated into their organizational structure. Outlaw motorcycle clubs (OMC) have a bureaucratic style of organization, but their (illegal) business activities are not under the control and direction of the organizational hierarchy. Instead, members engage in crime in association with other members—persons in whom they have trust—and use their OMC membership for purposes of intimidation and networking. Thus, while an OMC may not be a criminal organization per se, it facilitates the criminal activities of its members. At the other end of this structure–business spectrum are the Colombian cocaine cartels whose business structure and organizational structure are one and the same.

Finally, members of an organized crime group may engage in a variety of criminal activities for which membership is neither necessary nor of any particular advantage. For example, they may commit theft or robbery of cash or cybercrime. These crimes can be and are engaged in by persons having no connection to organized crime—a 16-year-old sitting at his computer in Nigeria can be involved in hacking or advance-fees schemes without any organizational affiliation.

With this in mind, let us review the "goods and services" of organized crime. In this chapter we will examine gambling, loansharking, theft and fencing, commercial sex, and trafficking in persons and arms. In Chapter 13, we will look at the business of drugs, and in Chapter 14, we will examine organized crime in labor and business.

GAMBLING

Gambling includes a wide array of games of chance and sporting events on which wagers are made. Some of these are legal, for example, state licensed horse- and dog-racing tracks, casinos, and government-operated off-track betting parlors. Most states operate lotteries, and licensed casino gambling is often operated by Native Americans on Indian land. State, county, and municipal governments earn a great deal of money from these authorized gambling activities. At the same time, there are unauthorized (illegal) gambling operations whose control is the responsibility of these same governments. In such an ambiguous environment, it is easy to understand why gambling

"Of all of the various scams and operations orchestrated by wiseguys, none is as profitable and as dependable as illegal gambling. . . . It is a 365-day-a-year proposition" (Pistone 2004: 40).

enforcement may not generate a great deal of public support. The estimated amount of illegal betting increased tenfold between 1983 and 1995, while arrests for illegal gambling declined significantly, particularly in urban centers. In 1960, 123,000 persons were arrested for illegal gambling, but by 1995 that number was down to about 15,000 (McGraw 1997; McMahon 1992).

The low priority given to gambling enforcement adds to its attractiveness. Although profits from drug trafficking are quite substantial, so are enforcement activities and penalties, whereas sentences for illegal gambling are minimal. Lack of enforcement resources due to competing demands for police services, combined with advanced telephonic communications—for example, the cell phone and the Internet—explain why enforcement has declined. There is an absence of public pressure to improve gambling enforcement. The relatively light sentences for gambling violations is highlighted by the case of the Gambino soldiers Ronnie ("One Arm") Trucchio (52) and his son Alphonse who, at 26, is reputed to be the youngest Mafia member in New York. In 2004, they pled guilty to running a $30 million a year sports betting operation and received sentences of one to three years. That same year, Gambino Family captain, Joseph ("Sonny") Juliano, 65, received a sentence of one-and-a-half to three years for a sports betting and numbers operation that collected more than $3 million in bets annually. Sentences for wholesale drug convictions are typically decades.

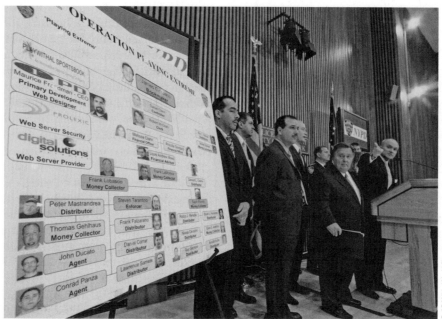

© AP/Wide World Photos

New York Police Commissioner Raymond Kelly, right, is joined by Queens District Attorney Richard Brown, second from right, as he speaks to reporters during a news conference at New York City Police Department headquarters in 2006. Prosecutors brought charges against twenty-seven people in connection with a billion-dollar-a-year Internet sports gambling ring.

Bookmaking

Bookmakers "book" bets on two types of events—horse and sometimes dog races and sporting events such as football, basketball, baseball, and boxing. In earlier days, "horse parlors" or "wire rooms," neighborhood outlets, were often set up in the back of a legitimate business. Results coming in over the wire service were posted on a large chalkboard for waiting bettors. Today, most bets are placed by telephone directly or through a roving "handbook," "runner," or "sheetwriter" who transmits the bet to the bookmaker. To maintain security, some bookmakers change locations frequently, often monthly, or they may use cellular telephones. Many use a "call back" system. The bettor calls an answering service or answering machine and leaves his or her number. The bookmaker returns the call from a variety of locations, and the bet is placed.

Bets are written down and may also be tape-recorded by a machine attached to the phone. This helps avoid any discrepancies about what arrangements were actually made over the phone. The bookmaker usually employs clerks and handbooks, runners, or sheetwriters. The clerks handle the telephone, record the bets, and figure out the daily finances. The runners call the clerks and are given the day's totals for the bets they booked. Based on this information, the clerks either collect or pay off. The runners receive a portion of the winnings, usually half, and they must also share in the losses (Rubinstein and Reuter 1977).

Horse-Race Wagering[1]   The oldest of the major bookmaking activities, illegal horse-race wagering, ranks behind sports wagering. This discrepancy has increased with the advent of legalized off-track betting in places such as New York, Connecticut, and Illinois. The typical bettor is middle-aged or older, and wagers are usually modest. Information on the horses running at each track on a given day may be obtained from a local newspaper or a "scratch sheet" such as the *Armstrong Daily News*

Review, Turf and Sports Mirror, or the *Daily Racing Form*. Voluminous data are available in the *Daily Racing Form*, and the scratch sheets provide information on the time and nature of each race, the jockeys, the post positions, the weights carried, the probable odds, and the handicapper's estimates of horses' finishing position. This information, especially what is gleaned from the scratch sheet, is the basic data needed by the bookmaker in handling wagers.

Payoffs at the track are the basis for a bookmaker's profits (a net of between 10 and 15 percent), except where a bookmaker's limits are reached. The bookie's cut is obtained in the following manner: Before the track makes a payoff under the pari-mutuel system (in which the track acts as a broker to pay the winners from the money it collects from the losers), it deducts for taxes and operational expenses. The bookmaker, by keeping the allocation of wagers roughly equal to the track's, realizes a profit from the portion that at the track goes to expenses and taxes. Because this deduction is generally from 15 to 20 percent, there is comfortable room for maneuvering. A bookmaker who has booked too much money on one horse, lays off the excess. This layoff process continues wherever a lack of balance exists until it reaches the top layoff operation, which has its agents stationed near major tracks. Upon being given their orders, the agents make an ultimate layoff by placing large wagers at the track's pari-mutuel window. If the wager is a winning one, money to assist in making payoffs comes from the track winnings. Also, by placing large wagers at the track, the track's payoff, and consequently the bookmaker's, is reduced because the odds are determined by the amount of money bet on each entry.

The bookmaker cannot, of course, know precisely what percentage of money will be wagered on each horse at the track. However, information supplied by the scratch sheet or the *Daily Racing Form* is generally an acceptable guide. In the event of a high track payoff, the bookmaker invokes limits: generally 15 or 20 to 1 for a "win" bet, 6 or 8 to 1 for a "place" bet, and 3 or 4 to 1 for "show"; for multihorse events such as the "daily double," it will usually be 50 to 1.

---

[1]Unless otherwise cited, material in this section has been taken from Boyd (1977).

FIGURE 12.1   *Common Wagers as Recorded by a Bookmaker*

Win—choose the horse that will finish first.

1 NY JOEY' BOY 2/1
6 L# 85-0-0

(First race, New York [e.g., Aqueduct], $2 to win on Joey Boy
(Sixth race, Laurel horse with post position 8. $5 to win)

Place—choose the horse that will finish first or second.

4 G5 MARY MARY X-10-X

(Fourth race, Gulfstream, $10 to place on Mary Mary)

Show—choose the horse that will finish first, second, or third.

9 S/A 65/3

(Ninth race, Santa Anita, horse #6, $5 to show)

Combo (Across-the-Board)—a single bet encompassing equal amounts for win, place, and show.

B 6 2 2/2/2

(Sixth race, Bowie, horse #2, $2 to win, $2 to place, $2 to show)

Wagers shown in Figure 12.1 are commonly recorded by a bookmaker: The information includes a bettor's identity (often in code), the racetrack, the identity of the horse, the type of wager, and the amount of the wager. The name of the track is almost always abbreviated (either by name or location). The identity of the horse may be written out fully or represented by its post position or the handicapper's number as found on the scratch sheet.

Sports Wagering   From a gross dollar volume standpoint, sports wagering is the king of bookmaking, although the net profit for the bookmaker is typically less than 5 percent. As in other forms of bookmaking, the sports bookmaker seeks to act as a broker, not a gambler. To achieve equality between teams, one which the bookmaker hopes will attract like sums of money on each contestant, a handicapping process takes place through the use of a *line* or *spread*, the expected point difference between the favored team and the underdog:

> The line theoretically functions as a handicap to balance relative strengths of the opposing teams. It consists of points either added to the underdog teams' final scores or subtracted from the favorite teams' final

scores. Then again, theoretically having balanced the relative strengths of the teams, wagers are accepted by bookmakers usually at eleven to ten odds. Thus, for instance, if a bettor desires to bet $500 on the Washington Redskins at -6 (meaning Washington is favored by 6 points and, thus, 6 points are subtracted from Washington's final score to determine the result of the wager), he would actually risk $550 to the bookmaker's $500.

> The line is only theoretically a balancing of the strengths of the teams. However, as a practical matter, the line is really a number of points, either added to the underdogs' scores or subtracted from the favorites' scores, which the bookmakers feel will tend to attract relatively even amounts on wagering on both sides of the contest. If the bookmaker achieves an even balance of wagering on a game and he has no gamble or risk, his profit is assured of being 10 percent, the "juice" or "vigorish" of the losing wages. (Harker 1977: 2)

That is because bookmakers build in a profit by requiring a bettor to risk $11 to win $10—the $1 is called vigorish. Thus, to break even, a bettor would have to win 52.38 percent of the time. In the case of the Washington Redskins bet, if bettors won by more than 6 points, the bookmaker would pay out $500. He would receive $550 from someone who bet that amount on the losing team—a profit of $50, or 10 percent.

To make any necessary line changes, major booking operations continuously track changes in the Las Vegas line by computer. Sports betting and the use of the point spread (line) are illegal except in Nevada. Professional gamblers—who bet for income, not fun—also track line changes in an effort to "middle": They shop around for the most advantageous lines and bet opposite sides of a contest, thus ensuring that the only possible loss is vigorish, while possible earnings will be many times that amount. The bookmaker's profits depend on an ability to alter the point spread so that bets keep coming in for both teams. Even though the bookmaker sets the opening line, it shifts largely in response to what bettors do. Too much money on one team and the vigorish is endangered and the bookmaker becomes a gambler—unless he can lay off his out-of-balance bets (discussed later).

When there are attempts to fix the outcome of sporting events, the approach is to have key players "shave points."[2] That is, their play will reflect the need to keep the score within the point spread favored by the fixers. The National Football League has been extremely outspoken in its opposition to the legalization of sports betting. Pete Rozelle (quoted in Tuite 1978: B21), speaking for the NFL, stated: "The league believes legalized gambling on professional sports will dramatically change the character of the fan's interests in the sports. No longer will sports fans identify their interests with the success or failure of their favorite teams, but with the effect of their team's performance in the winning or losing of bets." The NFL's real fear, of course, is that legalized gambling will greatly increase the security problems confronting professional sports. Actually, the incomes of professional athletes make the fix more likely in college sports.[3]

When the state of Delaware experimented very briefly with football wagering in 1976, the NFL sued that state but lost the suit. The league's chief security officer explained why the suit was brought: "We are not naive. We are not unaware of the fact that there is a great deal of gambling going on, but we don't think that the state or any governmental authority rightfully should come in and impose a gambling situation on our game" (Marshall 1978: 21). Delaware gave up football wagering "after it found out that state officials were less adept at setting odds than the underworld. Professional gamblers realized they could take advantage of Delaware's inexperience in bookmaking and collect a lot of easy money" (Marshall 1978: 21).

How difficult is the bookmaking business? An experienced investigator responds: "Well you have day games and night games. So you're bookin' from twelve to one during the day, and five-thirty to six-thirty at night—we're talkin' maybe four hours. Then if you use voice mail, you're not even bookin', you're at the golf course. So at night you call up and get all your bets. . . . Where's the work? There's not much. All you have to worry about is who's winnin' and who's losin'. You pay someone $500 a week to take care of the collecting and payouts. He should set it up where he has a pattern, where he meets the guys at a set time. They usually get retired guys to do this, and these guys don't think they're doing anything wrong. You can't even arrest him—for what, for givin' someone money?" (Herion 1998). (See Figure 12.2.)

Organized Crime and Bookmaking In an earlier period, bookmaking was an important source of income for organized crime. Organized crime units ran the operation directly, or "licensed" syndicate bookmakers, and the wire service that provided instant race results was an important source of organized crime control over bookmaking.

---

[2]For a discussion of point shaving, see Whalen (1995). If a bookmaker suspects a fix—experiences an influx of bets ("smart money") on a particular underdog, for example—he may "circle" or "scratch" the game. A circle means he will limit the amount any one bettor can wager; a scratch means he will accept no further bets.

[3]For an inside look at the effect of gambling on college basketball, see Cohen (1977), Hill (1981), and Rosen (1978).

FIGURE 12.2 *Sports Betting Lines*

Latest Line
Sports Features Syndicate Inc.

College Basketball Tonight Preseason NIT Quarterfinals					
Favorite	*Pts.*	*Underdog*	San Jose St.	3	at Nevada
At Arkansas	1 1/2	Arizona	Southern Miss.	6	at SW Louisiana
At Georgia Tech	3	Oklahoma	At Stanford	9	California
At Michigan	10 1/2	Weber St.	Tennessee	25 1/2	at Kentucky
College Football Tomorrow			At Texas	17 1/2	TCU
			Texas Tech.	19	Ohio
Favorite	*Pts.*	*Underdog*	At Utah St.	9 1/2	Pacific
At Baylor	15	Rice	At Virginia	4	Virginia Tech
At BYU	5 1/2	Utah	At Washington	13 1/2	Washington St.
At Brown	7 1/2	Columbia	At W. Michigan	8	C. Michigan
Cincinnati	4 1/2	at Tulsa	At Wisconsin	7	Iowa
Clemson	4	at S. Carolina	At Wyoming	4 1/2	Fresno St.
At E. Carolina	13	Memphis			
E. Michigan	13 1/2	at Kent	**NBA Tonight**		
At Florida	42	Vanderbilt			
At Illinois	6	Minnesota	*Favorite*	*Pts.*	*Underdog*
Kansas	9 1/2	at Oklahoma St.	At Boston	4 1/2	Washington
At LSU	1 1/2	Arkansas	At Atlanta	3 1/2	Miami
At Louisiana Tech	3 1/2	N. Illinois	At Chicago	14	New Jersey
At Louisville	26	N. Texas	Dallas	4 1/2	at LA Clippers
At Miami (Fla.)	12	W. Virginia	At Denver	1	New York
At Miami (Ohio)	30 1/2	Akron	LA Lakers	7 1/2	At Vancouver
At Missouri	3 1/2	Iowa St.	Minnesota	1 1/2	at Toronto
At Navy	6 1/2	Tulane	At Philadelphia	3	Cleveland
At UNLV	6 1/2	New Mex. St.	Phoenix	3	at Sacramento
New Mexico	13	at UTEP	Seattle	1 1/2	at Charlotte
At N. Carolina	15	Duke	Utah	4	at Detroit
N.C. State	6	at Wake Forest			
Northwestern	4 1/2	at Purdue	**NHL Tonight**		
At Ohio St.	32 1/2	Indiana			
At Oregon	16	Oregon St.	*Favorite*	*Gls.*	*Underdog*
At Penn	5	Cornell	At Anaheim	1-1 1/2	NY Islanders
Princeton	1 1/2	at Dartmouth	Colorado	1-1 1/2	at Calgary
Rutgers	3	at Temple	At Dallas	1 1/2-2	San Jose
San Diego St.	8 1/2	at Hawaii	Detroit	1/2-1	at Edmonton
			NY Rangers	E-1/2	at Winnipeg
			Pittsburgh	E-1/2	at Washington
			E-Even		

However, most illegal wagering today involves sports, rather than horse racing, and bets are made by telephone—or over the Internet. Payoffs are made the day after the event, so the prompt results provided by the wire service are no longer relevant. The almost-exclusive use of the telephone provides greater security and has reduced the need for police protection, often an important syndicate service.

Bookmakers (and numbers operators) frequently find their bets sufficiently unbalanced to require that they be laid off (or else the bookmaker becomes a gambler, not a broker). The bookmaker may use legal bookmakers in Las Vegas to accomplish this layoff, or he may contract with a layoff service. The layoff service is actually a bookmaker's bookmaker, accepting bets nationally, and is thereby better able to balance teams from different cities. For example, if a New York team is playing a Chicago team, bookmakers in New York are likely to have too many bets on the hometown favorite. The layoff service can balance those bets with excess ones from Chicago, where bookmakers have the same hometown-team problem. Because of its scale, the layoff is typically a service provided by organized crime.

Bookmaking involves many transactions and generates a great deal of paperwork. The wagers are recorded when received, and clerks have to review their receipts to determine winners and losers. In 1995, police raided a major bookmaking operation—estimated gross $65 million, net of 20 percent—where they found all data entries on computers using a custom-made sports betting program. The computers were also linked to an online service from Las Vegas that provided the latest line on sporting events. The operation was connected to the Colombo and Gambino Families (Raab 1995e).

Technical changes have also made it harder to find bookmakers, who have insulated themselves by the routine use of mobile telephones, pagers, and call back services. A gambling investigator explains:

> I've been trying to find a guy [bookmaker]. An informant would give me this phone number. I would check it out and it [the address] would be a vacant lot; the bill would go to a Post Office box in some other county. Suppose you're the bookmaker. You pay me $500 a week. You give me the phone and people call up. I don't know who they are, they all have [ID] numbers. So a guy would call up and say, "Give me $2,000 on the Bulls minus two" . . . whatever. I write it down, but I don't know them. You're in the background and you're the only one who knows. But you are not involved in bookmaking. You're the bookmaker, but you're not involved in the actual booking itself. You just figure out who won and who lost, and pay or collect. So you meet him [the bettor]. But, if you're real sharp, you have another guy meet him. Now you just meet

your guy on a street corner and he hands you an envelope. You meet the guy in a different place all the time. You call him on the phone and give him ten minutes to meet you. Now how am I [as a gambling enforcement officer] supposed to find you? (Herion 1998)

Competition is difficult to control because bookmaking can involve operations outside the United States. Bookmakers frequently advertise in sports publications, through radio programs, and on the Internet.

Lotteries/Numbers The American colonies authorized lotteries. "In 1612, King James I authorized a lottery to promote the colony of Virginia. The colonies themselves used lotteries, and such outstanding men as George Washington bought and sold lottery tickets." The lottery was used (unsuccessfully) to help finance the Revolutionary War. Many of America's outstanding institutions of higher learning were supported through the use of lotteries—Rhode Island College (now Brown), Columbia, Harvard, University of North Carolina, William and Mary, and Yale (Chafetz 1960: 20–21).

During the nineteenth century, lotteries under state license or control were found throughout the United States. Because of the negative publicity surrounding problems with the Louisiana lottery, in 1890, the United States enacted legislation prohibiting lotteries from using the mails and even prohibited newspapers that carried lottery advertisements from using the mails (Chafetz 1960). This prohibition opened the way for the illegal exploitation of the desire to bet on lotteries through such devices as "numbers" or "policy" betting.

Policy is based on drawing numbers from 1 to 78 by spinning a wheel. Twelve to fifteen numbers are drawn, and players bet that from one to four numbers in various sequences will be among those drawn. Bets are typically small, but when a policy operation is controlled by a syndicate, the total profits can be quite large. In the past, bets were placed in "policy shops" or, in more contemporary times, through runners. "Dream books" are sold to help players choose their lucky numbers. During the 1920s, *numbers* were introduced as competition with policy.

In numbers, a player selects one, two, or three digits from 0 to 9 with the odds of winning running from 10 to 1, 100 to 1, and 1,000 to 1. For a single-digit ("single action") play, the payoff is 6 or 7 to 1; for two digits ("double action"), the payoff is between 50 and 64 to 1; for three digits, the payoff is between 550 and 600 to one. On certain popular combinations (for example, 711), the payoff may be reduced to 500 to 1 or even lower. A player can also "box" numbers—bet all the possible three-digit combinations. Although this increases the chances of winning, it also lowers the payoff to about 100 to 1.

A variety of elaborate schemes are available for determining the winning numbers, for example, using the amounts for win, place, and show of the first race at a particular racetrack or the last three digits of the racetrack's "handle" (total gross receipts)—figures that are readily available in the daily newspapers. In some games the numbers are selected before an audience of bettors at a central location. Today, in the 42 states having a legal lottery, the illegal lottery will often use the same numbers as the state lottery, although the odds in the illegal lottery may be higher than those offered by the state. In the Chicagoland area, the legal lottery pays $500 for each dollar wagered on a three-number bet, but the illegal lottery pays $600; payment for a four-number bet is the same as the state's, but winners are paid cash and no taxes are withheld.

The structure of the illegal lottery requires a great deal of coordination and is labor intensive, providing many jobs for unskilled individuals, making it an important source of employment in poor communities. At the bottom of the hierarchy are those who accept wagers directly from the bettors, such as writers, runners, and sellers. These are generally individuals with ready access to the public, such as elevator operators, shoeshine boys, newspaper vendors, bartenders, and waiters.[4] Customarily they are paid a percentage of the wagers they write (unlike sports bookmaking, numbers wagering is done on a cash basis), usually from 15 to 30 percent, and frequently are given a 10 percent tip from winning bettors.

It is essential that wagers reach trusted hands before the winning number or any part of it is known. Sometimes this is done by telephone; other times wager records (commonly known as work, action, or business) are physically forwarded to a higher echelon by a pickup man. In a small operation the wagers may go directly to the central processing office (commonly called the bank, clearinghouse, or countinghouse). More often, in large enterprises they are given to management's field representative (known as the field man or controller), who may be responsible for making a quick tally to determine the existence of any heavily played numbers that should be laid off. At such levels of operation one frequently finds charts consisting of 1,000 spaces numbered 000 to 999

---

[4]The proliferation of small grocery stores in some neighborhoods is explained by the illegal lottery.

where tallies can be made for only certain wagers meeting minimum dollar values.

Near the top of the hierarchy is the *bank* where all transactions are handled. During the collection process the bank will be making decisions as to whether or not to lay off certain heavily played numbers.[5] After the winning number is known, the bank will meticulously process the paperwork to determine how much action has been written, how many hits are present, and the controllers or writers involved. (For a look at the details of the numbers game and its historical relationship to organized crime, see Liddick [1998].)

Decreasing organized criminal opportunity was one argument for the legalization of certain types of gambling, in particular the state lottery, beginning in New Hampshire in 1964, followed by New York in 1967. The first financially successful lottery, however, was the 50-cent weekly established by New Jersey in 1971 (Gambling Commission 1976). Most lottery states have a variety of games: instant winners, daily drawings, weekly drawings, and multistate lotteries with pay-offs in the millions of dollars. This form of gambling was originally offered as a way of reducing the income of the illegal lottery—numbers—and capturing those monies for public use, particularly education. Without doubt, the lottery has added billions of dollars to the public coffers without generating the political heat that raising taxes would: about $12 billion annually (from wagers of about $35 billion). "State sponsorship reflected a lifting of social and moral barriers and initiated an expansion of gambling that continues today" (Wellford 2001: 15).

There is no evidence, however, that the legal lotteries have diminished the revenues of their illegal counterparts. In fact, publicity may have actually increased illegal revenues along with those of state lotteries. The introduction of a legal lottery educates persons who heretofore did not know the intricacies of numbers gambling (Blount and Kaplan 1989). Illegal operators typically provide better odds—and do not report the winnings to tax officials. Furthermore, the daily lottery provides illegal operators with a winning number in which bettors have confidence and offers a free lay-off service so that numbers banks can always balance their bets. The illegal lottery, however, does not encourage people to gamble by an unseemly spate of advertising (about $400 million a year). In America's poorest communities, "the [legal] lottery is a dominant force and many poor and modest-income residents are devoted to an endless search for winning numbers in an unswerving belief that a jackpot waits for them" (Pulley 1999: 12).

More than three decades ago, a federal commission warned: "The availability of legal gambling creates new gamblers." Therefore, "a government that wishes merely to legitimize illegal wagering must recognize the clear danger that legalization may lead to unexpected and ungovernable increases in the size of the gambling clientele" (Gambling Commission 1976: 2). In the constant quest for new revenues, states such as New York have introduced new forms of lottery such as Keno, an electronic game in which bettors pick one or more numbers and win if the computer selects their numbers. Instead of a weekly or daily drawing, Keno picks a new number every five minutes—the compulsive gambler's nightmare—and scratch-off tickets selling for as much as $50 each offer instant payouts to people who can ill-afford to gamble.

Off-track betting (OTB) in New York has been less than a resounding success and is struggling to cover its expenses, although it has created plenty of patronage jobs. In 2008, the mayor announced his intention to discontinue OTB. Off-track betting did succeed in reducing illegal betting on horses, because few bookmakers in New York accept bets on horse racing. As in a number of other states, OTB in New York is considering the introduction of sports betting. Some fear that introducing sports betting will serve to educate more persons on the intricacies of gambling. Because illegal operators typically provide better odds (their overhead is significantly lower), do not report the winnings to tax officials, and accept bets

---

[5]In games using state lottery numbers, the layoff can be accomplished by purchasing large quantities of lottery tickets, although illegal operators will have to absorb some loss on the transaction, because they usually pay winners more than the state.

on credit and over the telephone, legalized sports betting may succeed in recruiting new bettors for the bookmakers.

Casino Gambling and Related Activities

Casino gambling (with a wide array of games of chance including roulette, chuck-a-luck, blackjack, and craps) requires a great deal of planning, space, personnel, equipment, and financing. In the past, casino gambling was available in "wide-open towns" such as Newport, Kentucky, and Phenix City, Alabama,[6] and on a more discreet level in Saratoga Springs, New York, and Hot Springs, Arkansas. Some cities have a tradition of holding "Las Vegas Nights," events often run under the auspices of, or with the approval and protection of, an organized crime unit, using the legitimate front of a religious or charitable organization. The operators provide gambling devices, personnel, and financing, and they share some of the profits with the sponsoring organization.

Organized crime operatives may also organize or sponsor card or dice games, taking a cut out of every pot for their services. These may be in a permanent location such as a social club or veterans' hall, or for security reasons, may "float" from place to place. The games may be operated in the home

of a person in debt to a loan shark as a form of paying off the loan. In certain cities, gambling activities not operated under organized crime protection, "outlaw games," run the risk of being raided by the police or being held up by independent criminals or robbery teams sponsored by an organized crime unit. Vincent Siciliano (1970: 50), an armed robber with organized crime connections, reports: "The organization knows there is this game and when some friend in the police needs an arrest, to earn his keep as a protector of the people against the bad gamblers, the organization guy tells the police and off they go with sirens wailing." During the raid, Siciliano notes, the police can also help themselves to much of the game's proceeds. He points out that even the dumbest thief knows which are syndicate games and recognizes the consequences of disregarding the organized crime connection. A career armed robber expresses concern with the possibility of "knocking over" a "connected" operation: "I don't think the Mafia'd read me my rights and let me go consult with an attorney. And I said [to my partners], 'Is this thing connected?' I said, 'Look, if this is the Mafia's money I don't want any part of it. I don't want some guys to come gunnin' for me'" (Greenberg 1981: 93).

Las Vegas and New Jersey In 1931, the state of Nevada, desperate for tax revenue during the Great Depression, legalized gambling and established licensing procedures for those wanting to operate gambling establishments. Las Vegas "served principally as a comfort station for tourists fleeing the

---

[6]On June 15, 1954, Albert L. Patterson, a Phenix City reformer who had been nominated Alabama attorney general, was murdered. His son Gordon was subsequently elected governor of Alabama. He declared martial law in Phenix City and sent in the National Guard to "close it down." These events inspired the movie *The Phenix City Story* (Wright 1979).

desert heat" (Reid and Demaris 1964: 12). Then came Bugsy Siegel, the first important criminal to recognize the potential from legalized gambling in Nevada. Operating out of California, "from about 1942 until the time of his death, Siegel controlled the wire-service in Las Vegas through Moe Sedway, an ex-convict, gambler, and longtime associate of many New York mobsters, who Siegel brought to Las Vegas. Through control of the wire service, Siegel controlled the operations of all handbooks operating in Las Vegas. He refused wire service to any book unless he or his agents operated and managed it" (Kefauver 1951a: 91).

With financing from organized crime leaders throughout the country, including Frank Costello, Meyer Lansky, Tony Accardo, Longie Zwillman of New Jersey, and Moe Dalitz of the Cleveland syndicate, Siegel built the Flamingo Hotel, the first of the elaborate Las Vegas gambling establishments. Until then, gambling consisted of a "few ancient one-armed bandits and a couple of homemade crap tables," and most of the action was at the poker table (Reid and Demaris 1964: 12). The former bootleggers were ideally suited to exploit Las Vegas: They had available capital that they were used to pooling, expertise in gambling, and business acumen developed during Prohibition. "Without the ex-bootleggers to found and staff the first generation of hotel casinos," argues Mark Haller (1985a: 152), "Las Vegas might not have been possible."

After Siegel's murder in 1947, the Flamingo and a number of plush hotels were controlled (through hidden interests) by organized crime units. Typically, funds were "skimmed" before being counted for tax purposes, and the money was distributed to organized crime bosses in proportion to their amount of (hidden) ownership. According to federal officials, from 1973 to 1983 at least $14 million was skimmed from just one hotel, the Stardust. In 1983, several Stardust employees were prosecuted and the owners (of record) were forced to sell the hotel. The Stardust was originally licensed to Moe Dalitz. In 1983, two Kansas City, Missouri, organized crime figures and an executive of the Tropicana Hotel-Casino were sentenced to long prison terms for skimming operations (Turner

1984). As noted in Chapter 5, the top leaders of organized crime in Chicago, Kansas City, Cleveland, and Milwaukee were sentenced to prison in 1986 for skimming the profits of Las Vegas casinos (depicted in the book and movie *Casino*).

Las Vegas is no longer a mob-controlled playground—casinos are major corporate entities—and organized crime has been moved to the fringes of the Las Vegas scene. In 1998, for example, federal agents arrested six men from the Gambino Family for planning to use violence against several "out-call" operators. The intended victims provide nude dancers for hotel room sessions (prostitution, though legal in some parts of Nevada, is illegal in Las Vegas and Clark County). The operators were competing with organized crime–affiliated services and, as one of the Gambinos told an undercover agent, the competing firms were being sent an "aspirin"—an enforcer known as "Vinnie Aspirins." Mr. Aspirins is known for using a cordless power drill to bore holes in victims' heads; he was arrested in Las Vegas with a former military mercenary, an expert on explosives.

In Atlantic City, New Jersey, the second state to authorize casino gambling, there were intensive efforts to keep organized crime out of the casinos. The New Jersey State Police, which has extensive experience in dealing with organized crime, and the New Jersey Casino Control Commission, were put in charge of overseeing casino operations to prevent organized crime infiltration. "While it may be true that mobsters haven't yet found their way into the casino counting rooms—as they once did in Las Vegas—almost anywhere you look in the city you'll find a wiseguy or one of his associates. The mob is on the floor of every casino in the city. It's in the restaurants and the casino lounges. It controls the labor unions whose workers make the big casino-hotels go" (Anastasia 1991: 163). In Atlantic City, organized crime has been able to influence the purchase of goods and services through control over key unions, particularly Local 54 of the Hotel Employees and Restaurant Employees Union. Local 54, which represents 22,000 casino hotel employees, has long been dominated by the Bruno Family of Philadelphia. In 1990, the federal government, under provisions of the Racketeer Influenced and Corrupt Organizations (RICO) statute, sued to have Local 54 placed in receivership. In 1991, the government reached an agreement with the union, and Local 54 was placed into receivership. Its leaders accepted voluntary "banishment" (Sullivan 1991).

There is increasing evidence that the easy availability of legalized gambling is attracting young persons at an alarming rate. Lottery scratch cards contain cartoon graphics, video poker machines resemble video machines that many have grown up with, and video arcades on the Atlantic City boardwalk feature slot machines for children that dispense prizes instead of money. Casino operators encourage parents to bring their children, and they sponsor amusement parks to keep the children busy while their parents gamble. The entry of underage gamblers into casinos without detection continues to be a problem (Pulley 1998).

Miscellaneous Gambling

Bingo is legal in forty-six states. Although purportedly played to raise funds for charitable causes, bingo is also a source of profits for organized crime. Persons connected to organized crime may run the operations for the front (charity) or merely be connected through "licensure." In a number of localities, coin-operated video poker machines are very popular, often a staple in many bars or taverns. These machines operate like slot machines but are legal because they do not dispense money. Payoffs are provided by the proprietor (or bartender) surreptitiously. In Chicago, the Outfit provides the machines and splits the profits, which can be several thousand dollars per week per machine. Net profits from the poker machines are typically split fifty-fifty between the distributors of the machine and the proprietor, and each machine can generate $2,000 per week.

In the Chicagoland area:

They're all over the place. And the poker machines themselves are not illegal. . . . Mostly snack bars, blue-collar places. Let's say the owner hears about the money you can make. He contacts a guy and the guy explains that they will be partners. He will put a machine in, maybe more. "Whatever you net for the week we'll split down the middle." He can't lose. The machine will take up to $20 at a time; it's got different slots for different denominations. You get so many units for a winning hand. They're not supposed to pay out in cash, but the rule of thumb is every forty units is worth $10. You wave over the clerk or the bartender and he pays $10 for every forty points. The machine adds it up and you can add units by adding more money. . . . The distributor can set it to pay out whatever he wants. There's no skill, strictly chance. When they first put in the machine, they will maybe set it to pay out up to 80 or 85 percent [of the times]. Then they get people hooked and the distributor reduces the payout. [And the profits?] Some places, like a truck stop I know, they had ten machines and were making $100,000 a month. Some mom and pop operations couldn't stay open without the machines. They've taken seats out of restaurants so they could make room for more of these machines. (Herion 1998)

A sheriff's investigator reports: "About five months ago our vice unit hit a truck stop somewhere in the Calumet City [just south of Chicago] area, an oasis just off the Calumet Expressway. They brought in ten or twelve machines that had been running for two days, and there was $8,500 registered on them. I think a lot of mom and pop type taverns in the city are probably paying their overhead with the income from the machines" (Scaramella 1998). In 2002, the former mayor of suburban Stone Park was sentenced to 18 months' imprisonment for taking bribes from the Chicago Outfit to protect video poker machines in the town's taverns.

Although there is no evidence of any attempts to restrict market entry—competition—the video poker appears to be totally an Outfit business. People know how to contact Outfit guys, and in many neighborhoods, the owners of small businesses would rather do business with the Outfit than someone unknown to them (who could be an undercover officer).

Cyber-Gambling

There is also online casino gambling whose connection to organized crime is uncertain. With an Internet connection, gamblers can access virtual bingo, poker, roulette, and other casino games 24 hours a day. Although it is illegal in the United States, online gambling is permitted to operate in a number of countries. Participants set up an account using a credit or debit card. Money is added or subtracted from the account according to the bettor's success, or lack of it. And, despite their dubious legality in the United States, the Internet is replete with gambling sites, up from 6 in 1996 to more than 2,400 in 2006, many of them legal in their country of origin, for example, Costa Rica. Internet gaming includes casino gambling, sports betting, and the lottery that generate about $12 billion dollars in annual revenue (Healey and Hagenbaugh 2005; Miller, 2006). "Cyber-bookie" Calvin Ayre is headquartered in Costa Rica where he operates an online casino with 145,000 customers, most of them in the United States. He is not an American citizen, has no physical presence in the United States, and pays no U.S. taxes on a net worth of about $1 billion (Miller 2006).

Although credit card companies often refuse to process payments for Internet gambling, a bettor can open an account by sending a cashier's check, money order, or wire transfer to a licensed bookmaker in the Caribbean; a minimum balance of $500 is usually required. Each bettor is given a personal identification number, bets are placed on a special long-distance toll-free number or the Internet, and money is added or subtracted from the account. A bettor can withdraw money, receiving his or her winnings in the mail via check or wire transfer (Dretzka 2001; Financial Crimes Enforcement Network 2000). And while gamblers are supposed to declare their winnings on their 1040, cyber-bookies do not file reports with the IRS (Miller 2006).

Although the 1994 Federal Wire Wager Act (18 U.S.C. § 1084) makes it a crime to operate a betting or wagering business using telephone lines or other wire communication facility, if the business is legal where it is licensed, the bookmakers are beyond U.S. jurisdiction. But if they enter the United States, they could be in trouble. In 1998, the federal government charged executives of fourteen offshore betting firms with illegally using interstate phone lines to facilitate betting. Three of the defendants were subsequently arrested while visiting the United States (Weiser 1998a). In 2000, a man who operated a sports betting business on the Internet was convicted by a federal jury in what is believed to be the first case of its kind to go to trial. He headed an operation based in Antigua and was among twenty-two defendants charged who operated offshore companies that took bets from Americans via the Internet or toll-free telephone numbers. He was sentenced to twenty-one months and a federal appeals court subsequently upheld his conviction (Neumeister 2000; "Man Loses Federal Appeal in Internet Gambling Case" 2001). The Internet Gambling Enforcement Act of 2006 makes it is illegal for American financial institutions to process transactions originating from or directed toward any online gambling operator, prohibiting businesses, including banks, credit card companies, interactive computer service providers, and telecommunications services, from accepting or transferring money to offshore gambling sites. This includes credit cards, checks, and electronic fund transfers.

LOANSHARKING (USURY)

The generally negative view of money lending is highlighted in the Bible, which on three separate occasions cautions against charging interest—*neshek* (to "bite"): "If thou lend money to any of My people, even to the poor with thee, thou shalt not be to him as a creditor; neither shall ye lay upon him interest" (*Exodus* 22: 24); "And if thy brother be waxen poor . . . thou shalt not give him thy money upon interest nor give him thy victuals for increase" (*Leviticus* 25: 36–37). However, "Unto a foreigner thou mayest lend upon interest [for business investment purposes]; but upon thy brother thou shalt not lend upon interest." Thus, the Hebrews could not charge interest on a loan to another Hebrew.[7] Later, the Church adopted a similar interpretation: Christians could not charge interest on loans to other Christians. This prohibition created problems for commercial enterprises and led to a paradoxical situation.

Within organized Jewish communities, the Hebrew Free Loan Society developed to loan money to Jews without interest, and laws and regulations restricting the ability of Jews to purchase land and enter guilds resulted in Jews becoming moneylenders to Christians. William Shakespeare's character Shylock, in the *Merchant of Venice* (1596), is based on this historical irony. Shakespeare depicted the unsavory Shylock as a money-lending Jew demanding a pound of flesh from a hapless borrower as repayment for a delinquent loan. At the time Shakespeare was writing, there were no Jewish moneylenders in England— all Jews had been expelled from that country by Edward I in 1290, and they did not return until the 1650s. And Shakespeare's father had twice been accused of violating usury laws (Greenblatt 2004). The name "Shylock" reportedly became slurred by illiterate criminals into "shark," and the word *loanshark* was born. As noted earlier, the Hebrew term for interest is *neshek*, to bite, something for which sharks are noted.

Between 1880 and 1915 a practice known as "salary lending" thrived in the United States. This quasi-legal business provided loans to salaried workers at usurious rates. The collection of debts was ensured by having the borrower sign a variety of complicated legal documents that subjected him or her to the real possibility of being sued and losing employment. Through the efforts of the Russell Sage Foundation, states began enacting small-loan acts to combat this practice. Massachusetts was the first in 1911. These laws, which licensed small lenders and set ceilings on interest, eventually brought salary lending to an end; credit unions, savings banks, and similar institutions began to offer small loans. However, this also led to the wholesale entry of organized crime into the illicit credit business (Goldstock and Coenen 1978).

Loansharking embodies two central features: "The assessment of exorbitant interest rates in extending credit and the use of threats and violence in collecting debts" (Goldstock and Coenen 1978: 2). As noted in Chapters 4 and 5, as Prohibition was drawing to a close, and with the onset of the Great Depression, persons in organized crime began

---

[7]According to the Talmud (*Baba Metzia* 5: 4), even though charging interest on personal loans is prohibited, Jews can lend money to other Jews for business purposes and receive an equity stake in the enterprise.

searching for new areas of profit. These criminals found themselves in the enviable position of having a great deal of excess cash in a cash-starved economy, which gave them an important source of continued income. "Contemporary loansharking is marked by the dominance of organized crime. This pervasive influence is hardly surprising. Syndicate access to rich stores of capital allows the underworld to pour substantial amounts of cash into the credit market. The strength and reputation of organized operations lends credence to threats of reprisals, thus augmenting the aura of fear critical to success in the loansharking business. Moreover, organized crime's aversion to competition militates strongly against successful independent operations" (Goldstock and Coenen 1978: 4).

Persons in organized crime may insulate themselves from direct involvement in loansharking by using nonmember associates. For example, Gambino Family soldier Tony Plate (Piatta) employed—actually funded—his associate Charles ("the Bear") Calise. Calise, in turn, employed others as lenders and collectors. The connection with Tony Plate gave the whole operation an umbrella of protection from other criminals and credibility to debtors. Without this connection, a borrower who is a "made guy" or associate of a crime Family could easily avoid paying back the loan, and violence used to collect the debt could bring retaliation from the Family.

Many loan sharks provide loans to other criminals. "There is strong evidence for specialization by loan sharks. Some deal with legitimate businessmen only, some with illegal entrepreneurs. One medium-level loan shark specialized in fur dealers, though he might make loans to other small businessmen. Some specialize in lending to gambling operators" (Rubinstein and Reuter 1978b: Appendix 3-5). Genovese Family soldier Joseph Valachi (Maas 1968) worked as a loan shark and reported that most of his customers were themselves involved in illegal activities such as numbers and bookmaking. Loan sharks "frequently provide capital for a bookmaker who is in financial difficulty" (Rubinstein and Reuter 1978b: 53).

Individual gamblers may also borrow from a loan shark who stays around card and dice games or accepts "referrals" from a bookmaker. In Chicago, the street crew headed by Sam Carlisi "would require that delinquent debtors obtain a juice loan at an interest rate of 5 percent per week to pay off the gambling debt" (*United States v. Carlisi* [1990]). In one New York case, a young gambler borrowed from a loan shark to pay his bookmaker. He continued to gamble and borrow and eventually was unable to pay his loan shark. As a result, he embarked on a series of illegal activities that led to a prison term. He ran high-stakes poker games, at which his wife played hostess, and secured fraudulent loans from numerous banks. On one occasion, he decided to use some of this money to continue gambling and missed his loan shark payment. He was severely beaten in a parking lot, leaving him with two black eyes and a broken nose. The loan shark obviously has methods of collection not typically employed by other lending institutions. When a debtor fell behind on his juice payments to Joseph DiFronzo, brother of Chicago mob boss John DiFronzo, he was given an offer he could not easily refuse: grow marijuana. DiFronzo was arrested in 1998, at age 63, for overseeing the largest indoor marijuana growing operation ever discovered in Illinois.

The case of Louis Bombacino, a collector for the Chicago Outfit's 26th Street crew, who routinely carried a firearm, vividly reveals the intimidation involved in loansharking. The government intercepted a telephone conversation between Bombacino and a debtor who indicated he could make no further payments. The debtor said he was afraid of the federal government because he had engaged in criminal activity to pay back the loan. Bombacino introduced his associate, known as "Pete," and told the victim: "Pete can be ten times worse than the 'G' [federal government]. The 'G' could only put you in jail; Pete could destroy your whole family." He then put Pete on the phone. Pete made threats of violence against the debtor and his family, and then returned the phone to Bombacino: "I'm glad you talked to this guy, [because] this will be the same guy that'll probably come looking for you. . . . You know I love you like a brother. You know what? I don't need no more kids to adopt and you got three beautiful daughters. And I really love 'em, that's why I keep protecting you."

> *Debtor*: What, I, I, what are they gonna do? They gonna kill me for that [paying late]?
> *Bombacino*: Yeah, yeah. Ya know why?
> *Debtor*: Why?
> *Bombacino*: It ain't the money; it's the principle. The money don't mean a fuckin' thing.

In 1997, Bombacino, 54, pleaded guilty to racketeering and received a 12-year sentence.

However, loan sharks are not in the "muscle" business; they are in the credit business, and thus "they lend money to customers whom they expect will pay off and eventually return as customers again. The loan shark is not attempting to gain control of the customer's business" (Rubinstein and Reuter 1978b: Appendix 3-4). A loan shark obviously has the money to be in a legitimate business. Loansharking, however, requires very little time and can be engaged in by those with limited intelligence and ability. Some persons in organized crime are very bright, but many others would lose an argument with a fire hydrant. In the American Mafia, there is even a term for wiseguys who have a difficult time making a living; they are derisively referred to as "brokesters."

But sometimes a loan shark finds himself involved with a debtor's business. Joseph Valachi lent money to a legitimate businessman, the owner of a dress and negligee company, and became a partner when the loan could not be repaid. With Valachi's financial backing, however, and his ability to keep labor unions from organizing the factory, the business prospered (Maas 1968). Research into loansharking in New York revealed that collection rarely involves violence or even the threat of violence: "Loan sharks are interested in making credit assessments in the manner of legitimate lenders. Often they secure collateral for the loan, though it may be in an illiquid form. Sometimes a borrower will have to produce a guarantee. In many cases the loan is very short term, less than a month, and collection is simply not an issue. Repeat business is the backbone of those operations we have studied. A good faith effort to make payments will probably guarantee the borrower against harassment,

particularly if he has made substantial payment of interest before he starts to have repayment problems" (Rubinstein and Reuter 1978b: Appendix 4).

There are two basic types of usurious loan: the *knockdown* and the *vig*. The knockdown requires a specified schedule of repayment, including both principal and interest. For example, $1,000 might be repaid in fourteen weekly installments of $100. The vig is a "six-for-five" loan: for every $5 borrowed on Monday, $6 is due on the following Monday. The $1 interest is called *vigorish* or *juice*, and loansharking is frequently referred to as the "juice racket." If total repayment of the vig loan, principal plus interest, is not forthcoming on the date it is due, the borrower must pay the interest, and the interest is compounded for the following week. Thus, for example, a loan of $100 requires repayment of $120 seven days later. If this is not possible, the borrower must pay the vig, $20, and this does not count against the principal or the next week's interest. The debt on an original loan of $100 will increase to $120 after one week, to $144 after two weeks, to $172.80 after three weeks, to $207.36 after four weeks, and so on.

The insidious nature of the vig loan is that the borrower must keep paying interest until the principal plus the accumulated interest is repaid at one time. It is quite easy for the original loan to be repaid many times without actually decreasing the principal owed. The loan shark is primarily interested in a steady income and is quite willing to let the principal remain outstanding for an indefinite period.

THEFT AND FENCING

Members of *Cosa Nostra* do not usually engage directly in theft, burglary, or robbery, although many have criminal records for such activities that typically precede their entry into organized crime. However, members will provide information and financing, arrange for necessary firearms or stolen cars, and help link up criminals to carry out more predatory crimes such as payroll robberies, large-scale commercial burglaries, hijackings, and thefts of stocks and bonds. They will finance frauds, swindles, and any conventional criminal activity that can bring in a profit substantial enough to make the effort worthwhile. *Cosa Nostra* members will help market stolen merchandise such as securities, checks, and credit cards. Members of organized crime are in a unique position to provide these services. Their widespread connections to both legitimate and illegitimate outlets provide a link between conventional criminals and the business world. Organized crime serves as a catalyst for a great deal of "disorganized" crime. In 1997, for example, an FBI sting resulted in the videotaping of members and associates of a Gambino Family crew in Canarsie, Brooklyn, disposing of $6 million worth of stolen merchandise, much of it hijacked over a two-year period (Raab 1997b).

Stolen Securities

The late 1960s and early 1970s saw a dramatic increase in the volume of securities being traded, which provided a lucrative source of income for organized crime. Because of the large volume of trade, security grew lax. Paperwork began to back up, and brokerage houses and banks were frequently totally unaware that hundreds of thousands of dollars worth of securities were being taken from their vaults. Thus, the securities were not even reported as missing for several months. The securities industry employs a great many persons—clerks, runners—whose pay is relatively low. Employees with gambling or loan shark debts or those merely seeking to supplement their incomes found a ready market for such "paper." All that was needed was an organized crime connection. In some cases, armed robbery or "give ups" (faked robberies) of messengers were used.

Although many people may have access to valuable securities, few can put stolen securities to immediate use. Organized crime groups serve as the intermediate link in the criminal enterprise. Bookmakers and loan sharks who may have exerted the pressure that induced the thief to take the securities frequently serve as the conduit by which the stolen securities get into the hands of other organized crime figures. Passing through the network of organized crime, the stolen securities will eventually reach the hands of someone

who does have the expertise, the capital, and the personnel to effect a profitable disposition.

The bull market of the late 1990s led to another addition to the dynamic repertoire of organized crime, the "pump and dump." High-ranking members of the Bonanno and Genovese Families cooperated in a scheme that duped investors in seven states of millions of dollars. The crime Family members bribed a group of brokers to use high-pressure tactics to sell shares of stock owned by the conspirators, who then dumped the inflated securities before the prices plummeted. In 1999, several members of the conspiracy were sentenced to imprisonment for their role in the scheme (Weiser 1999).

Fencing

The fence provides a readily available outlet for marketing stolen ("hot") merchandise. He thus provides an incentive for thieves and may also organize, finance, and direct their operations. In her research on fences, Walsh (1977: 13) found that about 13 percent of the fences she studied were part of organized crime. "For these individuals fencing appeared to be just another enterprise in a varied and totally illegal business portfolio." In addition to fencing, she notes, these persons were active in loansharking and gambling, and some were enforcers. In the Genovese Family, for example, Anthony ("Figgy") Ficcorata (or Ficcarata) forced jewel thieves to deal only with certain fences, from whom Ficcorata would receive a commission (Abadinsky 1983). In Chicago, eight "independent" burglars "were murdered for refusing to dispose of their loot through syndicate-connected fences" (Nicodemus and Petacque 1981: 5). Because of his connection with criminals and (otherwise) legitimate businessmen, the wiseguy is in a unique position to arrange for the disposition of stolen goods.

THE BUSINESS OF SEX

Organized crime's involvement in sex as a business has changed with the times. House prostitution (whorehouses or bordellos) was an important social phenomenon during the days of large-scale immigration; immigrants were most often unattached males, single or traveling without their wives (Light 1977). Commercial sex, usually confined to infamous vice ("red light") districts in urban areas, was a target of social and religious reformers. The campaign against this activity became known as the war on the "white slavery" trade, which at the turn of the century was an international problem. In a book entitled *War on the White Slave Trade* (Bell 1909: 48), Edwin W. Sims, U.S. attorney for Chicago, states: "The recent examination of more than two hundred 'white slaves' by the office of the United States district attorney at Chicago has brought to light the fact that literally thousands of innocent girls from the country districts are every year entrapped into a life of hopeless slavery and degradation because parents in the country do not understand conditions as they exist and how to protect their daughters from the 'white slave' traders who have reduced the art of ruining young girls to a national and international system."

In 1904, an international treaty was signed in Paris by all of the governments of Western Europe and Russia. The respective governments, as the treaty preamble states, were "desirous to assure to women who have attained their majority and are subjected to deception or constraint, as well as minor women and girls, an efficacious protection against the criminal traffic known under the name of trade in white women (*Traite des Blanches*)."[8] The U.S. Senate ratified the treaty in 1908. In 1910, the "White Slave Act," called the Mann Act after its sponsor, Congressman James R. Mann of Illinois, prohibited the interstate transportation of women "for the purpose of prostitution, or debauchery or for any other immoral purpose." Nevertheless, the practice flourished.

In the United States, there was an elaborate system for procuring and transporting women between New York, Milwaukee, St. Louis, and Chicago (Landesco 1968). The constant transfer of women provided "new faces" and was good for business. The syndicates that dominated the trade included one headed by Big Jim Colosimo and Johnny Torrio in Chicago. Madams opened brothels, attracted prostitutes and customers, and secured protection from the police. The most famous of these establishments was owned and operated by the Everleigh sisters, who left their brutal husbands in Kentucky and traveled to the Windy City at the turn of the century. In 1900, the two sisters opened the lavish Everleigh Club in the downtown area. Despite the high cost of political protection, the establishment netted $10,000 a month. The club was closed in a flush of reform in 1911 (Washburn 1934). The madam also acted as a "housemother," preventing quarrels and providing advice; she was both friend and employer: "Her work made it almost inevitable that she would assume traditionally maternal functions" (Winick and Kinsie 1971: 98).

Organized crime's interest in prostitution waned during Prohibition because money could be made more easily in bootlegging. With Prohibition drawing to a close, and with the advent of the Great Depression, organized crime groups began looking for new areas of income. In many cities they "organized" independent brothels: The madams were forced to pay organized crime middlemen for protection from the police and from violence. Gangsters such as David ("Little Davey") Betillo, a member of the Luciano crime Family, organized previously independent brothels in New York, which, as noted in Chapter 4, eventually resulted in Luciano's imprisonment.

The normalization of the gender ratio—immigrants were predominantly male—and changes in sexual mores led to a reduction in the importance of house prostitution. The brothel industry reached its peak in 1939. During World War II, and more significantly after 1945, the importance of brothels as a source of income for organized crime steadily declined but did not entirely disappear (Winick and Kinsie 1971). Organized crime members may organize or finance or be involved in an extortionate relationship with the proprietors of commercial sex establishments, ranging from brothels to bars that feature sexually explicit entertainment. In some of the Chicago

---

[8]Later we will look at criminal organizations involved in global trade in sex workers, a situation paralleling that which led to the Paris treaty of 1904.

suburbs, such establishments pay "street taxes" to the Outfit for the privilege of operating. And there is also pornography.

The pornography business, like prostitution, suffers from a great deal of "amateur" involvement. Pornography, which at one time was under the almost exclusive control of organized crime, is widely available throughout the United States. Liberal court decisions have virtually legalized the genre and legitimate entrepreneurs have entered the market. Organized crime involvement today may simply be parasitic—extorting "protection" money. In Los Angeles, the entire hierarchy of the Dragna crime Family was convicted of, among other crimes, extorting money from the owners of porn shops. Because they were no longer illegitimate entrepreneurs, porn operators in Los Angeles were able to go to the authorities and complain about the extortion attempt.

TRAFFICKING IN PERSONS

Trafficking in persons includes two broad categories: indenture of undocumented workers who are brought into bonded servitude; and trade in persons for the commercial sex industry. Both often involve the manipulation of persons with promises of legitimate employment. As Phil Williams (2006: 1) points out, "one of the most pernicious and demeaning aspects of trafficking in women and children is that it reduces people to the status of commodities."

Central to the trade is the "principle of captivity, applied upon arrival, through seizure of travel documents such as passports and tickets of the trafficked person" (Truong 2003: 62). Wages may be withheld until the employer recovers an advance and the victim is without papers or funds. Trafficking organizations operate through a specialized network of persons— recruitment, passage, documents, workplace—and those at the front end may not even know those at the receiving end (Truong 2003). Trafficking differs from alien smuggling, which seeks short-term gain by aiding undocumented persons to gain entry to a country—the relationship with the smuggler ends when the alien reaches his or her destination; human trafficking seeks a continuing exploitive relationship. "Buying women who are trafficked is a limited once off investment; the sale of their services continues to generate profits long after the initial outlays have been covered" (Williams 2006: 7).

Debt is one of the most common means of control. A woman must pay her expenses from future earnings, and the debt is passed from one trafficker to the next until she ends up in the destination country. Inflated housing and living expenses soon leave the victim unable to pay off the debt. Her earnings are taken and the woman becomes

"One of the most striking aspects of this business is the parallels with 'the white slave trade' at the end of the nineteenth century and the beginning of the twentieth. Then, as now, Russia and Ukraine were among the major source countries, while Western Europe, the United States and Turkey were among the major destination countries. Then the trade was facilitated by the expansion of railways, the steamship, and the telegraph; now it is facilitated by airline travel, by the mass mobility of people and by global communications systems such as the telephone and the Internet" (Williams 2006: 1).

totally dependent on her exploiters because she has no financial means to escape. It is also normal to confiscate passports and travel papers. In most European countries, it is almost impossible for the victims to avoid immediate deportation, and that effectively prevents the women from approaching the authorities even in the most aggravated cases of abuse (Lehti and Aromaa 2003).

Trafficking in persons "is a form of modern-day slavery" (Women's Bureau 2002: 1). Trafficking organizations prey on individuals who are poor, often women who are lured with false promises of good jobs and better lives and, instead, are forced to work under brutal conditions. Under federal law, the technical term is "severe forms of trafficking in persons." In the United States, the government estimates that approximately 50,000 women and children are trafficked annually. In Europe, the victims of human trafficking are not only from the most economically deprived and socially and politically unstable areas, but also typically belong to the most disadvantaged social and economic groups in these areas (Lehti and Aromaa 2003).

Child sex tourism (CST) is a dark side of globalization, with some two million children exploited in the global commercial sex trade. CST involves people who travel from their own country to another to engage in commercial sex acts with children. Tourists typically travel to developing countries looking for anonymity and the availability of children in prostitution. The crime is typically fueled by weak law enforcement, corruption, and poverty in many tourist destinations and, increasingly, technology that facilitates this predatory behavior.

The explosion of the Internet and the growing use of digital cameras and cell phone cameras have given perpetrators additional tools to victimize children. Predators are going online to share stories, trade child pornography, and plan sex tours. Sex tourists use chat rooms, message boards, peer-to-peer file-sharing servers, news groups, and specialized websites to obtain information on potential destinations. One disturbing activity is the establishment of "cyber-sex" dens where some children may be sexually abused by a foreign pedophile and the images beamed via a webcam to the Internet. Payment to watch these live "shows" is often made by a credit card via an Internet connection (U.S. Department of State information).

While human trafficking can be accomplished by individual amateurs or small "mom and pop" operations, the involvement of transnational criminal organizations may simply be part of their broad business portfolio, for example, the Moscow-based *Solntsevo* discussed in Chapter 10, the Mafia, Camorra, *'Ndrangheta*, and *Sacra Corona Unita* of southern Italy, Albanian clans, and Japan's *yakuza* (Williams 2006). International trafficking in women for the sex industry has been a characteristic of modern transnational organized crime. In the states of the former Soviet Union and the volatile Balkans region, women are recruited for lawful foreign employment only to find themselves in the hands of criminals who force them into the sex trade (Hughes and Denisova 2001). As part of a nefarious web that spreads across the Balkans and into Western Europe, "tens of thousands of women have been caught up by the traffickers and have suffered rape, extreme violence and slavery at the hands of criminal groups renowned for their brutality and greed" (Gall 2001: 1). Even traditional enemies such as Albanians and Slavs readily deal with one another in this trade. Women are recruited through ads in newspapers, magazines, and the Internet offering employment as dancers, waitresses, maids, and babysitters in nonspecified western countries.

Many countries grant "artistic" or "entertainer" visas that facilitate the movement and exploitation of trafficking victims. Women are granted these temporary visas upon presentation of a work contract or offer of engagement by a club owner, proof of financial resources, and/or medical test results. Employment agencies, often licensed under the laws of the origin and destination countries, play a key role in the deception and recruitment of these women. On arrival at their destination, victims are stripped of their passports and travel documents and forced into situations of sexual exploitation or bonded servitude. Having overstayed or otherwise violated the terms of the visa, victims are coerced by their exploiters with threats to turn them over to immigration authorities (U.S. Department of State 2004). Turkey, where prostitution is legal, has lax visa requirements and a growing sex trade in Slavic women from the former Soviet Union (C. Smith 2005).

People in the Balkans find it inherently attractive to travel abroad, and although the women in general are aware that the offers for certain types of work abroad in reality means prostitution, a nonspecified number of women are nevertheless misled. The women who are aware that they are going to work as prostitutes consider present living conditions and earning potential as considerably poorer than the prospects held out to them by the sex trade (Task-Force on Organized Crime in the Baltic Sea Region 2001). Thus, even in the absence of deception and physical coercion, "trafficking must be seen as part of the world-wide feminization of poverty and of labour migration. When women are structurally denied access to the formal and regulated labour market, they are increasingly pushed into unprotected or criminalized labour markets, such as sexual and exploitive domestic work" (International Organization for Migration 1998: 14). And at the center of this

exploitation is organized crime. In the Ukraine, for example, the highly organized criminal networks that traffic in women "are also involved in other criminal activities. They traffic drugs, stolen cars, and guns; conduct robberies; and are frequently involved in murders or contract killings" (Hughes and Denisova 2001: 47).

In Southern and Eastern Europe kidnapping is rare, and traffickers instead exploit the desire to emigrate for well-paying employment: "At recruitment, traffickers generally promise traditionally female service sector jobs, such as waitress, salesperson, domestic worker and au pair/babysitter. However, recruiters also often adapt to the local labour market, promising work similar to that offered by legal agencies, thereby deflecting suspicion." They frequently "use contracts and legal documentation as a means of deflecting concerns about trafficking and masking the intended exploitation" (Surtees 2008: 50, 51). In Albania, women are frequently recruited through promises of marriage that never materialize. Traffickers often use legal travel documents to move victims who do not realize the real purpose of their trips. The documents are subsequently confiscated, making it difficult for the victim to escape (Surtees 2008).

Human trafficking is a serious problem in Myanmar, where transnational criminal organizations and the country's ruling military junta are at the center of the trade. About 27 percent of Myanmar's population lives below the poverty line, making the country one of the poorest in Southeast Asia. Many victims of transnational crime in Myanmar are the poor, becoming commodities themselves as they are trafficked to be child soldiers for the junta or slaves for sexual exploitation. Junta officials are directly involved in trafficking for forced labor and the unlawful conscription of child soldiers. Women and girls, especially those of ethnic minority groups and those among the thousands of refugees along Myanmar's borders, are trafficked for sexual exploitation in urban centers and commercial centers, truck stops, border towns, and mining and military camps (Wyler 2007).

In West Africa, Nigerians have been at the center of a flourishing trade in prostitutes who are sent to Europe, especially Italy, and the Middle

East. Organizers are often women, sometimes former prostitutes themselves, who have succeeded in making money and graduating to the status of madams, although they depend on men for forging travel documents and escorting the girls to their destination. Many girls initiated into prostitution are obliged to undergo quasi-traditional religious rituals that bind them to secrecy, before being provided with forged papers and sent abroad, often via other West African countries. They may be initiated into their new trade through rape and other violence.

Successful madams organize the recruitment of prostitutes in West Africa, often on the pretext that they will find jobs in agriculture or the hotel business in Europe, and procure false or forged travel documents. They bribe immigration officials, both in Nigeria and in transit countries. The madam has a network of operators of hotels or hostels and guides, referred to as "trolleys"; she will use fetish priests, who administer an oath of secrecy on prospective prostitutes, and lawyers who can draft agreements binding a prostitute to a madam. Typically, a madam will claim to have invested $40,000 to $50,000 for the costs of travel to Europe, and the prostitute is required to repay that money (United Nations Office on Drugs and Crime 2005).

ARMS TRAFFICKING

"The extent and type of weaponry currently available to terrorists, insurgents, and other criminals are enormous. These groups have exploited and developed local, regional, and global supply channels to traffic in munitions and equipment worldwide. Their access to weaponry is facilitated through covert transfers by governments and by legal and quasi-legal commercial dealers, outright black-market sales, and the theft or diversion of both state-owned and privately owned arms and weapons stores" (Cragin and Hoffman 2003: iii).

There are two basic explanations for the affinity of organized crime for arms trafficking: They have already established routes for drug and human trafficking, and the obvious need for firearms.

Thus, "parallel to, and closely associated with illicit arms trafficking, is increasing trafficking in drugs, people and other contraband, as organised criminal gangs employ the same routes and partnerships to smuggle various illicit commodities across Europe" (Davis, Hirst, and Mariani 2001: 5). The movement of drugs and arms is often connected or overlapping (Curtis and Karacan 2002). The vessels and vehicles that deliver arms can carry drugs on their return. While arms smuggling often involves institutions and individuals who are not parts of criminal organizations—national defense ministries, national security agencies, banks, legitimate arms dealers—both terrorist and organized crime groups are active participants. Organized crime groups often act as middlemen facilitating the illegal trade in arms.

The dissolution of the Soviet Union and the Warsaw Pact left vast stockpiles of arms. Ineffective inventory monitoring, export controls, and official corruption have made such stockpiles available to arms traffickers, helping to fuel armed conflict in the Caucasus and nearby Balkans. This has served to attract established criminal organizations looking to take advantage of the profits to be made in arms trafficking. Russian and Italian criminal organizations have operated in the midst of the conflicts in the former Yugoslavia, and weapons from Balkans have been used by terrorist organizations such as the Basque Fatherland and Liberty organization (ETA) and the Real Irish Republican Army (Curtis and Karacan 2002; Davis, Hirst, and Mariani 2001).

During the Cold War governments on both sides of the Iron Curtain used private arms brokers to facilitate covert arms deals. With the end of the Cold War, these brokers remained in the arms business in the void of communist or democratic ideologies. They continue to use their existing networks that also serve to move drugs, diamonds, and other valuable commodities. To facilitate their enterprises, these brokers use legitimate or counterfeit documents and develop corrupt ties with government officials. They often disguise arms shipments as humanitarian aid and use circuitous routes through "friendly" transshipment countries (Stohl 2005).

"Terrorist groups from other parts of the world, especially Asia and Africa, have obtained significant armaments from traffickers based in Western Europe or using Western Europe as part of the delivery route" (Curtis and Karacan 2002: 6). Turkish/Kurdish groups, criminal and terrorist—there is often overlap—have been part of a drugs-for-arms trade in Europe. Drugs from the Golden Crescent are exchanged for arms that remain part of the group's arsenal or are trafficked again: "Although illegal trafficking in arms frequently coexists with illegal trafficking in narcotics, the two activities do not necessarily have a symbiotic relationship; rather, conditions that promote one type of trafficking very often promote the other. Thus organized crime groups in Italy, Albania, and the former Yugoslavia trade in both types of commodity, taking advantage of available resources as well as favorable conditions. Often, narcotics and arms are items of exchange in a complex deal that involves third and fourth parties," and the exchange may also include diamonds and ivory (Curtis and Karacan 2002: 21).

In Latin America, arms dealers have been attracted to areas of conflict such as Nicaragua, El Salvador, Guatemala, and, of course, Colombia. Arms are stolen from military supplies and production facilities and moved into the black market. The tri-border area discussed in Chapter 1 is a source of illegal weapons. Vast stockpiles of arms have their origins in the Cold War, supplied by the United States and the Soviet Union to proxy combatants (Cragin and Hoffman 2003).

While the United States and Russia had dominated the small-arms market, this is no longer true. Indeed, most law enforcement officers in the United States are armed with foreign-made weapons, mostly Glock, but also Walther, Beretta, and Sig Sauer. Governments in Africa, Asia, and Latin America frequently manufacture their own small arms for security forces and also sell them to both legitimate merchants and less scrupulous "merchants of death" who can camouflage their enterprises within the network of legitimate arms trading (Cragin and Hoffman 2003).

In 2008, Thai authorities arrested a former Russian air force major who was the inspiration for the 2005 Nicholas Gage motion picture *Lord of War*. Victor Bout, 40, was the successful target of a U.S. Drug Enforcement Administration sting operation during which he offered an enormous supply of arms to undercover agents he believed to be representatives of Colombia's FARC guerillas. With his own airline, Bout supplied arms to, among other groups, the Taliban. This made him a high-priority target for the United States to which he was subsequently extradited.

That same year, international arms dealer Monzer al Kassar ("Abu Munawar," "El Taous") was extradited from Spain to New York to face federal terrorism charges. He is accused of offering to provide military weapons to the FARC in Colombia. According to the U.S. Drug Enforcement Administration (DEA), al Kassar developed an international network of criminal associates as well as front companies and bank accounts in various countries. He engaged in money-laundering transactions in bank accounts throughout the world to disguise the nature of his proceeds (DEA press release, June 13, 2008).

The problem of illicit arms trafficking is complicated by the ambivalent position of the United States, a prominent supplier of small arms to volatile regions. "In doing so, it has at times bought and transported arms through the same gray networks and dealers that in Europe have been accused of illegal trafficking" (Chivers 2008b: 5).

SUMMARY

- The business of organized crime often includes activities that are neither "goods" nor "services" but are clearly parasitic, although the boundary between providing a good or a service and being parasitic is not clearly delineated.
- Organized crime may limit competition and provide collection and/or arbitration services in return for tribute.
- Bookmakers and numbers operators act as brokers between bettors and may need to lay off bets that are unbalanced—organized crime often provides a layoff service.

- Gambling, usually numbers and sports book-making, is attractive to organized crime because penalties are relatively light as compared with drug trafficking.
- Technology, such as cell phones and the Internet, has made it harder for law enforcement to act against unlicensed operators, and widespread legalized gambling has increased the number of persons who gamble.
- Many prefer illegal gambling operations because they do not report winnings to tax authorities and offer credit.
- Although numbers operators may use the numbers of the legal lottery, they are able to offer better odds to bettors.
- Though Las Vegas has been able to rid its casinos of organized crime, and Atlantic City has been able to keep them out, organized crime still has influence in related and peripheral industries such as unions, hotel supplies, and loansharking. There is also organized crime control over miscellaneous gambling such as poker machines.

- After Prohibition, criminals were cash-rich in a depressed economy, so loansharking was a natural avenue for them—and they had the means to collect on usurious debts.
- Although they do not usually engage directly in theft, burglary, or robbery, organized crime members will provide information and arrangements for criminals to carry out more predatory crimes. They will finance frauds and swindles, and will help market stolen merchandise.
- Organized crime's involvement in sex as a moneymaker has changed with the times. Today they are more likely to be involved in Internet sex—cramming—than providing pornography, which is such a competitive industry.
- A related business involves the procuring of women from overseas for the sex industry; these women are often tricked by offers of legitimate employment.
- Much as they traffic in persons, criminal organizations are often part of the vast illegal trade in arms, often part of a nexus between terrorism and organized crime, and sometimes part of a "dope-for-guns" arrangement.

REVIEW QUESTIONS

1. In addition to providing "goods and services" that happen to be illegal, what important criminal activity is part of the business of organized crime? How does this activity operate?
2. How does the concept of *rispetto* enable a member of organized crime to act as an arbitrator?
3. Why is it often important for a professional criminal to have ties to organized crime?
4. How can traditional organized crime act as a catalyst for a great deal of conventional crime?
5. What are the various roles of organized crime in bookmaking?
6. In sports betting, what is the "line"?
7. What was the role of organized crime in Las Vegas?
8. What factors led to the heavy involvement of organized crime in loansharking?
9. Why has organized crime involvement in the sex industry in the United States waned in recent years?
10. What is the nature of the international trade in women for the sex industry?
11. What is the connection between trafficking in arms and trafficking in drugs?

CHAPTER
13

The Drug Business

To fully appreciate the relationship between drug trafficking and organized crime, it is necessary to examine the history of how drug trafficking, like bootlegging during the Prohibition era, became an important criminal enterprise. Concern about opium products, morphine and heroin led to the most important piece of drug legislation, the Harrison Act, so our historical review will center on that substance. We will then move to other drugs, in particular, cocaine.

HISTORICAL BACKGROUND

The earliest "war against drugs" in the United States was in response to opium, an analgesic (pain reliever) and central nervous system depressant that can provide relief from stress. Its source is the *Papaver somniferum*, or opium poppy, of which there are many species. There is some dispute about when opium was first used. Wherever the poppy plant is found, the young leaves have been used as potherbs and in salads; its small, oily seeds are high in nutritional value. The seeds can be eaten; they can be pressed to release an edible oil, baked into cakes, and ground into flour, and the oil may be burned in lamps. As a source of vegetal fat, "the seed oil could have been a major factor attracting early human groups to the opium poppy" (Merlin 1984: 89). Wherever it was found, opium was used both medicinally and recreationally.

Explaining the popularity of opium is easy when we realize that the chief end of medicine until the beginning of the nineteenth century was to relieve pain and therapeutic agents were directed at symptoms rather than at causes. Therefore, "it is not difficult to understand the wide popularity of a drug which either singly or combined so eminently was suited to the needs of so many medical situations" (Terry and Pellens 1928: 58). At a time when the practice of medicine was quite primitive, opium became the essential ingredient in innumerable remedies dispensed in Europe and America for the treatment of diarrhea, dysentery, asthma, rheumatism, diabetes, malaria, cholera, fevers, bronchitis, insomnia, and pain of any kind (Fay 1975).

As the primary ingredient in many "patent" medicines—actually, secret formulas that carried no patent at all—opiates were readily available in the United States until 1914. Doctors and others prescribed them for general symptoms as well as for specific diseases. The smoking of opium was popularized by Chinese immigrants who brought the habit with them to California, which became part of the United States in 1848. During the latter part of the nineteenth and early twentieth centuries, Chinese in the United States also operated commercial "opium dens" that often attracted the attention of the police not because of the use of drugs but because they became gathering places for criminals.

Around the turn of the eighteenth century, a German pharmacist poured liquid ammonia over opium and obtained an alkaloid, a white powder that he found to be many times more powerful than opium. He named the substance *morphium* after Morpheus, the Greek god of sleep and dreams. Ten parts of opium can be refined into one part of morphine (Bresler 1980). It was not until 1817, however, that the publication of articles in scientific journals popularized the new drug, resulting in its widespread use by doctors. Quite incorrectly, as it turned out, the medical profession viewed morphine as an opiate without negative side effects.

By the 1850s, morphine tablets and a variety of morphine products were readily available without prescription. In 1856, the hypodermic method of injecting morphine directly into the bloodstream was introduced to American medicine. The popularity of morphine rose dramatically during the Civil War when it was used intravenously in an indiscriminate manner to treat battlefield casualties (Terry and Pellens 1928). Following the war, the increase in morphine use was so marked among ex-soldiers as to give rise to the term *army disease*. "Medical journals were replete with glowing descriptions of the effectiveness of the drug during wartime and its obvious advantages for peacetime medical practice" (Cloyd 1982: 21). Hypodermic kits became widely available, and the use of unsterile needles by many doctors and laypersons led to abscesses or disease (Morgan 1981).

In the 1870s, morphine was exceedingly cheap, cheaper than alcohol. Pharmacies and general stores carried preparations that appealed to a wide segment of the population. Physicians commonly prescribed morphine for any complaint, from a toothache to consumption (Latimer and Goldberg 1981), and widely abused the substances themselves. Until the late 1870s, the concept of addiction was not widely known or understood (Morgan 1981). Although it eventually became associated with the underworld elements of urban America, morphine abuse in the latter part of the nineteenth century was apparently most prevalent in rural areas (Terry and Pellens 1928). At the turn of the twentieth century, diacetylmorphine was synthesized, creating the most powerful of the opiates—*heroin*—marketed as a non-habit-forming analgesic to take the place of morphine (Bresler 1980; Nelson et al. 1982). Opiates, including morphine and heroin, were readily available in the United States until 1914. In 1900 alone, 628,177 pounds of opiates were imported into the United States (Bonnie and Whitebread 1970). Morphine, albeit highly regulated, is available in the United States for the treatment of chronic pain. It is essential for treating traumatic battlefield injuries.

China and the Opium Wars

The American response to drugs in the twentieth century is directly related to international affairs and trade with China. Until the sixteenth century, China was a military power whose naval fleet surpassed any that the world had ever known. A power struggle ultimately led to a regime dominated by Confucian scholars. In 1525, they ordered the destruction of all oceangoing ships and set China on a course that would lead to poverty, defeat, and decline (Kristof 1999). In 1626, a British warship appeared off China and its captain bombarded Canton. In response to the danger posed by British ships, the emperor opened the city of Canton to trade.

The British East India Company enjoyed a government-granted monopoly over the China trade. Shipments of tea to England were particularly important. By the 1820s a trade imbalance existed between England and China. Although the British consumer had an insatiable appetite for Chinese tea, the Chinese desired few English goods. The exception was opium (Beeching 1975). Poppy cultivation had been an important source of revenue for the Mughal emperors (Muslim rulers of India, 1526–1857). When the Mughal empire fell apart, the British East India Company salvaged and improved upon the system of state control of opium. In addition to controlling the domestic market, the British supplied Indian opium to China.

Opium was first prohibited by the Chinese government in 1729, a time when only small amounts of the substance were reaching China. Ninety years earlier, tobacco had been similarly banned as a pernicious foreign good. Opium use was strongly condemned in China as a violation of Confucian principles, and for many years the imperial decree against opium was supported by the population (Beeching 1975). In 1782, an attempt by a British merchant ship to sell 1,601 chests of opium resulted in a total loss, for no purchasers could be found. By 1799, however, a growing traffic in opium led to an imperial decree banning the trade.

The ban was not successful (official corruption was endemic in China). As consumption of imported opium increased and the method of ingestion shifted from eating to smoking, official declarations against opium increased, as did smuggling. "When opium left Calcutta, stored in the holds of country ships and consigned to agents in Canton, it was an entirely legitimate article. It remained an entirely legitimate article all the way up to the China Sea. But the instant it reached the coast of China, it became something different. It became contraband" (Fay 1975: 45).

Opium provided the British with the silver needed to buy tea. Because opium was illegal in China, however, its importation—smuggling— brought China no tariff revenue. Before 1830, opium was transported to the coast of China, where it was offloaded and smuggled inland by the Chinese themselves. The outlawing of opium by the Chinese government led to the development of an organized underworld. Gangs became secret societies—Triads (discussed in Chapter 9)—that continue to smuggle heroin to destinations all over the world (Latimer and Goldberg 1981). The armed British opium ships were safe from Chinese government intervention, and the British were able to remain aloof from the actual smuggling.

In the 1830s the shippers grew bolder, entering Chinese territorial waters with their opium cargo. The British East India Company, now in competition with other opium merchants, sought to flood China with cheap opium and drive out the competition (Beeching 1975). In 1837, the emperor ordered his officials to move against opium smugglers, but the campaign was a failure, and the smugglers grew even bolder. In 1839, in a dramatic move, Chinese authorities laid siege to the port city of Canton, confiscating and destroying all opium waiting offloading from foreign ships. The merchants agreed to stop importing opium into China, and the siege was lifted. The British merchants petitioned the Crown for compensation and retribution. The reigning parliamentary Whig majority, however, was very weak, and compensating opium merchants was not politically or financially feasible. Instead, the cabinet, without Parliament's approval, decided to wage a war that would result in the seizure of Chinese property (Fay 1975).

In 1840, a British expedition attacked the poorly armed and organized Chinese forces. The emperor was forced to pay $6 million for the opium his officials had seized and $12 million as compensation for the war, and Hong Kong became a crown colony. Opium was not mentioned in the peace (surrender) treaty, but the trade resumed with new vigor. By the mid-1840s, in a remarkable reversal of the balance of trade, China had a significant opium debt (Latimer and Goldberg 1981). In the wake of the First Opium War, China was laid open to extensive missionary efforts by Protestant evangelicals, who, although they opposed the opium trade, viewed saving souls as their primary goal. Christianity, they believed, would save China from opium (Fay 1975).

The Second Opium War began in 1856, when the balance of payments once again favored China. A minor incident between the British and Chinese governments was used as an excuse to force China into making further treaty concessions. This time, the foreign powers seeking to exploit a militarily weak China included the French, Russians, and the Americans. Canton was sacked, and a combined fleet of British and French warships sailed right up the Grand Canal to Peking and proceeded to sack and burn the imperial summer palace. The emperor was forced to indemnify the British in an amount more than enough to offset the balance of trade that had actually caused the war. A commission was appointed to legalize and regulate the opium trade (Latimer and Goldberg 1981). In the 1870s, the British opium monopoly in China was challenged by opium imported from Persia and cultivated in China itself. Because British colonial authorities were heavily dependent on a profitable opium trade, they increased the output of Indian opium. This caused a decline in prices, driving the competition out of business. This oversupply resulted in an increase in the amount of opium entering the United States for the Chinese population.

The "Chinese Problem" and the American Response

Chinese workers were originally encouraged to emigrate to the United States in 1848 to labor in the gold mines, doing the dangerous work refused by most white men, such as blasting shafts, putting beams in place, and laying track lines in the mines. Chinese immigrants also helped build the Western railroad lines at "coolie wages"—pay few whites would accept. After their work was completed, the Chinese were often banned from the area. By the 1860s they were clustering in Pacific Coast cities, where they established Chinatowns—and smoked opium.

In 1883, Congress raised the tariff on the importation of smoking-grade opium. In 1887, Congress responded to obligations imposed on the United States by a Chinese American commercial treaty by banning the importation of smoking opium by Chinese subjects. Americans were still permitted to import the substance, and many did so, selling it to both Chinese and U.S. citizens (PCOC 1986a). The typical American opiate addict during the nineteenth century was a middle-aged white woman of the middle or upper class (Courtwright 1982). Compared with the Chinese, however, this addict did not smoke opium but rather ingested it as medicine. During

the nineteenth century, opiates were not associated in the public mind with crime. While opium use may have been frowned upon by some as immoral, employees were not fired for addiction. Children were not taken from their homes and lodged in foster homes or institutions because one or both parents were addicted. "Addicts continued to participate fully in the life of the community. Thus, the nineteenth century avoided one of the most disastrous effects of current narcotic laws and attitudes—the rise of a deviant addict subculture, cut off from respectable society and without a 'road back' to respectability" (Brecher 1972: 6–7).

Domestic anti-Chinese legislation raised the ire of China against the United States. In an effort to increase American influence in China, and thus improve its trade position, the United States supported the anti-opium efforts of the International Reform Bureau (IRB). A temperance organization representing more than thirty missionary societies in the Far East, the IRB sought a ban on opiates, which was also the position of the Chinese government. In 1901, Congress enacted the Native Races Act, which prohibited the sale of alcohol and opium to "aboriginal tribes and uncivilized races." The provisions of the act were later expanded to include "uncivilized elements" in the United States proper: Indians, Eskimos, and Chinese (Latimer and Goldberg 1981).

In 1898, as a result of the Spanish-American War, the Philippines were ceded to the United States. At the time of Spanish colonialism, opium smoking was widespread among Chinese workers on the islands. The Reverend Charles Henry Brent (1862–1929), a supporter of the IRB, arrived in the Philippines as the Episcopal bishop. His arrival coincided with a cholera epidemic that began in 1902 and that reportedly led to an increase in the use of opium. As a result of his efforts, in 1905 Congress banned the sale of opium to Filipino natives except for medicinal purposes and three years later banned sales to all Philippines residents. "Reformers attributed to drugs much of the appalling poverty, ignorance, and debilitation they encountered in the Orient. Opium was strongly identified with the problems afflicting an apparently moribund China. Eradication of drug abuse was part of America's white man's burden and a way to demonstrate the New World's superiority" (Morgan 1974: 32).

The Reverend Brent proposed the formation of an international opium commission to meet in Shanghai in 1909. This plan was supported by President Theodore Roosevelt, who saw it as a way to assuage Chinese anger at the passage of the Chinese Exclusion Act (Latimer and Goldberg 1981). The International Opium Commission, chaired by Brent and consisting of representatives from thirteen nations, convened in Shanghai on February 1. Brent successfully rallied the conferees around the American position that opium was evil and had no use outside of medical applications. The commission unanimously adopted a number of vague resolutions (Terry and Pellens 1928).

Only the United States and China, however, were eager for future conferences, and strong anti-opium legislative efforts in the United States following the conference were generally unsuccessful. Southerners distrusted federal enforcement, and the drug industry was opposed to any new regulations. Attempts to gain southern support for anti-drug legislation focused on the alleged abuse of cocaine by blacks, which reputedly made them "uncontrollable." On February 14, 1914, a *New York Times* headline screamed: "Negro Cocaine 'Fiends' Are a New Southern Menace." This caused many southern police departments to change from .32 caliber revolvers to more powerful .38 caliber revolvers (Kinder 1992).

A second conference was held in The Hague in 1912, with representatives from the United States, China, and ten other nations. A number of problems stood in the way of an international agreement: Germany wanted to protect her burgeoning pharmaceutical industry and insisted on a unanimous vote before any action could be agreed upon; Portugal insisted on retaining the Macao opium trade; the Dutch demanded to maintain their opium trade in the West Indies; Persia and Russia wanted to continue growing opium poppies. Righteous American appeals to the delegates were rebuffed with allusions to domestic usage and the lack of laws in the United States (Latimer and Goldberg 1981). Nevertheless, the conference

resulted in a patchwork of agreements known as the International Opium Convention, which was ratified by Congress in 1913. The signatories committed themselves to enacting laws designed to suppress the abuse of opium, morphine, and cocaine, as well as any drugs prepared or derived from these substances (PCOC 1986a). In 1914, the Harrison Act, representing the U.S. attempt to carry out the provisions of The Hague Convention, was approved by President Woodrow Wilson.

The Harrison Act

The Harrison Act provided that persons in the business of dealing in drugs covered by the act—including opium derivatives and cocaine—were required to register yearly and to pay a special annual tax of $1. The statute made it illegal to sell or give away opium or opium derivatives and coca or its derivatives without a written order on a form issued by the Commissioner of Internal Revenue. Persons who were not registered were prohibited from engaging in interstate drug trafficking, and anyone who possessed drugs without first registering and paying the tax faced a penalty of as long as five years' imprisonment and a fine of as much as $2,000. Rules promulgated by the Treasury Department permitted only medical professionals to register, and they had to maintain records of the drugs they dispensed. Within the first year, more than 200,000 medical professionals registered, and the small staff of treasury agents could not scrutinize all the prescription records generated (Musto 1973).

Concern over federalism—constitutional limitations on the police powers of the central government—led Congress to use the taxing authority rather than the police authority of the federal government to respond to the problem of drug control. At the turn of the twentieth century, federal authority to regulate narcotics and the prescription practices of physicians was generally thought to be unconstitutional (Musto 1973). In 1919, the use of taxing authority to regulate drugs was upheld by the U.S. Supreme Court in *United States v. Doremus*, 249 U.S. 86.

The Harrison Act was supported by the American Medical Association (AMA), which by that time "was well on its way to consolidation of American medical practitioners" (Musto 1973: 56), and by the American Pharmaceutical Association, which, like the AMA, had grown more powerful and influential in the first two decades of the twentieth century. The medical profession had been granted a monopoly over the dispensing of opiates and cocaine. The Harrison Act also effectively imposed a stamp of illegitimacy on most narcotics use, fostering an image of the degenerate "dope fiend" with immoral proclivities (Bonnie and Whitebread 1970). At this time, there were an estimated 300,000 opiate addicts in the United States (Courtwright 1982).

But the addict population was already changing. The medical profession had, by and large, abandoned its liberal use of opiates. Imports of medicinal opiates declined dramatically during the first decade of the twentieth century. The public mind came to associate heroin with urban vice and crime. Unlike the (often female and) "respectable" opiate addicts of the nineteenth century, opiate users of the twentieth century were increasingly male habitués of pool halls and bowling alleys, denizens of the underworld. As in the case of minority groups, this marginal population was an easy target of drug laws and drug-law enforcement.

The Commissioner of Internal Revenue was in charge of upholding the Harrison Act. In 1915, 162 collectors and agents of the Miscellaneous Division of the Internal Revenue Service were given the responsibility of enforcing drug laws. In 1919, a narcotics division was created within the Bureau of Prohibition, with a staff of 170 agents and an appropriation of $270,000. The narcotics division, however, suffered from its association with the notoriously inept and corrupt Prohibition Bureau and from a corruption scandal of its own: There was "public dissatisfaction with the activities of the Narcotics Division, which was tainted by its association with the country's anti-liquor laws" (PCOC 1986a: 204).

In 1916, the Supreme Court ruled in favor of a physician who had provided maintenance doses of morphine to an addict (*United States v. Jin Fuey Moy*, 241 U.S. 394). Three years later, however, the Court ruled (*Webb v. United States*, 249 U.S. 96) that a prescription for morphine that was issued to an habitual user who was not under a physician's care and that was intended not to cure but to maintain the habit was not a prescription and thus violated the Harrison Act. Private physicians found it impossible to handle the sudden upsurge in their drug clientele: They could do nothing "more than sign prescriptions" (Duster 1970: 16). In *United States v. Behrman* (258 U.S. 280 [1922]), the Court ruled that a physician was not entitled to prescribe large doses of proscribed drugs for self-administration *even if* the addict was under the physician's care. The Court stated: "Prescriptions in the regular course of practice did not include the indiscriminate doling out of narcotics in such quantity as charged in the indictments." In 1925 the Court limited the application of *Behrman* when it found that a physician who had prescribed small doses of drugs for the relief of an addict did not violate the Harrison Act (*Linder v. United States*, 268 U.S. 5).

The powers of the narcotics division were clearly limited to the enforcement of registration and record-keeping regulations. "The large number of addicts who secured their drugs from physicians were excluded from the Division's jurisdiction." Furthermore, the public's attitude toward drug use "had not much changed with the passage of the Act—there was some opposition to drug use, some support of it, and a great many who did not care one way or the other. The Harrison Act was actually passed with very little publicity or news coverage" (Dickson 1977: 39). Richard Bonnie and Charles Whitebread (1970: 976) note similarities between the temperance and anti-narcotics movements. "Both were first directed against the evils of large scale use and only later against all use. Most of the rhetoric was the same: These euphoriants produced crime, pauperism, and insanity." However, "the temperance movement was a matter of vigorous public debate; the antinarcotics movement was not. Temperance legislation was the product of a highly organized nationwide lobby; narcotics legislation was largely ad hoc. Temperance legislation was designed to eradicate known evils resulting from alcohol abuse; narcotics legislation was largely anticipatory."

Writing in 1916, Pearce Bailey (1974: 173–74) noted that the passage of the act spread dismay among heroin addicts. The price of heroin soared 900 percent, and was sold in adulterated form, putting it beyond the easy reach of the majority of users. Beginning in 1918, narcotic clinics opened in almost every major city. Information about them is sketchy (Duster 1970), and there is a great deal of controversy surrounding their operations. While they were never very popular with the general public, most clinics were well run and under medical supervision (Morgan 1981).

Following World War I and the Bolshevik Revolution, xenophobia and prohibitionism began to sweep the nation. The United States severely restricted foreign immigration, and alcohol and drug use were increasingly associated with an alien population. In 1922, federal narcotic agents closed the drug clinics and began to arrest physicians and pharmacists who provided drugs for maintenance. At issue was section eight of the Harrison Act, which permitted the possession of controlled substances if prescribed "in good faith" by a registered physician, dentist, or veterinarian in accord with "professional practice." The law did not define "good faith" or "professional practice." Under a policy developed by the federal narcotics agency, thousands of persons, including many physicians, were charged with violations: "Whether conviction followed or not mattered little as the effects of press publicity dealing with what were supposedly willful violations of a beneficent law were most disastrous to those concerned" (Terry and Pellens 1928: 90). "After this initial burst of arrest activity directed against registrants, the Narcotics Division turned its attention to closing clinics that had been established to conduct research and treat large numbers of addicts who could not afford private care" (PCOC 1986a: 202). They were declared illegal by the drug agency and were closed down (Terry and Pellens 1928).

The medical profession stopped dispensing drugs to addicts, forcing them to look to illicit sources and giving rise to an enormous illegal drug business. Those persons addicted to opium smoking eventually found their favorite drug unavailable—the bulky smoking opium was difficult to smuggle—and they turned to the more readily available heroin, which was prepared for intravenous use (Courtwright 1982). The criminal syndicates that resulted from Prohibition added heroin trafficking to their business portfolios. When Prohibition was repealed in 1933, profits from bootlegging disappeared accordingly, and drug trafficking remained an important source of revenue for organized criminal groups.

THE BUSINESS OF HEROIN

The opium poppy,[1] *Papaver somniferum*, requires a hot, dry climate and very careful cultivation (Wishart 1974). Poppy seeds are scattered across the surface of freshly cultivated fields. Three months later when the poppy is mature, the green stem is topped by a brightly colored flower. Gradually the flower petals fall off leaving a seedpod about the size of a small egg. Incisions are made in the seedpod just after the petals have fallen but before it is fully ripe. A milky-white fluid oozes out and hardens on the surface into a dark brown gum—raw opium. The raw opium is collected by scraping the pod with a flat, dull knife—a labor-intensive process.

The raw opium is dissolved in drums of hot water and lime (calcium oxide). Fertilizer is added, precipitating out organic wastes and leaving morphine suspended near the surface. After residual waste is removed, the morphine is transferred to other drums, where it is heated and mixed with concentrated ammonia. The morphine solidifies and falls to the bottom of the drum where it is filtered out in the form of chunky white kernels. In this form, morphine weighs about one-tenth as much as the original raw opium. To produce 10 kilograms (one kilogram = 2.2046 pounds;

---

[1]Sales of poppy seeds for cultivation, not culinary use—they often appear on bagels—have been illegal in the United States since 1970. The Drug Enforcement Administration has been conducting an ineffectual campaign against the cultivation of the pretty red flower, which looks elegant when dried (Vest 1997).

hereafter kilo) of almost pure heroin, the chemist mixes 10 kilos of morphine and 10 kilos of acetic anhydride and heats it at exactly 185 degrees for six hours, producing an impure form of heroin. Although this step is not complex, it can be dangerous: "If the proportion of morphine to acetic acid is incorrect or the temperature too high or too low the laboratory may be blown up." Acetic acid is also highly corrosive, attacking both skin and lungs (Lamour and Lamberti 1974: 17).

Next, the solution is treated with water and chloroform until the impurities precipitate out. The heroin is drained off into another container, to which sodium carbonate is added until crude heroin particles begin to solidify and drop to the bottom. The particles are filtered out and purified in a solution of alcohol and activated charcoal. This mixture is heated until the alcohol begins to evaporate, leaving granules of almost pure heroin at the bottom. In the final step, the granules are dissolved in alcohol, and ether and hydrochloric acid are added to the solution. Tiny white flakes begin to form. These flakes are filtered out under pressure and dried in a special process, the result being a powder between 80 and 99 percent pure, known as *No. 4 heroin*.

For street sale, the white crystalline powder (the Mexican product contains impurities that give it a thick oily "black tar" or a more refined brown powder color) is typically diluted ("stepped on" or "cut") with any powdery substance that dissolves when heated, such as lactose, quinine, flour, or cornstarch. Until the 1990s, consumer-available heroin prepared for intravenous use usually had a purity of less than 5 percent. In recent years, purity levels of retail heroin sold in parts of New York City have approached 90 percent, revealing that heroin is being subjected to little if any cutting before it reaches the consumer level. Increased purity makes smoking and sniffing feasible. The increased purity and the concern about AIDS caused a shift from injecting to smoking and sniffing among many heroin users. Heroin can be sniffed like cocaine and even smoked. When smoked—"chasing the dragon"—heroin is heated and the fumes inhaled, usually through a small tube.

Like any other business that is international in scope, heroin trafficking requires extensive transportation networks, but since the commodity is illegal, these operate in the shadows of global trade. Consolidation and vertical integration, cherished buzzwords of multinational corporations, are impossible. Instead, drug barons base their operations in remote safe havens, "the more war-torn and chaotic the better" (Brzezinski 2002: 26). Most of the heroin smuggled into the United States originates in such areas where the opium poppy thrives—parts of Asia known as the Golden Triangle, the Golden Crescent, Mexico, and, more recently, Colombia. (See Figure 13.1.)

The Golden Triangle

The Golden Triangle of Southeast Asia encompasses approximately 150,000 square miles of forested highlands, including the western fringe of Laos, the four northern provinces of Thailand, and the northeastern parts of Burma—Burma is the world's second largest producer of opium and accounts for about 90 percent of the total heroin production of the Golden Triangle. A nation slightly smaller than Texas, with a population of more than 47 million, since a coup in 1962, poverty-ridden Burma has been dominated by a repressive military dictatorship—the world's longest-running military regime (Pepper 2008). In 1989 the country changed its name to Myanmar, but brutality against ethnic minorities and collaboration with drug trafficking continued. In 2003, rights organizations and the U.S. State Department accused the Myanmar military of a policy of systematic rape of ethnic minority women (Mydans 2003a). Transnational organized crime groups in Myanmar operate a multibillion-dollar criminal industry that stretches across Southeast Asia. Humans, drugs, wildlife, gems, timber, and other contraband flow through Myanmar where collusion between traffickers and the country's ruling military junta allows organized crime groups to function with virtual impunity and bolsters a regime that fosters a culture of corruption and disrespect for the rule of law and human rights

FIGURE 13.1 *Major Asian Opium Regions*

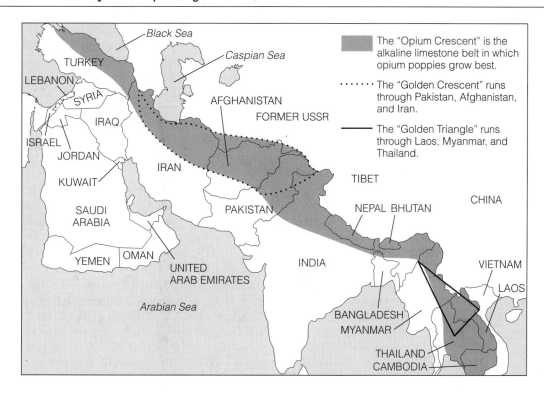

(Wyler 2007). The United States bans all imports from Myanmar.

In 1826, the British introduced opium use into their colony of Burma. In the strongly Buddhist south, use of the drug was considered a violation of religious principles and was not widespread. In the northern Kachin and Shan tribal areas, opium was valued, particularly as a medicine, and its use was acceptable to the mostly non-Buddhist population. The British managed the different ethnic groups in their colony by dividing them into discrete states that, as a result, began to develop aspirations of autonomy. When the colonial regimes retreated, these aspirations intensified (Renard 2003).

French colonial officials in the Golden Triangle used paramilitary organizations and indigenous tribes against various insurgent groups, particularly those following a Marxist ideology. As support for overseas colonies dwindled at home, French officials in Southeast Asia utilized the drug

trade to finance their efforts. The French would buy the raw opium from Hmong tribesmen in Vietnam and provide it to criminal organizations that administered red-light districts in Saigon (today Ho Chi Minh City) and aided in the suppression of Communist opposition to French rule (Schulte-Bockholt 2006). Some Golden Triangle opium was also shipped to Marseilles, where the Corsican underworld processed it into heroin for distribution in the United States—the "French Connection." The French withdrew from Southeast Asia in 1955, and several years later the United States took up the struggle against Marxist groups—the Vietnam War is part of this legacy. The U.S. Central Intelligence Agency (CIA) waged its own clandestine war and, again, heroin played a role, for many of the indigenous tribal groups recruited and armed by the CIA cultivated opium. In Laos and South Vietnam, corrupt governments were heavily involved in heroin trafficking, making the substance easily available to American soldiers

(McCoy 1972: 1991). This longstanding tradition of using drugs to help finance military efforts continues in this part of the world.

With the end of colonial rule, countries emerged with relatively weak central governments, their rural areas inhabited by bandits and paramilitary organizations such as the Kuomintang.

Kuomintang With the defeat of the Chinese Nationalist forces in 1949, the Third and Fifth Armies of Chiang Kai-shek stationed in the remote southern province of Yunnan escaped over the mountainous frontier into Burma's Shan States. Although part of this army dispersed and became integrated with the local population, "more than 6,000 of them remained together as a military entity, their numbers being swollen by indigenous tribesmen" (Lamour and Lamberti 1974: 94). By 1952, the Kuomintang (KMT), numbering about 12,000, became the de facto power in the eastern part of the Shan States. In 1951 and 1952, with support from the United States, the KMT was rearmed and resupplied and, with additional troops from Taiwan and recruits from the Hmong hill tribesmen–poppy cultivators, attempted to invade China. When its attempts failed, U.S. interest and support waned, and the KMT settled permanently in Burma. For several years the Burmese military attempted to evict the KMT and finally succeeded in 1954, forcibly escorting them to the Thai border, from which the Nationalist government evacuated about 6,000 troops to Taiwan. Nevertheless, the strength of the KMT grew, through secret reinforcements from Taiwan and/ or through recruitment among indigenous tribes, to about 10,000 troops.

In 1961, a resentful government in Rangoon (now called Yangon), perhaps with assistance from the People's Republic of China, finally drove the KMT into the Thai portion of the Golden Triangle (Lamour and Lamberti 1974), where it sold its military skills to a joint Central Intelligence Agency and Thai Army command fighting communist insurgents in the Shan States. This force tried to prevent the Laotian communist Pathet Lao from linking up with local insurgents. In 1961 and 1969, U.S.-backed airlifts of KMT troops to Taiwan were the last official contacts between the KMT remnants on the mainland and Chiang Kai-shek's government, but unofficial ties remained strong (Lamour and Lamberti 1974). The remaining troops, about 4,000 strong, became known as the Chinese Irregular Forces (CIF). While the KMT had always dabbled in opium, it now became the sole support of the CIF. Despite this fact, the CIF was tolerated on the Thai border as a barrier against Communist insurgents.

Shan United Army/Mong Tai Army The Shan States, an area somewhat larger than England, lie on a rugged, hilly plateau in the eastern part of central Burma, flanking the western border of China's Yunnan Province. They contain an array of tribal and linguistic groupings. The largest group is the Shans, who speak Thai and thus have more in common with their neighbors in Thailand than those in Myanmar. The Shans are lowland rice cultivators, but hill tribes on the mountain ridges around them cultivate opium. During British colonial rule (1886–1948), the Shan States were administered independently from Burma, and the Shan princes enjoyed a great deal of autonomy. Burma won independence in 1948: The Shans, with great misgivings, agreed to join the Union of Burma in return for statehood and guarantees of a number of ministry posts. As a final incentive, the Shans were given the right to secede after 1957.

The Burmese government's heavy-handed approach to the Shan States set the stage for revolution. Official Burmese financial policies were devastating to many hill farmers, who turned increasingly to poppy cultivation as a cash crop outside of central government control (Delaney 1977). Shan princes (known as *sawbwas*) "had been encouraged to introduce the opium poppy to their fiefdoms by the British as far back as 1866 and opium shops had been opened . . . to retail the narcotics to licensed addicts" (Bresler 1980: 67). In later years, the British made a number of efforts to abolish opium cultivation in the Shan States, although they were never completely successful (McCoy 1972). In any event, many Shans blamed their princes for accommodating the central government, and traditional systems of authority deteriorated.

Originally known as the Shan United Army (SUA), the Mong Tai Army (MTA; Mong Tai is Shan for "Shan State"), under the leadership of Chang Chifu, who is half-Chinese, half-Shan and better known as *Khun Sa*, resorted to opium trafficking in order to purchase arms and support its independence movement (Delaney 1977). Khun Sa had military experience, serving in the Kuomintang military discussed earlier. He was authorized by the Burmese military to set up militias as a way of fighting groups rebelling against the central government. He eventually rebelled against Burma and was imprisoned from 1969 to 1974. After his release, he established the SUA (Fuller 2007a).

The SUA/MTA came to dominate the opium trade along the Thai-Burma border where about 400,000 hill tribesmen had no source of income other than heroin (Permanent Subcommittee on Investigations 1981a). In 1965, an opium war broke out between the CIF and the indigenous Shan United Army (SUA), and the CIF drove SUA leader Khun Sa into Laos. Khun Sa returned and in 1981 defeated the CIF. The SUA/MTA was able to control both the shipments of opium and the production of heroin in its laboratories.

In the 1980s the Thai government succeeded in driving the MTA out of Thailand and back into Burma, but the group continued to dominate opium traffic, taxing drug caravans crossing their territory. In 1990, the Shans suffered significant setbacks: Khun Sa was indicted for drug trafficking by a federal grand jury, and the United States offered a $3 million reward for his capture and conviction in an American court. And his Mong Tai Army suffered defeats by the primitive but ferocious Wa tribesmen (Schmetzer 1990).

Golden Triangle traffickers began to recognize the value of switching from heroin to amphetamines: It made unnecessary the cultivating of vast fields of poppies, and the manufacturing could be accomplished in small one-room laboratories. Khun Sa also recognized that, as compared to the rather stable and fixed heroin market, a drug that could be taken orally instead of by injection, and energize

its user, would have a greater potential market. As a result, early in the 1990s, opium producers began manufacturing amphetamines (Renard 2003). The amphetamine precursor for amphetamine production is ephedrine, the principal alkaloid of ephedra, a shrub that grows wild throughout Yunnan, the Chinese province bordering on the Golden Triangle (Finckenauer and Chin 2007).

In 1994, a joint U.S.-Thai operation ("Tiger Trap") closed the Thai-Myanmar border in areas where the MTA operated. This cut off Khun Sa's ability to move heroin into Thailand and curtailed purchases of supplies for his forces. Later that year, Thai police arrested thirteen major MTA brokers who had been indicted by a federal grand jury in New York. The squeeze was complete when in 1995 the Myanmar army moved against Khun Sa, whose forces were low on food, ammunition, and medical treatment for their wounded. Shortly afterward, ethnic strife broke out: The rank-and-file ethnic Shans mutinied against the MTA, whose top officers are ethnic Chinese (Shenon 1996). Khun Sa began secret negotiations with Myanmar, and in 1996 a deal was made. In front of reporters from Thailand, Khun Sa submitted his resignation (he was retiring to raise chickens, he told them), disbanded the MTA, and closed MTA laboratories. The 15,000-strong MTA disintegrated, many soldiers returning home whereas others shifted to banditry or joined other rebel groups such as *Ywet Sit*/Shan State Army-South (SSA-S) (Lintner 2002).

As a result, the amount of Southeast Asian heroin entering the United States dropped dramatically (replaced by heroin from Colombia). The Myanmar government refused to extradite Khun Sa, and until his health deteriorated, he regularly golfed with the generals against whom he fought a protracted guerrilla war (Wren 1998c). The former warlord died in 2007 at age 73. Nevertheless, the Shan States continue to be a major area for heroin production and the increasing production of methamphetamine (U.S. State Department 2008; Wyler 2007).

United Wa State Army Until 1989, another formidable private army in the Golden Triangle served the Burmese Communist Party (BCP). The BCP force had in the past received support from the People's Republic of China. After Beijing cut off this aid in order to improve relations with Burma, the BCP, following a long-established precedent in the region, went into the opium business. The BCP controlled much of the poppy-producing area and received opium as a form of tax and tribute from local farmers, which it then refined into heroin in its own laboratories.

In 1989, its ethnic rank-and-file Wa tribesmen—fierce warriors whose ancestors were headhunters—rebelled, and the BCP folded as an armed force (Haley 1990). Most Wa political groups reached an accommodation with the Myanmar ruling junta, but one faction of the Wa reorganized as the United Wa State Army (UWSA), also referred to as the Red Wa. Headquartered on the border of China's Yunnan Province, the UWSA uses heroin—and more recently methamphetamine—trafficking as a means of funding efforts against Burmese control (U.S. Department of State 2003; Witkin and Griffen 1994). Nearly one million Wa straddle the border between Myanmar and China, and the UWSA operates freely along the China and Thailand borders, controlling much of the Shan State with a militia estimated to have about 18,000 members, well armed with ground-to-air missiles and modern communications equipment. Ironically, the Wa routinely executes anyone caught dealing drugs for local use. "Since the surrender of the SUA/MTA, the USWA has reigned supreme in narcotics production in Burma," the world's largest producer of heroin (NNICC 1998: 50; Wyler 2007). But for the Wa, profits from methamphetamine production and smuggling have surpassed heroin.

In 2000, Myanmar negotiated a truce with the Wa which gave them autonomy in their state, and the Wa reached an accommodation with China. In return for sophisticated weapons and expertise from China, the Wa moved their people, their army, and their drug laboratories into the Thai-Myanmar border area known as Doi Lang. The Chinese were concerned with their own drug problem and preferred the Wa to be a Thai rather than a Chinese problem. But the situation has grown complex and volatile. Thailand supports the SSA-A, which is in rebellion against Myanmar. Myanmar supports the Wa, who police the border against Shan incursions. China supports Myanmar and the Wa, and the United States supports Thailand. In 2001, the United States moved about 5,000 troops into northern Thailand where Myanmar and Thailand have exchanged threats and artillery shells along their Doi Lang border (Schmetzer 2001). In 2005, eight senior leaders of the United Wa State Army (UWSA) were indicted in the United States on charges of heroin and methamphetamine trafficking. The Myanmar government has not acted against any of those indicted, but one has died and another was arrested by the police in Hong Kong (U.S. Department of State 2008).

Thailand Whether the source is the BCP, CIF, MTA, SSA-A, or the UWSA, opium in the form of morphine base or of almost pure heroin, as well as methamphetamine, is usually brokered in Thailand, which has modern communications and transportation systems. A nation of 50 million persons, Thailand is almost as large as France. A staunch anti-Communist ally of the United States, Thailand sent troops to fight alongside American soldiers in Korea and Vietnam. In addition to its role in drug trafficking, Thailand, with an estimated 50,000 active brothels, has a reputation of being the "world's biggest whorehouse" with a law enforcement apparatus permeated with corruption (Mydans 2003b; Schmetzer 1991b). Thailand enjoys a close relationship with Myanmar's military regime with whom they share important commercial interests (Kaplan 2008).

In 1991 a military coup—one of seventeen since 1932—overthrew the democratically elected Thai government. In 2001, a democratically elected prime minister initiated a vigorous campaign against the trade in methamphetamine, a major drug problem in Thailand. Critics allege that this effort has been excessive with many questionable killings by the police and vigilante forces allied with the government (Phongpaichit and Baker 2003). In a two-month period in 2003, there was an average of thirty such killings a day (Mydans 2003c). Political unrest continues pitting rural Thais in the northwest against their urban countrymen in Bangkok (Mydans 2008).

"Once the sourcing and processing stages are complete, isolated countries like Myanmar or Afghanistan [discussed later] lose their competitive advantage" because they simply do not have the sophistication or international networks to get their product to market. This is what the foreign syndicates, who reap the greatest profits, provide (Brzezinski 2002: 27). At the center of much of Thai drug trafficking are ethnic Chinese organizations such as the Triads, discussed in Chapter 9. They dominate a major part of the world heroin market. "In Southeast Asia, not only did the British and French opium monopolies create massive addict populations, but they also inadvertently formed a smuggling network that was crucial to the post–World War II heroin epidemic. Although the colonial administrations reaped huge profits, they never became involved in the drug's distribution and sale. That work was left to each colony's licensed opium merchant. Invariably they were Chinese" (Posner 1988: 66).

According the U.S. Department of State (2008), ethnic Chinese groups dominate the drug syndicates operating in areas controlled by the UWSA and the SSA-S.

Bangkok has a large population of Thai-born Chinese, called *Haw*, who are known by Thai names but maintain close ties with compatriots in Hong Kong, Yunnan province,[2] Amsterdam, and British Columbia. From Bangkok, Chinese criminal organizations have flooded their "China White" into major cities of Europe, Canada, and the United States. But there are other players, particularly Nigerians who are "by far the most organized and entrenched group. Their job in heroin's ever-lengthening supply chain is also among the riskiest: to get the heroin into the United States" (Brzezinski 2002: 28–29). It is those who control the sophisticated networks that dominate transportation and distribution who reap the huge profits in heroin.

The central role that the Golden Triangle played in the heroin trade has been significantly diminished, in part because of economic pressure from China. The UWSA publicly pledged to eliminate opium poppy cultivation, there have been crackdowns on opium farmers, and, as noted above, traffickers have switched from opium cultivation to manufacturing methamphetamines ("ice"), turning the Golden Triangle into a new "Ice Triangle." As a result, Golden Triangle heroin has been largely eclipsed by that from the Golden Crescent (Fuller 2007b).

The Golden Crescent

The Golden Crescent of Southwest Asia includes parts of Iran, Afghanistan, and Pakistan. The region has limestone-rich soil, a climate and altitude ideal for poppy cultivation, and, like the Golden Triangle, a ready abundance of cheap labor for the labor-intensive production of opium. Afghan

---

[2]Because it is located next to the Golden Triangle, China's Yunnan ("south of the clouds") province, with a population that includes 20 of the country's minority groups, has been a center for drug trafficking. High-quality heroin passes easily over borders that were opened for trade decades ago, supported by rampant corruption among the police and other officials.

opium is processed into heroin in local laboratories or shipped—generally aboard donkeys, but sometimes aboard jeeps bought with U.S. funds—to processing plants in Pakistan (NNICC 1998).

Pakistan has been a producer of opium for export since the earliest time of Muslim rule and the later British Empire. In Pakistan, the typical poppy farmer lives in a semi-autonomous northern tribal area outside the direct control of the central government in Islamabad. The Pakistani authorities have little control in these areas and must appeal to tribal leaders to move against the region's dozens of illegal processing laboratories. In northwest Pakistan's Karakorum Mountains, one acre of poppies yields about a dozen kilos of opium gum; ten kilos of opium gum can be converted into one kilo of base morphine. The wholesaling is accomplished in lawless border towns such as Landi Kotal, which is about three miles from the Afghan border. Much of the heroin trade in and from Pakistan is controlled by a consortium of three Quetta-based families, referred to as the Quetta Alliance. Quetta, a border city of more than 1 million persons, is filled with Afghan refugees, poverty, and drug addicts.

Although these groups appear to be independent, they cooperate with each other when such cooperation is to their mutual benefit. Extensive corruption efforts shield them from law enforcement, and many family members hold provincial-level political offices (NNICC 1998). As a result of eradication efforts in recent years, the amount of opium production has been greatly reduced. Instead, opium products are often processed into morphine base or heroin in Afghanistan and then shipped through Pakistan to world markets by Pakistan-based traffickers.

Unlike Southeast Asia, Afghanistan's rugged terrain and the martial tradition of its tribes kept it free of colonialism. Western interest in this nation of about 27 million was limited until the Soviet invasion. The Pashtuns, a tribal group that founded Afghanistan and ruled it for all but about four years of its history, populates Pakistan's Northwest Frontier Province and composes almost half of the inhabitants of Afghanistan (Waldman 2003). The border dividing Pashtuns in Pakistan from their tribal brethren in Afghanistan was drawn by the British more than a century ago, and is generally ignored—there are few border patrols in the

Afghan villagers tend to opium poppies in Helmand province, in southern Afghanistan.

Afghanistan

"Poppy growing is so uncontrolled that despite millions of aid dollars spent to train anti-drug forces and to help farmers grow other crops, Afghanistan is showing no signs of leaving its position as the world's biggest producer of opium. It accounts for almost three-quarters of global opium production" (Gall 2006: 4; also United Nations Office on Drugs and Crime 2008b).

Between a Rock and a Hard Place

"In Afghanistan, a weak government has produced a security vacuum that in turn inhibits economic development and diversification, forcing impoverished farmers to grow lucrative crops like the opium poppy for cash. Any deliberate crop destruction carried out by the Afghan government often drives poor farmers to sympathize with the insurgency" (B. Powell 2007: 37).

Golden Crescent "Oil"

"What crude oil is to the Middle East, poppies are to Afghanistan" (B. Powell 2007: 31).

Afghan Hashish

In 2008, Afghan officials working with U.S. Drug Enforcement Administration (DEA) agents seized 262 tons of hashish, the largest of any known drug seizure. The drugs were being stored in underground bunkers in a Taliban-controlled area of Kandahar Province (DEA press release, June 13, 2008).

region (Ahmed-Ullah 2001). Known as exceptional warriors, the Pashtuns are also the major drug traffickers in the region. Along with other Islamic groups, many Pashtuns fought a guerrilla war against the Soviet-backed regime in Kabul. In late 1979, the Soviets rolled their tanks into the opium provinces of Afghanistan. "Suddenly, the tribes which had spent the last decade maneuvering their heavily armed drug caravans past the increasingly troublesome patrols of the U.S. Drug Enforcement Administration's agents found themselves flung into the limelight as the new anti-communist 'crusaders'" (Levins 1980: 20).

United States anti-Soviet efforts in Afghanistan were orchestrated by the CIA, and the agency adopted a benign attitude toward drug trafficking. As the conflict wound down, the United States became increasingly concerned with rebel drug activity. Opium is the cash crop that has traditionally enabled feuding tribes in Afghanistan and in Pakistan's Northwest Frontier Province to purchase weapons and ammunition. In 1991, U.S. officials announced that they would no longer provide military assistance to Afghan rebels. Prior to its disintegration, the Soviet Union also agreed to stop aiding the Afghan government. The following year, *mujahedin* forces entered Kabul without encountering any resistance, and the war officially ended, but warfare between rebel groups continued, supported by heroin. By 1998, the Islamic fundamentalist Taliban movement, made up primarily of Pashtuns, controlled most of the country, and Afghanistan became one of the world's largest producers of heroin (Wren 1998a).

Until 2001, Afghanistan was the world's second largest grower of the opium poppy, producing about one-third of the heroin entering the United States, and about 80 percent of the heroin consumed in Europe. Despite the severe economic ramifications, in 2001, the Taliban leadership

Gettin' hi v. *Semper fi*

Several companies from the 24th Marine Expeditionary Unit walk through vast poppy fields as Afghan laborers scrape the plant's gooey resin—opium. This is the southern Helmand Province, a Taliban stronghold, and to destroy the poppy crop would alienate Afghans who depend on it for their income, and thereby strengthen the Taliban who exchange daily fire with the Marines. The Marines need a helicopter-landing zone, but this would ruin a poppy field, so it is not built. Of course, the opium provides the Taliban with funds to continue fighting the Marines (Straziuso 2008).

banned the growing of poppies as a sin against the teachings of Islam. Compliance was immediate and thorough (Bearak 2001). In the wake of the September 11, 2001, terrorist attacks and U.S. military action, the Taliban government told farmers they were once again free to grow the opium poppy, and in Taliban strongholds they levy a tax on the harvest (Anderson 2007).

With the collapse of the Taliban government, the poppy once again became an indispensable crop in parts of Afghanistan. Anti-drug efforts are hampered by a lack of alternative crops for impoverished farmers—poppy prices are ten times those for wheat (Rohde 2007). Afghanistan now produces 90 percent of the world's opium, and the drug trade represents more than half of the country's gross domestic product (GDP). So critical is opium to the Afghan economy that American officials have been reluctant to engage in an anti-drug war that could conflict with efforts to deal with terrorism. Wealth from the drug trade has increased the power of local warlords whose militias are a threat to the central government (Schmitt 2004). In 2005, an Afghan tribal leader with close ties to both the Taliban and the United States was arrested in New York to which he had been lured by U.S. officials and charged with importing more than $50 million in heroin into the United States (B. Powell 2007). High-ranking members of the government are reportedly profiting from the drug trade (Moreau and Yousafzai 2006). In a downtown Kabul neighborhood, there are dozens of gaudy "poppy palaces" owned by former warlords and senior Afghan government officials (J. L. Anderson 2007).

Afghan heroin destined for Europe is frequently transported across the forbidding Margo desert. Heavily armed convoys traveling at high speeds move their supplies into Iran where thousands of police officers have been killed battling the trade (Gall 2005). Turkey, which serves as a land bridge to markets in the West for heroin from the Golden Crescent, is fighting a similar battle. Kurdish separatists and Turkish criminal groups (*babas*) have important connections in the Western drug market. They move heroin across the highways of Turkey and into Europe where other criminal organizations, in particular Mafia and Camorra groups, distribute the drug throughout the European market.

The United States has pressured Pakistan to move against poppy cultivation, but the infusion of hundreds of thousands of Afghan tribesmen into Pakistan has made this difficult, if not impossible. Tribesmen in Pakistan are now armed with rocket-propelled grenade launchers and automatic weapons to protect miles of poppy plants, pledging to die fighting rather than give up their best cash crop. Furthermore, there is a growing domestic market for heroin in Pakistan: although most poppies now grow on the Afghan side of the border and are shipped to Europe and America in the form of powdered heroin, Pakistan's heroin-smoking population has grown, with estimates as high as one million users.

The nations of Central Asia that surround Afghanistan, such as Tajikistan, have a predominantly young, rapidly growing and poverty stricken population. Add heroin to this mix and you get an expanding addict population and drug organizations taking advantage of porous borders and easily bribed officials. "The drug business sustains up to 50 percent of the Tajik economy and props up its currency, if only because of the great number of people it employs" (Orth 2002: 168). For many of the warlords who are part of the post-Taliban Afghan government, heroin was the way they supported their armed followers. Islamic terrorist groups also operate in this region, and heroin provides them with an invaluable source of funds. And the corruption-drug connection reaches into the highest ranks of the Russian military (Orth 2002).

Mexico

Mexico is the source of "black tar" or brown heroin, which gained a foothold in the American drug market after the demise of the "French Connection." In the five years after the collapse of the French connection, Mexico became the major source of U.S. heroin. "Mexico's rise was logical: the country contains extensive regions suitable for both opium cultivation and refining and shares a lightly guarded 2,000 mile border with the United States. Mexicans could manufacture heroin and smuggle it into the United States with little risk of detection. This simplified trafficking system resulted in increased Mexican heroin availability in the United States" (PCOC 1986a: 107).

Black tar heroin is a less refined but more potent—and very popular—form of the substance. The conversion of the opium gum to black tar—No. 3—heroin is more convenient and requires only simple equipment that can be readily dismantled if law enforcement is detected in the area. In addition, almost anyone can be trained to perform the conversion process, making it unnecessary to pay the higher salary that would most certainly be demanded by skilled chemists. The process is more rapid and more economical than that required to produce the higher purity—No. 4—white heroin (DEA 1991b). White heroin from the Golden Triangle and the Golden Crescent can approach 100 percent purity, but Mexican black tar or brown generally ranges from 65 to 85 percent pure.

The poppy is not native to Mexico but was brought into the country at the turn of the twentieth century by Chinese laborers who were helping to build the railroad system. Chinese immigrants dominated heroin trafficking until anti-Chinese riots and property confiscations during the 1930s caused the trade to pass into Mexican hands (Lupsha 1991).

Poppy fields are generally small and difficult to detect, although larger fields cultivated by more sophisticated growers have been discovered. The poppies are grown in remote areas of the Sierra Madre states of Durango, Sinaloa, and Chihuahua, as well as Sonora (the Mexican state just south of Arizona). Opium gum is then transported to nearby villages. *Acaparadores,* or gatherers, travel around the countryside buying large quantities of opium gum, which is flown to secret laboratories owned and operated by major heroin organizations.

The conversion process for Mexican heroin takes about three days (although with special equipment and trained personnel it can be accomplished in one day). Once the chemists are finished, the heroin is moved to large population centers. From there, Mexican couriers transport the heroin to members of the trafficking organization in the United States (PCOC 1986a).

The drug trade is big business in poverty-wracked Mexico. Large traffickers (discussed in Chapter 7) have traditionally received protection from the highest levels of government and law enforcement. Indeed, some important traffickers have backgrounds in law enforcement. As Peter Lupsha notes, "For some of Mexico's top enforcement officials entrance into drug trafficking has simply been a lateral transfer" (1990: 12). This ugly facet of the drug trade was dramatically revealed when several Mexican law enforcement officers were implicated in the torture-murder of a U.S. drug agent. They were acting on orders from drug kingpin Rafael Caro-Quintero. When Quintero and other members of his Guadalajara cartel were arrested, they were carrying credentials identifying them as agents of the Dirección Federal de Seguridad, the Mexican equivalent of the FBI. Alberto Sicilia Falcón, another leading Mexican trafficker, carried similar credentials (Lupsha 1991). In Rafael's hometown of Sinaloa, just south of Arizona, he and other members of the Caro-Quintero clan are revered and are even the subjects of songs and legends (Bowden 1991). In 2004, a local Mexican police unit killed seven people in one

Since authorities began keeping records in 1990, dozens of dope tunnels have been found along the Mexican border with the United States. In 2006, federal agents discovered a tunnel 60 feet below ground that stretched from a warehouse near the international airport in Tijuana to a vacant industrial building in Otay Mesa, California, about 20 miles southeast of downtown San Diego. The tunnel was outfitted with a concrete floor, electricity, lights, ventilation, and ground-water pumping systems. On the Mexican side, officials found a pulley system at the entrance and several thousand pounds of marijuana (Archibold 2006). In 2007, authorities uncovered a 1,300-foot tunnel some 50 feet below the ground linking Tecate, Mexico, with the city of the same name in California. The tunnel began in the floor of a building in Mexico and ended in a large shipping container in California. Passages were illuminated by fluorescent light, and carefully placed pumps kept the tunnel dry. "The neatly squared walls, carved through solid rock, bear the signs of engineering skill and professional drilling tools" (Archibold 2007: 18).

family in a mistaken attempt to assassinate rival drug traffickers (McKinley 2004b). As noted in Chapter 7, Mexican organizations are now transporting cocaine into the United States for Colombian traffickers.

The vast and remote border between Mexico and the United States makes patrolling very difficult and facilitates the transportation of drugs into Texas, California, Arizona, and New Mexico. Drugs are also secreted in a variety of motor vehicles and smuggled past official border entry points. Private aircraft make use of hundreds of small airstrips that dot the U.S.-Mexican border and dozens of larger airstrips on the Yucatán Peninsula to move heroin north. Since September 11, 2001, however, the use of private aircraft to smuggle drugs into the Unites States has declined—any plane trying to fly under radar is likely to trigger a fighter-plane scramble.

Colombia

As noted in Chapter 7, since the 1980s Colombia has become a major poppy grower and Colombians have become major heroin wholesalers. On the mountain slopes of Colombia's Andean rain forests, guerrillas and drug traffickers have become major poppy growers (McGuire 1993). Coca is a lowland crop; the poppy thrives in the Andes. On the hillsides of a reservation in the southern Colombian state of Cauca, 9,000 feet high,

Guambiano Indians cultivate their most precious crop—gum from their poppies brings about $115 a pound and represents the difference between food and hunger. Nine other states are known to have poppy plantations (Tamayo 2001).

At the end of 1991, police raids in Colombia disclosed thousands of acres of poppy plants ("Colombian Heroin May Be Increasing" 1991). By 1998, Colombian heroin accounted for more than 50 percent of the drug smuggled into the United States. The purity level of Colombian heroin—it passes through fewer hands from "the farm to the arm" than the Asian variety—enables ingestion by sniffing and smoking, methods much safer than injection which is the only way to gain a potent high with weaker versions of the drug. By 1999, Colombia was believed the source of 70 percent of the heroin sold on the East Coast. In New York, Colombians caused a glut on the heroin market, with declining prices and street-sale purity as high as 90 percent—in the early (pre-Colombian) 1980s, it was barely 5 percent (Wren 1999a).

COCAINE

Cocaine is an alkaloid found in significant quantities only in the leaves of two species of coca shrub. One species grows in the Andes of Ecuador, Peru, and Bolivia; the other is found in the mountainous regions of Colombia, along the Caribbean coast of South America, on the northern coast of Peru, and in the dry valley of the Marañòn River in northeastern Peru. The practice of chewing coca leaves has been carried on by Indians in Peru for at least twenty centuries. The leaves are used as a poultice for wounds and to brew a tea, *mate de coca*, said to cure the headaches of tourists bothered by the 12,000-foot altitude of La Paz. Although cash crops raised on the mountain slopes of Peru require a great deal of care—the nutrient-poor soil needs continuous fertilization—coca is a hardy jungle plant with abundant seeds that needs little or no fertilizer. "Once a coca field is planted, it will yield four to five crops a year for thirty to forty years, needing little in return but seasonal weeding" (Morales 1989: xvi).

Spanish explorers observed indigenous people chewing coca leaves during their colonization of South America, although they did not adopt the practice. In the middle of the nineteenth century, scientists began experimenting with the substance, noting that it showed promise as a local anesthetic and had an effect opposite that of morphine. At first cocaine was used to treat morphine addiction, but the result was often a morphine addict who also became dependent on cocaine (van Dyke and Byck 1982). "Throughout the late nineteenth century, both coca itself (that is, an extract from the leaf including all its alkaloids) and the pure chemical cocaine were used as medicines and for pleasure—the distinction was not always made—in an enormous variety of ways" (Grinspoon and Bakalar 1976: 19). By the late 1880s, a feel-good pharmacology based on the coca plant and its derivative cocaine was promoted for everything from headaches to hysteria. The most famous beverage containing coca, however, was first bottled in 1894 (Helmer 1975). Coca-Cola continues to use non-psychoactive residue from the coca plant for flavoring.

After the first flush of enthusiasm for cocaine in the 1880s, there was a decline in its use. Although it continued to be used in a variety of notions and tonics, cocaine did not develop a separate appeal as did morphine and heroin (Morgan 1981). Indeed, cocaine gained a reputation for inducing bizarre and unpredictable behavior. After the turn of the century, cocaine, like heroin, became identified with the urban underworld. From 1930 until the 1960s there was limited demand for cocaine and, accordingly, only limited supply. Cocaine use was associated with deviants—jazz musicians and the denizens of the underworld—and supplies were typically diverted from medical sources. Cocaine has limited medical use. It constricts blood vessels when applied topically, the only local anesthetic that has this effect. Because of this quality, cocaine is used in surgery of the mucous membranes of the ear, nose, and throat, and for procedures that require the passage of a tube through the nose or throat (van Dyke and Byck 1982).

During the late 1960s and early 1970s, attitudes toward recreational drug use became more relaxed, a spin-off of the wide acceptance of marijuana. Cocaine was no longer associated with deviants, and the media played a significant role in shaping public attitudes: "By publicizing and glamorizing the lifestyle of affluent, upper-class drug dealers and the use of cocaine by celebrities and athletes, all forms of mass media created an effective advertising campaign for cocaine, and many people were taught to perceive cocaine as chic, exclusive, daring, and nonaddicting. In television specials about cocaine abuse, scientists talked about the intense euphoria produced by cocaine and the compulsive craving that people (and animals) develop for it. Thus, an image of cocaine as being extraordinarily powerful, and a (therefore desirable) euphoriant was promoted" (Wesson and Smith 1985: 193).

Cocaine soon became associated with a privileged elite. The new demand was sufficient to generate new sources, refining, and marketing networks outside of medical channels and the development of the international cocaine organizations discussed in Chapter 7 (Grinspoon and Bakalar 1976). Greater availability of cocaine led to a corresponding increase in use. Enormous profits accrue at each level of the cocaine business. These profits have proved so alluring that criminal organizations that have traditionally avoided direct involvement in drug trafficking have become involved in the cocaine business.

The Business of Cocaine

Coca is a flowering bush or shrub that in cultivation stands three to six feet tall. Each shrub yields at most four ounces of waxy, elliptical leaves that are about 1 percent cocaine by weight. Pulverized leaves of the coca bush are soaked and shaken in a mixture of alcohol and benzol (a petroleum derivative). The liquid is then drained, sulfuric acid is added, and the solution is again shaken. Sodium carbonate is added, forming a precipitate, which is washed with kerosene and chilled, leaving behind crystals of crude cocaine known as coca paste. Between 200 and 500 kilos of leaves are made into 1 kilo of paste; 2.5 kilos of coca paste are converted into 1 kilo of cocaine base—a malodorous, grainy, greenish yellow powder of more than 66 percent purity. Cocaine base is converted into cocaine hydrochloride by being treated with ether, acetone, and hydrochloric acid. One kilo of cocaine base is synthesized into 1 kilo of cocaine hydrochloride, a white crystalline powder that is about 95 percent pure.

In the United States cocaine hydrochloride is cut for street sale by adding sugars such as lactose, inositol, or mannitol, or talcum powder, borax, or other neutral substances, and local anesthetics such as procaine hydrochloride (novocaine) or lidocaine hydrochloride. (Novocaine is sometimes mixed with mannitol or lactose and sold as cocaine.) After cutting, the cocaine typically has a consumer sale purity of less than 20 percent. Huge increases in the availability of cocaine have resulted in consumer sale purity levels as high as 50 percent—and a concomitant increase in the number of emergency room admissions for cocaine overdose.

The most common method of using cocaine is "snorting"—inhaling it into the nostrils through a straw or rolled paper or from a "coke spoon." Some abusers take it intravenously, which is the only way to ingest 100 percent of the drug. When the drug is inhaled, its effects peak in 15 to 20 minutes and disappear in 60 to 90 minutes. Intravenous use results in an intense feeling of euphoria that crests in 3 to 5 minutes and wanes in 30 to 40 minutes. Cocaine causes the release of the natural substance adrenaline: "In essence the cocaine-stimulated reactions in the body are mimicking a natural physiological stress response." The body prepares for "fight" or "flight," but the brain sends the message that everything is better than fine (Gold et al. 1986). In small doses, cocaine will bring about a sensation of extreme euphoria and indifference to pain, along with illusions of increased mental and sensory alertness and physical strength. At higher doses, the drug has the potential to produce megalomania and feelings of omnipotence in most individuals (Gold et al. 1986).

For many decades, coca leaf was converted to cocaine base in Bolivia and Peru, and then smuggled by small aircraft or boat into Colombia where it was refined into cocaine in jungle laboratories. Laboratories have relocated to cities far from cultivation sites to be closer to sources of precursor chemicals and also because improved law enforcement methods facilitate the detection of jungle laboratories. Essential precursor chemicals are usually manufactured in the United States and Germany, and Panama and Mexico serve as major transit sources. Colombian cartels, using dummy companies and multiple suppliers, pay as much as ten times the normal prices for these chemicals.

Some Colombian traffickers have set up laboratories in other Latin American countries and even the United States in response to increased law enforcement in Colombia and the increasing cost of ether, sulfuric acid, and acetone in Colombia. Although sulfuric acid and acetone have wide industrial use in Colombia, ether does not, and each kilo of cocaine requires 17 liters of ether. The Cali cartel pioneered setting up coke labs in rural parts of the United States in order to have a ready source of precursor chemicals (Chepesiuk 2003). The cost of these chemicals has increased because of controls imposed by the Colombian government on their importation and sale and because of U.S. Drug Enforcement Administration efforts to disrupt the supply of chemicals essential in the cocaine refinement process. Acetone, sulfuric acid, and ether, however, are widely available for commercial purposes in the United States (Hall 2000).

In the past, because the quality of Colombian coca was significantly less than that grown in Peru and Bolivia, Colombia was not a major coca producer; but success in eradicating coca in Bolivia and Peru led to a major increase in Colombian coca cultivation, and in 1998, Colombia became the world's leading coca producer (Goering 1998; Krauss 2000). Colombian traffickers achieved extraordinary levels of efficiency in extracting cocaine from their coca crops (*International Narcotics Control Strategy Report, 1999* 2000). By 2002, however, coca was making a comeback in Peru, driven by a combination of poverty and soaring prices for coca. In Bolivia, coca production shot up in 2005, the result of a backlash against U.S.-financed eradication programs that helped to destabilize the country and topple several governments; and at the end of the year, Bolivia elected a coca-growing socialist president (Forero 2002, 2005b, 2005c).

In Colombia, about three-quarters of the coca is grown in six rural provinces about the size of Kansas, southwest of Bogatá, with a population of about six million. The area is desperately poor and plagued by left- and right-wing paramilitary groups (Forero 2001b). Indeed, Colombia is the only country in Latin America still fighting a major guerilla insurgency (discussed in Chapter 7).

DISTRIBUTION OF HEROIN AND COCAINE

The organizers who arrange for the importation and wholesale distribution of heroin and cocaine typically avoid physical possession. "The key figures in the Italian heroin establishment never touched heroin. Guys who were in the business for twenty years and had made millions off it had never seen it. After all, does a commodities trader on Wall Street have to see hog bellies and platinum bars?" (Durk and Silverman 1976: 49). Importation often entails little or no risk of arrest—heroin or cocaine can be secreted in a variety of imported goods, and possession cannot be proven. Furthermore, although a single shipment may be detected and confiscated, smugglers often divide their supplies so that other shipments arrive unimpeded—"shotgunning." Colombian dealers have been known to offer to insure their shipments through a joint arrangement. The cost of insurance is passed on to the import buyer, who is then financially protected in the event of interdiction by American authorities.

After importation, heroin is sold in 10- to 50-kilo quantities to wholesalers—"kilo connections." The heroin is then "stepped on" or diluted several times. The wholesaler, basically a facilitator, arranges for the cutting (diluting) of the almost-pure heroin. The actual work is often done by women brought together for the task. Between ten and twenty women cut from 10 to 50 kilos in an apartment rented for this purpose. Under guard, often working without any clothes on (as a precaution against theft of the precious powder), and wearing surgical masks to avoid inhaling heroin dust, they mix the heroin with quinine, lactose, and dextrose, usually four or five parts of the dilutant to one part of heroin. They work through the night and receive several thousand dollars each, making the risk and embarrassment worthwhile.

Residual Profits

When cocaine-transporting fast boats run into patrols from the United States or Nicaragua along that country's Mosquito Coast, the traffickers throw the bales overboard. Sometimes they run out of fuel or have an accident. In any event, tons of cocaine wash up on the coast of one of the Caribbean's most desolate regions where villagers wait to recover the valuable cargo. Colombian traffickers or Nicaraguan middlemen offer them about $4,000 a kilo, which has allowed many indigenous fishermen to move out of their huts and into multi-story homes with satellite dishes (Carroll 2007).

When the cutting is complete, jobbers—"weight dealers"—who have been waiting for a telephone call arrive with the necessary cash, which they exchange for 2 to 5 kilos of the cut heroin. The jobbers move it to wholesalers, who cut it again. From there it moves to street wholesalers, then to street retailers, and finally to consumers. At each step of the process, profits increase as the kilo of pure heroin increases in bulk, the result of further cutting.

The enormous profits that accrue in the business of drugs are part of a criminal underworld where violence is always an attendant reality. Transactions must be accomplished without recourse to the formal mechanisms of dispute resolution that are usually available in the world of legitimate business. This reality leads to the creation of private mechanisms of enforcement. The drug world is filled with heavily armed and dangerous persons in the employ of the larger cartels, although even street-level operatives are often armed. These private resources for violence limit market entry, ward off competitors and predatory criminals, and maintain internal discipline and security within an organization.

Below the multi-kilo wholesale level, cocaine or heroin is an easy-entry business, requiring only a source, clientele, and funds. A variety of groups deal heroin and cocaine, including street gangs in many urban areas. In several parts of the country, particularly New York City and Los Angeles, the relatively stable neighborhood criminal organizations who dominate the heroin and cocaine trade have found new competitors: youthful crack dealers. Crack requires only a small investment for entry to the trade. Street gangs or groups of friends and relatives have entered the market, often touching off explosive competitive violence that frequently involves the use of high-powered handguns and automatic weapons. The sharp decline in murder in some major cities such as New York is believed to be related to a stabilizing of the crack market, much as post-Prohibition organized crime–related murder dipped significantly in Chicago in the absence of competition.

The sale of heroin and cocaine/crack is carried out by thousands of small-time operators who dominate particular local markets—a public housing complex, a number of city blocks, or simply a street corner location. Control is exercised through violence. For most participants at the street level, however, the net profits are rather modest. Even though dealers typically work long hours and subject themselves to substantial risk of violence and incarceration, their incomes generally range from $1,000 to $2,000 a month. Less successful participants eke out a living that rivals minimum wage. Many are involved to support their own drug habits, to supplement earnings from legitimate employment, or both. In the crack business young men often work for less than minimum wage—for example, $30 a day for acting as a lookout, or 50 cents for each vial of crack sold. They can expect $100 to $200 per week for working long hours under unpleasant conditions and are without unemployment insurance, medical insurance, or any of the usual benefits of legitimate employment.

Many retail operators sell more than one drug—they are often "walking drug stores." The lower down on the distribution chain, the more likely the person or organization will be involved in the sale of more than one substance. And the

Crack

Although cocaine hydrochloride cannot easily be smoked, freeing the alkaloid from the hydrochloride attachment produces purified crystals of cocaine base that can be crushed and smoked in a special glass pipe or sprinkled on a tobacco or marijuana product. Cocaine hydrochloride powder is easily converted into crack by cooking it in a mixture of sodium bicarbonate (baking soda) and water, and then removing the water. The soap-like substance is then cut into bars or chips, sometimes called "quarter rocks," and smoked. It is generally sold on the street in small glass vials. The nickname "crack" comes from the crackling sound the drug makes when it is smoked in a glass pipe. Smoking crack produces a short but very powerful euphoria that lasts 10 to 15 minutes.

business of drugs includes substances other than heroin and cocaine/crack.

METHAMPHETAMINE

Amphetamines are synthetic drugs, and their effects are similar to those of cocaine. Amphetamines mimic the naturally occurring substance adrenaline and cause a biochemical arousal—being "turned on"—without the presence of sensory input to cause such arousal. The body becomes physiologically activated. Because they ward off sleep, amphetamines have proven popular with college students cramming for exams and long-haul truck drivers.

First synthesized in 1887, amphetamines were introduced into clinical use in the 1930s and were eventually offered as a "cure-all" for just about every ailment (D. E. Smith 1979). Between 1932 and 1946 there were thirty-nine generally accepted medical uses ranging from the treatment of schizophrenia and morphine addiction, to low blood pressure and caffeine and tobacco dependence. It was believed that the substance had no abuse potential (*Drug Abuse and Drug Abuse Research* 1987). Because amphetamines appear to act on the hypothalamus to suppress the appetite, they were once widely prescribed to treat obesity. Compared with more natural forms of dieting, however, the appetite returns with greater intensity after withdrawal from the drug. Only as a "last resort" is methamphetamine hydrochloride (Desoxyn) now used to treat obesity as one component of a weight-reduction regimen, and even then the treatment is limited to only a few weeks.

Legally produced amphetamine is taken in the form of tablets or capsules. Some abusers crush the substance, dissolve it in water, and ingest it intravenously. Illegally produced amphetamine is available in tablet and powdered form (called "ice") that is sometimes smoked. There are three basic types of amphetamine, but the methyl-amphetamines have the greatest potential for abuse because they are fast acting and produce a "rush." Methamphetamine hydrochloride, one of the methyl group, is a widely abused drug known on the street simply as "meth"; in liquid form it is often referred to as "speed." As with cocaine, methamphetamine in small doses will bring about a "rush," a sensation or euphoria often described in sexual terms, along with indifference to pain and illusions of increased mental and sensory alertness, and physical strength.

The main active ingredient in methamphetamine, phenyl-2-propanone, referred to as P2P, is widely available in Europe, and bulk shipments of P2P from Germany are often the source of illegal methamphetamine produced in the United States. But the dynamics of illicit methamphetamine production and trafficking have been changing with P2P as the primary precursor being replaced by ephedrine. Mexican manufacturers typically produce the drug in three phases, using such precursor chemicals as ephedrine, pseudoephedrine, red phosphorus, and hydriodic acid. Canada has been

The Law of Unintended Consequences

In 2005, Iowa, like about thirty other states, enacted a law restricting the sale of cold medicines whose pseudoephedrine can be used to make methamphetamine. As a result, during the first seven months, there was a significant decrease in home-cooked methamphetamine: Lab seizures went from 120 to 20 and, while $2.8 million dollars had been spent in 2004 on treating people at the University of Iowa Burn Center whose skin had been scorched by toxic chemicals, there was a virtual absence of victims.

But the bad news: More methamphetamine-dependent patients were under treatment, and the seizure of the drug increased as the homemade powdered version was replaced by the more powerful Mexican crystal methamphetamine (Zernike 2006).

the source of pseudoephedrine that is imported in powder form, mostly from China, for use as a decongestant (Krauss 2002).

Although most of the chemicals needed are easily obtained or manufactured clandestinely, they also present numerous hazards both during the production process and after when they are discarded because of their caustic, flammable, or reactive nature. The danger of chemical fires and explosions extends beyond manufacture. After producing the finished methamphetamine, clandestine lab workers are typically left with 5 to 6 pounds of hazardous waste for each pound of the finished drug produced. Most of this waste consists of corrosive sodium hydroxide solution often discarded in Freon cans, which may become a hazard due to temperatures and internal pressure. In addition, traces of red phosphorous will likely remain on discarded materials and equipment, presenting a flammable hazard for three to four decades.

The illegal activities associated with methamphetamine production and hazardous waste encompass more than the clandestine lab cooks and workers. Just as legitimate industries generate secondary services, clandestine lab site "brokers," property owners, and "oil barons" support and profit from the manufacture of methamphetamine, with the former two negotiating or allowing the use of property and the latter recycling hazardous waste material.

Even when law enforcement is able to arrest and prosecute the individuals involved, there can be staggering costs associated with removing the containers, contaminated apparatus, and chemical waste. Depending on the extent of the contamination and whether the area affected is a structure, soil, or water, costs can range from thousands of dollars to do the initial cleanup to hundreds of thousands of dollars to cleanse a water supply or make a dwelling re-habitable. Contaminated areas undetected will continue to do incalculable damage to the environment (Nieves 2001).

The distribution of methamphetamine has been a main staple of outlaw bikers. Although there has been an increase in the involvement of Mexican gangs operating in southern California, where they produce methamphetamine in unpopulated desert areas, Mexican organizations have saturated the Western market with high-purity methamphetamine, so that even outlaw motorcycle clubs "are finding it more cost effective to purchase this stimulant from Mexican sources" (DEA 1995a: 1). By using previously established networks, Mexican organizations are producing and distributing d-methamphetamine, a drug twice as potent as its predecessor (dl-methamphetamine) and with a longer lasting high than cocaine provides.

As Mexican d-methamphetamine producing and trafficking organizations seek to further expand their controlling interest in this emerging, lucrative market, the incidence of clandestine lab and dump sites has increased, although it remains primarily a West Coast phenomenon.

In the seventeen counties of California's Central Valley area—Bakersfield to Sacramento—there are vast, unpopulated areas with ready access to interstate roads, and chronic unemployment in the area makes recruiting drug workers relatively easy, despite the hazards of methamphetamine production. Mexican organizations have set up laboratories throughout the area. Labs that are discovered are easily replaced, as are the workers who are arrested—they are viewed as a "renewable resource" (Nieves 2001).

CANNABIS/MARIJUANA

The biggest influence on marijuana legislation has been racism. State laws against marijuana were often part of a reaction to Mexican immigration (Bonnie and Whitebread 1970). By 1930, sixteen states with relatively large Mexican populations had enacted anti-marijuana legislation. "Chicanos in the Southwest were believed to be incited to violence by smoking it" (Musto 1973: 65). Because of marijuana's association with suspect marginal groups—Mexicans, artists, intellectuals, jazz musicians, bohemians, and petty criminals—it became an easy target for regulation (Morgan 1981). By 1931, twenty-two states had marijuana legislation, often part of a general-purpose statute against narcotics (Bonnie and Whitebread 1970). In 1937, Congress passed the Marijuana Tax Act, which put an end to lawful recreational use of the substance. Despite being outlawed, marijuana was never an important issue in the United States until the 1960s: "It hardly ever made headlines or became the subject of highly publicized hearings and reports. Few persons knew or cared about it, and marihuana laws were passed with minimal attention" (Himmelstein 1983: 38).

The source of marijuana, the hemp plant, grows wild throughout most of the tropical and temperate regions of the world, including parts of the United States. Hemp has been cultivated for several useful products: The tough fiber of the stem is used to make rope, the seed as part of feed mixtures, and the oil as an ingredient in paint. The psychoactive part of the plant is a substance called Delta9THC, or simply THC. It is most highly concentrated in the leaves and resinous flowering tops of the plant. The THC level of marijuana cigarettes varies considerably: Domestic marijuana typically has had less than 0.5 percent, because the plants were originally introduced to produce hemp fiber. More recently developed strains, however, exhibit considerably higher levels, the result of careful cross breeding by outlaw horticulturalists. The domestic cultivation of marijuana has spawned a significant market in horticultural equipment. These suppliers advertise in *High Times*, a magazine devoted to marijuana use.

Jamaican, Colombian, and Mexican marijuana ranges from 0.5 to 4.0 percent THC. The most select product, sinsemilla (Spanish *sin semilla*, "without seed"), is prepared from the unpollinated female cannabis plant. Sinsemilla has been found to have as much as 8.0 percent THC. Hashish, which is usually imported from the Middle East, contains the drug-rich resinous secretions of the cannabis plant, which are collected, dried, and then compressed into a variety of forms—balls, cakes, or sheets. Hashish has a potency as high as 10 percent. Hashish is usually mixed with tobacco and smoked in a pipe. "Hashish oil" is a dark, viscous liquid, the result of repeated extractions of cannabis plant materials. It has a THC level as high as 20 percent. A drop or two on a cigarette has the effect of a single marijuana cigarette. Marijuana prepared for street sale may be diluted with oregano, catnip, or other ingredients and may contain psychoactive substances such as lysergic acid diethylamide (LSD).

In the United States, marijuana is usually rolled in paper and smoked. The user typically inhales the smoke deeply and holds it in the lungs for as long as possible. This tends to maximize the absorption of the active THC, about one-half of which is lost during smoking. The psychoactive reaction occurs in 1 to 10 minutes and peaks in about 10 to 30 minutes, with a total duration of 3 to 4 hours. The most important variables with respect to the drug's impact are the individual's experiences and expectations and the strength of the marijuana ingested. Thus, the first-time user may not experience any significant reaction. In general, low doses tend to induce restlessness and an increasing sense of well-being and gregariousness, followed by a dreamy state of relaxation; hunger, especially a craving for sweets, frequently accompanies marijuana use. Higher doses may induce changes in sensory perception—heightening the senses of smell, sight, hearing, and taste—which may be accompanied by subtle alterations in thought formation and expression.

There is little or no pattern to marijuana trafficking in the United States, although some areas have apparently gotten hooked on the business. In Kentucky, most cultivation takes place in the eastern region: the mountainous and inaccessible Appalachia. The impoverished region has a high unemployment rate. In the region's rugged hills, poverty—and thus incentive—is widespread. Although the rest of the nation prospered amid record economic growth, the region's endemic poverty and ideal growing climate feeds the industry. Appalachia's rugged terrain also provides a natural camouflage for the marijuana. Much of the cultivation occurs on federal lands to avoid forfeiture laws (discussed in Chapter 15). In Boone National Forest, 192,685 plants worth $384 million were eradicated in 1999. The marijuana business has a positive impact on the legitimate economy supported by the cultivators—everything from grocery stores to car dealerships depends on marijuana (Hefling 2000).

BARBITURATES

There are about 2,500 derivatives of barbituric acid and dozens of brand names for these derivatives. Lawfully produced barbiturates are found in tablet or capsule form. Illegal barbiturates may be found in liquid form for intravenous use because lawfully produced barbiturates are poorly soluble in water. "Barbiturates depress the sensory cortex, decrease motor activity, alter cerebralar function, and produce drowsiness, sedation, and hypnosis" (*Physicians' Desk Reference* 1987: 1163). They inhibit seizure activity and can induce unconsciousness in the form of sleep or surgical anesthesia. Unlike opiates, barbiturates do not decrease one's sense of pain. They can produce a variety of mood alterations, ranging from mild sedation to hypnosis and deep coma. A high dosage can induce anesthesia, and an overdose can be fatal. Barbiturates are used primarily as sedatives for the treatment of insomnia and as anticonvulsants (Mendelson 1980), although in some persons, they produce excitation (*Physicians' Desk Reference* 1988). The euphoria that follows barbiturate intake makes them appealing as intoxicants (Wesson and Smith 1977).

Barbiturates are classified according to the speed with which they are metabolized (broken down chemically) in the liver and eliminated by the kidneys: slow, intermediate, fast, and ultra fast. The fast-acting forms—the best known is sodium pentothal—are used to induce unconsciousness in a few minutes. At relatively high dosages, they are used as anesthetics for minor surgery and to induce anesthesia before the administration of slow-acting barbiturates. In low dosages, barbiturates may actually increase a person's reaction to painful stimuli. The fast-acting barbiturates, particularly Nembutal (sodium pentobarbital), Amytal (amobarbital sodium), Seconal (secobarbital sodium), and Tuinal (secobarbital sodium and amobarbital sodium combined), are the abuse risks (O'Brien and Cohen 1984).

There is no apparent pattern to the illegal market in barbiturates, and traffickers may sell them as part of their portfolio.

METHAQUALONE

Methaqualone was first synthesized in 1951 in India, where it was introduced as an antimalarial drug but found to be ineffective. At the same time its sedating effects resulted in its introduction in Great Britain as a safe, nonbarbiturate sleeping pill. The substance subsequently found its way into street abuse: A similar sequence of events occurred in Germany and Japan. In 1965, methaqualone was introduced into the United States as the prescription drugs Sopors and Quaalude. Methaqualone was not listed as a scheduled (controlled) drug. By the early 1970s, "ludes" and "sopors" were part of the drug culture. Physicians overprescribed the drug for anxiety and insomnia, believing that it was safer than barbiturates. The supplies for street sales came primarily from diversions of legitimate sources.

Eight years after it was first introduced into the United States, methaqualone's dangers became evident. The drug was placed on Schedule II—high potential for abuse, limited medical use—in 1973. Although the drug is chemically unrelated to barbiturates, methaqualone intoxication is similar to barbiturate intoxication. Addiction develops rapidly, and an overdose can be fatal. Although similar to barbiturates in its effects, methaqualone produces an even greater loss of motor coordination, which explains why it is sometimes referred to as a "wallbanger." Methaqualone is now illegally manufactured in Colombia and smuggled into the United States.

PHENCYCLIDINE (PCP)

Phencyclidine is reported to have received the name PCP—"peace pill"—on the streets of San Francisco. The drug was reputed to give illusions of everlasting peace. Frequently referred to as "angel dust," PCP was first synthesized in 1956 and found to be an effective surgical anesthetic when tested on monkeys. Experiments on humans were carried out in 1957, and although PCP proved to be an effective surgical anesthetic, it had serious side effects. Some patients experienced agitation, excitement, and disorientation during the recovery period. Some male surgical patients became violent, and some females appeared to experience simple intoxication (Linder, Lerner, and Burns 1981). "When PCP was subsequently given to normal volunteers in smaller doses, it induced a psychotic-like state resembling schizophrenia. Volunteers experienced body image changes, depersonalization, and feelings of loneliness, isolation, and dependency. Their thinking was observed to become progressively disorganized" (Lerner 1980: 14).

There are more than one hundred variations (analogs) of the substance. Unlike other anesthetics, PCP increases respiration, heart rate, and blood pressure, qualities that make it useful for patients endangered by a depressed heart rate or low blood pressure. In the 1960s, PCP became commercially available for use in veterinary medicine as an analgesic and anesthetic, but diversion to street use led the manufacturer to discontinue production in 1978. It is now produced easily and cheaply in clandestine laboratories in tablet, capsule, powder, and liquid form and sometimes sold as LSD. Its color varies, and there is no such thing as a standard dose. As with any drug sold on the street, PCP is often mixed with other psychoactive substances. Most commonly, PCP is applied to a leafy vegetable, including marijuana, and smoked. "Street preparations of phencyclidine have continuously changed in name, physical form and purity" (Lerner 1980: 15).

A moderate amount of PCP produces a sense of detachment, distance, and estrangement from one's surroundings within 30 to 60 minutes of ingestion, and the effects last as long as hours. Numbness, slurred speech, and a loss of coordination also occur. These symptoms are often accompanied by feelings of invulnerability. "A blank stare, rapid and involuntary eye movements, and an exaggerated gait are among the more common observable effects" ("Drugs of Abuse" 1979: 30). Users may also experience mood disorders, acute anxiety, paranoia, and violent behavior. Some reactions are similar to LSD intoxication: auditory hallucinations and image distortion, similar to fun-house mirror images. "PCP is unique among popular drugs of abuse in its power to produce psychoses indistinguishable from schizophrenia" ("Drugs of Abuse" 1979: 30).

Like methamphetamine, PCP has been distributed by outlaw motorcycle clubs.

ECSTASY

Ecstasy, the common name for 3, 4-Methylene-DioxyMethAmphetamine or MDMA, is a synthetic drug with a chemical structure similar to the stimulant methamphetamine and the hallucino-gen mescaline (Grob et al. 1996). Some therapists used it in the 1970s to help patients explore their feelings for each other. In a controlled setting, MDMA was reputed to promote trust between patients and physicians (Karch 1996). In 1985, scheduling hearings on MDMA were conducted and the administrative law judge expressed his view that there was sufficient evidence for safe use under medical supervision and recommended Schedule III status. He was overruled by the direc-tor of the Drug Enforcement Administration who placed MDMA in Schedule I—high potential for abuse, no medically accepted use.

MDMA is usually ingested orally in tablet or capsule form. It is also available as a powder and is sometimes snorted and occasionally smoked. Ecstasy did not receive a great deal of attention until its "rediscovery" in the late 1970s because of its purported ability to produce profound pleasur-able effects: acute euphoria and long-lasting posi-tive changes in attitude and self-confidence, with some symptoms resembling those caused by LSD but without the severe side effects typically associ-ated with methamphetamine.

"The effects of MDMA usually become apparent twenty to sixty minutes following oral ingestion of an average dose (100–125 milligrams) on an empty stomach. The sudden and intense onset of the high experienced by many users is commonly referred to as the 'rush' (also the 'wave' or 'weird period')." This phase is often (particu-larly during initial use) experienced with a certain degree of trepidation, tension, stomach tightness, or mild nausea. Discomfort is generally transi-tory and melts away into a more relaxed state of being. "Although novice users occasionally experi-enced some apprehension during this initial onset, anxiety levels typically decreased with subsequent use, allowing for increased enjoyment" (Beck and Rosenbaum 1994: 63). The total effects last from three to six hours.

The drug's rewarding effects vary with the individual taking it, the dose and purity, and the environment in which it is taken. In high doses, ecstasy may cause the body's temperature to mark-edly increase (malignant hyperthermia) leading to muscle breakdown and kidney and cardiovascu-lar system failure, which has proven fatal in some cases. Drinking water does not reduce the effects of ecstasy, but prevents dehydration. Drinking too much water, however, may lead to serious health complications in some people. Ecstasy may also produce a hangover effect: loss of appetite, insom-nia, depression, and muscle aches. It can also make concentration difficult, particularly on the day after ecstasy is taken. Higher doses of ecstasy can produce hallucinations, irrational behavior, vomit-ing, and convulsions. Some evidence suggests that long-term use of ecstasy may cause damage to the brain, heart, and liver.

Although most MDMA/ecstasy consumed domestically is produced in Europe—primarily the Netherlands and Belgium—a limited number of MDMA labs operate in the United States. In recent years, Israeli crime syndicates, some com-posed of Russian émigrés associated with Russian organized crime, have forged relationships with Western European traffickers and gained control over a significant share of the European market. The Israeli syndicates are currently the primary source to U.S. distribution groups.

Overseas ecstasy trafficking organizations smuggle the drug in shipments of 10,000 or more tablets via express mail services, couriers aboard commercial airline flights, or through air freight shipments from several major European cities to cities in the United States. Ecstasy costs as little as 25 cents per pill to produce, but wholesale prices range from $5 to $20 and retail prices range from $10 to $50 a dose. Ecstasy traffickers use brand names and logos as marketing tools and to dis-tinguish their product from that of competitors. The logos are produced to coincide with holidays or special events. Among the more popular logos are butterflies, lightning bolts, and four-leaf clo-vers (*National Synthetic Drugs Action Plan* 2004).

LYSERGIC ACID DIETHYLAMIDE (LSD)

In 1949, LSD was introduced into the United States as an experimental drug for treating psychi-atric illnesses, but until 1954 it remained relatively rare and expensive, because its ingredients were difficult to cultivate. In that year the Eli Lilly Company announced that it had succeeded in creating a completely synthetic version of LSD (Stevens 1987). LSD ("acid") affects the body in a variety of ways. The visual effects range from blurring to a visual field filled with strange objects; three-dimensional space appears to contract and enlarge, and light appears to fluctuate in intensity. Auditory effects occur but to a lesser degree. All of these changes are episodic throughout the "trip." Temperature sensitivity is altered, and the environment is perceived as being abnormally cold or hot. Body images are altered—out-of-body experiences are common, and body parts appear to float. Perceptions of time are affected: Sometimes time is perceived as running fast-forward or fast-backward.

There are "good acid trips" and "bad acid trips." This appears to be controlled by the attitude, mood, and expectations of the user and often depends on suggestions of others at the time of the trip. Favorable expectations produce "good trips," but excessive apprehension is likely to produce the opposite. The substance appears to intensify feelings, so the user may feel a magnified sense of love, lust, and joy, or anger, terror, and despair: "The extraordinary sensations and feelings may bring on fear of losing control, paranoia, and panic, or they may cause euphoria and even bliss" (Grinspoon 1979: 13). Ingesting LSD unknowingly can result in a highly traumatic experience, since the victim may feel that he or she has suddenly "gone crazy" (Brecher 1972), and it only takes 0.01 milligram to have an effect.

LSD is colorless, odorless, and tasteless, and it is relatively easy to produce. One ounce contains about 300,000 human doses (Ray 1978). Although LSD has been used experimentally to treat a variety of psychological illnesses, it currently has no accepted medical use. It may be taken orally in a pure form as a white powder, mixed with a number of other substances, or absorbed on paper ("blotter acid"), sugar, or gelatin sheets ("window panes"). A trip begins between 30 to 60 minutes after ingestion, peaks after 2 to 6 hours, and fades out after about 12 hours.

LSD was popular for a time during the 1960s, when it became part of the "hippie" culture. Current use appears limited, and distribution patterns are not well known.

ANALOGS AND DESIGNER DRUGS

There are many chemical variations, or analogs (also called "designer drugs"), of the drugs discussed in this chapter, for example, semi-synthetic opiates such as hydromorphine, oxycodone, etorphine, and diprenorphine, as well as synthetic opiates such as pethidine, methadone, and propoxyphene (Darvon). The synthetic drug fentanyl citrate, which is often used intravenously in major surgery, works exactly like opiates: It kills pain, produces euphoria, and leads to addiction if abused. The substance is easily produced by persons skilled in chemistry. Fentanyl compounds are often sold as "China White," the street name for the finest Southeast Asian heroin, to addicts who cannot tell the difference. Those who know the difference may actually prefer fentanyl because it is usually cheaper than heroin and some users believe it contains less adulterants than heroin (Roberton 1986). In fact, fentanyl compounds are quite potent and difficult for street dealers to cut properly, a situation that can lead to overdose and death. Fentanyl has been used (illegally) to "dope" racehorses, because the substance is very difficult to detect in urine or blood.

Synthetic substances chemically similar to cocaine, such as lidocaine and procaine (novocaine), will eliminate all feeling when applied topically, as dental patients recognize. Single small doses of lidocaine, when taken intranasally by experienced cocaine users, produced the same euphoric response as cocaine—they could not distinguish between the two substances (van Dyke and Byck 1982). Other tests indicate that laboratory animals will work as hard for procaine as they will for cocaine. Since the passage of the Antidrug Abuse Act of 1986, all analogs of controlled substances have themselves become controlled substances.

SUMMARY

- Until the 1914 Harrison Act—the result of efforts to enhance America's trade position with China—drugs such as heroin were legally available in the United States.
- Enforcement efforts by federal agents led to a thriving black market.
- The four main sources for heroin are the Golden Triangle, the Golden Crescent, Mexico, and, more recently, Colombia. In these areas a volatile mixture of politics and poverty support poppy cultivation and provide wealth and resources to political insurgents and criminal organizations.
- The popularity of cocaine is more recent, and as the market expanded in the 1960s, the criminal organizations of Colombia (discussed in Chapter 7) came to dominate the trade.

- After heroin and cocaine are smuggled into the United States, the drugs move through a distribution network during which the substances are usually diluted with various inert powders until they reach the retail-consumer level.
- At each step, the enormous profits that accrue can give rise to violence because transactions must be accomplished without recourse to the formal mechanisms of dispute resolution.
- The drug world is filled with heavily armed and dangerous persons in the employ of the larger cartels, although even street-level operatives are often armed.
- In addition to heroin and cocaine, methamphetamine and ecstasy trafficking are often part of the world of organized crime, and some organizations traffic in more than one drug.

REVIEW QUESTIONS

1. Until they were made illegal in the United States, why were opium products so popular?
2. What was the real cause of the Opium Wars?
3. How did the Chinese opium problem affect the United States?
4. What was the relationship between Chinese immigrants and the legislation against opium?
5. What was the direct cause of the passage of the Harrison Act?
6. How did the Supreme Court rule with respect to the Harrison Act?
7. How did the federal drug enforcement agency respond to the Harrison Act?
8. What are the similarities and differences between trafficking in alcohol during Prohibition and drug trafficking after the Harrison Act?
9. Why is it difficult, if not impossible, for an organized crime unit to control the drug market?
10. What political elements result in the enormous production of Golden Triangle heroin?
11. Why has it been difficult to curtail the cultivation of poppies and the manufacturing of heroin in the Golden Crescent?
12. What led to the widespread popularity of cocaine during the late 1960s and early 1970s?
13. What are designer drugs?

CHAPTER

14

Labor, Business, and Money Laundering

There are more than fifteen million persons who belong to labor unions in the United States. The unions to which they belong provide representation through collective bargaining that is guaranteed by federal law—the National Labor Relations (Wagner) Act of 1935 (upheld by the Supreme Court in the 1937 case *National Labor Relations Board v. Jones and Laughlin Steel Corporation*, 301 U.S. 1).

Labor racketeering is the infiltration, domination, and use of a union for personal benefit by illegal, violent, and fraudulent means. Ronald Goldstock points out that the "sometimes bewildering array of labor rackets assume three basic forms: the sale of 'strike insurance' in which the union threatens a walkout and the employer pays to assure a steady supply of labor; the 'sweetheart deal' in which management pays the labor representative for contract terms unobtainable through arm's-length bargaining; and the direct or indirect siphoning of union funds" (PCOC 1985a: 658). An employer may be tempted into a corrupt relationship with labor unions because "he may hope that through a payment to the union officers he can persuade them not to organize his shop, thereby allowing for payment of less than the

going union wage. Such an arrangement is particularly beneficial when his competitors are organized." If he cannot stifle organization, "he may at least be able to get a lenient 'sweetheart' agreement with the union." Furthermore, the "union itself can be used for the benefit of the employer through the limitation of competition. Competition can be limited by the union in several ways— either through the refusal to work on goods or by directly enforcing price agreements" (Newell 1961: 79). Although labor and related business racketeering can be conducted by anyone, the history of the labor movement shows that the most substantial corruption of unions is conducted by organized crime.

Labor and business racketeering distinguish the American Mafia and its predecessor groups from later forms of organized crime. Irish, Jewish, and Italian organized crime groups helped shape the economic life of the United States. The rise of organized labor and the subsequent reaction of American business generated a conflict that provided fertile ground for the seeds of racketeering and organized crime. The leaders of organized crime provided mercenary armies to unions that were willing to use violence to organize workers and thwart strikebreakers. In the spirit of ideological neutrality, they also provided private violence to business for use in its efforts against organized labor and also its dealings with the demanding competition of a capitalistic marketplace.

ORGANIZED LABOR IN AMERICA

The Civil War led to the dramatic industrialization of America. War profiteers accumulated large amounts of capital, enabling them to invest in the trusts: oil, coal, iron, steel, sugar, and railroads. Congress imposed protective tariffs, and industry blossomed during the Gilded Age of the Robber Barons. "Within twenty-five years of the assassination of Abraham Lincoln, America had become the leading manufacturing nation in the world" (Brooks 1971: 39).

At the bottom of this industrial world was labor, often immigrants who spoke English with foreign accents, if they spoke English at all. Children of both sexes often labored 12 hours a day, 6 days a week, under conditions that threatened life and limb. Labor's struggle for better working conditions and wages resulted in what Sidney Lens calls *The Labor Wars* (1974: 4): "The labor wars were a specific response to a specific set of injustices at a time when industrial and financial capitalism was establishing its predominance over American society. In a sense the battles were not different from the hundreds of other violent clashes against social injustices, as normal as the proverbial apple pie in the nation's annals."

During the first half of the nineteenth century until the Civil War, criminal conspiracy statutes were used against labor's efforts to organize and strike. This approach was replaced by the use of equity—a civil procedure—in the form of injunctions restraining unions from striking. The unions sought relief from Congress, but in 1908 the Supreme Court declared that Congress had no power with respect to union activities (*Adair v. United States*, 208 U.S. 161). It was not until the Great Depression that Congress stripped the federal courts of their power to issue injunctions

in labor disputes (1932 Norris-La Guardia Act). In 1935, the Wagner Act gave explicit protection to the rights of workers to organize and engage in collective bargaining.

From the earliest days of our republic until the passage of the Wagner Act, labor confrontations with employers often took on a particular scenario: Company spies, often from the Pinkerton Private Detective Agency, would identify union leaders, who were then fired by management. The guard force would be increased and strikebreakers secured. Company lawyers would secure injunctions from friendly judges prohibiting a strike. The union would organize "flying squadrons" to guard against the influx of strikebreakers and plan for mass picketing. If the guard force proved inadequate, hired thugs, deputy sheriffs, policemen, National Guard, and even U.S. Army troops would be used to deal with strikers.

LABOR RACKETEERING: IN THE BEGINNING . . .

The first step away from union democracy was a response to power wielded by employers. In order to avoid the problem of company spies reporting to management, some unions employed the "walking delegate" or business agent, who was empowered to call a strike without any formal vote by the union membership. As an employee of the union, he was immune from management intimidation, and his power enabled the union to strike quickly and at the most opportune time, for example, at a construction site during the height of the building season. The men chosen for this position were usually tough, and it was this quality rather than intelligence, integrity, and commitment to labor that characterized business agents. Before long some of these men began abusing their power, calling needless strikes and engaging in extortionate practices (Seidman 1938). In 1928, for example, two racketeers set up the United Lathing Company and hired the Lathers Union walking delegate. He would appear at job sites and issue a strike order. When contractors asked for an explanation, he would refer them to the United Lathing Company, where, for a fee, the strike would be called off (Nelli 1976). These types of racketeers intimidated union members and employers but were usually not connected to a syndicate (Newell 1961).

In the early days, labor unions provided "muscle" from the ranks of their membership to deal with Pinkerton agents and strikebreakers. In the first decade of the twentieth century, however, a need arose for a more systematic and professional approach. Enter Benjamin ("Dopey") Fein. A leader of the Lower East Side gang once headed by Monk Eastman (discussed in Chapter 4), Fein became an integral part of the Jewish labor movement (Joselit 1983: 109): Whenever a strike was called under the auspices of the umbrella organization called United Hebrew Trades (UHT), "Dopey and his men were given union cards as pickets and union delegates." They protected fellow pickets against management goons—strong-arm personnel who were employed by licensed detective agencies.

Fein formed alliances with New York street gangs such as the Hudson Dusters, assigning territories and working out businesslike arrangements and patterns of operation. He also assisted the union in keeping its members in line. It soon became clear, however, that it was easier to hire gangsters than it was to fire them (Seidman 1938). Racketeers such as Lepke Buchalter and Gurrah Shapiro came to dominate many of the industries into which they were invited (see Chapter 4). "The introduction of armed hoods as 'finks' (strikebreakers) or as 'nobles' (armed guards) by industry, facilitated the entry of the Arnold Rothsteins and Capones into the lucrative business of industrial racketeering" (Brooks 1971: 147).

When Max ("The Butcher") Bloch tried to organize a union, the Wholesale Butcher Drivers, and called a strike, he found himself meeting with some fearsome representatives of the meatpacking houses: Harry ("Pittsburgh Phil") Strauss and his fellow partners in Murder, Inc. (discussed in Chapter 4). Max the Butcher's background as an ex-con and professional boxer allowed him to "sweet talk" the "Boys from Brooklyn," and he

was left alone. "So the wholesalers couldn't break the strike. They'd gone to the toughest and lost. They saw they couldn't shake us, that nobody would go against us" (Bloch and Kenner 1982: 72). The business agent for the Chicago local of the Bartenders International League (which later merged with the Hotel and Restaurant Employees Union) was not so lucky. In 1939, representatives of the Capone syndicate ordered him to step aside and appoint one of their men to the local's presidency. When he returned to his office and, after consultation with the other officers of the local, it was decided that the honest union leader's life was worth more than resisting the syndicate—he resigned (Newell 1961).

Labor racketeers "didn't target steel mills and auto factories and foundries, the giant pool of workers who truly needed the protection of a collective bargaining agreement." Instead, they "picked on small, vulnerable mom-and-pop operations such as dry cleaners, taverns, and bakeries." Or they exploited their control over labor to extort money from vulnerable businesses such as those selling wholesale fish. Because of the perishable nature of the product, seafood wholesalers depend on speed for display and delivery, which makes them vulnerable to threats of delay (Neff 1989: 20).

An Example: The Fulton Fish Market

New York's Fulton Fish Market represents a classic saga in the power of organized crime to control an industry. While the market was established in 1833, the organized crime connection began during Prohibition, when some innovative criminals—in this case Joseph ("Socks") Lanza—avoided bootlegging for the less competitive rewards of labor and business racketeering. At age 14, Lanza began working as a fish handler at the giant wholesale market along the East River near Fulton Street in lower Manhattan. He became a member of the crime Family of Lucky Luciano (now known as the Genovese Family), and in 1923 organized his fellow workers into Local 359 of the United Seafood Worker's Union. As head of the local and subsequently a *caporegime* in the

Genovese Family, Lanza extorted money from every dealer in the market. "Lanza influenced the price of fish not only in New York but throughout much of the nation. The union served as the principal basis of Lanza's $20-million-a-year racket" (Nelli 1976: 245). He and his brother, also a Genovese captain, determined which businesses could operate in the market. Through his leadership of the union, Lanza asserted control over fishing boats because he could withhold the labor needed to unload the vessels. He also controlled the Fulton Market's Watchmen's Protective Association: "Dealers who visited the market and failed to have a Lanza watchman look after their vehicles usually found their tires slashed" (Peterson 1983: 173).

In 1938, Lanza was convicted of racketeering, and in 1943 he was convicted of extortion involving local Teamster union officials (Carroll 1991). Paroled in 1950, Lanza was arrested as a parole violator seven years later in a case that touched off a scandal. New York State parole officers recommended returning Lanza to prison as a major racketeer, but the parole board member in charge of his case released the "Fish Market Czar." A subsequent investigation revealed that high-level political pressure had led to the decision to release. The parole board subsequently overruled the decision, and Lanza was returned to prison to finish out his unexpired term. Convictions and imprisonment notwithstanding, Lanza continued to control the Fulton Market until his death in 1968, when domination passed into other Genovese Family hands (Nelli 1976).

Despite the fact that the market operated on city property, government controls remained absent for decades, creating a lawless atmosphere in which rules of operation evolved through violence and intimidation—an ideal atmosphere for organized crime (Carroll 1991). In 1988, as a result of a civil action brought by the U.S. Department of Justice, an outside administrator was appointed to monitor the market and rid it of illegal activities—U.S. Attorney Rudolph Giuliani convinced a federal judge that the market was dominated by the Genovese Family (Glaberson 1989). Two years later, however, the administrator stated that the

market continued to operate "in a frontier atmosphere, in that the Fulton Fish Market is a sovereign entity where the laws of economic power and physical force, not the laws of New York City, prevail" (Raab 1990: B12).

The market is a vital economic asset to the city, generating sales of 125 million tons of seafood annually and providing about 1,000 jobs. It is the source of most seafood sold in retail outlets and served in restaurants throughout the New York region. When they come to pick up supplies, merchants are assigned parking spots by unlicensed loaders who charge a fee and retain the right to transport supplies to the purchaser's vehicle. Many firms seek to avoid the high prices at the market, shopping instead in Philadelphia and Boston, which has cost New York City as much as $2 billion in lost sales annually (Raab 1995d, 1995e).

When the former U.S. attorney became Mayor Giuliani, he asserted city control over the market through the power to license, regulate, and investigate who does business or works in the market. The city evicted six unloading companies allegedly affiliated with the Genovese Family and hired an outside firm to replace them. In response, in 1995, a wildcat strike threw the market into chaos. The strike soon ended and a strained sense of calm prevailed, only to be upset again in 1996 with more wildcat strikes. Reforms established by the city of New York have reduced, if not eliminated, the influence of organized crime, but this is seen as a mixed blessing by the market's wholesale dealers, who have complained of rigid rules and increased overhead costs (Raab 1996a, 1996f).

In 2005, the market moved to a new 450,000-square-foot facility that is the length of the Empire State Building, in the Hunts Point section of the Bronx. Like other public food markets, Hunts Point is under the licensing jurisdiction of the New York City Business Integrity Commission. At the end of 2006, the Commission was responsible for uncovering a gambling and loansharking operation that included numbers and sports betting being run at the market by members and associates of the Genovese Family.

"Every union member who wanted to work or sought a better assignment was expected to pay; every unionized employer who wanted to be left alone ('labor peace') or granted a little slack on the strict terms of the collective bargaining agreement to thereby cut costs and gain a competitive advantage ('sweetheart deal') was expected to pay; every outside vendor on every job site was expected to pay—the lunchwagon, the landscaper, the electrician, the painting contractor, the supplier of spare parts for the company inventory—and every vendor for the union and its benefit plans was expected to pay—the contractor who remodeled the union hall at a huge inflated cost, the dentist and attorney and every other service provider to the welfare plan, and the actuary and investment manager and especially the banker who had custody of the millions or tens of millions in pension plan assets, all were expected to pay" (Stewart 2006: 62–63).

LABOR RACKETEERING AND THE "BIG FOUR"

Unions fought not only with management, but also with each other. In 1938, a number of industrial unions led by John L. Lewis broke with the American Federation of Labor (AFL) and formed the Congress of Industrial Organizations (CIO). During struggles over jurisdiction and representation between the AFL and the CIO, both sides resorted to "muscle" from organized crime. But for whatever reason, whoever utilized organized crime was "playing with the devil." Many locals and some internationals were delivered into the hands of organized crime.

Leaders of industrial unions working alongside hundreds or even thousands of other workers in factories or mines proved difficult to intimidate. In contrast, unions whose members worked in geographically dispersed locations for numerous small employers, such as restaurant workers, teamsters, and construction workers, or those representing workers whose employment was sporadic or seasonal, longshoremen, for example, proved susceptible to racketeering (Jacobs 2006). In 1983, a congressional committee concluded: "At least four international unions are completely dominated by men who either have strong ties to or are members of the organized crime syndicate. A majority of the locals in most major cities of the United States in the International Brotherhood of Teamsters (IBT), Hotel and Restaurant Employees Union (HRE), Laborers' International Union of North America (Laborers), and International Longshoremen's Association (ILA) are completely dominated by organized crime" (Permanent Subcommittee on Investigations 1982: 5).

Laborers' International Union

Formed in 1903, the Laborers' International Union of North America (LIUNA) is one of fifteen unions that belong to the Building Construction Trades Department of the AFL-CIO. Representing about 800,000 laborers in hundreds of locals in the United States and Canada, LIUNA members perform the dirtiest, most strenuous, and most dangerous work associated with building construction. Control over laborers provides control over many construction sites. The Laborers' Union "is classic Chicago old-time unionism. It was headed for years by Peter Fosco,[1] an Italian immigrant whose association with Capone-era hoodlums did not prevent him from winning public office and once earning an Italian-American award at a dinner addressed by Richard Nixon. The Laborers' Union has always had a healthy treasury, kept brimming with hard-working workers' dues" (Kilian, Fletcher, and Ciccone 1979: 247).

In Chicago, the Laborers' Union has always had close ties to the Outfit. For more than a decade, the 19,000-member Chicago District Council

---

[1]Peter Fosco was succeeded by his son Angelo in 1975. Angelo was acquitted of union corruption charges and remained president of the LIUNA until his death in 1993 at age 71.

of the Laborers' Union was headed by Ernest Kumerow, who is married to the daughter of the late Outfit boss Tony Accardo. Until his death in 1992, Accardo spent winters in a coach house in the rear of Kumerow's home. Street boss Vincent Solano was president of Local 1 until his death from natural causes in 1992, and his son remained a LIUNA official. Street boss Alfred Pilotta was president of Local 5 until he was convicted in 1982 for his role in a kickback scheme involving the union's welfare benefit fund. In 1992, a veteran LIUNA official and Outfit boss in charge of the southern suburbs was sentenced to 32 years for extorting money from bookmakers in northwest Indiana. His codefendant, a Laborers' Union field representative, received 36 years (Jackson 1990). In 1997, the $90,000-a-year LIUNA secretary-treasurer of Local 5, a top lieutenant for the South Side Outfit boss, was charged with the 1988 murder of the owner of a pallet company who refused to pay a $100,000 juice loan—he had been shot six times. In 2000, while awaiting trial for murder, the LIUNA official died of natural causes. In 2001, John Serpico, a former international vice president of LIUNA and reputed Outfit associate, was convicted of receiving kickbacks for using his union influence to arrange for millions of dollars in loans from the union.

Surveillance tapes contain conversations involving New Jersey Family boss Sam DeCavalcante, during which he discussed how control of Laborers' Union locals enabled him to "shake down" building contractors who wanted to avoid using expensive union labor. When DeCavalcante retired, the man he chose to replace him, John Riggi, was business agent for LIUNA Local 394 in Elizabeth, New Jersey (G. Smith 2003). For much of his adult life, until he was voted out in 1992, Matthew ("Mikey") Trupiano, head of the St. Louis *Cosa Nostra*, led the Laborers' Union Local 110.[2] In 1985, the President's Commission on Organized Crime concluded that in New York,

several LIUNA locals are controlled by members of the five crime Families.

In 1995, the U.S. Department of Justice reached a consent agreement with the union under which the federal government would monitor efforts to purge LIUNA officials connected to organized crime. As part of the agreement, LIUNA agreed to hold direct elections for the union's top posts; previously they had been chosen by delegates at the annual convention. In only one instance did an opposition candidate ever challenge the union slate, and he was physically beaten on the floor of the 1981 convention (Johnson 1996). Chicago's Bruno Caruso lost the government-monitored election to Arthur Coia.

Coia is the son of a former secretary-treasurer of LIUNA who allegedly had close ties with New England crime boss Raymond Patriarca. A native of Rhode Island, Arthur Coia first headed the Laborers' local in Providence and later throughout New England. He admitted knowing Raymond Patriarca, Jr., who took over the crime Family after his father died of natural causes in 1984. Coia has also admitted that he met with mob figures in Chicago—he denied knowing they were connected to the Outfit. He stated that he was told to meet with them in order to get permission to take the top spot in the union (Greenhouse 1997, 2000c).

Under an arrangement with the Department of Justice, the union conducted an internal investigation led by a former federal organized crime prosecutor. As a result, the Justice Department dropped a 1995 civil complaint that sought to remove Coia and place the union under receivership. One of those suspended in the subsequent union purge was president of the Chicago LIUNA Local 225 who in 1999 was convicted of syndicated gambling—accepting $200,000 in sports wagers over a three-week period—for which he was placed on probation. In 1999, the president of LIUNA Local 2 in Chicago was removed for his alleged role in the Outfit's North Side crew. In 2001, a federal hearing officer removed the business managers of Local 1001 and 1006 in Chicago; according to the government, the brothers Bruno and Leo Caruso, along with Outfit members, rigged union elections (Possley 2001). The Caruso

---

[2]In 1997, Trupiano, at 58, died of a heart attack. The criminal organization he headed was considerably weakened by internal strife—and bombings—after the death of Trupiano's uncle, Anthony Giordano, under whose leadership the St. Louis *Cosa Nostra* was a unit of some local stature.

brothers are the sons of Frank ("Skids") Caruso, for many years the Outfit boss of Chinatown who died in 1983, and nephews of a convicted First Ward alderman.

A civil RICO (discussed in Chapter 15) action was taken to rid the Buffalo, New York, LIUNA local from organized crime control. In 1996, the government concluded that eleven Buffalo LIUNA officials were made members of the Buffalo crime Family, and they were barred from the union. The Buffalo local was subsequently placed in trustee-ship under the provisions of RICO (Office of Inspector General 2000).

In 2000, a hearing officer cleared Coia of associating with members of organized crime but fined him $100,000 for buying a $450,000 Ferrari with help from a supplier to the union. The hearing officer's ruling was criticized by the Department of Justice, union dissidents, and Republican lawmakers (Franklin 1999; Greenhouse 1999; Kaiser 1999). Under Coia, the union was one of the three biggest contributors to President Bill Clinton's 1997 inauguration. The union has also been one of the biggest contributors to the Democratic Party and (as senator) Hillary Rodham Clinton has spoken before the LIUNA convention (Greenhouse 1997). On the first day of 2000, Coia, after agreeing to plead guilty to defrauding Rhode Island of about $100,000 in taxes, retired as LIUNA president (Greenhouse 2000a). Later that year, the Justice Department agreed to relax its oversight of LIUNA; this, after the union removed 220 corrupt officials from union positions, 127 of them found to be members or associates of organized crime (Office of Inspector General 2000).

Hotel Employees and Restaurant Employees International Union (HEREIU)

HEREIU was established in Chicago in 1891: "At first, only workers from pubs and restaurants were represented. Yet as America's cities began to grow so did the international, and soon hotel workers as well as food and beverage workers were represented. Thwarted only by prohibition in the 1920s, the international became the fastest growing union in the United States in the 1930s. By 1941,

the international was the seventh largest union in North America" (Permanent Subcommittee on Investigations 1982: 4). Today the HEREIU is the largest service union in the United States, with about 260,000 members in 235 locals in 48 states and 8 Canadian provinces.

HEREIU charters often provided the basis for extortion from restaurants in Chicago, as U.S. Senator John L. McClellen explained (1962: 141–42):

> If an owner knew what was good for him, he agreed to have his place unionized upon the first visit of the organizer. The workers were not consulted in this organizing drive; they rarely knew it was going on. The restaurant owner was told that the union wasn't greedy, a compromise figure would always be accepted. If the owner had forty employees, then twenty memberships would be given to the union. The owner paid the initiation fees and the dues for twenty names that he gave the organizer. That arrangement usually continued for years. It didn't make any difference to anyone concerned in the deal that, after a period of time, possibly ten or more of the twenty union members may no longer be employees. . . . Dues continued to be collected for twenty names.

In return, there "were no sudden fires in the middle of the night, no beatings, no sugar poured into gas tanks, no tires slashed, no vandalism" (1962: 142). The restaurant owners did not have to worry about workers' salaries or working conditions—conditions of employment that are the concerns of legitimate unions.

Many of the HEREIU locals were/are reputed to be under the domination of organized crime. Local 450 in Chicago was chartered in 1935 by Joey ("Doves") Aiuppa, a top leader in the Outfit. For forty years, the Outfit wielded power in Chicago area HEREIU locals and their joint executive board. "Their actions took on national proportions when Edward Hanley [a former bartender from Chicago's West Side], who began his career in Local 450 as a business agent in 1957, was elected to the HEREIU presidency in 1973"

(PCOC 1986b: 73). When Hanley, who has never been convicted of any crime, appeared before a U.S. Senate investigating committee, he refused to answer any questions, invoking the Fifth Amendment thirty-six times (Franklin 1995a). In Illinois, the 40,000-member union local has made significant political contributions, and Hanley has been feted by the Cook County Democratic organization.

HEREIU Local 54 in New Jersey has about 22,000 members, most of them employed in the Atlantic City casino business. The local has been controlled by the Philadelphia crime Family once headed by Angelo Bruno. As a result, Bruno Family members were able to force hotels in Atlantic City to buy supplies and provisions from companies they own. In 1980, when the president of the Philadelphia Roofers Union Local 30 attempted to organize bartenders in Atlantic City—even though they belonged to Local 54—he was murdered at his home. Two union officials were convicted of ordering the murder and are serving life sentences. In 1981, the New Jersey Casino Control Commission concluded that Local 54 was controlled by Philadelphia crime boss Nicky Scarfo, and legal action eventually forced the local's president to resign. In 1991, the local was placed in government receivership, which has since been lifted.

In New York, HEREIU Locals 6 and 100 have long been under the control of organized crime. The locals were used to dictate the way in which restaurants "could do business in New York. In return for payoffs, restaurant owners could pay reduced wages and pension and welfare fund contributions, or buy a lease on a restaurant shut down because it owed money to the union, or hire and fire without regard to grievance procedures, or operate without regard to union work rules" (PCOC 1986b: 83–84). At one point, there appeared to be a jurisdictional dispute between the two locals, something that is not unusual in organized labor. However, intercepted conversations between union officials and important organized crime figures revealed that the split was in fact "a market allocation of New York's entire restaurant business between the Colombo and Gambino crime families" (PCOC 1986b: 84).

In 1995, as the result of a settlement of a civil RICO lawsuit, the U.S. Department of Justice placed the HEREIU under supervision and appointed a monitor with disciplinary and oversight authority (Franklin 1995a). In 1998, faced with another federal investigation, Edward Hanley, who ran the union for 25 years, was forced to retire—with a guaranteed $267,000 a year salary for the rest of his life. In 2000, at age 67, Hanley was killed in a traffic accident. The government-appointed monitor expelled seventeen union officials and at the end of 2000, the Justice Department agreed to end five years of intensive monitoring—according to the government, the union has been largely purged of ties to organized crime (Greenhouse 2000b).

International Longshoremen's Association (ILA)

New York City's premier position as a commercial capital is due in large part to its deep-water harbor, the finest in North America. The New York waterfront encompasses over 700 miles of wharves and shoreline and 1,900 piers. Combined, the New York–New Jersey waterfront is an integrated commercial marketplace composed of several separate ports, including the Port of New York and the Port of New Jersey, occupying a common harbor and encompassing some 1,500 square miles and 234 municipalities. The waterfront harbor plays a critical role in the movement of manufactured, agricultural, and other goods throughout the Eastern seaboard and has a major impact on this nation's commerce. With government regulation absent, organized crime was able to assert control over this lucrative piece of geography.

With the able assistance of men such as Antonio Vaccarelli, better known as Paul Kelly, the ILA was organized in the 1890s and gained complete control over the New York waterfront by 1914 (Nelli 1976). Kelly, leader of the notorious Five Points Gang (discussed in Chapter 4), became vice president of the International Longshoremen's Association. Until the twentieth century, about 95 percent of the longshoremen in the New York City area were Irish. By 1912, Italians comprised about 35 percent, and by 1919, they accounted for about 75 percent of the area's longshoremen. The Irish controlled the notoriously violent West Side ("Hell's Kitchen") docks, and those in Hoboken and Jersey City, while the Italians dominated the East Side, Brooklyn, and most New Jersey docks. By the end of World War II, the ILA had 40,000 members in the Port of New York. Today, the union represents nearly 65,000 dockworkers and other employees at three dozen ports from Maine to Texas.

For poorly educated and often illiterate immigrants, the waterfront provided attractive employment opportunities. It was also attractive to racketeers for its lucrative illegal opportunities. The "shape up," vividly portrayed in the Academy Award–winning film *On the Waterfront*, provided corrupt ILA officials with kickbacks from workers eager for a day's wage. Loansharking, large-scale pilfering, smuggling, and deals with employers eager for "labor peace" profited the criminals who dominated the waterfront. The "necessity for speed, plus the lack of rail connections to the piers, gave rise to the coveted 'loading' racket, which involved moving cargo from the pier floor to waiting trucks. Since demand for cargo loading was inelastic and dependent upon immediate need when ships arrived, loading generated extraordinary profits, and was a principal incentive for organized crime to infiltrate the ILA" (PCOC 1986b: 33). Whoever controls waterfront labor controls the waterfront.

While Paul Kelly led an influx of criminals to the waterfront, it was under Joseph P. Ryan that organized crime control of the waterfront became complete (Nelli 1976). As union president, Ryan dispensed union charters to groups of workers to form their own ILA locals. Ryan—a strident anti-communist—served as ILA president from 1927 to 1953, when he was convicted of embezzling union funds. On the West Coast, where organized crime was much weaker, Australian-born Alfred Reuton ("Harry") Bridges withdrew from the ILA and formed the International Longshoremen and Warehousemen's Union (ILWU), which became part of the rival CIO. Bridges, who was born in 1901 and came to the United States as a merchant

seaman in 1920, went to work as a longshoreman in San Francisco. He reactivated a dormant ILA local in 1933 and led a successful strike in 1934, a strike opposed by ILA president Joe Ryan. Ryan attacked Bridges for his leftist views and close association with communists (Lens 1974). During the 1940s, the House of Representatives voted to have Bridges deported as an undesirable alien, an order that was overturned by the Supreme Court. In marked contrast to the ILA, always a strongly anti-communist union, the ILWU has been free of organized crime influence. Nevertheless, the ILWU was expelled from the CIO in 1950 for "following the communist line." A variety of unions, including the Teamsters, unsuccessfully attempted to raid the ILWU membership (Kimeldorf 1988). Bridges headed the ILWU until his retirement in 1977. He died in 1990 (Saxon 1990). Today, the ILWU has about 25,000 members employed at twenty-nine West Coast ports.

Once in control of the union, organized crime found the shipping industry an attractive and easy target for the more traditional types of racketeering (PCOC 1986b: 34–35): "When a ship docks, it must be emptied quickly. The cargo may include perishable foodstuffs, and in any event, the owner gathers no return for his capital investment—the ship—while it is in port. Ship turnaround time is thus a crucial key to profitability." Pier bosses regularly shook down shippers by threatening walkouts. "Time pressures also encouraged owners to maintain an oversupply of labor so that all ships, even on the busiest days, could be unloaded at once. The lucrative and commonly used 'kickback' racket also arose from time pressures. Because the number of ship arrivals fluctuated, the hiring boss (usually a union officer) selected the necessary number of workers from the surplus of men at the daily 'shape up.' The criterion for selection on many piers was the willingness, evidenced by a prearranged signal, such as a toothpick by the ear, to 'kickback' a part of the day's wages to the boss."

Other traditional rackets ran rampant on the ILA-controlled waterfront: gambling, loansharking, and cargo theft. Organized crime–corrupted port employees provided "access to

Waterfront Commission

The New York–New Jersey Waterfront Commission, created in 1953, has subpoena power and investigative authority in New York and New Jersey. The Commission employs investigators who possess full police powers in both states. With a budget of about $7.5 million, financed from a 2 percent assessment on gross wages of port employers, the Commission regulates waterfront employees and licenses stevedoring concerns that contract with shipping companies to unload their ships. The stevedoring firms own or rent the heavy equipment needed and hire longshoremen who provide the labor. Companies seeking to hire waterfront workers must submit applicants' names to the Commission, which does a thorough background investigation. The Commission also limits the number of waterfront employees.

The Commission has banned persons with serious criminal records from the docks, and the notorious "shape-up" has been eliminated. Convicted criminals are prohibited from holding office in waterfront unions, and the Commission audits the books and records of the licensed stevedore firms to guard against illegal payoffs and other violations of law.

As a result of containerization (cargo shipped in large corrugated containers), shipping into the ports of Manhattan and Brooklyn, which have only limited room for such mechanization, has been significantly reduced, as has the number of dockworkers who now number about 7,000.

cargo shipments and storage areas, security for the movement of contraband, such as narcotics, falsification of invoices and shipping documents in insurance scams, and collusion in the expropriation of stolen property, such as luxury vehicles and construction equipment" (PCOC 1986b: 35).

In 1953, the AFL convention voted to revoke the ILA charter because of rampant corruption. Shortly afterward, under indictment for misappropriating union funds, Ryan stepped down and William Bradley was elected president. The AFL attempted to wrest control of longshoremen from the ILA by setting up a rival union, the International Brotherhood of Longshoremen (IBL). In 1955, the AFL and CIO merged into the AFL-CIO. And, in 1959, after a series of often bloody physical battles between the rival longshoremen's unions, the IBL and ILA merged. Shortly afterward the ILA was admitted to the AFL-CIO.

Bradley, however, failed to cooperate with organized crime, and taped conversations between leading waterfront racketeers indicate that he "was visited by mob members who told him he'd have to give up his position to Teddy Gleason or he'd be killed" (Permanent Subcommittee on Investigations 1981b: 447). In 1963, after Bradley declined to run for reelection, Thomas W. ("Teddy") Gleason was unanimously elected president of the ILA, a post he held until his retirement in 1987; he stepped down at age 87 because of poor health. Gleason died of natural causes in 1992. Without any opposition, the post went to his associate and ILA executive vice president, John Bowers.

In 1952, it was revealed that organized crime, using its control of the ILA, "had for years been levying the equivalent of a 5 percent tax on all general cargo moving in and out of the harbor" (Goddard 1980: 35). The outrage that was generated led to the 1953 establishment of the Waterfront Commission.

In 1963, Anthony Scotto, a *caporegime* in the Gambino Family, took over Local 1814 in Red Hook, Brooklyn, when his father-in-law, Anthony ("Tough Tony") Anastasio, a member of the Gambino Family (and brother of crime Family boss Albert Anastasia), died of natural causes. In 1953, Michael Clemente, president of ILA Local 856 in Manhattan and a member of the Genovese Family, was convicted of extorting money from waterfront employers and perjury before the New York State Crime Commission (PCOC 1986b). Upon his release from prison, however, Clemente resumed his control of the Manhattan waterfront.

Another Genovese Family member, Tino Fiumara, exercised similar control on the New Jersey side.

An exception were the piers in Hudson County, New Jersey, where the Irish had been entrenched for decades. William Murphy headed Longshoremen's Local 2 in Hoboken until 1973 when he was shot by two masked gunmen while stopped at a traffic light. A few months later, Frank Murray, the head of ILA Local 1247 in Jersey City, vanished while en route to a union-related meeting in Manhattan. The Jersey side of New York harbor then came completely under the control of the American Mafia (Stewart 2006).

As a result of more stringent law enforcement efforts in the ports of New York and New Jersey, notes Donald Goddard (1980: 66), "ILA racketeers moved operations to Florida, where they plundered the booming Port of Miami." The ILA shifted from exploiting its members to "carving up the cargo traffic among the port's stevedores and 'taxing' them on their shares." The ILA used its domination of the port to establish a system whereby competition among stevedoring companies and other waterfront firms was significantly reduced. Goddard points out that ship owners, agents, stevedores, contractors, and service companies were caught up in a web of corrupt practices with the ILA—and few wanted to escape. "They only had to pay their 'rent' in order to enrich themselves with guaranteed profits." Louis J. Freeh of the FBI noted before a congressional committee (Permanent Subcommittee on Investigations 1981b: 183): "You do not have extortion, you do not have threats, you do not have violence. What you have is a businessman who is as corrupt as the ILA official who he pays looking for additional business, looking for an advantage against his competitors and using his organized crime connection to have that union official contact another businessman to extend an economic advantage."

The FBI's UNIRAC investigation (1975–1979) was accomplished with the help of stevedore Joe Teitelbaum, who was approached by ILA officials for a $3,000 payoff as a down payment for continuing to do business in Miami. When he declined to pay, shipping clients began to receive calls from the union officials indicating Teitelbaum was having labor problems, and he could not guarantee that he could provide longshoremen when their cargo needed offloading in Miami. Teitelbaum went to the FBI and agreed to serve in an undercover capacity. The investigation resulted in 117 convictions, including that of Tino Fiumara,[3] Michael Clemente, and Anthony Scotto. (This did not stop New York's governor and two former New York City mayors from acting as character witnesses at Scotto's trial.)

The investigation revealed that ports along the East Coast from New York to Florida had been divided between the Genovese and Gambino Families into spheres of interest. Scotto and the others were convicted of a number of corrupt practices, including:

- Payoffs in lieu of employer contributions to ILA pension and welfare plans
- Payoffs to secure "labor peace" and avoid adhering to costly ILA rules that amounted to "featherbedding"
- Payoffs by businessmen to secure union contracts that were necessary to qualify for maritime work in ports under ILA control
- Payoffs to help firms secure new business and to keep the business they had without competitive bidding

The relationship between racketeers and employers has frequently been mutually beneficial: "Convicted union officers have gone back to the ports working for industries closely associated with the port, thus enabling them to circumvent the provisions of the Landrum-Griffin Act" that bars them from holding union office (PCOC 1986b: 44).

Organized crime activities on the waterfront have continued into the twenty-first century, with the Genovese Family asserting influence in New Jersey and the Gambinos in Brooklyn and Staten Island (Marzulli 2004b). In 2001, the imprisoned acting boss of the Genovese crime Family was indicted for laundering money he siphoned from

---

[3]When Fiumara, born in 1941, was released from prison in 1994, he became the head of the Genovese Family's New Jersey operations. In 1999, he was returned to prison for parole violation and released in 2005.

the ILA benefit fund (Rashbaum 2001b). The following year, Gambino Family members including Richard Gotti, a captain and one of John Gotti's brothers, and Peter Gotti, acting Family boss, were indicted for controlling the appointment of union officials and extorting money from dockworkers and the union's managed care system (Rashbaum 2002). All were subsequently convicted.

International Brotherhood of Teamsters (IBT)

The IBT is the largest labor union in the United States, representing more than 1.4 million truckers, delivery drivers, warehouse workers, flight attendants, and other workers.[4] In 1899, the Team Drivers International Union, headquartered in Detroit, received a charter from the AFL for its membership of 1,200 drivers. In 1902, Chicago members of the Team Drivers established a rival Teamsters National Union with 18,000 horse handlers. The following year, Samuel Gompers, president of the AFL, arranged for a merger of the two, which became the IBT. The union was marked by violence from its inception. When the Teamsters went on strike, the public suffered and therefore supported efforts against the drivers. Allen Friedman, IBT vice president and former strong-arm for the union, reports: The Teamsters' "answer was to fight back, sending their own men to do battle with baseball bats, knives, guns, blackjacks, and any other weapon they owned or could make. They also teamed up with local gangsters who enjoyed being paid to break heads for either side." Unfortunately, the influx of neighborhood gangsters marked a major change in the Teamsters. "Suddenly there were men involved who had neither loyalty nor ideology. They began changing the face of organized labor in many communities, taking control and becoming extortionists" (Friedman and Schwartz 1989: 9).

Although the Teamsters remained a relatively weak union, by 1933 they had about 125,000 members concentrated in industrial centers such as

Detroit and Chicago. In 1907, Dan Tobin became IBT president and served without major scandal until 1952. He was succeeded by Dave Beck of Seattle who controlled the Western Conference of Teamsters. Because of the support he received from Jimmy Hoffa, head of the Teamsters in Detroit, Beck awarded Hoffa with an IBT vice presidency. In 1957, before a U.S. Senate (McClellan) Committee, Beck took the Fifth Amendment 142 times. That year he was convicted of state charges and in 1959 of federal charges—embezzling union funds and income-tax violations—for which he received a five-year prison sentence. Beck died at the end of 1993, at age 99.

At the 1957 IBT convention in Miami, James R. Hoffa, who had been accused of dozens of improper activities by the McClellen Committee (see Chapter 3), was elected president. That same year, the IBT was expelled from the AFL-CIO (Moldea 1978). In 1987, the AFL-CIO readmitted the IBT to its ranks. At the time, the Teamsters were struggling against a Justice Department effort to place them under the control of a court-appointed trustee under provisions of the Racketeer Influenced and Corrupt Organizations (RICO) statute.

Jimmy Hoffa   James Riddle Hoffa was born in Brazil, Indiana, in 1913 and moved to Detroit with his family in 1924. A high school dropout, Hoffa eventually became a warehouse worker and developed a reputation as a tough street fighter who always stood up for his fellow workers against management. Because of this, Hoffa was fired from his warehouse job and hired as an organizer for Local 299 of the IBT, a troubled local—misuse of funds, rigged elections—that had to be taken into receivership by the IBT. He and other IBT organizers battled management goons in their organizing efforts throughout Detroit. Hoffa also used organized crime connections to shake down an association of small grocery stores, leading to his first criminal conviction, for which he paid a fine. After he had risen to a leadership position in Local 299, Hoffa continued to work with organized crime in Detroit, using the threat of labor trouble to force businesses to use a mob-controlled overalls supply firm (Friedman and Schwarz 1989).

---

[4]The union has lost considerable membership since the 1970s, when it represented 2.2 million workers.

In 1941, Hoffa found himself in a battle with the CIO that began a "raid" to represent Detroit's teamsters. The CIO action was backed by a small army of goons, and the AFL-affiliated IBT was literally being beaten in the streets of Detroit. Hoffa turned to his friends in the Detroit underworld and secured the assistance of the powerful Meli crime Family. "The CIO raiders were defeated by the end of the year. And considering the new players on Hoffa's team, it was a miracle that the CIO survived at all in Detroit" (Moldea 1978: 38). The victory was not without cost: "The CIO's defeat, brought about by Hoffa's ringers, became the major factor in his rapid plunge from union reformer to labor racketeer. His pact with the underworld, no matter how tenuous at the time, took him out of the running as a potentially great leader of the Teamsters' rank and file" (1978: 38).

Hoffa's road to power and the presidency of the IBT was strewn with scandal—for example, his alliance with Anthony Provenzano: "The Hoffa-Provenzano alliance was typical of the bargains Hoffa struck with gangsters around the country; they helped push him to the top, and he helped them use their union posts for a series of money-making schemes: extortion from employers, loan-sharking, pension-fund frauds, and anything else that control of union muscle and money offered" (Brill 1978: 125).

Tony Provenzano and Local 560 Born in 1917, Anthony ("Tony Pro") Provenzano was one of six sons of a Sicilian immigrant couple living on the Lower East Side of New York. He dropped out of school at age 15 to become a truck helper and later a driver. He had aspirations of becoming a professional boxer, and his reputation for violence brought him to the attention of a next-door neighbor, Anthony Strollo ("Tony Bender," born in 1899). Bender was a *caporegime* in the Genovese Family and a powerful waterfront racketeer. As a result of Bender's patronage, Provenzano became a member of the Genovese Family and an organizer for IBT Local 560 in New Jersey. By 1941, Provenzano was a shop steward. In 1959, with the help of Jimmy Hoffa, Provenzano was elected president of the local. In 1960, Hoffa

appointed Provenzano to fill a vacancy among IBT vice presidents. He also rose in the ranks of the Genovese Family, reportedly becoming a *caporegime* (McFadden 1988).

Union opponents of Provenzano found themselves subjected to threats, beatings, or (in at least two instances) murder. In 1961, a rival was beaten and garroted by mob executioners led by the infamous ex-fighter Harold ("Kayo") Konigsberg (Konigsberg 2001). In 1963, another Provenzano rival was shot to death in Hoboken, New Jersey. By 1963, Provenzano's union salaries totaled $113,000—at the time he was the highest-paid union official in the world. That same year, he was convicted of extorting $17,000 from a trucking company to end a discipline problem the firm was having with its union employees. During the four and one-half years he was in prison and the five years he was disqualified from holding union office (as per the 1959 Landrum-Griffin Act), his brothers Salvatore ("Sammy") and Nunzio headed the local while Tony ran its affairs. In 1978, Tony Pro was convicted of the 1961 murder and sentenced to life imprisonment.

In 1981, Nunzio Provenzano, president of Local 560, was sentenced to 10 years' imprisonment. He was convicted of accepting $187,000 from four interstate trucking companies to ensure "labor peace," and he permitted the companies to avoid contract rules for hiring Local 560 drivers. Brother "Sammy Pro" became president of Local 560. In 1984, Sammy Pro went to prison, and a close Provenzano aide, Michael Sciarra, became interim president; Tony Pro's daughter became the secretary-treasurer at a salary of $71,000. That same year, the federal government invoked the civil racketeering provision of the RICO statute, and a federal judge in New Jersey removed Local 560's executive board and put the local into trusteeship "until such time as the membership can freely nominate and elect new officers" (PCOC 1986b: 123).

After more than two years under government trusteeship, the members of Local 560 voted in the local's first contested election in twenty-five years. Sciarra was barred from seeking his former position as the local's president after a federal judge released tapes indicating that Matthew ("Matty the Horse") Ianiello, a *caporegime* in the Genovese Family, wanted Sciarra to head the local. In 1988, when the mailed ballots were counted by government monitors, Danny Sciarra—running as a surrogate for his brother Michael—won by a vote of 2,842 to 1,535 (Sullivan 1988). Four days later, at age 71, Anthony Provenzano died of a heart attack in a California hospital near the federal prison where he was incarcerated. At the end of 1998, a former truck driver running on a reform platform was elected president of the 4,400-member local, and the following year the local was released from a court-ordered federal trusteeship (McFadden 1999).

John Dioguardi and Anthony Corallo   Elections were scheduled to be held in 1956 to choose officers for the IBT's Joint Council 16 in New York City. If Jimmy Hoffa could affect the outcome of the Joint Council 16 elections, it would enable him to win control of the IBT national presidency. Accordingly, in 1955 Hoffa had seven new Teamster charters issued to his friend John ("Johnny Dio") Dioguardi.

Born on the Lower East Side in 1914, Dioguardi was the nephew of James Plumeri (better known as "Jimmy Doyle"), a *caporegime* in the Lucchese Family. Dioguardi also became a member of that crime Family and in 1937 was convicted for extorting money from the trucking industry. In 1956, Dioguardi was indicted for ordering the acid-throwing attack that blinded labor reporter Victor Reisel—Reisel had been critical of union racketeering. The charges were dropped when a witness refused to testify. In 1967, Dioguardi received a five-year sentence for bankruptcy fraud ("scam") discussed later. When he finished that term he was convicted of stock fraud involving a car-leasing company and died in prison in 1979 (Kihss 1979).

Along with Anthony ("Tony Ducks") Corallo, also a member of the Lucchese Family, Dioguardi filled the IBT locals for which he had charters with a number of gangsters who could then vote in the 1956 union election. Five of the seven locals did not have a single legitimate member—they were "paper locals." Corallo had already gained control of five other Teamster locals, although he held office in only one. Dioguardi and Corallo brought into the newly chartered locals forty men with an aggregate record of 178 arrests and 70 convictions. Corallo was subsequently described by Robert F. Kennedy (1960: 84) as "an underworld figure of great influence whose unusual nickname stems from his reputation for 'ducking' convictions in court cases in which he is arrested. Tony Ducks, whose police record includes drug and robbery charges and who is on the Treasury Department's narcotic list, lost only one bout with the law." In 1941, Corallo was sentenced to six months for unlawful possession of narcotics. In 1962, he received a two-year sentence for bribing a judge in a fraudulent bankruptcy case. In 1968, Corallo was convicted for his part in a kickback scheme that involved a New York City water commissioner and received a three-year sentence. He subsequently became boss of the Lucchese Family.

While Hoffa was interested in winning over the locals and their votes in his quest for the IBT presidency, Dioguardi and Corallo were interested in the financial rewards that control of the locals promised. The newly "elected" officers would approach various nonunion employers with an offer they could not easily refuse: pay the union initiation fees and membership dues for your employees (who usually did not even know they were members of a union) and you keep your business free of all labor problems, including demands by legitimate unions; fail to pay, and labor problems, or worse, will result. By the time Hoffa gained control of the IBT in New York, twenty-five of the men Dio and Ducks brought into their locals had already been convicted of crimes, including bribery, extortion, perjury, and forgery (Brill 1978; Sheridan 1972). According to the federal government, Lucchese crime Family control over IBT Local 295 continued into the 1990s. In 1992, a special trustee was appointed by a federal judge to monitor the local's activities (Fried 1992).

An important part of Hoffa's Teamster legacy involves his connection to Allen Dorfman and the looting of the IBT pension fund.

Allen Dorfman   Born in 1923, Allen Dorfman was awarded the Silver Star during his World War II service with the Marine Corps. In 1948 he was a physical education teacher at the University of Illinois, earning $4,000 a year; by 1953 he was a millionaire. Allen's stepfather, Paul ("Red") Dorfman, was a professional boxer and a close friend of Chicago crime boss Tony Accardo. In 1928, Red Dorfman was indicted for rigging election ballots and terrorist tactics in a local election, although there is no record of the disposition. In 1940, the founder and secretary-treasurer of the Chicago Waste Handlers Union was murdered. Red Dorfman, who had never been a member of the union or a waste handler, showed up at a union meeting, paid his dues, and on the same night became the new secretary-treasurer. In 1942, he was arrested as the result of a dispute with the chairman of the waste handlers employers' association—the two disagreed over wages to be paid to men in Dorfman's union. Using brass knuckles concealed in a glove, Dorfman severely beat the man in his office. The charges were dropped when the victim refused to prosecute. In 1949, Red Dorfman assisted Jimmy Hoffa by introducing him to important people in the Outfit and gaining their help in Hoffa's organizing drive for the Teamsters (Brill 1978).

Allen Dorfman established an insurance agency, and in 1950 and 1951, Hoffa successfully maneuvered the insurance business of the Teamsters health and welfare funds to Red and Allan Dorfman. Subsequently, the Dorfmans, with absolutely no experience in the insurance field, "received more than $3 million in commissions and service fees on Teamsters insurance over an eight year period" (Permanent Subcommittee on Investigations 1983: 83).

In 1955, Jimmy Hoffa negotiated the IBT's first pension plan, into which each employer was to contribute $2 per week per Teamster employee: the Central States, Southeast and Southwest Areas Pension Fund and Health and Welfare Fund (usually referred to simply as the Central States Pension Fund). Allen Dorfman was appointed as a consultant to the fund's board of trustees and turned it into "a bank for the underworld and their cronies in the 1960s and early 1970s" (Frantz and Neubauer 1983: 1). Dorfman had the trustees lend millions of dollars to Las Vegas casinos, organized crime–connected resorts, and speculative hotel and land ventures, projects that conventional lending institutions would not finance. Investments in Las Vegas casinos were directed by organized crime bosses in Chicago, Kansas City, Milwaukee, and Cleveland, who were then able to skim casino profits.

In 1972, as a result of the FBI's PENDORF investigation, Dorfman was convicted of taking $55,000 in kickbacks to secure a $1.5 million loan from the pension fund, and he served 10 months in federal prison. In 1974, he was indicted along with Irwin Weiner, and Outfit members Joey Lombardo and Anthony Spilotro, on charges of fraud in connection with another pension fund loan. They were subsequently acquitted after the chief government witness was gunned down outside his business establishment. In 1977, the federal government forced the trustees of the Central States Pension Fund to relinquish financial control to an independent management firm (Frantz and Neubauer 1983).

On December 15, 1982, Dorfman, Lombardo, and Teamster president Roy L. Williams were found guilty of attempting to bribe U.S. Senator Howard Cannon of Nevada in return for his help in delaying legislation that would substantially deregulate the trucking industry. Dorfman, Lombardo, and Williams were scheduled for sentencing on February 10, 1983.[5] On January 20, 1983, Dorfman was walking with Irwin Weiner in a motel parking lot in suburban Lincolnwood, just outside Chicago. Two men approached from behind. One carried a sawed-off shotgun under his coat, and the other drew a .22 caliber automatic with a silencer attached and fired five shots, point blank, into Dorfman's head. Weiner ducked down between two cars and the gunmen made no effort to harm him. The two men then pulled on ski masks and fled in a car driven by a third person. The murder remains (officially) unsolved.

---

[5]In 1982, Senator Cannon was defeated in his bid for a fifth term; Williams received a 10-year sentence and was paroled in 1989.

Hoffa versus Kennedy During the 1950s, the activities of the Teamsters Union gained the attention of the U.S. Senate, in particular, the Permanent Subcommittee on Investigations, which for many years was chaired by John L. McClellen of Arkansas. IBT officials, however, refused to cooperate with the committee. They "would not produce records; they repeatedly challenged the jurisdiction of the Permanent Subcommittee to probe the inner workings of the union; they exerted considerable and constant pressure upon members of Congress in both houses to have Teamster activities rest in the traditionally gentle hands of the Senate's Labor Committee" (McClellen 1962: 14).

"The response of the Senate," notes Senator McClellen (1962: 19), "was prompt and decisive." With a unanimous vote, on January 30, 1957, an eight-member bipartisan Senate Select Committee on Improper Activities in the Labor or Management Field was established. The senator wrote of his experiences with the IBT in a 1962 book entitled *Crime Without Punishment*. Robert Kennedy, who was chief counsel to the committee, also authored a book on his experiences with the committee: *The Enemy Within* (1960). The first IBT target of the committee was its president, Dave Beck of Seattle. The committee spotlight shone very brightly on Beck, and within months of his appearance he was convicted of embezzling union funds and of income-tax violations. The spotlight then turned to James R. Hoffa.

Subpoenaed to appear before the Select Committee, Jimmy Hoffa was sometimes blunt, sometimes evasive, in his testimony (McClellen 1962). At times the Teamster leader referred to Kennedy as "Bob" or "Bobby" and as "nothing but a rich man's kid." Law professor Monroe Freedman states: "From the day that James Hoffa told Robert Kennedy that he was nothing but a rich man's kid who never had to earn a nickel in his life, Hoffa was a marked man" (quoted in Navasky 1977: 395).

In 1957, FBI surveillance cameras recorded Hoffa giving $2,000 in exchange for confidential McClellen Committee documents to a New York attorney who was cooperating with the government. Hoffa had recruited the attorney to serve as a plant on the committee. When FBI agents arrested Hoffa the following day, he had confidential committee reports on him. Nevertheless, Hoffa was acquitted in a jury trial. The following year, Hoffa was tried for illegally wiretapping the phones of some Teamster officials. The first trial resulted in a hung jury, the second in an acquittal.

In 1960, John F. Kennedy was elected president of the United States and appointed his brother Robert attorney general. Robert Kennedy made the Labor Racketeering Unit of the Criminal Division his personal "Get Hoffa Squad." The unit was headed by former FBI special agent Walter Sheridan, who was actually on the attorney general's payroll as a "confidential assistant" (Navasky 1977). Sheridan subsequently wrote a book, *The Fall and Rise of Jimmy Hoffa* (1972), on the IBT and the government's efforts to prosecute Hoffa.

Soon federal grand juries across the country began investigating the IBT. Several important convictions were secured, including that of Anthony Provenzano. In 1962, Hoffa was charged with a conflict-of-interest violation of the Taft-Hartley Act—a misdemeanor. Victor Navasky (1977: 417) comments: "Never in history had the government devoted so much money, manpower, and top-level brainpower to a misdemeanor case." The trial lasted two months and ended in a hung jury—7 to 5 for acquittal. Hoffa was subsequently accused of trying to bribe jurors in the first trial. In 1964, he was convicted of jury tampering and sentenced to eight years' imprisonment.

In 1971, Hoffa was released from prison after President Richard Nixon approved his application for executive clemency—the IBT had supported Nixon for president. Despite a condition added to the pardon that Hoffa abstain from union affairs for ten years, by 1975, he was actively seeking the Teamster presidency, and IBT officials loyal to him were holding fund-raising dinners to prepare for the campaign. Hoffa began attacking Frank Fitzsimmons, the man who had replaced him as IBT president. Ironically, Hoffa criticized Fitzsimmons as a tool of organized crime. On

July 30, 1975, Hoffa arrived at a suburban Detroit restaurant to meet with several persons, including his friend Anthony ("Tony Jack") Giacalone, a *caporegime* in the Detroit crime Family, and Anthony Provenzano. Giacalone had arranged the meeting ostensibly to mediate differences between Provenzano and Hoffa over Hoffa's quest for the IBT presidency.[6] None of the principals were at the restaurant, and Hoffa has not been seen since. Fitzsimmons died of natural causes in 1981. In a biography published after his death, Frank Sheeran, an associate of the crime Family in Pittson, Pennsylvania, and long-time confidant of the ex-Teamster president, admits to killing Hoffa on orders from the Family boss Russell Bufalino (Brant 2004).

Organized crime Families maneuvered behind the scenes to ensure that Roy L. Williams of Kansas City, Missouri, would become the new IBT president. At the same time, "the Senate Permanent Subcommittee on Investigations rushed out a report spotlighting William's LCN [*La Cosa Nostra*] ties. The senators revealed a portion of the Justice Department's evidence that Williams was getting kickbacks of cash skimmed from Las Vegas casinos bought with Teamster pension loans, kickbacks funneled through Nick Civella's Kansas City Mafia family" (PCOC 1985a: 42).

Nevertheless, the IBT executive board chose Williams to fill the unexpired term of Frank Fitzsimmons, and the Teamster convention subsequently elected him to a full term. After his 1982 conviction, Williams testified before the President's Commission on Organized Crime that his election had been engineered by organized crime bosses and that he himself was under the control of Kansas City boss Nick Civella. When Williams resigned, Jackie Presser of Cleveland was chosen to head the IBT, despite (or because of) his close ties to organized crime.

Jackie Presser   Born in Cleveland in 1926, Jackie Presser learned about organized labor at an early age from his father, Bill Presser, a Teamster Union

official and close associate of the Cleveland crime Family. Large for his age, Jackie was an unruly, brawling student who dropped out of school at 16 and joined the Navy: He was honorably discharged in 1947. As expected, Jackie went into the union business, securing a position with the Teamsters. He was joined by his uncle, Allen Friedman, an ex-convict and juice loan collector. Jackie soon showed that he lacked the tact necessary for successful labor racketeering: His threats, shakedowns, and embezzlements attracted so much attention that he had to temporarily bow out of union activities. Using IBT pension fund loans, Jackie opened up several bowling alleys, but they failed due to mismanagement, and the Teamster money was lost.

Nevertheless, Bill Presser had a new IBT local chartered for his son, and Jackie teamed up with two relatives, Allen Friedman and his brother Harry—both stalwart union organizers and ex-convicts—to organize warehouse workers for the IBT. With Bill Presser's help, they raided other IBT locals, and Jackie's local prospered, moving beyond warehousemen and adding other workers to Local 507's membership. Part of the local's success was due to the sweetheart contract: Employers fearful of other (legitimate) unions organizing their workers agreed to recognize the local and signed a contract with Jackie.

When Jimmy Hoffa went to prison and Frank Fitzsimmons became acting president of the IBT, Bill Presser filled a vacancy on the executive board, becoming a union vice president. Bill organized a political action committee called DRIVE to raise money and support political candidates, and Jackie was given a major role in DRIVE efforts. Jackie Presser was astute enough to recognize the value of good public relations. He began a major effort to clean up the image of the IBT, hiring a public relations firm and personal publicist. However, he continued to cheat his union members.

When Bill Presser fell seriously ill, Jackie replaced him as an IBT vice president. When IBT president Fitzsimmons became terminally ill, Roy Williams became acting president. Williams's conviction in the PENDORF case (discussed earlier) cleared the way for Jackie Presser to become IBT president. Jackie was supported by leaders of

---

[6]At the time of his death in 2001, Giacalone, 82, was awaiting trial for racketeering and extortion.

Cleveland's organized crime Family who lobbied organized crime chieftains in Chicago and New York on Presser's behalf (Neff 1989).

With Jackie's backing, DRIVE and the IBT supported Ronald Reagan's successful candidacy for president. After the election, Allen Friedman reports: My brother-in-law, Bill Presser, "handed me a briefcase he said was filled with cash and told me to take it to [Attorney General] Edwin Meese in Washington. This was back in late November or early December after Ronald Reagan became president. I don't know how much was in that case; Bill knew I would never open it. But after Reagan got in, he named Bill's son, Jackie Presser, to his transition cabinet. Then he wanted to make Jackie undersecretary of labor, though I guess cooler heads prevailed. Jackie's presence would have been just one more scandal for the administration. After all, though Jackie never did time in jail as Bill and I did, that was only because his father and I covered his ass, not because he was ever an honest man" (Friedman and Schwarz 1989: 3).

Jackie Presser died of cancer in 1988. In 1989, as part of a RICO case against the IBT, court records revealed that he had been providing information to the FBI for nine years (Serrin 1989). The Chicago Outfit informed Anthony ("Fat Tony") Salerno, boss of the Genovese Family, that Presser was an informant, but Salerno refused to believe them.

In 1988, Rudy Giuliani, then U.S. attorney for the Southern District of New York, filed a RICO complaint against the IBT, the first time it had been used against an entire union. In addition to union officers, named as defendants were the heads of New York's five Families, as well as those in Chicago and Milwaukee. That same year, William J. McCarthy became IBT president, and the following year he reached an agreement with the Department of Justice to a settle a RICO suit against the union. McCarthy became the last Teamster president chosen at a national convention by delegates from the various locals; he died of natural causes in 1998. In 1991, for the first time, the union's international officials were elected by the rank-and-file in a secret ballot supervised by the government; Ronald R. Carey was elected president.

Carey headed the United Parcel Service local in Long Island City, New York, and is a longtime IBT dissident. Despite his reform credentials, Carey was criticized in 1992 by a federal judge overseeing the consent decree that helped elect him; the judge accused the IBT of dragging its feet on reform. Fifteen months after taking office, Carey suspended six of the top officers of the 14,000-member IBT Local 705 in Chicago—the local has long been linked to organized crime—and appointed trustees to run the local. In 1995, he brought a lawsuit against the former officers, alleging that they had defrauded the local (Franklin 1993, 1995b). He also placed more than two dozen locals in the New York City area under trusteeship control.

Carey's enemies in the union alleged that he had ties to organized crime and had engaged in improper financial deals. These accusations were supported by a former acting boss of the Lucchese crime Family ("Gaspipe" Casso) when he became a government witness. A three-member panel created by a federal court order, however, found no evidence to support the allegations (Raab 1994c).[7] Carey's most serious challenge, however, came from Jimmy Hoffa, Jr., son of the missing Teamster leader and five years younger than Carey. Hoffa, Jr., a labor lawyer with backing from much of the union's "old guard," challenged Carey for the union's presidency in 1996, but lost. Carey was reelected to a second five-year term with about 52 percent of the vote.

The following year, the election was declared invalid because Carey had received more than $220,000 in illegal contributions. He was subsequently barred from running in the new election—a rematch against Jimmy Hoffa, Jr.—because it was discovered that he had backed a plan to divert union funds for his campaign. A court-appointed review board subsequently expelled Carey from the Teamsters Union, and a new election in 1998 pitted Hoffa against a leader of the reformist wing of the IBT. Hoffa, who has never been a truck driver or laborer, easily beat the reform candidate.

---

[7]Jeffrey Goldberg (1995) presents a less flattering portrait of Carey and the report that cleared him.

In 1999, under Hoffa the Teamsters hired Edwin Stier, a former federal prosecutor who had succeeded in reforming the corrupt New Jersey IBT Local 560, to investigate and help rid the union of organized crime influence. Citing recalcitrance on the part of Jimmy Hoffa, Jr., in 2004 Stier resigned (Jacobs and Alford 2005).

In 2005, the IBT and six other unions withdrew from the AFL-CIO and formed a rival federation.

BUSINESS RACKETEERING[8]

As we have already seen with respect to the waterfront, there is no hard-and-fast line separating labor racketeering from business racketeering—one is often an integral part of the other. In many schemes involving corrupt union officials, "legitimate" businessmen have willingly cooperated in order to derive benefits such as decreased labor costs, inflated prices, or increased business in the market (PCOC 1986b). Jonathan Kwitny (1979) describes the machinations of racketeer-extraordinaire Moses ("Moe") Steinman, who dominated the wholesale meat industry in New York City. Because of his connections with important organized crime figures such as John Dioguardi and Paul Castellano, Steinman was able to deal with racketeer-controlled unions and thus affect labor relations in the meat industry. This ability secured him a position as a supermarket chain executive who led industry-wide negotiations with meat industry unions. Utilizing under-the-table payments to the union leaders, Steinman determined from whom the supermarkets purchased their meat. Supermarket officials bought from firms recommended by Steinman, overpaying for their beef; they were rewarded with kickbacks, and Steinman was paid handsome commission fees by the beef companies for these sales.

Steinman's greatest achievement was his relationship with the founder of Iowa Beef, the largest meat processing firm in the world. The patrician Midwestern businessman and the hard-drinking, inarticulate New York racketeer had something in common—greed. In return for opening up New York markets for Iowa Beef and assisting the company with "labor relations," Iowa Beef gave millions of dollars to Steinman and his friends and relatives (Kwitny 1979). Two former FBI agents (O'Brien and Kurins 1991) allege a similar relationship between Gambino Family boss Paul Castellano and chicken tycoon Frank Perdue.

Certain industries and their associated businesses are more attractive, and thus more vulnerable to organized crime. These are relatively easy businesses to enter—they do not require a large cash investment—and highly competitive. Other characteristics include an intense need for timely action, for example, businesses dealing with perishable foods and industries where any disruption of work or deliveries can be quite costly, such as the construction industry. Organized crime is drawn to labor-intensive industries that provide an opportunity to control related component businesses through a "choke point strategy." For

---

[8]For a look at case studies involving organized crime infiltration of legitimate business, see Kelly (1999).

example, domination of the concrete business provides influence over widely divergent construction activities dependent on a steady and predictable delivery of concrete supplies. Or control over the supply of labor—through control of a union local—enables domination of an industry dependent on a predictable supply of workers (Edelhertz and Overcast n.d.). The role of trucking in New York's garment center provides an example.

The Garment Center

Extensive business racketeering in New York's garment industry dates back to the days of Lepke Buchalter who, in addition to his influence over key unions, controlled interstate trucking from the garment center (Kavieff 2006). Its more contemporary manifestation has centered on the ability of racketeers to control local trucking: Whoever controls trucking controls the industry. The fast-paced nature of the fashion industry cannot countenance even short delays in shipping garments. "In New York City, garment manufacturers do not, as a rule, actually cut cloth and sew it into a dress, shirt, or other garment. They design clothes, order cloth, and arrange for the cutting and sewing to be done in smaller shops, called contractors. As a result, cloth is constantly being shipped by truck from manufacturer to contractor, from contractor to contractor, and from contractor back to manufacturer" (Mass 1991: 38–39).

Until 1992, control over garment-center trucking was exercised by the multimillionaire sons of Carlo Gambino, Thomas and Joseph. Crime Family boss Gaetano Lucchese had been introduced to the garment center by Lepke Buchalter himself, and Thomas Gambino is Lucchese's son-in-law. Residing in an 1881 mansion in the exclusive Lenox Hill neighborhood, Thomas Gambino, a graduate of Manhattan College, is known for his charitable contributions; he is also known as a *caporegime* in the crime Family that bears his father's name.

The Gambino brothers owned Consolidated Carriers, the major garment-center cartage firm. Together with a trucking firm owned by a Lucchese Family member, they divided manufacturers and contractors among a limited number of truckers and assigned one to each shop: "None of these truckers will carry garments for a shop not assigned to him. If a shop uses a gypsy trucker and is caught, it is required to pay its regular trucker for the goods shipped, just as if the assigned trucker had carried them. Elaborate rules govern the trading of shops among the cartel members and the allocation of a trucker to a company leasing space that was formerly occupied by another company serviced by a cartel member" (Mass 1991: 39). Manufacturers and contractors knew who they were dealing with, which was usually enough to ensure compliance with the allocation scheme.

Because there was an absence of competition, trucking prices remained high, while service remained poor. Some companies fled the garment center, and others refused to move in. The number of people employed in the industry declined substantially, and this impacted negatively on the New York City economy.

Evidence against the Gambinos was compiled through an elaborate sting operation orchestrated by investigators from the office of Manhattan District Attorney Robert M. Morgenthau. First, an undercover state police officer drove around Chinatown posing as a gypsy trucker soliciting business from companies that had been serviced by the Gambino cartel. He quickly found that no matter how competitive his prices, he could not secure any accounts. One manufacturer whispered the reason: "the Mafia." Another undercover officer succeeded in being hired by Consolidated Carriers.

On Halloween night 1989, investigators disguised as Consolidated Edison workers broke into the Gambino trucking company headquarters and planted a court-authorized "bug." State police investigators opened up their own garment manufacturing firm which was the ultimate weapon in the Gambino sting. In 1992, in exchange for not being imprisoned, the Gambino brothers pled guilty to restraint of trade violations and agreed to quit New York City's garment center and pay a fine of $12 million (Blumenthal 1992; Mass 1991). After three years without the Gambino brothers, shipping costs in the garment center fell dramatically, taking about 7 percent off the price of a finished garment. The fine paid by the Gambinos has financed a government-appointed monitor for the garment center, as well as providing funds for the district attorney's office and the state police, and compensation to several overcharged companies (Raab 1995b). In 1993, Thomas Gambino, at 64, was found guilty of racketeering charges stemming from his control of a Connecticut gambling operation and sentenced to five years' imprisonment. He entered a federal prison in 1996 and was released in 2000.

The end of the Gambino brothers' operations did not end racketeering in the garment center. In 1998, the acting boss of the Lucchese Family and eleven others, including members of the Gambino and Genovese Families, were indicted for an extortion scheme that netted $30,000 to $40,000 a month. In return for payments, garment makers (sewing, cutting, and dyeing plants) were given "protection" and guaranteed labor peace; if they were not unionized, they were allowed to remain so (Weiser 1998b). Most of the defendants subsequently pleaded guilty.

Robert Stewart (2006: 65) points out that organized crime can bring stability to the potentially chaotic world of *laissez-faire* capitalism, and it is stability that the employer craves because it almost always results in a decent profit. The employer makes a cost-benefit evaluation: "The Mafia racketeer is always there for the employer, with a sympathetic ear, ready to intervene in any problem as an expediter. As long as the unionized employer pays, he can expect the trucks to operate on schedule, production will never be disrupted, and potential competitors will be discouraged for a moderate surcharge."

Restraint of Trade

Bid rigging and customer allocation are Sherman Act violations and carry a maximum sentence of 10 years' imprisonment and a maximum fine of $1 million for individuals and $100 million for corporations. While organized crime may aid in the policing of illegal contracts, organized crime involvement in a restraint of trade scheme may simply be through the use of private resources for coercion and violence, something relatively easy to accomplish, since the participants are operating outside of the law and cannot easily complain to the authorities. In New Jersey, for example, the organizer of a waste haulers association that had effectively restrained competition found himself being pushed out by an emissary from Gerardo ("Jerry") Catena, who ran New Jersey operations for the Genovese Family. The head of the association described his response: "I had a feeling, fear, that if I did not just put my tail between my legs and allow myself to be pushed out, they would find another way to get me out" (Abadinsky 1981a: 30).

Following a pattern set in Chicago, in Detroit during the 1920s cutthroat competition among the owners of dry cleaning plants led to the formation of the Wholesale Cleaners and Dyers Association. Soon afterward, the association ruled that retail cleaning shops could not switch from one plant to another. Wholesalers were now free to increase prices without worrying about losing customers. The Purple Gang, a group of notorious Jewish gangsters, was employed to police this restraint of trade. Independent wholesalers and retailers who balked were terrorized: "Bricks destroyed plant windows at night and shops were stench bombed—a practice that ruined thousands of dollars worth of clothing" (Kavieff 2000: 58). If more were required, there would be arson and bombs. Eventually, Purple Gang leader Abe Bernstein declared himself the head of the retail cleaners association, and his gunman would attend meetings until all member dues were collected. In 1928, a representative of the association sided with a decision to take Bernstein off the payroll—a subsequent coroner's examination revealed he had been beaten to death.

Organized crime is not necessarily a crucial element in restraint of trade schemes. The pattern of racketeering may precede the involvement of organized crime and would likely continue in its absence. In 1980, thirty-seven manufacturers admitted to being part of an 18-year nationwide conspiracy to fix the prices of corrugated containers and sheets, a multibillion-dollar scheme. They settled out of court. From May 1983 through June

1992, the U.S. Department of Justice initiated 102 prosecutions for price fixing involving 100 corporations: 96 pled guilty or were found guilty after trial (Ross 1992). In 1993, it was revealed that in at least twenty states executives of the nation's largest dairy companies had conspired, some for decades, to rig bids on milk products sold to schools and military bases. Dozens of dairy executives pled guilty (Henriques, with Baquet 1993). In 1996, Archer Daniel Midlands (ADM), one of the world's leading grain processors, with about $13 billion in annual sales, pled guilty to price fixing and agreed to pay $100 million, the largest fine ever in a federal antitrust case (Millman 1996). In 2008, several airlines, including Air France, British Airways, KLM Royal Dutch Airlines, and SAS, pled guilty in the U.S. District Court for the District of Columbia to fixing prices on air cargo. Airline executives had conversations and held meetings for the purpose of monitoring and enforcing adherence to the agreed-upon cargo rates (U.S. Department of Justice 2008a). In 2008, three leading electronics manufacturers pled guilty and agreed to pay a fine of $585 million for conspiring to fix the price of Thin-Film Transistor-Liquid Display panels that are used in computer monitors, televisions, notebooks, and other electronic devices, a $70 billion a year market (U.S. Department of Justice 2008b).

As discussed at the beginning of Chapter 12, organized crime is sometimes a provider of illegal goods and services—helping to arrange and enforce collusive bidding arrangements, for example—while at other times it is simply a predator imposing itself on those involved in such activities. With this in mind, we will examine business racketeering in the construction and private waste hauling industries.

Construction Industry

Construction is both a lucrative and highly competitive industry. While competition is advantageous to the builder, it reduces the profits of construction firms. Organized crime can play a crucial role in limiting competition by enforcing a system of collusive bidding. The President's Commission reports: "Participating construction contractors, with the guidance of union officials and LCN family members, allocate construction jobs among themselves and exclude non-cartel contractors whose entry into the New York market might threaten the stability, predictability and control of construction work that the cartels offer their members. Under such a system, the participant companies are beneficiaries, not victims, since the benefits of the cartel may totally offset the increased costs it imposes" (PCOC 1986b: 219).

In New York City, the construction industry is huge and fragmented, "with over one hundred thousand workers, many hundreds of specialty subcontractors, hundreds of general contractors, and dozens of major developers. There are also a large number of one-time or infrequent builders ranging from large corporations to small entrepreneurs" (New York State Organized Crime Task Force 1988: 3; hereafter NYSOCTF). Construction businesses range from those building private single-family dwellings to those putting up shopping centers and high-rise buildings. Construction workers are organized into approximately one hundred local unions for building trades, who engage in collective bargaining with the approximately fifty employer associations formed by contractors in the same type of construction work.

"Traditionally, unions have had a great deal of leverage in high-rise construction because they have had a monopoly over the skilled workers needed to carry out this highly complex type of building" (NYSOCTF 1988: 44). Through collective bargaining agreements, construction unions typically control access to skilled labor: "Some pre-hire contracts contain clauses requiring contractors to hire all or part of their employees from union hiring halls. Even where there is no hiring hall provision, the union's designation as exclusive bargaining agent gives its elected officials control over who works for that contractor" (NYSOCTF 1988: 45–46). Through control over labor unions, racketeers are able to offer benefits to or impose prohibitive costs on contractors. The ability to assign (or not assign) workers to jobs is a powerful tool that can be used against union members who might wish to challenge racketeer leadership. There is also the very real threat of violence.

The New York State Organized Crime Task Force reported that the industry's structure creates fragmentation and fragility: "An organized crime syndicate can use its network of relationships throughout the construction industry to reduce uncertainties and promote needed stability. For example, if more than one union has a jurisdictional claim over a particular construction task, an organized crime syndicate in return for a payoff can work out a reasonable arrangement between the contractor and the affected unions. In this role, the syndicate serves the same functions, albeit by criminal means, as a highly effective, legitimate labor consultant" (1988: 66).

Writing in 1985, the President's Commission reported that in "New York City organized crime controls all construction contracts of a half-million dollars or more extending up to amounts of approximately $100 million. . . . The prime source of influence and the prime point of contact for organized crime are the 20 or so largest contractors in New York City who from time to time, through collusive bidding, decide among themselves who will get a particular project." After winning the rigged bid, an emissary of organized crime or a union official approaches the general contractor and informs him "who his suppliers will be, who his subcontractors will be, from whom he will purchase materials, and at what price those materials will be purchased, and, on occasion, designating to the general contractor which unions he will use during the course of the construction of the building and other construction jobs in the New York City area" (PCOC 1985a: 71–72).

Bidding on concrete-contracting work, for example, was rigged so that big jobs were rotated among a small group of contractors and suppliers. For this service there was a "tax" of 1 or 2 percent. Jobs under $2 million required "1 point"; "2 points" were required for jobs over $2 million. In return, construction firms got guaranteed contracts and good workers who did not have to be paid according to the full union contract. Failure to pay meant the company was out of business (Owen 2003).

The agreement was policed by Ralph Scopo, a member of the Colombo Family and president of the Cement and Concrete Workers District Council of the Laborer's Union. He would "go to a building site, and the owner of the construction company would come out and sit with him in his car, and Scopo would talk about how 'the family' needs this money, and how you want to be sure that your wife and kids are OK" (Owen 2003: 72). The rigged bidding inflated costs and drove up the price of everything from raw materials to finished office space.

In 1987, Scopo and a *caporegime* in the Colombo Family were convicted of racketeering. (Scopo died in 1993 while serving a 100-year sentence.) In 1988, ten union officials and contractors were convicted in Brooklyn federal court for accepting or extorting payoffs from contractors in return for labor peace and rigging bids on projects to reward companies that paid bribes and to punish those that did not (Rangel 1988). In 1991, a federal jury convicted the *consiglieri* of the Genovese and Colombo Families for heading a 12-year bid-rigging scheme involving contracts for installing windows in New York City Housing Authority projects (Lubasch 1991b). In Sicily, the *mafioso* serves as a guarantor for price rigging and collusive bidding on building projects, and "any businessman who defects from the collusive agreement or refuses to take part in it, exposes himself to violent retaliation from a Mafia protector" (della Porta and Vannucci 1999: 229).

In 1996, a major New York City contractor who had designed and helped build scores of Manhattan skyscrapers, in addition to working on the Javits Convention Center and a new federal courthouse, admitted to being a *caporegime* in the Colombo crime Family. In the courthouse he helped build, the 62-year-old contractor pled guilty to being the Colombo Family representative on the mob council that oversaw activities in the construction industry ("Contractor Admits Double Life" 1996). Nevertheless, racketeering continued in the construction industry as evidenced by a 2000 indictment of thirty-eight persons, including the acting boss of the Lucchese Family, for bid rigging and associated crimes (Rashbaum 2000a). In 2005, labor racketeering expert and law professor James Jacobs and Kristin Stohner reported that a key construction union, the New York City District Council of Carpenters, was still being influenced by organized crime. That view was reinforced by a federal judge in 2008 when he ordered an extension of the government oversight over the union, which has spent fourteen years under supervision (Greenhouse and Rashbaum 2008).

Payments to organized crime may be direct, or by making a racketeer (or one of his relatives) a business partner, or by employing "ghost employees," names of persons on a construction payroll who receive salaries but do not work. When two union construction workers began complaining about ghost employees on the payroll of a contractor helping to build the World Trade Center in New York, one of the "ghosts," the boss of the Genovese Family, referred the problem to his private "police force," headed by Anthony ("Figgy") Ficarotta, a former professional boxer:

> Figgy, Joey, Louie and me went over to the Twin Towers construction site. The building was up about eleven stories and there were no walls, just the frames and concrete floors. The elevator was in an open shaft, and that's how the workers got up and down. We went up to the top floor and Figgy sees these two guys working. "Follow me," he says and we start walking around the floor. Figgy is telling the other workers: "Why don't youse go to lunch, go ahead." One of the workers says: "Who are you? We take our orders from Phillie." "Well I'm over Phillie," Figgy says, "so just go down and when you see him tell him who sent you—a short guy with the funny nose."
>
> We walked around telling guys to go downstairs until we got to the two guys and they start to walk toward the elevator shaft. "You guys goin' to lunch?" Figgy asks. They are standing by the shaft for the lift to come back and Figgy picks up a two-by-four and pushes it under the chin of this guy. The guy grabs onto the shaft to keep from fallin' in: "So you want a fuckin' check too, huh?

> Well it's waitin' for you on the ground. I'm gonna see that you get it—in a hurry." The guy is hanging on for his life and Figgy keeps pushing him further into the shaft. The second guy doesn't know what to do—there's nowhere to run. Joe and Louie start backing him up—and there's nowhere to go except down eleven stories.
>
> The guy with Figgy is yelling: "No, no, please, I don't want no check." "Why? You been bitchin' about some checks and I'm gonna send you down to get one." "Please no. I don't want no check." Joey and Louie back the other guy up to the edge and he yells out: "I don't want no check either." "Then just do your fuckin' work and shut the fuck up. Or we'll be back." Figgy threw the piece of wood down and we went onto the lift. There was no further trouble. (Abadinsky 1983: 131)

In New Jersey, firms owned by Philadelphia crime boss Nicky Scarfo and his underboss were able to gain lucrative construction contracts because of their influence over a few key labor unions, particularly Concrete Workers Local 33 and Ironworkers Local 350. Contractors subcontracting work to the Scarfo firms were guaranteed labor peace, and the two firms were able to underbid rivals by violating the union contract with respect to pension and other benefits (New Jersey Commission of Investigation 1987). In fact, the construction industry is quite inefficient, characterized by various unions having overlapping jurisdictions and a great deal of featherbedding. "The existence of so much inefficiency provides a strong incentive to pay off union officials not to press their jurisdictional claims or to reach out to racketeers who can dictate accommodations between competing unions" (NYSOCTF 1988: 50).

Private Solid Waste Carting

If there is a legitimate business activity that conjures up an image of organized crime, it is the private collection of solid waste—it is "Tony

Soprano's" business. Back in 1931, Walter Lippman (1962: 61) noted that "racketeering in many of its most important forms tends to develop where an industry is subjected to exceedingly competitive conditions." Companies "faced with the constant threat of cutthroat competition are subject to easy temptation to pay gangsters for protection against competitors." Peter Reuter (1987) offers additional insight into an industry's attractiveness to organized crime. When the entrepreneurs have a low-status (for example, limited education) background, and the enterprises are small, local, and family-based, the industry is vulnerable to organized crime infiltration.

The solid waste collection industry meets these criteria. It is characterized by numerous, relatively small competing firms that are often family-based. It is an easy-entry enterprise, requiring only some trucks and a willingness to work hard. Competition for a customer's business drives down profits until, at some point, with or without help from organized crime, an association is formed. Association members divide up the industry, usually allocating geographic areas (territories) or specific customers. The members (illegally) agree not to compete for another member's business. Each is thereby free to charge whatever the market will bear for its services (State Commission of Investigation 1989). The New York [Manhattan] District Attorney's Office estimated that because of organized crime, customers paid an overcharge of 30 to 40 percent or more; $500 million a year more than they should have, according to a study by Salomon Smith Barney (Gerlat 2002).

Organized crime may become involved if there is a need to police the (illegal) agreement. In 1956, New York City began requiring all commercial enterprises to arrange for their own garbage collection services. Prior to that, businesses operating in residential blocks had their garbage hauled for free by the Department of Sanitation. "Overnight, more than 50,000 businesses were up for grabs" (Cowan and Century 2002: 14). Within months, restraint of trade cartels were in place, formed around waste hauling trade associations (Behar 1996). A made guy would sit on the grievance committees that settle disputes between members of the associations "using the basic rule that whoever serviced the site first has continuing rights to any customer that occupies the site. While there is little evidence of either threats or actual violence,[9] it seems reasonable to infer that the racketeers provide a credible continuing threat of violence that ensures compliance with the ruling of the committee" (Reuter et al. 1983: 11; also Fried 2005). James ("Jimmy Brown"—partial to brown clothes) Failla, a *caporegime* in the Gambino Family, headed the Association of Trade Waste Removers of Greater New York for thirty years, organizing and facilitating restraint of trade agreements (Fried 1993b). In 1999, Failla, 80, died while serving a seven-year sentence for his role in the 1985 murder of Gambino Famiily boss Paul Castellano.

In New York City, about 300 trash haulers served 250,000 businesses. In 1995, four waste hauling associations (as well as individual firms and their owners) affiliated with the Gambino and Genovese Families were accused of having "carved out a system of *property rights*: a carter

---

[9]But there has been violence: In 1989, two owners of a family-run private waste hauling business on Long Island, brothers-in-law Robert Kubecka and Donald Barstow, were murdered for refusing to participate in an organized crime price-fixing cartel (Carlo 2008; Fried 2005).

'owns' the building where his customer is located. If the customer leaves or goes out of business, the carter has the right to service the new customer. If the carter loses a stop to another carter, the 'owner' of the stop has the right to be compensated for his loss either by receiving a stop of comparable value or through the payment of a multiple of the monthly charges the 'owner' had charged. The multiple is frequently '40 to 1' or more, meaning 40 times the monthly fee charged by the 'owner.' Disputes over which carter has the 'right' to service a particular stop are mediated by the associations" (District Attorney of New York County and the New York City Police Department 1995: 2). Carters not belonging to the associations—"outlaws"—faced economic and physical intimidation if they attempted to compete with association members.

The investigation that broke this cartel began when the Manhattan district attorney received a complaint from the second-largest waste hauling company in the country, Browning-Ferris Industries (BFI) of Houston.[10] The company was attempting to compete in the New York market but found it virtually impossible to win and maintain customers despite submitting lower bids. Company officials were subjected to intimidation—one received the freshly severed head of a German shepherd with a note that read: "Welcome to New York." In the ensuing investigation, a detective worked three years undercover as an executive for an "outlaw" firm—one that refused to join the cartel. His role began inadvertently. Detective Richard Cowan was investigating the arson of an empty garbage truck. As he was interviewing the owner, two thugs burst in and threatened the trash firm's owner, who said the detective was his cousin. As the "cousin," Detective Cowan successfully infiltrated the trash hauling industry and helped break the organized crime–dominated cartel. His work led to the conviction of fourteen persons, including its two leaders, a *caporegime* in the Genovese Family and a soldier in the Gambino Family—both headed trash collecting trade associations (Raab 1997a, 1997d). Cowan authored a book on his undercover activities that provides an insider's view of the process (Cowan and Century 2002).

As a result of these efforts, cartel customers who (often with great trepidation) switched to BFI saved as much as 60 percent on their trash hauling contracts (Behar 1996). With the cartel broken, members scrambled to keep customers, lowering their fees to become more competitive. One of the largest privately owned buildings in Manhattan had been paying $1.2 million for garbage pickup; Browning-Ferris bid $120,000. In 1996, New York put a cap on what businesses could be charged for waste hauling and created a Trade Waste Commission, which can deny a license to any firm with ties to organized crime (Goozner 1996). Dozens of persons were convicted of restraint of trade–related charges, and dozens of small firms were driven out of business.

In 2001, New York City created the Organized Crime Commission to, among other responsibilities, regulate the private solid waste hauling industry. Renamed the Business Integrity Commission (BIC), in addition to solid waste hauling, the agency has both regulatory and law enforcement authority over seafood distribution areas, public

---

[10]BFI has been accused of price fixing in several markets and has paid millions of dollars in fines for such activities (Myerson 1995).

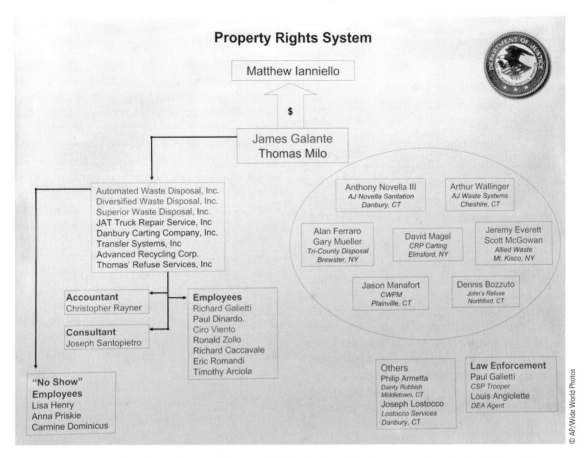

Property Rights System

Matthew Ianniello

$

James Galante
Thomas Milo

Automated Waste Disposal, Inc.
Diversified Waste Disposal, Inc.
Superior Waste Disposal, Inc.
JAT Truck Repair Service, Inc
Danbury Carting Company, Inc.
Transfer Systems, Inc
Advanced Recycling Corp.
Thomas' Refuse Services, Inc

Anthony Novella III
AJ Novella Sanitation
Danbury, CT

Arthur Wallinger
AJ Waste Systems
Cheshire, CT

Alan Ferraro
Gary Mueller
Tri-County Disposal
Brewster, NY

David Magel
CRP Carting
Elmsford, NY

Jeremy Everett
Scott McGowan
Allied Waste
Mt. Kisco, NY

Accountant
Christopher Rayner

Employees
Richard Galietti
Paul Dinardo.
Ciro Viento
Ronald Zollo
Richard Caccavale
Eric Romandi
Timothy Arciola

Consultant
Joseph Santopietro

Jason Manafort
CWPM
Plainville, CT

Dennis Bozzuto
John's Refuse
Northford, CT

**"No Show"
Employees**
Lisa Henry
Anna Priskie
Carmine Dominicus

Others
Philip Armetta
Dainty Rubbish
Middletown, CT
Joseph Lostocco
Lostocco Services
Danbury, CT

Law Enforcement
Paul Galietti
CSP Trooper
Louis Angiolette
DEA Agent

© AP/Wide World Photos

This government graphic shows the organization and individuals involved in an investigation in which trash haulers used the Mafia as a silent partner for more than a decade. In New Haven, Connecticut, in 2006, twenty-nine people, including a reputed mob boss, a former Waterbury mayor, and the region's largest garbage hauler, were indicted by federal prosecutors.

wholesale markets, and shipboard gambling. The agency has more than sixty employees who are supported by city police officers. As a condition of granting a license or registration, BIC can impose a monitor to oversee the activities and affairs of the applicant business. Additionally, BIC has investigative, audit, and subpoena powers at its disposal, allowing the commission to conduct searches pursuant to warrants and arrests for criminal activities. Lastly, BIC enforces the laws and regulations governing the regulated businesses and industries and issues civil or administrative violations for offenses against such laws and regulations.

The reduction of organized crime influence has had some unintended consequences. Price cuts for trash removal engineered by national firms are driving the remaining small companies out of business, significantly limiting competition.

CRIMINALS IN A LEGITIMATE BUSINESS

In addition to their illegal business activities, persons involved in organized crime often own or invest in legitimate enterprises. One popular activity of government officials has been to decry the "infiltration" of organized crime into legitimate business. Michael Maltz (1975: 83) states that the "alternative to penetration of legitimate business is the reinvestment of the ill-gotten gains into some criminal enterprises, which may cause greater social harm." Annelise Anderson (1979: 77) points out, however, that funds from illegal business activities cannot easily "be profitably reinvested in illegal market enterprises without aggressive expansion of the territory controlled by the group." Thus, organized crime members may have an oversupply of illegally derived funds that cannot be profitably used to expand their illegal activities. Maltz (1975) concludes that the penetration of organized crime into legitimate business can be viewed as the equivalent of the legitimation of family fortunes by the robber barons discussed in Chapter 2.

However, Mark Moore (1987: 51) points out that the features of the organized crime group, rather than the substantive offenses committed, make it a societal menace. "What is bad about organized crime is that the criminal groups seem resistant to law enforcement measures, that they seem to become rich as a result of their crimes, that they coolly calculate how best to make money without worrying about whether a planned enterprise is illegal and violent, and that they threaten additional criminal activity in the future even if their current conduct is tolerable." In other words, organized crime groups would pose a threat to society "even if they were engaged largely in legitimate activities and even if their criminal activities produced relatively insignificant levels and kinds of victimization" (1987: 52). Moore suggests that the organized crime group should be viewed as a business firm pursuing profit with a portfolio that encompasses illicit as well as licit enterprises and that poses a serious societal threat. Activities of a Genovese Family crew in New Jersey provide an example of Moore's observations. In addition to more traditional activities—gambling, loansharking, and labor racketeering—the Hoboken-based crew controlled a firm that arranged managed group health care for employers and locals of the Teamsters, Laborers, and Hotel Workers unions. According to the New Jersey attorney general, the firm increased its profit margin by coercing plan administrators into approving inflated fees for service (Raab 1996d).

Anderson provides six reasons for organized criminal involvement in legitimate business:

1. *Profit.* For persons in organized crime, profit provides motivation; not all members of organized crime are able to make a "respectable" income from illicit activities. In an intercepted conversation, New Jersey underboss Anthony Russo complained to boss Sam de Cavalcante that the *amici nostri* could not even support themselves. In another incident, de Cavalcante arranged for the removal of a local union official, who was also a *caporegime* in his crime Family, because the official was not providing *legitimate* employment to the *amici nostri* as construction laborers. Jimmy Fratianno's biography, *The Last Mafioso* (Demaris 1981), contains very little discussion of his business activities. Indeed, it appears that Fratianno's most successful enterprise was a legitimate trucking firm he owned in California.

2. *Diversification.* A legitimate business provides the organized crime member with security of income. While it may be subject to market and other business conditions, a legitimate enterprise is usually not a target of law enforcement efforts. (As will be discussed in Chapter 15, since Anderson wrote her book in the late 1970s, federal and local governments have become increasingly active in the civil seizure of the assets of members of criminal organizations, including those derived from legitimate businesses.)

3. *Transfer.* Illegitimate enterprises are difficult, if not impossible, to transfer to dependents (particularly if they are female). Investing in legitimate enterprises such as a business or real estate ensures that an estate can be legally inherited.

4. *Services.* An organized crime member with a legitimate business is in a position to act as a patron for a person in need of legitimate employment— for example, persons on probation or parole or relatives he wants to shield from the stigma and risks associated with criminal enterprises.

5. *Front.* A legitimate business can provide a front or a base of operations for a host of illegal activities such as loansharking, gambling, fencing, and drug trafficking.

6. *Taxes.* A legitimate business can provide a tax cover, thereby reducing the risk of being charged

with income-tax evasion. Funds from illegitimate enterprises can be mixed with those from the legitimate business, particularly if it is a "cash" business.

Obviously, these categories are not mutually exclusive. It is quite likely that organized crime involvement in legitimate business involves a combination of these six reasons. Persons in organized crime may also use a legitimate business as part of a scam.

The Scam

The scam is a bankruptcy fraud that victimizes wholesale providers of various goods and sometimes insurance companies. The business used as the basis for a scam may be set up with that scheme as its purpose, or it may be an established business that has fallen into organized crime control as a result of gambling or loan shark debt. Scam operations are popular in industries with merchandise that has a high turnover potential, is readily transportable, and is not easy to trace. There are three basic variations (De Franco 1973: 5–7).

Three-Step Scam A new corporation is formed and managed by a front man, or "pencil," who has no prior criminal or bankruptcy record. This person may owe money to a loan shark and may participate in the scam to help pay off the debt. A large bank deposit, known as the "nut," is made to establish credit. This money, plus other money subsequently deposited, is later withdrawn. A large store is rented, and orders for merchandise are placed with as many companies as possible. The size of these orders appears to indicate a successful operation to the suppliers. The owners then proceed with the three steps:

1. Smaller orders are placed during the first month, and such orders are paid for in full. During the second month, larger orders are placed, and about a quarter of the balance due on such orders is paid.
2. During the third month, using credit established as a result of the payments

made for the previous orders, very large orders are placed. Items easily converted into cash, such as jewelry and appliances, usually constitute a large proportion of these orders. Thereafter, merchandise is converted into cash through a fence or a surplus-property operator, normally one with a sufficiently large legitimate inventory to easily intermix the scam merchandise into the normal inventory.
3. The company is then forced into bankruptcy by creditors because, according to plan, all cash has been appropriated by the scam operators.

One-Step Scam Since the three-step scam requires several months for completion, the more rapid one-step scam may be used. A successful business with good credit references is purchased or falls into the hands of a loan shark. No notice of the change in management is provided to Dun and Bradstreet or other credit agencies, thus enabling the new management to trade on the previous owner's reputation for good credit. Manufacturers are approached in person or at trade shows to arrange for the purchase of merchandise. The orders are usually large, and suppliers who did not sell to the company before are very politely informed by the scam operator that if they do not want to fill the order, some other company will be glad to do so. This technique is known as the "sketch." Orders then include many items not previously purchased by the company. After the orders have been received, the merchandise is sold, as in the three-step scam. The money is milked from the business, and the company is forced into bankruptcy.

Same-Name Scam In a variation of the one-step scam, a company is organized with a name deceptively similar, and often almost identical, to that of a successful company in the same area. Large orders are placed with suppliers, who fill them assuming the legitimacy of the company based on the similarity in firm names. The merchandise is then sold in the same fashion as with the other types of scam.

A popular time for the scam operator is just before a seasonal increase in the popularity of particular merchandise, when rush deliveries are commonplace and thorough credit checks are often overlooked. In some scams, arson is the final step: The business is "torched" for the insurance instead of declaring bankruptcy.

Stock Fraud

The entry of organized crime into the stock market is not new. It was noted earlier that John Dioguardi, who died in prison in 1979, was convicted of stock fraud involving a car-leasing company. During the late 1960s and early 1970s, there was a dramatic increase in the volume of securities being traded, providing a lucrative source of income for organized crime. Paperwork began to back up, and brokerage houses and banks were frequently unaware that hundreds of thousands of dollars worth of securities were being taken from their vaults. Thus, the securities were not even reported as missing for several months.

The securities industry employs a great many persons—clerks, runners—whose pay is relatively low. Employees with gambling or loan shark debts or those merely seeking to supplement their incomes found a ready market for such "paper." All that was needed was an organized crime connection. Although many people may have access to valuable securities, few can put stolen securities to immediate use. Organized crime groups serve as the intermediate link in the criminal enterprise. Bookmakers and loan sharks who may have exerted the pressure that induced the thief to take the securities frequently serve as the conduit by which the stolen securities get into the hands of other organized crime figures. Passing through the network of organized crime, the stolen securities eventually reach the hands of someone who does have the expertise, the capital, and the personnel to effect a profitable disposition.

Stolen securities can be transferred to a country with strict bank secrecy laws regarding such transactions, such as Panama. The securities are deposited in a bank, which issues a letter of credit, which is used to secure loans that are eventually defaulted. They can be used as collateral for bank loans from "cooperative" loan officials or "rented" to legitimate businessmen in need of collateral for instant credit. Panama's strategic location between the Atlantic and Pacific Oceans, North and South America, its dollar-based economy, and its modern international trade and financial sectors, makes the country a magnet for such schemes.

More recently, the organized crime foray into the stock market has added elements—intimidation and violence—to widely known scams. With the entry of organized crime, and the "boiler room" and "pump and dump" schemes, in addition to financial dangers, unsuspecting customers can now face physical dangers. In 2000, the federal government accused 120 persons throughout the United States, including members of the Colombo and Bonanno Families, of involvement in a Manhattan brokerage and investment bank that bilked investors of at least $50 million. The indictment alleged that brokers who refused to cooperate were assaulted. Some of the principals in the case were part of a defunct brokerage, one of whose officers was found dead in his New Jersey mansion in 1999. His body was found with that of another broker—both had been shot execution style.

Brokers for the firm used traditional high-pressure—"boiler room"—tactics to sell worthless stocks, created phony stock trades, and bribed brokers from other firms to push the stock in an effort to inflate the price. The wiseguy stock would then be sold off at enormous profits. Brokers who had a change of heart or refused further cooperation in the scheme were threatened with violence and assaulted (Roane 2000; Sullivan and Berenson 2000).

In 2001, another indictment alleged that twenty persons working with members of the Gambino Family bilked thousands of investors of more than $50 million; two victims lost at least $12 million. Investors identified from lists of retirees and businesspersons would receive a "cold call" from a broker promoting shares in several companies. The brokers would then drive up the price—the "pump"—and demand that the victims hold on to their stocks, refusing to execute sell orders, and threatening some with violence if they did anything that could drive the price down. The brokers would then sell off their shares of the stocks—the "dump"—at huge profits (Christian 2001).

MONEY LAUNDERING

Money laundering is "to knowingly engage in a financial transaction with the proceeds of some unlawful activity with the intent of promoting or carrying on that unlawful activity or to conceal or disguise the nature, location, source, ownership, or control of these proceeds" (Genzman 1988: 1). According to the U.S. Treasury Department, money laundering is "the process by which criminals or criminal organizations seek to disguise the illicit nature of their proceeds by introducing them into the stream of legitimate commerce and finance" (Motivans 2003: 1).

Ever since Al Capone was imprisoned for income-tax evasion, financially successful criminals have sought ways to "launder" their illegally secured "dirty" money. The practice has developed its own lexicon: "Getting currency into the bank, around the reporting system, at home or abroad, is called *placement*. Once the money is in the form of a bank entry, the launderer hides its criminal origins through a series of complex transactions. Police call it *layering*. The launderer then makes the proceeds available to the criminals in an apparently legitimate form. The term for this is *integration*" (Blum 1999: 59).

Some use a cash business, such as a vending machine firm, to mingle cash from illegitimate sources with legally earned money. Some criminals use casinos for the same purpose or to convert cash from small denominations to $100 bills. In New Jersey, one drug trafficking ring opened a casino account for $118,000, stayed several days, but did not gamble. They then left the hotel with checks payable to third parties, who deposited the checks in a securities firm. The money was later withdrawn—"laundered" (PCOC 1984a). Casinos were made subject to the Bank Secrecy Act in 1985 (discussed later), so purchasing large amounts of chips while engaging in minimal gambling attracts unwanted casino attention. In response, collusive pairs began betting large amounts on both "red and black" or "odd and even" on roulette, or both with and against the bank in baccarat, or both the "pass line" or "come line" and the "don't pass line" or "don't come line" in craps. The "winning partner" then cashes in his or her chips and gets a casino check. The jewelry business also provides money laundering opportunities. In 1991, for example, several men from Lebanon and Argentina were convicted of laundering $1 billion in Colombian drug profits through the purchase and sale of gold, using jewelry companies in Houston, Miami, Los Angeles, and New York City as fronts.

In elaborate money laundering schemes, the first step is to convert large quantities of cash into one or more cashier's checks. In addition to being easier to carry—450 bills weigh about one pound—they are difficult to trace because they do not bear the receiver's name or address. Transactions involving the proceeds of drug trafficking often consist of large amounts of cash in small denominations. In such instances, the first step is to convert the small bills into hundreds—$1 million in $20 bills weighs 110 pounds; in $100 bills, it weighs only 22 pounds. To avoid IRS reporting requirements under the Bank Secrecy Act, transfers of cash to cashier's checks or $100 bills must take place in amounts under $10,000 or through banking officials who agree not to fill out a Currency Transaction Report (CTR). A CTR is required for each deposit, withdrawal, or exchange of currency or monetary instruments in excess of $10,000. It must be submitted to the IRS within 15 days of the transaction. In 1984, tax amendments extended the reporting requirements to anyone who receives more than $10,000 in cash in the course of a trade or business. More than 13 million CTRs are filed each year, and an additional half-million are filed by casinos. A CMIR (Currency and Monetary Instrument Report) must be filed for cash or certain monetary instruments exceeding $10,000 in value that enter or leave the United States. Federal Reserve regulations require banks to file a suspicious activity report (SAR) when they suspect possible criminal wrongdoing in transactions.

Attempts to strengthen these regulations have met vigorous opposition from the banking industry (Wahl 1999a). In the wake of the September 11, 2001, terrorist attacks, money laundering regulations have been strengthened. In 2002, a small Manhattan bank that accepted duffel bags filled with cash totaling at least $123 million pled guilty to violating federal anti–money laundering statutes (discussed in Chapter 15). Bank tellers frequently complained to their supervisors how long it took to count the deposits. Once the money was deposited, it was quickly wired to accounts in Latin America and the Middle East (Worth 2002).

In 1985, it was revealed that the Bank of Boston, the city's oldest and biggest bank, had helped launder money for the underboss of the Patriarca Family. From 1979 to 1983, Jerry Angiulo and his brothers would convert paper bags stuffed with tens of thousands of dollars in small bills into $100 bills and more than $7 million in cashier's checks. None of the transactions were reported to the IRS. Two real estate companies controlled by the Angiulos in the Italian neighborhood of Boston's North End had been placed on the "exempt" list, so their cash transactions in excess of $10,000 did not have to be reported to the IRS.

The only businesses legally entitled to such exemptions are retail outlets such as supermarkets that do a great deal of business in large amounts of cash on a daily basis. Money launderers may utilize car dealerships, whose managers accept cash for automobile purchases and fail to file the required CTRs.

Currency exchanges (*casas de cambio*) have sprouted up along the Texas-Mexico border. These poorly regulated enterprises accept (illegally) large amounts of cash. They pool many customers' funds into one account and deposit the money in a domestic or foreign bank, keeping records on what is owed to each customer. When a foreign drug trafficker wants to send money to his own country, the *casa* operator wires the funds from the bank to the trafficker's foreign account(s). Even when a U.S. bank completes a CTR, it names the *casa* as the owner of the funds, not the actual owner. In 2007, the Union Bank of California was fined $10 million by the Financial Crimes Enforcement Network of the U.S. Department of the Treasury because the bank failed to adequately monitor Mexican *casa de cambio* accounts which allowed the movement of millions of dollars of suspected proceeds of drug sales without detection or reporting of the suspicious transactions. In the Houston area, in addition to *casas*, there are *giro* (wire) houses. In general, the *giros* move drug money to Colombia, while the *casas* move Mexican drug money (Webster and McCampbell 1992).

Elmhurst-Jackson Heights, a Colombian section of the New York City borough of Queens, has many storefront shops for wiring money outside of the country. In response to their use for money laundering, the Treasury Department imposed a $750 per transaction limit on twelve firms with 1,600 outlets suspected of wiring drug money. If they wish to avoid the transaction limit, customers must provide picture identity cards, which have to be copied by the store and submitted to the Treasury Department (McFadden 1997). The Cali cartel (discussed in Chapter 7) have used their aircraft fleet, the same planes they use to bring in cocaine, to fly millions of dollars out of the United States (Chepesiuk 2003). Traffickers also use nontraditional methods to transport their drug proceeds from the United States back to Colombia, for example, $100 bills are rolled into a cylinder shape, pressed, and then swallowed by couriers.

In some schemes, money launderers use dozens of persons (called "smurfs") to convert cash into money orders and cashier's checks that do not specify payees or that are made out to fictitious persons. Each transaction is held to less than $10,000 (called "structuring") to avoid the need for a CTR. One ring operating out of Forest Hills, New York, employed dozens of persons who used about thirty banks in New York and New Jersey to launder about $100 million a year for the Cali cartel. The checks were pasted between the pages of magazines and shipped to Cali; from there the money was transferred to banks in Panama. In 1989, sixteen persons were indicted when one of the banks became suspicious of the unusual amount of cash transactions and reported them to federal authorities (Morgan 1989). "Smurfing" has now been made a federal crime, and increased bank scrutiny has made tellers suspicious of cash transactions just under $10,000. In response, smurfs have reduced transactions to as low as $5,000 and often make dozens of transactions in a day, typically in banks that do not usually have long wait lines (Walter 1990).

One ring working for the Cali cartel was centered in a small New York City law firm that specialized in international banking. They used a number of persons, including the owner of a trucking firm, a firefighter, a police officer, and two rabbis. Whenever $1 million in street sales had been accumulated, the law firm would be notified and a courier sent to pick up the money. The courier would take the money to a bank, which wired the money on behalf of the firm to Zurich (Treaster 1994). Other legitimate companies have been involved in money laundering. In 1994, a banking arm of American Express paid the federal government $32 million to settle a money laundering case involving the Gulf cartel drug organization of Juan Garcia Abrego (discussed in Chapter 7). In response, the government agreed not to seek criminal charges against the corporation (Myerson 1994). Two American Express employees were convicted of playing a role in the scheme ("Bank Officer Is Convicted of Laundering" 1994).

Money laundering has been greatly facilitated by advances in banking technology. It has become increasingly difficult for the government to effectively monitor banking transactions. "An alternative to physically removing money from the country is to deposit the cash, then transfer the funds electronically to other domestic and foreign banks, financial institutions, or securities accounts. Swiss law enforcement officials report that when money is transferred by wire to Switzerland, it seldom comes directly from the country of origin; rather it is 'prewashed' in a third country such as Panama, the Bahamas, the Cayman Islands, or Luxembourg" (Webster and McCampbell 1992: 4). The sheer volume of wire transfers makes accounting difficult—one major bank in New York handles about 40,000 wires each business day.

A customer can instruct his or her personal computer to direct a bank's computer to transfer money from a U.S. account to one in a foreign bank. The bank's computer then tells a banking clearinghouse that assists in the transfer—no person talks to another. While depositing more than $10,000 in cash into an account requires the filing of a CTR, the government receives more than

A Complex Island Laundry

As the result of an undercover money laundering investigation, in 1998, federal agents seized $1.8 million from several Citibank accounts in New York City. The accounts were held by a Cayman Islands bank that never had an office in that country; its listed corporate headquarters in Uruguay was an accounting firm that processed its correspondence. Despite the seizure, for almost two years an additional $300 million moved through the accounts. Part of the money wired into the accounts was paid out in cash in Argentina to a local real estate agent reputed to be a representative of Mexican drug traffickers (Golden 2001).

Black Market Peso Exchange ("BMPE")

BMPE is an informal currency exchange system in which one or more "peso brokers" serve as middlemen between, on one hand, narcotics traffickers who control massive quantities of drug money in cash in the United States, and, on the other, companies and individuals in Colombia who wish to purchase U.S. dollars outside the legitimate Colombian banking system so that they can, among other things, avoid the payment of taxes, import duties, and transaction fees owed to the Colombian government.

The BMPE system involves three steps. First, narcotics traffickers enter into contracts with peso brokers in which the brokers deliver pesos in Colombia in return for cash drug money in the United States and Canada. Second, the peso brokers use accounts in the United States or other countries outside Colombia to place the narcotics proceeds into the international banking system. Finally, the peso brokers enter into contracts with Colombian companies or individuals who deliver pesos to the brokers in Colombia in exchange for a wire transfer of dollars. Both transactions are verbal, without any paper trail, and the disconnection between the peso transactions (which generally all occur in Colombia) and the dollar transactions (which generally all occur outside Colombia) make discovery of the money laundering by international law enforcement extremely difficult. Because of these inherent advantages, the BMPE system has become one of the primary methods by which Colombian narcotics traffickers launder their illicit funds (DEA press release, May 4, 2004).

12 million such reports annually and is hopelessly behind in reviewing them.

The Internet has also facilitated money laundering. A launderer establishes a company—the Abadinsky Computer Co.—offering high-end products over the Internet. The launderer purchases products from the Abadinsky Computer Co. over the Internet using credit cards. The Abadinsky Computer Co. invoices the credit card company that, in turn, forwards payment for the purchases. "The credit card company, the Internet service provider, the Internet invoicing service, and even the bank from which the illegal proceeds begin this process would likely have no reason to believe there was anything suspicious about the activity, since they each only see one part of it" (Financial Action Task Force on Money Laundering 2001: 4).

In 1989, a Panamanian bank pled guilty to money laundering charges in the largest such case to end in a conviction. Although the bank (*Banco de Occidente*) had no operations in the United States, it held several accounts in Continental Illinois Bank's

New York branch that were used to launder money. Drug dealers in New York, Miami, Houston, and Los Angeles distributed money from cocaine sales to bogus jewelry firms that acted as fronts. The cash was sent by Wells Fargo armored truck to other phony jewelry operations in Los Angeles, where it was counted by high-speed machines. The cash was then shipped by armored courier to Los Angeles banks that were told it was being used to purchase gold bullion, something common in the jewelry business. The Los Angeles banks made an electronic transfer to New York, and from there the funds were electronically transferred to Europe or directly to Latin America, eventually winding up in Colombia. The operators were paid 7 percent of the funds they laundered. The scheme ended when Wells Fargo became suspicious and informed federal authorities of the unusually large amounts of cash that were being deposited— $25 million in three months (Labaton 1989b).

As part of an overseas laundering scheme, a lawyer acting on behalf of a client creates a "paper" (or "boilerplate") company in any one of a number of countries that have strict privacy statutes, for example, Panama. In 2001, Panama had 373,701 registered offshore banks and companies (James 2001). The funds to be laundered are transferred physically or wired to the company's account in a local bank. The company then transfers the money to the local branch of a large international bank. The paper company is then able to borrow money from the United States (or any other) branch of this bank, using the overseas deposit as security (Walter 1990). Or an employment contract is set up between the launderer and his or her "paper" company for an imaginary service for which payments are made to the launderer. In some cases, the lawyer may also establish a "boilerplate bank"— like the company, this is a shell. Not only does the criminal get his money laundered, but he also earns a tax write-off for the interest on the loan. Under the Bank Secrecy Act, wiring or physically transporting cash or other financial instruments out of the country in excess of $10,000 must be reported to the Customs Service. Once the money is out of the United States, however, it may be impossible for the IRS to trace it. In some schemes, the money is returned to the United States or other destination via the purchase of life insurance policies from the British Isle of Man, a center for international insurance firms. The policies frequently taken out in the name of relatives are then cashed out prematurely, the 25 percent penalty being part of the cost of the operation.

Another method of laundering funds without actually moving cash out of the country involves otherwise legitimate companies that import goods from the United States. Representatives of the Cali cartel in the United States paid for imported goods with dollars that went to the exporters. In return, the participating companies paid the cartel in Colombia at slightly less than the true exchange rate (Krauss and Frantz 1995). Or drug proceeds are used to purchase easily sold goods such as expensive liquor or electronic products. These are shipped to Colombia and sold at a 20 to 30 percent discount (Sanger 1995). In a more elaborate scheme, a currency exchange broker in the United States receives dollars in exchange for pesos at 30 to 40 percent below the actual market rate which he promises to deliver to the trafficker's accounts in Colombia—the broker's life provides collateral. The broker's "smurfs" deposit the cash into hundreds of U.S. bank accounts in amounts below $10,000. The dollars are sold to businessmen in Colombia for pesos at a 20 percent discount. The pesos are transferred to the trafficker's accounts. The Colombian businessmen use the dollars to import American goods (Leonhardt and Whitaker 2000).

A more recent laundering scheme involves the use of prepaid cards such as gift cards and phone cards. They provide a compact, easily transportable way of moving money. Profits from crime are used to buy cards that can be used to connect to ATMs or for debit purposes. Cash is loaded onto the cards and then sent out of the country (Associated Press 2006).

Private Banking

Money laundering is facilitated by a variety of private banking operations, formal and informal. In the United States, commercial banks and securities firms may offer special banking services to wealthy persons who deposit $1 million or more. The bank then assigns a private banker or broker-dealer in securities who facilitates complex wire transfers throughout the world and creates offshore accounts. An investment manager for a major securities firm in New York pled guilty in 2005 to laundering $15 million in Mexican drug proceeds generated by the Gulf cartel. Using a system known as layering, she coordinated the establishment of offshore corporations as well as offshore accounts in the names of third parties with the funds ultimately winding up back in the firm's accounts under the names of fictitious persons (Berkeley 2002a; Preston 2005c). In 2003, a small securities firm in Manhattan was indicted for illegally transmitting more than $3 billion for private clients in two years—the firm was accused of doing this for nine years. This case developed as part of an investigation into the use of debit cards issued by offshore banks. In 2001, they had 115,000 debit card accounts that were used to access more than $100 million in the Bahamas and Cayman Islands (Saulny 2003).

Chinese criminals are aided by an underground banking system operating through gold shops, trading companies, commodity houses, travel agencies, and money changers, managed in many countries by the same extended Chinese family. "The method of moving money is the *chop*, which is in effect a negotiable instrument. A *chop* can be cashed in Chinese gold shops or trading houses in many countries. The value and identity of the holder of the chop is a secret between the parties. The form of chop varies from transaction to transaction and is difficult to identify. In effect, the chop system allows money to be transferred from country to country instantaneously and anonymously" (Chaiken 1991: 495). For example, cash to finance a heroin deal is deposited in a San Francisco Chinatown gold shop in return for a *chop*. The *chop* is sent by courier to Hong Kong and is cashed. The owner of the *chop* receives his money from the original issuer, who is fronting for the drug deal.

A similar system, the *hawala*, is used in South Asia, where the size of the underground economies is estimated to be 50 to 100 percent the size of the documented economies. Similar to the modern practice of "wiring money," the ancient system of *hawala* was the primary money transfer mechanism used in South Asia prior to the introduction of Western banking. "Hawala operates on trust and connections ('trust' is one of the several meanings associated with the word 'hawala'). Customers trust hawala 'bankers' (known as hawaladars) who use their connections to facilitate money movement worldwide. Hawala transfers take place with little, if any, paper trail, and, when records are kept, they are usually kept in code" (U.S. Department of State 1999: 22). In Pakistan, for example, $100,000 (plus a transaction fee) is given to a hawaladar who provides a code term. Via the Internet, the hawalader informs his broker in the Cayman Islands, where someone who provides the code term is given $100,000 to deposit in an island account. Money is never actually moved, and periodically hawaladars/brokers balance their respective transactions, usually by wire transfers using goods and invoices as a cover. In the United States, there are an estimated 20,000 informal remittance businesses working out of a variety of convenience stores, restaurants, and small shops whose owners speak languages unfamiliar to Westerners such as Arabic, Urdu, Hindu, and a variety of Chinese dialects (Freedman 2005).

Taking advantage of bank secrecy laws to avoid disclosure of ownership has drawbacks: It may be difficult, if not impossible, to pass on these assets to one's heirs.

SUMMARY

- Labor and business racketeering distinguish the American Mafia and its predecessors from other forms and makes the former more influential than the latter.
- The rise of organized labor and the subsequent reaction of American business generated a conflict that provided fertile ground for the seeds of racketeering and organized crime.
- The leaders of organized crime provided mercenary armies to unions that were willing to

Cayman Islands

Located south of Cuba, an easy flight from either Florida or Colombia, this small West Indian island is only 100 miles square and has a population of only 23,400. Yet there are 570 banks and 20,000 registered companies on the Cayman Islands. The Georgetown financial district has the highest density of banks and fax machines in the world. Most banks are simply "plaques" or box offices—no vaults, tellers, or security guards—with transactions recorded by Cayman booking centers. In 1984, the United States and Great Britain signed an agreement that gives American officials investigating drug cases information about secret bank accounts in the Cayman Islands. The Caymans, which are administered by Britain, can maintain secrecy in all other cases unless there is proof of an offense under their law. Virtually anyone can still "establish his or her own shell company for a few thousand dollars in legal fees, open a local bank account and, because the required disclosure is minimal and business operates behind a wall of strict secrecy, no one need know about the company or what funds are stashed there. The few slips of paper that constitute the company records may be held in the office of a Cayman lawyer" (Lohr 1992: 28; Silverstein 2000).

Western and South Pacific

The Western and Pacific islands of Cook, the Marshalls, Nauru, Niue, Samoa, and Vanuatu have seen the development of offshore financial centers (OFC). Together, these tiny entities have more than 18,000 registered banks and companies (James 2001). Naura, with a population of about 12,000, has 450 banks registered to a single post office box. These islands have a laissez-faire approach to their banking rules and regulations—a regulatory philosophy that was created especially to prevent effective oversight of the offshore sector. As a result, governments in most of these nations have little or no control over their OFCs.

"Isolated as they are, these OFCs demonstrate the globalization of international finance. Via the Internet and wire transfer, many U.S.-based Asians are now using banking facilities of Nauru's OFC. There is significant use by Russian organized crime of the OFCs of Vanuatu, Samoa and Nauru. One increasingly common scheme is to employ non-Russian middlemen to open accounts or charter shell banks or shell companies (all with the same post office box in Nauru) to give the impression of legitimate business with non-Russian entities" (U.S. State Department 1999: 11). Vanuatu is the best established South Pacific OFC: Port Vila, its one-street capital, has nearly 80 private banks and 2,000 trust companies, but the "identity of bank owners and the nature of their assets remain secret to both the public and foreign investors" (Lintner 2002: 7).

use violence to organize workers and thwart strikebreakers.

- Craft and large industrial unions have generally been free of organized crime, and while the locals of a variety of unions have been linked to organized crime, four unions have historically had the closest relationship: International Brotherhood of Teamsters, Hotel and Restaurant Employees Union, Laborers' International Union of North America, and International Longshoremen's Association.

- There is no hard-and-fast line separating labor racketeering from business racketeering. Corrupt union officials and "legitimate" businessmen have willingly cooperated in order to derive such benefits as decreased labor costs and restraint of trade agreements; organized crime can police these illegal agreements.

- Certain industries, such as construction and private solid waste hauling, are more vulnerable to organized crime because they are relatively easy businesses to enter—they do not require a large cash investment—and highly competitive. Other characteristics include an intense need for timely action, such as those that deal with perishable foods and industries where any disruption of work or deliveries can be quite costly.

- An organized crime group should be viewed as a business firm pursuing profit with a portfolio that encompasses illicit as well as licit enterprises.

- Reasons for being in a legitimate business include profit, diversification, transfer, services, front, and taxes. Successful criminals need to be able disguise the illicit nature of their proceeds by introducing them into the stream of legitimate commerce and finance.

- There are both simple and complex methods for accomplishing this money laundering that range from converting large quantities of cash into one or more cashier's checks to depositing the funds and having them wired to an overseas account. Of particular interest are private banking systems that depend on trust and can move funds without a paper trail.

REVIEW QUESTIONS

1. What are all of the possible advantages for an employer who enters into a corrupt relationship with a labor union?
2. What historical factors led to the entry of organized crime into labor unions?
3. How did "Dopey" Benny Fein rationalize labor's relationship with criminals?
4. What four international unions have reputedly been under the control of organized crime?
5. Why were stevedoring firms often willing partners in corruption with organized labor?
6. What are "paper locals," and how were they used by labor racketeers?
7. How does business racketeering differ from labor racketeering?
8. What are the elements that make a particular industry, such as private waste hauling, susceptible to racketeering?
9. How did the election of John F. Kennedy lead to the demise of Jimmy Hoffa?
10. What is a scam, and how is it used by organized crime figures?
11. What are the six reasons for organized crime involvement in legitimate business?
12. What is the typical role of organized crime in a restraint of trade agreement?
13. What is money laundering, and how can it be accomplished?
14. What is a Currency Transaction Report (CTR)?
15. What are the advantages of using offshore banking facilities for money laundering?
16. What are the similarities between the *chop* and the system of *hawala*?

CHAPTER
15
Organized Crime Statutes and Law Enforcement

ORGANIZED CRIME STATUTES

The business of organized crime involves the violation of numerous laws. Many are routinely enforced by municipal police departments, including laws against gambling, drugs, prostitution, extortion, assault, and murder. The investigation and prosecution of organized crime per se, however, has largely been a responsibility of the federal government, which has a number of specialized statutes to carry out this purpose. Chief among them are the Internal Revenue Code, the Controlled Substances Act, the Hobbs Act, the Racketeer Influenced and Corrupt Organizations (RICO) statute, the Continuing Criminal Enterprise statute, the Consumer Credit Protection Act, statutes against conspiracy, and the anti–money laundering provision of Title 18.

Internal Revenue Code

In 1927, the U.S. Supreme Court decided the case of *United States v. Sullivan* (274 U.S. 259), which denied the claim of self-incrimination (Fifth Amendment) as an excuse for failure to file income tax on illegally gained earnings: It would be ridiculous if legitimate persons had to file income tax returns but criminals did not. This decision enabled the federal government to successfully prosecute Al Capone and members of his organization. Because persons in organized crime have obligations as taxpayers, they can be prosecuted for several acts:

1. Failing to make required returns or maintain required business records
2. Filing a false return or making a false statement about taxes
3. Willful failure to pay federal income tax or concealment of assets with intent to defraud
4. Helping others evade income taxes
5. In gambling operations, failing to file a "Special Tax Return and Application for Registry-Wagering"

"Acts which do not comprise a violation or attempt to violate any of these substantive sections may be punishable as part of a conspiracy 'to impair, defeat, and obstruct the functions of the Commissioner of Internal Revenue' by concealing matters relevant to collection of federal taxes" (Johnson

1963: 17). An employer can be prosecuted for not complying with Social Security withholding requirements relative to employees. Thus, the manager of an illegal enterprise, a gambling operation, for example, could be prosecuted for such evasions.

The Internal Revenue Service of the Department of the Treasury employs about 2,800 special agents in the Criminal Investigation (CI) division. While the primary role of the IRS is collection of revenue and compliance with tax codes, CI seeks evidence of criminal violations for prosecution by the Department of Justice. In particular, agents seek out information relative to income that has not been reported: "Additional income for criminal purposes is established by both direct and indirect methods. The direct method consists of the identification of specific items of unreported taxable receipts, overstated costs and expenses (such as personal expenses charged to business, diversion of corporate income to office-stockholders, allocation of income or expense to incorrect year in order to lower tax, etc.), and improper claims for credit or exemption. The advantage of using this method is that the proof involved is easier for jurors and others to understand" (Committee on the Office of Attorney General 1974: 49–50).

Persons in organized crime have devised methods for successful evasion of taxes—dealing in cash, keeping minimal records, setting up fronts, and using a *zapper*. A zapper is an automated sales suppression software program often on a flash drive that is attached to a cash register to facilitate removing cash without leaving a record for tax audit purposes. A dollar amount or percentage is entered and the program calculates which receipts to erase to get close to the cash the person wants to remove. The device then suggests how much cash to remove and erases enough entries so the register balances (Furchgott 2008).

These evasion schemes are countered by the indirect method known as the *net worth theory*: "The government establishes a taxpayer's net worth at the commencement of the taxing period [which requires substantial accuracy], deducts that from his or her net worth at the end of the period, and proves that the net gain in net worth exceeds the income reported by the taxpayer" (Johnson

1963: 17–19). In effect, the Internal Revenue Service reconstructs a person's total expenditures by examining the person's actual standard of living and comparing it with reported income. The government can then maintain that the taxpayer did not report his or her entire income. The government does not have to show a probable source of the excess unreported gain in net worth. Earl Johnson (1963: 18) points out that the Capone case taught many criminals a lesson: "management-level persons in organized crime scrupulously report their income—at least the part of it that they spend."

In 2002, a federal judge ruled that money paid to organized crime—$1.7 million a year to a captain in the Gambino Family—for protection of coin-operated video pornographic booths was not a deductible business expense. The judge found that although such payments might qualify as "ordinary and necessary" payments in this industry, the defendant had attempted to hide the payments from the IRS, and the judge ruled that this disqualified the deductions (Johnston 2002).

Controlled Substances Statutes

In 1914, the Harrison Act made it illegal to sell or give away opium or opium derivatives and coca or its derivatives without written order on a form issued by the Commissioner of Revenue. Persons who were not registered were prohibited from engaging in interstate traffic in the drugs, and no one could possess any of the drugs who had not registered and paid the special tax under a penalty of up to five years' imprisonment and a fine of no more than $2,000.

By 1970, the issue of federal police authority had been largely resolved, and the Comprehensive Drug Abuse Prevention and Control Act of 1970 represented a new legal approach to federal drug policy—it was predicated not on the constitutional power to tax but on federal authority over interstate commerce. This shift had enormous implications for the way in which the federal government would approach drug enforcement in the future. The act "set the stage for an innovation in Federal drug law enforcement techniques. That innovation was the assigning of large numbers of Federal narcotic

Anti-Diversion Law

The principal statute to control the diversion of precursor and essential chemicals for the manufacture of drugs is the Chemical Diversion and Trafficking Act, Subtitle A of the Anti-Drug Abuse Amendments of 1988. The act established record-keeping requirements and enforcement standards for more than two dozen precursor and essential chemicals. State and federal statutes make the unauthorized trade in any of the listed substances equivalent to trafficking in the actual illegal drugs.

agents to work in local communities. No longer was it necessary to demonstrate interstate traffic to justify Federal participation in combating illegal drug use" (PCOC 1986a: 28). The new approach was sustained by decisions of the Supreme Court. The 1970 legislation establishes five schedules into which all controlled substances could be placed according to their potential for abuse (see Figure 15.1).

The Comprehensive Crime Control Act of 1984 supplemented the 1970 drug statute by authorizing the doubling of a sentence for drug offenders with prior domestic or foreign felony drug convictions. The Anti-Drug Abuse Act of 1986 imposes mandatory prison sentences for certain drug offenses and a mandatory doubling of the minimum penalties for offenders with prior felony drug convictions. In 1988, the military's role in drug-law enforcement was substantially increased, and Congress enacted another drug abuse act that mandates greater control over precursor chemicals and devices used to manufacture drugs, such as encapsulating machinery.

FIGURE 15.1   *DEA Schedules of Controlled Substances*

SCHEDULE I

A. The drug or other substance has a high potential for abuse.
B. The drug or other substance has no currently accepted medical use in treatment in the United States.
C. There is a lack of accepted safety for use of the drug or other substance under medical supervision.

SCHEDULE II

A. The drug or other substance has a high potential for abuse.
B. The drug or other substance has a currently accepted medical use in treatment in the United States or a currently accepted medical use with severe restrictions.
C. Abuse of the drug or other substances may lead to severe psychological or physical dependence.

SCHEDULE III

A. The drug or other substance has a potential for abuse less than the drugs or other substances in Schedules I and II.
B. The drug or other substance has a currently accepted medical use in treatment in the United States.
C. Abuse of the drug or other substance may lead to moderate or low physical dependence or high psychological dependence.

SCHEDULE IV

A. The drug or other substance has a low potential for abuse relative to the drugs or other substances in Schedule III.
B. The drug or other substance has a currently accepted medical use in treatment in the United States.
C. Abuse of the drug or other substance may lead to limited physical dependence or psychological dependence relative to the drugs or other substances in Schedule III.

SCHEDULE V

A. The drug or other substance has a low potential for abuse relative to the drugs or other substances in Schedule IV.
B. The drug or other substance has a currently accepted medical use in treatment in the United States.
C. Abuse of the drug or other substances may lead to limited physical dependence or psychological dependence relative to the drugs or other substances in Schedule IV.

Anti-Drug Abuse Amendments of 1988 created a complex and extensive body of civil penalties aimed at casual users. These include withdrawal of federal benefits, such as mortgage guarantees, and loss of a pilot's license or stockbroker's license at the discretion of a federal judge. Fines of up to $10,000 can be imposed for illegal possession of even small amounts of controlled substances. There are special penalties for the sale of drugs to minors. The statute permits imposition of capital punishment for murders committed as part of a continuing criminal enterprise or for the murder of a law enforcement officer during an arrest for a drug-related felony. The statute also established an Office of National Drug Policy headed by a director appointed by the president. The director is charged with coordinating federal drug supply reduction efforts, including international control, intelligence, interdiction, domestic law enforcement, treatment, education, and research.

The Hobbs Act

The earliest statutes designed to deal with "racketeering" are collectively known as the Hobbs Act (18 U.S.C. §§ 1951–1955). Since 1946 they have been amended several times. The Hobbs Act makes it a federal crime to engage in criminal behavior that interferes with interstate commerce:

> Whosoever in any way or degree obstructs, delays, or affects commerce or the movement of any articles or commodity in commerce, by robbery or extortion or attempts or conspires to do so, or commits or threatens physical violence to any person or property in furtherance of a plan or purpose to do anything in violation of this section shall be fined not more than $10,000 or imprisonment for not more than twenty years or both.

The statute has been broadly interpreted so as to permit the successful prosecution of more than sixty Chicago police officers for extorting payoffs from the owners of saloons. The six-year investigation (1970–1976) by the U.S. Department of Justice was based on the part of the Hobbs Act that makes extortion that in any way affects interstate commerce a federal crime: Federal attorneys "reasoned that because taverns sold beer and liquor, much of which was either delivered from or manufactured in states other than Illinois, extortion of a tavern owner would be a violation of the Hobbs Act" (Biegel and Biegel 1977: 7).

The Hobbs Act also prohibits foreign or interstate travel or the use of interstate facilities, such as the mails or telephones, to advance illegal activities such as gambling, drug trafficking, extortion, and bribery. This permitted the federal government to prosecute corrupt officials and lawyers in Cook County, Illinois—"Operation Greylord"—in the late 1980s and early 1990s. Section 1954 defines as criminal a union official who misuses an employee benefit plan. "An official who receives or agrees to or solicits any fee, kickback, commission, gift, loan, money, or thing of value because of or with intent to be influenced with respect to, any of the actions, decisions, or other duties relating to any question or matter concerning such plan or any persons who directly or indirectly gives or offers, or promises to give or offer, any fee, kickback, commission, gift, loan, money, or thing of value prohibited by this section, shall be fined not more than $10,000 or imprisoned for not more than three years, or both."

Conspiracy

The United States does not criminalize participation in a criminal organization, as such, since to do so might implicate constitutional prohibitions against measures inhibiting freedom of association. However, both at the federal level and in most of the states, conspiracies to commit offenses are punishable. Conspiracy is an agreement between two or more persons to commit a criminal act; it is *the agreement* that becomes the *corpus* (body) of the crime. To prove a conspiracy, it is not necessary that it be shown that the offense was actually committed. Indeed, in 2003, the Supreme Court, in a unanimous decision (*United States v. Recio*, 537 U.S. 270), ruled that even when the object of the conspiracy (drug distribution) had been frustrated by the police, who turned it into a sting operation, the conspiracy charge is still valid.

Federal conspiracy statutes generally require the government to prove that two or more persons agreed to commit an offense and that one or more of these persons did at least once act to carry out the agreement. In some cases, for example, money laundering, it is not necessary to prove that conspirators did anything concrete to carry out the scheme (*Whitfield v. United States*, 543 U.S. 209, 2005). In 1994, the Supreme Court (*United States v. Shabani*, 513 U. S. 10) ruled that conspiring to violate federal drug laws can be a crime even in the absence of overt acts. Withdrawing from a conspiracy requires the defendant to show *actual* withdrawal—merely ceasing to participate does not meet the burden of proof (Diener and T. Johnson 2005).

Conspiracy statutes provide valuable tools for prosecuting persons in organized crime because:

- Intervention can occur prior to the commission of a substantive offense.
- A conspirator cannot shield him- or herself from prosecution because of a lack of knowledge of the details of the conspiracy or the identity of co-conspirators and their contributions.
- An act or declaration by one conspirator committed in furtherance of the conspiracy is admissible against each co-conspirator (an exception to the hearsay rule).
- Each conspirator is responsible for the substantive crimes of his or her co-conspirators (vicarious liability); even late joiners can be held liable for prior acts of co-conspirators if the agreement by the latecomer is made with full knowledge of the conspiracy's objective.

The charge of conspiracy, which federal prosecutors generally include whenever a case involves multiple defendants (Campane 1981a), is particularly effective against upper-echelon organized crime figures: "The fundamental essence of a conspiracy obviates the necessity of establishing that the organization leader committed a physical act amounting to a crime or that he even committed an overt act in furtherance of the object of the conspiracy. It is sufficient if he can be shown to have been a party to the conspiratorial agreement" (Johnson 1963: 2). Its usefulness can be seen in the following incident:

> Two young men entered an Italian restaurant and approached the table of an elderly gentleman who was sipping anisette with a large, burly individual. After he acknowledged them, the two sat down at the table. They were members of the Genovese crime Family; he was the boss. The young men explained that they had just discovered a large-scale gambling operation that was not tied to organized crime—an "outlaw" game. They wanted to "license" the operation and asked for his approval. The boss gestured with his hands and face, saying nothing, but conveying approval. The two young men excused themselves and left. With several other members of the Family, they proceeded to assault and threaten to kill the owner of the gambling operation, extorting several thousand dollars from him. They returned and shared the money with their boss, who knew nothing of the details of what had occurred and never asked.

There are three basic types of conspiracy:

1. *Wheel conspiracies.* One person at the "hub" conspires individually with two or more persons who make up the "spokes" of the wheel. For the conspiracy to be (legally) complete, the wheel needs a "rim": each of the spokes must be aware of and agree with each other in pursuit of at least one objective.

2. *Chain conspiracies.* Like the lights on a Christmas tree, each conspirator is dependent on the successful participation of every other member. Each member is a "link" who understands that the success of the scheme depends upon everyone in the chain.

3. *Enterprise conspiracies.* The RICO enterprise conspiracy avoids the practical limitations inherent in proving wheel and chain conspiracies. The statute makes it a separate crime to conspire to violate state or federal law as the result of an agreement to participate in an *enterprise* by engaging in a *pattern*

of racketeering activity. Members of the conspiracy need not know each other or even be aware of each other's criminal activities. All that needs to be shown is each member's agreement to participate in the organization—the *enterprise*—by committing two or more acts of racketeering such as gambling or drug violations within a 10-year period (a pattern of racketeering). The enterprise conspiracy facilitates mass trials with each member of the enterprise subject to the significant penalties—20 years' imprisonment on each count—that can result from a conviction.

Prosecuting criminal conspiracy cases can be problematic. In a 1974 case (*United States v. Sperling*, 506 F.2d 1323, 1341, 2d Cir.), the court noted that "it has become too common for the government to bring indictments against a dozen or more defendants and endeavor to force as many of them as possible to trial in the same proceeding on the claim of a single conspiracy when the criminal acts could more reasonably be regarded as two or more conspiracies, perhaps with a link at the top. This creates the risk of 'guilt by association,' wherein a jury, confronted by a large number of defendants and a great volume of evidence, is unable to give each defendant the individual consideration that due process requires. In such situations, a finding of guilty brings with it the risk of being reversed on appeal." Constitutional guarantees of a fair trial "make it imperative to determine whether the evidence establishes one large conspiracy as opposed to multiple smaller ones" (Campane 1981b: 30).

Another considerable problem is that conspiracy cases usually require direct testimony of eyewitnesses; these are often participants in the conspiracy who agree to testify ("flip") against their co-conspirators in exchange for leniency or immunity from prosecution. "An investigator should therefore be prepared to locate witnesses (often immunized co-conspirators) who are willing to testify and are able to explain the complicated or intricate nature of the unlawful activity, and as a consequence, the stake in the venture or mutual dependence each participant has with each other" (Campane 1981b: 29).

RICO

The *Racketeer Influenced and Corrupt Organizations* statute (18 U.S.C. §§ 1961–1968), usually referred to as RICO, is the most important single piece of legislation ever enacted against organized crime. Title IX of the Organized Crime Control Act of 1970, RICO defines *racketeering* in an extremely broad manner, and it includes many offenses that do not ordinarily violate any federal statute: "any act or threat involving murder, kidnapping, gambling, arson, robbery, bribery, extortion, or dealing in narcotic or other dangerous drugs, which is chargeable under State law and punishable by imprisonment for more than one year." In addition, there is a "laundry list" of offenses that are defined as "racketeering":

- Hobbs Act violations
- Bribery
- Sports bribery
- Counterfeiting
- Embezzlement from union funds
- Loansharking
- Mail fraud
- Wire fraud
- Obstruction of (state or federal) justice
- Contraband cigarettes
- White slavery (Mann Act violations)
- Bankruptcy fraud (scam)
- Drug violations
- Obscenity (added in 1984)

RICO provides the federal government with jurisdiction that heretofore had been exclusively that of state and local law enforcement, which are often ineffective in dealing with organized crime because, in contrast to "street crime," it is a low priority. As a result, the FBI became the lead agency in organized crime law enforcement.

Under traditional conspiracy statutes, prosecution for engaging in "organized crime" requires agreement among the participants about the specific crime(s). Given the diverse and often unrelated crimes committed by members of organized crime, use of conspiracy statutes proved difficult. The thrust of RICO is to prove a pattern of crimes conducted through an organization—an *enterprise*: "any individual, partnership,

Civil RICO Decrees

Under the provisions of RICO, a U.S. attorney names as defendants union officers and organized crime figures. They are charged with having violated RICO by acquiring or aiding and abetting the acquiring influence in the union through a pattern of racketeering activity, typically by means of violence and intimidation; and conducting union affairs through a pattern of racketeering activity, typically extortion, theft, and fraud. The government asks that the union defendants be removed from their positions and for the organized crime figures to sever all contacts with the union. Finally, the judge is asked to appoint a trustee empowered to initiate disciplinary charges against union officials who violate the decree, the union constitution, or bylaws. The trustee is also empowered to administer union affairs and to organize and monitor a fair election (Jacobs 2006).

corporation, association, or other legal entity, and any union or group of individuals associated in fact, although not a legal entity." In place of having to prove a series of separate conspiracies, under RICO it is a crime to belong to an enterprise, for example, an organized crime Family or outlaw motorcycle club, that is involved in a "pattern of racketeering," even if the racketeering was committed by other members. "It shall be unlawful for any person employed by or associated with any enterprise engaged in, or the activities of which affect, interstate or foreign commerce, to conduct or participate, directly or indirectly, in the conduct of such enterprise's affairs through a pattern of racketeering activity or collection of an unlawful debt." The enterprise must contain some structure distinct from the "pattern of racketeering" (J. Bourgeois et al. 2000).

In order for racketeering to be a RICO violation, there must be a "pattern," which requires the commission of at least two of the specified crimes within a ten-year period, although, in ruling against anti-abortion activists, the Supreme Court has determined that RICO does not require defendants to have an economic motive. Isolated criminal acts, however, do not constitute a "pattern." Instead, there must be a relationship between the two (or more) predicate crimes over a substantial period of time (J. Bourgeois et al. 2000). However, section 904(a) of RICO states that "the provisions of this title shall be liberally construed to effectuate its remedial purposes."

The criminal penalties for violating RICO are substantial: "Whoever violates any provision of section 1962 of this chapter shall be fined not more than $25,000 or imprisoned not more than twenty years, or both." In addition to the criminal penalties, there are civil forfeiture provisions, requiring the violator to forfeit to the government any business or property he or she has acquired in violation of RICO. The government can also freeze a defendant's assets before trial.

Under the provisions of RICO, the government can file a petition in federal district court seeking to have a branch (local) of a labor union, or even the leadership of the union itself, removed and the entity placed in receivership. Since this is a proceeding in equity (see Abadinsky 2008), there is no right to a trial by jury. As noted in Chapter 14, this was done with Local 560 of the International Brotherhood of Teamsters (the "Tony Pro local") and Local 54 of the Hotel and Restaurant Employees Union. By 2006, there were twenty successful RICO suits resulting in court-appointed trustees responsible for eliminating the influence of organized crime and establishing union democracy (Jacobs 2006).

While RICO has as its stated purpose "the eradication of organized crime in the United States," the "broad wording of the statute has allowed it to be used in a vast array of situations totally unrelated to organized crime. For example, RICO's authorization for civil suits is frequently invoked in commercial and business litigation, particularly when there is a claim of fraud" (Chemerinsky 2000: 1). RICO has provisions by which private citizens can sue for damages: "Any person injured in his business or property by reason of a violation of section 1962 of this chapter may sue therefore in any appropriate United States district court and shall recover threefold damages he sustains and the cost of the suit, including a reasonable attorney's fee." In *NOW v. Scheidler* (510 U.S. 249, 1994), the Supreme Court ruled unanimously that abortion clinics can invoke RICO to sue violent anti-abortion protest groups for damages.[1] In 1998, a federal jury in Chicago found three leading anti-abortion activists liable under RICO and awarded $85,000 to two abortion clinics, an amount tripled by the judge as per the statute (Pallasch and Peres 1998). In an editorial, the *New York Times* noted: "The use of RICO has raised legitimate concern that this precedent could be expanded to obstruct free speech and political protest" ("Abortion Harassers as Racketeers" 1998).

While it took some time for federal prosecutors to fully understand and incorporate RICO into their array of prosecutorial tools, it has become clear that the use of the statute has been quite effective. By 1990, more than 1,000 major and minor organized crime figures had been convicted and given lengthy prison sentences. "The hierarchies of the five New York LCN Families have been prosecuted, and similar prosecutions have dented the LCN hierarchies in Boston, Cleveland, Denver, Kansas City, Milwaukee, New Jersey, Philadelphia, Pittsburgh and St. Louis" (Pennsylvania Crime Commission 1990: 18). In fact, the threat of lengthy imprisonment under RICO provides a "stick" that has been used to gain the cooperation of defendants. Rudolph W. Giuliani (1987: 106), former U.S. attorney for the Southern District of New York, who successfully used RICO in prosecuting organized crime cases, points out that "the federal prosecutor derives a variety of benefits from the RICO statute's definitions of enterprise and racketeering activity. For example, it is the only criminal statute that enables the Government to present a jury with the whole picture of how an enterprise, such as an organized crime family, operates. Rather than pursuing the leader of a small group of subordinates for a single crime or scheme, the Government is able to indict the entire hierarchy of an organized crime family for the diverse criminal activities in which that 'enterprise' engages. Instead

of merely proving one criminal act in a defendant's life, it permits proof of a defendant's whole life in crime." Giuliani provides an example, the successful prosecution of the Colombo Family.

Criticism of RICO   Four basic criticisms of RICO have been raised:

1. RICO is overreaching, leading to the prosecution of persons who, although they may have been involved in criminal behavior, are not by any stretch of the imagination connected to organized crime.
2. Invoking RICO can result in assets being frozen even before a trial begins, an action that can effectively put a company out of business. The threat of freezing assets can induce corporate defendants to plead guilty even when they believe themselves to be innocent.
3. A RICO action brings with it the stigma of being labeled a "racketeer," which may be inappropriate given the circumstances at issue.
4. RICO permits lawsuits for triple damages when ordinary business transactions, not organized crime or racketeering, are at issue.

The Organized Crime Control Act (of which RICO is a part) fails to define *organized crime*, and RICO fails to define *racketeer*. This lack of precision coupled with the substantial penalties makes RICO a tempting tool for federal prosecutors to use against persons who are not connected to organized crime, no matter how widely that term is defined. In Chicago, for example, a deputy sheriff and clerk in traffic court were convicted under RICO for helping to fix parking tickets. In New York, the U.S. attorney used RICO against a small commodities firm for a transaction so commonplace that on some days such transactions account for a third of the volume on the New York Stock Exchange (Epstein 1988b). In 1988, the government brought a RICO indictment against a securities firm, seeking $500,000 in illegal profits. Prosecutors insisted, however,

---

[1] For a discussion of this case, see Randolph (1995) and Vitielo (1995).

RICO and the Colombo Crime Family

Fourteen defendants were indicted as either leaders, members, or associates of the Colombo Family of *La Cosa Nostra*. In setting forth the "enterprise," the indictment identified the three "Bosses" of the Family and five *capos*, who were all charged with supervising and protecting the criminal activities of the subordinates of the Family. The leadership as well as the lower-ranking members were included within the Family "enterprise" as a group of individuals associated in fact. The ongoing nature of the enterprise was demonstrated by the fact that the Family selected an acting boss to direct its criminal activities while the Boss was in jail. Reliance entirely upon traditional conspiracy law without RICO would not have enabled the government to include all of these individuals within a single prosecution or to identify each of their specific roles within the enterprise.

In addition, RICO's requirement of proving a "pattern of racketeering activity" and its broad definition of "racketeering activity" allowed the prosecution to join in a single indictment of the widely diverse state and federal crimes the Colombo Family had engaged in over the past fifteen years. Thus, the indictment included charges that the Family had engaged in extortion, labor racketeering, drug trafficking, gambling, loansharking, and both state and federal bribery violations. The prosecution was also able to include as predicate acts of racketeering the prior federal bribery convictions of three of the defendants.

Moreover, venue in RICO cases permits the prosecution of a continuing offense in any district in which such offense was begun, continued, or completed. Thus, the prosecution was able to include crimes committed in the Southern and Eastern Districts of New York, as well as in Florida and New Jersey.

Finally, because of RICO's broad definition of a pattern of racketeering activity, it was possible for the prosecutors to include predicate offenses in which the criminal conduct occurred at a time beyond the reach of the general federal five-year statute of limitations. In this regard, all that RICO requires is that one act of racketeering occurred after the effective date of the statute (October 15, 1970), and that the last or most recent predicate act occurred within ten years of a prior act of racketeering. Given these provisions, the prosecution was permitted to charge a 1970 heroin transaction as well as extortions that took place in 1975 (Giuliani 1987).

---

on a bond of $24 million, forcing the company to liquidate before a trial even began (Nocera 1988). Similar criticism has been leveled at the USA PATRIOT Act enacted in the wake of 9/11 to deal with terrorism. The law has frequently been used in cases having little or nothing to do with terrorism (Lichtblau 2003c).

Supporters argue that RICO has been very effective in combating corporate crime that has traditionally proven difficult to prosecute successfully (Waldman and Gilbert 1989). Illegal business practices—crime—can certainly be defined as organized if they are sufficiently large in scale and are continuously performed by specialists, even in the absence of violence and/or corruption. For example, securities violations involving prestigious

brokerage firms have been successfully prosecuted using RICO.

About 1,000 civil racketeering suits are filed each year by private plaintiffs (the government averages about one hundred a year) seeking to recover triple their damages from a variety of defendants—business competitors, swindlers, securities brokers, and unions, or, as noted earlier, anti-abortion activists. There are so many cases that the practice has spawned its own publication: *RICO Law Reporter*.

While private cases have generally proven hard to win, critics argue that the threat of triple damages—and of being referred to as a "racketeer"—causes many defendants to settle. Furthermore, the triple-damage provision encourages contingency lawyers to sue when under ordinary circumstances the potential reward would not be worth the commitment of time. The courts, however, have fined lawyers for bringing frivolous racketeering claims (Diamond 1988). One critic (O'Brien 1986) argues that in contract disputes attorneys routinely add RICO violations, thereby removing their cases from state court and overloading federal courts. Law professor Robert Blakey (1986), author of RICO, argues that the civil sections provide a powerful tool for persons victimized by swindlers to recover their losses and also serve as a deterrent. To avoid the problem of inappropriate labeling, some recommend that the term *racketeer* be removed from the civil aspects of the statute (Waldman and Gilbert 1989). In 2008, Blakey represented a major hog processing company using a RICO suit against an employee union critical of the company for labor, environmental, and safety issues. What Mr. Blakey calls racketeering, notes *New York Times* legal reporter Adam Liptak (2008: 14), "sounds quite a bit like free speech."

In the first case to limit the scope of a state RICO law—some states have laws patterned after RICO—the Supreme Court ruled that the inventory of a Fort Wayne, Indiana, adult bookstore could not be subjected to seizure in advance of an obscenity conviction. In a unanimous decision, the Court referred to prohibitions against "prior restraint" of publications that have not been judged to be obscene. In a 6–3 vote, however, the Court rejected a claim that the First Amendment prohibits the use of RICO to prosecute obscenity cases and left open the possibility that the materials could be confiscated after obscenity is proven at trial (*Fort Wayne Books, Inc. v. Indiana, et al.*, 488 U.S. 445, 1989). That same year, the Supreme Court unanimously refused to limit the scope of RICO with respect to private suits (*H.J., Inc. v. Northwestern Bell Telephone Co.*, 492 U.S. 229).

Continuing Criminal Enterprise

The Continuing Criminal Enterprise (CCE) statute (21 U.S.C. § 848) is similar in purpose to RICO but targets only illegal drug activity. The statute makes it a crime to commit or conspire to commit a continuing series of felony violations of the 1970 Drug Abuse Prevention and Control Act when the violations are undertaken in concert with five or more persons. The courts have ruled that *series* requires three or more violations. "For conviction under this statute, the offender must have been an organizer, manager, or supervisor of the continuing operation and have obtained substantial income or resources from the drug violations" (Carlson and Finn 1993: 2). In 1999, the Supreme Court ruled (*Richardson v. United States*, 526 U.S. 813) that juries must agree on which specific illegal

Use of the RICO statute resulted in one of the most important prosecutions ever brought against organized crime in the United States. A task force of personnel from federal, state, and local law enforcement agencies targeted the commission of organized crime Families in New York. Electronic surveillance was used on an unprecedented scale—bugs were planted in cars, homes, and social clubs. In addition, the Bonanno Family was penetrated by an FBI agent to the point of his being proposed for membership (see Pistone 1987). "The theory of the government's case was that the Cosa Nostra commission constituted a criminal enterprise, that each defendant had committed two or more racketeering acts in furtherance of the commission's goals. According to the prosecution, the defendant's predicate racketeering acts fell into three categories: first, management of a multifamily bid-rigging and extortion scheme in the New York concrete industry; second, conspiracy to organize loansharking territories in Staten Island; and, third, the murders of Bonanno family boss Carmine Galente and two of his associates [discussed in Chapter 2] in furtherance of the commission's effort to resolve a Bonanno family leadership dispute" (Jacobs 1994: 81).

During the course of the trial, the defense admitted the existence of *Cosa Nostra* and the commission. They denied, however, the commission's involvement in criminal activity, but to no avail: In 1986 all of the defendants, including Carmine Persico, boss of the Colombo Family, Anthony Salerno, boss of the Genovese Family, and Anthony Corallo, boss of the Lucchese Family, were found guilty. Charges against Paul Castellano, boss of the Gambino Family, were dropped after his murder (*United States v. Salerno*, 85 Cr. 139, SDNY 1985).

acts were committed by a defendant, rather than simply finding that he or she committed a series of drug violations without specifying which ones. The 6–3 decision makes it harder to convict persons for violating the CCE.

Consumer Credit Protection Act (CCPA)

The 1968 Consumer Credit Act (18 U.S.C. §§ 891–894) was designed to combat loansharking. It provides a definition of a *loan shark debt* as any extension of credit with respect to which is the *understanding* of the creditor and the debtor at the time the loan is made that delay in making repayment or failure to make repayment could result in the use of violence or other criminal means to cause harm to the person, reputation, or property of any person. The statute chose the term *understanding*, note Ronald Goldstock and Dan Coenen (1978: 65), "in an obvious effort to catch the many loansharks who operate purely on the basis of implication and veiled suggestion." The critical element of the offense is the understanding that violence "could result" if repayment is not timely.

The statute even provides for an alternative to direct evidence. An implied threat can be assumed: "The state must show the debtor's reasonable belief that the creditor had used, or had a reputation for using, 'extortionate means' to collect or punish nonpayment. Second, if direct evidence of this sort is unavailable (as when the victim is dead or too frightened to testify) and certain other prerequisites are met, the court may allow evidence tending to show the creditor's reputation as to collection practices to show the 'understanding' element" (Goldstock and Coenen 1978: 110–11).

The CCPA also contains a provision intended to make it possible to prosecute upper levels of the organized crime hierarchy who, although they may not make the loans themselves, are often the original source of funding for extortionate credit transactions made directly by underlings (18 U.S.C. § 893): "Whoever willfully advances money or property, whether as a gift, as a loan, as an investment, pursuant to a partnership or profit-sharing agreement, or otherwise, to any person, with the reasonable grounds to believe that it is the intention of that person of making extortionate extensions of credit, shall be fined not more than $10,000 or an amount not to exceed twice the value of the money or property so advanced, whichever is greater, or shall be imprisoned not more than 20 years, or both." The same penalties hold for both the loan shark actually making the loan and those who assist in attempting to collect an extortionate extension of credit.

Forfeiture

For obvious reasons—funds without taxation—governments have found forfeiture very attractive. In 1972, Hawaii enacted civil RICO legislation with the seizure and forfeiture provision, and by 1989, twenty-five other states had enacted similar legislation. Interest in forfeiture has generated several periodicals. The Treasury Department's Assets Forfeiture Fund was created by the Comprehensive Crime Control Act of 1984 to receive the proceeds of forfeiture. A portion of the money from the fund is given to state and local law enforcement agencies that contributed directly to the seizure or forfeiture.

In addition to the civil procedures contained in RICO, section 881 of the Comprehensive Drug Abuse Prevention and Control Act of 1970 provides for the seizure of assets under certain conditions. The reach of section 881 was extended through amendments in 1978 and 1984: The statute now permits forfeiture of all profits from drug trafficking and all assets purchased with such proceeds or traded in exchange for controlled substances. It authorizes the forfeiture of all real property used in any manner to facilitate violations of drug statutes, including entire tracts of land and all improvements regardless of what portion of the property facilitated the illegal activities. Currency, buildings, land, motor vehicles, and airplanes have all been confiscated (Stahl 1992). The government also has the right to seize untainted assets as a substitute for tainted property disposed of or otherwise made unavailable for forfeiture (Greenhouse 1994).

A seizure can be made incident to an arrest or customs inspection or upon receipt of a seizure order. To obtain a seizure order (actually a warrant), the government must provide sworn testimony in an affidavit spelling out the property to be seized and why there is reason to believe that it is being used to commit crimes or was acquired with money from criminal activity—the same process used in securing a search warrant. The filing of criminal charges against the owner is not required. The owner of the property has a right to contest the seizure only after it has occurred; he or she must prove that the money or property was earned through legal enterprise. In 1993, the Supreme Court (*United States v. Good Real Property*, 510 U.S. 43) ruled that the government cannot seize real estate without providing the owner with a notice and opportunity to contest the proposed seizure. This decision applies only to real estate and not portable possessions.

Civil forfeiture is an *in rem* proceeding in contrast to the *in personam* proceedings used in criminal forfeiture (see Figure 15.2). As such, the action is against the property, not the person, so that even an acquittal on the criminal charges does not preclude civil forfeiture. In 1996, the Supreme Court ruled in *United States v. Ursery* (518 U.S. 267) that a criminal prosecution and civil forfeiture in the same case does not violate the constitutional prohibition against double jeopardy[2]: Ordinary forfeiture is not punishment but a device for denying someone the fruits of their criminal behavior.

Although forfeiture laws vary, two legal theories have evolved: *facilitation* and *proceeds*:

> The *facilitation* theory allows the government to seize property when it facilitates certain criminal conduct. For example, in drug investigations, any property involved in the manufacture, delivery, and sale of controlled substances can be subjected to seizure. This includes real estate used to store drugs, automobiles and boats used to transport drugs, and other facilitating property, such as cash and firearms. The *proceeds* theory allows the government to seize property that represents the proceeds of certain specified unlawful

---

[2]The Supreme Court has long interpreted the Fifth Amendment as prohibiting multiple punishments as well as multiple prosecutions for the same offense (Greenhouse 1996).

FIGURE 15.2   *Verified Complaint for Forfeiture*

IN THE UNITED STATES DISTRICT COURT
NORTHERN DISTRICT OF ILLINOIS
EASTERN DIVISION

UNITED STATES OF AMERICA Plaintiff v. A 1987 ROLLS-ROYCE CORNICHE VIN SCAZDO2A4HCX20937, $152,645.00 in UNITED STATES CURRENCY seized from SAFE DEPOSIT BOX 6265 at CLYDE FEDERAL $30,040 in UNITED STATES CURRENCY seized from SAFE DEPOSIT BOX 5660 at WESTERN NATIONAL BANK $22,400 in UNITED STATES CURRENCY seized from SAFE DEPOSIT BOX 8805–N AT OAK PARK TRUST AND SAVINGS BANK, and UNITED STATES CURRENCY in THE AMOUNT OF $120,023.00 Defendants	NO. **89C1250** FEB 16 1989 JUDGE JUDGE NORGLE MAGISTRATE LEFKOW

VERIFIED COMPLAINT FOR FORFEITURE

The United States of America, by its attorney, Anton R. Valukas, United States Attorney for the Northern District of Illinois for its complaint states:

1.) This is a forfeiture action under Title 21, United States Code, Section 881 (a) (6) and this Court has jurisdiction under Title 28, United States Code, Sections 1345 and 1355.

2.) The defendants named in the caption were seized on land within the Northern District of Illinois and will remain within this Court's jurisdiction throughout the pendency of this action.

3.) On February 7, 1989, a search warrant arising from a narcotics investigation of an individual known as Rufus Sims was executed at a residence at 2606 South Boeger in Westchester, Illinois. The search resulted in the seizure of a large quantity of weapons and twenty-three (23) bags containing cocaine repackaged for sale commingled with United States Currency in the amount of $4,301.00.

4.) During the execution of the warrant at the residence, the police discovered title to the defendant 1987 Rolls Royce Convertible, VIN SCAZDO2A4HCX20937. Review of records at Steve Foley Cadillac revealed that the purchase price of the car was $176,681, of which $129,461 was paid in currency and the remainder of the purchase price came from Sims' trade-in of another Rolls-Royce owned by him.

activities. This can be quite complex because before seizure can occur, the government must identify property and prove ownership. The government also must trace the asset to the criminal activity, and each time the subject converts the proceeds from one form to another, the more complicated this becomes. (Hartman 2001: 1)

Under federal statutes, before an order to seize property can be issued, the government must show there is a substantial connection between the property and the crime by *a preponderance of the evidence*, the legal standard of proof for civil cases. (Prior to 2000, the standard of proof was *probable cause*, a lower level of evidence required for search warrants and summary arrests.) This is done without notice to the defendant at an *ex parte* (defendant not present) hearing. After seizure, if forfeiture is contested, there is a shift in the burden of proof that diminishes the Fifth Amendment privilege against self-incrimination because the defendant cannot pursue the claim to seized property without explaining its ownership. The Supreme Court has refused to apply the Fifth Amendment's double jeopardy clause or the Sixth Amendment's guarantee of the right to confront witnesses to *in rem* forfeiture (Stahl 1992). Since the process is quasi-criminal, however, the exclusionary rule is applicable, and evidence seized in violation of the Constitution cannot be considered (*One 1958 Plymouth Sedan v. Pennsylvania*, 380 U.S. 691, 701, 1965).

Section 881 provides for an innocent owner's defense: The violation occurred without the owner's knowledge. The burden is on the owner to prove innocence by a preponderance of the evidence. The government can overcome claims of innocence by showing that it would be reasonable to believe that the owner was aware. In addition, some courts have required the owner to prove that he or she took all reasonable steps to prevent the violation (Stahl 1992). There is also a remission procedure—the claimant can file a petition with the attorney general, who can order the return of property if there are mitigating circumstances. However, remission is a discretionary act. In 1996,

the Court determined that property can be seized even when the owner is innocent of any wrongdoing. In this case, *Bennis v. Michigan* (517 U.S. 1163), a couple's jointly owned car was impounded after the husband used it to solicit a prostitute.

In 1988, the Supreme Court, in a 5–4 decision, ruled that under the Comprehensive Forfeiture Act, the government can freeze the assets of criminal defendants before trial (*Caplin and Drysdale, Chartered v. United States*, 491 U.S. 617; *United States v. Monsanto*, 491 U.S. 600). Legislation enacted in 2000, in addition to raising the standard of evidence, allows federal judges to release property to the owner pending trial if confiscation causes him or her substantial hardship. The statute also shifted the burden of proof from property owners to the government.

Criticism of Forfeiture   A great deal of criticism has been leveled at forfeiture. The normally conservative *Chicago Tribune*, for example, in an editorial (April 1, 1993), stated that while forfeiture, when used appropriately, can be an effective punishment for crime, "a growing number of innocent parties and two-bit players are being swept up in the net. And those who are unfairly trapped find that forfeiture laws turn due process on its head." In 1993, the Supreme Court ruled unanimously that the Eighth Amendment's protection against "excessive fines" requires that there be a relationship between the gravity of the offense and the value of the property seized (*Austin v. United States*, 506 U.S. 602). In 1998, the Court extended *Austin*, ruling 5–4 against the forfeiture of $357,144 in cash that was not the proceeds of crime. The money had been seized from someone who attempted to take cash out of the country to pay debts without filing a Currency Transaction Report (*United States v. Bajakajian*, 524 U.S. 321).

There is criticism that forfeiture can distort the purpose of drug law enforcement, for example, police delaying raids until drug caches are depleted and cash maximized (Worrall and Kovandzic 2008). Or it can result in a "get out of jail free" card, a plea-bargaining device for drug kingpins. They negotiate lighter sentences by promising to reveal hidden assets and not put up court challenges to their seizure. Law enforcement agencies eager for additional funds allegedly promote leniency for those at the top of the drug trafficking ladder, while those down below, without significant hidden assets, face significant penalties (Navarro 1996).

Until 1988, the act permitted the Department of Justice to prosecute attorneys and seize fees from tainted sources. Defense attorneys argued that this created a situation "in which a defendant cannot retain an attorney because of the government's threat of criminal and civil sanctions against any attorney who takes the case" (Weinstein 1988: 381). The defendant is left without a free choice of attorneys and dependent upon a public defender, who is not always able to defend against the often-complex nature of RICO prosecutions. Supporters of this legislation argue that criminals who have grown wealthy from crime are not entitled to any greater consideration with respect to legal representation than their less successful criminal colleagues, who are often represented by a public defender. In 1988, President Ronald Reagan signed an anti-drug abuse bill that contained an amendment to 18 U.S.C. section 1957. The amendment excluded defense attorneys' fees from the criminal money laundering provisions. Thus, while criminal defense fees could still be subject to forfeiture, attorneys who accept tainted fees are exempt from criminal prosecution.

Forfeiture statutes of some states permit all seized assets to be returned to the initiating agency; others provide for distribution to all law enforcement agencies involved and the prosecutor's office; still others permit no proceeds to be returned to law enforcement and, instead, require that they be placed in an education fund. Law enforcement agencies in these states are able to bypass the requirement by having the case "adopted" by a federal agency such as the DEA or FBI, which then passes it off to the U.S. Attorney. The adoption procedure can result in up to 80 percent of the proceeds being returned to the initiating department (Worrall and Kovandzic 2008). Increased police assets via forfeiture provide an incentive for local governments to reduce their allocations for policing (Skolnick 2008).

Money Laundering

In 1970, in response to increasing reports of people bringing bags full of illegally obtained cash into banks for deposit, Congress enacted the statute commonly referred to as the Bank Secrecy Act (BSA). (Technically, the BSA is Titles I and II of Public Law 91-508, as amended. Title II is also called the Currency and Foreign Transactions Reporting Act.) The BSA contains two basic sets of authorizing provisions that are put into effect by implementing regulations. The first set authorizes the Secretary of the Treasury (and in some places, the Secretary and the Federal Reserve Board jointly) to require banks and other financial institutions to retain records to ensure that the details of financial transactions can be traced if investigators need to do so.

The second set of provisions authorizes the Secretary of the Treasury to require financial institutions, and in some cases other businesses and private citizens, to report financial transactions of certain kinds. The two most important reporting rules authorized in 1970 were the reporting by financial institutions of transactions in currency in excess of $10,000 (using the Currency Transaction Report [CTR]) and the reporting of the transportation of currency and bearer instruments (in amounts initially in excess of $5,000—now in excess of $10,000) into or out of the United States (using the Report of International Transportation of Currency or Monetary Instruments [CMIR]).[3] A specific prohibition was added to the BSA against "structuring" transactions, breaking larger transactions into smaller exchanges, to avoid the impact

---

[3]The constitutionality of the BSA was challenged on a number of grounds. In *California Bankers Association v. Shultz*, 416 U.S. 21 (1974), the U.S. Supreme Court rejected claims that various parts of the BSA violated constitutional due process requirements, the Fourth Amendment protection against unreasonable searches and seizures, and the Fifth Amendment privilege against self-incrimination. The Court emphasized that the information sought from the reporting banks concerned transactions to which the banks themselves had been parties. A later Supreme Court decision, *United States v. Miller*, 425 U.S. 435 (1976), settled a question reserved in *California Bankers Ass'n* by ruling that bank customers possess no privacy interests protected by the Fourth Amendment in records of their affairs maintained by the banks with which they deal.

of the BSA's reporting thresholds. This system generates about 18 million CTRs annually.

The act authorizes the IRS to issue regulations requiring banks and other financial institutions to take a number of precautions against financial crime, including setting up anti–money laundering programs and filing reports that have been determined to have a high degree of usefulness in criminal, tax, regulatory investigations and proceedings, and certain intelligence and counterterrorism matters.

Prior to the passage of the Money Laundering Control Act of 1986, money laundering was not a federal crime, although the Department of Justice had used a variety of federal statutes to successfully prosecute money laundering cases. The act consolidated these statutes with the goal of increasing prosecutions for this offense. Money laundering was made a separate federal offense punishable by a fine of $500,000 or twice the value of the property involved, whichever is greater, and 20 years' imprisonment (Weinstein 1988). Title 18 U.S.C. section 981 provides for the civil confiscation of any property related to a money laundering scheme. Legislation enacted in 1988 allows the government to file a suit claiming ownership of all cash funneled through operations intended to disguise their illegal source. The courts can issue an order freezing all contested funds until the case is adjudicated. An amendment to the Drug Abuse Act of 1988 requires offshore banks to record any U.S. cash transactions in excess of $10,000 and to permit U.S. officials to have access to the records. Offshore banks that fail to comply can be banned from holding accounts in U.S. banks and denied access to U.S.-dollar clearing and money-transfer systems.

The Annunzio-Wylie Money Laundering Act of 1992 and the Money Laundering Suppression Act of 1994 (the "MLSA") gave the Treasury Department a wider variety of regulatory tools to combat money laundering. Annunzio-Wylie amended the BSA in several respects. Most important, it authorizes the Secretary of the Treasury to require financial institutions and gambling casinos to submit a "Suspicious Activity Report" (SAR) relevant to a possible violation of law or

regulation. More than 1 million are filed annually. The statutory SAR authorization includes a "safeharbor" provision to protect financial institutions from civil liability to their clients and third parties that might otherwise be claimed to have arisen from the designation of transactions as suspicious by reporting institutions. Annunzio-Wylie authorizes the Secretary to require financial institutions to carry out anti–money laundering programs and authorize special record keeping. Finally, Annunzio-Wylie made operation of an illegal money transmitting business a crime (information from the U.S. Department of the Treasury).[4] In 1985, Arizona became the first state to enact an anti–money laundering statute, and since that time at least thirty-five more states have done the same (Motivans 2003).

Under the Currency and Foreign Transactions Reporting Act (31 U.S.C. § 5311, as amended), the United States can compel other countries to maintain certain financial records similar to those required under the Bank Secrecy Act. The Treasury Department's Financial Crimes Enforcement Network (discussed later) works with bank regulators to ensure compliance with the act. If a country fails to negotiate an acceptable records system, its financial institutions can be denied access to the U.S. banking system. There are problems implementing this legislation: Apart from developed countries with exchange control laws, few countries have legislation requiring their banks and other financial institutions to collect and report such information to a government (Chaiken 1991). Anti-terrorism legislation enacted in 2001 permits the Treasury Department to impose sanctions on countries that refuse to provide information on depositors. The legislation also bars American banks from doing business with offshore ("shell") banks having no connection to any regulated banking industry.

A person is guilty of money laundering if he or she knows that the property involved represents

---

[4]Because this statute requires proof of "willfulness," in 1994 the Supreme Court ruled that persons who structured their transactions to avoid the CTR, by keeping transactions at $9,500, for example, did not violate the law unless they *knew* such action was illegal (*Ratzlaf v. United States*, 510 U.S. 135).

the proceeds of some illegal activity; attempts to conceal or disguise the nature, the location, the source, the ownership, or the control of the proceeds; or attempts to avoid a transaction-reporting requirement. Furthermore, a person is guilty of money laundering if he or she transports or attempts to transport a monetary instrument or funds out of the United States with the intent to carry out an unlawful activity. If a person knows that the monetary instrument or funds involved represent the proceeds of some form of unlawful activity or attempts to conceal or disguise the nature, location, source, ownership, or control of the proceeds or to avoid a transaction-reporting requirement, he or she is guilty of money laundering.

The International Emergency Economic Powers Act allows the president to take extraordinary actions in the case of an "unusual threat to national security." In 1995, President Bill Clinton issued a directive under the act, requiring financial institutions to search for and freeze accounts held in the name of persons or companies determined by the government to assist or play a significant role in international drug trafficking. The order also forbids American businesses and officials to trade with those individuals and their front companies (Mitchell 1995).

In 1999, two of Mexico's biggest banks pled guilty to money laundering in an effort to stave off sanctions that would include not being able to do business in the United States; they had to forfeit millions of dollars seized by federal officials. As part of a vast undercover operation in Mexico by the U.S. Customs Service, dozens of Mexican bankers, businessmen, and suspected drug traffickers were indicted. Controversy surrounds the investigation, which drew the wrath of Mexico—U.S. agents operating in that country without informing the Mexican government—and criticism that the Clinton administration ordered the investigation terminated early in order not to further embarrass Mexico (Golden, 1999a, 1999b).

In the wake of 9/11, statutes were enacted permitting the Department of Justice to seize accounts in foreign banks that do business in the United States. Typically, when suspect source accounts are discovered, federal authorities work through international law enforcement treaties to request that the home country of a foreign bank freeze the money and turn it over to the United States. Some countries, however, do not have treaties with the United States, although most foreign banks maintain "correspondent accounts" in American banks enabling them to exchange U.S. currency and manage other financial transactions in this country. The law permits prosecutors to seize such accounts without the need to trace the money back to the target of the investigation (Lichtblau 2003b).

"Trafficking in Persons" Statutes

Trafficking in persons (discussed in Chapter 12) is prohibited by the Thirteenth Amendment that outlaws slavery and involuntary servitude—holding persons for service/labor through force or the threat of force. Existing statutes that enforce the Thirteenth Amendment have been supplemented by the Victims of Trafficking and Violence Prevention Act (VTVPA) of 2000 and the Prosecutorial Remedies and Other Tools to End the Exploitation of Children Today (PROTECT) Act of 2003.

Under VTVPA slavery and peonage, sex trafficking in children and adults, and the confiscation of a victim's documents are felonies. Prior to VTVPA, statutes were already in place outlawing human smuggling, kidnapping, transportation for prostitution or any criminal sexual activity, and importation of aliens for unlawful activities. The act was passed virtually unanimously by both houses of Congress and addresses issues of worker exploitation resulting from trafficking in persons. The law expands the definition of *forced labor* to reach forms of coercion occurring in contemporary times. The statute:

- Creates new laws that criminalize trafficking with respect to slavery, involuntary servitude, peonage, or forced labor
- Permits prosecution where nonviolent coercion is used to force victims to work in the belief they would be subject to serious harm
- Permits prosecution where the victim's service was compelled by confiscation

of documents such as passports or birth certificates

- Increases prison terms for all slavery violations from 10 years to 20 years and adds life imprisonment where the violation involves the death, kidnapping, or sexual abuse of the victim
- Requires courts to order restitution and forfeiture of assets upon conviction
- Enables victims to seek witness protection and other types of assistance
- Gives prosecutors and agents new tools to get legal immigration status for victims of trafficking during investigation and prosecution (U.S. Department of Justice information)

PROTECT authorizes the prosecution of Americans whose behavior involves the commercial sexual exploitation of children (CSEC) anywhere in the world. The Sex Tourism Prohibition Improvement Act of 2002 removed the intent requirement for individuals and criminalized the actions of sex tour operators. CSEC traffickers who exploit children under age 14 using force or fraud can be sentenced to life imprisonment. If the crimes do not involve force or fraud and the victim is between ages 14 and 18, the maximum sentence is 20 years.

In 2000, the United Nations General Assembly adopted "The Protocol to Prevent, Suppress and Punish Trafficking in Persons." The protocol includes a range of cases where human beings are exploited by organized crime groups and where there is an element of duress involved and a transnational aspect, such as the movement of people across borders or their exploitation within a country by a transnational organized crime group such as the Mafia, Triads, or *yakuza*. It is designed to facilitate international cooperation against such trafficking. The protocol provides for criminal sanctions, control and cooperation measures against traffickers, and provides some measures to protect and assist the victims. The United States has not ratified this protocol.

ORGANIZED CRIME LAW ENFORCEMENT

In this section we will look at the various agencies responsible for responding to organized crime and the techniques they use. But first we need to consider three constraints on law enforcement efforts in general, and on organized crime law enforcement in particular: constitutional restraints, jurisdictional limitations, and the intertwining problems of corruption and informants.

Constitutional Restraints

Law enforcement in the United States operates under significant constitutional constraints. Important protections against government, while they protect individual liberty, also benefit the criminal population: the right to remain silent (Fifth Amendment); the right to counsel (Sixth Amendment); the right to be tried speedily by an impartial jury (Sixth Amendment); and the right to confront witnesses (Sixth Amendment). Particularly important for organized crime law enforcement are the Fourth Amendment and the exclusionary rule. The Fourth Amendment provides that "the right of the people to be secure in their persons, houses, papers and effects, against unreasonable searches and seizures shall not be violated, and no Warrants shall issue, but upon probable cause, supported by Oath or affirmation, and particularly describing the place to be searched, and the persons or things to be seized." In practice, information sufficient to justify a search warrant in organized crime cases is difficult to obtain because unlike conventional crimes such as robbery and burglary, there are often no innocent victims to report the crime. The *exclusionary rule* provides that evidence obtained in violation of the Fourth Amendment cannot be entered as evidence in a criminal trial (*Weeks v. United States*, 232 U.S. 383, 1914; *Mapp v. Ohio*, 357 U.S. 643, 1961), although there are a number of exceptions that are beyond the scope of this book.

Intercepting confidential information is a prerequisite to moving against organized crime. However, the Fourth Amendment and Title III of the Omnibus Crime Control and Safe Streets Act of 1968 (18 U.S.C. §§ 2510–2520) place restrictions on the way the government can secure this information. In order to surreptitiously intercept conversations by wiretapping telephones or using electronic ("bugging") devices, a court order must be secured. Like a search warrant, it must be based upon information sufficient to prove the legal standard of probable cause. When an order to intercept electronic communications is secured (generally referred to as a Title III), it is quite limited, requires extensive documentation, and the persons monitored must be notified after the order expires. These requirements make electronic surveillance quite expensive (in terms of personnel hours expended) and difficult to accomplish. (Electronic surveillance is discussed in more detail later.)

Jurisdictional Limitations

The Constitution provides for a form of government in which powers are diffused horizontally and vertically. There are three branches—legislative, judicial, and executive—and four levels of government—federal, state, county, and municipal. Although each level has responsibilities for responding to organized criminal activities, there is little or no coordination between them—each level of government responds to the problem largely independent of the others. Federalism was part of a deliberate design to help protect us against tyranny; it also provides us with a level of inefficiency that significantly handicaps efforts to deal with organized criminal activity.

On the federal level, a host of executive branch agencies, ranging from the military to the Federal Bureau of Investigation (FBI), have responsibility for combating organized crime. There is also a separate federal judicial system responsible for trying organized crime cases and a legislative branch responsible for enacting organized crime legislation and allocating funds for federal enforcement efforts. The jurisdiction of many federal enforcement agencies overlaps, and efforts are often competitive rather than cooperative (see Dannen 1992a). At the municipal level, there are about 20,000 police agencies. Each state has state-level enforcement agents (state police or similar agency), and the state is responsible for operating prisons and the parole system (if one exists). County government usually has responsibility for prosecuting defendants, and a county-level agency, typically the sheriff, is usually responsible for operating jails. The county may also have a department with general policing responsibilities, independent of or as part of the sheriff's office. Almost every municipality has a police department whose officers enforce laws involving organized criminal activity. Each of these levels of government has taxing authority and allocates resources with little or no consultation with other levels of government. The result is a degree of inefficiency that surpasses that of most democratic nations.

American efforts against drug trafficking also are limited by national boundaries: Cocaine and heroin originate where U.S. law enforcement has no jurisdiction. The Bureau of International Narcotics Matters, within the U.S. Department of State, is the primary agency responsible for coordinating international programs and gaining the cooperation of foreign governments in anti-drug efforts. But the bureau has no authority to force governments to act in a manner most beneficial to U.S. efforts in dealing with cocaine or heroin. The State Department collects intelligence on policy-level international drug developments, while the Central Intelligence Agency (CIA) collects strategic narcotics intelligence and is responsible for coordinating foreign intelligence on narcotics. The CIA, however, has often shielded drug traffickers who have provided foreign intelligence information useful to that agency. United States efforts against drug trafficking are often sacrificed to foreign policy (Golden 1995a; Sciolino and Engelberg 1988). For example, the U.S.-backed contras in Nicaragua trafficked in cocaine, allegedly with the knowledge if not the assistance of the CIA (Harmon 1993). Similar relationships in Southeast Asia were discussed in Chapter 13.

Corruption

Two basic strategies are available to law enforcement agencies—reactive and proactive—and many use a combination of both. *Reactive law enforcement* has its parallel in firefighting: Firefighters remain in their stations, equipment at the ready, until a call for service is received. Reactive law enforcement encourages citizens to report crimes; the agency then responds. This type of law enforcement is used for dealing with conventional crimes such as murder, rape, assault, robbery, burglary, and theft—crimes that are likely to be discovered by or

reported to the police. (It should be noted, however, that with the exception of murder and auto theft, studies indicate that most of these crimes do not come to the attention of the police.) *Proactive law enforcement* requires officers/agents to seek out indications of criminal behavior, a necessity when the nature of the criminal violation includes victim participation such as in gambling, prostitution, and drugs. These crimes are often referred to as "victimless" because victims are unlikely to report the crime to the police.

In order to seek out criminal activity in the most efficient manner possible, proactive law enforcement officers must conceal their identities and otherwise deceive the criminals they are stalking. James Q. Wilson (1978: 59) points out that both reactive and proactive law enforcement officers are exposed to opportunities for graft, but the latter are more severely tested: The reactive law enforcement officer, "were he to accept money or favors to act other than as his duty required, would have to conceal or alter information about a crime already known to his organization." The proactive enforcement agent, however, "can easily agree to overlook offenses known to him but to no one else or to participate in illegal transactions (buying or selling drugs) for his own rather than for the organization's advantage." Undercover officers pretending to be criminals are difficult to supervise; the agency for which they work often knows about their activities only to the extent that the agents inform it. And if they are able to fool wary criminals. . . .

In 1996, prosecutors in New York City had to throw out cases against 98 drug defendants because the police officers involved in their cases were from the Uptown Manhattan 30th Precinct where 33 officers were convicted of drug corruption charges (Kocieniewski 1997). The following year, prosecutors in Chicago had to drop charges in 120 drug cases because police officers involved in the cases had been indicted for taking payoffs and extorting money from drug dealers (Warnick 1997). In 1998, 44 officers from five law enforcement agencies in the Cleveland, Ohio, area were charged with taking bribes to protect cocaine dealers in northern Ohio (Belluck 1998).

Probably the most egregious episode of the nexus between organized crime and corruption was disclosed in 2005 when two retired NYPD detectives were accused of having been on the payroll of Lucchese Family underboss Anthony ("Gaspipe") Casso. According to a federal indictment, the detectives received $4,000 a month each for confidential information and additional money for specific acts; $65,000, for example, for murdering a Gambino soldier in 1992. Information provided by the two also led to the death of an innocent telephone installer who happened to share the same name as the intended victim. One of the detectives was assigned to the Organized Crime Homicide Unit, giving him access to confidential intelligence; the other had a father who was a member of the Gambino Family (Feuer and Rashaum 2005; Marzulli 2005b; Marzulli and O'Shaughnessy 2005).

There is also the problem of corruption in foreign countries that grow, process, or serve as transshipment stations for illegal substances. "The corrupt official," notes the President's Commission on Organized Crime (1986a: 178), "is the *sine qua non* of drug trafficking." The commission concluded that "corruption linked to drug trafficking is a widespread phenomenon among political and military leaders, police and other authorities in virtually every country touched by the drug trade. The easily available and enormous amounts of money generated through drug transactions present a temptation too great for many in positions of authority to resist."

A problem related to proactive law enforcement and corruption involves the use of informants.

***Informants*[5]** The "snitch" or confidential informant (CI) comes in two basic forms, the "good citizen" and the "criminal." The former is so rare, particularly in organized crime law enforcement, that we will deal only with the criminal informant, an individual who provides help to law enforcement in order to further his or her own ends.

These include financial rewards, vengeance, an effort to drive competition out of business, and, most frequently, "working off a beef"—securing leniency for criminal activities that have become known to the authorities.

While serving as informers, criminals may be unofficially allowed to engage in illegal activity (Goldstein 1982)—we will examine a particularly egregious case later. The more involved is the informer in criminal activity, the more useful is his or her assistance. This raises serious ethical and policy questions. Should the informant be given immunity from lawful punishment in exchange for cooperation? If so, who is to make that determination: the agent who becomes aware of the informant's activities, his or her supervisor, the prosecutor who is informed of the situation, or a trial judge? Should a murderer be permitted to remain free because he or she is of value to organized crime law enforcement efforts?

Los Angeles intelligence detective Mike Rothmiller (1992: 89–90) points to a problem with using informants. He was sharing an informant with a DEA agent. On one occasion he arranged to meet the DEA agent at the informant's home. When the detective walked in, he found the informant in the living room with at least a pound of cocaine on a glass table, dividing it up into sale packages—as the DEA agent looked on. Rothmiller motioned the agent into another room.

"What's going on here?" he said. The federal agent explained that his informant was helping him take down some other dealers and that he also claimed to have information on a major hydroponic marijuana-growing operation in Colorado. "You gotta do what you gotta do." The agent shrugged apologetically.

There are other dangers: "Given the number of law enforcement agencies and given their heavy dependence on intelligence, it is inevitable that there are informants who inform on other informants, who are probably informing on them. A consequence of that is selective prosecution: arbitrary decisions made by police officers and agents as to who will go to jail and who will be allowed to remain on the street. Given the vast amounts of money at stake in the drug business,

---

[5]For a discussion of legal issues involving informants, see Schreiber (2002).

Nick Mitola, Jr.—Informant

Raised in middle-class circumstances and college educated, Nick Mitola, Jr., became a career criminal at an early age. He moved from gambling to credit card scams to drugs and, after being convicted for drug trafficking, to informer. In return for his freedom, Mitola worked for the FBI, developing evidence against a crew from the New Jersey branch of the Lucchese Family headed by *caporegime* Anthony ("Tumac") Accetturo. At the same time—without the knowledge of his FBI handler—Mitola continued in the drug business. In this capacity, he began dealing with a DEA informant: "Not only was an undercover FBI informant dealing with an undercover DEA informant without either agency realizing that the other was an informant, but the DEA informant was cheating the DEA. In the spirit of true American entrepreneurs, the DEA informant claimed to be buying drugs from Mitola at a higher price than Mitola was actually selling them and, apparently, pocketing the difference" (Rudolph 1992: 341). In 1991, Mitola, who had entered the Witness Protection Program, was imprisoned for the stabbing death of an Iranian immigrant (Possley 1996).

selective prosecution raises the specter of corruption" (Eddy, Sabogal, and Walden 1988: 85). In 2008, several New York City police officers assigned to drug enforcement were charged with paying informants with confiscated drugs.

This raises the problem of informant veracity. With strong incentives to produce information, how reliable is an informant? Journalist Jack Newfield (1979) quotes an FBI agent who specialized in organized crime cases: "I once had an informant who told me all sorts of stories. Later on I found out the guy was simultaneously an informant to the New York City Police Department, only I didn't know. What he was telling the police was completely different than what he was telling the bureau. And we were both paying him for his bullshit." In Chicago, the FBI paid an informant $10,000 a month for his work in ferreting out corrupt union officials. Unfortunately, the money was wasted and, in at least one case, an innocent union official was framed by the informant. In 1999, the informant was convicted of lying to a grand jury and sentenced to 2.5 years in prison (M. O'Connor 1999b). In 1989, an informant in Los Angeles admitted that he had committed perjury in several cases and suggested that some men may have gone to death row based, at least in part, on his false testimony. The informant said he received prison furloughs, a recommendation for parole, a reduction of bail, and $2,700 for his efforts ("Jail Informer's Admissions Spur Inquiry"

1989; Reinhold 1989). One high school dropout began working as a paid informant for the DEA in 1984, after a hitch in the Marines. Despite the fact that the DEA was aware that he had compromised dozens of prosecutions by falsely testifying under oath and concealing his own arrest record, the agency continued to use—and pay—him until 2000, by which time he had earned $1.8 million (Thompson 2001).

Furthermore, working closely with informants is a potentially corrupting influence. The informant helps the agent enter an underworld filled with danger—and great financial rewards. Under such circumstances, there is always concern that the law enforcement agent may become something else to the informer—a friend, an employee, an employer, or a partner. The rewards can be considerable: The agent can confiscate money and drugs or receive payment for not arresting gamblers or traffickers and at the same time improve his or her work record by arresting competing or unaffiliated criminals. It is often only a small step from using criminals as informants to entering into business with them.

In 1982, FBI special agent Daniel A. Mitrione, an eleven-year veteran of the bureau, was assigned to an undercover operation involving drug trafficking. In his undercover role the agent began working with an informant. Arnold Trebach (1987: 343) reports: "In a familiar scenario that sometimes seems to flow naturally from the dynamics of the situation, one day the informer asked for the privilege of being a real dealer on the side while he was acting like one for the government. Agent Mitrione allowed the man to take a small load of cocaine to Miami and simply failed to tell his FBI supervisors about it. For this small initial courtesy, the appreciative informant-trafficker gave him $3,500 and a $9,000 Rolex watch. Over the next few years, the agent received more than $850,000 and eventually a ten-year prison term."

Criminal informants who testify against former colleagues present problems for any prosecutor. These persons typically have serious criminal histories that may equal or surpass those of the defendants. They are almost invariably provided with significant incentives to provide testimony. Acquittals occur in such cases when the informant is key to successful prosecution and juries do not accept the credibility of the witness(es). In the 2005 trial of John Gotti, Jr., the government's two most important witnesses admitted a total of six murders, crimes more serious than the charges for which the son of the Gambino Family boss was being tried (Preston 2005b).

The "Grim Reaper" One of the more bizarre agent–confidential informant (CI) relationships involves the case of Gregory Scarpa of the Colombo crime Family and his FBI handler. Known as the "Grim Reaper" because of his penchant for violence, Scarpa was a wealthy man who ran an important Colombo crew out of his social club in Bensenhurst, Brooklyn. Although arrested ten times from 1950 to 1985, his only jail time was 30 days for attempting to bribe a police officer.

After a six-week jury trial in 1995, two Colombo captains and five soldiers were acquitted of murder and firearms charges. Their defense centered on the relationship between Scarpa and his FBI handler, who was accused of giving the CI information to help his faction of the Colombo Family track down its opponents in a mob war. Defense attorneys argued that the FBI agent used Scarpa to foment the war between rival factions of the crime Family that led to ten dead and fourteen wounded. The defendants claimed that their actions were an effort to avoid being killed (Raab 1994a, 1995f).

Scarpa's bizarre relationship with the FBI actually dates back to 1964. In that year, reportedly at the behest of J. Edgar Hoover, he traveled to Mississippi, where the FBI had been unable to solve the disappearance of three young civil rights workers. The Bensenhurst wiseguy quickly got to the heart of the case—he kidnapped a Philadelphia, Mississippi, klansman and placed a gun in his mouth while starting to cut off the man's penis. Within 72 hours the FBI had uncovered the three bodies and seven men had been arrested, including the deputy sheriff who had arrested the three young victims (Dannen 1996; Robbins and Capeci 1994).

Scarpa's colleagues occasionally suspected his close relationship with the FBI. One crew member recalls (Connolly 1996: 50): "We all suspected something, but a few days later we were in the club with Greg and a guy he hated. We're talking and joking, and out of nowhere, Greg whips out a piece and shoots the guy in the head. . . . [T]he guy's brains were all over me! My ears were ringing from the gunshot. Cool as he can be, he told us to roll the body in the rug and get rid of it. Nobody distrusted Greg after that day."

Before he died of AIDS in 1994, Scarpa had committed at least four murders while an informant for the FBI. In 1992, during a struggle for control of the Colombo Family, a joint FBI-NYPD team conducting an ongoing surveillance of one of Scarpa's enemies was suddenly withdrawn, allowing Scarpa and two associates to murder the man. In 2006, a retired FBI supervisory agent was accused of aiding in the murder of a member of the Colombo Crime Family. The agent was the exclusive handler of Greg Scarpa.

The potential dangers of involvement with criminal informants are exemplified by the actions of the FBI in Boston.

Boston Until the 1930s, much of organized crime in Boston was dominated by the Irish Gustin Gang, named after a street in South Boston. When they attempted to move into territory in the Italian North End, three of the gang were gunned down. The Irish eventually made their peace with the Italians, whose leader, Raymond Patriarca, operated out of Providence, Rhode Island. Despite the power of the Italians, local Irish-led gangs continued to have a presence in the Boston area and one, the Winter Hill gang—Winter Hill is a neighborhood in the Boston suburb of Somerville, maintained a close working relationship with the Patriarca Family.

From "Southie," as the insular Irish neighborhood of South Boston is known, emerged the Bulger brothers, who grew up in a public housing project. William M. Bulger was president of the state senate for longer than anyone in history, until he stepped down to assume the presidency of the University of Massachusetts. Brother James ("Whitey") Bulger (b. 1929) was the vicious and widely feared crime boss of Southie. A delinquent in his youth, at 27 Whitey was serving federal time for bank robbery. When he returned home in 1965, to satisfy the conditions of his parole, he took a political job as a courthouse custodian. His parole completed, Bulger became an enforcer and debt collector for a local bookmaker. When his boss became embroiled in a dispute with Howie Winter, head of the Winter Hill gang, Bulger abandoned him and allied himself with the predominantly Irish gang. With the backing of Howie Winter, Whitey became the leading gangster in Southie (Lehr and O'Neil 2000). "Like a neighborhood godfather from long ago, Bulger doled out turkeys to the needy on Thanksgiving and Christmas, lent money to school kids, did favors for his 'constituents,' and settled disputes" (English 2005: 2).

In 1976, Whitey Bulger became a government informant. Unbeknownst to Whitey at the time, his partner, Steve ("The Rifleman")[6] Flemmi (b. 1934)—who had declined an invitation to become a made guy in the Patriarca Family, had already been providing information to the FBI. According to Sean Flynn (1998), this arrangement resulted from an attempt by Jerry Angiulo, Patriarca Family underboss in charge of Boston, to use law enforcement authorities to take out the Winter Hill group; they were too dangerous for a more violent approach. Bulger and Flemmi

succeeded in turning the tables—aiding the FBI to take out Angiulo. But, for the government, it was a bargain with the devil. Starting in 1965, more than twenty people were murdered by FBI informants, often with the help of FBI agents (Butterfield 2003).

FBI field offices were under pressure to wage an effective war against the Italian mob, known in New England as the "Office." So, in return for informing on the Patriarca Family, Bulger and Flemmi were given virtually unbridled freedom to conduct their criminal business safe in the knowledge that they were protected by the FBI. If Bulger's victims complained to the FBI, his case agent would see to it that nothing happened, as when vending machine executives complained that Bulger and Flemmi were shaking them down. When the husband and wife owners of a liquor store complained that Bulger and Flemmi had threatened to kill them if they would not sell it to the pair at a "bargain" price, the FBI asked the frightened couple to wear a wire—and tipped off Bulger. Other victims who insisted on action were told of the need to testify and enter the Witness Protection Program. When the Massachusetts State Police conducted their own investigation, which included electronic surveillance, Bulger and Flemmi were tipped off by the FBI. They were also tipped off about DEA and local police attempts at electronic surveillance. Despite being told that they could not be involved in murder, Bulger and Flemmi were responsible for at least nineteen, including those of two women with whom the pair were romantically involved (English 2005).

Emboldened by their FBI protection, Bulger and Flemmi engaged in a systematic shakedown of independent bookmakers and loan sharks in the south Boston area. When Howie Winter was imprisoned in 1978, Bulger took over the Winter Hill gang. When cocaine became popular in the 1980s, Bulger and Flemmi extended their shakedowns to include drug dealers. And then there were murders. In 1981, to protect an embezzling accountant, Bulger had the notorious Winter Hill hit man John Martorano kill a business executive in Tulsa, Oklahoma. Martorano was then sent to Florida, and the accountant was found stuffed into the trunk of a car at the Miami airport.

---

[6]Flemmi served as a paratrooper during the Korean War.

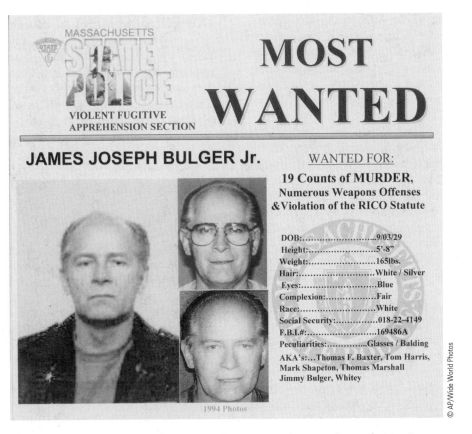

Massachusetts state police wanted poster of James J. ("Whitey") Bulger, a fugitive Boston gangster who was at the center of a scandal in which the FBI was found to have protected Bulger in return for his providing information about the New England Mafia.

In 1982, Bulger was the executioner of a Winter Hill member who had turned informant (Butterfield 2003; Lehr and O'Neil 2000).

Raymond Patriarca was indicted in 1980 for labor racketeering, and in 1981 for ordering a double execution. In 1984, while charges were still pending, he died of natural causes. Raymond Patriarca, Jr., claimed the position and, with the approval of the New York Families, became boss of the Office. By 1989, Junior's reign was in trouble. Information being provided by Bulger and Flemmi and electronic bugs led to the convictions of almost every member of the Boston branch of the Office. Replacements chosen by Junior irritated the Providence branch, and a war broke out.

In an effort to restore peace, in 1989, an initiation ceremony was staged to allow four new members, three from Boston and one from Providence, to be made. The ceremony was recorded by two electronic eavesdropping devices placed in the basement ceiling of a house in a Boston suburb. It was the first time that the FBI had been able to record a Mafia initiation. In 1991, Patriarca pleaded guilty to racketeering and was sentenced to eight years. Another two years were added as the result of a government appeal of the original sentence. He was released on parole in 1998. Further prosecutions decimated the New England crime Family.

In 1995, Bulger and Flemmi were indicted by a federal grand jury for racketeering and extortion;

the Rifleman was arrested and Whitey became a fugitive. In 1999, during his trial, Flemmi's attorney argued that the federal government cannot prosecute crimes it effectively authorizes informers to commit (C. Goldberg 1999; especially *United States of America v. Stephen J. Flemmi*, U.S. Court of Appeals for the First Circuit, No. 99-2292, 2000). The chief witness against Flemmi was John Martorano, 62, who admitted to twenty murders in return for a sentence of 10 to 12.5 years. Since Bulger and Flemmi were informants, it is believed that Martorano felt he had no obligation to be loyal to them. In 2001, in exchange for a plea of guilty, Flemmi was sentenced to 10 years for extortion and money laundering, and in 2003, he pled guilty to ten murders in exchange for a life sentence.

The success of the FBI in prosecuting the Patriarca Family was marred by revelations concerning the activities of some of its agents. In 1999, a federal grand jury indicted a retired FBI agent on charges of conspiring with Bulger and Flemmi, receiving gifts and protecting their criminal activities. As a result of disclosures from this case, it was revealed that in order to protect their informants, the FBI allowed three men to be convicted and imprisoned for a murder they did not commit. Furthermore, the FBI knew of the murder plan and did not intervene. One of the three falsely convicted men died in prison; another had his sentence commuted and was released from prison in 1997; and the third had his conviction vacated and was released from prison in 2001 after serving more than 33 years, four of them on death row (Butterfield 2003; C. Goldberg 2001). In 2002, the FBI agent who was Bulger's handler received a 10-year sentence for racketeering—for essentially becoming part of Whitey Bulger's organization (Butterfield 2002; Carr 2006; Spinale 2004). In 2005, he was indicted in Florida for the 1982 murder of a man believed to be cooperating with authorities (Associated Press 2005c).

In the wake of the Boston disclosures, the attorney general toughened the requirements on the use of informants, but a 2005 report by the Justice Department's inspector general revealed that they were routinely violated by FBI agents (Lictblau 2005a).

LAW ENFORCEMENT AGENCIES

Before we examine the law enforcement agencies responding to organized crime and the techniques they use to enforce the statutes reviewed earlier, certain issues must be noted. General police responsibility is the function of a "full-service" municipal department—there is no national police force in the United States—while the primary responsibility of state police forces is highway traffic enforcement. Most of the resources of a municipal police department go into uniformed services such as patrol; only a small portion goes into plainclothes or detective units. In larger cities, such units include specialties such as "vice" (gambling and prostitution) and drug enforcement. In this function, local police do apprehend some of the participants in organized criminal activity. Organized crime, however, is rarely a priority item for a municipal department. Resources devoted to organized crime detract from the department's ability to respond to citizen demands for police services.

> Few local departments have the luxury of developing a sophisticated organized crime control program. Obviously, the daily realities of police work at the grassroots level militate against a well-developed execution of an organized crime control strategy. Since organized crime is often synonymous with vice enforcement—gambling, prostitution, narcotics, and loansharking—there are few incentives for a police administrator to allocate limited and valuable resources toward this particular form of criminality. Often the investment of personnel to enforce laws which govern "consensual relationships" between customer and supplier are met with judicial indifference and public apathy; and as demonstrated through numerous studies and investigations, it is highly questionable from a purely cost-benefit analysis whether the benefits outweigh the costs incurred. Accordingly, most investigative and law-enforcement efforts against organized crime are found at the federal level. (Dintino and Martens 1980: 67)

Primary Federal Law Enforcement Agencies

Department of Justice

- Bureau of Alcohol, Tobacco, Firearms and Explosives
- Drug Enforcement Administration
- Federal Bureau of Investigation
- Marshals Service

Department of the Treasury

- Internal Revenue Service

Department of Homeland Security

- Coast Guard
- Customs Service and Border Protection
- Immigration and Customs Enforcement
- Secret Service

The New York State Organized Crime Task Force has been responsible for developing important cases against persons involved in organized crime, and the New York Police Department has its own organized crime bureau. New Jersey and New Mexico have established commissions in response to organized criminal activity.

Because the police are the most visible agents of governmental power, and because Americans have historically distrusted government in general and the federal government in particular, there has never been serious consideration of a federal police force. Over the decades, however, necessity has led to the creation of a number of specialized federal enforcement agencies in an unplanned and uncoordinated manner. Thus, while they all have the same nominal boss—the president—federal law enforcement is fragmented. The result is a confusing number of agencies in several departments—Justice, Treasury, Labor, Defense, and, since 9/11, Homeland Security—whose responsibility for organized crime law enforcement lacks systematic coordination.

Department of Justice (DOJ)

Clearly the most important federal department dealing with organized crime, the Department of Justice is headed by the attorney general, a member of the president's cabinet. Each of the 94 federal judicial districts has a U.S. attorney appointed by the president for a period of four years. The U.S. attorneys and about 2,000 assistant U.S. attorneys prosecute cases for all federal enforcement agencies. Within the DOJ is the Organized Crime and Racketeering Section (OCRS) responsible for coordinating and developing nationwide programs for responding to organized crime.

Federal Bureau of Investigation (FBI)   The FBI is the closest thing to a federal police force in the United States. Its origins date back to the establishment of the Department of Justice in 1870. Until 1908, the department used private detectives or borrowed men from the Secret Service. In that year, President Theodore Roosevelt directed the attorney general to develop an investigative unit within the Justice Department; it was named the Bureau of Investigation. In 1935, Congress renamed it the Federal Bureau of Investigation, and special agents were given authority to carry weapons and make arrests, a response to the "Kansas City Massacre of 1933" when unarmed bureau agents were gunned down.

After World War I, the bureau was involved in a great deal of "antiradical" activity at the direction of Attorney General A. Mitchell Palmer. The FBI conducted raids and arrested thousands of people in what became known as the "Red Scare of 1919." The "Palmer Raids" were the subject of a congressional investigation and were strongly defended by the bureau's assistant director, John Edgar Hoover, who was appointed director in 1924 and remained head of the FBI until his death in 1972.

Over the years, the bureau was given responsibility for investigating interstate shipment of stolen vehicles, kidnapping, bank robbery, interstate fugitives, espionage, and sabotage. After World War II, FBI resources were directed toward the perceived threat posed by domestic communism, while the problem of organized crime was left unattended—in 1956, there were four agents assigned to the New York office to investigate "Crime, Organized" (Volkman 1998). Stanford Ungar (1975: 391) argues that "the Director was simply clever enough to steer clear of the toughest problems—the ones less likely to produce prompt and stunning results, that might test conflicts of loyalty among agents, or that would require them to be exposed to the seamier side of life (and, as with many policemen, tempt them into corruption)."[7] This changed when President John F. Kennedy appointed his brother Robert attorney general.

The FBI has become the major law enforcement agency combating organized criminal activity and the lead agency in using the RICO statute discussed earlier. In 1982, its broad investigative mandate was expanded when the FBI was given concurrent jurisdiction with the Drug Enforcement Administration for drug-law enforcement and investigation. While the FBI usually does not initiate a drug investigation, if one is uncovered in the course of an investigation, the agency may follow up without having to involve the DEA.

Since 9/11, there is concern that the increased focus on terrorism could detract from FBI efforts to respond to organized crime. A study by a research organization associated with Syracuse University (http://www.trac.syr.edu) revealed that prosecutions in organized crime cases brought by the FBI dropped from 498 in fiscal year 2001 to 163 in fiscal year 2006, and they have continued to drop.

Drug Enforcement Administration (DEA)

In 1919, a Narcotics Division was created within the Bureau of Prohibition with a staff of 170 agents and an appropriation of $270,000. The Narcotics Division was tainted by its association with the country's anti-liquor laws. "Public dissatisfaction intensified because of a scandal involving falsification of arrest records and charges relating to payoffs by, and collusion with, drug dealers" (PCOC 1986a: 204). Responding in 1930, Congress removed drug enforcement from the Bureau of Prohibition and established the Federal Bureau of Narcotics (FBN) as a separate agency within the Department of the Treasury. "Although the FBN was primarily responsible for the enforcement of the Harrison Act and related drug laws, the task of preventing and interdicting the illegal importation and smuggling of drugs remained with the Bureau of Customs" (PCOC 1986a: 205). In 1973, responsibility for enforcing federal drug statutes was given to the DEA, which was placed in the Department of Justice.

The DEA is a single-mission agency responsible for enforcing federal statutes dealing with controlled substances by investigating alleged or suspected major drug traffickers. The DEA is also responsible for regulating the legal trade in controlled substances such as morphine, methadone, and barbiturates. Diversion agents conduct accountability investigations of drug wholesalers, suppliers, and manufacturers. They inspect the records and facilities of major drug manufacturers and distributors, and special agents investigate instances where drugs have been illegally diverted from legitimate sources. DEA special agents are also stationed in other countries, where their mission is to gain cooperation in international efforts against drug trafficking and to help train foreign enforcement officials.

The basic approach to DEA drug-law enforcement is the "buy and bust" or the "controlled buy." Typically, a drug agent is introduced to a seller by an informant. The agent arranges to buy a relatively small amount of the substance and then attempts to move further up the organizational ladder by increasing the amount of drugs purchased. "The agent prefers to defer an arrest until he can seize a large amount of drugs or can implicate higher-ups in the distribution system or both" (Wilson 1978: 43). When arrests are made, DEA agents attempt the "flip"—convince a

---

[7]Anthony Summers (1993) presents a more sinister set of explanations for Hoover's lack of activity against organized crime.

defendant to become an informant, particularly if the person has knowledge about the entire operation so that a conspiracy case can be effected. As discussed earlier, the use of informants is problematic. The DEA, usually with the aid of customs agents and state and local enforcement agencies, monitors airports in an effort to interdict drugs being smuggled by "mules."

Marshals Service The Marshals Service is the oldest federal law enforcement agency, dating back to 1789. During the period of westward expansion, the U.S. marshal played a significant role in the "Wild West," where he was often the only symbol of law and order. In the past marshals have also been used in civil disturbances as an alternative to military intervention. Today, they provide security for federal court facilities; transport federal prisoners; serve civil writs issued by federal courts, which can include the seizure of property under the provisions of RICO; and investigate and apprehend certain federal fugitives. Their most important task relative to organized crime, however, is responsibility for administering the *Witness Security Program*.

Witness Security Program[8] Because of the potentially undesirable consequences for a witness who testifies in an organized crime case, efforts have been made to protect such witnesses from retribution. The Witness Security Program was authorized by the Organized Crime Control Act of 1970:

> The Attorney General of the United States is authorized to rent, purchase, modify or remodel protected housing facilities and to otherwise offer to provide for the health, safety, and welfare of witnesses and persons intended to be called as Government witnesses, and the families of witnesses and persons intended to be called as Government witnesses, in legal proceedings instituted against any person alleged to have

participated in an organized criminal activity whenever, in his judgment, testimony from, or a willingness to testify by, such a witness would place his life or person, or the life or person of a member of his family or household, in jeopardy. Any person availing himself of such an offer by the Attorney General to use such facilities may continue to use such facilities for as long as the Attorney General determines the jeopardy to his life or person continues.

The program was given over to the U.S. Marshals Service to administer, an arrangement designed to enhance the value of witness testimony: "Law enforcement officers wanted the protecting and relocating agency to be in the criminal justice system but to be as far removed as possible from both investigating agents and prosecution. That way the Government could more readily counter the charge that cooperating witnesses were being paid or otherwise unjustifiably compensated in return for their testimony" (Permanent Subcommittee on Investigations, hereafter PSI, 1981c: 54).

However, the Marshals Service was not prepared for these new responsibilities—its typical duties were related to support of the judicial system. Moreover, the educational requirements and training of deputy U.S. marshals were not rigorous. This has changed. Marshals Service personnel are better trained, and a new position, that of inspector, was created specifically for the Witness Security Program. Nevertheless, officials had not anticipated the number of persons who would enter the program. They had expected about two dozen annually, and not the more than 500 principals brought into the program each year—by 2005, the program was protecting more than 17,000 witnesses and their dependents.

Some critics of the program have charged that the Marshals Service shields criminals not only from would-be assassins but also from debts and lawsuits. In an attempt to remedy this, an amendment to the 1984 Comprehensive Crime Control Act directs the Justice Department to stop hiding witnesses who are sued for civil damages and to

---

[8]For an examination of the program by its founder, see Early and Shur (2002).

drop from the program participants linked to new crimes. But the program still provides career criminals with "clean" backgrounds that they can use to prey on or endanger an unsuspecting public.

The problem is obvious: "The marshals are often dealing with men and women who have never done an honest day's work in their lives. Many of them were skilled criminals—burglars, embezzlers, arsonists, physical enforcers—accustomed to lucrative financial rewards and a high standard of living" (PSI 1981c: 53–54), a standard that is not going to be duplicated by the program, which typically provides about $2,000 to $3,000 monthly for seventeen months; participants may also receive help with job training. Once the immediate physical danger has passed, some of these protected witnesses begin to yearn for the excitement and, for some, the status and financial rewards that crime brought to their lives. Government witness Sammy Gravano, former underboss of the Gambino Family, was relocated to Arizona. He soon grew bored with his new life and, while keeping his new name, told neighbors his real identity and signed autographs for people who stopped him on the street. In 2000, Gravano was arrested for involvement in an ecstasy drug ring that also included his son, who apparently introduced his father to the trade (Murr 2000). Having few if any noncriminal skills, it is not surprising that some of these protected witnesses return to criminal activity even if it places both their freedom and their lives, and the lives of their families, at risk. While about thirty witnesses who left the program have been murdered, none following program guidelines have been harmed (Sabbag 1996).

In some cases, estranged spouses have been unable to visit their own children. This was dramatically portrayed in the 1980 movie *Hide in Plain Sight*, starring James Caan. In 1983 the government relocated the ex-wife and young daughter of Anthony Prisco to a secret location. His ex-wife was married to a drug trafficker who became a government witness. Prisco hired a private investigator, who found out that she and their daughter were in the Witness Protection Program. In 1984, Congress amended the law to provide greater rights to parents in such cases. They permit Prisco monthly visits monitored by marshals, but he has no input into his daughter's upbringing (Tulsky 1987).

Bureau of Alcohol, Tobacco, Firearms and Explosives (ATFE)

On January 24, 2003, the Bureau of Alcohol, Tobacco and Firearms (ATF) was transferred from the Treasury Department to the Department of Justice. The tax and trade functions of ATF remain in the Treasury Department with the new Alcohol and Tobacco Tax and Trade Bureau. In addition, the agency's name was changed to the Bureau of Alcohol, Tobacco, Firearms and Explosives (ATFE) to reflect its new mission in the Department of Justice.

ATFE traces its origins to 1791, when a tax was placed on alcoholic spirits. Eventually, the Prohibition Bureau evolved. With the repeal of Prohibition, this became known as the Alcohol Tax Unit. In 1942, the bureau was given jurisdiction over federal firearms statutes and, in 1970, over arson and explosives. ATFE agents are empowered to seize and destroy contraband and illegal liquor production facilities, and they are responsible for combating contraband cigarette smuggling from a low-tax state to a high-tax state—North Carolina to New York, for example—and the bootlegging of untaxed tobacco products, activities often engaged in by persons in organized crime who, through their extensive networks, have readily available outlets for such products. Through enforcement of federal firearms and explosives statutes and regulations, ATFE has been involved in the investigation of outlaw motorcycle clubs. The Anti-Arson Act of 1982 increased the bureau's jurisdiction over arson. (The FBI has jurisdiction in arson or bombings that occur at federal buildings or other institutions that receive federal funds and in incidents that fit the Department of Justice's definition of terrorism.) ATFE's National Response Teams investigate cases of arson and bombings in conjunction with state and local agencies. Each team is composed of special agents, a forensic chemist, and an explosives specialist and is equipped with sophisticated, state-of-the-art equipment.

Department of the Treasury

The primary responsibility of the Department of the Treasury is the collection of revenues due the federal government. In carrying out these responsibilities, the Treasury Department employs law enforcement personnel in the Internal Revenue Service who have an important role in dealing with organized crime. The mission of the IRS is to encourage and achieve the highest possible degree of voluntary compliance with tax laws and regulations. When such compliance is not forthcoming or not feasible, as in the case of persons involved in organized criminal activity, the Criminal Investigation division (CI), which employs about 3,000 special agents, receives the case. Agents examine bank records, canceled checks, brokerage accounts, property transactions, and purchases, compiling a financial biography of the subject's lifestyle in order to prove that proper taxes have not been paid (according to the net worth theory discussed earlier).

As a result of the excesses revealed in the wake of the Watergate scandal during the presidency of Richard Nixon, Congress enacted the Tax Reform Act of 1976. The act reduced the law enforcement role of the IRS and made it quite difficult for law enforcement agencies other than the IRS to gain access to income tax returns. Amendments in 1982 reduced the requirements and permit the IRS to better cooperate with the efforts of other federal agencies investigating organized crime, particularly drug traffickers. In addition to investigating criminal violations of the Internal Revenue Code, the CI division special agents' jurisdiction includes money laundering and Bank Secrecy Act laws. Only the IRS can investigate criminal violations of the IRS code. Due to the increased use of automation for financial records, CI special agents are trained to recover computer evidence and use specialized forensic technology to recover financial data that may have been encrypted, password protected, or hidden by other electronic means. The CI division's conviction rate is one of the highest in federal law enforcement. Not only do the courts hand down substantial prison sentences, but those convicted must also pay fines, civil taxes, and penalties (IRS website).

Financial Crimes Enforcement Network (FinCEN) Established in 1990 in the Treasury's Office of Terrorism and Financial Intelligence, FinCEN administers the Bank Secrecy Act (BSA) of 1970, as amended, the USA PATRIOT Act of 2001, and other laws. FinCEN is a key component of the U.S. international strategy to combat terrorism and organized crime using counter–money laundering laws, and provides intelligence and analytical case support to federal, state, local, and international investigators and regulators. Its 200 employees include intelligence analysts and criminal investigators as well as specialists in the financial industry and computer field. In addition, approximately 40 long-term detailees are assigned to FinCEN from twenty-one different regulatory and law enforcement agencies. FinCEN maintains a database in Detroit that documents every suspicious-activity report filed since they were initiated in 1996.

Department of Homeland Security

As a result of the Homeland Security Act of 2002, several Treasury agencies have been transferred to the Department of Homeland Security (DHS).

Immigration and Customs Enforcement (ICE) Immigration and Customs Enforcement (ICE) is the result of a post-9/11 restructuring of the Immigration and Naturalization Service and the Customs Service. The primary role of the immigration enforcement arm of ICE is to prevent illegal entry into the United States and to apprehend those who have entered illegally. DHS uniformed Border Patrol officers check suspicious individuals within 100 miles of border areas that are likely to be used as illegal crossing points, and they often arrest people who are transporting drugs.

The Customs Service was established in 1789 to collect duties on various imports. Inspectors examine cargoes and baggage, articles worn or carried by individuals, and vessels, vehicles, and aircraft entering or leaving the United States. The frontiers of the United States, to the north and the south, "are the longest undisputed, undefended borders on earth" (Weiner 2002b: 14).

Drug Smuggling Interceptions

- A light gray spray-painted bust of Jesus composed of molded cocaine
- 5 pounds of cocaine packed in condoms surgically implanted in a sheepdog
- 37 pounds of cocaine packed in condoms and inserted in the rectums of live boa constrictors
- 1,000 pounds of cocaine packed in hollow plaster shells shaped and painted to resemble yams
- 6,000 pounds of cocaine packed in kilo bricks inside ice-packed cases of broccoli
- 2,000 pounds of cocaine in the soles of a shipment of sneakers

- 16 tons of cocaine inside concrete fence posts
- 3,000 pounds of cocaine hidden beneath a shipment of iced fish fillets
- Cocaine, smuggled into the United States by Mexican drug organizations, secreted in tombstones engraved with the Virgin Mary
- 12 pounds of heroin discovered by customs officials at Newark Airport in more than 100 candy bars that had been individually wrapped and packaged

Source: Associated Press (1999c, 2007); Lambert (2006); Speart (1995).

Special teams of inspectors and canine enforcement officers concentrate on cargo and conveyances that are considered to be at high risk. In 1981 the Customs Service established the Office of Intelligence to better manage information and target suspects; it participates in several multiagency programs designed to combat organized criminal activities in drug trafficking. ICE works with commercial carriers, often signing cooperative agreements, to enhance the carriers' ability to prevent their equipment from being used to smuggle drugs. Special agents are responsible for carrying out investigations into drug smuggling and currency violations as part of money laundering schemes.

ICE and the Border Patrol are not bound by Fourth Amendment protections that typically restrain domestic law enforcement. Agents do not need probable cause or warrants to engage in search and seizure at ports of entry; certain degrees of suspicion will suffice. The typical case is a "cold border bust," the result of an entry checkpoint search. Because it is impractical if not impossible to thoroughly search most vehicles and individuals entering the United States, agents have developed certain techniques for minimizing inconvenience to legitimate travelers and shippers while targeting those who are most likely to be involved in smuggling activity. Besides being alert to various cues that act as tip-offs, the officials at border-crossing points have computers containing information such as license plate numbers and names of known or suspected smugglers. People arrested by ICE become targets for offers of plea bargaining in efforts to gain their cooperation in follow-up enforcement efforts by the Drug Enforcement Administration; they are pressured to become informants in return for some form of leniency. As the result of the 9/11 attacks, ICE priorities have shifted to intercepting potential terrorists seeking to enter the United States.

ICE is hampered by the need to patrol more than 12,000 miles of international boundary, which more than 420 billion tons of goods and 270 million people cross each year. About half the drugs entering the United States come through commercial ports, where they are secreted in tightly sealed steel containers, 20 or 40 feet long, 12 feet high, and 8 feet wide, millions of which enter the country every year. Officials can inspect only a small number (about 10 percent) of these containers, and without advance information, the drugs typically pass right through the ports. Drugs that are intercepted are easily replaced.

Homeland Security has been plagued by charges of corruption on the U.S.-Mexico border. In part, this is the result of dramatic increases in the number of agents and tougher enforcement that has driven smugglers to engage in greater efforts at compromising security. There is concern that smugglers are sending operatives to take jobs in border enforcement (Archibald and Becker 2008).

Coast Guard   The Coast Guard is responsible for drug interdiction on the seas. Its vessels conduct continuous surface patrols and frequent surveillance flights over waters of interest, and its personnel board and inspect suspect vessels at sea. Coast Guard personnel are law enforcement officers who do not have to establish probable cause prior to boarding a vessel. "The Coast Guard conducts both continuous surface patrols and frequent surveillance flights over waters of interest, and boards and inspects vessels at sea. In the past major Coast Guard resources have been concentrated in the 'choke points' traditionally transversed by traffickers. Cutters now more frequently patrol the Bahamas, the eastern passes of the Caribbean, and the Gulf, Atlantic and Pacific coastal areas" (PCOC 1986a: 313).

A typical seizure begins with the sighting of a suspect plane by a Coast Guard radar plane 250 miles away. The radar plane informs an intelligence center, where the suspect plane's flight track is compared with flight plans submitted to the Federal Aviation Administration. If a flight plan has not been filed, a two-engine Coast Guard tracking plane is dispatched. The tracking plane picks up the suspect plane on radar and then turns the radar off to avoid being detected by a "fuzz-buster." The tracker follows behind and above the suspect aircraft, maintaining surveillance with an infrared device that senses heat but does not send out an electronic beam.

When the suspect plane prepares to land, the tracker notifies officers aboard a waiting helicopter, and they move in to make arrests. If the plane makes a drop at sea for pickup by boat, a Coast Guard helicopter or patrol boat makes the seizure. Coast Guard personnel are sometimes assigned to U.S. Navy ships assigned to drug interdiction, because military personnel are prohibited from making arrests of civilians by the Posse Comitatus Act.

The Coast Guard and ICE are hampered by the need to patrol more than 12,000 miles of international boundary, over which more than 420 billion tons of goods and 270 million persons cross each year. The Coast Guard has been deploying 150 mph MH-68A Stingray helicopters to intercept "cigarette boats," also known as "go fasts," used to transport drugs from South America or northern Mexico. These slim 30- to 40-foot vessels propelled by 800-horsepower engines can reach speeds of 50 mph on open seas and carry a cargo of up to three tons. The helicopters are equipped with machine guns and high-impact .50 caliber sniper rifles whose rounds are as thick and long as a hot dog and can disable a boat engine, at which time a high-speed Coast Guard cutter effects a seizure (Kilian 2002). This tactic has been so successful that traffickers have resorted to using crude submarine-like vessels to move cocaine from Colombia to Mexico (Franklin and Logan 2008).

Department of Labor

The Office of the Inspector General (OIG), Office of Investigations, Division of Labor Racketeering, conducts investigations in three general areas: employee benefit plans, labor-management relations, and internal union affairs. Within this broad investigative area, top priority is given to traditional organized crime domination of labor unions and/or employee benefit plans. Second priority is given to organized crime influence or manipulation of labor unions and/or employee benefit plans. The OIG employs special agents to carry out these responsibilities (OIG information).

Department of Defense (DOD)

The primary role of the Department of Defense is obviously to protect the security of the United States from hostile military activities of foreign powers. Prior to U.S. military involvement in Afghanistan and Iraq, the DOD had been drawn into the fight against drug trafficking, and this role is quite controversial. In the wake of the Reconstruction era, when the Union Army occupied the states of the Confederacy, Congress enacted the 1878 Posse Comitatus Act prohibiting the U.S. Army from performing civilian law enforcement. In 1956, Congress added the Air Force to the Posse Comitatus Act, while the Navy and Marines promulgated administrative restrictions.

The prohibition on military involvement in domestic law enforcement, particularly drug enforcement, is based on fear that DOD involvement could:

- Compromise American security by exposing military personnel to the potentially corrupting environment of drug trafficking; in 1993, for example, Army personnel were accused of smuggling hundreds of pounds of cocaine from Panama into the United States using military transport
- Impair the strategic role of the military
- Present a threat to civil liberties: "The very nature of military training precludes any considerations of due process or civil rights" (Marsh 1991: 63)

Until 1981, the DOD limited its involvement in law enforcement to lending equipment and training civilian enforcement personnel in its use. In that year, as part of a new "War on Drugs," Congress amended the Posse Comitatus Act, authorizing a greater level of military involvement in civilian drug enforcement, particularly the tracking of suspect ships and airplanes and the use of military pilots and naval ships to transport civilian enforcement personnel. As a result of this legislation, the DOD provides surveillance and support services, using aircraft to search for smugglers and U.S. Navy ships to tow or escort vessels seized by the Coast Guard to the nearest U.S. port. The 1981 legislation authorized the military services to share information collected during routine military operations with law enforcement officials and to make facilities and equipment available to law enforcement agencies.

Further amendments to the 1981 legislation led to the use of military equipment and personnel in interdiction efforts against cocaine laboratories in Bolivia. These amendments permit the use of such personnel and equipment if the secretary of state or the secretary of defense and the attorney general jointly determine that emergency circumstances exist—the scope of specific criminal activity poses a serious threat to the interests of the United States. Combined operations involving U.S. Army Special Forces, DEA agents, U.S. Border Patrol officers, and Bolivian police and military officers have been successful in destroying hundreds of coca-paste laboratories in the coca-growing Champare region. The U.S. Department of State uses former military pilots to fly helicopter gunships, transport planes, and cropdusters used by U.S. and foreign drug agents in countries where U.S. military operations are barred.

Until 1988, federal efforts against airborne drug smuggling were coordinated by the Customs Service and the Coast Guard, with the DOD using radar to help detect smugglers. The following year, Congress designated the DOD as the lead agency in these efforts, but a report by the General Accounting Office stated that the equipment used was costly, operated poorly in bad weather, and required frequent maintenance. Furthermore,

Corrupting the Army

In 2005, five United States soldiers, part of a 500-member unit training Colombian security forces combating drug traffickers, were accused of smuggling 35 pounds of cocaine into Texas aboard a military aircraft. Later that year, two other American soldiers were charged with diverting thousands of rounds of ammunition for paramilitary squads aligned with drug traffickers (Forero 2005a).

airborne smugglers responded to the DOD activities by switching airports and finding other ways of entering the country (Berke 1989). In 1999, the United States negotiated a ten-year agreement with Ecuador to allow the basing of Air Force radar surveillance aircraft in Manta to monitor Colombian drug shipments on the Pacific Ocean. In response, the traffickers started to rely less on speedboats and instead began using low-tech submarines built for $1 million in Colombia's jungles. In 2008, Ecuador's president, whose father had been imprisoned in the United States for smuggling, demanded a closing of the base (Romero 2008b).

DOD support roles include air and ground observation and reconnaissance, environmental assessments, intelligence analysts and linguists, and transportation and engineering support. Mobile training teams teach civilian law enforcers such skills as combat lifesaving, advanced marksmanship, and tactical police operations that can be used in counterdrug operations.

Using night vision gear and thermal imaging equipment, U.S. service members man observation posts and patrol the rugged terrain along the 2,000-mile border between the United States and Mexico. Their job is to watch and listen; if they spot suspicious activity, they radio for the Border Patrol or local law enforcement. Since November 1989, U.S. forces have helped law officers in their counterdrug activities in Texas, New Mexico, Arizona, and California, an area covering about 580,000 square miles. By the end of 1995, the mission expanded to provide support throughout the continental United States, Puerto Rico, and the U.S. Virgin Islands (American Armed Forces Information Service information).

United States military officials have traditionally opposed involvement of the armed forces in law enforcement: It has been viewed as inappropriate because the goal of military operations is to kill and destroy, and law enforcement could potentially undermine its primary mission. Other fears have included a threat to civil liberties and the potentially corrupting influence of drug traffickers on the military. Furthermore, civilian casualties ("collateral damage") are often a by-product of military operations (Marsh 1991). Despite this fear, in 1988, legislation was overwhelmingly approved to dramatically expand the role of the military and allow the arrest of civilians under certain circumstances.

Other Federal Enforcement Agencies

In addition to the agencies already discussed, a number of other federal agencies have an investigative or law enforcement role that at times may involve their personnel with organized crime. The *Secret Service* in the Department of Homeland Security, in addition to its primary role of providing executive protection, is responsible for investigating counterfeiting of money and credit cards; and the *Postal Inspection Service* has the responsibility of ensuring the integrity of the mails, and in this role investigates the use of the mails to further racketeering or the unlawful shipment of controlled substances.

INTERPOL

The International Police Organization, known by its radio designation INTERPOL, assists law enforcement agencies with investigative activities that transcend national boundaries. It was founded in 1923 through the efforts of the police chief of Vienna. The organization became dormant during

World War II but was reorganized at a conference in Brussels in 1946. A stormy relationship existed between the director of the FBI and leaders of INTERPOL, and in 1950 the FBI withdrew from participation. The Treasury Department, anxious to maintain international contacts to help with its drug enforcement responsibilities, continued an informal liaison with INTERPOL.

Until 1968, "INTERPOL meant very little to the United States law enforcement community and was virtually unknown" (Fooner 1985: 19). In that year, Iran announced that it was going to end its ban on opium production. At the same time, there appeared to be an epidemic of drug use in the United States. A U.S. National Central Bureau (NCB) with a connection to INTERPOL was quickly activated in Washington, and by 1970 the NCB was handling about three hundred cases a year. In the mid-1970s, a turf battle ensued between the Treasury Department and the Justice Department: The attorney general, after decades of neglect, decided that he wanted the United States to be part of INTERPOL, but the Treasury Department resisted. An agreement—a memorandum of understanding—was effected between the two departments in 1977; they would share the responsibility of representing the United States to INTERPOL and of operating the NCB.

There are currently more than 180 INTERPOL members. A country merely announces its intention to join in order to become a member. In each country, there is an NCB that acts as a point of contact and coordination with the General Secretariat in Lyon, France, where INTERPOL has a headquarters staff of about 250, about 60 of whom are law enforcement officers from nearly 40 different countries. The president of INTERPOL is chosen for a four-year term at its General Assembly, although the organization is under the day-to-day direction of a secretary general. The General Assembly, INTERPOL's supreme governing body, meets once a year to take all major decisions affecting general policy. It is composed of delegates appointed by the governments of member countries. Each member country represented has one vote, and all votes have equal standing.

INTERPOL is a coordinating body and has no investigators or law enforcement agents of its own. At its headquarters there are databases containing records of people linked to international crime (Imhoff and Cutler 1998). The number of messages exchanged through the INTERPOL global police communication exceeded 3 million for the first time in 2003. In that year, INTERPOL began its high-security Internet-based communications infrastructure known as I-24/7. The system provides for swift and efficient cooperation to combat all forms of serious international crime. INTERPOL's communication system links the General Secretariat, National Central Bureaus, and police officers in member countries so that they can send and receive police information, including images, throughout the world on a secure, real-time basis, 24 hours a day, 7 days a week. It also provides access to INTERPOL's secure web pages that enables the organization to share crime-related information more easily. The system gives immediate interactive access to crime data held at the General Secretariat. This means that real-time checks can be made of any suspect's fingerprints, passports, or vehicles, anywhere in the world, by any police force linked to the system (*INTERPOL at Work* 2003).

Requests for assistance from federal, state, and local law enforcement are checked and coded by technical staff and entered into the INTERPOL Case Tracking System (ICTS), a computer-controlled index of persons, organizations, and other crime information items. The ICTS conducts automatic searches of new entries, retrieving those that correlate with international crime. The requests are forwarded to senior staff members who serve as INTERPOL case investigators, usually veteran agents from a federal agency whose experience includes work with foreign police forces. Each investigator is on loan from his or her principal agency, and each state, the District of Columbia, Puerto Rico, territories, and New York City, has a designated liaison office through which state and local agencies can connect to NCBs throughout the world (Imhoff and Cutler 1998).

Requests for investigative assistance range "from murder, robbery, narcotics violations, illicit firearms traffic, and large frauds, to counterfeiting, stolen works of art, bank swindles, and locating fugitives for arrest and extradition. The bureau also receives investigative requests for criminal histories, license checks, and other ID verifications. Sometimes locations of persons lost or missing in a foreign country are also requested" (Fooner 1985: 6). The Financial and Economic Crime Unit at INTERPOL headquarters facilitates the exchange of information stemming from credit card fraud, airline ticket counterfeiting, computer crime, offshore banking, commodity futures, and money laundering schemes. The monitoring of this type of activity can sometimes lead to the identification of suspects involved in drug trafficking or other types of organized crime who had previously escaped detection.

INVESTIGATIVE TOOLS IN ORGANIZED CRIME LAW ENFORCEMENT

Enforcing the law against organized criminal activity requires highly trained agents and prosecutors using sophisticated investigative and enforcement tools. In this section we will examine these tools—their advantages, disadvantages, and limitations.

Intelligence

The collection of information about organized crime, its evaluation, collation, analysis, reporting, and dissemination, is referred to as "intelligence" (Dintino and Martens 1983). It is laborious and usually unexciting work that requires a great deal of expertise. The *American Heritage Dictionary* (2000) defines *intelligence* as the work of gathering secret information about an actual or potential enemy. Justin Dintino and Frederick Martens (1983: 9) conceive of intelligence as "(1) a process through which information is managed which (2) will hopefully increase our knowledge of a particular problem (3) resulting in preventive and/or informed public policy."

Intelligence data are collected for two main purposes—tactical and strategic. At times, these two categories overlap (Godfrey and Harris 1971). *Tactical intelligence* is information that contributes directly to the achievement of an immediate law enforcement objective, such as arrest and prosecution. *Strategic intelligence* is information that contributes to producing sound judgment with respect to long-range law enforcement objectives and goals. The information is collected over time and put together by an intelligence analyst to reveal new (or newly discovered) patterns of organized crime activity. The information may be unsubstantiated ("raw") data requiring further investigation for confirmation—to become "hard" data.

Robert Stewart (1980: 54) notes the common sources of intelligence data:

- Court records
- Other public agency documents such as real estate, tax, and incorporation records
- Business records
- Old case records in the intelligence unit's files
- Investigative and intelligence files of other law enforcement agencies
- Newspapers, periodicals, books
- Utility company records
- Documents and items recovered during searches or subpoenaed by the grand jury, administrative agencies, and legislative committees
- Electronic surveillance
- Information and material produced voluntarily by citizens
- Statements and/or testimony obtained from accomplices, informants, victims, and law enforcement personnel

This material can be collected overtly or covertly. Covert collection involves the accumulation of information from subjects who are unaware that they are being observed or overheard. Since this type of collection is usually quite expensive in terms of the personnel required, it is usually tied directly to the goal of securing evidence that can be used in prosecution; that is, it is more tactical than strategic.

Drexel Godfrey and Don Harris (1971) refer to analysis as the "heart" of the intelligence

Regional Information Sharing Systems (RISS)

Established in 1974, and funded by the Bureau of Justice Assistance of the U.S. Department of Justice, RISS is a multijurisdictional criminal intelligence system that supports the sharing of intelligence information among over 7,000 federal, state, and local agencies in the fifty states, Canada, the District of Columbia, Australia, Guam, the U.S. Virgin Islands, England, and Puerto Rico. The vast majority of member agencies are at the municipal and county levels, but over 465 state and hundreds of federal agencies are also members. The Drug Enforcement Administration, Federal Bureau of Investigation, U.S. Attorneys' Offices, Internal Revenue Service, Secret Service, U.S. Immigration and Customs Enforcement, and the Bureau of Alcohol, Tobacco, Firearms and Explosives are among the federal agencies participating in the RISS program. Agencies join their regional RISS center through an application process established by the center.

RISS is designed to enhance the ability of state and local criminal justice agencies to identify, target, and remove criminal conspiracies and activities spanning jurisdictional boundaries. The executive director and policy board chairperson of each of six regional centers compose the RISS Directors National Policy Group, which has direct control over the policies and operations of the secure nationwide law enforcement communications and information sharing network (RISSNET) and related resources.

The regional centers are staffed by intelligence and analytical personnel, field representatives, and technical systems personnel. They provide controlled input and dissemination, rapid retrieval, and systematic updating of criminal justice information, as well as data analysis. Centers may also provide investigative support and technical assistance, training, and the loan of specialized equipment.

system. An analyst uses the methods of social science research, and central to this approach is the hypothesis. The analyst develops a hypothesis, an "educated guess," about the relevance of the information that has already been collected, collated, and stored. The investigators are then told to seek data that will permit "hypothesis testing." If the hypothesis does not withstand an adequate test, alternative hypotheses must be developed and tested. A hypothesis that has been supported by the data after rigorous testing becomes the basis for an intelligence report. The report guides tactical and/or strategic law enforcement efforts.

Intelligence gathering lacks many of the exciting aspects of law enforcement—there are no television series based on the adventures of intelligence analysts. The results produced by strategic intelligence are never immediate and seldom dramatic. They fail to impress those who allocate funds for law enforcement agencies, and intelligence personnel often have little status in agencies such as the DEA. There have been abuses as well: "A basic principle in collecting information for a

criminal intelligence file is that such information should be restricted to what an agency needs to know in order to fulfill its responsibility to detect and combat organized crime in its jurisdiction." Therefore, "the ethnic origin or the political or religious beliefs of any individual, group, or organization should never be the reason for collecting information on them. Criminal activities or associations must be the key factors. If associations are found not to be criminal in nature, the data collected on them should be dropped from the files" (Task Force on Organized Crime 1976: 122).

For several decades this was not the practice. In many urban police departments and the FBI, extensive intelligence efforts were directed against political groups and personalities. In Los Angeles, this type of activity was accomplished under the cover of the Organized Crime Intelligence Division, which "maintained secret Stalinesque dossiers, some of them kept in privately rented units; there were files on virtually every mover and shaker in Southern California" (Rothmiller and Goldman 1992: 9). "Red squads" and similar units

Electronic Surveillance

- *Telephone tap*: An extension hooked into a line at a telephone switching station.
- *Transmitter*: A microphone about the size of a small wooden matchbox. The batteries need to be changed every forty-eight hours. More sophisticated devices can be turned on and off from a remote location using a microwave signal.
- *Telephone transmitter*: A microphone wired inside a telephone, from which it draws its power. Some devices are activated by an outside telephone call and can transmit voices as well as telephone conversations.

- *Laser interceptors*: These devices can be pointed at a window to record vibrations on the glass caused by indoor conversations. A computer converts the vibrations into conversations.
- *Satellite relays*: Some microphones can transmit by way of a space satellite to a ground receiver.
- *Fiber optics*: Microsized fiber optic filaments embedded into walls draw power from a building's electrical system and can be used to intercept conversations.

would sometimes "leak" raw data whose source was untrustworthy. However, when such data move through a respected law enforcement agency, there is a "cleansing" effect, and the now "laundered" information takes on new importance, particularly when reported by the news media. Law enforcement intelligence files frequently contain news clips whose source is the agency itself—known as "circular sourcing."

During the late 1960s and early 1970s, lawsuits were brought against law enforcement intelligence units who were maintaining files on people without any evidence of criminality. As a result, the courts ordered intelligence files to be purged from police records, and in many cases police agencies had to pay damage awards. Restrictions on what information may be kept in intelligence files and "Freedom of Information" statutes have resulted to correct such abuses (Carter 2005).

Electronic Surveillance

The vast majority of law enforcement officials believe that evidence necessary to bring criminals from the higher echelons of organized crime to justice will not be obtained without the aid of electronic surveillance. The Task Force on Organized Crime (1976: 148) points out that "because of their organization and methods of organization, organized criminal activities require sophisticated means of evidence gathering. Often witnesses will not come forward, and members are bound by either an oath of silence or threats of violence. Often the use of informants is of limited value, and many organizations are difficult, if not impossible, for undercover agents to penetrate to the point where they can obtain useful evidence." One way to break through these conspiratorial safeguards, notes the Task Force, is through the use of electronic surveillance.

As the technology to accomplish electronic surveillance became increasingly sophisticated, the temptation to use it to gain information that is none of the government's business has proven quite strong. Legal definitions of just what may be part of law enforcement's business have been evolving since the first wiretap case confronted the U.S. Supreme Court in 1928. In *Olmstead v. United States* (277 U.S. 438), telephone wiretaps were used to prosecute persons involved in large-scale Prohibition violations. The interception of Olmstead's telephone line was accomplished without trespass. Chief Justice William Howard Taft, writing for the majority, determined that since telephone conversations are not tangible items, they cannot be the subject of an illegal seizure, and thus wiretapping is not prohibited by the Fourth Amendment. Shortly after the *Olmstead* decision, Congress prohibited interception of telephonic communication without judicial authorization.

The first case to reach the Supreme Court under the congressional restrictions was *Goldman v. United States* (316 U.S. 129) in 1942. The Court, consistent with *Olmstead*, ruled that a dictaphone placed against an office wall did not violate the Fourth Amendment because there was no trespass. In *Silverman v. United States* (365 U.S. 505, 1961), a foot-long spike with a microphone attached was inserted under a faceboard and into the wall until it made contact with a heating duct that ran through Silverman's house. The Court found this activity unconstitutional, not because of trespass but because of actual intrusion into "a constitutionally protected area."

In 1967, the Supreme Court ruled (*Berger v. New York*, 388 U.S. 41) that a New York State law authorizing "eavesdropping" was unconstitutional. The case involved a Chicago public relations man who was convicted of conspiracy to bribe the chairman of the New York State Liquor Authority. The evidence consisted of conversations intercepted by bugs and wiretaps pursuant to a court order. According to the Court, the statute failed to require warrants to state the specific crime being committed and the place or the persons to be surveilled. Also, no time limits were placed on the order once incriminating conversation was secured.

Later in 1967, the case of *Katz v. United States* (389 U.S. 347) came before the Supreme Court. In violation of the Hobbs Act, Katz transmitted wagering information on the telephone (McGuinness 1981: 27):

> In *Katz*, the Government, acting without a warrant or other judicial authorization, intercepted defendant's end of telephone conversations by means of two microphones attached by tape to the top of two adjoining public telephone booths from which Katz regularly made calls. Katz was subsequently prosecuted for the interstate transportation of wagering information by telephone in violation of a Federal statute, and tape recordings of the intercepted telephone calls were introduced in evidence over his objection. The Government argued that since no

physical intrusion was made into the booth and since it was not a "constitutionally protected area" (the defendant having no possessory interest as such in the booth), a search for Fourth Amendment purposes did not occur. In holding that there was a search, the Court stated that it was erroneous to resolve questions of Fourth Amendment law on the basis of whether a constitutionally protected area is involved, "[f]or the Fourth Amendment protects people, not places." This being the case, the reach of the "Amendment [also] cannot turn upon the presence or absence of a physical intrusion into any given enclosure." The Court thus concluded that the Government's activities "violated the privacy upon which [the defendant] justifiably relied while using the telephone," and hence a search within the meaning of the Fourth Amendment had taken place.

The keys to understanding *Katz* and subsequent decisions concerning surveillance and the Fourth Amendment are the phrases "reasonable expectation of privacy" or "legitimate expectation of privacy" and "justifiable expectation of privacy" (McGuinness 1981). As Kimberly Kingston (1988: 22–23) notes, the Supreme Court "redefined the term 'search' to include any governmental action which intrudes into an area where there is a reasonable expectation of privacy." However, she points out (1988: 24), it is not the subjective expectation of privacy that is protected but rather "only those that society as a whole is willing to recognize and protect." Thus, while a drug trafficking defendant may have had a subjective expectation that his trash was private, it was not an expectation of privacy that society was willing to recognize and protect—the defendant had exposed his garbage to the public and that included the police (*California v. Greenwood*, 486 U.S. 35, 1988). During the 1960s, the FBI used electronic surveillance extensively, often without the benefit of judicial authorization. "Numerous Congressional committees and criminal court judges in the 1960s found that the FBI and local police had for decades used illegal electronic surveillance to supplement their investigations. And, worse, they had used taps and bugs to spy on and disrupt the activities of law-abiding citizens and organizations. Civil rights leader Martin Luther King, Jr., for one, was the subject of extensive electronic surveillance in the 1960s" (Krajick 1983: 30). Furthermore, private wiretapping received greater coverage in the press: "The publicity continued to grow, and by the mid-1960s there were regular exposures of industrial espionage and of electronic surveillance operations by private detectives" (National Commission for the Review of Federal and State Laws Relating to Wiretapping and Electronic Surveillance 1976: 39; hereafter National Wiretap Commission).

As a result of this activity, and in order to bring some uniformity into the use of electronic surveillance, Congress enacted Title III of the Omnibus Crime Control and Safe Streets Act in 1968 (18 U.S.C. §§ 2510–2520). It was the first time in history that Congress had sanctioned electronic surveillance (Lapidus 1974). "Pressures had been mounting on Congress to enact legislation regulating electronic surveillance, but the scope of the controls could not be agreed to. *Berger* and *Katz* not only forced some legislative action by ruling out law enforcement use of electronic microphones without judicial warrant, but also outlined the scope of the privacy which was protected by the Fourth Amendment and sketched the guidelines for adequate warrant protection" (National Wiretap Commission 1976: 38).

Title III bans all private eavesdropping and authorizes federal officials and prosecutors in states whose laws conform to the federal statute to petition for court authorization to intercept wire or oral communications provided that:

1. There is probable cause for belief that an individual is committing, has committed, or is about to commit a particular offense that is enumerated in Title III.
2. There is probable cause for belief that particular communications concerning that offense will be obtained through such interception.
3. Normal investigative procedures have been tried and have failed, or reasonably

appear unlikely to succeed if tried, or are too dangerous.
4. There is probable cause for belief that the facilities in which, or the place where, the oral communications are to be intercepted is being used, or is about to be used, in conjunction with the commission of such offense, or is leased to, listed in the name of, or commonly used by persons believed to commit such offenses.

The Title III judicial order terminates in thirty days or less, unless extended by the issuing judge:

No order entered under this section may authorize or approve the interception of any wire or oral communication for any period longer than necessary to achieve the objective of the authorization, nor in any event longer than thirty days. Extensions of an order may be granted, but only upon the application for an extension made in accordance with subsection (1) of this section [essentially the four points listed earlier]. . . . The period of extension shall be no longer than the authorizing judge deems necessary to achieve the purposes for which it was granted and in no event for longer than thirty days. Every order and extension thereof shall contain a provision that the authorization to intercept shall be executed as soon as practicable, shall be conducted in such a way as to *minimize the interception of communications not otherwise subject to interception under this chapter*, and must terminate upon attainment of the authorization objective, or in any event in thirty days. (Emphasis added)

The *minimization* noted above requires that great care be taken to avoid intercepting conversations that are not relevant to the judicial order. In order to ensure that an unauthorized interception does not occur, the eavesdropping equipment must be monitored at all times. Each time a conversation is intercepted, the agent is permitted to listen only briefly, long enough to establish whether the nature of the conversation is within the scope of the judicial order. If the monitoring agent should hear a privileged conversation between doctor and patient or attorney and client or a personal conversation between husband and wife unrelated to the judicial order, he or she must discontinue the interception—hit the DNR, Dialed Numbered Recorder button. The recorder stops and an audible tone starts; the DNR prints out the time and date the minimization occurred and whether the monitor went back to the conversation or the conversation ended in the minimization mode. A monitoring agent who allows the recording of a privileged conversation jeopardizes the results of the investigation.

Judges and prosecutors are required to file reports on their use of Title IIIs with the Administrative Office of the United States Courts (AOUSC) in Washington, DC, and the AOUSC must submit an annual report on Title III to Congress. Title III requires that the target(s) of the judicial order be notified that their conversations have been intercepted within ninety days after termination of the order.

Although Title III regulates the interception of wire and oral communications, Congress did not explicitly provide any authority for the surreptitious placement of a listening device ("bug") to intercept oral communication—a "black bag job." Federal courts remained in conflict over the issue until *Dalia v. United States* (441 U.S. 238, 1979). FBI agents pried open a window in the New Jersey office of Lawrence Dalia in order to install a bug in his ceiling. As a result of the intercepted conversations, Dalia was convicted of violating the Hobbs Act by receiving property stolen from an interstate shipment. The Supreme Court concluded that a Title III warrant for eavesdropping implicitly grants authority for covert entry. Amendments to Title III in 1986 authorize "roving surveillance" of suspects using a number of different telephones or sites.

Title III is sometimes criticized by law enforcement officials because of the extensive investigation and documentation required to secure a warrant, although there are emergency exceptions built into the statute:

> Any investigative or law enforcement officer, specially designated by the Attorney General, or by the principal prosecuting attorney of any State or subdivision thereof acting pursuant to a statute of that State, who reasonably determines that (a) an emergency situation exists with respect to conspiratorial activities threatening the national security interests or to conspiratorial activities characteristic of organized crime that requires a wire or oral communication to be intercepted before an order authorizing such interception can with due diligence be obtained, and (b) there are grounds which an order could be entered under this chapter to authorize such interception may intercept such wire or oral communication if an application for an order approving the interception is made in accordance with this section within forty-eight hours after the interception has occurred, or begins to occur.

Any wire or oral communication may be intercepted legally by federal agents (while some states, such as Illinois, have local restrictions) without a court order if one of the parties to the communication gives prior consent. Thus, law enforcement officers and informants may be "wired" to secure incriminating conversation without a court order. In 1979, the Supreme Court (by a 5–3 vote) ruled that the police do not need a search warrant to record the numbers dialed from a particular telephone—there is an absence of a "reasonable expectation of privacy" because the telephone company routinely maintains such information for billing purposes. In *Smith v. Maryland* (442 U.S. 735), the Court affirmed the robbery conviction of a man linked to the crime by a pen register, which, when installed at a telephone company switching station, can record the numbers dialed from a particular phone.

Since Title III was enacted in 1968, more than thirty states have passed statutes permitting electronic surveillance, although some place restrictions beyond those contained in the federal statutes. Some states rarely make use of the law, and cost is a major reason. In addition to the investigative costs of securing the order, monitoring ties up at least two law enforcement officers over three shifts for thirty days or more on a continuous basis, at an average cost in excess of $40,000. There have been cases in which the cost exceeded $2 million—and less than 20 percent of all electronic surveillance actually produces incriminating evidence. Persons in organized crime frequently limit conversations that could be subjected to interception to code phrases. John Gotti, boss of the Gambino Family, was recorded as advising a young associate about telephone conversations: "Don't ever say anything you don't want played back to you some day"—advice he frequently disregarded (Mustain and Capeci 1988: 115). Conversations may be in a foreign language, so monitors have to be fluent in that language, or the conversation may be in a dialect or contain colloquial expressions that are difficult for outsiders to translate.

Material from electronic bugs must often be enhanced by specialists to reduce background noise from radios or televisions. The conversations then need to be transcribed and usually only the monitoring agents are familiar enough with the subjects' manner of speech to be able to accomplish this tedious task, which can take months of effort.

In addition to the wire and oral communications covered in Title III, the Electronic Communications Privacy Act (ECPA) of 1987 created a third category, "electronic communications," governing conversations over a broader array of technology including cellular (but not cordless) telephones and electronic (e-) mail. The ECPA also regulates the use of pen registers, devices that can record the phone numbers of outgoing calls, and trap-and-trace devices that can record the numbers of incoming calls—they are usually used in tandem. A simplified court order is required to install these devices (Colbridge 2000).

In recent years, electronic surveillance has been complicated by technological advances in communications. Conversations via high-capacity digital lines (human voices translated into numbers) and fiber optic lines (using pulses of light), for example, cannot be intercepted using conventional wiretap equipment. Advances in encryption technology allow for communication virtually impossible for eavesdroppers to decipher; they would need access to the code (or an impossible expenditure of time—years). Inexpensive computer programs and hardware can now scramble telephone calls and computer e-mail. In response, the Department of Justice (DOJ) has requested a weakening of the systems so they can be subjected to law enforcement surveillance. Authority for this is based on a DOJ interpretation of the 1994 Communications Assistance for Law Enforcement Act intended to help law enforcement agencies intercept telephone calls. This has engendered strong opposition from many members of Congress and telephone companies. They argue that making communication devices more susceptible to FBI surveillance would also make them more vulnerable to illegal penetrations while retarding advances in communications technology. In 1998, the Federal Communications Commission moved the deadline for complying with the law to 2007, but it is still being litigated.

Typo Technology

In 1999, federal agents seized a computer from Nicodemo S. Scarfo, Jr., son of the imprisoned Philadelphia crime boss, who was running a $5 million-a-year bookmaking operation under the Gambino Family in the Newark, New Jersey, area. However, they were unable to access information because it was stored in an encrypted file. The agents subsequently requested another search warrant (but not a Title III wiretap order) to break in and install a "key logger" or "keystroke recorder," a device the size of a sugar cube that conveys the keys pressed on a computer keyboard to a remote location. This device, which heretofore had been used only in national security cases, enabled the FBI to figure out the password and, thereby, decrypt Scarfo's files which contained records of gambling and loansharking operations (Anastasia 2002; Salkowski 2001; Schwartz 2001). In 2001, after courts ruled against suppressing the computer evidence, Scarfo, 36, pled guilty to bookmaking.

In the meantime, additional methods for avoiding electronic surveillance have surfaced, such as the use of anonymous remailers. Messages sent over the Internet are received by the remailer, which automatically strips off all traces of the sender's identity and forwards the message to an electronic mailbox (or to other remailers to further bury the identity of the source). Since messages are remailed in random sequence different from the order in which they arrive, anyone monitoring the remailer cannot match outgoing messages with incoming messages to identify who sent which message (Lohr 1999). Internet phones present a challenge to wiretapping because solutions are expensive, ultimately to the consumer, and may threaten the privacy of innocent parties (Belson 2004).

Additional problems arise with the widespread use of cellular phones. Based on the 1994 Communications Assistance for Law Enforcement Act, the DOJ requires the installation of devices that will make it easier for the government to intercept cellular calls. The cellular industry is resisting and has filed suit to avoid compliance. There is further controversy over the use of devices to track cellular callers—cellular companies have been installing them to be able to locate callers in the event of emergencies—that would be an aid to law enforcement. Should the caller have control over giving out his or her location? In addition, there are readily available radios that can hop frequencies—"spread spectrum"—and are nearly impossible to track.

Grand Jury

In the federal system, a grand jury is a body of 23 citizens empowered to operate with a quorum of 16 and requiring 12 votes for an indictment. In the state system, the minimum number of jurors varies considerably, although nowhere does the maximum number of grand jurors exceed 23. While some states adhere to the federal rule of 12 for an indictment, in others the range is anywhere from 4 to 9. Like those serving on a petit or trial jury, grand jurors are selected from the voting rolls; however, they meet in secret to consider evidence presented by the prosecutor.

Since the members of a grand jury are not agents of the government—they act as direct representatives of the citizenry, the extensive due process rights typically enjoyed by a criminal defendant are not necessarily relevant to grand jury proceedings. Their activities are secret, and only sixteen states permit the subject of a grand jury inquiry to have an attorney present, and then only to give advice. In the remaining states and the federal system, an attorney is not even permitted to accompany his or her client at a grand jury hearing. There is no right to present evidence or to cross-examine adverse witnesses. While the subject can refuse to answer any questions whose answers may be incriminating, he or she can be granted immunity and required to testify under the threat of being jailed for contempt.

The grand jury can receive virtually any type of information, even that which would not be admissible at a trial, such as certain types of hearsay and evidence that was secured in violation of the Fourth Amendment—the exclusionary rule does not apply to the grand jury (*United States v. Calandra*, 414 U.S. 338, 1974). In every state and in the federal system, the grand jury may be utilized for investigative purposes, and when so used it has broad investigative authority, including the power to subpoena persons and documents. In those states where statutes permit and in the federal system, the grand jury is used to investigate the operations of law enforcement and other government agencies, particularly when corruption is suspected, and to investigate the activities of organized crime.

The Organized Crime Control Act of 1970 requires that a special grand jury be convened at least every 18 months in federal judicial districts of more than 1 million persons. It can also be convened at the request of a federal prosecutor. Its typical life, 18 months, may be extended to 36 months. The special grand jury and grand juries of several states have the power to publish reports at the completion of their terms on certain types of noncriminal misconduct by public officials. While such reports cannot command any particular action, the widespread publicity they typically enjoy usually encourages action by government officials.

According to Robert Stewart (1980: 124), the investigative grand jury is:

> the single most useful tool by which to attack the traditional forms of organized crime. For example, convicted drug pushers, bookmakers, numbers writers and runners, prostitutes, weapons offenders and petty thieves can be summoned before the grand jury, immunized and questioned about the higher-ups in a particular enterprise or activity. If the witness is not already under charges, there is little likelihood that the grant of immunity will jeopardize any prosecution. If the witness testifies truthfully, that witness will be ostracized from the criminal community

and thereby neutralized as an organized crime operative. Moreover, the defection of one member of an organization may serve as a catalyst forcing others within the organization to defect and cooperate with the state. Whenever any appreciable number of lower-level offenders are summoned before an investigative grand jury, the higher-ups in the organized crime structure can never be sure what, if anything, is being said. This alone is sufficient to generate severe tensions within the organized crime structure. The grand jury can also request a grant of immunity for witnesses who refuse to testify on Fifth Amendment grounds.

Immunity

The Fifth Amendment to the U.S. Constitution provides that no person "shall be compelled in any criminal case to be a witness against himself." This is an important protection for the individual against the coercive powers of the state, and it can be partially neutralized by a grant of immunity. There are two types of immunity:

1. *Transactional immunity* provides blanket protection against prosecution for crimes about which a person is compelled to testify.
2. *Use immunity* prohibits the information provided by a person from being used against him or her, but the person can still be prosecuted using evidence obtained independently of his or her compelled testimony.

In many states and the federal system, the court or the prosecutor may grant immunity to reluctant witnesses. Legislative or administrative bodies investigating criminal activity can also request a grant of immunity. A witness who, after being granted immunity, refuses to testify can be subjected to civil or criminal contempt.

> The *civil contempt* proceeding is summary in nature and relatively simple. First the witness is immunized. Upon refusing to answer in the grand jury [or other authorized body]

the witness appears before the court. The prosecutor makes an oral application and the court instructs the witness to testify. The witness returns to the grand jury room; and, if recalcitrant, is directed to reappear before the court. The prosecutor then makes an oral application for the court to enforce its previous order, which the witness has disobeyed. The prosecutor explains what has occurred before the grand jury, and the foreperson or reporter testifies about these facts. The witness is given an opportunity to be heard; and thereafter the court decides whether the witness is in contempt and should be remanded. (Stewart 1980: 239)

"The remand order normally specifies that the witness shall remain confined until he offers to purge himself of the contempt by agreeing to testify or for the life of the grand jury, whichever is shorter" (1980: 240). The term of a grand jury is usually 18 months. Legislative committees and administrative bodies, of course, have indefinite terms. In 1970, as a result of his refusal to testify before a New Jersey investigating committee after being immunized, Jerry Catena (then acting boss of the Genovese Family) was imprisoned for contempt. He remained imprisoned for five years, never testifying.

The *criminal contempt* proceeding is quite different, since it requires a formal trial, and the witness is entitled to the full array of due process rights enjoyed by any criminal defendant. Being found guilty of criminal contempt, however, can result in a substantial sentence of imprisonment: "The purpose of the remand is coercive [to compel testimony], while the purpose of the criminal contempt sentence is punitive and deterrent" (Stewart 1980: 246). Of course, a witness, whether immunized or not, is subject to the laws against perjury.

In 1972, the Supreme Court decided the case of *Kastigar v. United States* (406 U.S. 441), which involved several persons who had been subpoenaed to appear before a federal grand jury in California in 1971. The assistant U.S. attorney, believing that the petitioners in *Kastigar* were likely to assert

their Fifth Amendment privilege, secured from the federal district court an order directing them to answer all questions and produce evidence before the grand jury under a grant of immunity. Nevertheless, the persons involved refused to answer questions, arguing that the "scope of the immunity provided by the statute was not coextensive with the scope of the privilege against self-incrimination, and therefore was not sufficient to supplant the privilege and compel their testimony."

The Supreme Court, in upholding the immunity order, quoted from the federal immunity statute: "The witness may not refuse to comply with the order on the basis of his privilege against self-incrimination; but no testimony or other information compelled under the order (or any information directly or indirectly derived from such testimony or other information) may be used against the witness in any criminal case, except a prosecution for perjury, giving a false statement, or otherwise failing to comply with the order." The Court concluded that since the statute prohibited the prosecutorial authorities from using the compelled testimony in any respect, it therefore ensured that the testimony could not lead to the infliction of criminal penalties on the witness. In a dissenting opinion, Justice Thurgood Marshall pointed to the possibility of using the testimonial information for investigative leads designed to secure evidence against the witness. The Court majority agreed that the statute barred such use of the testimony.

Civil action against a criminally immunized witness, however, is possible and has been upheld by the appellate courts (Rhodes 1984). In addition, a grant of immunity does not protect the witness from a loss of social status, employment, and, most important, revenge from those against whom he or she is forced to testify. Rufus King (1963: 651) raises additional issues:

> The immunity bargain is a somewhat unsavory device per se, inaccurate and potentially very unfair; it should be used only sparingly and where it is absolutely required. Immunity grants are always exchanges, a pardon for crimes that would otherwise be

punishable, given in return for testimony that could otherwise be withheld. In every case the interrogating authority must enter into a special "deal" with a wrongdoer to buy his testimony at the price of exoneration for something [for which] he would otherwise deserve punishment.

Such bargains are always somewhat blind. Ordinarily the witness will be hostile, so that his examiners cannot be sure in advance exactly what value the withheld testimony will have. And at the same time, especially in broad legislative or administrative inquiries, it is impossible to tell beforehand just what crimes are likely to be exonerated. Conceivably, the witness may have a surprise ready for his questioners at every turn of the proceedings.

Because of the potentially undesirable repercussions, some prosecutors have developed guidelines for consideration when making an immunity decision. The following guidelines are from the New Jersey Division of Criminal Justice (quoted in Committee on the Office of Attorney General 1978: 27):

- Can the information be obtained from any source other than a witness who wants to negotiate immunity?
- How useful is the information for the purposes of criminal prosecution?
- What is the likelihood that the witness can successfully be prosecuted?
- What is the relative significance of the witness as a potential defendant?
- What is the relative significance of the potential defendant against whom the witness offers to testify? In other words, is the witness requesting immunity more culpable than those against whom she or he is agreeing to testify? Are they in a position to provide evidence against the witness or superior evidence against others?
- What is the value of the testimony of the witness to the case (is it the core evidence upon which the prosecution is based)?

- What impact will immunity have on the credibility of the witness at trial? Are the terms of the immunity agreement so favorable to the witness that the jury will not accept the testimony?
- What impact will immunity have on the prosecutor's personal credibility and that of his or her office?

Rhodes notes, however, "that a grant of immunity has a favorable impact on a jury. It makes a defendant's testimony more credible. A prosecutor can point to the witness with a sordid record and say to the jury, 'What reason does Mr. X have to lie? His immunity is assured and if he lies he will be prosecuted for perjury!'" (1984: 193).

SUMMARY

- Part of the Organized Crime Control Act of 1970, RICO defines *racketeering* in an extremely broad manner, and it includes many offenses that do not ordinarily violate a federal statute.
- In place of having to prove a series of separate conspiracies, under RICO it is a crime to belong to an enterprise, for example, an organized crime Family or outlaw motorcycle club, that is involved in a "pattern of racketeering," even if the racketeering was committed by other members.
- Lack of precision coupled with the substantial penalties make RICO a tempting tool for federal prosecutors to use against persons who are not connected to organized crime.
- Civil provisions of RICO have been criticized for threatening triple damages and referring to defendants as "racketeers" in cases unrelated to organized crime.
- The 1968 Consumer Credit Act does not require proving violence or threats of violence to prove loansharking. Instead, the term *understanding* allows prosecutors to offer proof of the loan shark's reputation for violence.
- In civil forfeiture, the action is against the property, not the person, so that even an acquittal on the criminal charges does not preclude civil forfeiture.

- The Bank Secrecy Act (BSA) requires financial institutions to retain records to ensure that the details of financial transactions can be traced if investigators need to do so. They are also required to report transactions in currency in excess of $10,000 and transportation of currency and bearer instruments in excess of $10,000 into or out of the United States.
- There is a specific prohibition against "structuring" transactions to avoid the impact of the BSA's reporting thresholds.
- The Victims of Trafficking and Violence Prevention Act (VTVPA) makes peonage, sex trafficking in children and adults, and the confiscation of a victim's documents felonies.
- Related statutes also outlaw human smuggling, kidnapping, transportation for prostitution or any criminal sexual activity, and importation of aliens for unlawful activities.
- PROTECT authorizes the prosecution of Americans whose behavior involves the commercial sexual exploitation of children anywhere in the world.
- The Sex Tourism Prohibition Improvement Act of 2002 removed the intent requirement for individuals and criminalized the actions of sex tour operators.
- There are three constraints on organized crime *law enforcement:* constitutional restraints, jurisdictional limitations, and the intertwining problems of corruption and informants.
- Since resources devoted to organized crime detract from a police department's ability to respond to citizen demands for police services, responding to organized crime is primarily a federal responsibility.
- The lead agency is the Federal Bureau of Investigation (FBI), while a number of other federal agencies also have important roles: the Drug Enforcement Administration (DEA); U.S. Marshal's Service (Witness Protection Program); Internal Revenue Service (IRS); the Bureau of Alcohol, Tobacco, Firearms and Explosives (ATFE); Immigration and Customs Enforcement (ICE); Coast Guard; and the Department of Labor. And there is INTERPOL, which assists law enforcement agencies with investigative activities that transcend national boundaries.
- United States military officials have traditionally opposed involvement of the armed forces in law enforcement, as that could potentially undermine its primary mission, threaten civil liberties, and expose personnel to the potentially corrupting influence of drug traffickers.
- Intelligence data are collected for two main purposes, and at times these two categories overlap: *Tactical intelligence* is information that contributes directly to the achievement of an immediate law enforcement objective, such as arrest and prosecution; and *strategic intelligence* is information that contributes to producing sound judgment with respect to long-range law enforcement objectives and goals.
- During the 1960s, the FBI used electronic surveillance extensively, often without the benefit of judicial authorization and for political purposes.
- As a result, Congress enacted Title III of the Omnibus Crime Control and Safe Streets Act in 1968, the first time in history that Congress sanctioned electronic surveillance. Title III bans all private eavesdropping and authorizes federal officials and prosecutors in states whose laws conform to the federal statute to petition for court authorization to intercept wire or oral communications.
- Electronic surveillance has been complicated by technological advances in communications, and advances in encryption technology allow for communication that is virtually impossible for eavesdroppers to decipher.
- In response, the Department of Justice, based on the 1994 Communications Assistance for Law Enforcement Act, has requested a weakening of the systems so they can be subjected to law enforcement surveillance.
- This has engendered strong opposition from many members of Congress and telephone companies. They argue that making communication devices more susceptible to FBI surveillance would also make them more vulnerable to illegal penetrations while retarding advances in communications technology.

- A grand jury is a body of citizens that in the federal and some state systems is empowered to investigate corruption and organized crime.

- Through the use of immunity, *use* or *transactional*, witnesses can be compelled to testify under threat of imprisonment.

REVIEW QUESTIONS

1. What are the most important federal statutes used in organized crime control?
2. What historically significant changes were instituted by the drug control legislation of 1970?
3. What are the major provisions of the Hobbs Act?
4. How is the Consumer Credit Protection Act used against organized crime?
5. What is a conspiracy and what three forms can a conspiracy take?
6. How can "guilt by association" become a problem in a conspiracy prosecution?
7. Why does a conspiracy prosecution usually require an informant to testify?
8. What are the required elements for a RICO prosecution?
9. Why has RICO been criticized?
10. According to forfeiture statutes, under what conditions can the government seize property?
11. What are the levels of evidence applicable in a forfeiture proceeding?
12. What are the provisions of anti–money laundering statutes?
13. What is the purpose of the Victims of Trafficking and Violence Protection Act of 2000?
14. How is organized crime law enforcement limited by constitutional restraints and jurisdictional limitations?
15. Why is corruption a problem associated with organized crime law enforcement?
16. What is the problem inherent in using informants in organized crime law enforcement?
17. Why does most organized crime law enforcement take place at the federal level?
18. What are the two primary responsibilities of the Drug Enforcement Administration?
19. What agencies of the Department of Justice are responsible for organized crime law enforcement?
20. What agencies of the Department of the Treasury have responsibilities for organized crime law enforcement?
21. What unusual powers are enjoyed by Immigration and Customs Enforcement agents?
22. What are the responsibilities and special powers of the Coast Guard?
23. Why is the use of military personnel to fight drug trafficking controversial?
24. What is meant by "intelligence" in law enforcement and what are the two types of intelligence?
25. What does federal law (Title III) require with respect to electronic surveillance?
26. What are the advantages of using the grand jury to investigate organized crime?
27. What are the advantages and disadvantages of using immunity in organized crime cases?
28. Why is the Witness Security Program both necessary and controversial?
29. What is the role of the grand jury in responding to organized crime?
30. How has technology impacted on the ability of government to intercept electronic communications?

CONCLUSION

Responding in a rational manner to organized crime requires a sense of proportion and an appreciation of American history. Organized crime in America can be understood as one stage along a continuum. Our colonial forebears exhibited many of the activities currently associated with organized crime: bribery, usury, and monopoly, not to mention seizure of land by force, indentured servitude, and slavery. Early American adventurers cheated and killed Native Americans, and chartered pirates—privateers—plundered the high seas. During the War of 1812, and later during the Civil War, profiteers accumulated fortunes while the less fortunate suffered and died. The range wars in the West and the frauds, bribery, violence, and monopolistic practices of the "Robber Barons" discussed in Chapter 3 are all part of the context in which we must understand modern forms of organized crime. The cost of organized crime must be measured against the cost of corporate crime, which has the potential to harm far more persons, both financially and physically (see, for example, Clinard et al. 1979; Eichenwald 2002; Mokhiber 1988; Tillman and Pontell 1995). Indeed, corporate America often appears as eager as any Mafia Family to engage in restraint of trade/price fixing.

Organized crime has provided economic opportunity for certain groups, allowing them to move into legitimate society on a level that would otherwise not be readily available. There are, of course, ethical and moral objections to "blasting" or "thieving" into the middle or upper strata, even though this has been a feature of U.S. history from the earliest days. Very few management-level members of organized crime have been able to escape either assassination or significant prison terms. Indeed, law enforcement efforts against organized crime are impressive, constrained as they are by the requirements of a democratic system that provides a great deal of legal protection to even its criminal citizens. With this in mind, we should proceed with a great deal of caution when contemplating changes in policy with respect to organized crime.

Organized crime evolved out of moralistic laws that created opportunity for certain innovative actors. As circumstances changed, so did available opportunity, and organized crime exhibited great flexibility. Beginning as essentially a provider of "goods and services," it entered racketeering and legitimate business, adapting to changing laws and social and economic conditions. Policy for responding to organized crime must be based on an appreciation of history, an understanding of the side effects of proposed policy changes, and the realization that organized crime has proven to be a dynamic phenomenon.

In the future we can expect that in the Darwinian world of organized crime, weaker components will die either literally or figuratively, while the survivors will improve on their style of

Restraint of Trade

In 2004, the Bayer Corporation pled guilty and agreed to pay $33 million for taking part in a criminal conspiracy to fix the price of certain chemicals essential for consumer products such as grocery bags (Associated Press 2004b).

organization and the sophistication of their operations. Impacting on this process will be government, helping to "trim the herd" while occasionally dealing shattering blows to organized criminals and their organizations. We can expect that *Cosa Nostra* will continue indefinitely, at times limping along, while others, such as Russian organized crime, will become more structured—and more threatening. Organized crime differs in many significant ways from the nonorganized variety. Organization permits a scope of activities unavailable to conventional criminals, while providing a vehicle for criminal interaction and coordination on a regional, national, and international level. For these reasons, organized crime, like threatening diseases, will always be part of the global community, requiring vigilance and international cooperation to limit its destructive potential.

REFERENCES

Abadinsky, Howard
  2008 *Drug Abuse: An Introduction*, 5th ed. Belmont, CA: Wadsworth.
  1987 "The McDonald's-ization of the Mafia." Pages 43–54 in *Organized Crime in America Concepts and Controversies*, edited by Timothy S. Bynum. Monsey, NY: Criminal Justice Press.
  1983 *The Criminal Elite: Professional and Organized Crime.* Westport, CT: Greenwood.
  1981a *The Mafia in America: An Oral History.* New York: Praeger.
  1981b *Organized Crime.* Boston: Allyn and Bacon.
"Abortion Harassers as Racketeers"
  1998 *New York Times* (April 23): 20.
Abrahamson, Mark
  1996 *Urban Enclaves: Identity and Place in America.* New York: St. Martin's Press.
Ackerman, Kenneth D.
  1988 *The Gold Ring: Jim Fisk, Jay Gould, and Black Friday, 1869.* New York: Harper & Row.
Agence France-Press
  1997 "Japan Fears Reprisals After Mob Boss Is Slain." *New York Times* (August 29): 5.
Ahmed-Ullah, Noreen S.
  2001 "Pashtun Identity Defies Colonial Line." *Chicago Tribune* (November 6): 15.
Aichhorn, August
  1963 *Wayward Youth.* New York: Viking Press.
Albini, Joseph L.
  1971 *The American Mafia: Genesis of a Legend.* New York: Appleton-Century-Crofts.
Albini, Joseph L., R. E. Rogers, Victor Shabalin, Valery Kutushev, and Vladmir Moiseev
  1995 "Russian Organized Crime: Its History, Structure and Function." *Journal of Contemporary Criminal Justice* 11 (December): 213–43.
Alexander, Herbert E. and Gerald E. Caiden
  1985 *The Politics and Economics of Organized Crime.* Lexington, MA: D. C. Heath.
Alexander, Shana
  1988 *The Pizza Connection: Lawyers, Money, Drugs, Mafia.* New York: Weidenfeld and Nicolson.
Ali, Lorraine
  2002 "The Tunes You Can't Refuse." *Newsweek* (August 26): 54–55.
Allen, Frederick
  1998 "American Spirit." *American Heritage* (May/June): 82–92.
Allsop, Kenneth
  1968 *The Bootleggers: The Story of Prohibition.* New Rochelle, NY: Arlington House.
Allum, P. A.
  1973 *Politics and Society in Post-War Naples.* Cambridge: Cambridge University Press.

American Heritage Dictionary, 4th ed.
  2000 Boston: Houghton Mifflin.
Anastasia, George
  2002 "Big Brother and the Bookie." *Mother Jones* (January/February): 63–67.
  1998 *The Goodfella Tapes.* New York: Avon.
  1991 *Blood and Honor: Inside the Scarfo Mob—The Mafia's Most Violent Family.* New York: William Morrow.
Anbinder, Tyler
  2001 *Five Points: The 19th-Century Neighborhood That Invented Tap Dance, Stole Elections, and Became the World's Most Notorious Slum.* New York: Free Press.
  1992 *Nativism and Slavery: The Northern Know-Nothings and the Politics of the 1850s.* New York: Oxford University Press.
Anderson, Annelise Graebner
  1979 *The Business of Organized Crime: A Cosa Nostra Family.* Stanford, CA: Hoover Institution Press.
Anderson, John Lee
  2007 "The Taliban's Opium War." *New Yorker* (July 9 and 16): 60–71.
Anderson, Robert T.
  1965 "From Mafia to Cosa Nostra." *American Journal of Sociology* 71 (November): 302–10.
Andrews, Edmund L.
  1995 "The Mob's Truly Sorry: Killing Upsets the Police." *New York Times* (September 6): 4.
Andrews, Wayne
  1941 *The Vanderbilt Legend.* New York: Harcourt, Brace.
"Anti-Drug Efforts Encounter Resistance in Colombia"
  1995 *New York Times* (December 12): 4.
Arax, Mark and Tom Gorman
  1995 "The State's Illicit Farm Belt Export." *Los Angeles Times* (March 13): 1, 16, 17.
Archibald, Randal C. and Andrew Becker
  2008 "Border Agents Lured by the Other Side." *New York Times* (May 27): 1, 18.
Archibold, Randal C.
  2007 "Along the Border, Smugglers Build a World Below Ground." *New York Times* (December 7): 18.
  2006 "Officials Find Surprise Tunnel with Surprising Amenities." *New York Times* (January 27): 14.
  2004 "Writing a Field Guide to Dominican New York." *New York Times* (December 28): B2.
Argentine, Adolfo Beria di
  1993 "The Mafias in Italy." Pages 19–30 in *Mafia Issues*, edited by Ernesto U. Savona. Milan, Italy: United Nations.
Arie, Sophie
  2004 "Neapolitans Take Stand Against Mafia Turf War." *Christian Science Monitor* (December 22): 7.
Arlacchi, Pino
  1993 *Men of Dishonor: Inside the Sicilian Mafia.* New York: William Morrow.

1986   *Mafia Business: The Mafia Ethic and the Spirit of Capitalism*. London: Verso.

Aronson, Harvey
1978   *Deal*. New York: Ballantine Books.
1973   *The Killing of Joey Gallo*. New York: Putnam's.

Asbury, Herbert
1950   *The Great Illusion: An Informal History of Prohibition*. Garden City, NY: Doubleday.
1942   *Gem of the Prairie: An Informal History of the Chicago Underworld*. Garden City, NY: Knopf.
1928   *Gangs of New York*. New York: Knopf.

Associated Press
2008a   "Afghan Tribal Leader Convicted on NY Drug Charges." *USA Today* (September 23): Internet.
2008b   "Miami Jury Convicts Ex-FBI Agent in 1982 Killing." *USA Today* (November 7): Internet.
2007   "Feds Seize Candy Bars Filled with 5M in Heroin." *New York Daily News* (February 24): 10.
2006   "Gift Cards Are Increasingly Used to Launder Money, Report Says." *New York Times* (January 12): 19.
2005a   "Dutch Police Arrest 45 Hell's Angels." *Seattle Post Intelligencer* (October 12): Internet.
2005b   "8 From Marsh Are Indicted in Bidding Case." *New York Times* (September 16): C5.
2005c   "Imprisoned F.B.I. Agent Indicted in Killing of Gambling Executive." *New York Times* (May 5): 32.
2005d   "Texas Killings Bring New Fear in Drug War." *New York Times* (February 21): 15.
2004a   "'Amphetamine King' Gets 50-Year Sentence." *USA Today* (September 22): Internet.
2004b   "Bayer Unit Plea-Bargains in Price Fixing." *New York Times* (October 1): C1.
1998a   "Italy Arrests Scores of Mafia Suspects." *New York Times* (June 27): 4.
1998b   "12 Convicted in Prison Plot to Control Drug Gangs." *New York Times* (May 31): 8.
1997   "'Wino Willie' Forkner; Inspired 'The Wild One.'" *Chicago Tribune* (June 26): Sec. 2: 10.
1996   "Hell's Angels Center Explodes in Denmark." *New York Times* (October 7): 4.

Attorney General's Commission on Pornography
1986   *Final Report*. Washington, DC: U.S. Government Printing Office.

Audett, James Henry
1954   *Rap Sheet: My Life Story*. New York: William Sloane.

Bailey, Pearce
1974   "The Heroin Habit." Pages 171–76 in *Yesterday's Addicts: American Society and Drug Abuse, 1865–1920*, edited by Howard Wayne Morgan. Norman: University of Oklahoma Press.

Baker, Russell
1996   "Taking the Saps." *New York Times* (June 15): 11.

"Bank Officer Is Convicted of Laundering"
1994   *Chicago Tribune* (June 3): 10.

Barboza, David
1999   "$1.1 Billion to Settle Suit on Vitamins." *New York Times* (November 4): C1.

Barboza, Joe and Hank Messick
1976   *Barboza*. New York: Dell.

Barger, Ralph "Sonny" with Keith and Kent Zimmerman
2000   *Hell's Angels*. New York: William Morrow.

Barger, Sonny
2004   "Foreword" to *Hells Angels Motorcycle Club*. Photographs by Andrew Shaylor. London: Marrell.

Barker, Tom
2005   "One Percent Bikers Clubs: A Description." *Trends in Organized Crime* 9 (Fall): 101–112.

Barnes, Leroy and Tom Folsom
2007   *Mr. Untouchable: The Rise, Fall, and Resurrection of Heroin's Teflon Don*. New York: Rugged Land.

Barzini, Luigi
1977   "Italians in New York: The Way We Were in 1929." *New York* (April 4): 34–38.
1972   *The Italians*. (Paperback ed.) New York: Bantam.
1965   *The Italians*. New York: Atheneum.

Basler, Barbara
1988   "Hong Kong Gangs Wield Vast Power." *New York Times* (December 12): 4.

Bearak, Barry
2001   "At Heroin's Source, Taliban Do What 'Just Say No' Could Not." *New York Times* (May 24): 1, 12.

Beck, Jerome and Marsha Rosenbaum
1994   *Pursuit of Ecstasy: The MDMA Experience*. Albany, NY: State University of New York Press.

Becker, Andrew
2008   "Border Inspector Is Accused in Big Cocaine Case." *New York Times* (November 10): 17.

Becker, Maki and Thomas Zambito
2004   "Corral Coke Kingpin." *New York Daily News* (December 5): 6.

Beeching, Jack
1975   *The Chinese Opium Wars*. New York: Harcourt Brace Jovanovich.

Beers, Rand and Francis X. Taylor
2002   "The Worldwide Connection Between Drugs and Terror." Testimony Before Senate Committee on the Judiciary Subcommittee on Technology, Terrorism and Government Information, March 13: Internet.

Behan, Tom
1996   *The Camorra*. London: Routledge.

Behar, Richard
1996   "How Bill Ruchelshaus Is Taking on the New York Mob." *Fortune* (January 15): 91–100.

Bell, Daniel
1964   *The End of Ideology*. Glencoe, IL: Free Press.
1963   "The Myth of the Cosa Nostra." *The New Leader* 46 (December): 12–15.

Bell, Ernest A., ed.
1909   *War on the White Slave Trade*. Chicago: Thompson.

Belluck, Pam
1998   "44 Officers Are Charged After Ohio Sting Operation." *New York Times* (January 22): 14.

Belsamo, William and George Carpozi
1995   *Under the Clock: The Mafia's First Hundred Years*. Far Hills, NJ: New Horizon Press.

Belson, Kem
2004   "The Call Is Cheap—The Wiretap Is Extra." *New York Times* (August 23): C1, 3.

Bendavid, Naftali
1999   "Vitamin Price-Fixing Draws a Record $755 Million in Fines." *Chicago Tribune* (May 21): 3.

Bennett, David H.
1988 *The Party of Fear: From Nativist Movements to the New Right in American History*. Chapel Hill: University of North Carolina Press.

Bequai, August
1979 *Organized Crime: The Fifth Estate*. Lexington, MA: D. C. Heath.

Berger, Meyer
1957 "Anastasia Slain in a Hotel Here: Led Murder, Inc." *New York Times* (October 26): 1, 12.
1944 "Lepke's Reign of Crime Lasted Over 12 Murder-Strewn Years." *New York Times* (September 21): 1, 20.
1940 "Gang Patterns: 1940." *New York Times Magazine* (August 4): 5, 15.
1935 "Schultz Reigned on Discreet Lines." *New York Times* (October 25): 17.

Bergreen, Laurence
1994 *Capone: The Man and His Era*. New York: Simon and Schuster.

Berke, Richard L.
1989 "U.S. Attack on Airborne Drug Smuggling Called Ineffective." *New York Times* (June 9): 10.

Berkeley, Bill
2002a "Code of Betrayal, Not Silence, Shines Light on Russian Mob." *New York Times* (August 19): 1, 14.
2002b "A Glimpse into a Recess of International Finance." *New York Times* (November 12): C1, 14.

Betts, Kate
2004 "The Purse-Party Blues." *Time* (August 2): 68–70.

Bey, Lee
1995 "Police Don't Buy Hoover's Reform." *Chicago Sun-Times* (September 1): 23.

Biegel, Herbert and Allan Biegel
1977 *Beneath the Badge: A Story of Police Corruption*. New York: Harper & Row.

"Biker Club House Blasted in Norway"
1997 *New York Times* (June 5): 5.

Bilefsky, Dan
2008 "In Feuds, Isolation Engulfs Families." *New York Times* (July 10): 6, 8.

Bishop, Jim
1971 *The Days of Martin Luther King, Jr*. New York: Putnam's.

Black, Donald W. with C. Lindon Larson
1999 *Confronting Antisocial Personality Disorder*. New York: Oxford University Press.

Blakey, G. Robert
1986 "RICO's Triple Damage Threat: The Public's Secret Weapon vs. Boesky." *New York Times* (December 7): F3.

Blakey, G. Robert, Ronald Goldstock, and Charles H. Rogovin
1978 *Rackets Bureau: Investigation and Prosecution of Organized Crime*. Washington, DC: U.S. Government Printing Office.

Blau, Peter M.
1964 *Exchange and Power in Social Life*. New York: Wiley.

Bloch, Max with Ron Kenner
1982 *Max the Butcher*. Secaucas, NJ: Lyle Stuart.

Block, Alan A.
1979 *East Side–West Side: Organizing Crime in New York, 1930–1950*. Swansea, Wales: Christopher Davis.

Block, Alan A. and Frank R. Scarpitti
1985 *Poisoning for Profit: The Mafia and Toxic Waste*. New York: William Morrow.

Blok, Anton
1974 *The Mafia of a Sicilian Village, 1860–1960: A Study of Violent Peasant Entrepreneurs*. New York: Harper & Row.

Blount, William E. and H. Roy Kaplan
1989 "The Impact of the Daily Lottery on the Numbers Game: Does Legalization Make a Difference?" Paper presented at the Annual Meeting of the Academy of Criminal Justice Sciences, March 29, Washington, DC.

Blum, Howard
1993 *Gangland: How the FBI Broke the Mob*. New York: Pocket Books.

Blum Jack A.
1999 "Offshore Money." Pages 57–84 in *Transnational Crime in the Americas*, edited by Tom Farer. New York: Routledge.

Blumenthal, Ralph
1992 "When the Mob Delivered the Goods." *New York Times Magazine* (July 26): 22–23, 31–34.
1988 *Last Days of the Sicilians: At War with the Mafia; the FBI Assault on the Pizza Connection*. New York: Times Books.

Bohlen, Celestine
1999 "To Sicilians, Russia Has No Mafia. It's Too Wild." *New York Times* (January 19): WK 5.
1998 "Russian Lawmaker's Killing Stirs Anger." *New York Times* (November 22): 14.
1997 "Officially, Sicily Is Desperately Short of Jobs, But Sub Rosa, Things Are Rosier." *New York Times* (June 17): 6.
1996a "Italian Police Arrest a Top Mafia Boss in Sicily." *New York Times* (May 22): 1, 6.
1996b "Italy's North-South Gap Widens, Posing Problem for Europe Too." *New York Times* (November 15): 1, 8.
1996c "Italy Treats a Mafia Leader's Repentance with Caution." *New York Times* (August 24): 5.
1995a "Killings in Sicily Raise Fears of Mafia Campaign." *New York Times* (March 9): 4.
1995b "As Omerta Crumbles, the Mafia Changes the Rules." *New York Times* (October 11): 3.
1995c "Uffizi Blast 2 Years Ago Laid to Mafia." *New York Times* (August 7): 2.
1995d "Vatican Draws Criticism for Embrace of Andriotti." *New York Times* (December 20): 7.
1994 "Graft and Gangsterism in Russia Blight the Entrepreneurial Spirit." *New York Times* (January 30): 1, 6.
1993 "Russia [sic] Mobsters Grow More Violent and Pervasive." *New York Times* (August 16): 1, 4.

Boissevain, Jeremy
1974 *Friends of Friends: Networks, Manipulators and Coalitions*. Oxford: Basil Blackwell.

"Bomb Kills 1 at Biker Gang Headquarters"
1997 *Chicago Tribune* (June 6): 14.

Bonanno, Bill
1999 *Bound by Honor: A Mafioso's Story*. New York: St. Martin's Press.

Bonanno, Joseph with Segio Lalli
1983   *A Man of Honor: The Autobiography of Joseph Bonanno.* New York: Simon and Schuster.
Bonavolonta, Jules and Brian Duffy
1996   *The Good Guys: How We Turned the FBI 'Round—And Finally Broke the Mob.* New York: Simon and Schuster.
Bonner, Raymond
1999   "Russian Gangsters Exploit Capitalism to Increase Profits." *New York Times* (July 25): 1, 4.
Bonner, Raymond and Christopher Drew
1997   "Cigarette Makers Are Seen as Aiding Rise in Smuggling." *New York Times* (August 25): 1, C12.
Bonner, Raymond and Timothy L. O'Brien
1999   "Activity at Bank Raises Suspicions of Russia Mob Tie." *New York Times* (August 19): 1, 6.
Bonnie, Richard J. and Charles H. Whitebread II
1970   "The Forbidden Fruit and the Tree of Knowledge: An Inquiry into the Legal History of American Marijuana Prohibition." *Virginia Law Review* 56 (October): 971–1203.
Booth, Martin
1990   *The Triads: The Growing Global Threat from the Chinese Criminal Societies.* New York: St. Martin's Press.
Bopp, William J.
1977   *O. W. Wilson and the Search for a Police Profession.* Port Washington, NY: Kennikat Press.
Borger, Julian
2001   "Bodies Pave the Way to Jamaican Polls." *Guardian* (July 12): 6.
Bourgeois, Richard L., Jr., S. P. Hennessey, Jon Moore, and Michael E. Tschupp
2000   "Racketeer Influenced and Corrupt Organizations." *American Criminal Law Review* 37 (Spring): 879–91.
Bourne, Peter
1990   "Our Dubious Crusade in Colombia." *Chicago Tribune* (July 2): 11.
Bowden, Charles
1991   "La Virgen and the Drug Lord." *Phoenix* (March): 96–103.
Bowden, Mark
2001   *Killing Pablo: The Hunt for the World's Greatest Outlaw.* New York: Atlantic Monthly Press.
Boyd, Kier T.
1977   *Gambling Technology.* Washington, DC: U.S. Government Printing Office.
Brant, Charles
2004   *"I Heard You Paint Houses."* Hanover, NH: Steerforth Press.
Brant, Martha
1997a "Liposuctioned to Death." *Newsweek* (July 21): 43.
1997b "Most Wanted Kingpin?" *Newsweek* (March 10): 36.
Brashler, William
1981   "Two Brothers from Taylor Street." *Chicago* (September): 150–56, 194.
1977   *The Don: The Life and Death of Sam Giancana.* New York: Harper & Row.
Brecher, Edward M. and the Editor of *Consumer Reports*
1972   *Licit and Illicit Drugs.* Boston: Little, Brown.

Brenner, Marie
1990   "Prime Time Godfather." *Vanity Fair* (May): 109–15, 176–81.
Bresler, Fenton
1980   *The Chinese Mafia.* New York: Stein and Day.
Briley, Ron
1997   "Hollywood and the Rebel Image in the 1950s." *Social Education* (October): 352–58.
Brill, Steven
1978   *The Teamsters.* New York: Simon and Schuster.
Bristow, Edward J.
1982   *Prostitution and Prejudice: The Jewish Fight Against White Slavery 1870–1939.* New York: Schocken Books.
Broder, Jonathan
1984   "As a Tradeoff, Soviets Let Afghan Heroin Flow." *Chicago Tribune* (September 2): 12.
Brodt, Bonita
1981a "'Royal Family' Are Kings of Killing." *Chicago Tribune* (September 6): 5.
1981b "'Royal Family Boss Gets Death Sentence for Killing." *Chicago Tribune* (September 10): 14.
Brooke, James
1995   "Colombia Marvels at Drug Kingpin: A Chain-Saw Killer, Too?" *New York Times* (June 21): 7.
1993   "In a 'Dirty War,' Former Drug Allies Are Terrorizing Escobar." *New York Times* (March 4): 4.
1992a "How Escobar, a Rare Jailbird, Lined His Nest." *New York Times* (August 5): 1, 2.
1992b "Trafficker Is Still Feared in Colombia." *New York Times* (January 2): 5.
1991a "Cali, the 'Quiet Cocaine Cartel,' Profits Through Accommodation." *New York Times* (July 14): 1, 6.
1991b "Colombia's Rising Export: Fake U.S. Money." *New York Times* (April 21): 4.
1990   "In the Capital of Cocaine, Savagery Is the Habit." *New York Times* (June 7): 4.
Brooks, Thomas R.
1971   *Toil and Trouble: A History of American Labor.* New York: Dell.
Brzezinski, Matthew
2004   "Hillbangers." *New York Times Magazine* (August 15): 38–43.
2002   "Re-Engineering the Drug Business." *New York Times Magazine* (June 23): 24–46, 54–55.
Buckman, Robert T.
2004   *Latin America.* Harpers Ferry, WV: Sryker-Post Publications.
Buenker, John D.
1973   *Urban Liberalism and Progressive Reform.* New York: Scribner's.
"Bugs Moran Dies in Federal Prison"
1957   *New York Times* (February 26): 59.
Bullough, Vern L.
1965   *The History of Prohibition.* New Hyde Park, NY: University Books.
Burnett, Stanton H. and Luca Mantovani
1998   *The Italian Guillotine.* Lanham, MA: Rowman and Littlefield.
Burnstein, Scott M.
2006   *Motor City Mafia: A Century of Organized Crime in Detroit.* Charleston, SC: Arcadia Publishing.

Buse, Renee
1965 *The Deadly Silence*. Garden City, NY: Doubleday.

Bussey, Jane
2008 "Drug Lords Rose to Power When Mexicans Ousted Old Government." *Kansas City Star* (September 17): Internet.

Butterfield, Fox
2003 "Committee Details F.B.I.'s Reliance on Killers." *New York Times* (November 21): 22.

"By Order of the Mafia"
1888 *New York Times* (October 22): 8.

California Department of Justice
2007 "Organized Crime in California." *Trends in Organized Crime* 10 (September): Internet.

Campane, Jerome O.
1981a "Chains, Wheels, and the Single Conspiracy: Part 1." *FBI Law Enforcement Bulletin* (August): 24–31.
1981b "Chains, Wheels, and the Single Conspiracy: Conclusion." *FBI Law Enforcement Bulletin* (September): 24–31.

Campbell, Rodney
1977 *The Luciano Project*. New York: McGraw-Hill.

Campo-Flores, Arian
2005 "The Most Violent Gang in America." *Newsweek* (March 28): 22–25.

Cantalupo, Joseph and Thomas C. Renner
1990 *Body Mike*. New York: Saint Martin's Press.

Capé, Kevin
2005 "Where Organized Crime Still Thrives." *The* [Eugene, OR] *Register-Guard* (November 23): Internet.

Capeci, Jerry
2003 *Gangland*. New York: Alpha.

Capeci, Jerry and Gene Mustain
1996 *Gotti: Rise and Fall*. New York: Onyx.

"Capone Dead at 48; Dry Era Gang Chief."
1947 *New York Times* (January 26): 7.

Caputo, David A.
1976 *Organized Crime and American Politics*. Morristown, NJ: General Learning Press.

Cardwell, Diane
2001 "Fugitive Gang Enforcer Arrested in Push-In Robberies." *New York Times* (March 2): Internet.

Carlo, Philip
2008 *Gaspipe: Confessions of a Mafia Boss*. New York: William Morrow.

Carlson, Kenneth and Peter Finn
1993 *Prosecuting Criminal Enterprises*. Washington, DC: Bureau of Justice Statistics.

Carr, Howie
2006 *The Brothers Bulger: How They Terrorized and Corrupted Boston for a Quarter Century*. New York: Warner Books.

Carroll, Brian
1991 "Combating Racketeering in the Fulton Fish Market." Pages 183–98 in *Organized Crime and Its Containment: A Transatlantic Initiative*, edited by Cyrelle Fijnaut and James Jacobs. Deventer, Netherlands: Kluwer.

Carroll, Rory
2007 "Villagers Seek High Life." *Globe and Mail* (October 9): 2.

"Cartel Leader Captured"
2005 *New York Times* (November 22): 14.

Carter, David L.
2005 "Brief History of Law Enforcement Intelligence: Past Practice and Recommendations for Change." *Trends in Organized Crime* 8 (Spring): 51–62.

Casey, James
2007 "Dealing with Hawala: Informal Financial Centers in the Ethnic Community." *FBI Bulletin* (February) 10–14.

Cashman, Sean Dennis
1981 *Prohibition*. New York: Free Press.

Catanzaro, Raimondo
1992 *Men of Respect: A Social History of the Sicilian Mafia*. New York: Free Press. Translated by Raymond Rosenthal.

Ceccarelli, Alessandra
2007 "Clans, Politics and Organized Crime in Central Asia." *Trends in Organized Crime* 10: 19–36.

Center for Strategic and International Studies (CSIS)
1997 *CSIS Task Force Report: Russian Organized Crime*. Internet.

Chafetz, Henry
1960 *Play the Devil: A History of Gambling in the United States from 1492 to 1955*. New York: Clarkson Potter.

Chaiken, David A.
1991 "Money Laundering: An Investigatory Perspective." *Criminal Law Forum* 2 (Spring): 467–510.

Chalidze, Vallery
1977 *Criminal Russia: Crime in the Soviet Union*. New York: Random House.

Chambliss, William
1975 "On the Paucity of Original Research on Organized Crime: A Footnote to Galliher and Cain." *American Sociologist* 10 (August): 36–39.
1973 *Functional and Conflict Theories of Crime*. New York: MSS Modular Publications.

Chapman, Stephen
1991 "Prohibition—From Alcohol to Drugs—Is a Costly Failure." *Chicago Tribune* (September 1): Sec. 4: 3.

Cheloukhine, Serguei
2008 "The Roots of Russian Organized Crime: From Old-Fashioned Professionals to the Organized Criminal Groups of Today." *Crime, Law and Social Change* 50 (June): 353–374.

Chemerinsky, Erwin
2000 "Plaintiff's Use of Rico Limited." *Trial* 36: 123–125.

Chepesiuk, Ron
2007 *Gangsters of Harlem*. Fort Lee, NJ: Barricade Books.
2003 *The Bullet or Bribe: Taking Down Colombia's Cali Drug Cartel*. Westport, CT: Praeger.

Chepesiuk, Ron and Anthony Gonzalez
2007 *Superfly: The True-Untold Story of Frank Lucas*. New York: Street Certified Entertainment.

Cherry, Paul
2005 *The Biker Trials: Bringing Down the Hells Angels*. Toronto, Canada: ECW Press.

Chin, Ko-lin
1990   *Chinese Subculture and Criminality: Non-Traditional Crime Groups in America.* Westport, CT: Greenwood.

Chin, Ko-lin, Robert J. Kelly, and Jeffrey Fagan
1994   "Chinese Organized Crime in America." Pages 213–43 in *Handbook of Organized Crime in the United States*, edited by Robert J. Kelly, Ko-lin Chin, and Rufus Schatzberg. Westport, CT: Greenwood.

Chin, Ko-lin, Sheldon Zhang, and Robert J. Kelly
1998   "Transnational Chinese Organized Crime Activities: Patterns and Emerging Trends." *Transnational Organized Crime* 4 (Autumn/Winter): 127–154.

"Chinatown's New Enforcer"
1995   *New Yorker* (April 3): 36.

Chivers, C. J.
2008a   "Medvedev Takes Oath in Russia, but Putin Dominates Much of the Day." *New York Times* (May 8): 16.
2008b   "U.S. Position Complicates Global Effort to Curb Illicit Arms." *New York Times* (July 19): 5.

Chrisafis, Angelique
2005   "Spotlight Turns to Slick IRA Money-Making Machine." *Guardian* (February 19): Internet.

Christian, Nichole M.
2001   "Officials Say Stock Scheme Raised Money for the Mob." *New York Times* (March 9): 19.

Christian, Shirley
1992   "Why Indulge Drug Lord? Colombia Pressed to Tell." *New York Times* (July 29): 3.

Chu, Yiu Kong
2005   "Hong Kong Triads After 1997." *Trends in Organized Crime* 8 (Spring): 1–12.

Chubb, Judith
1982   *Patronage, Power, and Poverty in Southern Italy.* Cambridge: Cambridge University Press.

Cilluffo, Frank
2000   "The Threat Posed from the Convergence of Organized Crime, Drug Trafficking, and Terrorism." Testimony before the U.S. House Committee on the Judiciary Subcommittee on Crime, December 13. Internet.

Cilluffo, Frank J. and George Salmoiraghi
1999   "And the Winner Is . . . the Albanian Mafia." *The Washington Quarterly*, 22 (Autumn): 21–25.

Cimino, Tonia N.
2005   "Illegal Gambling Ring Busted." *Queens Courier* (May 25): 12.

Clarke, Donald Henderson
1929   *In the Reign of Rothstein.* New York: Grosset and Dunlap.

Clinard, Marshall B., Peter C. Yeager, Jeanne Brissette, David Petrashek, and Elizabeth Harries
1979   *Illegal Corporate Behavior.* Washington, DC: Government Printing Office.

Cloninger, Susan C.
2004   *Theories of Personality: Understanding Persons*, 4th ed. Upper Saddle River, NJ: Prentice-Hall.

Cloward, Richard A. and Lloyd E. Ohlin
1960   *Delinquency and Opportunity.* New York: Free Press.

Cloyd, Jerald W.
1982   *Drugs and Information Control: The Role of Men and Manipulation in the Control of Drug Trafficking.* Westport, CT: Greenwood.

"Cocaine Cartel Leader to Face Charges in the United States"
2008   U.S. Department of Justice press release (August 22): Internet.

Coffey, Joseph and Jerry Schmetterer
1991   *The Coffey Files: One Cop's War Against the Mob.* New York: St. Martin's Press.

Coffey, Thomas A.
1975   *The Long Thirst: Prohibition in America: 1920–1933.* New York: Norton.

Cohen, Mickey
1975   *Mickey Cohen: In My Own Words.* Englewood Cliffs, NJ: Prentice-Hall.

Cohen, Stanley
1977   *The Game They Played.* New York: Farrar, Straus and Giroux.

Colbridge, Thomas D.
2000   "Electronic Surveillance: A Matter of Necessity." *FBI Law Enforcement Bulletin* (February): 25–32.

Collins, Randall
1975   *Conflict Sociology.* New York: Academic Press.

"Colombian Heroin May Be Increasing"
1991   *New York Times* (October 27): 10.

Colombia's New Armed Groups
2007   Bogotá, Colombia: International Crisis Group.

Combs, Cindy C.
2003   *Terrorism in the Twenty-First Century*, 3rd ed. Saddle River, NJ: Prentice-Hall.

Commission on the Review of the National Policy Toward Gambling
1976   *Gambling in America.* Washington, DC: U.S. Government Printing Office.

Committee on the Office of Attorney General
1978   *Witness Immunity.* Raleigh, NC: National Association of Attorneys General (NAAG).
1974   *Prosecuting Organized Crime.* Raleigh, NC: NAAG.

Comptroller General
1989   *Nontraditional Organized Crime: Law Enforcement Officials' Perspectives on Five Criminal Groups.* Washington, DC: U.S. Government Printing Office.

Connable, Alfred and Edward Silberfarb
1967   *Tigers of Tammany: Nine Men Who Ruled New York.* New York: Holt, Rinehart and Winston.

Connolly, John
1996   "Who Handled Who?" *New York* (December 2): 46–49.

Constantine, Thomas A.
1999a   "Statement Before the Subcommittee on Criminal Justice, Drug Policy and Human Resources." March 4.
1999b   "Statement Before the U.S. Senate Drug Caucus." February 24.

"Contractor Admits Double Life"
1996   *New York Times* (May 2): 13.

Cook, Fred J.
1973   *Mafia!* New York: Fawcett.
1972   "Purge of the Greasers." Pages 89–109 in *Mafia, U.S.A.*, edited by Nicholas Gage. New York: Dell.

Cooley, Robert with Hillel Levin
2004 *When Corruption Was King*. New York: Carroll and Graf Publishers.

Corbitt, Michael with Sam Giancana
2003 *Double Deal*. New York: William Morrow.

Costanzo, Ezio
2007 *The Mafia and the Allies: Sicily 1943 and the Return of the Mafia*. New York: Enigma Books.

Courtwright, David T.
1982 *Dark Paradise: Opiate Addiction in America Before 1940*. Cambridge, MA: Harvard University Press.

Cowan, Rick and Douglas Century
2002 *Takedown: The Fall of the Last Mafia Empire*. New York: Putnam.

Cowell, Alan
1994 "Gunmen Linked to the Mafia Kill a Priest in Italy." *New York Times* (March 20): 3.
1993 "Busting the Mafia: Italy Advances in War on Crime." *New York Times* (June 27): 3.
1992a "Inquiry into Sicilian Slaying Looks for Mafia Link to Colombia Drug Cartel." *New York Times* (June 21): 3.
1992b "Italians Defying Shakedowns Pays with Lives." *New York Times* (November 12): 5.
1992c "Italy Arrests 75 in Mafia Roundup." *New York Times* (November 18): 3.
1992d "Mafia Throws the Gauntlet in Italy's Face." *New York Times* (July 21): 5.
1992e "Sicilian Symbolizes Mob's Survival." *New York Times* (August 2): 8.
1992f "A Top Sicilian Politician Is Slain; Pre-Election Mafia Warning Seen." *New York Times* (March 12): 2.

Crack Cocaine
1994 Washington, DC: Drug Enforcement Administration.

Cragin, Kim and Bruce Hoffman
2003 *Arms Trafficking in Colombia*. Santa Monica, CA: RAND.

Cressey, Donald R.
1972 *Criminal Organization: Its Elementary Forms*. New York: Harper & Row.
1969 *Theft of the Nation*. New York: Harper & Row.

Criminal Intelligence Service Canada (CISC)
2004 *Annual Report on Organized Crime in Canada*. Ottawa: CISC.

Crisanti, Layla
2008 "A Battle Against the Mob." *Tandem* [Canada] (June 15–June 22): Internet.

Crouse, Russel
1947 "The Murder of Arnold Rothstein: 1928." Pages 184–200 in *Sins of New York*, edited by Milton Crane. New York: Grosset and Dunlap.

Curtis, Glenn E., John N. Gibbs, and Ramón Miró
2004 "Nations Hospitable to Organized Crime and Terrorism." *Transnational Organized Crime* 8 (Fall): 5–23.

Curtis, Glenn E. and Tara Karacan
2002 *The Nexus Among Terrorists, Narcotics Traffickers, Weapons Proliferators, and Organised Crime Networks in Western Europe*. Washington, DC: Library of Congress.

Daley, Dave
2000 "Biker Is Convicted of '93 Killings of Richmond Couple." *Chicago Tribune* (June 16): Sec. 2: 3.

Daley, Robert A.
1978 *Prince of the City*. Boston: Houghton Mifflin.

Dannen, Federic
1996 "The G-Man and the Hit Man." *New Yorker* (December 16): 68–81.
1995 "Hong Kong Babylon." *New Yorker* (August 7): 30–38.
1992a "The Untouchable? How the FBI Sabotaged Competing Prosecution Teams in the Race to Nail Alleged Mob King John Gotti." *Vanity Fair* (January): 27–44.
1992b "Revenge of the Green Dragons." *New Yorker* (November): 76–99.

Danner, Mark
2005 "Taking Stock of the Forever War." *New York Times Magazine* (September 11): 45–68, 86–87.

David, John J.
1988 "Outlaw Motorcycle Gangs: A Transnational Problem." Paper presented at the Conference on International Terrorism and Transnational Crime, Chicago, August.

Davis, Ian, Chrissie Hirst, and Bernardo Mariani
2001 *Organised Crime, Corruption and Illicit Arms Trafficking in an Enlarged EU*. London, UK: Saferworld.

Davis, John H.
1993 *Mafia Dynasty: The Rise and Fall of the Gambino Crime Family*. New York: HarperCollins.

DEA. See Drug Enforcement Administration

Decker, Scott, Tim Bynum, and Deborah Weisel
1998 "A Tale of Two Cities: Gangs as Organized Crime Groups." *Justice Quarterly* 15 (September): 395–425.

De Franco, Edward J.
1973 *Anatomy of a Scam: A Case Study of a Planned Bankruptcy by Organized Crime*. Washington, DC: U.S. Government Printing Office.

Defus, R. L.
1928 "The Gunman Has an Intercity Murder Trade." *New York Times* (July): XX 3.

de Gennaro, G.
1995 The Influences of Mafia Type Organizations on Government, Business and Industry." *Trends in Organized Crime* 1 (Winter): 36–42.

Deitche, Scott M.
2004 *Cigar City Mafia: A Complete History of the Tampa Underworld*. Fort Lee, NJ: Barricade Books.

de la Garza, Paul
2000 "Mexico Striking Back at Top Drug Cartel." *Chicago Tribune* (June 1): 4.
1998 "With Drug War, Anarchy Reigns in Mexican City." *Chicago Tribune* (October 31): 4.
1997a "The Scent of Scandal Has Church Scrambling." *Chicago Tribune* (October 6): 8.
1997b "In Tijuana, War on Drugs Is Lost." *Chicago Tribune* (March 31): 1, 13.

de Lama, George
1988 "Besieged Colombia Becoming the Lebanon of Latin America." *Chicago Tribune* (November 20): 5.

Delaney, William P.
1977 "On Capturing an Opium King: The Politics of Law Sik Han's Arrest." Pages 67–88 in *Drugs and Politics*, edited by Paul E. Rock. New Brunswick, NJ: Transaction Books.

della Porta, Donatella and Alberto Vannucci
1999 *Corrupt Exchanges: Actors, Resources, and Mechanisms of Political Corruption*. New York: Walter de Gruyter.

Dellios, Hugh
1998 "Once Just a Supplier, Nigeria Develops Heroin Woes." *Chicago Tribune* (July 29): 4.

Demaris, Ovid
1981 *The Last Mafioso: The Treacherous World of Jimmy Fratianno*. New York: Bantam.
1969 *Captive City: Chicago in Chains*. New York: Lyle Stuart.

DeStefano, Anthony M,
2006 *King of the Godfathers: "Big Joey" Massino and the Fall of the Bonanno Crime Family*. New York: Pinnacle Books.

de Tocqueville, Alexis
1966 *Democracy in America*. New York: Harper & Row. Translated by George Lawrence.

Diamond, Stuart
1988 "Steep Rise Seen in Private Use of Federal Racketeering Law." *New York Times* (August 1): 1, 15.

Diapoulos, Peter and Steven Linakis
1976 *The Sixth Family*. New York: Dutton.

Dickie, John
2004 *Cosa Nostra: A History of the Sicilian Mafia*. New York: Palgrave Macmillan.

Dickson, Donald T.
1977 "Bureaucracy and Morality: An Organizational Perspective on a Moral Crusade." Pages 31–52 in *Drugs and Politics*, edited by Paul E. Rock. New Brunswick, NJ: Transaction Books.

Diener, Kathy and Teisha C. Johnson
2005 "Federal Criminal Conspiracy." *American Criminal Law Review* (Spring): 463–99.

Dillon, Sam
1999a "Mexico's Troubadours Turn From Amor to Drugs." *New York Times* (February 19): 4.
1999b "Ruling Party, at 70, Tries Hard to Cling to Power in Mexico." *New York Times* (March 4): 1, 12.
1998a "Gunmen Kill 3 Families in Mexico Over Drugs." *New York Times* (September 18): 6.
1998b "Mexico Arrests Two Accused of Flooding the U.S. with 'Speed.'" *New York Times* (June 3): 7
1998c "Mexico Drug Trafficker Slain; Major Figure Near U.S. Border." *New York Times* (September 12): 3.
1998d "Mexico Jails 2 Drug Agents and U.S. Sees Graft." *New York Times* (September 25): 12.
1998e "Mexico Says Rivalry Between Gangs Led to Mass Murders." *New York Times* (November 11): 10.
1997 "Mexico Editor Hurt in Ambush; His Bodyguard and Gunman Die." *New York Times* (November 28): 5.
1996a "Bribes and Publicity Mark Fall of Mexican Drug Lord." *New York Times* (May 12): 1, 6.
1996b "Canaries Are Singing, But Uncle Juan Won't." *New York Times* (February 9): 4.
1996c "Mexican Aide's Millions; U.S. Charges Drug Link." *New York Times* (November 12): 5.
1996d "Mexico Arrests a Top Suspect in Drug Trade." *New York Times* (January 16): 1, 2.
1996e "Mexican Drug Gang's Reign of Terror." *New York Times* (February 4): 24.
1996f "Mexicans Tire of Police Graft as Drug Lords Raise Stakes." *New York Times* (March 21): 3.
1996g "Mexican Trafficker Plans to Cooperate in FBI's Inquiries." *New York Times* (January 20): 1, 5.

Dillon, Sam and Craig Pyes
1997a "Court Files Say Drug Baron Used Mexican Military." *New York Times* (May 24): 1, 4.
1997b "Drug Ties Taint 2 Mexican Governors." *New York Times* (February 23): 1, 4.

Dintino, Justin J, and Frederick T. Martens
1983 *Police Intelligence Systems and Crime Control*. Springfield, IL: Charles C. Thomas.
1980 "Organized Crime Control in the Eighties." *Police Chief* (August): 66–70.

District Attorney of New York County and the New York City Police Department
1995 "Press Release, June 22." New York: Photocopied.

Dobyns, Fletcher
1932 *The Underworld of American Politics*. New York: Fletcher Dobyns.

Dorsett, Lyle W.
1968 *The Pendergast Machine*. New York: Oxford University Press.

Douglas, Paul H.
1974 "Introduction." *Bosses in Lusty Chicago*, by Lloyd Wendt and Herman Kogan. Bloomington: Indiana University Press.

Downey, Patrick
2004 *Gangster City: The History of the New York Underworld 1900–1935*. Fort Lee, NJ: Barricade Books.

Dretzka, Gary
2001 "Rolling the Dice on Internet Gambling." *Chicago Tribune* (June 15): Sec. 5: 1, 3.

Drew, Christopher
1998 "RJR Subsidiary Pleads Guilty to Smuggling." *New York Times* (December 23): 1, 25.

Driehaus, Bob
2008 "Some States Set Caps to Control Payday Loans." *New York Times* (September 8): 17.

Droban, Kerrie
2007 *Running with the Devil: The True Story of the ATF's Infiltration of the Hells [sic] Angels*. Guilford, CT: Lyons Press.

Drug Abuse and Drug Abuse Research
1987 Rockville, MD: National Institute on Drug Abuse.

Drug Enforcement Administration (DEA)
1995a *Illegal Drug Price/Purity*. Washington, DC: DEA.
1995b *LSD in the United States*. Washington, DC: DEA.
1991a *Worldwide Cocaine Situation*. Washington, DC: DEA.
1991b *Worldwide Heroin Situation*. Washington, DC: DEA.
1988 *Crack Cocaine Availability and Trafficking in the United States*. Washington, DC: DEA.

"Drugs of Abuse"
1979 *Drug Enforcement* (July), entire issue.

Dryomin, Viktor
2003 "Organised Crime and Corruption in Ukraine as a System Phenomenon." Pages 49–59 in *Organised Crime, Trafficking, Drugs: Selected Papers Presented at the Annual Conference of the European Society of Criminology*, Helsinki, edited by Sami Nevala and Kauko Armomaa.

Dubocq, Tom and Manny Garcia
1997 "'Redfellas': Cops Say Strip Club Was Hangout for Russian Mob." *Miami Herald* (February 8): 1, 6.

Duggan, Christopher
1989 *Fascism and the Mafia*. New Haven, CT: Yale University.

Durk, David and Ira Silverman
1976 *The Pleasant Avenue Connection*. New York: Harper & Row.

Durkheim, Émile
1951 *Suicide*. New York: Free Press.

Duster, Troy
1970 *The Legislation of Morality: Law, Drugs, and Moral Judgment*. New York: Free Press.

Duzán, Maria Jimena
1994 *Death Beat: A Colombian Journalist's Life Inside the Cocaine Wars*. New York: HarperCollins.

Early, Pete and Gerald Shur
2002 *Inside the Federal Witness Protection Program*. New York: Bantam.

Eaton, Leslie
1997 "Russian Émigrés Run Afoul of Stock Regulators." *New York Times* (January 14): C1, 7.

Edberg, Mark C.
2001 "Drug Traffickers as Social Bandits." *Journal of Contemporary Criminal Justice* 17 (August): 259–77.

Eddy, Paul, Hugo Sabogal, and Sara Walden
1988 *The Cocaine Wars*. New York: Norton.

Edelhertz, Herbert and Thomas D. Overcast
n.d. *The Business of Organized Crime*. Loomis, CA: Palmer Press.

"Editorial"
1995 *Chicago Tribune* (January 2): 12.

Edwards, Peter and Michel Auger
2004 The *Encyclopedia of Canadian Organized Crime*. Toronto: McClelland and Stewart.

Eichenwald, Kurt
2002 "White-Collar Defense Stance: The Criminal-less Crime." *New York Times* (March 3): WK 3.

Elliott, Delbert S., David Huizinga, and Suzanne S. Ageton
1985 *Explaining Delinquency and Drug Use*. Beverly Hills, CA: Sage.

Elliott, Dorinda
1992 "Russia's Goodfellas: The Mafia on the Neva." *Newsweek* (October 12): 50, 52.

Engelmann, Larry
1979 *Intemperance: The Lost War Against Liquor*. New York: Free Press.

English, T. J.
2005 *Paddy Whacked: The Untold Story of the Irish American Gangster*. New York: HarperCollins.
1995a *Born to Kill*. New York: William Morrow.
1995b "Where Crime Rules." *New York Times* (June 26): 11.
1990 *The Westies: Inside the Hell's Kitchen Irish Mob*. New York: Putnam's.

Epstein, Edward Jay
1988a "The Dope Business." *Manhattan, Inc.* (July): 25–27.
1988b "Marrying the Mob to Wall Street." *Manhattan, Inc.* (October): 43–47.
1977 *Agency of Fear: Opiates and Political Power in America*. New York: Putnam's.

Epstein, Leon D.
1986 *Political Parties in the American Mold*. Madison: University of Wisconsin Press.

Erie, Steven P.
1988 *Rainbow's End: Irish-Americans and the Dilemmas of Urban Machine Politics, 1840–1985*. Berkeley: University of California Press.

Eskridge, Chris
1998 "The Mexican Cartels: A Challenge for the 21st Century." *Criminal Organizations* 12 (1 & 2): 5–15.

Fackler, Martin
2007 "Mayor's Death Forces Japan's Crime Rings Into the Light." *New York Times* (April 21): 3.

Fahim, Kareem
2006 "Albanian Groups Are Muscling Into Mob Land, Officials Say." *New York Times* (January 3): B1, 3.

Faison, Seth
1995a "Charges Against President Threaten Chinatown Tong." *New York Times* (June 1): 16.
1995b "U.S. Indicts 2 Businessmen as Gang Lords in Chinatown." *New York Times* (September 10): 11.
1993 "How Betrayal Snagged a Chinatown Gang Leader." *New York Times* (August 31): 12.

Farrell, Amy, Jack McDevitt, and Stephanie Fahy
2008 "Understanding and Improving Law Enforcement Responses to Human Trafficking." Boston: Northeastern University Institute on Race and Justice.

Farrell, Ronald A. and Carole Case
1995 *The Black Book and the Mob*. Madison: University of Wisconsin Press.

Fay, Peter Ward
1975 *The Opium War: 1840–1842*. Chapel Hill: University of North Carolina Press.

"FBI Says Los Angeles Gang Has Drug Cartel Ties"
1992 *New York Times* (January 10): 8.

Federal Bureau of Investigation
1988 "Debriefing of Gerald H. Scarpelli." Investigative File # CG183B-2272.

Federal Research Division
2002 "Asian Organized Crime and Terrorist Activity in Canada, 1999–2002." *Trends in Organized Crime* 7 (Spring): 3–18.

Feiden, Douglas
2004 "The Fat Cats on the Waterfront." *New York Daily News* (January 4): 6–7.

Feinberg, Alexander
1959 "Genovese Is Given 15 Years in Prison in Narcotics Case." *New York Times* (April 18): 1, 15.
1944 "Lepke Is Put to Death, Denies Guilt to Last; Makes No Revelation." *New York Times* (March 5): 1, 30.

Ferkenhoff, Eric and Heather Vogell
2001 "Cops Seize $2 Million in Goods." *Chicago Tribune* (February 24): 5.

Fernandez, Manny
  2007 "Onetime Mob Stronghold Hears Echo of the Old Days." *New York Times* (June 11): B3.
Feuer, Alan
  2001a "Reporter's Notebook: Violent Testimony in Staccato Language." *New York Times* (May 13): Internet.
  2001b "7 Are Charged in Running Bank That Was Front for Mob Crimes." *New York Times* (November 7): 19.
Feuer, Alan and William K. Rashbaum
  2005 "Blood Ties: 2 Officers' Path to Mob Indictments." *New York Times* (March 12): 1, B4.
Fijnaut, Cyrelle and James Jacobs, eds.
  1991 *Organized Crime and Its Containment: A Transatlantic Initiative.* Deventer, Netherlands: Kluwer.
Financial Action Task Force on Money Laundering (FATF)
  2001 *Report on Money Laundering Typologies, 2000–2001.* Paris: FATF.
Financial Crimes Enforcement Network
  2000 A *Survey of Electronic Banking, and Internet Gambling.* U.S. Department of the Treasury: Internet.
Finckenauer, James O. and Ko-lin Chin
  2007 *Asian Transnational Organized Crime.* Washington, DC: National Institute of Justice.
Finckenauer, James O. and Yuri A. Voronin
  2001 *The Threat of Russian Organized Crime.* Washington, DC: National Institute of Justice.
Finckenauer, James O. and Elin J. Waring
  2001 "Challenging the Russian Mafia Mystique." *NIJ Journal* (April): 2–7.
  1999 *Russian Mafia in America: Immigration, Culture, and Crime.* Boston, MA: Northeastern University Press (advance page proofs).
Finkelstein, Katherine Eban
  1998 "The Brighton Beach Swindle." *New York* (February 2): 39–43, 78.
Finley, M. I., Denis Mack Smith, and Christopher Duggan
  1987 *A History of Sicily.* New York: Viking.
Fiorentini, Gianluca and Sam Peltzman, eds.
  1995 *The Economics of Organized Crime.* Cambridge: Cambridge University Press.
Fisher, Ian
  2007 "Breaking All the Rules, With a Shrug and a Sigh." *New York Times* (February 14): 3.
  2005 "Italian Police Arrest Fugitive Crime Leader in Naples Gang War." *New York Times* (September 17): 5.
  2004 "New Blood on Naples Streets Brings Back Old Fears." *New York Times* (December 13): 3.
Fisher, Ian and Danielle Pinto
  2008 "Italy's Trash Crisis Taints Reputation of Prized Cheese." *New York Times* (March 26): 7.
"Fishy Haul, A"
  2004 *New York Daily News* (September 28): 5.
Flinn, John J.
  1973 *History of the Chicago Police.* New York: AMS Press. Originally published in 1887.
Flynn, Sean
  1998 "Good Guy, Bad Guy." *Boston Magazine* (Internet).
Fogelson, Robert M.
  1977 *Big City Police.* Cambridge, MA: Harvard University Press.

Foglesong, Todd S. and Peter H. Solomon, Jr.
  2001 *Crime, Criminal Justice, and Criminology in Post-Soviet Ukraine.* Washington, DC: National Institute of Justice.
Fong, Mak Lau
  1981 *The Sociology of Secret Societies: A Study of Chinese Secret Societies in Singapore and Peninsular Malaysia.* Oxford, England: Oxford University Press.
Fooner, Michael
  1985 *A Guide to Interpol.* Washington, DC: U.S. Government Printing Office.
Forero, Juan
  2006 "Commanders Recast Old Militias of Colombia as Syndicates for Drugs and Extortion." *New York Times* (March 5): 4.
  2005a "Ammo Seized in Colombia; 2 G.I. Suspects Are Arrested." *New York Times* (May 5): 10.
  2005b "Bolivia's Newly Elected Leader Maps His Socialist Agenda." *New York Times* (December 20): 8.
  2005c "Turbulent Bolivia Is Producing More Cocaine, the U.N. Reports." *New York Times* (June 15): 5.
  2005d "U.S. Voicing Fears of Tampered Elections, Is Rebuked by Colombia." *New York Times* (December 18): 25.
  2004a "Attack by Colombia Rebels Threatens Fragile Talks." *New York Times* (June 17): 3.
  2004b "With Chief Missing, Colombia Militias Gain Leverage." *New York Times* (May 19): 16.
  2004c "Colombia's Landed Gentry: Coca Lords and Other Bullies." *New York Times* (January 21): 4.
  2004d "Paramilitary Chief Tied to Drug Trade Gains Power in Colombia." *New York Times* (April 25): 15.
  2004e "Rightist Militias Are a Force in Colombia's Congress." *New York Times* (November 10): 3.
  2004f "Rightist Militias in Colombia Offer to Disarm 3,000 of Their Fighters." *New York Times* (October 9): 5.
  2002 "Farmers in Peru Are Turning Again to Coca Crop." *New York Times* (February 14): 3.
  2001a "Europe Expands as Market for Colombian Cocaine." *New York Times* (May 29): 1, 9.
  2001b "New Challenge to the Bogotá Leadership." *New York Times* (May 6): 8.
  2001c "No Crops Spared in Colombia's Coca War." *New York Times* (January 31): 1, 8.
  2001d "Ranchers in Colombia Bankroll Their Own Militia." *New York Times* (August 8): 1, 6.
  2001e "Rightist Chief in Colombia Shifts Focus to Politics." *New York Times* (June 7): Internet.
  2001f "Union Says Coca-Cola in Colombia Uses Thugs." *New York Times* (July 26): 6.
  2001g "In the War on Coca, Colombian Growers Simply Move Along." *New York Times* (March 17): 1, 5.
  2001h "Where a Little Coca Is as Good as Gold." *New York Times* (July 8): Sec. 4: 12.
Forte, Elisa
  2008 "Thousands in Italy Rally Against the Mafia." Reuters, Internet.
"$4,000,000 in Narcotics Seized Here Tied to Rothstein Ring."
  1928 *New York Times* (December 19): 1.

Fox, Ben
2001 "Record Cocaine Cache Seized." *Chicago Tribune* (May 15): 9.

Fox, Stephen
1989 *Blood and Power: Organized Crime in the Twentieth Century.* New York: William Morrow.

"Frank Costello Dies of Coronary at 82; Underworld Leader."
1972 *New York Times* (February 19): 1, 21.

Franklin, Jonathan and Samuel Logan
2008 "Birds of Prey." *Men's Vogue* (June/July): 31–34.

Franklin, Stephen
1999 "Laborers' President Cleared by Union." *Chicago Tribune* (March 10): Sec. 3: 1, 3.
1995a "Hotel Workers' Union, U.S. Reach Oversight Accord." *Chicago Tribune* (August 20): Sec. 3: 1, 4.
1995b "Teamsters Aim at Corruption." *Chicago Tribune* (February 10): Sec. 3: 1, 3.
1993 "Teamsters Move on Local." *Chicago Tribune* (June 17): Sec. 2: 1, 2.

Franks, Lucinda
1977 "An Obscure Gangster Is Emerging as the New Mafia Chief in New York." *New York Times* (March 17): 1, 34.

Frantz, Douglas and Chuck Neubauer
1983 "Teamster Pension Fund Just Fine After Surgery." *Chicago Tribune* (May 29): 1, 10.

Frantz, Douglas with Vivian S. Toy
1995 "Portrait of Man as Mobster Stirs Community's Disbelief." *New York Times* (July 11): 1, B15.

Franzese, Michael and Dary Matera
1992 *Quitting the Mob.* New York: Harper Paperbacks.

Freedman, Michael
2005 "The Invisible Bankers." *Forbes* (October 17): 94–104.

Freeman, Ira Henry
1957 "Anastasia Rose in Stormy Ranks." *New York Times* (October 26): 12.

French, Howard W.
2001 "Even in Ginza, Honor Among Thieves Crumbles." *New York Times* (October 10): 4.

Fried, Albert
1980 *The Rise and Fall of the Jewish Gangster in America.* New York: Holt, Rinehart and Winston.

Fried, Joseph P.
2005 "Family of 2 Victims Finds Satisfaction." *New York Times* (February 13): 42.
1995 "Civic Pillar Pleads Guilty in Slaying Plot." *New York Times* (October 31): B15.
1993a "Government Sues to Seize Gotti's Remaining Assets." *New York Times* (January 15): 16.
1993b "Indictment Links the Mafia to Trash-Hauling Industry." *New York Times* (April 20): B16.
1992 "Inside Man for U.S. Oversees Union at Kennedy in War on Airport Rackets." *New York Times* (May 17): 21.

Friedman, Allen and Ted Schwarz
1989 *Power and Greed: Inside the Teamsters Empire of Corruption.* New York: Watts.

Friedman, Robert I.
2000 *Red Mafia: How the Russian Mob Has Invaded America.* Boston: Little, Brown.

1996 "The Money Plane." *New York* (January 22): 25–33.

Friel, Frank and John Gunther
1990 *Breaking the Mob.* New York: Warner Books.

Frisby, Tanya
1998 "The Rise of Organised Crime in Russia: Its Roots and Social Significance." *Europe-Asia Studies* 50 (January): 27–50.

Fuller, Thomas
2007a "Khun Sa, Golden Triangle Drug King, Dies at 73." *New York Times* (November 5): B7.
2007b "No Blowing Smoke: Poppies Fade in Southeast Asia." *New York Times* (November 16): WK 3.

Furchgott, Roy
2008 "With Software, Till Tampering Is Hard to Find." *New York Times* (August 30): C6.

Gage, Nicholas
1975 "Carlo Gambino Dies in His Long Island Home at 75." *New York Times* (October 16): 26.
1974 "Questions Are Raised on Lucky Luciano Book." *New York Times* (December 17): 28.
1971a *The Mafia Is Not an Equal Opportunity Employer.* New York: McGraw-Hill.
1971b "Gallo-Colombo Feud Said to Have Been Renewed." *New York Times* (June 29): 21.

Gage, Nicholas, ed.
1972 *Mafia, U.S.A.* New York: Dell.

Gall, Carlotta
2008a "Afghanistan's Opium Harvest Shrinks After Record Crop, U.N. Says." *New York Times* (August 27): 10.
2008b "Bush Ex-Official Says Corrupt Afghan and a Hesitant Military Hinder Drug Fight." *New York Times* (July 24): 12.
2006 "Another Year of Drug War, and the Poppy Crop Flourishes." *New York Times* (February 17): 4.
2005 "Armed and Elusive, Afghan Drug Dealers Roam Free." *New York Times* (January 2): 3.
2001 "Macedonia Village Is Center of Europe Web in Sex Trade." *New York Times* (July 28): 1, 6.

Gallagher, James P.
1995a "In Chechnya, Vendetta Is a Way of Life, Death." *Chicago Tribune* (March 5): 1, 12.
1995b "Corruption Touches Many Lives in Russia." *Chicago Tribune* (August 13): 15, 18.
1994 "Russian Gangs Send the Dead Out in Style." *Chicago Tribune* (November 20): 29.
1992a "Chechens Stir Bloody Cauldron in Caucasus." *Chicago Tribune* (January 10): 20.
1992b "As Law Enforcement Crumbles, Russian Crime, Gangs Proliferate." *Chicago Tribune* (September 2): 6.

Galliher, John F. and James A. Cain
1974 "Citation Support for the Mafia Myth in Criminology Textbooks." *American Sociologist* 9 (May): 68–74.

Gallo, Patrick J.
1981 *Old Bread, New Wine: A Portrait of the Italian-American.* Chicago: Nelson-Hall.

Galvan, Manuel
1982 "Capone's Yacht Sails Calmer Seas Today." *Chicago Tribune* (February 16): Sec. 2: 1.

Gambetta, Diego
1993 *The Sicilian Mafia: The Business of Private Protection.* Cambridge, MA: Harvard University Press.

Gambino, Richard
    1977   *Vendetta*. Garden City, NY: Doubleday.
    1974   *Blood of My Blood: The Dilemma of the Italian-American*. Garden City: Doubleday.
"Gamblers Hunted in Rothstein Attack"
    1928   *New York Times* (November 6): 1.
Gambling Commission. See Commission on the Review of the National Policy Toward Gambling
"Gang Kills Suspect in Alien Smuggling"
    1931   *New York Times* (September 11): 1.
"Gang Linked to Union Charged at Trial"
    1934   *New York Times* (January 31): 8.
"Gangster Shot in Daylight Attack"
    1928   *New York Times* (July 2): 1.
Gardiner, John A.
    1970   *The Politics of Corruption: Organized Crime in an American City*. New York: Russell Sage Foundation.
Gately, William and Yvette Fernandez
    1994   *Dead Ringer*. New York: Donald I. Fine.
Gender, Alison
    2005   "Feds Hook King of Coke." *New York Daily News* (August 20): 5.
Genzman, Robert W.
    1988   "Press Release." October 11.
Gerlat, Allan
    2002   "Mob Mentality—NYC Breaks Longtime Grip." *Waste News* 7 (April 15): 12.
Giancana, Antoinette and Thomas C. Renner
    1985   *Mafia Princess: Growing Up in Sam Giancana's Family*. New York: Avon.
Giancana, Sam and Chuck Giancana
    1992   *Double Cross: Inside Story of the Mobster Who Controlled America*. New York: Warner Books.
Gilinsky, Yakov
    2004   "Contemporary Russian Corruption." Pages 60–69 in *Organized Crime, Trafficking, Drugs: Selected Papers Presented at the Annual Conference of the European Society of Criminology, Helsinki*. Helsinki, Finland: European Institute for Criminal Prevention and Control.
Giuliani, Rudolph W.
    1987   "Legal Remedies for Attacking Organized Crime." Pages 103–30 in *Major Issues in Organized Crime Control*, edited by Herbert Edelhertz. Washington, DC: U.S. Government Printing Office.
Gjoni, Ilir
    2004   "Organized Crime and National Security: The Albanian Case." Master's Thesis. Monterey, CA: Naval Postgraduate School.
Glab, Michael G.
    1997   "Gang Green." *Chicago Reader* (November 14): 1, 16–34.
Glaberson, William
    1989   "U.S. Loses Round in Bid to Curb Mob at Fish Market." *New York Times* (January 25): 12.
Glenny, Misha
    2008   *McMafia: A Journey Through the Global Criminal Underworld*. New York: Knopf.
Glonti, Georgi
    2003   "Human Trafficking: Concept, Classification, and Questions of Legislative Regulation." Pages 70–80

in *Organised Crime, Trafficking, Drugs: Selected Papers Presented at the Annual Conference of the European Society of Criminology*, Helsinki, edited by Sami Nevala and Kauko Armomaa.
Goddard, Donald
    1988   *Undercover: The Secret Lives of a Federal Agent*. New York: Times Books.
    1980   *All Fall Down*. New York: Times Books.
    1978   *Easy Money*. New York: Farrar, Straus and Giroux.
    1974   *Joey*. New York: Harper & Row.
Godfrey, E. Drexel, Jr. and Don R. Harris
    1971   *Basic Elements of Intelligence*. Washington, DC: U.S. Government Printing Office.
Godson, Roy and William J. Olson
    1995   "International Organized Crime." *Society* (January/February): 18–29.
Goering, Laurie
    2001   "Colombia Caught in a Struggle for Power." *Chicago Tribune* (May 27): 1, 12.
    1998   "In Peru, Battle Against Flow of Drugs Moves to Amazon River Maze." *Chicago Tribune* (June 30): 6.
Gold, Mark S., Charles A. Dackis, A. L. C. Pottash, Irl Extein, and Arnold Washton
    1986   "Cocaine Update: From Bench to Bedside." *Advances in Alcohol and Substance Abuse* 5 (Fall/Winter): 35–60.
Goldberg, Carey
    2001   "An Innocent Man Goes Free 33 Years After Conviction." *New York Times* (February 2): 12.
    1999   "At Stake in a Messy Boston Trial: How to Handle Informers' Crimes." *New York Times* (March 13): 1, 7.
Goldberg, Jeffrey
    1999   "The Don is Done." *New York Times Magazine* (January 31): 24–31, 62–66, 71.
    1995   "Hoffa Lives!" *New York* (July 31): 27–35.
Golden, Tim
    2001   "The Citibank Connection: Real Money, Shadow Banks." *New York Times* (February 27): 6.
    2000a   "Killing Raises Doubts on Mexico's War on Drugs." *New York Times* (June 5): 3.
    2000b   "Mexican Gang Still on Loose Despite Search." *New York Times* (January 10): 1, 9.
    1999a   "Top Mexican Off-Limits to U.S. Drug Agents." *New York Times* (March 16): 1, 10.
    1999b   "2 Mexican Banks to Plead Guilty in Laundering Case." *New York Times* (March 30): 3.
    1998a   "In Breakthrough, Mexican Official Testifies in Texas." *New York Times* (July 15): 1, 6.
    1998b   "Elite Mexican Drug Officers Said To Be Tied to Traffickers." *New York Times* (September 16): 1, 10.
    1998c   "Salinas Brother Is Tied by Swiss to Drug Trade." *New York Times* (September 19): 1, 6.
    1998d   "Saying Salinas Aided Traffickers, Swiss Seize $90 Million." *New York Times* (October 21): 3.
    1997a   "Mexico and Drugs: Was the U.S. Napping?" *New York Times* (July 11): 1, 10.
    1997b   "Pakistan's Jailing of a Drug Agent Sours U.S. Ties." *New York Times* (November 17): 1, 10.
    1995a   "To Help Keep Mexico Stable, U.S. Soft-Pedaled Drug War." *New York Times* (July 31): 1, 4.
    1995b   "Mexican Connection Grows as Cocaine Supplier to U.S." *New York Times* (July 30): 1, 8.

Goldstein, Joseph
1982 "Police Discretion Not to Invoke the Criminal Process." Pages 33–42 in *The Invisible Justice System: Discretion and the Law*, 2d ed., edited by Burton Atkins and Mark Pogrebin. Cincinnati, OH: Anderson.

Goldstock, Ronald and Dan T. Coenen
1978 *Extortionate and Usurious Credit Transactions: Background Materials*. Ithaca, NY: Cornell Institute on Organized Crime.

Goozner, Merrill
1996 "New York Trying to Trash Mob Hold on Waste-Hauling." *Chicago Tribune* (December 6): 1, 16.
1992 "Thugs Avenge a Movie's Insults." *Chicago Tribune* (June 4): 4.

Gordon, Michael R.
1996 "Key Russian Legislator Accuses Leading Military Officers of Graft." *New York Times* (July 10): 1, 4.

Gosch, Martin and Richard Hammer
1974 *The Last Testament of Lucky Luciano*. Boston: Little, Brown.

Gosnell, Harold
1977 *Machine Politics: The Chicago Model*. Chicago: University of Chicago. Originally published in 1937.

Gottschalk, Marie
2006 *The Prison and the Gallows: The Politics of Incarceration in America*. New York: Cambridge University Press.

Gottfried, Alex
1962 *Boss Cermak of Chicago*. Seattle: University of Washington Press.

Graham, Fred
1977 *The Atlas Program*. Boston: Little, Brown.

Graham, Hugh Davis and Ted Robert Gurr, eds.
1969 *The History of Violence in America: A Report to the National Commission on the Causes and Prevention of Violence*. New York: Bantam.

Grann, David
2004 "The Brand." *New Yorker* (February 16 & 23): 157–71.

Greenberg, Norman
1981 *The Man with a Steel Guitar: Portrait of Desperation, and Crime*. Hanover, NH: University Press of New England.

Greenblatt, Stephen
2004 "Shakespeare's Leap." *New York Times Magazine* (September 12): 50–55.

Greenhouse, Steven
2000a "Ex-Union Leader to Admit Ferrari Fraud." *New York Times* (January 28): 10.
2000b "U.S. Is Easing Close Scrutiny of Hotel Union." *New York Times* (December 3): 31.
2000c "Union Cleanup Praised; U.S. Oversight Is Eased." *New York Times* (January 21): 20.
1999 "Laborers' Union President Is Cleared of Links to Mob." *New York Times* (March 10): 9.
1997 "An Overseer Bars Teamster Leader from Re-election." *New York Times* (November 18): 1, 16.

Greenhouse, Steven and William K. Rashbaum
2008 "Judge Continues Oversight of the Carpenter's Union." *New York Times* (August 13): B3.

Griffin, Dennis and Frank Cullotta
2007 *Cullotta: The Life of a Chicago Criminal, Las Vegas Mobster, and Government Witness*. Las Vegas: Huntington Press.

Griffin, Sean Patrick
2003 *Philadelphia's Black Mafia: A Social and Political History*. Dordrecht, Netherlands: Kluwer.

Grinspoon, Lester
1979 *Psychedelic Drugs Reconsidered*. New York: Basic Books.

Grinspoon, Lester and James B. Bakalar
1985 *Cocaine: A Drug and Its Social Evolution*, Revised ed. New York: Basic Books.
1976 *Cocaine: A Drug and Its Social Evolution*. New York: Basic Books.

Griswold, Eliza
2005 "Medellín: Stories From an Urban War." *National Geographic* (March): 72–91.

Grob, Charles S., Russell E. Poland, Linda Chang, and Thomas Ernst
1996 "Psychobiologic Effects of 3,4-methylenedioxymethamphetamine in Humans: Methodological Considerations and Preliminary Observations." *Behavioral Brain Research* 73: 103–107.

Grutzner, Charles
1969 "Genovese Dies in Prison at 71; 'Boss of Bosses' of Mafia Here." *New York Times* (February 15): 1, 29.

Gugliotta, Guy and Jeff Leen
1989 *Kings of Cocaine: Inside the Medellín Cartel—An Astonishing True Story of Murder, Money, and International Corruption*. New York: Simon and Schuster.

Gunst, Laurie
1996 *Born Fi' Dead: A Journey Through the Jamaican Posse Underworld*. New York: Henry Holt and Company.

Haberman, Clyde
1985 "TV Funeral for Japan's Slain Godfather." *New York Times* (February 1): 6.

Hagan, Frank
2006 "'Organized Crime' and 'Organized Crime': Indeterminate Problems of Definition." *Trends in Organized Crime* 9 (June): 127–137.

Haley, Bruce
1990 "Burma's Hidden Wars." *U.S. News and World Report* (December 10): 44–47.

Hall, Kevin G.
2000 "Drug Chemicals Difficult to Target." *Chicago Tribune* (November 23): 36.

Haller, Mark H.
1991 *Life under Bruno: The Economics of an Organized Crime Family*. Conshohocken, PA: Pennsylvania Crime Commission.
1990a "Illegal Enterprise: A Theoretical and Historic Interpretation." *Criminology* 28 (May): 207–35.
1990b "Policy Gambling, Entertainment, and the Emergence of Black Politics: Chicago from 1900 to 1940." *Journal of Social History* 24: 719–38.
1985a "Bootleggers as Businessmen: From City Slums to City Builders." Pages 139–57 in *Law, Alcohol, and Order: Perspectives on National Prohibition*, edited by David E. Kyvig. Westport, CT: Greenwood.
1985b "Philadelphia Bootlegging and the Report of the Special Grand Jury." *Pennsylvania Magazine of History and Biography* 109 (April): 215–33.

1974 "Bootlegging in Chicago: The Structure of an Illegal Enterprise." Paper presented at the annual meeting of the American Historical Association, Chicago, December 28.

1971–72 "Organized Crime in Urban Society: Chicago in the Twentieth Century." *Journal of Social History* 5: 210–34.

Hamilton, Don
1998 "For Motorcyclists, It's the Black Hills or Bust." *Chicago Tribune* (July 26): Sec. 12: 1, 7.

Hamm, Richard F.
1995 *Shaping the 18th Amendment.* Chapel Hill: University of North Carolina Press.

Handelman, Stephen
1995 *Comrade Criminal: Russia's New Mafiya.* New Haven, CT: Yale University Press.

Hapgood, Norman and Henry Moskowitz
1927 *Up from the Streets: Alfred E. Smith.* New York: Harcourt, Brace.

Harker, R. Phillip
1978 "Sports Bookmaking Operations." *FBI Law Enforcement Bulletin* (September): FBI reprint.
1977 "Sports Wagering and the 'Line.'" *FBI Law Enforcement Bulletin* (November): FBI reprint.

Harmon, Dave
1993 "Ex-Agent: Drug Sales Aided Contras." *Chicago Tribune* (January 26): 3.

Hartman, Victor E.
2001 "Implementing an Asset Forfeiture Program." *FBI Law Enforcement Bulletin* (January): 1–7.

Hartocollis, Anemona
2006 "Enforcer Paints Picture of Gotti as Powerful Don." *New York Times* (February 23): B6.
2005 "Albanian Gang Portrayed as Aspiring Mafiosi." *New York Times* (December 20): B3.

Hawley, Chris
2008 "Beer's Outlaw Image Leaves Bad Taste in Critic's Mouths." *USA Today* (September 3): Internet.

Hayde, Frank R.
2008 *The Mafia and the Machine: The Story of the Kansas City Mob.* Fort Lee, NJ: Barricade Books.

Hayes, Bill
2005 *The Original Wild Ones: Tales of the Boozefighters Motorcycle Club.* St. Paul, MN: MBI Publishing Co.

Hayner, Don
1990 "Chinatown Gambling: Inside Story." *Chicago Sun-Times* (September 2): 1, 20–21.

Healey, James R. and Barbara Hagenbaugh
2005 "Online Bettors Furiously Ante Up for March Madness." *USA Today* (March 18): B1, 2.

Healy, Patrick
2003 "Investigators Say Fraud Ring Staged Thousands of Crashes." *New York Times* (August 13): 1, B5.

Hefling, Kimberly
2000 "Pot Crop Thrives in Appalachia." Associated Press (May 14): Internet.

Helmer, John
1975 *Drugs and Minority Oppression.* New York: Seabury Press.

Henriques, Diana B. with Dean Baquet
1993 "Investigators Say Bid-Rigging Is Common in Milk Industry." *New York Times* (May 23): 1, 12.

Herguth, Robert
2004 "Sons of the Mob Step Up in Family Business—Unions." *Chicago Sun-Times* (July 4): 18.

Herion, Don
1998 Director of the Vice Enforcement Unit of the Cook County (IL) Sheriff's Police Department. Personal interviews.

Hersh, Seymour M.
1994 "The Wild East." *Atlantic Monthly* (June): 61–85.

Hess, David, Kenneth Meyers, Michele Gideon, Sal E. Gomez, and John Daly
1999 "Italian Organized Crime and Money Laundering." Pages 345–405 in *Organized Crime: Uncertainties and Dilemmas,* edited by Stanley Einstein and Menachem Amir. Chicago: Office of International Criminal Justice of the University of Illinois at Chicago.

Hess, Henner
1973 *Mafia and Mafiosi: The Structure of Power.* Lexington, MA: D. C. Heath.

Hibbert, Christopher
1966 *Garibaldi and His Enemies.* Boston: Little, Brown.

Hill, Henry, with Douglas S. Looney
1981 "How I Put the Fix In." *Sports Illustrated* (February 16): 14–21.

Hill, Peter B. E.
2003 *The Japanese Mafia: Yakuza, Law, and the State.* Oxford, England: Oxford University Press.

Himmelstein, Jerome L.
1983 *The Strange Career of Marijuana: Politics and Ideology of Drug Control in America.* Westport, CT: Greenwood.

Hirsch, Michael and Hideo Takayama
1997 "Big Bang or Bust?" *Newsweek* (September 1): 44–45.

Hirschi, Travis
1969 *Causes of Delinquency.* Berkeley: University of California Press.

"History of Antagonism, A"
1994 *New York Times* (December 13): 3.

Hobsbawm, Eric J.
1976 "Mafia." Pages 90–98 in *The Crime Society,* edited by Francis A. J. Ianni and Elizabeth Reuss-Ianni. New York: New American Library.
1971 *Bandits.* New York: Dell.
1969 "The American Mafia." *The Listener* 82 (November): 685–88.
1959 *Social Bandits and Primitive Rebels.* Glencoe, IL: Free Press.

Hockstader, Lee
1995 "Crime Atop Chaos: In Post Communist Russia, the Strong Arm of the Mafiya is Everywhere." *Washington Post,* National Weekly Edition (March 20–26): 6–9.

Hoffman, Paul
1976 *To Drop a Dime.* New York: Putnam's.

Hofstadter, Richard
1956 *The Age of Reform: From Bryan to F.D.R.* New York: Knopf.

Hofstadter, Richard and Michael Wallace, eds.
1971 *American Violence: A Documentary History.* New York: Vintage.

Hohimer, Frank
1975 *The Home Invaders.* Chicago: Chicago Review Press.

Homans, George C.
1961 *Social Behavior: Its Elementary Forms.* New York: Harcourt, Brace and World.

Homer, Frederic D.
1974 *Guns and Garlic.* West Lafayette, IN: Purdue University Press.

Hopton, Isobel
1996 "On the Triad Trail." *CJ International* 12 (July–August): 5–6.

Horne, Louther
1932 "Capone's Trip to Jail Ends a Long Battle." *New York Times* (May 8): IX 1.

Horowtiz, Jason
2005 "Italy: 46 Held in Mafia Raids." *New York Times* (January 26): 6.
2004 "Italy's Worrisome South Erupts as Mob Killings Rise in Naples." *New York Times* (November 26): 5.

Howe, Benjamin Ryder
2000 "Out of the Jungle." *Atlantic Monthly* (May): 32–38.

Hughes, Donna M. and Tatyana Denisova
2001 "The Transnational Political Criminal Nexus of Trafficking in Women from Ukraine." *Trends in Organized Crime* 6 (Spring/September): 43–67.

Humphries, Drew and David F. Greenberg
1981 "The Dialectics of Crime Control." Pages 209–54 in *Crime and Capitalism*, edited by David F. Greenberg. Palo Alto, CA: Mayfield.

Hundley, Tom
1998a "Anti-Mafia Sweep Helps Sicilian Capital Clean Up Its Act." *Chicago Tribune* (April 22): 7.
1998b "Euro Conversion Could Be Mafia's Big Chance." *Chicago Tribune* (November 8): 4.
1998c "Sicilian Women Lift Past Veil to Take Charge." *Chicago Tribune* (September 20): 5.
1997 "Violence Tempers Naples' Return to Glory." *Chicago Tribune* (March 1): 7.

Huston, Peter
2001 *Tongs, Gangs, and Triads: Chinese Crime Groups in North America.* San Jose, CA: Authors Choice Press.

Ianni, Francis A. J.
1974 *The Black Mafia: Ethnic Succession in Organized Crime.* New York: Simon and Schuster.
1972 *A Family Business: Kinship and Social Control in Organized Crime.* New York: Russell Sage Foundation.

Iannuzzi, Joseph
1993 *Joe Dogs: The Life and Crimes of a Mobster.* New York: Simon and Schuster.

Ibrahim, Youssef M.
1997 "Sweden's Courteous Police Spoil a Hell's Angels Party." *New York Times* (March 3): 1, 6.

Iliff, Laurence
2005 "Nuevo Laredo Officers Charged With Organized-Crime Activities." *Dallas Morning News* (September 6): Internet.

Imhoff, John J. and Stephen P. Cutler
1998 "INTERPOL: Extending Law Enforcement's Reach Around the World." *FBI Law Enforcement Bulletin* (December): 10–16.

Inciardi, James A.
1986 *The War on Drugs: Heroin, Cocaine, Crime, and Public Policy.* Palo Alto, CA: Mayfield.

1975 *Careers in Crime.* Chicago: Rand McNally.

Intelligence Bulletin Colombia
1995 Washington, DC: Drug Enforcement Administration.

International Narcotics Control Strategy Report, 1999
2000 Bureau for International Narcotics and Law Enforcement Affairs, U.S. Department of State. Washington, DC, March 2000.

International Organization for Migration (IOM)
1998 *Information Campaign Against Trafficking in Women from Ukraine.* IOM.

INTERPOL at Work
2003 Lyon, France: Interpol General Secretariat.

Irey, Elmer L. and William T. Slocum
1948 *The Tax Dodgers.* Garden City, NY: Doubleday.

Israely, Jeff
2004 "Sicily's Invisible Man." *Time International* (September 6): 50.

"Italy: Mafia Boss Returns to Rome Amid Tight Security"
2008 *Adnkronos International* (August 20): Internet.

Iwai, Hiroaki
1986 "Organized Crime in Japan." Pages 208–33 in *Organized Crime: A Global Perspective*, edited by Robert J. Kelly. Totowa, NJ: Rowman and Littlefield.

Jackson, David
1990 "Bad Company." *Chicago* (February): 91–95, 109–10.

Jacobs, D. Lea
2002 *Friend of the Family.* Washington, DC: Compass Press.

Jacobs, James B.
2006 *Mobsters, Unions, and Feds: The Mafia and the American Labor Movement.* New York: New York University Press.

Jacobs, James B. and R. P. Alford
2005 "The Teamsters Rocky Road to Recovery—The Demise of Project RISE." *Trends in Organized Crime* 9 (Fall): 5–23.

Jacobs, James B. with Colleen Friel and Robert Raddick
1999 *Gotham Unbound: How New York City Was Liberated From the Clutches of Cosa Nostra.* New York: New York University Press.

Jacobs, James B. and Elizabeth A. Mullin
2003 "Congress' Role in the Defeat of Organized Crime." *Criminal Law Bulletin* (May–June): 269–312.

Jacobs, James B. with Christopher Panarella and Jay Worthington
1994 *Busting the Mob: United States v. Cosa Nostra.* New York: New York University Press.

Jacobs, James B. and Kristin Stohner
2005 "Ten Years of Court-Supervised Reform: A Chronicle and Assessment." *California Criminal Law Review* 3 (Vol. 6): Internet.

Jacobson, Mark
2000 "The Return of Superfly." *New York* (August 14): 36–45.

"Jail Informer's Admissions Spur Inquiry"
1989 *New York Times* (January 3): 10.

"Jamaican Murders Hit an All-Time High"
2005 *New York Daily News* (November 26): 6.

James, Frank
2001 "Tax Havens an Evasive Issue." *Chicago Tribune* (July 22): Sec 5: 1, 6.

Jamieson, Alison
2000 *The Antimafia: Italy's Fight Against Organized Crime.* New York: St. Martin's.
Jenkins, Philip and Gary W. Potter
1985 *The City and the Syndicate: Organizing Crime in Philadelphia.* Lexington, MA: Ginn Custom Publishing.
Jennings, Dean
1967 *We Only Kill Each Other.* Englewood Cliffs, NJ: Prentice-Hall.
Joe, Karen
1992 "Chinese Gangs and Tongs: An Exploratory Look at the Connection on the West Coast." Paper presented at the annual meeting of the American Society of Criminology, New Orleans, November 4–7.
"Johnny Torrio, Ex-Public Enemy 1, Dies; Made Al Capone Boss of the Underworld"
1957 *New York Times* (May 8): 32.
Johnson, Earl, Jr.
1963 "Organized Crime: Challenge to the American Legal System." *Criminal Law, Criminology, and Police Science* 54 (March): 1–29.
Johnson, Kirk
1996 "Laborers' Union Agrees to Open Up Elections." *New York Times* (February 2): 12.
1986 "Manhattan Gang Is Tied to 30 Unsolved Killings." *New York Times* (December 17): 19.
Johnson, Malcolm
1972 "In Hollywood." Pages 325–38 in *Mafia, U.S.A.,* edited by Nicholas Gage. New York: Dell.
Johnston, David Cay
2002 "Loophole Is Too Small for an Ex-Convict." *New York Times* (March 17): 8.
Johnston, Michael
1982 *Political Corruption and Public Policy in America.* Monterey, CA: Brooks/Cole.
Jones, Marilyn
2002 "Policy Paradox: Implications of U.S. Drug Control Policy for Jamaica." *Annals* 582 (July): 117–147.
Jordon, Mary and Kevin Sullivan
1999 "Exploiting Weakness, Japanese Mobsters Go Mainstream." *Philadelphia Inquirer* (April 25): 17.
Joselit, Jenna Weissman
1983 *Our Gang: Jewish Crime and the New York Jewish Community, 1900–1940.* Bloomington: Indiana University Press.
Josephson, Matthew
1962 *The Robber Barons.* New York: Harcourt, Brace and World. Originally published in 1934.
Kaban, Elif
1998 "Russian Mafia Suspect Goes on Swiss Trial." Reuters (November 30): Internet.
Kaiser, Rob D.
1999 "Laborers Union Ousts Local Chief." *Chicago Tribune* (May 18): Sec. 3: 1, 2.
Kalfus, Ken
1996 "Far From Normal: Scenes from the New Moscow." *Harper's* (December): 53–62.
Kaplan, David E.
1998 "Yakuza, Inc." *U.S. News and World Report* (April 13): 40–47.

Kaplan, David E. and Alec Dubro
1986 *Yakuza: The Explosive Account of Japan's Criminal Underworld.* Reading, MA: Addison-Wesley.
Kaplan, Robert D.
2008 "Lifting the Bamboo Curtain." *The Atlantic* (September): 84–95.
Karch, Steven B.
1996 *The Pathology of Drug Abuse,* 2d ed. Boca Raton, FL: CRC Press.
Katcher, Leo
1959 *The Big Bankroll: The Life and Times of Arnold Rothstein.* New York: Harper & Brothers.
Katel, Peter
1996 "Handing Off a Hot Case." *Newsweek* (January 29): 41.
Katz, Leonard
1973 *Uncle Frank: The Biography of Frank Costello.* New York: Drake Publishers.
Kavieff, Paul R.
2006 *The Life and Times of Lepke Buchalter.* Fort Lee, NJ: Barricade Books.
2000 *The Purple Gang: Organized Crime in Detroit, 1910–1945.* Fort Lee, NJ: Barricade Books.
Keefe, Joseph D.
2001 "Testimony Before the U.S. House of Representatives Committee on Government Reform Subcommittee on Criminal Justice, Drug Policy and Human Resources," July 12.
Kefauver, Estes (Special Committee to Investigate Organized Crime in Interstate Commerce)
1951a *Third Interim Report.* Washington, DC: U.S. Government Printing Office.
1951b *Crime in America.* Garden City, NY: Doubleday.
Kelly, Robert J.
1999 *The Upperworld and the Underworld: Case Studies of Racketeering and Business Infiltrations in the United States.* Hingham, MA: Kluwer.
1986 *Organized Crime: An International Perspective.* Totowa, NJ: Rowman and Littlefield.
Kelly Robert J., Ko-lin Chin, and Jeffrey A. Fagan
1993 "The Dragon Breathes Fire: Chinese Organized Crime in New York City. *Crime, Law and Social Change* 19: 245–69.
Kelly, Robert J., Ko-lin Chin, and Rufus Schatzberg, eds.
1994 *Handbook of Organized Crime in the United States.* Westport, CT: Greenwood.
Kennedy, David M.
1999 "Victory at Sea." *Atlantic Monthly* (March): 51–76.
Kennedy, Randy
1996 "Drugs Stir Neighborhood Worries." *New York Times* (October 3): B12.
Kennedy, Robert F.
1960 *The Enemy Within.* New York: Popular Library.
Kerr, Peter
1988a "Chinese Criminals Move to Broaden Role in U.S." *New York Times* (January 4): 1, 12.
1988b "Cocaine Glut Puts New York in Drug Rings' Tug-of-War." *New York Times* (August 24): 14.
1988c "Cocaine Ring Holding Fast in Colombia." *New York Times* (May 21): 1, 5.

Kershaw, Sarah
2006 "Through Indian Lands, Drugs' Shadowy Trail." *New York Times* (February 19): 1, 26–27.

Kidner, John
1976 *Crimaldi: Contract Killer.* Washington, DC: Acropolis Books.

Kihss, Peter
1979 "John Dioguardi (Johnny Dio), 64, a Leader in Organized Crime, Dies." *New York Times* (January 16): B6.

Kilgannon, Corey
2005 "Phone Executive Admits Conspiracy in Mob Fraud." *New York Times* (January 9): 28.

Kilian, Michael
2002 "Seizure of Drugs at Sea Soaring." *Chicago Tribune* (March 18): 9.

Kilian, Michael, Connie Fletcher, and Richard P. Ciccone
1979 *Who Runs Chicago?* New York: St. Martin's Press.

Kimeldorf, Howard
1988 *Reds or Rackets? The Making of Radical and Conservative Unions on the Waterfront.* Berkeley: University of California Press.

Kinder, Douglas Clark
1992 "Shutting Out the Evil: Nativism and Narcotics Control in the United States." Pages 117–42 in *Drug Control Policy: Essays in Historical and Comparative Perspective*, edited by William O. Walker. University Park: Pennsylvania State University.

King, Rufus
1969 *Gambling and Organized Crime.* Washington, DC: Public Affairs Press.
1963 "The Fifth Amendment Privilege and Immunity Legislation." *Notre Dame Lawyer* 38 (September): 641–54.

Kingston, Kimberly A.
1988 "Reasonable Expectation of Privacy Cases Revive Traditional Investigative Techniques." *FBI Law Enforcement Bulletin* (November): 22–29.

Kinzer, Stephan
1996a "Biker Wars in the Land of Vikings." *New York Times* (May 6): 5.
1996b "In Germany, Vietnamese Terrorize Vietnamese." *New York Times* (May 23): 4.

Kirk, Donald
1981 "Death of Japan Crime Boss Breeds Fear." *Miami Herald* (July 27): 17.
1976 "Crime, Politics and Finger Chopping." *New York Times Magazine* (December 12): 60–61, 91–97.

Kleemans, Edward R. and Christianne J. de Poot
2008 "Criminal Careers in Organized Crime and Social Opportunity Structure." *European Journal of Criminology* 5 (1): 69–98.

Klein, Malcolm, Cheryl L. Maxson, and Lea C. Cunningham
1991 "'Crack,' Street Gangs, and Violence." *Criminology* 29 (November): 623–50.

Klein, Maury
1986 *Life and Times of Jay Gould.* Baltimore, MD: Johns Hopkins University Press.

Kleinfield, N. R.
1995 "Chinatown Officers Said to Forge a Partnership of Vice and Greed." *New York Times* (June 19): 1, B12.

Kleinknecht, William
1996 *The New Ethnic Mobs: The Changing Face of Organized Crime in America.* New York: Free Press.

Klepper, Michael, Robert Gunther, Jeanette Baik, Linda Barth, and Christine Gibson
1998 "The American Heritage 40." *American Heritage* (October): 56–60.

Kobler, John
1971 *Capone: The Life and World of Al Capone.* Greenwich, CT: Fawcett.

Kobrin, Solomon
1966 "The Conflict of Values in Delinquency Areas." Pages 151–60 in *Juvenile Delinquency: A Book of Readings*, edited by Rose Giallombardo. New York: Wiley.

Kocieniewski, David
1997 "New York Pays a High Price for Police Lies." *New York Times* (January 5): 1, 16.

Konigsberg, Eric
2001 "Blood Relation." *New Yorker* (August 6): 46–59.

Koziol, Ronald and Edward Baumann
1987 "How Frank Nitti Met His Fate." *Chicago Tribune* (June 29): Sec. 5: 1, 7.

Koziol Ronald and George Estep
1983 "Fresh Insight into February 14 Killings." *Chicago Tribune* (February 14): 13.

Krajicek, David J.
2007 "Rhode Island Rumrunner." *New York Daily News* (August 5): 38.

Krajick, Kevin
2004 "Officer Billy Club." *New York Daily News* (January 18): 47.
1983 "Should Police Wiretap?" *Police Magazine* (May): 29–32, 36–41.

Kramer, Andrew
2008a "Chechnya's Capital Rises from the Ashes, Atop Hidden Horrors." *New York Times* (April 30): 9.
2008b "Russian Police Arrest a Suspected Racketeer." *New York Times* (January 26): C4.

Kramer, Jane
1992 "Letter from Europe." *New Yorker* (September 21): 108–24.

Krauss, Clifford
2002 "U.S. Moves to Close Canadian Drug Route for Illegal Stimulant." *New York Times* (March 5): 5.
2000 "Bolivia Wiping Out Coca, at a Price." *New York Times* (October 23): 10.

Krauss, Clifford and Douglas Frantz
1995 "Cali Drug Cartel Using U.S. Business to Launder Cash." *New York Times* (October 30): 1, 13.

Kristof, Nicholas D.
1999 "A Sexy Economic Feud of No Interest to the I.M.F." *New York Times* (June 17): 4.
1995a "Japanese Outcasts Better Off Than in Past But Still Outcast." *New York Times* (November 30): 1, 8.
1995b "Mob Takes a Holiday as V.I.P.'s Tour Osaka." *New York Times* (November 19): 6.
1995c "The Quake That Hurt Kobe Helps Its Gangs Get Richer." *New York Times* (June 6): 1, 4.

Kurtis, Bill
1976 "The Caviar Connection." *New York Times Magazine* (October 26): 132–33, 136–37, 141.

Kwitny, Jonathan
1979 *Vicious Circles: The Mafia in the Marketplace.* New York: Norton.

Labaton, Stephen
  2001   "The World Gets Tough on Price Fixers." *New York Times* (June 3): Sec. 3: 1, 7.
  1997   "100 Are Arrested as Drug Ring with 'Speed' Is Broken Up." *New York Times* (December 6): 7.
  1989a "Banking's Technology Helps Drug Dealers Export Cash." *New York Times* (August 14): 1, 10.
  1989b "Bank to Plead Guilty to Laundering Drug Money." *New York Times* (August 11): 1, 10.
Labaton, Stephen and David Barboza
  1999   "U.S. Outlines How Makers of Vitamins Fixed Global Prices." *New York Times* (May 21): 1, C6.
Lacey, Mark
  2008a "Tijuana's New Police Chief Touts an Achievement: Survival." *New York Times* (August 23): A8.
  2008b "In Mexico, Sorting Out Good Guys From Bad." *New York Times* (November 2): 6.
  2008c "Officials Say Drug Cartels Infiltrated Mexican Law Unit." *New York Times* (October 28): 10.
Lacey, Mark and Antonio Betancourt
  2008   "A Boy's Killing Prods a City to Stand Up to Kidnappers." *New York Times* (August 14): Internet.
Lacey, Robert
  1991   *Little Man: Meyer Lansky and the Gangster Life.* Boston: Little, Brown.
Lambert, Bruce
  2006   "Law Enforcement Agencies Break 2 Major Drug Rings." *New York Times* (March 31): B3.
Lamothe, Lee and Adrian Humphreys
  2006   *The Sixth Family: The Collapse of the New York Mafia and the Rise of Vito Rizzuto.* Mississauga, Ontario, Canada: John Wiley and Sons.
Lamour, Catherine and Michael R. Lamberti
  1974   *The International Connection: Opium from Growers to Pushers.* New York: Pantheon.
Landesco, John
  1968   *Organized Crime in Chicago.* Chicago: University of Chicago Press. Originally published in 1929.
  1933   "The Life History of a Member of the '42' Gang." *Journal of Criminal Law, Criminology, and Police Science* 23: 964–998.
Landler, Mark and Ian Fisher
  2007   "German Police Link 6 Dead Men to an Italian Mob Feud." *New York Times* (August 16): 8.
Langlais, Rudy
  1978   "Inside the Heroin Trade: How a Star Double Agent Ended Up Dead." *Village Voice* (March 13): 13–15.
Langton, Jerry
  2006   *Fallen Angel: The Unlikely Rise of Walter Stadnick in the Canadian Hells Angels.* Mississauga, Ontario, Canada: Wiley.
Lapidus, Edith J.
  1974   *Eavesdropping on Trial.* Rochelle Park, NJ: Hayden Book Co.
Lardner, James and Thomas Reppetto
  2000   *NYPD: A City and Its Police.* New York: Henry Holt.
Lasswell, Harold D. and Jerimiah B. McKenna
  1972   *The Impact of Organized Crime on an Inner-City Community.* New York: Policy Sciences Center.

Latimer, Dean and Jeff Goldberg
  1981   *Flowers in the Blood: The Story of Opium.* New York: Franklin Watts.
LaVerle, Berry, Glenn E. Curtis, John N. Gibbs, Rex A. Hudson, Tara Karacan, Nina Kollars, and Ramón Miró
  2003   *Nations Hospitable to Organized Crime and Terrorism.* Washington, DC: Library of Congress.
Lavigne, Yves
  1996   *Hells Angels: Into the Abyss.* New York: HarperCollins.
  1987   *Hells Angels: Taking Care of Business.* Toronto, Canada: Deneua and Wayne.
LeDuff, Charlie
  2005   "100 Members of Immigrant Gang Are Held." *New York Times* (March 15): 18.
Ledwith, William E.
  2000   "Testimony Before the House of Representatives Subcommittee on Criminal Justice, Drug Policy, and Human Resources," February 15.
Lee, Denny
  2003   "Years of the Dragon." *New York Times* (May 11): CY 1, 16.
Lee, Henry
  1963   *How Dry We Were: Prohibition Revisited.* Englewood Cliffs, NJ: Prentice-Hall.
Lee, Jennifer
  2005   "Crime Ring Is Crushed Police Say." *New York Times* (April 28): B6.
Lehmann, Daniel J. and Tom McNamee
  1995   "Gang Busted." *Chicago Sun-Times* (September 1): 1, 22.
Lehr, Dick and Gerard O'Neil
  2000   *Black Mass: The Irish Mob, the FBI, and a Devil's Deal.* New York: Public Affairs.
Lehti, Martil and Kauko Aromaa
  2003   "Trafficking in Women and Children in Europe." Pages 114–128 in *Organised Crime, Trafficking, Drugs: Selected Papers Presented at the Annual Conference of the European Society of Criminology,* Helsinki, edited by Sami Nevala and Kauko Armomaa.
Lens, Sidney
  1974   *The Labor Wars.* Garden City, NY: Doubleday.
Leonard, John
  1996   "Bandit King." *New York* (August 19): 55–56.
Leonhardt, David with Barbara Whitaker
  2000   "U.S. Companies Tangled in Web of Drug Dollars." *New York Times* (October 10): 1, 20.
Lerner, Steven E.
  1980   "Phencyclidine Abuse in Perspective." Pages 13–23 in *Phencyclidine Abuse Manual,* edited by Mary Tuma McAdams, Ronald L. Linder, Steven E. Lerner, and Richard Stanley Burns. Los Angeles: University of California Extension.
Lev, Michael A.
  1997   "Meeting Protection Racket Snares Mitsubishi." *Chicago Tribune* (October 24): Sec. 3: 1, 2.
Levine, Edward M.
  1966   *The Irish and Irish Politicians.* Notre Dame, IN: University of Notre Dame Press.
Levine, Gary
  1995   *Jack "Legs" Diamond: Anatomy of a Gangster.* Fleishmanns, NY: Purple Mountain Press.

Levine, Michael
1990 *Deep Cover.* New York: Delacorte.

LeVine, Steve, Betsy McKay, and Natasha Lebedeva
1993 "A Long Bloody Summer." *Newsweek* (August 30): 38–39.

Levins, Hoag
1980 "The Kabul Connection." *Philadelphia* (August): 114–20.

Levy, Clifford J.
1995 "Russian Émigrés Are Among 25 Named in Tax Fraud in Newark." *New York Times* (August 8): 1, 8.

Lewis, Norman
1964 *The Honoured Society.* New York: Putnam's.

Library of Congress (LC)
2003 *Organized Crime and Terrorist Activity in Mexico, 1999–2002.* Washington, DC: LC.

Lichtblau, Erie
2005a "F.B.I. Found to Violate Its Informant Rules." *New York Times* (September 13): 14.
2005b "Justice Dept. Defends Patriot Act Before Senate Hearings." *New York Times* (April 5): 19.
2003a "Mexico and U.S. Hold 240 and Seize 13 Tons of Cocaine." *New York Times* (August 1): 12.
2003b "U.S. Cautiously Begins to Seize Millions in Foreign Banks." *New York Times* (May 30): 16.
2003c "U.S. Uses Terror Law to Pursue Crimes From Drugs to Swindling." *New York Times* (September 28): 1, 32.

Liddick, Don
1998 *The Mob's Daily Number: Organized Crime and the Number's Gambling Industry.* Lanham, MD: University Press of America.

Lieven, Anatol
1998 *Chechyna: Tombstone of Russian Power.* New Haven, CT: Yale University Press.

Light, Ivan
1977 "The Ethnic Vice Industry, 1880–1944." *American Journal of Sociology* 42 (June): 464–79.

Lindberg, Richard C.
1991 *To Serve and Collect: Chicago Politics and Police Corruption from the Lager Beer Riot to the Summerdale Scandal.* New York: Praeger.

Linder, Ronald L., Steven E. Lerner, and R. Stanley Burns
1981 *PCP: The Devil's Dust.* Belmont, CA: Wadsworth.

Lintner, Bertil
2002 *Blood Brothers: The Criminal Underworld of Asia.* New York: Palgrave Macmillan.

Lippman, Walter
1962 "The Underworld as Servant." In *Organized Crime in America*, edited by Gus Tyler. Ann Arbor: University of Michigan Press. Article originally published in 1931.

Liptik, Adam
2008 "A Corporate View of Mafia Tactics: Protesting, Lobbying and Citing Upton Sinclair." *New York Times* (February 5): 14.

Liu, Jainhong, Dengke Zhou, Allen E. Liska, Steven F. Messner, Marvin D. Krohn, Lening Zhang, and Zhou Lu
1998 "Status, Power, and Sentencing in China." *Justice Quarterly* 15 (June): 289–300.

Lloyd, Henry Demerest
1963 *Wealth Against Commonwealth*, edited by Thomas C. Cochran. Englewood Cliffs, NJ: Prentice-Hall.

Logan, Andy
1970 *Against the Evidence: The Becker-Rosenthal Affair.* New York: McGraw-Hill.

Lohr, Steve
1999 "Privacy on Internet Poses Legal Puzzle." *New York Times* (April 19): C4.
1992 "Where the Money Washes Up: Offshore Banking in the Cayman Islands." *New York Times Magazine* (March 29): 26–29, 32, 46, 52.

Lombardo, Robert M.
2004 "The Black Hand: A Study in Moral Panic." *Global Crime* 6 (November): 267–84.
2002a "The Black Hand." *Journal of Contemporary Criminal Justice* 18 (November): 393–408.
2002b "The Black Mafia: African-American Organized Crime in Chicago, 1890–1960." *Crime, Law and Social Change* 38: 33–65.
1994 "The Organized Crime Neighborhoods of Chicago." Pages 169–87 in *Handbook of Organized Crime in the United States*, edited by Robert J. Kelly, Ko-lin Chin, and Rufus Schatzberg. Westport, CT: Greenwood.
1979 "Organized Crime and the Concept of Community." Unpublished paper, Department of Sociology, University of Illinois at Chicago.

Longstreet, Stephen
1973 *Chicago 1860–1919.* New York: McKay.

Lorch, Donatella
1990 "Mourners Shot Back at Funeral." *New York Times* (July 30): 9.

Loree, Don
2002 "Organized Crime: Changing Concepts and Realities for the Police." *Trends in Organized Crime* 7 (Summer): 73–78.

Loth, David
1938 *Public Plunder: A History of Graft in America.* New York: Carrick and Evans.

Lubasch, Arnold H.
1992a "Death Penalty Sought at a Trial in Brooklyn." *New York Times* (April 14): 16.
1992b "U.S. Moves to Break Up Trash Cartel." *New York Times* (August 18): B12.
1992c "U.S. Prosecutors Say That Gotti Is Still a Functioning Crime Boss." *New York Times* (September 16): 18.
1992d "Mobster Testifies of Bribing Juror." *New York Times* (November 5): 13.
1991 "Ex-Mob Leader Tells Court of Killings." *New York Times* (April 26): 16.

Luft, Kerry
1995 "For Bogotá's Street Children, Death Is Just Around the Corner." *Chicago Tribune* (January 15): 12.

Lupsha, Peter A.
1995 "Transnational Narco-Corruption and Narco Investment: A Focus on Mexico." *Transnational Organized Crime* 1 (Spring): 84–101.
1991 "Drug Lords and Narco-Corruption: The Players Change But the Game Continues." *Crime, Law and Social Change* 16: 41–58.
1990 "The Geopolitics of Organized Crime: Some Comparative Models from Latin American Drug Trafficking Organizations." Paper presented at the annual meeting of the American Society of Criminology, Baltimore, MD, November.

1983   "Networks Versus Networking: Analysis of an Organized Crime Group." Pages 59–87 in *Career Criminals*, edited by Gordon P. Waldo. Beverly Hills, CA: Sage.

1981   "Individual Choice, Material Culture, and Organized Crime." *Criminology* 19: 3–24.

Lupsha, Peter A. and Kip Schlegel
1980   "The Political Economy of Drug Trafficking: The Herrera Organization (Mexico and the United States)." Unpublished paper, Department of Political Science, University of New Mexico at Albuquerque.

Maas, Peter
1997   *Underboss: Sammy the Bull Gravano's Story of Life in the Mafia*. New York: HarperCollins.

1968   *The Valachi Papers*. New York: Putnam's.

MacDougall, Ernest D., ed.
1933   *Crime for Profit: A Symposium on Mercenary Crime*. Boston: Stratford.

Maffei, Stefano and Isabella Merzagora Betsos
2007   "Crime and Criminal Policy in Italy: Tradition and Modernity in a Troubled Country." *European Journal of Criminology* 4 (4): 461–82.

Maltz, Michael D.
1990   *Measuring the Effectiveness of Organized Crime Control Efforts*. Chicago: Office of International Criminal Justice, University of Illinois.

1976   "On Defining 'Organized Crime.'" *Crime and Delinquency* 22 (July): 338–46.

1975   "Policy Issues in Organized and White Collar Crime." Pages 73–95 in *Crime and Criminal Justice*, edited by John A. Gardiner and Michael A. Mulkey. Lexington, MA: D. C. Heath.

Manca, John and Vincent Cosgrove
1991   *Tin for Sale: My Career in Organized Crime and the NYPD*. New York: William Morrow.

Mangione, Jerre
1985   *A Passion for Sicilians: The World Around Danilo Dolci*. New Brunswick, NJ: Transaction Books.

Mangione, Jerre and Ben Morreale
1992   *La Storia: Five Centuries of the Italian American Experience*. New York: HarperCollins.

"Man Loses Federal Appeal in Internet Gambling Case"
2001   *New York Times* (August 1): 16.

Mann, Arthur
1965   *La Guardia Comes to Power: 1933*. Philadelphia: Lippincott.

Márquez, Gabriel García
1997   *News of a Kidnapping*. New York: Knopf.

Marquis, Christopher and Juan Forero
2004   "U.S. Government Gains in Eradicating Andean Coca." *New York Times* (March 23): 3.

Marsh, Harry L.
1991   "Law Enforcement, the Military, and the War on Drugs: Is the Military Involvement in the War on Drugs Ethical?" *American Journal of Police* 10: 61–75.

Marshall, Claire
2005   "'Durgaon' Escapes from Mexico Jail." Internet: news.bbc.co.uk.

Marshall, Donnie
2001   "Testimony Before the U.S. House of Representatives Committee on the Judiciary Subcommittee on Crime," March 29.

1999   "Testimony Before the U.S. House of Representatives Committee International Relations Subcommittee on the Western Hemisphere," March 3: 1–11.

Marshall, Eliot
1978   "State Lottery." *New Republic* (June 24): 20–21.

Martel, Ned
2006   "Taking a Long Look at a Latino Gang Named for Fire Ants." *New York Times* (February 11): B18.

Martin, Andrew
1996   "Even with Leaders in Jail, Gang's Drug Business Is Flourishing." *Chicago Tribune* (January 29): 1, 13.

Martin, Andrew and John O'Brien
1996   "Alleged Drug Hub Didn't Fit the Area." *Chicago Tribune* (October 13): 1, 21.

Martin, Andrew and Matt O'Connor
1996a   "Jeff Fort's Son Faces Drug Charges." *Chicago Tribune* (September 4): Sec. 2: 1, 2.

1996b   "Gang 'Prince' Stakes Claim to the Throne." *Chicago Tribune* (September 21): 1, 12.

Martin, Raymond V.
1963   *Revolt in the Mafia*. New York: Duell, Sloan, and Pearce.

Martinez, Michael
1995   "Hells Angels Pay Their Last Respects to Slaying Victim." *Chicago Tribune* (March 8): Sec. 2: 1, 4.

Marx, Gary
1991   "Drug Lord, or Ghost, Stalks Colombian Town." *Chicago Tribune* (July 28): 4.

Marzulli, John
2006   "The Baby Godfather." *New York Daily News* (November 15): 5.

2005a   "Feds Hunt Real-Life 'Luca Brasi.'" *New York Daily News* (February 10): 4.

2005b   "Name Got a Good Guy Whacked." *New York Daily News* (March 11): 7.

2005c   "$650M Porn Scam." *New York Daily News* (February 15): 5.

2003   "Son Is in Like Chin." *New York Daily News* (July 26): Internet.

Marzulli, John and Jonathan Lemire
2005   "Mobster on Run Nabbed Upstate." *New York Daily News* (March 20): 24.

Marzulli, John and Patrice O'Shaughnessy
2005   "Muscle and Brains Behind Mob Cops." *New York Daily News* (March 13): 4–5.

Mass, Robert
1991   "Law Enforcement Approaches to Organized Crime Infiltration of Legitimate Industry." Pages 37–47 in *Organized Crime and Its Containment: A Transatlantic Initiative*, edited by Cyrelle Fijnaut and James Jacobs. Deventer, Netherlands: Kluwer.

Massing, Michael
1990   "In the Cocaine War, the Jungle Is Winning." *New York Times Magazine* (March 4): 26, 88, 90, 92.

Mazzitelli, Antonio
2006   "Transnational Organized Crime in West Africa: The Additional Challenge." *International Affairs* 83 (6): 1071–1090.

McAlary, Mike
1998   "Breaking the Code." *New York* (April 13): 31–35, 74.

McCaffrey, Lawrence J.
1976   *The Irish Diaspora in America*. Bloomington: Indiana University Press.

McClellan, John L.
1962   *Crime Without Punishment*. New York: Duell, Sloan, and Pearce.

McConaughy, John
1931   *From Cain to Capone: Racketeering Down the Ages*. New York: Brentano's.

McCormick, John
1999   "Winning a Gang War." *Newsweek* (November 1): 46–49.

McCoy, Alfred W.
1991   *The Politics of Heroin: CIA Complicity in the Global Drug Trade*. Brooklyn, NY: Lawrence Hill.
1972   *The Politics of Heroin in Southeast Asia*. New York: Harper & Row.

McFadden, Robert D.
2005   "Drug Suspect in Afghan Ring Is Sent to U.S." *New York Times* (October 25): B1, 2.
1999   "Teamsters' Unit Regains Control." *New York Times* (February 26): 19.
1997   "Limits on Cash Transactions Cut Drug-Money Laundering." *New York Times* (March 11): 1, 11.
1988   "Anthony Provenzano, 71, Ex-Teamster Chief, Dies." *New York Times* (December 13): 22.
1983   "Meyer Lansky Is Dead at 81; Financial Wizard of Organized Crime." *New York Times* (January 16): 21.

McGraw, Dan
1997   "The National Bet." *U.S. News and World Report* (April 7): 50–55.

McGuinness, Robert L.
1981   "In the Katz Eye: Use of Binoculars and Telescopes." *FBI Law Enforcement Bulletin* (June): 26–31.

McGuire, Michael
1993   "Airborne Police Wage Losing Battle in Colombia Poppy Fields." *Chicago Tribune* (April 4): 6.

McGuire, Phillip C.
1988   "Jamaican Posses: A Call for Cooperation among Law Enforcement Agencies." *Police Chief* (January): 20–27.

McKinley, James C., Jr.
2008a "After Massacre, a Mexican Town Is Left in Terror of Drug Violence." *New York Times* (May 31): 1, 8.
2008b "Drug War Causes Wild West Blood Bath, Killing 210 in a Mexican Town." *New York Times* (April 16): 10.
2008c "Mexican Federal Agents Seize Millions and Arrest 6." *New York Times* (April 4): 8.
2008d "Mexican Forces Clash with Drug Cartel Gunmen in Tijuana." *New York Times* (January 18): 5.
2008e "Mexico Hits Drug Gangs with Full Fury of War." *New York Times* (January 22): 1, 9.
2008f "Mexico's War Against Drugs Kills Its Police." *New York Times* (May 26): 1, 9.
2008g "6 Charged in Shooting Death of a Police Chief in Mexico." *New York Times* (May 13): 8.
2008h "3 Americans Arrested in Gang Battle with Mexican Police." *New York Times* (January 9): 5.
2007a "In Mexico, a Fugitive's Arrest Captivates the Cameras." *New York Times* (October 12): 3.
2007b "Mexico Tries to Show Resolve with Big Drug Seizure." *New York Times* (November 29): 10.
2007c "Songs of Love and Murder, Silenced by Murder." *New York Times* (December 18): 1, 20.
2006a "A War in Mexico: Drug Runners Gun Down Journalists." *New York Times* (February 10): 6.
2006b "With Beheadings and Attacks, Drug Gangs Terrorize Mexico." *New York Times* (October 26): 1, 12.
2005a "Drug Lord, Ruthless and Elusive, Reaches High in Mexico." *New York Times* (February 9): 3.
2005b "Mexican Troops Seize Prison After Drug Lord Violence." *New York Times* (January 15): 3.
2005c "Mexico: 12 Found Dead in Drug Shootouts." *New York Times* (February 17): 8.
2005d "Scandals Shake Mexico's Confidence in Elite Police Unit." *New York Times* (December 28): 3.
2004a "Mexico Arrests Man Suspected of Leading Drug Cartel's Assassins." *New York Times* (October 30): 6.
2004b "7 in Family Slain in Mexico in Mix-Up Laid to Police Renegades." *New York Times* (November 9): 5.
1990   "17 Charged in Raids of Brooklyn 'Posse' Linked to Deaths." *New York Times* (December 8): 1, 7.

McMahon, Colin
1996   "Top Drug Suspect Seized in Mexico." *Chicago Tribune* (January 16): 4.
1995   "Mexicans Make Their Mark in Drug Game as Middlemen." *Chicago Tribune* (September 18): 1, 14.
1992   "Illegal Wagers Now Are Safer Than Ever." *Chicago Tribune* (November 15): 1, 17.

McPhaul, Jack
1970   *Johnny Torrio: First of the Gang Lords*. New Rochelle, NY: Arlington House.

McPhee, Michele
2003   "Capo, His Young Guns Face New Murder Rap." *New York Daily News* (December 5): 16.

Mendelson, Wallace B.
1980   *The Use and Misuse of Sleeping Pills: A Clinical Guide*. New York: Plenum.

Merlin, Mark David
1984   *On the Trail of the Ancient Opium Poppy*. Rutherford, NJ: Farleigh Dickinson University Press.

Merriam, Charles Edward
1929   *Chicago: A More Intimate View of Urban Politics*. New York: Macmillan.

Merton, Robert
1967   *On Theoretical Sociology*. New York: Free Press.
1964   "Anomie, Anomia, and Social Interaction." Pages 213–42 in *Anomie and Deviant Behavior*, edited by Marshall B. Clinard. New York: Free Press.
1938   "Social Structure and Anomie." *American Sociological Review* 3: 672–82.

Meskil, Paul
1977   "Meet the New Godfather." *New York* (February 28): 28–32.
1973   *Don Carlo: Boss of Bosses*. New York: Popular Library.

Messick, Hank
1973   *Lansky*. New York: Berkley.
1967   *The Silent Syndicate*. New York: Macmillan.

"Mexico Seizes Top Drugs Suspect"
2008   Internet: news.bbc.co.uk.

Mieczkowski, Thomas
1986   "Geeking Up and Throwing Down: Heroin Street Life in Detroit." *Criminology* 24 (November): 645–66.
Milhaupt, Curtis J. and Mark D. West
2000   "The Dark Side of Private Ordering: An Institutional and Empirical Analysis of Organized Crime." *University of Chicago Law Review* 67: 41–98.
Miller, Matthew
2006   "Catch Me If You Can." *Forbes* (March 27): 112–116, 125.
Millman, Nancy
1996   "$100 Million Fine in ADM Guilty Plea." *Chicago Tribune* (October 16): 1, 27.
Mitchell, Alison
1995   "U.S. Freezes Assets of Cartel in New Effort Against Drugs." *New York Times* (October 23): 5.
1992   "Russian Emigres Importing Thugs to Commit Contract Crimes in U.S." *New York Times* (April 11): 1, 18.
Mokhiber, Russell
1988   *Corporate Crime and Violence: Big Business Power and the Abuse of the Public Trust*. San Francisco: Sierra Club Books.
Moldea, Dan E.
1978   *The Hoffa Wars*. New York: Charter Books.
Moody, John
1991   "A Day with the Chess Player." *Time* (July 1): 34–36.
Moore, Mark H.
1987   "Organized Crime as a Business Enterprise." Pages 51–64 in *Major Issues in Organized Crime Control*, edited by Herbert Edelhertz. Washington, DC: U.S. Government Printing Office.
Moore, Robin with Barbara Fuca
1977   *Mafia Wife*. New York: Macmillan.
Moore, William Howard
1974   *The Kefauver Committee and the Politics of Crime*. Columbia: University of Missouri Press.
Morales, Edmundo
1989   *Cocaine: White Gold Rush in Peru*. Tucson: University of Arizona Press.
Moreau, Ron and Sami Yousafzai
2006   "A Harvest of Treachery." *Newsweek* (January 9): 32–35.
Morgan, Howard Wayne
1981   *Drugs in America: A Social History, 1800–1980*. Syracuse, NY: Syracuse University Press.
Morgan, Howard Wayne, ed.
1974   *Yesterday's Addicts: American Society and Drug Abuse, 1865–1920*. Norman: University of Oklahoma Press.
Morgan, John
1985   *Prince of Crime*. New York: Stein and Day.
Morgan, Thomas
1989   "16 Charged in Scheme to Launder Millions." *New York Times* (May 14): 24.
Mori, Cesare
1933   *The Last Struggle with the Mafia*. London: Putnam's.
Moriarity, Tom
1998   Special Agent, Criminal Investigation Division, Internal Revenue Service. Personal interview.

Moseley, Ray
1997   "Biker War Revving Up in Denmark." *Chicago Tribune* (July 3): 1, 14.
Motivans, Mark
2003   *Money-Laundering Offenders, 1994–2001*. Washington, DC: Bureau of Justice Statistics.
Mulvey, Erin
2008   "Associate of Colombian Narco-Terrorist Group Extradited to United States on Cocaine Importation Charges." Drug Enforcement Administration press release, April 22.
Murphy, Kate
2008   "Mexican Robin Hood Figure Gains a Kind of Notoriety in the U.S." *New York Times* (February 8): 12.
Murr, Andrew
2000   "Corralling Sammy 'The Bull.'" *Newsweek* (March 6): 36–37.
Murray, George
1975   *The Legacy of Al Capone*. New York: Putnam's.
Mustain, Gene and Jerry Capeci
1992   *Murder Machine: A True Story of Murder, Madness, and the Mafia*. New York: Dutton.
1988   *Mob Star: The Story of John Gotti, the Most Powerful Criminal in America*. New York: Franklin Watts.
Musto, David
1973   *The American Disease: Origins of Narcotic Control*. New Haven, CT: Yale University Press.
Mydans, Seth
2008   "In Thai Protests, a Divide Between Urban and Rural." *New York Times* (October 13): 6.
2003a   "Burmese Women Are Reporting Systematic Rapes by Military." *New York Times* (May 12): 12.
2003b   "Thai Vice-King's Lament: Police Don't Stay Bought." *New York Times* (July 30): 8.
2003c   "A Wave of Drug Killings Is Linked to Thai Police." *New York Times* (April 8): 3.
1995   "Racial Tensions on the Rise in Los Angeles Jail System." *New York Times* (February 6): 8.
Myers, Gustavus
1936   *History of Great American Fortunes*. New York: Modern Library.
Myers, Willard H., III
1995   "Orb Weavers—The Global Webs: The Structure and Activities of Transnational Ethnic Chinese Groups." *Transnational Organized Crime* 1 (Winter): 1–36.
Myerson, Allen R.
1995   "The Garbage Wars: Cracking the Cartel." *New York Times* (July 30): F1, 11.
1994   "American Express Bank Unit Settles U.S. Laundering Case." *New York Times* (November 22): 1, C8.
"Naples Police in Huge Mafia Sweep"
2004   *BBC News* (December 7): Internet.
Napoli, Antonio
2004   *The Mob's Guys*. College Station, TX: Virtualbookworm.com Publishing.
Naravane, Vaiju
2008   "Berlusconi Sparks Outrage." *The Hindu* (April 17): Internet.
National Advisory Commission on the Causes and Prevention of Violence
1969   *Staff Report: Crimes of Violence*. Washington, DC: U.S. Government Printing Office.

National Association of Attorneys General
1977 *Organized Crime Control Units*. Raleigh, NC: Committee on the Office of Attorneys General.
National Central Police University, Taipei, Taiwan
2005 "Organized Crime Gangs in Taiwan." *Trends in Organized Crime* 8 (Spring): 13–23.
National Commission on Law Observance and Enforcement
1931 *Report on Police*. Washington, DC: U.S. Government Printing Office.
National Commission for the Review of Federal and State Laws Relating to Wiretapping and Electronic Surveillance
1976 *Electronic Surveillance*. Washington, DC: U.S. Government Printing Office.
National Drug Intelligence Center
2008 *Indian Country: Drug Threat Assessment*. Washington, DC: U.S. Department of Justice.
National Police Agency of Japan
1996 "Promotion of Measures Against Organized Crime Groups." Excerpted in *Trends in Organized Crime* 1 (Spring): 49–57.
National Synthetic Drugs Action Plan
2004 Washington, DC: Office of National Drug Control Policy.
Navarro, Mireya
1998 "Upgraded Drug Traffic Flourishes on Old Route." *New York Times* (May 31): 14.
1997 "Russian Submarine Surfaces as Player in the Drug World." *New York Times* (March 7): 1, 9.
1996 "When Drug Kingpins Fall, Illicit Assets Buy a Cushion." *New York Times* (March 19): 1, C19.
Navasky, Victor S.
1977 *Kennedy Justice*. New York: Atheneum.
Needler, Martin C.
1995 *Mexican Politics: The Containment of Conflict*, 3d ed. Westport, CT: Praeger.
Neff, James
1989 *Mobbed Up: Jackie Presser's High Wire Life in the Teamsters, the Mafia, and the F.B.I.* New York: Atlantic Monthly Press.
Nelli, Humbert S.
1976 *The Business of Crime*. New York: Oxford University Press.
1969 "Italians and Crime in Chicago: The Formative Years: 1890–1920." *American Journal of Sociology* 74 (January): 373–91.
Nelson, Jack E., Helen Wallenstein Pearson, Mollie Sawyers, and Thomas J. Glynn
1982 *Guide to Drug Abuse Research Terminology*. Rockville, MD: National Institute on Drug Abuse.
Neumeister, Larry
2000 "Landmark Conviction in Web Gambling." Associated Press (February 28): Internet.
Newell, Barbara Warne
1961 *Chicago and the Labor Movement: Metropolitan Unionism in the 1930s*. Urbana: University of Illinois Press.
Newfield, Jack
1979 "The Myth of Godfather Journalism." *Village Voice* (July 23): 1, 11–13.
"New Gang Methods Replace Those of Eastman's Days"
1923 *New York Times* (September 9): Sec. 9: 3.

New Jersey Commission of Investigation (NJCI)
2004 The Changing Face of Organized Crime in New Jersey. Trenton, NJ: NJCI.
1987 *Report and Recommendations on Organized Crime-Affiliated Subcontractors at Casino and Public Construction Sites*. Trenton, NJ: NJCI.
New York State Organized Crime Task Force (NYSOCTF)
1988 *Corruption and Racketeering in the New York City Construction Industry*. Ithaca, NY: Cornell University School of Labor and Industrial Relations.
Nicaso, Antonio and Lee Lamothe
2005 *Angels, Mobsters and Narco-Terorists*. Ontario, Canada: John Wiley.
Nichols, Dave
2007 *One Percenter: The Legend of the Outlaw Biker*. St. Paul, MN: MBI Publishing Co.
Nicodemus, Charles and Art Petacque
1981 "Mob Jewel Fencing Investigated." *Chicago Sun-Times* (November 29): 5, 76.
Nietzel, Michael T., Douglas A. Bernstein, Geoffrey P. Kramer, and Richard Milich
2003 *Introduction to Clinical Psychology*, 6th ed. Upper Saddle River, NJ: Prentice-Hall.
Nieves, Evelyn
2001 "Drug Labs in Valley Feed Nation's Habit." *New York Times* (May 13): 1, 18.
Nigerian Advance Fee Fraud
1997 U.S. Department of State publication.
NNICC
1998 *The Supply of Illicit Drugs to the United States*. Washington, DC: National Narcotics Intelligence Consumers Committee (NNICC).
Nocera, Joseph
1988 "Drexel: Hanged Without a Trial." *New York Times* (December 30): 19.
O'Brien, Edward I.
1986 "RICO's Assault on Legitimate Business." *New York Times* (January 5): F2.
O'Brien, John
1996 "Chicago at Heart of Heroin Case." *Chicago Tribune* (October 12): 1, 9.
1993 "James J. D'Antonio, 65, Mob Driver." *Chicago Tribune* (December 15): Sec. 2: 11.
1988 "Car-Theft Figure Slain at His Home." *Chicago Tribune* (August 16): Sec. 2: 3.
O'Brien, John and Jan Crawford Greenburg
1996 "Raids Reveal How Little Guys Climb the Drug Ladder." *Chicago Tribune* (May 3): 1, 21.
O'Brien, John, Matt O'Connor, and George Papajohn
1995 "U.S. Goes Behind Bars to Indict 39 Gang Leaders." *Chicago Tribune* (September 1): 1, 12.
O'Brien, Joseph F. and Andris Kurins
1991 *Boss of Bosses: The FBI and Paul Castellano*. New York: Dell.
O'Brien, Robert and Sidney Cohen
1984 *Encyclopedia of Drug Abuse*. New York: Facts on File.
O'Connor, Anne-Marie
1999 "10 Alleged Leaders of Drug Ring Arrested." *Los Angeles Times* (February 2): Internet.
O'Connor, Len
1984 "Give Me That Old-Time Politics." *Chicago Magazine* (February): 114–19.

O'Connor, Matt
2000 "Gang Member Is Sentenced to 100 Years." *Chicago Tribune* (December 14): Sec 2: 5.
1999 "When a Bribe Isn't a Bribe: FBI Mole Lands Prison Term." *Chicago Tribune* (October 15): 1, 14.
1998 "Raiders Net Millions, Ton of Cocaine." *Chicago Tribune* (May 28): Sec. 2: 7.
1997 "Hoover, 6 Others Convicted; Seen as Blow to Gang." *Chicago Tribune* (May 10): 1, 12.
1996 "Gambling Manager for Mob Pleads Guilty to Racketeering." *Chicago Tribune* (September 25): Sec. 2: 3.
1994a "On Leong, Moy Plead Guilty to Running Long-time Casino." *Chicago Tribune* (February 12): 5.
1994b "Sentencing of 'Chinatown Mayor' Closes On Leong Case." *Chicago Tribune* (May 16): Sec 2: 1, 4.

O'Connor, Richard
1962 *Gould's Millions.* Garden City, NY: Doubleday.
1958 *Hell's Kitchen.* Philadelphia, PA: Lippincott.

Office of Inspector General
2000 *Semiannual Report to the Congress: October 1, 1999– March 31, 2000.* Washington, DC: U.S. Department of Labor.

Okada, Daniel W.
1992 "Asian Gangs: What Are We Talking About?" Paper presented at the annual meeting of the American Society of Criminology, New Orleans, November.

O'Neil, Gerard and Dick Lehr
1989 *The Underboss: The Rise and Fall of a Mafia Family.* New York: St. Martin's Press.

Orlando, Leoluca
2001 *Fighting the Mafia and Renewing Sicilian Culture.* San Francisco, CA: Encounter Books.

O'Rourke, John J.
1997 Special Agent, Federal Bureau of Investigation, retired. Personal interview.

Orth, Maureen
2002 "Afghanistan's Deadly Habit." *Vanity Fair* (March): 150–52, 165–77.

Ouagrham-Gormley, Sonia Ben
2007 "An Unrealized Nexus? WMD-Related Trafficking, Terrorism, and Organized Crime in the Former Soviet Union." *Arms Control Today* (July/August): Internet.

Overly, Don H. and Theodore H. Schell
1973 *New Effectiveness Measures for Organized Crime Control Efforts.* Washington, DC: U.S. Government Printing Office.

Owen, David
2003 "Concrete Jungle." *New Yorker* (November 10): 62–81.

Packer, Herbert L.
1968 *The Limits of the Criminal Sanction.* Stanford, CA: Stanford University Press.

Padgett, Tim
2005 "The Killers Next Door." *Time* (April 18): 140–41.

Padgett Tim and Ioan [sic] Grillo
2008 "Cocaine Capital." *Time* (August 25): 36–38.

Palacios, Marco
2007 *Between Legitimacy and Violence: A History of Colombia, 1875–2002.* Durham: Duke University Press. Translated by Richard Stoller.

Pallasch, Abdon and Judy Peres
1998 "Abortion Foes Suffer a Big Setback." *Chicago Tribune* (April 21): 1, 8.

Palley, Thomas I.
1996 "The Forces Making for an Economic Collapse." *Atlantic Monthly* (July): 44–45, 58.

Palsey, Fred D.
1971 *Al Capone: The Biography of a Self-Made Man.* Freeport, NY: Books for Libraries Press. Originally published in 1931.

Pantaleone, Michele
1966 *The Mafia and Politics.* New York: Coward and McCann.

Paoli, Letizia
2003 *Mafia Brotherhoods: Organized Crime, Italian Style.* New York: Oxford University Press.
2001 "Crime, Italian Style." *Daedalus* 130 (Summer): 157–70.
1999 "The Political-Criminal Nexus in Italy." *Trends in Organized Crime* 5 (Winter): 15–58.
1994 "An Underestimated Criminal Phenomenon: The Calabrian 'Ndrangheta." *European Journal of Crime, Criminal Law and Criminal Justice* 2 (3): 212–38.

Paoli, Letizia and Peter Reuter
2008 "Drug Trafficking and Ethnic Minorities in Western Europe." *European Journal of Criminology* 5 (1): 13–37.

Papajohn, George and Tracy Dell'Angela
1995 "Indictments Open Door for Next Gang." *Chicago Tribune* (September 3): 1, 16.

Paradis, Peter
2002 *Nasty Business: One Biker Gang's Bloody War Against the Hells Angels.* Toronto, Canada: HarperCollins.

Paterernostro, Silvana
2007 *My Colombian War: A Journey Through the Country.* New York: Henry Holt and Co.

Patterson, Orlando
2001 "The Roots of Conflict in Jamaica." *New York Times* (July 23): 21.

PCOC. See President's Commission on Organized Crime

Pennsylvania Crime Commission (PCC)
1990 *Organized Crime in Pennsylvania: A Decade of Change, 1990 Report.* Conshohocken, PA: PCC.
1988 *1988 Report.* Conshohocken, PA: PCC.

Pepper, Daniel
2008 "Aftermath of a Revolt: Myanmar's Lost Years." *New York Times* (October 5): 5.

Permanent Subcommittee on Investigations (PSI)
1983a *Crime and Secrecy: The Use of Offshore Banks and Companies.* Washington, DC: U.S. Government Printing Office.
1983b *Organized Crime in Chicago* (March 4). Washington, DC: U.S. Government Printing Office.
1982 *Hotel Employees and Restaurant Employees International Union: Part I* (June 22, 23). Washington, DC: U.S. Government Printing Office.
1981a *International Narcotics Trafficking.* Washington, DC: U.S. Government Printing Office.
1981b *Waterfront Corruption.* Washington DC: U.S. Government Printing Office.
1981c *Witness Security Program.* Washington, DC: U.S. Government Printing Office.

Petacco, Arrigo
1974   *Joe Petrosino*. New York: Macmillan.
Peterson, Virgil
1983   *The Mob: 200 Years of Organized Crime in New York.* Ottawa, IL: Green Hill Publishers.
1969   *A Report on Chicago Crime for 1968.* Chicago Crime Commission.
1963   "Chicago: Shades of Capone." *Annals* 347 (May): 30–39.
1962   "Career of a Syndicate Boss." *Crime and Delinquency* 8 (October): 339–49.
Phongpaichit, Pasuk and Chris Baker
2003   "Slaughter in the Name of a Drug War." *New York Times* (May 24): 15.
Physicians' Desk Reference
1988   Oradell, NJ: Medical Economics Co.
1987   Oradell, NJ: Medical Economics Co.
Pietrusza, David
2003   *Rothstein: The Life, Times, and Murder of the Criminal Genius Who Fixed the 1919 World Series.* New York: Carroll and Graf Publishers.
Pileggi, Nicholas
1995   *Casino.* New York: Pocket Books.
1990   *Wise Guy: Life in a Mafia Family.* New York: Pocket Books.
1985   *Wise Guy: Life in a Mafia Family.* New York: Pocket Books.
Pinkerton, James and Ioan [sic] Grillo
2005   "The Fight for Nuevo Laredo." *Houston Chronicle* (May 8): Internet.
Pistone, Joseph D.
2004   *The Way of the Wiseguy.* Philadelphia: Running Press.
1992   *The Ceremony: The Mafia Initiation Tapes.* New York: Dell.
1987   *Donnie Brasco: My Undercover Life in the Mafia.* New York: New American Library.
Pitkin, Thomas Monroe and Francesco Cordasco
1977   *The Black Hand: A Chapter in Ethnic Crime.* Totowa, NJ: Littlefield, Adams.
Plate, Thomas and the Editors of *New York*, eds.
1972   *The Mafia at War.* New York: New York Magazine Press.
Polgreen, Lydia
2005   "As Nigeria Tries to Fight Graft, a New Sordid Tale." *New York Times* (November 29): 1, 14.
Polgreen, Lydia and Tim Weiner
2004   "Drug Traffickers Find Haiti a Hospitable Port of Call." *New York Times* (May 16): 6.
"Police Tackle London's Yardies"
1999   *BBC News* (July 20): Internet.
Pomfret, John
2001   "Made Man in China Has Gangland Ties, Party Pals." *Seattle Times* (January 21): Internet.
Popiano, Willie with John Harney
1993   *Godson: A True-Life Account of 20 Years Inside the Mob.* New York: St. Martin's Press.
Porrello, Rick
1995   *The Rise and Fall of the Cleveland Mafia.* Ft. Lee, NJ: Barricade Books.
Posner, Gerald L.
1988   *Warlords of Crime: Chinese Secret Societies—The New Mafia.* New York: McGraw-Hill.

Possley, Maurice
2001   "Union Ousts 3 Leaders for Mob Ties." *Chicago Tribune* (January 12): Sec. 2: 1, 5.
1996   "U.S. Will Help Mole Set Up His New Digs." *Chicago Tribune* (January 22): 1, 16.
Possley, Maurice and Rick Kogan
2001   *"Everybody Pays": Two Men, One Murder, and the Price of Truth.* New York: Putnam.
Post, Henry
1981   "The Whorehouse Sting." *New York* (February 2): 31–34.
Potter, Gary
1994   *Criminal Organizations: Vice, Racketeering, and Politics in an American City.* Prospect Heights, IL: Waveland.
Potter, Gary, Larry Gaines, and Beth Holbrook
1990   "Blowing Smoke: An Evaluation of Marijuana Eradication in Kentucky." *American Journal of Police* 9: 97–116.
Povoledo, Elisabetta
2007   "A Top Sicilian Mafia Boss Is Held, Italy Says." *New York Times* (November 6): 14.
2006   "Police Seize Top Mafioso After 43 Years." *New York Times* (April 12): 3.
Powell, Bill
2007   "The Strange Case of an Afghan Warlord." *Time* (February 19): 28–37.
2005   "Generation Jihad." *Time* (October 3): 56–59.
Powell, Hickman
2000   *Lucky Luciano: The Man Who Organized Crime in America.* Ft. Lee, NJ: Barricade Books. Originally published in 1939.
Prall, Robert H. and Norton Mockridge
1951   *This Is Costello.* New York: Gold Medal.
Préfontaine, D. C. and Yvon Dandurand
2004   "Terrorism and Organized Crime: Reflections on an Illusive Link and Its Implications for Criminal Law Reform." Paper presented at the Annual Meeting of the International Society for Criminal Law Reform, Montreal, August 8–12.
President's Commission on Law Enforcement and Administration of Justice
1968   *The Challenge of Crime in a Free Society.* New York: Avon.
President's Commission on Organized Crime (PCOC)
1986a   *America's Habit: Drug Abuse, Drug Trafficking, and Organized Crime.* Washington, DC: U.S. Government Printing Office.
1986b   *The Edge: Organized Crime, Business, and Labor Unions.* Washington, DC: U.S. Government Printing Office.
1986c   *The Impact: Organized Crime Today.* Washington, DC: U.S. Government Printing Office.
1985a   "Materials on Ethical Issues for Lawyers Involved with Organized Crime Figures." Unpublished paper.
1985b   *Organized Crime and Labor-Management Racketeering in the United States.* Washington, DC: U.S. Government Printing Office.
1984a   *The Cash Connection: Organized Crime, Financial Institutions, and Money Laundering.* Washington, DC: U.S. Government Printing Office.

1984b *Organized Crime of Asian Origin.* Washington, DC: U.S. Government Printing Office.

1984c *Organized Crime and Cocaine Trafficking.* Washington DC: U.S. Government Printing Office.

"Press Release"
2000 U.S. Attorney for the Second District of New York (October 10).

1999 "Operation Impunity Dismantles Nationwide Drug Trafficking Operation." U.S. Department of Justice, September 22.

Preston, Julia and Craig Pyes
1997 "Mexican Tale: Drugs, Crime, Torture and the U.S." *New York Times* (August 18): 1, 5, 6.

"Profaci Dies of Cancer, Led Feuding Brooklyn Mob"
1962 *New York Times* (June 8): 32.

PSI. See Permanent Subcommittee on Investigations

Puente, Teresa and Paul de la Garza
1999 "Fear, Loathing and Drugs in Mexico." *Chicago Tribune* (December 5): 6.

Pulley, Brett
1999 "Living Off the Daily Dream of Winning a Lottery Prize." *New York Times* (May 22): 1, 12–13.

1998 "Those Seductive Snake Eyes; Tales of Growing Up Gambling." *New York Times* (June 16): 1, 23.

Putnam, Robert D.
1993 *Making Democracy Work: Civic Traditions in Modern Italy.* Princeton, NJ: Princeton University Press.

Quinn, James and D. Shane Koch
2003 "The Nature of Criminality Within One-Percent Motorcycle Clubs." *Deviant Behavior* 24 (3): 281–305.

Quirk, Matthew
2008 "How to Grow a Gang." *The Atlantic* (May): 23, 25.

Raab, Selwyn
2005 *Five Families: The Rise, Decline, and Resurgence of America's Most Powerful Mafia Empires.* New York: St. Martin's Press.

1997a "Arson Case Led to Inquiry of Mob Cartel." *New York Times* (June 23): 13.

1997b "FBI Agent Runs Brooklyn Club to Sting Mafia Stolen Goods Ring." *New York Times* (January 24): 1, 18.

1997c "Simone DeCavalcante, 84, Former Crime Figure in New Jersey." *New York Times* (February 12): 18.

1997d "Two Convicted as Masterminds of Mob's Hold on Private Garbage Collection." *New York Times* (October 22): 19.

1997e "2 Mob Suspects with Same Name Say U.S. Mixed Them Up." *New York Times* (October 19): 17.

1997f "Longtime Numbers King of New York Goes Public to Clear His Name." *New York Times* (July 6): Internet.

1996a "Crackdowns on Mob Seen as Mixed Blessing by Merchants of Fulton Fish Market." *New York Times* (March 31): 18.

1996b "End Gotti's Reign From Cell, Mafia Bosses Tell Gambinos." *New York Times* (October 26): 20.

1996c "Gotti Files 2d Appeal and Authorities Call It a Power Play." *New York Times* (January 21): 18.

1996d "New Jersey Officials Say Mafia Infiltrated Health-Care Industry." *New York Times* (August 21): 1, C19.

1996e "Trash Haulers Charged with Rigging Bids." *New York Times* (November 13): 17.

1996f "Walkout Disrupts Fish Market." *New York Times* (January 3): B12.

1995a "Brother of Mob Turncoat Is Gunned Down." *New York Times* (October 6): 8.

1995b "Crackdown on Mob Aids Garment Makers." *New York Times* (June 12): B12.

1995c "Jury Convicts Philadelphia Mob Leader." *New York Times* (November 22): 8.

1995d "Mayor Seeks Fulton Fish Market Takeover." *New York Times* (February 1): 16.

1995e "New York Bookies Go Computer Age But Wind Up Being Raided Anyhow." *New York Times* (August 25): 6.

1995f "The Thin Line Between Mole and Manager." *New York Times* (July 2): 15.

1994a "Court Disclosures Expose Mobster Who Died of AIDS as F.B.I. Mole." *New York Times* (November 20): 19.

1994b "New Groups of Russian Gangs Gain Foothold in Brooklyn." *New York Times* (August 23): 1, 3.

1994c "Panel Clears Teamsters' Chief of Mob Ties." *New York Times* (July 12): C20.

1992a "Mafia Family in New York Linked to Newspaper Fraud." *New York Times* (July 8): C3.

1992b "'Most Dangerous Mafioso' Left at Helm of Lucchese Crime Family." *New York Times* (November 28): 14.

1992c "Top Member of Colombo Crime Family Is Ambushed in Brooklyn." *New York Times* (December 30): 13.

1990 "Racketeering Held to Persist at New York's Fish Market." *New York Times* (August 9): B12.

"Racket Chief Slain by Gangster Gunfire"
1931 *New York Times* (April 16): 1.

Rakove, Milton L.
1975 *Don't Make No Waves, Don't Back No Losers.* Bloomington: Indiana University Press.

Randolph, Jennifer G.
1995 "RICO—The Rejection of an Economic Motive Requirement." *Journal of Criminal Law and Criminology* 85 (Spring): 1189–1222.

Rangel, Jesus
1988 "10 Are Convicted for Corruption." *New York Times* (November 20): 25.

Rashbaum, William K.
2005 "Three Longshoremen Not Guilty of Fraud and Other Charges." *New York Times* (November 9): B1, 12.

2004 "Officials Say Mob Stole $200 Million Using Phone Bills." *New York Times* (February 11): 1, B6.

2002 "Dock Rackets Tied to Gottis, U.S. Charges." *New York Times* (June 5): 21.

2001a "Mob Soldier Faces a Return to Jail for Parole Violations." *New York Times* (July 18): Internet.

2001b "Two Are Charged in Money-Laundering Scheme." *New York Times* (July 18): Internet.

2000 "A Smuggling Operation with a Russian Twist." *New York Times* (August 9): 1, 15.

Rashbaum, William K. and Juan Forero
2005 "Detective in New York vs. Drug Lord in Colombia." *New York Times* (October 5): B1, 5.

Rawlinson, Patricia
  1997 "Russian Organized Crime: A Brief History." Pages 28–52 in *Russian Organized Crime: The New Threat?* edited by Phil Williams. London, England: Frank Cass.

Ray, Oakley
  1978 *Drugs, Society, and Human Behavior.* St. Louis: Mosby.

Reagan, Ronald
  1986 "Declaring War on Organized Crime." *New York Times Magazine* (January 12): 26, 28, 47, 55–57, 62, 65, 84.

Reece, Jack
  1973 "Fascism, the Mafia, and the Emergence of Sicilian Separatism." *Journal of Modern History* 45 (June): 261–76.

Reedy, George E.
  1991 *From the Ward to the White House: The Irish in American Politics.* New York: Scribner's.

Reid, Ed
  1970 *The Grim Reapers.* New York: Bantam.

Reid, Ed and Ovid Demaris
  1964 *The Green Felt Jungle.* New York: Cardinal Paperbacks.
  1953 *The Shame of New York.* New York: Random House.

Reif, Rita
  1984 "Gould Jewels to Be Sold at Auction." *New York Times* (January 3): 21.

Reinhold, Robert
  1989 "California Shaken Over an Informer." *New York Times* (February 17): 9.

Remnick, David
  1995 "In Stalin's Wake." *New Yorker* (July 24): 46–62.

Renard, Ronald D.
  2003 "The Mandalay Connection: Drugs in Myanmar/Burma." Pages 119–132 in *Transnational Organized Crime: Myth, Power, and Profit,* edited by Emilio C. Viano, Jose Magallanes, and Laurent Bridel. Durham, NC: Carolina Academic Press.

Reppetto, Thomas A.
  2004 *American Mafia: A History of Its Rise to Power.* New York: Holt.
  1978 *The Blue Parade.* New York: Free Press.

Reuter, Peter
  1995 "The Decline of the American Mafia." *Public Interest* (Summer): 89–99.
  1987 *Racketeering in Legitimate Industries: A Study in the Economics of Intimidation.* Santa Monica, CA: RAND Corporation.
  1983 *Disorganized Crime.* Cambridge, MA: MIT Press.

Reuter, Peter and Carol Petrie, eds.
  1999 *Transnational Organized Crime: Summary of a Workshop.* Washington, DC: National Academy Press.

Reuter, Peter, Jonathan Rubinstein, and Simon Wynn
  1983 *Racketeering in Legitimate Industries: Two Case Studies. Executive Summary.* Washington, DC: U.S. Government Printing Office.

Reuters (News Service)
  2004a "Gunmen Free 29 Inmates From Mexico Jail." *New York Times* (January 6): 6.
  2004b "Mexican Drug Boss and 2 Others Slain." *New York Times* (September 13): 5.
  1999 "Italian Police Capture Calabrian Mafia Boss." (March 11): Internet.
  1996 "Hells Angels Convicted in Denmark Slaying." *New York Times* (December 21): 7.

Rey, Guido M. and Ernesto U. Savona
  1993 "The Mafia: An International Enterprise?" Pages 69–80 in *Mafia Issues,* edited by Ernesto U. Savona. Milan, Italy: United Nations.

Reynolds, Marylee
  1995 *From Gangs to Gangsters: How American Sociology Studied Organized Crime, 1918–1994.* Albany, NY: Harrow and Heston.

Rhodes, Robert P.
  1984 *Organized Crime: Crime Control vs. Civil Liberties.* New York: Random House.

Riding, Alan
  1987a "Colombian Envoy Shot in Budapest." *New York Times* (January 14): 5.
  1987b "Colombia Effort Against Drugs Hits Dead End." *New York Times* (August 20): 4.

Riordon, William L.
  1963 *Plunkett of Tammany Hall.* New York: Dutton.

Risley, Raymond
  1998 Commander, Organized Crime Division, Chicago Police Department. Personal interview.

Roane, Kit R.
  2000 "The Mob Goes Downtown." *U.S. News and World Report* (June 26): 16–17.

Robb, Peter
  1996 *Midnight in Sicily.* Boston: Faber and Faber

Robbins, Tom and Jerry Capeci
  1994 "Wiseguy Helped: Civil Rights Killings Solved by Snitch." *New York Daily News* (June 21): 12–13.

Roberton, Robert J.
  1986 "Designer Drugs: The Analog Game." Pages 91–96 in *Bridging Services: Drug Abuse, Human Services and the Therapeutic Community,"* edited by Alfonso Acampora and Ethan Nebelkopf. New York: World Federation of Therapeutic Communities.

Robinson, Linda
  1998a "Is Colombia Lost to Rebels?" *U.S. News and World Report* (May 11): 38–42.
  1998b "Land for Peace in Colombia." *U.S. News and World Report* (November 23): 37.

Robinson, Louis N.
  1933 "Social Values and Mercenary Crime." Pages 13–31 in *Crime for Profit: A Symposium on Mercenary Crime,* edited by Ernest D. MacDougall. Boston: Stratford Company.

"ROC." See "Russian Organized Crime in the United States"

Rockaway, Robert A.
  1993 *But—He Was Good to His Mother: The Lives and Crimes of Jewish Gangsters.* Jerusalem, Israel: Gefen Publishing House.

Roemer, William F., Jr.
  1995 *Accardo: The Genuine Godfather.* New York: Donald I. Fine.
  1994 *The Enforcer, Spilotro: The Chicago Mob's Man over Las Vegas.* New York: Ivy Books.

Rohde, David
  2007 "Taliban Push Poppy Production to a Record Again." *New York Times* (August 26): 3.

Rohter, Larry
1991   "A Cocaine Baron's Tales of Intrigue and Greed Liven Up Noriega's Trial." *New York Times* (November 24): E3.
1989   "Mexico Captures Top Drug Figure and 80 Policemen." *New York Times* (April 11): 1, 6.

Rohter, Larry and Clifford Krauss
1998a   "Dominican Drug Traffickers Tighten Grip on the Northeast." *New York Times* (May 11): 12, 17.
1998b   "Dominicans Allow Drugs Easy Sailing." *New York Times* (May 10): 1, 6.

Rome, Florence
1975   *The Tattooed Men*. New York: Delacorte.

Romero, Simon
2008a   "Union Killings Peril Trade Pact with Colombia." *New York Times* (April 14): 1, 8.
2008b   "Ecuador Opposes Outpost in American War on Drugs." *New York Times* (May 12): 8.
2008c   "Colombia Extradites 14 Paramilitary Leaders to the United States." *New York Times* (May 14): 6.
2008d   "Colombian Warlord Pleads Not Guilty to Drug Charges." *New York Times* (May 15): B3.
2008e   "Despite Rebel Losses, Cocaine Sustains War in Rural Colombia." *New York Times* (July 27): 1, 8.
2008f   "As U.S. Presses Drug War, Bolivia Is Antagonist and Uneasy Ally." *New York Times* (August 29): 1, 11.
2007   "Cocaine Wars Turn Port into Colombia's Deadliest City." *New York Times* (May 22): 3.

Romoli, Kathleen
1941   *Colombia*. Garden City, NY: Doubleday, Doran.

Rosen, Charles
1978   *Scandals of '51: How the Gamblers Almost Killed College Basketball*. New York: Holt, Rinehart and Winston.

Rosner, Lydia S.
1995   "Preface" to "Organized Crime IV: The Russian Connection." *Contemporary Criminal Justice* 11 (December): vi–viii.
1986   *Soviet Way of Crime*. South Hadley, MA: Bergin and Garvey.

Ross, Irwin
1992   *Shady Business: Confronting Corporate Corruption*. New York: Twentieth Century Fund Press.

Ross, Ron
2003   *Bummy Davis vs. Murder, Inc.* New York: St. Martin's Press.

Rothmiller, Mike and Ivan G. Goldman
1992   *L.A. Secret Police: Inside the LAPD Elite Spy Network*. New York: Pocket Books.

Rubinstein, Jonathan and Peter Reuter
1978a   "Fact, Fancy, and Organized Crime." *Public Interest* 53 (Fall): 45–67.
1978b   "Bookmaking in New York." New York: Policy Sciences Center. (Preliminary unpublished draft)
1977   "Numbers: The Routine Racket." New York: Policy Sciences Center. (Preliminary unpublished draft)

Rudolph, Robert
1992   *The Boys from New Jersey*. New York: William Morrow.

Ruggiero, Vincenzo
1993   "The Camorra: 'Clean' Capital and Organised Crime." Pages 141–61 in *Global Crime Connections: Dynamics and Control*, edited by Frank Pearce and Michael Woodiwiss. Toronto, Canada: University of Toronto Press.

Rugoff, Milton
1989   *America's Gilded Age: Intimate Portraits from an Era of Extravagance and Change, 1850–1890*. New York: Henry Holt.

Russell, Francis
1975   *A City in Terror—1919—The Boston Police Strike*. New York: Viking.

"Russian Organized Crime in the United States"
1996   Hearing Before the U.S. Senate Permanent Subcommittee on Investigations, May 15. Washington, DC: Committee on Governmental Affairs.

Ryan, Patrick J. and George E. Rush, eds.
1997   *Understanding Organized Crime in Global Perspective: A Reader*. Thousand Oaks, CA: Sage.

Sabbag, Robert
1996   "The Invisible Family." *New York Times Magazine* (February 11): 33–39.

Sack, John
2001   *The Dragonhead*. New York: Crown.

Salerno, Joseph and Stephen J. Rivele
1990   *The Plumber*. New York: Knightsbridge.

Salerno, Ralph and John S. Tompkins
1969   *The Crime Confederation*. Garden City, NY: Doubleday.

Salkowski, Joe
2001   "Encryption on Wrong Side of Law, Officers Say." *Chicago Tribune* (January 29): Sec. 4: 2.

Samuels, David
2008   "The New Dodge City." *Men's Vogue* (February): 20–28.

Sandoval, Ricardo
1998   "19 Mexicans Slain; Drug Feud Is Blamed." *Chicago Tribune* (September 18): 10.

Saney, Parviz
1986   *Crime and Culture in America: A Comparative Perspective*. New York: Greenwood.

Sanger, David E.
1997   "Japanese Near Pact with U.S. on Threat to Bar Their Ships from American Ports." *New York Times* (October 18): 5.
1995   "Money Laundering, New and Improved." *New York Times* (December 24): E4.
1992   "Top Japanese Party Leaders Accused of Links to Mobsters." *New York Times* (September 23): 1, 4.

Sann, Paul
1971   *Kill the Dutchman: The Story of Dutch Schultz*. New York: Popular Library.

Sante, Luc
1991   *Low Life*. New York: Vintage.

Saulny, Susan
2003   "Laundering of Billions Is Alleged." *New York Times* (June 27): B1, 3.

Saviano, Roberto
2007   *Gomorrah: A Personal Journey into the Violent Empire of Naples' Organized Crime System*. New York: Farrar, Strauss and Giroux. Translated by Virginia Jewiss.

Sawyers, June
1988   "A 'King' Who Had Us in His Pocket." *Chicago Tribune Magazine* (October 2): 10.

Saxon, Wolfgang
1990 "Harry Bridges, Docks Leader, Dies at 88." *New York Times* (March 31): 11.

Scaramella, Gene
1998 Investigator, Cook County (IL) Sheriff's Police. Personal interview.

Schatzberg, Rufus
1994 "African American Organized Crime." Pages 189–212 in *Handbook of Organized Crime in the United States*, edited by Robert J. Kelly, Ko-lin Chin, and Rufus Schatzberg. Westport, CT: Greenwood.
1993 *Black Organized Crime in Harlem: 1920–1930*. New York: Garland.

Schatzberg, Rufus and Robert J. Kelly
1996 *African-American Organized Crime: A Social History*. New York: Garland.

Schelling, Thomas C.
1971 "What Is the Business of Organized Crime?" *American Scholar* 40 (Autumn): 643–52.

Schemo, Diana Jean and Tim Golden
1998 "Bogotá Aid: To Fight Drugs or Rebels?" *New York Times* (June 2): 1, 12.

Schmetzer, Uli
2001 "U.S., China Take Sides in Border Skirmish." *Chicago Tribune* (May 19): 1, 6.
1991a "'Nigerian Connection' Ties Chicago to Asian Drugs." *Chicago Tribune* (December 21): 1, 11.
1991b "Slave Trade Survives, Prospers Across Asia." *Chicago Tribune* (November 15): 1, 18.
1990 "'Prince of Death' Is a Wanted Man." *Chicago Tribune* (March 21): 21.
1985 "A City Whose Kids Are Hired to Kill." *Chicago Tribune* (October 13): 4.

Schmidt, John R.
1992 *Mr. Capone*. New York: William Morrow.

Schmitt, Eric
2004 "Afghans' Gains Face Big Threat in Drug Traffic." *New York Times* (December 11): 1, 6.

Schneider, Jane, Peter Schneider, Stanley R. Barrett, Bojan Baskar, Henk Driessen, Chris Hann, Thomas Hauschild, Andrew Kipnis, Lutz Musner, Susana Narotzky, Gustavo Lins Ribeiro
2005 "Mafia, Antimafia, and the Plural Cultures of Sicily." *Current Anthropology* 46 (August–October): 501–521.

Schoenberg, Robert J.
1992 *Mr. Capone*. New York: William Morrow.

Schorr, Mark
1979 "The .22 Caliber Killings." *New York* (May 7): 43–46.

Schreiber, Amanda J.
2002 "Dealing with the Devil: The FBI's Troubled Relationship with Its Confidential Informants." *Columbia Journal of Law and Social Problems* 301 (Summer): Internet.

Schulte-Bockholt, Alfredo
2006 *The Politics of Organized Crime and the Organized Crime of Politics*. Lexington, MA: Lexington Books.

"Schultz Aide Slain; 7th in Five Months"
1931 *New York Times* (June 22): 2.

"Schultz Product of Dry Law Era"
1933 *New York Times* (January 22): 23.

"Schultz Succumbs to Bullet Wounds Without Naming Slayers"
1933 *New York Times* (October 25): 1.

Schwartz, John
2001 "U.S. Declines to Release Data in Trial." *New York Times* (August 25): B1, 2.

Schweich, Thomas
2008 "Is Afghanistan a Narco-State?" *New York Times* (July 27): 44–47, 60–62.

Sciascia, Leonard
1963 *Mafia Vendetta*. New York: Knopf.

Sciolino, Elaine and Stephen Engelberg
1988 "Narcotics Effort Foiled by U.S. Security Goals." *New York Times* (April 10): 1, 10.

Scott, W. Richard
1981 *Organizations: Rational, Natural, and Open Systems*. Englewood Cliffs, NJ: Prentice-Hall.

Seedman, Albert A.
1974 *Chief!* New York: Arthur Fields.

Seguin, Rheal
2005 "Bust Shattered Drug Network, Quebec Police Say." *Globe and Mail* (February 24): 46.

Seidman, Harold
1938 *Labor Czars: A History of Labor Racketeering*. New York: Liveright.

Semple, Kirk
2001 "Colombia's Cocaine Frontier." *Mother Jones* (November/December): 58–63.

Sengupta, Somini
2004 "Violence Jolts the Still Fragile Democracy in Nigeria." *New York Times* (May 24): 3.

Serao, Ernesto
1911a "The Truth about the Camorra." *Outlook 98* (July 28): 717–26.
1911b "The Truth about the Camorra: Part II." *Outlook* 98 (August 50): 778–87.

Serio, Joseph
2008 *Investigating the Russian Mafia*. Durham, NC: Carolina Academic Press.
1992a "Organized Crime in the Soviet Union and Beyond." *Low Intensity Conflict and Law Enforcement* 1 (Autumn): 127–51.
1992b "Shunning Tradition: Ethnic Organized Crime in the Former Soviet Union." *CJ International* 8 (November–December): 5–6.

Serrin, William
1989 "Jackie Presser's Secret Lives Detailed in Government Files." *New York Times* (March 27): 1, 11.

Servadio, Gaia
1976 *Mafioso: A History of the Mafia from Its Origins to the Present Day*. Briarcliff Manor, NY: Stein and Day.
1974 *Angelo LaBarbera: The Profile of a Mafia Boss*. London: Quartet Books.

Sexton, Joe
1995 "3 Men Accused of Running Chinatown Organized Crime." *New York Times* (June 2): 1, 16.

Seymour, Christopher
1996 *Yakuza Diary*. New York: Atlantic Monthly Press.

Shannon, Elaine
1991 "New Kings of Coke." *Time* (July 1): 29–33.
1988 *Desperados: Latin Drug Lords, U.S. Lawmen, and the War America Can't Win*. New York: Viking.

Shannon, William V.
1989 *The American Irish: A Political and Social Portrait.* Amherst: University of Massachusetts Press.

Shaw, Clifford and Henry D. McKay
1972 *Juvenile Delinquency and Urban Areas.* Chicago: University of Chicago Press. Originally published in 1942.

Shawcross, Tim and Martin Young
1987 *Men of Honour: The Confessions of Tommaso Buscetta.* London: Collins.

Shelley, Louise I.
2005 "The Unholy Trinity: Transnational Crime, Corruption, and Terrorism." *Brown Journal of World Affairs* 11 (Winter/Spring): 101–111.
2001 "Corruption and Organized Crime in Mexico in the Post-PRI Transition." *Journal of Contemporary Criminal Justice* 17 (August): 213–231.
1997 "Post-Soviet Organized Crime: A New Form of Authoritarianism." Pages 122–38 in *Russian Organized Crime, The New Threat?* edited by Phil Williams. London: Frank Cass.

Shelley, Louise I. and Sharon Melzer
2008 "The Nexus of Organized Crime and Terrorism: Two Case Studies in Cigarette Smuggling." *International Journal of Comparative and Applied Criminal Justice* 32 (Spring): 44–62.

Shelley, Louise I. and John T. Picarelli
2005 "Methods and Motives: Exploring Links Between Transnational Organized Crime and International Terrorism." *Trends in Organized Crime* 9 (Winter): 52–67.

Shelley, Louise I., John T. Picarelli, Allison Irby, Douglas M. Hart, Patricia A. Craig, Phil Williams, Steven Simon, Nabi Abdullaev, Bartosz Stanislawski, and Laura Covill
2005 *Methods and Motives: Exploring Links Between Transnational Organized Crime and International Terrorism.* Washington, DC: U. S. Department of Justice.

Shenon, Philip
1996 "Opium Baron's Rule May End with Surrender in Myanmar." *New York Times* (January 6): 4.
1986 "U.S. Crime Panel: Discord to the End." *New York Times* (April 6): 9.

Sher, Julian and William Marsden
2006 *Angels of Death: Inside the Biker Gang's Crime Empire.* New York: Carroll and Graf.

Sheridan, Michael
1997 "Triads Move on Hong Kong." *London Times* (July 13): 19.

Sheridan, Walter
1972 *The Fall and Rise of Jimmy Hoffa.* New York: Saturday Review Press.

Shipp, E. R.
1985 "Former Chief of Teamsters Ordered to Jail Next Month." *New York Times* (April 25): 12.

Short, James F., Jr., ed.
1968 *Gang Delinquency and Delinquent Subcultures.* New York: Harper & Row.

Siciliano, Vincent
1970 *Unless They Kill Me First.* New York: Hawthorn Books.

Siebert, Renate
1996 *Secrets of Life and Death: Women and the Mafia.* London: Verso.

"Siegel, Gangster, Is Slain on Coast."
1947 *New York Times* (June 22): 1.

Silverstein, Ken
2000 "Trillion-Dollar Hideaway." *Mother Jones* (November/December): 38–45, 94–96.

Simpson, Daniel
2002 "In Albanian Politics, Are the Changes Skin-Deep?" *New York Times* (November 21): 4.

Sims, Calvin
2000 "Feeling Pinch, Japan's Mobs Struggle for Control." *New York Times* (April 2): 6.

Sinclair, Andrew
1962 *The Era of Excess: A Social History of the Prohibition Movement.* Boston: Little, Brown.

Singer, Mark
2002 "The Gang's All Here." *New Yorker* (August 12): 56–61.

Sisk, Richard
2004 "Disabling Haiti Drug Cartels Is Job One." *New York Daily News* (March 4): 24.

Skolnick, Jerome H.
2008 "Policing Should Not Be for Profit." *Criminology and Public Policy* 7 (May): 257–62.

Skolnick, Jerome H., Theodore Correl, Elizabeth Navarro, and Roger Rabb
1990 "The Social Structure of Street Drug Dealing." *American Journal of Police* 9: 1–41.

Sloane, Arthur A.
1992 *Hoffa.* Cambridge, MA: MIT Press.

Sly, Liz
1999 "In a Hail of Bullets, Island of Macau Awaits a New Master." *Chicago Tribune* (February 18): 8.

Smith, Alson J.
1962 "The Early Chicago Story." Pages 138–46 in *Organized Crime in America*, edited by Gus Tyler. Ann Arbor: University of Michigan Press.

Smith, Craig S.
2005 "Turkey's Growing Sex Trade Snares Many Slavic Women." *New York Times* (June 26): 4.

Smith, David E., ed.
1979 *Amphetamine Use, Misuse, and Abuse.* Boston: G. K. Hall and Co.

Smith, Dwight C., Jr.
1982 "Paragons, Pariahs, and Pirates: A Spectrum-Based Theory of Enterprise." *Crime and Delinquency* 26 (July): 358–86.
1978 "Organized Crime and Entrepreneurship." *International Journal of Criminology and Penology* 6: 161–77.
1974 *The Mafia Mystique.* New York: Basic Books.

Smith, Dwight C., Jr., and Ralph Salerno
1970 "The Use of Strategies in Organized Crime Control." *Journal of Law, Criminology and Police Science* 61: 101–11.

Smith, Greg B.
2005 "Life and Times of New Donnie Brasco." *New York Daily News* (April 18): 20.
2004a "Albanian 'Mafiosi' in Feds' Net." *New York Daily News* (November 1): 24.
2004b "Moving In on the Mob." *New York Daily News* (October 27): 2.
2003 *Made Men.* New York: Berkeley Books.

Smith, John L.
1998   *The Animal in Hollywood: Anthony Fiato's Life in the Mafia*. New York: Barricade Books.

Smith, Peter H.
1999   "Semiorganized International Crime: Drug Trafficking in Mexico." Pages 193–216 in *Transnational Crime in the Americas*, edited by Tom Farer. New York: Routledge.

Smith, Richard Norton
1982   *Thomas E. Dewey and His Times*. New York: Simon and Schuster.

Smith, Sherwin D.
1963   "35 Years Ago Arnold Rothstein Was Mysteriously Murdered and Left a Racket Empire Up for Grabs." *New York Times Magazine* (October 27): 96.

"Smoking Gun, The"
1998   *New York* (November 22): 16.

Snedden, Christopher and John Visser
1994   *Financial and Organised Crime in Italy*. Commonwealth of Australia.

Sniffen, Michael J.
2000   "Mexico-Jamaica Drug Ring Broken." Associated Press (April 13): Internet.

Sondern, Frederic, Jr.
1959   *Brotherhood of Evil: The Mafia*. New York: Farrar, Straus and Cudahy.

Song, John Juey-Long
1996   "The Asian Factor: Methodological Barriers to the Study of Asian Gangs and Organized Crime." *American Journal of Criminal Justice* 21 (1): 27–41.

Spadolini, Giovanni
1993   "Foreword." Pages 7–9 in *Mafia Issues*, edited by Ernesto U. Savona. Milan, Italy: United Nations.

Speart, Jessica
1995   "The New Drug Mules." *New York Times Magazine* (June 11): 44–45.

Special Committee to Investigate Organized Crime in Interstate Commerce
1951   *Kefauver Crime Report*. New York: Arco.

Spector, Michael
1995   "Old-Time Boss for Russia's Showcase Port." *New York Times* (August 28): 1, 2.
1994   "New Moscow Mob Terror: Car Bombs." *New York Times* (June 10): 4.

Spergel, Irving
1964   *Racketville, Slumtown, Haulberg*. Chicago: University of Chicago Press.

Spiering, Frank
1976   *The Man Who Got Capone*. Indianapolis, IN: Bobbs-Merrill.

Spinale, Dominic
2004   *G-Men and Gangsters: Partners in Crime*. New York: MJF Books.

"Spotlight"
1981   *Chicago Crime Commission Searchlight* (October): 8.

Stahl, Marc B.
1992   "Asset Forfeiture, Burdens of Proof and the War on Drugs." *Journal of Criminal Law and Criminology* 83: 274–337.

Stanley, Alessandra
2001   "Where Hit Men Better Mean It When They 'Yes Ma'am' to the Boss." *New York Times* (January 11): 11.

1998   "The Army Is Leaving but the Mafia Probably Isn't." *New York Times* (June 26): 4.
1994   "Where Politicians Sometimes Tote Assault Rifles." *New York Times* (May 10): 4.

Starks, Carolyn
1999   "Witness Offers Inside Look at Biker Battle." *Chicago Tribune* (April 6): Sec. 2: 1, 4.

State Commission of Investigation
1989   *Solid Waste Regulation*. Trenton: New Jersey Commission of Investigation.

Steffens, Lincoln
1957   *The Shame of the Cities*. New York: Hill and Wang. Originally published in 1904.
1931   *The Autobiography of Lincoln Steffens*. New York: Chautauqua Press. Reprinted by Harcourt, Brace and World, 1958.

Steinberg, Alfred
1972   *The Bosses*. New York: New American Library.

Steinberg, Allen
2003   "The Public Prosecutor as Representational Image: The 'Lawman' in New York: William Travers Jerome and the Origins of the Modern District Attorney in Turn-of-the-Century New York." *University of Toledo Law Review* 34 (Summer): 753–82.

Sterngold, James
1995   "Organized Crime Puts Its Talent to Helping and Tokyo to Shame." *New York Times* (January 22): 7.
1994   "Gangster Ties to Banks Hurt Japan's Financial Recovery." *New York Times* (October 18): C1, C14.
1992a   "Corporate Japan's Unholy Allies." *New York Times* (December 6): 3: 1, 6.
1992b   "Japan Takes on Mob, and the Mob Fights Back." *New York Times* (June 15): 1, 6.
1992c   "Mob and Politics Intersect, Fueling Cynicism in Japan." *New York Times* (October 21): 1, 4.

Stevens, Jay
1987   *Storming Heaven: LSD and the American Dream*. New York: Atlantic Monthly Press.

Stevenson, James
2006   "Lost and Found New York." *New York Times* (February 25): 15.

Stewart, Robert C.
2006   "Reflections on Labor Racketeering and Interdisciplinary Enforcement." *Trends in Organized Crime* 9 (Summer): 60–101.
1980   *Identification and Investigation of Organized Criminal Activity*. Houston, TX: National College of District Attorneys.

Stille, Alexander
1995a   *Exquisite Cadavers: The Mafia and the Death of the First Italian Republic*. New York: Pantheon.
1995b   "Letter from Sicily: The Fall of Caesar." *New Yorker* (September 11): 68–83.
1993   "Letter from Palermo: The Mafia's Biggest Mistake." *New Yorker* (March 1): 60–73.

Stocckers, Sally W.
2000   "The Rise in Human Trafficking and the Role of Organized Crime." Transnational Crime and Corruption Center, American University. Internet.

Stohl, Rachel
2005   "Fighting the Illicit Trafficking in Small Arms." Center for Defense Information, Internet.

Stolberg, Mary M.
1995 *Fighting Organized Crime: Politics, Justice, and the Legacy of Thomas E. Dewey.* Boston: Northeastern University Press.

Stone, Michael
1992 "After Gotti." *New York* (February 3): 23–30.

Strauss, Neil
2002 "Mafia Songs Break a Code of Silence." *New York Times* (July 22): B1, B4.

Straziuso, Jason
2008 "Marines Ignore Taliban Cash Crop to Not Upset Afghan Locals." *Yahoo News* (May 6): Internet.

Strong, Josiah
1976 "Perils—The Boss, the Machine, the Immigrant: A Nineteenth-Century View." Pages 14–17 in *The City Boss in America: An Interpretive Reader*, edited by Alexander B. Callow, Jr. New York: Oxford University Press.

Sullivan, John and Alex Berenson
2000 "Brokers Charged With Crime Figures in Complex Scheme." *New York Times* (June 15): 1, C27.

Sullivan, Joseph F.
1991 "Casino Union Yields Power as Its Leaders Accept Curbs." *New York Times* (April 13): 7.
1988 "New Jersey Teamster Local Elects Slate Tied to the Mob." *New York Times* (December 8): 16.

Suo, Steve
2004 "Unnecessary Epidemic." *The Oregonian* (October 3): Internet.

Supreme Court of the State of New York
1942 *A Presentment Concerning the Enforcement by the Police Department of the City of New York of the Laws Against Gambling.* New York, reprinted by Arno Press, 1974.

Surtees, Rebecca
2008 "Traffickers and Trafficking in Southern and Eastern Europe: Considering the Other Side of Trafficking." *European Journal of Criminology* 5 (1): 39–68.

Sutherland, Edwin H.
1973 *Edwin H. Sutherland: On Analyzing Crime*, edited by Karl Schuessler. Chicago: University of Chicago Press.

Suttles, Gerald D.
1968 *The Social Order of the Slum.* Chicago: University of Chicago Press.

Swanberg, W. A.
1959 *Jim Fisk: The Career of an Improbable Rascal.* New York: Scribner's.

Taft, Philip and Philip Ross
1969 "American Labor Violence: Its Causes, Character, and Outcome." Pages 281–395 in *The History of Violence in America*, edited by Hugh Davis Graham and Ted Robert Gurr. New York: Bantam.

Tagliabue, John
1994 "Live by the Rules? An Italian Haven for Cigarette Smugglers Is Fuming." *New York Times* (March 7): 4.

Takahashi, Sadahiko and Carl B. Becker
1985 *Organized Crime in Japan.* Osaka, Japan: Kin'ki University, unpublished paper.

Talese, Gay
1971 *Honor Thy Father.* New York: World Publishing.
1965 *The Overreachers.* New York: Harper & Row.

Talmadge, Eric
1999 "Japanese Mob Raising Fears, Concern." Associated Press (April 20): Internet.
1988 "All Is Not Well Within Japan's Underworld." *Southtown Economist* (December 15): Sec. 2: 4.

Tamayo, Juan O.
2001 "Colombia's Heroin Trade Is Flourishing." *Chicago Tribune* (August 24): 6.

Task Force on Organized Crime
1976 *Organized Crime.* Washington, DC: U.S. Government Printing Office.
1967 *Task Force Report: Organized Crime.* Washington, DC: U.S. Government Printing Office.

Task-Force on Organized Crime in the Baltic Sea Region (TFOCBSR)
2001 *Report on the Fact-Finding Mission Conducted in November 2000 by the National Commissioner of Police for the Baltic Countries Regarding Ttrafficking in Women.* TFOCBSR: Internet.

Tayler, Jefferey
2001 "Russia Is Finished." *Atlantic Monthly* (May): 35–52.

Taylor, Ian, Paul Walton, and Jock Young
1973 *The New Criminology.* New York: Harper & Row.

Tendler, Stewart
2000 "Yardie Gangs Move into the Provinces." *London Times* (August 3): 4.

Teresa, Vincent, and Thomas C. Renner
1973 *My Life in the Mafia.* Greenwich, CT: Fawcett.

Terry, Charles E. and Mildred Pellens
1928 *The Opium Problem.* New York: The Committee on Drug Addictions, in collaboration with the Bureau of Social Hygiene, Inc.

Thomas, Jerry
1994a "Bombings in Chicago, Rockford Linked to Motorcycle Gang Merger." *Chicago Tribune* (November 9): Sec. 2: 4.
1994b "Biker War Erupts in Illinois." *Chicago Tribune* (November 20): Sec. 2: 1, 2.

Thomas, Ralph C.
1977 "Organized Crime in the Construction Industry." *Crime and Delinquency* 23: 304–11.

Thompson, Cheryl W.
2001 "DEA Shielded Tainted Informant." *Washington Post* (July 19): 1.

Thompson, Craig and Allan Raymond
1940 *Gang Rule in New York.* New York: Dial.

Thompson, Ginger
2005a "Drug Violence Paralyzes a City, and Chills the Border." *New York Times* (May 24): 4.
2005b "Mexico's Fallen Party Plans Its Revival with a New Star." *New York Times* (February 6): 12.
2005c "Rival Drug Gangs Turn the Streets of Nuevo Laredo into a War Zone." *New York Times* (December 4): 6.
2004 "Mexico Arrests Leading Figure in Drug Cartel." *New York Times* (August 24): 4.

Thompson, Ginger and James C. McKinley, Jr.
2005 "Mexico's Drug Cartels Wage Fierce Battle for Their Turf." *New York Times* (January 14): 3.

Thompson, Hunter S.
1966 *Hell's Angels: A Strange and Terrible Saga.* New York: Random House.

Thoumi, Francisco E.
1995 "The Size of the Illegal Drug Industry." Pages 77–96 in *Drug Trafficking in the Americas*, edited by Bruce M. Bagley and William O. Walker, III. New Brunswick, NJ: Transaction.

Thrasher, Frederic Milton
1968 *The Gang: A Study of 1,313 Gangs in Chicago*, abridged. Chicago: University of Chicago Press. Originally published in 1927.

Tillman, Robert and Henry Pontell
1995 "Organizations and Fraud in the Savings and Loan Industry." *Social Forces* 73 (June): 1439–63.

Tindall, George Brown
1988 *America: A Narrative History*, vol. 2. New York: Norton.

Toby, Jackson
1958 "Hoodlum or Businessman: An American Dilemma." Pages 542–50 in *The Jews: Social Patterns of an American Group*, edited by Marshall Sklare. Glencoe, IL: Free Press.

Tomass, Mark
1998 "Mafianomics: How Did Mob Entrepreneurs Infiltrate and Dominate the Russian Economy?" *Journal of Economic Issues* 32 (June): 565–75.

Tosches, Nick
2005 *King of the Jews*. New York: HarperCollins.

Touhy, Roger
1959 *The Stolen Years*. Cleveland, OH: Pennington.

Toy, Calvin
1992 "A Short History of Asian Gangs in San Francisco." *Justice Quarterly* 9 (December): 647–65.

Train, Arthur
1922 *Courts and Criminals*. New York: Scribner's.
1912 "Imported Crime: The Story of the Camorra in America." *McClure's Magazine* (May): 83–94.

Traub, James
1987 "The Lords of Hell's Kitchen." *New York Times Magazine* (April 5): 38, 40, 42, 44, 85.

Treaster, Joseph B.
1994 "U.S. Arrests Drug 'Laundry.'" *New York Times* (December 1): 1, 18.
1993 "U.S. Says Top Trafficker Is Seized in Puerto Rican Connection." *New York Times* (June 5): 7.
1991 "U.S. Seizes Suspect in New York in 40 Colombian Drug Slayings." *New York Times* (September 27): 1, 7.

Trebach, Arnold S.
1987 *The Great Drug War: Radical Proposals That Could Make America Safe Again*. New York: Macmillan.

Tricarico, Donald
1984 *The Italians of Greenwich Village*. Staten Island, NY: Center for Migration Studies of New York.

Tri-State Joint Soviet Émigré Organized Crime Project
1997 "An Analysis of Russian Émigré Crime in the Tri-State Region." Pages 177–210 in *Russian Organized Crime, The New Threat?* edited by Phil Williams. London: Frank Cass.

Truong, thanh-Dam
2003 "Organized Crime and Human Trafficking," Pages 53–69 in *Transnational Organized Crime*, edited by Emilio V. Viano, José Magallanes, and Laurent Bridel. Durham, NC: Carolina Academic Press.

Tucker, Richard K.
1991 *The Dragon and the Cross: The Rise and Fall of the Ku Klux Klan in Middle America*. Hamden, CT: Archon Books.

Tuite, James
1978 "Would Benefits of Legalized Betting on Sports Outweigh the Drawbacks?" *New York Times* (December 19): B21.

Tullis, LaMond
1995 *Unintended Consequences: Illegal Drugs and Drug Policies in Nine Countries*. Boulder, CO: Lynne Reinner.

Tully, Andrew
1958 *Treasury Agent: The Inside Story*. New York: Simon and Schuster.

Tulsky, Frederic N.
1987 "U.S. Witness Protection Program Hides a Daughter from Her Father." *Chicago Tribune* (March 5): Sec. 5: 3.

Turbiville, Graham H., Jr.
1995 "Organized Crime and the Russian Armed Forces." *Transnational Organized Crime* 1 (Winter): 57–104.

Turkus, Burton and Sid Feder
1951 *Murder, Inc.: The Story of the Syndicate*. New York: Farrar, Straus and Young.

Turner, Wallace
1984 "U.S. and Nevada Agents Crack Down on Casinos." *New York Times* (January 28): 1, 7.

Tyler, Gus
1975 "Book Review of 'The Black Mafia.'" *Crime and Delinquency* 21 (April): 175–80.

Tyler, Gus, ed.
1962 *Organized Crime in America*. Ann Arbor: University of Michigan Press.

Ungar, Sanford
1975 *The FBI*. Boston: Little, Brown.

"Unger Indicted in Drug Conspiracy"
1928 *New York Times* (December 11): 1.

United Nations Centre for International Crime Prevention
2000 "Assessing Transnational Organized Crime: Results of a Pilot Survey of 40 Selected Organized Criminal Groups in 16 Countries." *Trends in Organized Crime* 6 (Winter): 44–92.

United Nations Office on Drugs and Crime (UNODC)
2008a *Afghanistan: Opium Winter Rapid Assessment Survey*. UNODC.
2008b *Annual Report: 2008*. UNODC.
2008c *Illicit Drug Trends in the Russian Federation*. UNODC.
2007a *Cocaine Trafficking in Western Africa: Situation Report*. UNODC.
2007b *Cocaine Trafficking in West Africa: The Threat to Stability and Development (with a special reference to Guinea-Bissau)*. UNODC..
2005 *Transnational Organized Crime in the West African Region*. UNODC.

U.S. Department of Justice
2008a "Former Top SAS Cargo Group Executive Agrees to Plead Guilty to Participating in Price-Fixing Conspiracy." Press release (July 28).
2008b "LG, Sharp, Chunghwa Agree to Plead Guilty, Pay Total of $585 Million in Fines for Participating in LCD Price-Fixing Conspiracies." Press release (November 12).

U.S. Department of State (USDOS).
  2008 *International Narcotics Control Strategy Report.* USDOS.
  2005 *International Narcotics Control Strategy Report.* USDOS.
  2004 *Trafficking in Persons Report.* USDOS.
  2003 *Southeast Asia.* Internet.
  2001 *The Caribbean.* Bureau for International Narcotics and Law Enforcement Affairs. Internet.
  1999 *Money Laundering and Financial Crimes.* Washington, DC: Bureau for International Narcotics and Law Enforcement Affairs.

U.S. General Accountability Office (USGAO)
  2008 *Drug Control: Cooperation with Many Major Drug Transit Countries Has Improved, but Better Performance Reporting and Sustainability Plans Are Needed.* Washington, DC: USGAO.

Van Devander, Charles W.
  1944 *The Big Bosses.* New York: Howell, Soskin.

Van Duyne, Petrus and Alan A. Block
  1995 "Organized Cross-Atlantic Crime: Racketeering in Fuels." *Crime, Law and Social Change* 22: 127–47.

van Dyke, Craig and Robert Byck
  1982 "Cocaine." *Scientific American* 246 (March): 139–41.

Van Natta, Don, Jr.
  1998 "U.S. Indicts 26 Mexican Bankers in Laundering of Drug Funds." *New York Times* (May 19): 6.
  1996 "19 Indicted on U.S. Charges in Blow to Genovese Family." *New York Times* (June 12): B12.

Vaquera, Tony and David W. Bailey
  2004 "Latin Gang in the Americas: Los Mara Salvatrucha." *Crime and Justice International* 20 (November/December): 4–10.

Varese, Federico
  2006 "How Mafias Migrate: The Case of the 'Ndrangheta in Northern Italy." *Law and Society* 40 (2): 411–444.
  2001 *The Russian Mafia: Private Protection in a New Market Economy.* Oxford, United Kingdom: Oxford University Press.

Veno, Arthur
  2003 *The Brotherhoods: Inside the Outlaw Motorcycle Clubs.* Allen & Unwin: New South Wales, Australia.

Vest, Jason
  1997 "DEA to Florists: The Poppies Are Unlovely." *U.S. News & World Report* (March 17): 49.

Viano, Emilio C., José Magallanes, and Laurent Bridel, eds.
  2003 *Transnational Organized Crime: Myth, Power, and Profit.* Durham, NC: Carolina Academic Press.

Villalón, Carlos
  2004 "Cocaine Country." *National Geographic* (July): 34–55.

Villano, Anthony
  1978 *Brick Agent.* New York: Ballantine.

Villarreal, Andres
  2002 "Political Competition and Violence in Mexico: Hierarchical Social Control in Local Patronage Structures." *American Sociological Review* 67 (August): 477–99.

Violante, Luciano
  2000 "Foreword." Pages ix–xi in Alison Jamieson, *The Antimafia: Italy's Fight Against Organized Crime.* New York: St. Martin's Press.

Vitielo, Michael
  1995 "Has the Supreme Court Really Turned RICO Upside Down? An Examination of *Now v. Scheidler.*" *Journal of Criminal Law and Criminology* 85 (Spring): 1223–57.

Volkman, Ernest
  1998 *Gangbusters: The Destruction of America's Last Mafia Dynasty.* Boston: Faber and Faber.

Volkov, Vadim
  2000 "The Political Economy of Protection Rackets in the Past and the Present." *Social Research* 67 (Fall): Internet.

Von Lampe, Klaus and Per Ole Johansen
  2004 "Criminal Networks and Trust, On the Importance of Expectations of Loyal Behavior in Criminal Relations." Pages 102–113 in *Organised Crime, Trafficking, Drugs,* edited by Sami Nevala and Kauko Aromaa. Helsinki, Finland: European Institute for Crime Prevention and Control.

Voronin, Yuriy A.
  1997 "The Emerging Criminal State: Economic and Political Aspects of Organized Crime in Russia." Pages 53–62 in *Russian Organized Crime, The New Threat?* edited by Phil Williams. London: Frank Cass.

Wahl, Melissa
  2000 "Surge Puts Payday Loans Under Scrutiny." *Chicago Tribune* (May 7): 1, 11.
  1999a "Hitting a Wall of Opposition." *Chicago Tribune* (February 4): Sec. 3: 1, 4.
  1999b "Payday Loans Hit Pay Dirt." *Chicago Tribune* (November 18): 1, 6.
  1999c "Suspicions Mount About Secrecy Act." *Chicago Tribune* (March 26): Sec. 3: 1, 4.

Waldman, Amy
  2003 "Afghan Group, Once on Top, Again Makes Its Presence Felt." *New York Times* (December 21): 4.

Waldman, Michael and Pamela Gilbert
  1989 "RICO Goes to Congress: Keep the Teeth in the White-Collar Law." *New York Times* (March 12): F2.

Walker, Samuel
  1980 *Popular Justice: A History of American Criminal Justice.* New York: Oxford University Press.

Wallance, Gregory
  1982 *Papa's Game.* New York: Ballantine.

Walsh, Marilyn E.
  1977 *The Fence.* Westport, CT: Greenwood.

Walston, James
  1986 "See Naples and Die: Organized Crime in Campania." Pages 134–58 in *Organized Crime: A Global Perspective,* edited by Robert J. Kelly. Totowa, NJ: Rowman and Littlefield.

Walter, Ingo
  1990 *Secret Money: The World of International Financial Secrecy.* New York: Harper Business.

Walters, John
  2003 *Dialogue with John Walters, Director, White House Office of National Drug Control Policy.* Washington, DC: Center for Strategic and International Studies.

Warmbir, Steve, Robert C. Herguth, and Frank Main
  2005 "Mob on the Ropes After Indictment." *Chicago Sun-Times* (April 27): 1–2.

Warnick, Mark S.
1997 "City Cop Scandals Dash Drug Trials." *Chicago Tribune* (December 25): Sec. 2: 1, 2.

Washburn, Charles
1934 *Come into My Parlor: Biography of the Aristocratic Everleigh Sisters of Chicago*. New York: Knickerbocker Publishing Co.

Waugh, Daniel
2007 *Eagan's Rats. The Untold Story of the Prohibition Era Gang That Ruled St. Louis*. Nashville, TN: Cumberland House Publishing.

Webster, Barbara and Michael S. McCampbell
1992 *International Money Laundering: Research and Investigation Join Forces*. Washington, DC: National Institute of Justice.

Webster, Donovan
1994 "Chips Are a Thief's Best Friend." *New York Times Magazine* (September 18): 54–59.

Wedel, Janine R.
2001 "Corruption and Organized Crime in Post-Communist States: New Ways of Manifesting Old Patterns." *Trends in Organized Crime* 7 (Fall): 3–61.

Weiner, Tim
2002a "Drug Kingpin, Long Sought, Is Captured by Mexicans." *New York Times* (March 10): 15.
2002b "Border Customs Agents Are Pushed to the Limit." *New York Times* (July 25): 14.
2001 "Mexican Jail Easy to Flee: Just Pay Up." *New York Times* (January 29): 5.

Weinstein, Adam K.
1988 "Prosecuting Attorneys for Money Laundering: A New and Questionable Weapon in the War on Crime." *Law and Contemporary Problems* 51 (Winter): 369–86.

Weiser, Benjamin
2008 "Convictions Reinstated in Mob Case." *New York Times* (September 18): B1, 6.
2002 "Officials Say They Smashed International Ecstasy Ring." *New York Times* (November 6): 21.
1998a "14 Charged in Internet Betting in the First Case of Its Kind." *New York Times* (March 5): 1, 23.
1998b "Reputed Crime Family Head Indicted in Extortion Case." *New York Times* (April 29): Internet.

Weisman, Alan
1989 "Dangerous Days in the Macarena." *New York Times Magazine* (April 23): 40–48.

Weisman, Steven R.
1991 "Is Business Too Cozy with the Mob?" *New York Times* (August 29): 11.

Wellford, Charles
2001 "When It's No Longer a Game: Pathological Gambling in the United States." *National Institute of Justice Journal* (April): 14–18.

Wendt, Lloyd and Herman Kogan
1974 *Bosses in Lusty Chicago: The Story of Bathhouse John and Hinky Dink*. Bloomington: Indiana University Press. Originally published in 1943.

Werner, M. R.
1928 *Tammany Hall*. Garden City, NY: Doubleday, Doran.

Wesson, Donald R. and David E. Smith
1985 "Cocaine: Treatment Perspectives." Pages 193–203 in *Cocaine Use in America: Epidemiologic and Clinical Perspectives*, edited by Nicholas J. Kozel and Edgar H. Adams. Rockville, MD: National Institute on Drug Abuse.
1977 *Barbiturates: Their Use, Misuse, and Abuse*. New York: Human Sciences Press.

Wethern, George and Vincent Colnett
1978 *A Wayward Angel*. New York: Marek Publishers.

Whalen, David C.
1995 "Organized Crime and Sports Gambling: Point-Shaving in College Basketball." Pages 19–34 in *Contemporary Issues in Organized Crime*, edited by Jay Albanese. Monsey, NY: Criminal Justice Press.

White, Frank Marshall
1908 "The Bands of Criminals of New York's East Side." *New York Times* (November 8): V 9.

White, Jonathan
2006 *Terrorism and Homeland Security*, 5th ed. Belmont, CA: Wadsworth.

"Who Are the Yardies?"
1999 *BBC News* (June 19): Internet.

Whymant, Robert
2001 "Crime Bosses Killed in Funeral Attack." *London Times* (September 20): Internet.

Whyte, William Foote
1961 *Street Corner Society*. Chicago: University of Chicago Press.

Williams, Phil
2006 "Trafficking in Women: Markets, Networks and Organized Crime." *Criminal Trafficking and Slavery: The Dark Side of Global and Regional Migration*. Joint Annual Centers Annual Symposium, February 23–25. University of Illinois at Urbana-Champaign.
1997 "Introduction: How Serious a Threat Is Russian Organized Crime?" Pages 1–27 in *Russian Organized Crime, The New Threat?* edited by Phil Williams. London: Frank Cass.
1995a "The Geopolitics of Transnational Organized Crime." Paper presented at the annual meeting of the American Society of Criminology, Boston, November.
1995b "The New Threat: Transnational Criminal Organizations and International Security." *Criminal Organizations* 9 (3 and 4): 3–19.

Williams, T. Harry
1969 *Huey Long*. New York: Bantam.

Wilson, James Q.
1978 *The Investigators*. New York: Basic Books.
1975 *Thinking about Crime*. New York: Basic Books.

Wines, Michael
2002 "Politics in Moscow More Dagger Than Cloak." *New York Times* (August 24): 1, 4.

Winick, Charles and Paul M. Kinsie
1971 *The Lively Commerce*. Chicago: Quadrangle.

Winterhalder, Edward
2005 *Out in Bad Standings: Inside the Bandidos Motorcycle Club—The Making of a Worldwide Dynasty*. Owasso, OK: Blockhead City Press.

Wiretap Commission. *See* National Commission for the Review of Federal and State Laws Relating to Wiretapping and Electronic Surveillance

Wishart, David
1974 "The Opium Poppy: The Forbidden Crop." *Journal of Geography* 73 (January): 1425.
Withers, Kay
1982 "Cardinal Leads Drive to Crush Sicily's Mafia." *Chicago Tribune* (September 29): 5.
Witkin, Gordon
1991 "The Men Who Created Crack." *U.S. News and World Report* (August 19): 44–53.
Witkin, Gordon with Jennifer Griffen
1994 "The New Opium Wars." *U.S. News and World Report* (October 10): 39–44.
Witt, Howard
1996 "For Russians, Mafia Part of Everyday Life." *Chicago Tribune* (November 24): 1, 14.
1994 "Welcome to Vladivostok, Where Crime Is King." *Chicago Tribune* (November 21): 1, 19.
Woetzel, Robert K.
1963 "An Overview of Organized Crime: Mores versus Morality." *Annals* 347 (May): 1–11.
Wolf, Daniel R.
1991 *The Rebels: A Brotherhood of Outlaw Bikers.* Toronto: University of Toronto Press.
Wolf, Eric R.
1966 "Kinship, Friendship, and Patron-Client Relations in Complex Societies." Pages 1–22 in *The Social Anthropology of Complex Societies*, edited by Michael Banton. London: Tavistock.
Wolfgang, Marvin E. and Franco Ferracuti
1967 *The Subculture of Violence: Toward an Integrated Theory in Criminology.* London: Tavistock.
"Woman, 2 Men, Slain as Gang Raids Home in Coll Feud"
1932 *New York Times* (February 2): 1.
Women's Bureau
2002 *Trafficking in Persons: A Guide for Non-Governmental Organizations.* Washington, DC: U.S. Department of Labor.
Woodham-Smith, Cecil
1962 *The Great Hunger: Ireland 1845–1849.* New York: Old Town Books. Originally published by Harper & Row.
Woodiwiss, Michael
2005 *Gangster Capitalism: The United States and the Global Rise of Organized Crime.* New York: Carroll and Graff.
1988 *Crime, Crusades and Corruption: Prohibitions in the United States, 1900–1987.* Totowa, NJ: Barnes and Noble.
1987 "Capone to Kefauver: Organized Crime in America." *History Today* 37 (June): 8–15.
Worrall, John L. and Tomislav V. Kovandzic
2008 "Is Policing for Profit? Answers from Asset Forfeiture." *Criminology and Public Policy* 7 (May): 219–244.
Worth, Robert F.
2002 "Bank Failed to Question Huge Deposits." *New York Times* (November 28): C1, 9.

Wren, Christopher S.
1999 "Pipeline of Poor Smuggling Heroin." *New York Times* (February 21): 28.
1998a "Afghanistan's Opium Output Drops Sharply, U.N. Survey Shows." *New York Times* (September 27): 11.
1998b "Drug Officials Sense a Shift in Dominicans." *New York Times* (August 14): 16.
1998c "Road to Riches Starts in the Golden Triangle." *New York Times* (May 11): 8.
1997 "29 Held in Drug Smuggling to New York from Mexico." *New York Times* (August 12): C23.
1996 "Mexican Role in Cocaine Is Exposed in U.S. Seizure." *New York Times* (May 3): C19.
Wright, Michael
1979 "Phenix City, Ala., Leaves Ashes of Sin in the Past." *New York Times* (June 18): 14.
WuDunn, Sheryl
1996 "Uproar over a Bad Debt Crisis." *New York Times* (February 14): C1, 4.
Wyler, Liana Sun
2007 *Burma and Transnational Crime.* Washington, DC: Congressional Research Service.
Wyman, Mark
1984 *Immigrants in the Valley: Irish, Germans, and Americans in the Upper Mississippi Country, 1830–1860.* Chicago: Nelson-Hall.
Yarmysh, Alexander N.
2001 "A Behavioral Model for Ukrainian Organized Crime Groups." *Transnational Organized Crime* 6 (Spring): 143–49.
Yates, Ronald E.
1987 "Afghanistan Invasion Propels Pakistan to Top in Opium Trade." *Chicago Tribune* (February 12): 32.
1985 "Lawmen's Dispute on Gangs Rages Over Pacific." *Chicago Tribune* (December 8): 5.
Zaitseva, Lyudmila
2007 "Organized Crime, Terrorism and Nuclear Trafficking." *Strategic Insights* 6 (August): Internet.
Zalisko, Walter
2001 "Russian Organized Crime, Trafficking in Women, and Government's Response." PMC International Inc. (April): Internet.
Zambito, Thomas
2005 "Afghani Heroin King Denies Rap." *New York Daily News* (October 25): 8.
Zernike, Kate
2006 Potent Mexican Meth Floods in as States Curb Domestic Variety." *New York Times* (January 23): 1, 17.
Zimmermann, Tim and Alan Cooperman
1995 "Special Report." *U.S. News and World Report* (October 23): 56–67.
Zorbaugh, Harvey
1929 *The Gold Coast and the Slum.* Chicago: University of Chicago Press.

AUTHOR INDEX

SUBJECT INDEX